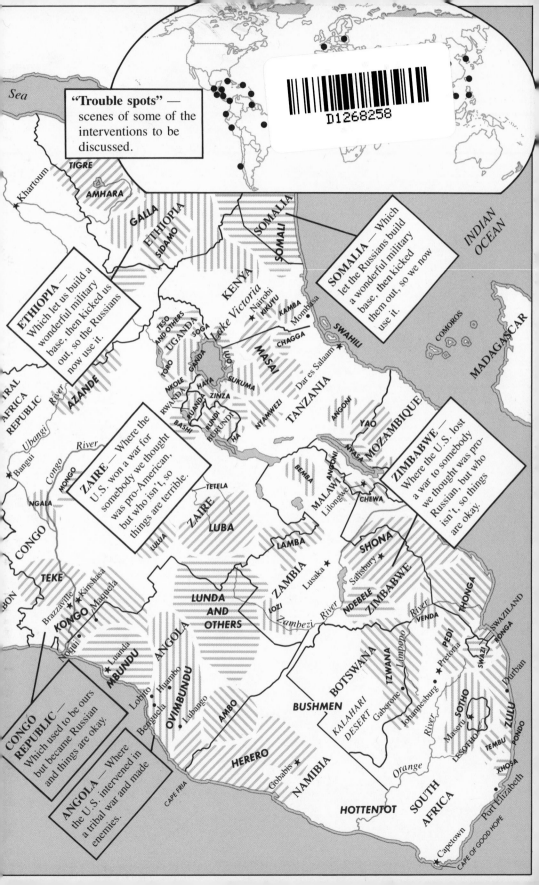

Sea

"**Trouble spots**" — scenes of some of the interventions to be discussed.

D1268258

TIGRE

Khartoum

AMHARA

GALLA

ETHIOPIA

SIDAMO

SOMALI

SOMALIA

INDIAN OCEAN

ETHIOPIA — Which let us build a wonderful military base, so the Russians kicked us out, so the Russians now use it.

SOMALIA — Which let the Russians build a wonderful military base, then kicked them out, so we now use it.

CENTRAL AFRICA REPUBLIC

Bangui

Ubangi River

AZANDE

KENYA

TESO AND OTHERS

UGANDA

TORO

SOGA

GANDA

NKOLE

RWANDA

HAYA

RUANDA

BASHI

ZINZA

RUNDI

BURUNDI

HA

Lake Victoria

Nairobi

KIKUYU

KAMBA

Mombasa

SWAHILI

LUO

SUKUMA

MASAI

CHAGGA

NYAMWEZI

Dar es Salaam

TANZANIA

ANGONI

YAO

COMOROS

MADAGASCAR

ZAIRE — Where the U.S. won a war for somebody we thought was pro-American, but who isn't, so things are terrible.

Congo River

MONGO

TETELA

NGALA

ZAIRE

LUBA

BEMBA

ANGONI

NYASA

MALAWI

MOZAMBIQUE

CHEWA

Lilongwe

ZIMBABWE — Where the U.S. lost a war to somebody we thought was pro-Russian, but who isn't, so things are okay.

CONGO

TEKE

LULUA

LAMBA

LUNDA AND OTHERS

ZAMBIA

Lusaka

SHONA

Satisbury

ZIMBABWE

NDEBELE

River

TONGA

VENDA

GABON

Brazzaville

Kinshasa

KONGO

Maquela

IOZI

Zambezi River

PEDI

SWAZILAND

TZWANA

Pretoria

RONGA

SWAZI

Noqui

Luanda

MBUNDU

Lobito

Huambo

OVIMBUNDU

Lubango

Benguela

ANGOLA

AMBO

BUSHMEN

BOTSWANA

KALAHARI DESERT

Gaborone

Johannesburg

River

SOTHO

Maseru

LESOTHO

Durban

ZULU

TEMBU

PONDO

CONGO REPUBLIC — Which used to be ours but became Russian and things are okay.

ANGOLA — Where the U.S. intervened in a tribal war and made enemies.

HERERO

Gobabis

NAMIBIA

Orange River

HOTTENTOT

SOUTH AFRICA

Capetown

CAPE FRIA

CAPE OF GOOD HOPE

Port Elizabeth

XHOSA

ENDLESS ENEMIES

ENDLESS ENEMIES

THE MAKING OF AN UNFRIENDLY WORLD

JONATHAN KWITNY

CONGDON & WEED, INC., New York

Copyright © 1984 by Jonathan Kwitny

Library of Congress Cataloging in Publication Data

Kwitny, Jonathan.
 Endless enemies.

 Includes index.
  1. United States—Foreign relations—1945–
2. Developing countries—Foreign relations—United States.
3. United States—Foreign relations—Developing countries.
4. Corporations, American—Developing countries—
History—20th century.   I. Title.
E840.K94   1984   327.730172'4   84-5806
ISBN 0-86553-124-2
ISBN 0-312-92178-0 (St. Martin's Press)

Published by Congdon & Weed, Inc.
298 Fifth Avenue, New York, N.Y. 10001
Distributed by St. Martin's Press
175 Fifth Avenue, New York, N.Y. 10010
Published simultaneously in Canada by Methuen Publications
2330 Midland Avenue, Agincourt, Ontario M1S 1P7

All Rights Reserved
Printed in the United States of America
Designed by Irving Perkins
First Edition

For my father
and mother,
who taught me
I had choices

To live bravely by convictions from which the free peoples of this world can take heart, the American people must put their faith in stable, long-range policies—political, economic, and military—programs that will not be heated and cooled with the brightening and waning of tension.

The United States has matured to world leadership; it is time we steered by the stars, not by the lights of each passing ship.

—General Omar Bradley

We have met the enemy and he is us.

—Pogo (Walt Kelly)

CONTENTS

AUTHOR'S NOTE

ADVANCE READERS have remarked on what seemed to them a frequent flattering mention of, and reliance on, the *Wall Street Journal*, especially coupled with occasional critical references to its main competitors, the *New York Times*, and the *Washington Post*. I have been employed by the *Journal* the past thirteen years, and my firsthand knowledge of the incredible care and integrity that goes into the reporting and editing of its contents leads me to rely on it more than on other newspapers. But I have not made it immune from criticism; several examples of misleading reporting cited in these pages are from the *Journal*, and one page-one *Journal* story is fairly ridiculed at length. I have tried also to put criticism of the *Times* and *Post* in the perspective of the fact that they are great newspapers, which is why their occasional failures are so important. If I have done this inadequately, let me note now: All three major national dailies, with hundreds of trained people working around the world, do a remarkable and generally reliable job of sorting through the billows of available information and obtaining, assembling, and packaging the important news. Whoever pays twenty-five, thirty or forty cents for any of them is probably getting by far the biggest bargain of his day, and whoever wants to be truly informed ought to plunk down a dollar and get all three; the recent addition of the *Washington Post Weekly* is a helpful contribution in areas where the *Post* isn't easily available. One wishes there were a similar weekly compendium of the best material from the *Los Angeles Times*, the *Philadelphia Inquirer*, the *Des Moines Register*, the *Miami Herald*, and a score of other top-flight newspapers around the country, too. At any rate, the purpose of the press criticism in this book is to highlight a common fallacy of approach in the reporting of foreign relations that has caused great harm to the country, and maybe even to inspire some correction; the purpose is certainly not to take pokes at vital institutions like our major newspapers.

As I began this book, I determined to respect the sensitivity of many Latin Americans to the usurpation by the United States of the word *American*. This determination to use *U.S.* when I meant to refer only to one country and its people quickly collapsed in the face of practical considerations, like being understood. I have still tried to use U.S. wherever the words seemed interchangeable, but there are many occasions where only *American* will do, and other occasions where that word provides added feeling or variety, and if Latins want to object they will need to come up with a graceful alternative. (Fidel Castro uses "North American," which is hardly fair to Canada, Mexico, and some smaller countries.)

—Jonathan Kwitny

‖CHAPTER ONE

A WORLD OF TROUBLES

=On Sunday, August 7, 1983, Mrs. Justine Eiseman of Belleville, Illinois, picked up her St. Louis *Post-Dispatch* and read about her country's latest foreign entanglement.* A threat from socialist Libya had been discovered at a lonely Sahara Desert oasis called Faya-Largeau, in the African country of Chad.

The more Mrs. Eiseman read, the less sense it made. Chad, a barren stretch of nothing if there ever was one, had been suffering a seesaw civil war for 15 years, between two culturally different groups of tribes. One group, supported by the U.S. Central Intelligence Agency, had won control of the capital and largest city (N'Djamena, population 240,000) a few years ago. But a rival group was supported by Libya—its members lived along the Libyan border and shared a cultural heritage with Libyans. And this Libyan-backed group had just retaken the northerly oasis of Faya-Largeau, which had changed hands several times in the previous few months. Suddenly, the State Department and the newspapers were saying that all of Africa would be imperiled if the Libyan-backed tribes weren't met with force and stopped now.

Mrs. Eiseman wasn't much up on her African geography. If she had been, the State Department story would have made even less sense, because on the other side of Chad lay Nigeria, Africa's biggest and second-richest country, a natural barrier to Libyan expansion. Nigeria had a superior, war-

*Facts are according to a telephone interview with Mrs. Eiseman, August 26, 1983.

toughened army, and was suspicious of the Libyans—who seemed to have all they could handle just taking Faya-Largeau anyway.

Nevertheless, on August 7, 1983, the State Department lurched into its arms deployment mode. Out to the desert oasis went some of our most sophisticated and expensive electronic aircraft, which everyone knew were not going to be flown and maintained by Chadian nomads.

That evening, Mrs. Eiseman drove her four-year-old Ford back to her first-floor garden apartment, and for the first time in all her fifty-seven years, she wrote a letter to the editor of an eastern newspaper—the *New York Times*. She had written to the *Post-Dispatch* before, but this was different.

Mrs. Eiseman lived alone, divorced, her children grown. She worked selling imprinted calendars, ballpoint pens and similar novelty promotional items around Belleville, representing a Chicago imprint firm. Her clients were banks, restaurants, and automobile dealerships that liked to give away mementos to customers. She was, by her count, picking up over $25,000 a year. She didn't have to stick with the old Ford much longer; she was ordering a new car. On the other hand, she was frequently confronted these days by people who weren't doing so well. Mrs. Eiseman liked to play bingo, and some friends she played with regularly—hard-working folk like her—were eating cheese distributed free by the government to the poor. Mrs. Eiseman was a bit shocked by that.

In 1980, Mrs. Eiseman had voted for Ronald Reagan. But she now considered that vote "a mistake." She explains, "I thought Carter was a phony, and that wife of his is absolutely awful. People back east, including our own congressmen, they live in another world. That is not America. This is America. They come back [to visit] and they stay in a $185 room."

When the handwritten draft of her letter satisfied her, she went to the typewriter and copied it. It appeared, as follows, in the *Times* of August 19, 1983:

> To the Editor:
>
> Extraordinary. Now military hardware is being sent to some country in Africa called Chad. I had never heard of Chad, and I couldn't care who governs it. What is the matter with this administration? They seem to want to rule the world. They want to monitor who governs every nation. If they spent more time and money helping the citizens of the United States, we wouldn't have this dreadful deficit or so many hungry people.

There was reason to believe that many of Mrs. Eiseman's countrymen shared her frustration. At about the time her letter appeared, leading opinion polls showed that the overwhelming majority of Americans couldn't even keep straight which side their blood and treasure was being spent on in Central America. In El Salvador, we were *for* the dictatorial government and *against* the rebel guerrillas; in Nicaragua, we were *against* the dictatorial government and *for* the rebel guerrillas. To make it even more confusing, the State Department, and often the newspapers, acted as if these conflicts had started in the past few years. It was somehow written out of history that the United States had been toppling and establishing the governments of Central America for decades, always to set things right, never with success.

In faraway Lebanon, U.S. marines were patrolling the streets, and occasionally dying. The newspapers said the marines were there to put an end to twenty-five years of bloody civil war, so Lebanon could "get back on its feet" and start a democracy. Nobody seemed to remember that Lebanon's twenty-five years of civil war began when the CIA sabotaged a democracy that was already in place. In 1957, the CIA had helped rig an election to load the Lebanese government with Christians, who it believed would better serve American interests. But the Christians we installed proved not terribly credible with their fellow Lebanese. The operation succeeded temporarily,* but the next year, 1958, the Moslem majority began fighting for control.

So U.S. marines were summoned in 1958—to help the young country get back on its feet and restart its democracy. But the marines couldn't stay forever, and the civil war the U.S. government had inadvertently touched off—maybe it would have started anyway, maybe not—wouldn't stop. As happens sometimes in foreign interventions, official Washington was eventually embarrassed to discover that partisans from "our side" in Lebanon were supporting themselves and their cause by smuggling dope into the United States. The cases weren't prosecuted. Many crimes against the American public have been incited, then covered up, by U.S. foreign policy designs around the globe.†

Like earlier missions, the 1983 U.S. mission to Lebanon was described as a one-time-only intervention, just temporary, until things were set right. It was also described as nonpartisan, although the government the marines were protecting was Christian, and the people shooting at the marines were Moslem. Planeloads of U.S. diplomats, led by the secretary of state himself, were hopping from Beirut to Jerusalem to Cairo, trying to negotiate settlements. But crisscrossing them in the sky, and undermining their work, were planeloads of arms salesmen, led by the secretary of defense. The one thing the Middle East never seemed to run out of was ammunition.‡

*For an account, see *Ropes of Sand* by former U.S. intelligence officer Wilbur Crane Eveland (W. W. Norton, 1980).

†Both the Treasury Department's Bureau of Alcohol, Tobacco, and Firearms and the Drug Enforcement Administration launched extensive investigations into narcotics dealing by Lebanese Christians during the 1970s. These investigations produced many accusatory field reports, but few prosecutions, before the investigations were ordered closed down by Washington. Some agents blame foreign policy considerations for the shutdown; proof isn't available. There is plenty of proof, though, for other instances to be cited in the pages ahead.

‡Thanks for this image to Michael Cooney.

* * *

THE American people have built a great country. Its prosperity is based in large part on the extraordinary ability of individual Americans to determine their own economic course, and this in turn is rooted in an extraordinary concept of liberty. However imperfectly at times, the United States still clings to the ideal that liberty requires the diffusion of power. Maybe nowhere, certainly not on such a scale, is there so much freedom to inquire, to speak, and to publish, coupled with so much genuine popular control of institutions. In Britain, newspapers are shackled in reporting many activities of government. In Belgium, giant trusts strangle the ambitions of small business in ways that U.S. law does not tolerate. In Japan, giant trusts are at times almost indistinguishable from government. Americans have been careful not to give anyone such power over their country. We have built a society hardly devoid of wrongs, but in which, perhaps uniquely, wrongs can be, and regularly are, righted by the independent actions of ordinary people.

Americans have a distinguished military history, too. It includes a much earlier war with the country that is now Libya. That earlier war wasn't fought in the Chadian desert to determine which tribe would manage a water hole. It was fought on the shores of the Libyan capital of Tripoli, to stop Libyan pirates from attacking U.S. commercial vessels on the high seas. We were clearly right, and we won, for all to see.

America's military history includes a successful war that stopped mighty totalitarian empires from Germany and Japan that were trampling over country after country, bombing our territory, sinking our ships, invading the traditional bastions of democracy, and stealing the productive output of our most important trading partners. We stood up against another mighty totalitarian empire, the Soviet Union, when it tried to cheat on our World War II truce lines in Berlin and Korea.

More recently, though, things haven't gone so well. Our efforts overseas have become more and more remote from the true interests of the American people, and the principles we stand for.

Americans have an interest in foreign affairs. They want and deserve security, peace, and prosperous trade. But these goals elude them. Their government's foreign policy has left them in constant peril of war with a seemingly unending list of enemies. Peril is found in places that neither Mrs. Eiseman nor most other Americans have ever heard of. Taxpapers are sacrificing nearly $1,000 a year for each member of each family, to support a military machine that does not allay the peril. And that doesn't include the hidden billions that the CIA is spending, or the cost of diplomatic missions. This expenditure is an enormous drain on the economy's ability to supply the goods and services that people want and that could make their lives more pleasurable.

Nearly a quarter century has passed since the Eisenhower administration stained the U.S. Constitution by overthrowing the legitimate government of the former Belgian Congo, now Zaire. We implanted a new government in the Congo that was thoroughly corrupted by Western business interests. Americans weren't told about the constitutional violations, or the corruption. They were just told that the good guys had won. Freedom would be preserved for Africans, and access to valuable minerals would be guaranteed for the American economy. But in 1983, the government we had established in the Congo continued to impose a murderous tyranny on its people. And instead of guaranteeing our mineral supplies, it daily held them hostage to a great economic and moral ransom. At considerable cost, we had achieved nothing and done great harm.

In August 1983, the month of Mrs. Eiseman's letter, Americans were shocked by the latest demonstration of what their government had wrought upon the Philippines. So very recently our relations in the Philippines had been wonderful. Americans had fought and died rescuing the islands from the Spanish and Japanese. After a shaky start early in the century, the U.S. appeared to have helped Filipinos obtain not only a genuine democracy, but also the liberal economic and educational institutions to make the democracy work. The U.S. had earned, and for a while actually *had*, the admiration and affection of millions of Filipinos.

But the State Department's global designs interfered, slowly at first, then radically during the Vietnam War. By August 1983, freedom and democracy in the Philippines had long been crushed, in the name of fighting communism. The Filipino people's friendship for the United States was squandered. Benigno Aquino, the most popular Filipino politician, lay dead under the wing of his commercial airliner at the Manila airport, only seconds after returning from refuge in the U.S. The long history of U.S. government cooperation with Philippine tyranny continued to unravel.

Ironically, just as in Zaire, one of the main freedoms the U.S. side had destroyed in the Philippines was freedom of the marketplace—free enterprise. We supported the nationalization of the Philippines' main industries. Where we can help it, we will not trust our allies with the economic liberty we say we are fighting for. And then we wonder at their ingratitude!

In Iran, the U.S. State Department had successfully overthrown a popular government that was not only anti-Communist, but led by a man who had successfully fought off the Soviet Union's attempt to occupy his country. This was done back in 1953, to protect an oil cartel whose interests were not at all synonymous with those of the American people. The result was a brutal tyranny for Iranians and high gasoline prices for Americans—then the almost inevitable revolution, the advent of a lunatic and rabidly anti-American government, the loss of Iranian oil altogether, and the seizure of American citizens as hostages. As if all this wasn't bad enough, it also allowed the Soviet Union to march into Afghanistan.

When U.S. foreign policy won, the American people lost. When the policy lost, we also lost, though often not quite as badly. When we were defeated in Southeast Asia, Indochina, wretchedly governed anyway, continued in agony. But the nearby nations, from Burma through Thailand, Malaysia, and on down to Australia—supposedly doomed to fall like dominoes—grew economically stronger and improved as trade partners. Politically, to the extent they changed at all, the domino countries became freer. Even the communist government of China, the supposed principal threat inspiring our enormous sacrifice in Vietnam, began behaving much more in accord with American desires, not only internationally, but even in its treatment of its own people. Then what was the sacrifice for?

As our policies betray us abroad, so they also do at home. The loss is not just in workers' hours, consumers' dollars, and soldiers' lives. The excuse of "national security" has been used to cloak a myriad of unconstitutional U.S. government invasions of our free society, from the break-in at Democratic party headquarters at the Watergate by Cuban CIA operatives to the clandestine manipulation of the AFL-CIO and many well-known businesses. Thugs have been secretly hired to perform unconstitutional acts for the U.S. government, then have carried on illegal activities that their government employers never contemplated, but dared not prosecute.

Corruption in American business has been not only tolerated, but, by much evidence, actively encouraged as an instrument of foreign policy. The result has been not just a moral stain, and the passing on to consumers of the cost of political bribery, but also the creation of monopolies and cartels that substantially elevate U.S. prices. Banks have been encouraged to alter their lending practices to the detriment of American borrowers. In the name of free markets, the U.S. has gone about the world rigging marketplaces.

As bad as anything, "national security" has provided a cloak under which the men who run a large part of the U.S. government have excused themselves from their responsibility to tell the truth to the people who elect them. U.S. citizens can't believe their leaders anymore, although some citizens in the press corps seem not to have learned that. We have been lied to through one war after another, the press often in naive complicity with the liars.

Forgotten are the words of Walter Lippmann, written after the disastrous U.S. invasion of Cuba at the Bay of Pigs: "A policy is bound to fail which deliberately violates our pledges and our principles, our treaties and our laws. . . . The American conscience is a reality. It will make hesitant and ineffectual, even if it does not prevent, an un-American policy. . . . In the great struggle with communism, we must find our strength by developing and applying our own principles, not in abandoning them."

All this did not need to be. It certainly does not need to continue.

WHAT follows is a reporter's view of the world as it relates to America. The view was formed during twenty years of traveling—some of it as a student tour leader, some of it as a Peace Corps volunteer, some of it as an unemployed, backpacking vagabond, and some of it, over the past thirteen years, as a reporter for the *Wall Street Journal*.

Much of that same twenty-year period has also been spent reporting on the domestic concerns of the American people. Those concerns—and the concerns of peoples overseas—are habitually ignored by the geopolitical strategists who for thirty-five years have committed us to endless and counterproductive entanglements abroad. And that is the reason for this book.

The book will dwell first on Zaire, for the American experience in Zaire seems to embody most of our characteristic foreign policy errors. What we could do wrong, we did in Zaire. It is an ultimate example, one that will make it easier to understand the errors we have committed at other crisis points around the world, and the ways in which they might be corrected.

CHAPTER TWO

THE BANKERS, THE BUSINESSMEN, AND THE LAWYERS

================IT IS September 24, 1980, in the Versailles Room of New York's St. Regis Hotel. Surrounded by marble walls, beneath chandeliers of cut Waterford crystal, forty-seven men and a sprinkling of women have gathered around white-linened tables at the invitation of the United States Chamber of Commerce. They have come to meet with some visiting officials from the far-off African republic of Zaire. Joining them, we may begin to learn why America's foreign relations have failed so.

Policy is being made here in the splendor of the St. Regis. Representatives from the great commercial banking houses are assembled here—Chase Manhattan, Citibank, Manufacturers Hanover Trust, and Irving Trust—as well as the more genteel Wall Street investment firms of Lehman Brothers Kuhn Loeb and Lazard Frères & Company. General Motors is represented. So are American Express, Texaco and Mobil oil companies, Newmont Mining Company, and a variety of shipping concerns.

Theodore Roosevelt IV of presidential blood is here representing Lehman Brothers, and Cyrus Vance, Jr., son of the recently departed secretary of state, is representing the worldwide shipowning and cargo-chartering interests of Skaarup Shipping Corporation. Orville L. Freeman, the former secretary of agriculture, is on the guest list representing Business International Corporation, a consulting firm.* Mary Lee Garrison, a foreign service careerist

*Freeman says he skipped the meeting and sent a subordinate.

8

who runs the Zaire (pronounced, "Zy-*ear*") desk at the State Department, is here representing the government.

Maurice Tempelsman, the international diamond magnate, prefers to keep a low business profile. He is represented at the St. Regis by several top aides. Recently, Tempelsman's low business profile has been threatened by gossip column items linking him romantically to Jacqueline Onassis. They have been photographed together on his yacht, and Mrs. Onassis is suing a photographer who harassed her daughter, Caroline Kennedy, outside Tempelsman's summer home.

Mrs. Onassis's son, John F. Kennedy, Jr., a college student, has spent the summer traveling in Africa in the employ of Tempelsman's operations. Her first husband's closest White House counselor, Theodore Sorensen, is Tempelsman's longtime lawyer. Sorensen has spent a bit of time in Zaire. One-fourth of all the world's diamonds come from there, and Tempelsman also has a stake in Zaire's rich copper lodes. Tempelsman, like many businessmen, has contributed generously to both major U.S. parties over the years. Belgian politics interest him as well; Belgium colonized Zaire, and arrangements made at the time of independence assured that the Belgians would retain considerable influence there. Tempelsman had the wife of the Belgian foreign minister on his payroll as a $20,000-a-year consultant before the foreign minister lost his job in a cabinet reshuffle a few months ago.

The Central Intelligence Agency may be represented in the Versailles Room, too, though, of course, we can't know by whom. Chase Manhattan and other big banks have provided cover for CIA operations at times by employing spies as bank officers.* Tempelsman has also employed at least one senior aide from CIA ranks (after the spy declared his retirement). Theodore Roosevelt's cousin Kermit Roosevelt spied for the CIA while working as a sales agent in the Middle East for big military contractors like Northrop. And Sorensen was President Carter's first, unsuccessful, choice to direct the CIA.

THIS is a tax write-off lunch. The guests at the St. Regis are mostly people accustomed to the tax write-off meal system. Companies pay for their senior employees' lunch, and often dinner, and then deduct the cost from taxable income as a business expense. The value of the meal isn't taxed as income to the eater himself, either. So 50 percent of the cost of dining, including the cost of the marble halls and cut Waterford crystal chandeliers required for the diner's comfort, is paid for out of the pockets of the millions of lathe operators, clerks, computer programmers, dirt farmers, druggists, and hod carriers who are harnessed collectively as the American taxpayer.

*There are numerous sources for this, including congressional investigators and former bank employees. It's been widely published and never denied.

But today's bill at the St. Regis is a little different, because when it is finally passed through the Chamber of Commerce to its member companies, much of the bill not covered by the American taxpayer will be forwarded in the form of fees and business costs to the citizens of Zaire. American taxpayers are having a rough time of it during these years of slow growth, high interest rates, and inflation. But next to their counterparts in Zaire, they have no complaints. A survey completed a few weeks earlier in this summer of 1980 by a team that included members of the United States Peace Corps concluded that malnutrition kills more than one-third of Zaire's citizens and leaves countless others with permanent brain damage, usually suffered in youth. The 25 to 28 million people of Zaire, half of them children, are literally starving to death in their mud huts.

Few Americans in the tax-free dining class, and certainly none of those at the St. Regis, consume three martinis with lunch. (Three martinis is the standard of extravagance that has been declared unacceptable by President Jimmy Carter.*) Even without the martinis, however, the vichyssoise, chicken florentine, strawberry tortes, and appropriate Italian wines served up by the St. Regis this day would leave the average Zairian walleyed. What's more, there is a final course to come for these financiers and industrialists, and it is far more expensive to the taxpaying citizens of the United States and Zaire than was the food that preceded it. That course is a vision of the world the way the tax-free dining class would like it to be.

AS the coffee is poured, Citoyen Namwisi Ma Koyi rises to read his prepared speech. ("Citoyen," or citizen, is the form of address that Namwisi's boss and Zaire's autocratic ruler, Mobutu Sese Seko, has decreed for his nation.) Citoyen Namwisi is the Zairian minister of finance, and his coal-black body is decked out in a well-tailored Western business suit.

"First of all," Namwisi says, "the government of Zaire wishes to keep its creditors and its current and potential economic partners informed of the progress made in the laborious process of rehabilitating and developing our country." He tells the creditors and economic partners around the Versailles Room that the laborious process is perking along fine. "Zaire is now doing noticeably better," he says. "The foundation for the improvement of the country's economic and financial condition is being strengthened daily.... Measures taken by the Zairian authorities, especially during the last twelve months, have begun to bear fruit."

Citoyen Namwisi admits his country still has a few problems. But he blames them on events beyond the control of him or his audience. He men-

---

*A reticent reformer, Carter was trying to ask Congress to end the government subsidy to luxury dining without directly embarrassing its rich, but usually sober, beneficiaries. So instead of attacking the actual $35 worth of viands and claret, he attacked the phony $7.50 worth of gin. He was thwarted by public apathy and the hotel-restaurant lobby.

tions "the sudden reversal of copper prices in 1974–1975," and "weather problems." And he complains about "the two foreign invasions of Shaba province." Shaba, formerly known as Katanga, holds most of Zaire's mineral wealth.

As everyone in the Versailles Room today knows, French and Belgian paratroopers, with U.S. military transport and logistical help, put down rebellions in Shaba in 1977 and again in 1978. These Western interventions, however, aren't the invasions to which Namwisi is referring. Nobody in the room likes to think of the arrival of French, Belgian, and American military forces in the middle of Africa to seize the world's richest copper and cobalt lodes as an "invasion." It is a "rescue mission." By "invasions," Namwisi is referring to alleged *prior* invasions from Soviet-influenced Angola. Invaders from Angola were the official justification for calling in Western troops.

At the time, the black invaders from Angola were reported in the American press as having carried out an indiscriminate massacre of hundreds of whites. It was also reported that only the arrival of U.S., French, and Belgian forces saved the entire white community of mining managers and their families and related personnel from similar execution. Most Americans who can remember the events—even most people in the Versailles Room—accept this story as true, because it's all they've heard.

For example, at the time of the 1978 conflict the Associated Press, quoting "survivors," reported, "Rebel tribesmen on a rampage of murder and rape slaughtered as many as 200 persons in a 'hunt for the white man.'" United Press International reported, "Rebel troops went into a frenzy of killing and looting in which they massacred at least 150 whites." The *Washington Post* said this "may turn out to have been the worst massacre of Europeans in modern African history." Then Walter Cronkite, perhaps the United States's most trusted news source, opened the "CBS Evening News" on May 19, 1978, with these words: "Good Evening. The worst fears in the rebel invasion of Zaire's Shaba province reportedly have been realized. Rebels being routed from the mining town of Kolwezi are reported to have killed a number of Europeans."*

What a judgment on the value of lives! It is clear now, and should have been then, that far more blacks died in the violence than did Europeans— and far more than that had been dying regularly for years from malnutrition and preventable disease. Big powers habitually discount the death of Third Worlders. This is a real problem, not just for the people dying, but also sometimes for the United States.

In this summer of 1980, even as Citoyen Namwisi speaks at the St. Regis, bodies of countless peasants litter the landscape of El Salvador. American

*Thanks to *Africa News* of Durham, North Carolina, which rounded up these quotes. They have been verified by the author.

support for the government there won't be broadly questioned until later, when three American nuns and another woman church worker are gunned down. All through 1979, Soviet weaponry was annihilating Afghan villagers. By much evidence, the weapons may have included poison gas that had been outlawed under international agreement. Few cared, until Soviet troops appeared in December, creating a crisis. When the same thing happened in Laos, and no Soviet troops appeared, few seemed to care at all.

Then there is Iran, a country to which Zaire is often compared. Like Iran, Zaire has resources the U.S. needs. Like Iran, Zaire was saddled long ago with an unpopular, Western-contolled government. And so Zaire is a candidate to have a very unpleasant revolution—like Iran's. In 1978 and 1979, countless thousands of Iranian civilians suffered brutalities from American-supplied weapons. U.S. guns killed them, U.S. cattle prods burned them, U.S. experts taught their oppressors how to torture them. American citizens remained largely unaware of this, and their president, Carter, went out of his way to embrace the Iranian shah. Now, in September 1980, the shah has been replaced, and the fate of the world is thought to hang on what happens to fifty American hostages—a relative handful, who will eventually be released unharmed.

Sympathy for the fifty hostages is not misplaced, of course, any more than sympathy for the four murdered church workers in El Salvador. But a refusal to see such events in their context leaves the United States perpetually unprepared for crises abroad, when these crises are the natural consequence not only of events long visible, but often, in part, of the U.S.'s own actions.

As for Walter Cronkite, his concern for fairness is usually exemplary. Most of his journalistic colleagues and most of his listeners—the American people—are likewise of good will, including a lot of the businessmen in the Versailles Room. But in the Shaba episode, journalists and their audiences alike were ready to plunge into action based on misunderstandings of local conditions—because the news stories about Shaba, like so many secondhand accounts of events in El Salvador, Afghanistan, Laos, Iran, and other Third World countries published in the American press, weren't true.

The *Washington Post* later made at least a partial retraction of the Shaba massacre story, though with considerably less visibility than the "massacre" got. It said that the original reports had come from Western and Zairian government sources, not from firsthand observation. These sources had "exaggerated," the *Post* explained.

Obviously, the government sources had lied, in order to gain sympathy for what is still generally described as a "rescue mission." It certainly was a rescue mission, but all the talk of rape and massacre merely obscured the fact that what was really being rescued were copper and cobalt mines, and a dictatorial government.

If you go to Kolwezi, the mining center that was at the heart of the fighting,* residents both black and white will tell you that the Shaba uprisings of 1977 and 1978 involved not so much invaders, but mostly local people, who are predominantly of the Lunda tribe, or ethnic group. These local Balunda ("Ba" is plural) were suffering under the same miserable conditions as other Zairians. In addition, they had long resented the domination of the central government by ethnic groups from the north and west of Zaire. (The Associated Press dispatch quoted above called the rebels "tribesmen," which conveys an inaccurate picture of painted savages; but the dispatch didn't explain the ethnic divisions of central Africa, which might have shed light on what was happening.)

The Shabans revolted when a small military force, mostly of fellow Balunda, arrived from across the nearby border with Angola. Ironically, most of this force had been trained not by the Soviets, as was being suggested, but by the West. That happened soon after Zaire (then the Congo) became independent in 1960. The Balunda had wanted to make their home province an independent country. Many Westerners with business interests there had encouraged them to secede and become independent. These European and American advisors feared that the central government might try to nationalize mineral resources, and they hoped to secure continued Western ownership of the mines through an alliance with an independent Shaba (then known as Katanga).

That early secession was put down by a force from the United Nations. Many defeated Balunda soldiers followed the Western mercenaries who had fought with them into Angola, which was then a Portuguese colony. These Western-trained secessionists and their sons were basically the same militiamen who entered Zaire in the Shaba incidents of 1977 and 1978. So they hardly qualify for the role of communist aggressors in which they were cast. Family and friends welcomed them back and joined them once more in rebellion against the central government.

In other words, practically all the "invaders" lived in the place they were "invading," and most had never left there. They were challenging the authority of a central government that had never been popular in Shaba. Now the government was unpopular throughout Zaire, for reasons wholly transcending socialism, capitalism, or Soviet or American alliances. The rebellion was overwhelmingly supported by the residents of Kolwezi.

Of course, the Zairian government of Mobutu Sese Seko put out a different story. To encourage Western intervention against the rebellion, Zaire said that Cuban troops—some 20,000 of whom were busy propping up the government of Angola—were fighting with the Shaba invaders. There has never been any evidence of this, and it almost certainly wasn't true. But President Carter immediately began accusing Cuba, first of equipping and training the

*My most recent visit to the area was in May 1980, four months before the luncheon in the Versailles Room.

rebels, then, failing evidence of that, just of not restraining them. (Carter's ultimate suggestion that Cuba had a moral responsibility to use its troops in the area to *prevent* the Balunda from rebelling against their dictatorial government certainly has an ironic touch.)

The administration line was widely accepted by an American people that, despite decades of being misled, still really wants to believe its government. The *Wall Street Journal* reported from Washington (not Kolwezi), "The invasion of Zaire's copper-rich Shaba province by guerrillas based in Angola...heightened administration concern about communist expansion in Africa. There is widespread disagreement over how to check Soviet and Cuban aggression, however."* By this time, it was almost hopeless to point out, spitting in the wind of accepted propaganda, that the problem in Zaire didn't involve Soviet or Cuban aggression—or racial massacres.

While the rebels controlled Kolwezi, according to interviews with people who lived through it, they conducted a house-to-house hunt-down of one or two dozen mining overseers, some white and some black, who were blamed for the death and mistreatment of miners. These men were singled out and murdered. But apparently even this didn't happen until after the town was attacked, first by Zairian government troops and then by the U.S.-supplied French and Belgians. (European reporters have written that the shooting of whites started when President Mobutu ordered Zairian government troops to kill some in order to ensure Western intervention, but this has never been substantiated.)

In the anarchy that prevailed as the rebellion crumbled, there was some looting and at least one widely reported case of multiple rape (of a white woman, which is no doubt why it was widely reported). It isn't clear whether the looters or rapists were rebels, Zairian government soldiers, civilians, or all three. There were reports of random shootings by unknown persons, and other atrocities attendant to war. There was also a lot of machine gun and mortar fighting, and many died in it. In all, of the several thousand whites who lived there, about 130 were killed.

But whites living in Kolwezi in 1980 recalled no indiscriminate massacre. Some whites said they were forced from their homes by French paratroops and made to fly to "safety" in Europe against their will. Some, including wives and children, even had to pay their own way back to Kolwezi. They did so, which was the ultimate demonstration of how unthreatened they felt.

All available evidence is that far more blacks were killed by the white "rescuers" than whites were killed by black rebels. Belgian soldiers reported seeing half a dozen whites die from gunfire from French troops. Before the Western forces arrived, most of the eighty-eight U.S. citizens in Kolwezi

---

*Three months later, another *Journal* reporter, Jonathan Spivak, actually went to Zaire, and did perhaps the year's best reporting from there. He avoided the official version of the Shaba episode, and told instead about conditions he observed in the country.

had been peacefully evacuated by truck and helicopter provided by Morrison-Knudsen Company, the construction firm that employed many of them. Fourteen chose to stay. One was killed, it's not clear by whom, apparently while driving through a combat zone trying to reach his German wife. She and the other Americans were unharmed.

Still, when the subject comes up, the Western press and people like Namwisi Ma Koyi speaking in the Versailles Room of the St. Regis Hotel continue to talk of Angolan invasions and massacres. To protect against this alleged Soviet-backed menace, the Zairian government persuaded its Western patrons to supply new arms and to station troops there (for "training purposes" only, of course). This new strength was then paraded before the bone-hungry pepole of Zaire to discourage them from further protesting their predicament.

The government of Zaire and the Western interests that use that government weren't the only ones exploiting the Shabans' plight. The international Left also found the invasion story convenient. A European-based group called the National Front for the Liberation of the Congo (Zaire is the name given by Mobutu) quickly claimed credit for leading the invading army, though it disclaimed any Balunda partisanship. This "liberation" group was largely unknown in Kolwezi or anywhere else in Zaire, and had no visible power. But its emissaries in Europe and the U.S. convinced leftists to endorse it as a kind of exile government. Much of the press also accepted the accuracy of these claims.

Thus the Shaba incidents became archetypal examples of Third World conflict. The truth vanished, as a local problem was translated into international melodrama. Local people suffered and nurtured their resentment, while the meolodrama suited vested interests elsewhere. Not a few of these suited vested interests were present in vested suits, in the Versailles Room of the St. Regis on September 24, 1980.

CITOYEN NAMWISI turns the subject from military invasion to money, and the International Monetary Fund. In 1978, an IMF team had taken up quarters in Zaire's central bank. It was and is a sort of minigovernment sent in from the U.S. and Western Europe, essentially to try to run Zaire's economy. The IMF operates such minigovernments in about forty countries.

Why would a country let an international outfit like the IMF take over an important function of national government? Namwisi tells his audience, "We recognize that Zaire should provide tangible proof to the international community as a whole of its serious efforts to redress its economy and finances. . . . Our relations with the International Monetary Fund offer proof of such resolve." What he means is, his government wants new loans, and it wants more time to pay the old ones. Installing an IMF team is the West's price for keeping credit lines open.

This is all part of a giant international flimflam, which accounts for a large part of the half a trillion dollars or so now owed by the poorer countries to the richer ones. Much of this debt is owed even though the poorer countries never received the money they supposedly borrowed. This debt is one of the most important unsettling factors in the world today. If you look beneath such boiling pots as Poland and Central America, you will find this debt, burning.

The debt system isn't as complicated as it sounds, and is worth a minute to understand. Theoretically, the IMF operates under the auspices of the United Nations, to promote international cooperation in keeping currencies stable and interchangeable. But the IMF is controlled by the West, because the West supplies most of the money that the IMF lends out.

The IMF lends to countries to help balance their international payments, if, for example, they import more than they export. A line of credit from the IMF guarantees that whoever is selling goods to such a country will get paid, even though the country that is buying the goods hasn't earned enough money on the world market to cover its debts. Such a loan can be looked at two ways. In one sense, it is an artificial device to help poor countries buy things beyond their current means. In another sense, it is an artificial device to allow businessmen in rich countries to sell things they otherwise couldn't sell. In any event, once the IMF makes such a loan, it often demands control over the borrowing country's importing and exporting, which can lead to control over the entire economy.

The IMF has a sister institution, the World Bank, that was originally intended to be much more important to Third World countries. The World Bank makes big loans for development projects like dams and airports. Of course, heavy development borrowing is a form of importing, and often leads to trade imbalances. So taking a loan from the World Bank is often a prelude to taking a loan from the IMF, which in turn often leads to the IMF's grabbing control of a country's financial management.

In the 1970s, the IMF role broadened. Much of the development lending that had been done by the World Bank and other international organizations was taken over by private banks in the United States and the former colonial countries of Western Europe. These private banks, flush with Arab oil money and other funds, have found big profits making direct loans to Third World governments. Yet the IMF has continued its role as regulator whenever a country can't pay its debts. So in a pracitcal sense, the IMF often acts as a U.N.-authorized collection agent for the big banks. By the end of 1981, the IMF exercised control not only in Zaire, but in such other large countries as the Philippines, Kenya, India, South Korea, Pakistan, Thailand, and Turkey.

At the St. Regis, Namwisi describes the IMF control of Zaire's finances in a way designed to please his audience. He says, "In order to be able to use the financial resources put at its disposal by the IMF, Zaire must adhere to a series of budgetary and monetary performance criteria." What Namwisi really means doesn't take a degree in economics to understand.

The IMF team will make sure that any money Zaire gets through sale of its resources is sent back out again to repay Western bankers. Enough spare parts and fuel will be allowed in to maintain the mining industry. And Zairian officials will be allowed to skim off enough in graft to keep them cooperative. Under this arrangement, much of the money paid for Zairian minerals never even arrives in Zaire except as a bookkeeping entry.

Zaire's external debt is in the neighborhood of six and a half billion dollars, or about $240 for every man, woman, and child in the country, against their average per capita income of about $127 a year.

The Western banks lend to Third World countries at relatively high interest rates. Details of the loans usually aren't made public, but overall profit records show that most banks get a higher rate of return from their Third World business than they do from their domestic loans. The ten U.S. banks with the biggest international lending business get, on average, about half of their profits from overseas loans. The biggest, Citibank, was getting about two-thirds of all its profits from these loans as Namwisi spoke in 1980. (The Citibank profit share from overseas loans reached 82.2 percent in 1977.) This shift in profit centers represents a tremendous diversion of lending resources, coinciding with the sharp rise in interest rates in the United States and a critical drying up of capital investment in basic U.S. industry.

If all this needed capital is being shipped overseas, one might expect that the Third World countries would at least *benefit* from it. And in some cases, they do. But in many others, maybe the majority, they don't, because this very expensive money isn't invested in sensible, productive ways. Although the money supposedly comes from the heartland of capitalism, almost none of the investment decisions are made by the free market. Most of the money is fed to central planners running Third World governments. Few of these planners are democratically chosen. Many, like Mobutu in Zaire, hold office because of U.S. intervention. Most are corrupt or naive or both, often to a mind-boggling degree.

To the bankers, it doesn't matter, because they have ways of collecting. When they lend at home, they must depend on the money's being invested productively in order to generate funds for repayment. Overseas, the repayment money is in the ground, in the form of minerals, and the taxpayer-funded IMF will see that it gets properly channeled. If necessary, the taxpayer-funded marines and paratroops will see to it. So the money flows, but instead of being guided by Adam Smith's "unseen hand," much of it is merely grabbed by sticky fingers. In Zaire's case, almost all of it has been.

Zaire now owes so much that its vast mineral exports barely meet the interest payments on its debt. When copper prices dip and interest rates rise, such as happened in the late 1970s, the exports don't quite do that. So the debt swells, and the IMF must be there at Zaire's central bank to seize any available spare change, lest Zaire try to spend some income feeding its people instead of fulfilling its international responsibilities.

It is the men in the Versailles Room who are getting paid. Namwisi announces: "I am happy to inform you that, overall, these diverse criteria have been scrupulously adhered to. . . . I can confirm to you that the government's budget is strictly controlled at a price you can well imagine."

Few in the audience really believe things are getting better for Zaire. The man from Citibank assures a reporter that he doesn't. But it's important to hear these things said. The men in this room depend on Zaire's reputation for solvency and reliability. Without that reputation, Western governments (including the one in Washington) might not be politically able to continue supplying their taxpayers' money and military force to support the system.

ONE justification is usually offered to Congress and the American voter for their continued support of the Mobutu government. That is the danger that Western industry might be cut off from Zaire's strategic minerals, say, by a leftist government. In fact, however, there really is not much danger of a cutoff at all.

War could halt production temporarily, in which event there are stockpiles. Or, as in the case of Iran, U.S. support for a hated dictatorship could engender an anti-Americanism so zealous that it might, for a while, override the economic impetus to trade. But that is a possibility the U.S. could still avoid in Zaire, and even in Iran such irrationalty may be short-lived. In the end, Zaire cannot eat its cobalt, diamonds, copper, and other minerals. Any Zairian government would have to be masochistic not to want to sell these items to whoever will pay for them.

Fox example, the government of Angola, which is the very prototype of the Soviet-influenced, socialist government from which it is thought Zaire must be protected, happily pumps Angolan oil into U.S. tankers. The Angolan government will likely continue doing so just as long as Gulf Oil Company keeps paying Angola more than $500 million a year, the going world price for the oil. Cuba and Vietnam would like to sell goods to the U.S., too, if the U.S. government would let them.

So the flow of minerals from Zaire is unlikely to stop, even if Zaire lands a new dictatorship of an extreme leftist sort, which it probably won't anyway. What *could* change, though, if Zaire changes leadership, is who gets the money. And in this, the interests of the Western banks and Western governments are intertwined in ways the public little realizes. In fact, if you analyze Zaire's $6.5 billion in debt, you find that almost *none* of it arises from anything that much benefited the Zairian people, who are being slowly starved to pay it off.

As the group meets in the St. Regis, for example, relatives of French president Valery Giscard d'Estaing and the companies they run, including large banks, are pulling literally billions of dollars out of the Zairian and other African economies. The banks connected to the Giscard d'Estaing family have lent a lot of money, secured by Africa's minerals. As a rule, this money never reached Africa, but rather was forwarded to European manufacturing companies connected to the Giscard d'Estaing family. With the money, the companies built high-priced showpiece items in Africa that Africans didn't really need, at what apparently was considerable profit for the Europeans. In the case of Zaire alone, contracts for skyscrapers and other lavish buildings, and a billion-dollar satellite and microwave communications system, all involving Giscard d'Estaing family interests, account for close to a third of the foreign debt (much of which is made up of mounting finance costs).

This is the money that the IMF is strangling the Zairian economy to collect. Most Zairians have never seen the fancy buildings. Most have never seen a telephone, and live a day or more's hard travel from the nearest electricity. So they don't need the ultrasophisticated communications system, which came complete with TV studios. Yet in December 1980, when the communications system was declared finished (it broke down almost immediately), its French manufacturer announced that Zaire was now "one of the first countries in the world to possess its own domestic satellite-communications network."

The president of that manufacturing concern was Philippe Giscard d'Estaing, the first cousin and lifelong close friend of the president of France. The contracts for the communications systems *and* the fancy buildings were awarded during the presidency of Valery Giscard d'Estaing, who twice sent French troops to Zaire to protect the Mobutu government. Members of his family, or companies in which they hold high positions, have had extensive business dealings in Gabon, Morocco, Chad, the Central African Republic, Cameroon, Ivory Coast, Mauritania, Niger, and Upper Volta. The governments of many of these countries are heavily obligated to the French government for the military support that keeps them in power.*

Belgium, another of the three countries whose military might regularly bails out Mobutu, also holds roughly a third of the Zairian debt. This mainly involves the banking and industrial trust called Société Général du Belgique, which in colonial days owned many of Zaire's mines and now runs them on contract. Société Général is in large part owned by the king of Belgium as a personal business venture. Its ties to other political leaders in Brussels are myriad. As one investigates these holdings, the availability of Western troops to support the government of Zaire becomes less wondrous.

The man from Manufacturers Hanover leans across the strawberries in the Versailles Room to tell a reporter how the system can work for a U.S. company. "We don't have any exposure in Zaire," he says. "It's all government guaranteed." What he means is that his bank has arranged for its

*Details may be found in a page-one article in the *Wall Street Journal*, April 23, 1981.

loans to Zaire to be guaranteed by the U.S. Export-Import Bank, a federal agency. So if Zaire doesn't repay the money it owes to Manufacturers Hanover, the U.S. taxpayer is obligated to repay it. Even though Manufacturers Hanover and its affiliates have lent hundreds of millions of dollars to Zaire, and are collecting interest, the bank doesn't have to worry about its investment.

The Export-Import Bank functions as a welfare arrangement for business that makes most government welfare programs for individuals look penurious by comparison. The Ex-Im bank uses tax revenues to make or guarantee loans that finance the sale of American goods and services abroad. This provides jobs, and profits, at home. The Ex-Im bank is considered necessary because competing industrialized countries like France and Japan have similar institutions that supply tax revenues to aid export businesses.

At the end of 1981, the Ex-Im bank reported $38.4 billion outstanding in direct loans and loan guarantees, including $624 million covering exports to Zaire. The bank is one of several loan and loan guarantee agencies the government operates to stimulate foreign sales. These agencies had close to $80 billion of taxpayer funds at risk in 1982. One such agency, the Commodities Credit Corporation, guaranteed loans to Poland of $680 million to buy American food. Early in 1982, this federal agency was called on to fork over $71.3 million to a group of ten big U.S. banks when Poland, under Soviet-ordered martial law, failed to pay for the food on schedule. In 1981, U.S. taxpayers had shelled out $158 million to bail out the banks on their bad loans to Poland. With things getting worse in Poland under martial law, that figure was expected to grow soon to nearly $400 million.

One might imagine that great care would go into parceling out these taxpayer guarantees to business. But a third such agency, the Overseas Private Investment Corporation,* with $4.9 billion in risks outstanding in 1982, is directed by a board including Maurice Stans, who, in 1975, pleaded guilty to three counts of campaign fund reporting violations and two counts of accepting illegal campaign contributions.

These transgressions involved contributions from businesses with big foreign investments, and there were strong suggestions that the implied promise of federal favoritism was used to help lure some of the money. Stans lived his life of crime while serving as President Nixon's secretary of commerce and reelection campaign financier. He was fined all of $5,000 for what he did, and six years later was chosen by President Reagan to supervise government support of private foreign investment.

MANUFACTURERS HANOVER got Export-Import Bank guarantees as lead lender on a project in Zaire that will cost something over $1 billion if

---

*So far, OPIC has prided itself on being profitable, even repaying to the Treasury some of its initial taxpayer seed money. Obviously, a turn of fortune could change that.

it's ever finished. (Most of the money is being supplied by other banks in various syndicates, and by direct loans from the Export-Import Bank.) The project is a power transmission line across eleven hundred miles of rugged, often jungly terrain. The line will carry electricity from the huge dam at Inga, on the Congo River near the Atlantic Ocean, to Shaba, the mining province in the interior. The Inga dam itself had to be expanded to provide extra electricity for the line.

The Inga-Shaba project is being billed as the longest power transmission line ever built, and it may be every bit of that. The problem, besides the fact that it's the better part of a decade behind schedule and the cost has risen to approximately double the original estimate, is that Shaba itself abounds with rivers whose hydroelectric potential is untapped.

Many people, including some American employees helping engineer and build the power line in Zaire, say that the Zairian mining industry could get all the power it needs from dams on these nearby rivers, and at a small fraction of the cost of the dazzlingly sophisticated Inga-Shaba line. That was exactly the conclusion of at least two engineering studies done for the government of Zaire before the power line was started. But the studies were discarded. It was also the opinion, stated in writing, of the Belgian-led company that ran the mines (an offshoot of Société Général). But that opinion was ignored.

New studies were undertaken, recommending the line. Significantly, an engineering technique was intentionally employed making it difficult or impossible for any electricity to be siphoned from the line before it gets to Shaba. So the line won't be able to light up the lives of the millions of Zairians who live along its 1,100-mile path, and who are totally without electricity. For them, the giant stanchions and droopy cables are at best an eyesore.

At worst, the line is a constant reminder of their political and economic servitude. Any one of them with a few sticks of dynamite could knock the power line out of commission. It presents an almost impossible security problem in a country with a long record of civil strife. Sabotage aside, some of the strung cables sag so low as to appear a safety hazard for unsophisticated people who might try to touch them.

With all these arguments against the line, one may reasonably ask why it was ever ordered. Plenty of Zairians and Americans, some in the State Department, say there are two real reasons the power line is being built: first, to provide a big construction contract for U.S. industry in return for U.S. support of the Mobutu regime; and second, to give Mobutu control over the flow of electricity to Shaba. Control of electricity by Mobutu might discourage secessionist movements, like the ones in the early 1960s, or further rebellions, like the ones in 1977 and 1978.

All this suggests that about $1.5 billion in mineral revenues that Zaire desperately needs to save the lives of its people is being wasted on the power line to feed the greed of Mobutu and his American supporters. There is ample evidence to support this conclusion.

A series of mostly secret cables between the U.S. embassy in Zaire and the State Department in 1965* reports the progress of a team of engineers from the United Nations Development Program. The team was headed by an American and included Italians, Frenchmen, and Belgians. The team was reported "opposed to the Inga project as too ambitious and improperly placed." A year later, the embassy reported that a second study, by the Belgian Institute of Economic and Social Research, had concluded, "The solution of refining the mineral products of Katanga [now Shaba] with Inga power is . . . rejected since the slightly lower price of electricity [at the Inga dam site] would not justify the transportation costs [of constructing and operating the power transmission line]." In a 1967 cable to Washington, the embassy itself argued against the project, and said, "Matters like the rehabilitation of transportation and agriculture would seem to have priority. . . ."

But after the Nixon administration took office in 1969, the new U.S. ambassador to Zaire, Sheldon Vance, began to boost the prospects of American companies wanting to build the power line. Encouraged from Washington, Vance apparently did quite an effective selling job.

Still, in 1971, the U.S. consul stationed in Shaba reported problems. He cabled Washington that Henri A. Liekens, the Belgian expatriate in charge of electrical services for the mining company, favored building a much cheaper dam and power station at nearby Busanga, right there in Shaba. The mining company went on record in favor of this local dam. The U.S. diplomatic cable also noted, however, that "Liekens believes that the Congolese governmnent might not approve the Busanga project for political reasons."

Apparently, Liekens, the Belgian electrical expert, was right about that. A few months later, Mobutu, as the U.S. suggested, decided to ignore the power potential of Busanga and build an 1,100-mile transmission line instead. Even then, the U.S. embassy in Brussels warned the State Department in a classified cable, "Neither World Bank nor Belgian government greatly interested in financing Inga-Shaba Transmission Line Project since it seemed based more on political than economic considerations."

But with U.S. taxpayers available to guarantee the money through the Export-Import Bank, and with Manufacturers Hanover and some affiliates willing to collect interest on a sure-thing loan, the project got under way. This was good news for several companies, including General Electric Company, which became a big subcontractor on the project—though not entirely by its own doing.

Ambassador Vance boasted in a cable to the State Department on July 11, 1972, "It was this embassy in the first instance last August that provided

*Declassified, and obtained by the author under the Freedom of Information Act, as were other cables referred to in this section.

G.E. with initial info [on] this project and urged them make effort obtain contract. Ambassador has followed matter in detail and has used his influence to fix appointments for G.E. on several occasions with top-level Govt. officials. No embassy in Kinshasa has given more all-out support to their national companies that we have. . . ."

The major contractor that got work on the line, with supplies coming from G.E., is Morrison-Knudsen Company, an engineering and construction concern based in Boise, Idaho. Both Vance himself and Morrison-Knudsen officials on the project say it was Vance who first called the project to Morrison-Knudsen's attention, and who guided the engineers from Idaho through the complexities of Zairian politics.

Thomas J. Hayes, then president of Morrison-Knudsen's international engineering subsidiary, and the executive who got the project going, recalled in a 1981 interview, "I hadn't been to Zaire before. I hadn't heard anything about it till we got a call from the American ambassador, Vance, [and] a note that Zaire was interested in getting American firms in there."

It turns out that Hayes of Morrison-Knudsen, and Vance, the ambassador, had been old friends, dating from the early 1960s when Vance worked in the U.S. embassy in Ethiopia and Hayes was in the Army Corps of Engineers there. "When I first went there [to Zaire], it was not with the idea of this line," Hayes said. "We got several small engineering contracts, and the line came up about six months later. I can't remember whether I talked first with Vance or Mobutu about it."

Morrison-Knudsen contends that the money for the Inga-Shaba project is not being wasted. It says that only such a power line can supply enough electricity for the Zairian copper industry to grow the way it should. The company makes this argument through the man who represents it in its Zairian dealings, a highly qualified Washington lawyer. He is that selfsame Sheldon Vance, erstwhile ambassador, now in private practice!

Vance won't say how much Morrison-Knudsen is paying him. Nor will he disclose whether G.E., for whom he boasted of doing so much, is also a client. He does say he represents other U.S. companies doing business in Zaire, but he declines to identify them. He also declines to say whether he used his influence as ambassador to win them contracts, or say how much he earns shooting trouble for companies on his trips to Africa. "In the legal profession, we don't discuss clients," he says. Nevertheless, if the power line does get finished, and Mobutu chooses to name it the Sheldon Vance Transmission Line, the honor may be considered appropriate.

IF Vance, on his business trips, asked enough questions at the U.S. embassy in Zaire, he might have heard an opinion different from his own about the Inga-Shaba project. Timothy Hauser, an officer in the economic section of the embassy, openly confessed to a visiting reporter in this summer of 1980 that Shaba had "a sufficient number of hydroelectric sites to tap" to meet its needs without the power line. He agreed that politics was "an element of" the decision to build the line, and he observed that the basis of Mobutu's decisions is "seldom on the cost-benefit analysis."

The embassy's chief political officer, Robert Boggs, told the same reporter this about the power line: "It's just costing more and more and more and more. It's taking so long that a lot of the equipment they're putting in at the two ends is deteriorating." Soon Boggs would be transferred to Washington and become State Department desk officer for Zaire. But the U.S. government would continue its support of the Inga-Shaba project. In the State Department, the people with the closest knowledge of local problems, and without an ax to grind in defense of an existing policy, often are the least listened to.*

In Shaba, a large copper mining expansion project had been a primary excuse for starting the power line a decade earlier. By 1980, the project had been indefinitely shelved, pending either higher copper prices or a cheaper refining process for the unusually rich ore. The mining project's big American backer is Maurice Tempelsman, the diamond magnate and Jacqueline Onassis's friend.

Project or no project, nobody seems worried about whether payment for the power line will be forthcoming—not Morrison-Knudsen or G.E., the contractors; nor Manufacturers Hanover, the lead financer; nor Vance, the lawyer. The good citizens of the U.S. and Zaire will tighten their belts as much as is necessary to see they get their money.

IN fact, for creditors of a basically bankrupt African nation, none of the luncheon guests at the St. Regis looks worried. The man from the Intercontinental Hotel chain (then a unit of Pan American World Airways, which sold it to a European group in 1981) tells a reporter, "At all times, the government [of Zaire] has done its very best to honor its obligations to us." The Intercontinental Hotel in Zaire is the only one in its class in the capital. For the traffic of visiting businessmen, it has no real competition. "It's been a very good one for us," the Intercontinental executive says. "They've made a profit every year since they've been open, since 1971."

On investigation, it turns out that the man Intercontinental hired to manage its hotel in Zaire is Tom D. Crowley. Crowley's wife's brother is Lannon Walker. Walker is deputy assistant secretary of state for African affairs, and is considered by some to be the most ardent advocate within the State Department for support of the Mobutu regime. In 1979, he pleaded successfully in congressional hearings for approval of continued financing by the Ex-Im Bank of the increasing cost overruns on the Inga-Shaba project. And he is

---

*Neither Hauser nor Boggs complained to me about that, but a lot of other foreign service officers have.

the boss of Mary Lee Garrison, the State Department desk officer for Zaire, who is at the Versailles Room of the St. Regis, representing the government. Small world.

AFTER Citoyen Namwisi finishes his speech, there are questions. People ask if debt payments are being made on schedule. They ask which foreign investment opportunities look good. Namwisi has a translator at his side (Zaire's national language is French). But he needs more than translation. After almost every question, Namwisi bends his ear down to the mouth of an eldery looking American seated nearby, who whispers to Namwisi. Then Namwisi replies.

The elderly looking American who seems to have all the answers is David A. Morse, seventy-three, a Washington lawyer, a former secretary of labor in the Truman administration, and a former director general of the International Labor Organization (a U.N. agency). Morse is now senior counsel to the U.N. Development Program and other organizations dispensing aid to the Third World. Simultaneously, he also hires himself out to countries, such as Zaire, that receive aid. He sells these countries adivce on how to handle their international relations.

Versatility is Morse's stock in trade. At one of the luncheon tables, for example, are a vice-president for government relations from International Harvester Company and a representative of Gaucher Pringle Limited, a Montreal-based engineering concern. In conversation, they disclose that International Harvester has taken on a Gaucher Pringle affiliate, Sofati, as a partner in bidding for a large transportation project in Zaire. It seems a wise choice of partners because the chairman of Sofati is David A. Morse, who is, after all, advising the Zairian government on how to spend its money. According to Gaucher Pringle, Sofati rakes in about $50 million a year running training programs and the like in Third World countries. (In 1981, Morse resigned as chairman of Sofati.)

Morse's law firm, Surrey & Morse, also represents Senegal, Egypt, Sudan, Romania, Venezuela, Botswana, China, and other countries. Before the people of Iran kicked the shah and the United States out of that country, Morse was vice-chairman of a company building a big dam and water project there.

Morse's law partner, Walter Surrey, was once profiled on page one of the *Wall Street Journal* as the very prototype of the Washington "rainmaker." That means, the *Journal* explained, that he is the kind of influential lawyer or lobbyist whose presence behind the scenes tends to make things happen "as if by magic," regardless of anything he does officially. Writing in *Inquiry* magazine, John Cummings, a *Newsday* reporter, described Surrey as "a charter member of the old boy network of U.S. intelligence . . . of the OSS [Office of Strategic Services] station in Stockholm during World War II . . . one of the capital's 'super lawyers'...and an expert on the Foreign Corrupt Practices Act." The Foreign Corrupt Practices Act forbids certain kinds of payments by U.S. companies overseas and permits others; businessmen being shaken down for bribes overseas would be worried about the act.

Surrey acknowledges he was in the OSS in World War II, but says he severed all ties with the intelligence community when he went to the State Department after the war as chief of the division of economic security controls. (He later went into private law practice.) Still, Surrey & Morse, the firm that whispers the answers in Zaire's ear as if it were pulling the strings of a puppet, seems to thrive on connections to countries caught up in the cold war.

Walter Surrey also is listed on documents as stockholder, director, and lawyer for a Miami-based concern called World Finance Corporation, beginning with its founding in 1970 by a group including CIA-connected, anti-Castro Cuban exiles. Surrey resigned his World Finance jobs in 1976, the year that several law enforcement agencies began long investigations of drug dealing and spying involving the company. By then it had offices in New York, Lima, Bogotá, Caracas, Panama, San José (Costa Rica), Mexico City, London, and the Ajman Arab Emirate in the Persian Gulf. Hundreds of millions, maybe billions, of dollars passed through its hands. Its ostensible businesses were banking, insurance, and real estate. Surrey says he came aboard mainly to help start a foreign-based mutual fund for an old client, a Cuban exile who helped found World Finance. He says he dropped out when the mutual fund deal fell through, and that he was unaware of any criminal or intelligence activities at the company.

Investigators, though, uncovered plenty of such activities before World Finance was finally shut down in 1980. The chief executive of the company, a Cuban exile, was convicted of income tax violations. Jerome Sanford, the assistant United States attorney in Miami who ran the Justice Department's part of the investigation, complains bitterly that the biggest crimes were never publicly exposed. He says the main investigation was halted by Washington in 1978, after the CIA objected that twelve of the Justice Department's chief targets were "of interest" to it. Sanford says he was told that this meant the men he was investigating were CIA operatives of one sort or another. Florida lawmen who worked with Sanford back up his story. Surrey laughs when told about this, and says it's a surprise to him.

The staff of the House Select Committee on Narcotics and Drug Abuse also investigated, and, in a secret report to Congress, said, "There is no question that the parameters of the WFC [World Finance] can encompass a large body of criminal activity, including aspects of political corruption, gun running, as well as narcotics trafficking on an international level....It is against this background that our investigation encountered a number of veiled or direct references to CIA and KGB [the Soviet intelligence agency] complicity or involvement in narcotics trafficking in South Florida." The committee took no public action. The mystery of World Finance remains.

But it seems reasonable to conclude that the law firm of Surrey & Morse at the very least gets along extraordinarily well with the U.S. government.

ZAIRE, like many other Third World countries, has found or been found by some very influential advisors. Besides the law firm of Surrey & Morse, Zaire is paying the Wall Street houses of Lazard Frères and Lehman Brothers Kuhn Loeb to counsel and represent it in dealing with Westerners.

Lazard Frères was originally the most blueblooded of French companies; it still has a large Paris home office, but now does most of its business in New York. Lehman Brothers, a U.S. company, has a penchant for recruiting State Department talent that is long on foreign connections and short on banking experience. By the late 1970s, both houses were doing a booming business advising countries faced with IMF problems. Often they worked together, and often also with S. G. Warburg. a British firm. This amounted to a kind of U.S.-French-British tripartite fix-it service for broke countries.

When a country was behind on its debts and faced with having an IMF finance team move in to take over its treasury, Lehman Brothers, Lazard Frères, and Warburg showed up to advise and try to straighten things out. The three companies have been reported working for not only Zaire, but also Costa Rica, Peru, Gabon, Sri Lanka, Turkey, Senegal, Panama, Jamaica, Ghana, and Cameroon. It's believed they have many other clients, but the business is highly secret. The companies won't say which countries they work for, or how much they charge, though it figures to be in the millions of dollars.

Jeffrey Garten, former head of the policy planning staff at the State Department, who went to work in 1978, as one of Lehman Brothers' top whizzes at this international advisory business, spent months excusing himself from an interview request. Finally cornered by a reporter for a two-hour lunch, he refused to be anymore specific about his travels and activities than to say they involved "Asia, Africa, and Latin America." When he wrote an op-ed page piece for the *New York Times* about international finance problems, he wrote only in the most general terms and his biographical note did not identify his banking firm. Other bankers approached were no more forthcoming.

BACK at the Versailles Room of the St. Regis, Namwisi tells his questioners that the "number one top priority" of his country is to "maintain relations with the West . . . trying to create the confidence of these Western countries." That is a strange number one top priority perhaps, considering that a public health survey of 20,000 typical central Zairian villagers, conducted in this summer of 1980 by expatriate missionaries, found a staggering 80 percent— four of every five people—suffering from serious but treatable maladies. Most prominent were worms, malaria, measles, whopping cough, and severe malnutrition. No such things are mentioned in the Versailles Room.

Namwisi says Zaire will "respect the agreement with the International Monetary Fund." It will control inflation and cut government spending. Namwisi doesn't say that Zairian government spending has already been cut to where the entire budget allocated that year to deal with the public health disaster is $6 million. He doesn't say that this $6 million is one-tenth of what the Zairian Ministry of Health had requested, and that most of this money went to maintain a single hospital in the capital city of Kinshasa, a city most Zairians have never visited. But Namwisi says his government will take "extraordinary measures" to make sure the foreign debt is serviced.

After the meeting he sits down for a requested interview with an American reporter, flanked by other Zairian officials including the head of the central bank. The former finance minister and now prime minister of Zaire, Ngouza Karl-i-bond, had been scheduled to appear today, but didn't show up. It is announced that he couldn't make it because of his new duties as prime minister. But three months later, he flees from Zaire upon learning that he is to be arrested by Mobutu.

Mobutu, a barefoot army sergeant when he first walked into the CIA office in Kinshasa in the 1950s, has since called himself one of the three richest men in the world, an estimate believed to be in the ballpark. He customarily jails or exiles anyone he thinks might be a threat to him. This is a recent reform of his administration. He used to kill such people. Now, under pressure from Western friends to clean up his act, more and more he gives his political enemies hints of their impending doom a few hours in advance so that they might take off by canoe across the Congo River to Brazzaville in the neighboring Republic of Congo, and thence by plane to Europe.

Ngouza Karl-i-bond got such a hint and made it all the way to Belgium, via Switzerland. Now he lives in a big house, with a big car and without any apparent source of income. He testifies before various commissions and parliamentary bodies in Europe and the United States, accusing Mobutu of corruption. He arrives for his testimony in chauffeur-driven limousines.

Back at the St. Regis, Namwisi and his Zairian colleagues aren't answering questions from the American reporter at the promised inverview. Seated at the table with them are five Western businessmen. *They* answer the questions. Henderson the Rain Kings they are, and they won't give their names, either. One says they represent, respectively, Lazard Frères, Lehman Brothers, Surrey & Morse, and Maurice Tempelsman. The others don't dispute it.

They explain that Zaire's debt payments have been rescheduled by Western creditors, a group known as "the Paris club" because Paris is where they often meet to reschedule the debt of various Third World nations. In 1980, Zaire has been scheduled to pay $500 million, and so far has made its payments on time. This, they say, amounts to 27 percent of Zaire's foreign exchange income—the proceeds from the sale of Zaire's minerals.

In 1981, Zaire is scheduled to pay $850 million, but the Western businessmen are confident that this, too, will be rescheduled. There is a simple reason the $850 million will be rescheduled. "It would be absolutely impossible for them to pay that," says a businessman-advisor. "What Zaire has tried to do is make a maximum effort to retire its debt service."

WHAT is happening here is obvious. The bankers have gotten Zaire in hock up to that country's maximum ability to repay, and they are keeping it there. Every year or so the bankers meet to determine how much more money can be squeezed out of that far-off, pathetic land where most of them personally dread to go. (If occasionally they must, they will conduct their business from the Intercontinental Hotel and get out. Paris is nicer.)

Zaire is not alone in this. The major banks have actually held weekly or monthly "country meetings," where experts at the home office figure out the maximum debt capacity of each overseas country. Loan officers around the empire are then instructed by cable to persuade the governments to borrow up to that capacity. At the height of this activity, during the 1970s, before most countries reached their capacities, bank officers were paid bonuses, and were promoted, based on how much debt they could sign up. Since the major banks were privy to the same basic information, they were after the same debt capacity. Vice-presidents assigned to foreign offices competed fiercely to find enticing projects to lend on. This still goes on when new capacity is found. Former bank officers and Third World government economists, in interviews, describe the competition in such countries as Indonesia, Brazil, and even Sri Lanka as frenzied at times.*

In 1981, a year after the St. Regis luncheon, the banks will decide that Namwisi and his friends have succeeded in upping production and holding down consumption to where Zaire can pay a little more. So the International Monetary Fund will increase Zaire's credit line another $1.1 billion. Zairians, of course, won't see it. The money is by and large kept in the West. It repays the old debt, and pays for a few spare parts to be shipped to Kinshasa to maintain production of export items.

Yet once again there is a campaign to convince the public that things are getting better. A reporter for a major American newspaper, after a brief visit to Lubumbashi, Zaire's second-largest city and the capital of Shaba, will actually write in 1981, "The economy has been improving, although hunger is increasingly widespread among the people."† The operation was a success; the patient died.

Probably no one sat down and plotted it that way, but in effect the system of international debt, as it operates in many Third World countries, has a

---

*Most sources for this talked (for obvious reasons) with the understanding that their names would not be used. The process has been described in detail for the author, however, by senior executives of two major New York banks and by loan officers of a third.

†An editor in New York perceptively wrote the sentence out of the story.

lot in common with Mafia loan sharking. The original loan is a snare, quickly lost sight of. The borrower is indebted up to his maximum ability to pay interest at a rate profitable to the lender, and is kept there for as long as the lender can control him. Thus the words of the anonymous advisor at the St. Regis were precise: "What Zaire has tried to do is make a maximum effort to retire its debt service"—not the debt, just the service.

Of course, the whole operation wears a three-piece suit and talks with all the refinement appropriate to its Harvard-Wharton-L'École National* background. The operators don't think of themselves as hoodlums. But to contemplate the analogy of roles, the construction or manufacturing firms who do the projects are the loan sharks. The World Bank and the IMF are the fellows they know who have some cash to put on the street. David Rockefeller (of Chase Manhattan) and Walter Wriston (of Citibank) are the godfathers, getting theirs cleanly by messenger, in plain brown envelopes. Lehman Brothers, Lazard Frères, and S. G. Warburg are the Mr. Niceguys who milk a little more out of the victim when things get bad by telling him that they are friends of the toughies he's in trouble with, and that they know how to smooth things over. And if worst comes to worst and the victim tries to rebel, then the U.S. C5A's fly in the French and Belgian paratroops, and they are the goons who will break both his legs.

THE reporter strains to get a question answered directly by one of the Zairians: "How long can your government carry on such a program before there is a revolution?" Sambwa Pida Mbagui, the governor of the Central Bank, replies: "That is not your problem." After this brief exposition, he is cut off by David Morse, who calls a quick halt to the interview. At the reporter's urging, Morse says he'll allow one more question, which must be submitted in writing.

The following question is submitted: "According to the résumé of Namwisi Ma Koyi [which has been distributed to the guests], he has been in the government service since leaving school in the late 1960s. How much money is he worth now and how did he get it? Does he control directly or indirectly any personal assets outside Zaire?"

The question is never answered.

Meanwhile, the assembled luncheon guests have returned to their offices or homes. Most are hard workers. They are loyal to their companies, loving of their families, and respected members of their communities. They would not in conscience steal. They oppose bloodshed. When they receive appeals on behalf of famine-stricken Africans, they write out checks, sometimes generous ones.

Many would openly acknowlege that there is something wrong with the system.

*The French equivalent.

CHAPTER THREE
FRIENDS IN FOREIGN LANDS

ABOUT NINE hours after Namwisi Ma Koyi finishes speaking at the St. Regis, day begins in the village of Yalifoka. It is 6 A.M. there. Three children emerge from their respective mud houses, walk swiftly in bare feet to the drum—a long, skin-covered, hollowed-out log in the center of the village—and beat their reveille. As it pulsates, hundreds of people rise from straw mats, a few from wood-frame beds. They don tattered shorts and shirts, mostly secondhand clothing, Salvation Army stuff from the West. They straggle out of their scattered houses and head into the bush for their fields before a visitor has finished brushing his teeth.

Yalifoka is about 90 miles southwest of Kisangani, Zaire's fourth-largest city and the metropolis of the northern half of the country. Back in the 1960s, when Kisangani was called Stanleyville, it was the scene of much fighting and at least one U.S.-European rescue mission. Zaire's national hero, Patrice Lumumba, had his main base of support around Stanleyville, before the United States paid to have him murdered in 1960. Food experts say this broad belt of jungle could be the breadbasket of Africa.

Among the Yalifokan villagers trekking to the fields are Afana Ongia and his three wives. Earlier this summer, the Afana family spent thirty days clearing and planting one hectare, about 2½ acres. It was backbreaking work. They whacked through dense jungle with machetes, then set the stumps and felled branches ablaze. Generations of Zairian farmers have cleared their fields with fire. Potential soil nutrients go up in smoke, but, without machines, burning seems the only way to plant. Since less than 2 percent of Zaire's potential farmland has been cultivated, nobody seems to mind the waste.

The field that remains is dotted with charred branches and stumps. But Afana and his wives plant around them. They needn't worry about sowing orderly rows. They have no machines to impose order, not even a mule to pull a plow. Beasts of burden haven't survived the climate and diseases of tropical Africa, and the Afana family probably couldn't afford an animal anyway.

Here and there among the charred stumps, they have planted equal quantities of rice to sell, manioc to eat, and plantain, a little for both. Manioc, called cassava in some countries, is a starchy root. It has the brown skin and white flesh of a potato, but grows more in the shape of a giant carrot, a foot or two long. Women husk it, dry it, grind it to powder, and boil it with water to make a gray, pasty gruel. Plantain is a big starchy banana, usually eaten mashed and cooked. Manioc and plantain are the dietary staples of Zaire.

Most of the actual clearing and planting is done by Afana's wives. He supervises. The women show the strain. His first two wives are only in their twenties, but already look old, with wrinkled faces and sagging breasts. In years of clearing jungle, they have also produced eight living children, all still too young to work the fields. Afana himself, in his early thirties, looks relatively fresh and youthful. So does the third wife he recently took.

Like most farm families in the area, the Afanas bring in a paltry $200 to $400 a year for their labor, plus the food they keep to eat. You don't see radios or bicyles in these villages, as you do across most of black Africa. Chairs, tables, and other furniture are homemade. Children play with sometimes elaborate homemade toys. Handcrafted guitars, and push-cars made of sticks and wire, are popular.

Electricity is unknown. Some homes have lamps, but kerosene is 66 cents for a beer-bottle-full, when it's available at all. So there is little light at night except for wood fires. Water is carried on women's heads from streams often more than a mile away. Most farmers in Africa—in Nigeria, Kenya, Ivory Coast, or even in poorer countries like Niger and Tanzania—have not lived in such primitive conditions for decades.

Afana's neighbor, Tikelake (his only name) is trying to raise his income by switching his crop to coffee under the tutelage of a government extension agent. Coffee is an export crop, unknown in Zaire as a beverage except to a few elite city-dwellers. (A Western visitor to these farms is left much in the conditon of Coleridge's Ancient Mariner, with coffee, coffee everywhere, nor any drop to drink.)

To encourage production, the government of Zaire has fixed a minimum price of $40 for an 80-kilo (176-pound) bag of coffee beans. But Tikelake can't bring the beans to market himself. He must sell to a *commerçant*, or trader. *Commerçants* dealing in coffee get to Yalifoka only about twice a year. When they show up with their trucks, Tikelake has little real choice but to accept their illegally low offers of $27 to $33 a bag. He and his wife grow between five and ten bags a year. The extension agent says they could easily double their production if they had a reliable market. Two of their six surviving children are old enough to farm now, but don't, because the marketing system offers little incentive for their added labor.

Unlike their father and his neighbor Afana, who grew up in colonial days and never went to school, Tikelake's children now attend class for up to six years. But the education doesn't seem much to brag about, even judged by standards elsewhere in black Africa. Children from several villages are crammed into one or two rooms. Among their subjects, they are supposed to be studying French, the national language. French was intended to open up communication among Zaire's hundreds of tribes, whose languages are often mutually unintelligible. But only a few of the children show even minimal knowledge of French after several years' study. Their teacher isn't much better. Despite the poor quality of the schools, school fees gobble up the largest part of the budget for many Zairian farm families. Each child attending requires yearly payment of about $31—$11 for tuition and $20 in bribes for admission.

In midafternoon, when the sun gets unbearable, the Afanas, the Tikelakes, and their neighbors return home from the fields. Naps are taken. Soon the women begin preparing the day's main, perhaps only, meal. It consists mostly of manioc gruel—pure, bulky starch that settles heavily into the stomach. Manioc root has miniscule nutritional value. Recent U.S. AID and United Nations studies show that it also contains more than a trace of cyanide, which may damage the brain, central nervous system, and other tissues over the years. According to AID, 50 percent of Zaire's cultivated land produces manioc, which provides 60 percent of the caloric intake for 70 percent of the people.* Sometimes boiled plantain is mashed into the manioc, a small nutritional spike. The mash is consumed with a bit of watery soup flavored with the leaves of the manioc plant, perhaps the most nutritious ingredient of all, plus, if available, a couple of hot peppers and a tomato or onion or two.

Scrawny chickens squawk about and one may occasionally be tossed into a soup to be shared among families. Such a chicken would bring $3.50 if sold, but buyers aren't always available because most people don't have $3.50. Sometimes there is fish for the soup. But even with animal flesh and some peppers, the mixture is pretty insipid—a far cry from the hearty, fiery broths of West Africa. Wild oranges provide dietary supplement. The main supplement, however, is sugar cane, which grows wild. Men, women, and

---

*Such figures cannot possibly be compiled so precisely, but from observation they seem accurate as a rough guide.

children chew cane all day, spitting out the pulp the way old-time cowboys or ballplayers spit their tobacco juice. Few would say the habit is healthful, but it beats hunger.

Stream water is the main beverage. To protect the water, great energy is expended digging sanitary pits at a safe distance from the stream, and building outhouses over the pits. There is an almost compulsive tidiness in villages throughout Zaire. Without it, the health situation would be even worse than it is. Dirt courtyards around the mud houses almost always bear fresh broom marks. Grassy spots or small gardens are neatly trimmed. Men are about here and there in the afternoons patching roofs with leaves.

In each village, rules are enforced that drinking water be drawn at the highest point in the stream, baths taken at midpoint, and clothes washed below. But a stream passes near many villages. So despite all these efforts, drinking water almost inevitable becomes contaminated—if not from the bodies or the clothes, then from the droppings of the animals that run about, or from the children who, prior to toilet training, empty themselves almost anywhere. Children, like most other people, are suffering from various diseases passed on through the dietary tract. A third of them don't make it to the age of five.

People complain, not so much about ill-health, to which there is no known alternative, but about continuing low incomes in the face of rising prices. New monetary controls demanded by the Western banks and the IMF have sent prices soaring up to 50 percent a year for clothes and other market goods. The cheapest cotton and polyester shirts cost $12 to $18, and pants about $17. But the economic complaints have a limit. There is a palpable fear of political discussion in the villages. With few exceptions, if you ask villagers about Mobutu Sese Seko, they will mutter uneasily that they don't want to talk about the president.

CONDITIONS are similar in farm villages throughout most of Zaire. Bi-pemba, for example, is a village in the south-central province of Western Kasai. Back at independence, in 1960, when the United States was helping murder the elected prime minister of Zaire and install a military government led by Mobutu, Kasai was much in the news. *Time* magazine referred to the rebellious province as the "dark interior" of the country where independence promised to bring "a running civil war of spears and poison arrows."

Katumba Mpoye was thirty-eight years old in 1960. He was farming in Kasai then, as he is now, and doesn't think the life has changed much. He doesn't recall dodging any spears or arrows—a few bullets back then, just flies and gnats now. "Agriculture is very difficult," he says, sweating heavily in the noon sun amid the corn and peanut patches. Kasai isn't dark. Most of it isn't even shady. "With the hoe, each day, each day, each day. The children won't accept the farm," Katumba says. Katumba and his wife have produced fourteen children. Of the eight who survived childhood without succumbing to disease or malnutrition, none farms. Only one still considers it. He is nineteen and in his third year of secondary school.

Most students don't get to secondary school. Most of those who do, like Katumba's son, have their studies interrupted several times when their families can't pay the high fees and bribes that are required. When money is scraped together they return to class, testament to the value placed on education. Two of Katumba's younger children are students. Three older ones call themselves students, but are out of school because of money, health, or scholastic performance. In other words, they are unemployed. One grown son is semiemployed as a small trader, and another, a high school graduate, is director of a primary school.

Katumba's farm is only about 4 miles from a market, so his wife can carry produce there on her head. Each time she carries a load, she has to pay a precious dollar to soldiers who have set up a roadblock on the only road. They call it "beer money." Commerical vehicles have to pay 100 Zaires (about $33) to pass the roadblock. Asked if there is justice in Zaire, Katumba replies, "If you have money, that is one justice. If you don't have money, that is another justice."

Because Kasai has most of Zaire's diamonds, Kasai's young people imagine that the gem trade is a means to wealth, And, in fact, diamond smuggling has made a few local Kasai men rich. Big Mercedeses sometimes roar past the bare mud houses of farmers like Katumba, their springs being tested on the dirt roads. Such flashes of opulence are an inspiration to many. Almost every day you can find men, women, even children, hoping to get in on the action, shoveling sand along the banks of the Sankuru River, looking for something bright and hard.

Kasai peasants often do find diamonds. But like Tikelake with his coffee, they seldom get fair value. One woman unwrapped a hanky for some inquiring visitors and revealed a handful of diamonds, some orange (industrial quality) and some clear. She boasted they were worth $65. An American who knew the diamond business, though, said they would bring thousands of dollars in New York. Zairians don't get Mercedeses by finding diamonds; they get Mercedeses by buying diamonds from peasants who *do* find them, and by paying less than the diamonds are worth. Only government influence decides who can get away with this.

Big international companies are supposed to have exclusive rights to the diamonds. A Zairian-Belgian combine known as MIBA mines them. Maurice Tempelsman's companies have rights to explore for and buy them. And the DeBeers syndicate marketed them, until several other European concerns were brought in to share the wealth in 1981.

Because the government has granted exclusive concessions to the big companies, freelance diamond digging is illegal. In July 1979, soldiers went to the bank of the Sankuru River, found an unusually large number of diggers, and opened fire. What happened next is argued about a lot. Local people say several hundred scavengers died, some from gunfire, most from drowning after they panicked and ran into the swift-running river (most Africans never learn to swim). Prominent citizens in town say they saw several dozen bodies. A government investigation organized by Mobutu reported only three deaths. Mobutu invited Amnesty International, the London-based human rights lobby, to investigate, but it declined. Amnesty said that the restrictions Mobutu imposed would prevent it from doing a thorough job.

Those few who are allowed to take diamonds out are assumed by nearly everyone to spread their profits, via bribery, among Mobutu's appointed local administrators and army officers. With the money they keep, the smugglers often buy trucks and become big-scale *commerçants*, hauling consumer goods in from the coast or the nearest airport or barge port and selling them to the transportationless masses.

The *commerçants* are not liked by the people who have to pay the high prices they charge. But because they have money, the *commerçants* often have friends in the white expatriate community. In Kisangani, you can see them sitting around the two big hotel dining rooms in the European section of town, topping off $20 meals with $5 snifters of imported brandy. In Mbuji-Mayi, a *commerçant* kept public company with the attractive young regional administrator for the United States Peace Corps.

MANY thousands of Zairians* work on plantations owned by big multinational companies, like Unilever, raising coffee, palm oil, sugar, or rubber. For this they are paid $10 to $13 a month. That is $120 to $156 a year. Their wives and children who don't work on the plantation can garden to fill the family table. But generally, workers must promise the plantation owner that they won't sap their energies by raising cash crops. This promise, of course, is almost universally broken. Anyone receiving so little money is going to try to improve his income by farming his own land. Energies *are* sapped, and that's one reason expatriates continue to accuse Zairians of laziness.

Some menials at the huge Unilever† palm oil plantation at Lokutu, about 120 miles into the bush west of Kisangani, get only $7 a month. Of the 50,000 Zairians Unilever says it employs, about 5,000 work at Lokutu. From their salaries, the company deducts several dollars a month for living quarters.

*I will try in this book to avoid offering precise statistics that have no reliable base. Plenty of agencies at the U.N. and elsewhere try to satisfy the curiosity of those who want to know how many thousands in such and such a country are starving or working or whatever, but such figures become ludicrous when you get to the scene and find no accurate means of measuring.

†Though Unilever stock is traded on the New York Stock Exchange, it is best known in the U.S. by its U.S. subsidiary, Lever Brothers.

This means that in cash, menials may get as little as $4 a month, and farmers $7 to $10 a month. The quarters consist of a 6-by-7-foot room for a single man, a bit more if the employee has a wife and children and can prove they're his. A Unilever executive from England on temporary assignment in Zaire describes all this, and his own life as well:

"I have a cook, a houseboy, a chauffeur, and a gardener and I get change from 200 Zaires [about $65 a month," the executive says. He laughs. It is not a laugh of disdain, but rather an expression of helplessness over a situation so obviously unfair that his own advantage is an embarrassment to him. He has a nice house in Lokutu, and on trips to Kisangani he enjoys a $30-a-night air-conditioned hotel room and spends $11 for a meal of pork chops, french fries, cole slaw, and beer. A single evening's expenses consume more than four times the monthly pay of the farm workers his company employs. The executive is ferried about by private plane. (Unilever ships its goods out by river, so it has not built a decent road to Kisangani.) He makes the usual expatriate complaints that Zairian workers are lazy. But then he laughs again, and adds, "If that was what they paid me, I wouldn't work either."

The daughter of another Unilever executive, also a Britisher, grew up in the Kisangani area. She has married a Portuguese, the branch manager of a European-owned chain of import-export stores. Over coffee in their Kisangani home, she agrees to talk about the import-export operation on condition that the business not be identified.

The operation sells mostly to Zairian *commerçants*, who in turn sell to market women, who then sell to customers. "The owners never put anything into the country," the woman says. "They never build anything. They are here to make as much money as they can while things are good, and then they get out."

You can hear such cynicism from a lot of expatriates, but this woman discloses more. She reveals that her husband's firm makes its money on the black market. It smuggles goods and currency into and out of the country in evasion of the controls established by the Zairian government at the direction of the IMF. Like other privileged concerns here, the company operates boats on the Congo River. The boats stop on the north bank in the neighboring Republic of Congo and off-load smuggled diamonds or coffee.

The company exchanges this Zairian wealth for hard foreign currency, which is forwarded directly to the company's European accounts. The boats also pick up Western goods and bring them back to Zaire illegally. And the firm has cargo aircraft that come and go pretty much unaccounted for. The money sucked out of the Zairian economy by the sale of illegally imported goods is not reflected on Zaire's international balances. The IMF, reporting on Zairian insolvency, never includes this sort of sneaking out of resources by Westerners, which is both immense and profitable.

The woman's husband enters, and flatly denies that his firm does illegal business. He says that all the coffee and other goods it exports are sold through government sales agencies, which adhere to currency controls. He praises Mobutu's government and says Zaire is in trouble only because Zairians are lazy. The British woman is embarrassed.

As her husband talks, an American working for UNESCO (the United Nations Educational, Scientific, and Cultural Organization) enters and pulls from his pockets several hundred U.S. dollars. He lays them on the table. The husband sweeps them into a box, and changes them at a rate of 5 Zaires to the dollar. The legally controlled rate is just under 3 Zaires to the dollar. There is no way the husband can pay this rate unless he is exporting the dollars on the sly, in flagrant violation of exchange controls. With no indication that he senses he is proving the charges against him, he offers to do the same for a reporter.

Like the diamonds, and coffee, and cobalt, and other goods, even this little bit of hard cash—UNESCO wages—is hustled out of the country. The Zairian people get no income from it. They get no roads, no schools, no hospitals. The hard Western currency that pays for all the smuggled goods stays outside the country. It goes into the pockets of Western businessmen and buys off influential Zairians. The elite may bring a few million dollars of the stolen wealth back into Zaire in the form of Mercedeses, and other goods for their private use. But the development capital their countrymen need to pull themselves into the twentieth century never makes it home.

THE tragedy of Zaire is not just that wealth is siphoned out by bankers big and small, operating with the open sanction of a crooked government installed and protected by the United States. The tragedy is that almost nothing has been left behind. The spirit as well as the wealth of the country has been raped. Life moves pathetically.

Mama Singa, a small *commerçant*, embodies the problem. She must do for Zaire what Continental Grain, the A & P, and several large railroads do in the U.S.: get food to the people. As a one-woman enterprise, she is anything but lazy. She is, in fact, impressively industrious. But as a national food distribution system, she is a mess.

It is a sizzlingly hot Friday afternoon, and in almost the geographical center of the continent the dusty town plaza broils in the sun's headachey glare. Mama, who isn't tall but easily weighs 180 pounds, has leased a bright red diesel truck from a big *commerçant* in Kisangani who owns five such trucks. For one money-making trip into the bush, the truck cost her 2,000 Zaires, or about $675. Within its slatted wooden sides wait 700 cubic feet of cargo space, about one-fifth the capacity of an American semi. Mama plans to go about 100 miles, to some of the prime crop land on the continent. If she's lucky, she'll get there and back in four or five days.

Mama picks up the truck, with driver, mechanic, and helper-apprentice, on the "right bank" of the Congo River. The right, or northern, bank, is the modern, pretty section of Kisangani. Its streets are paved, lined with trees, and well lit at night. Its buildings are stucco and masonry, neatly painted. It is inhabited by expatriates, *commerçants*, government officials, army officers, and others of the privileged.

After a forty-five-minute wait, a ferry crosses the river a few miles below Stanley Falls, and deposists Mama and the truck on the "left bank." The bulk of Kisangani's population lives there. The houses are of unpainted mud, and are ranged along dirt footpaths instead of boulevards. Women haul water on their heads from public spigots as much as a half-mile away. There's no electricity. Nights are dark except for wood fires. Some lucky residents pay 33 cents round-trip on the ferry every day to go to right-bank jobs that earn them $50 to $75 a month. Others walk to meager farms outside town.

Mama's truck faces two roads on the left bank. Neither road is paved. Both are gooey with mud. Mama takes the right road, leading southwest, toward a string of farming villages. Before she gets 200 yards, the clutch gives out. The truck stops four hours while the driver and a mechanic fix it. The truck goes on.

Mama isn't starting out empty. The back of the truck is loaded with about fifty market women carrying baskets. They have paid about $3.50 each for a one-way ride to Yatolema, a market town 58 miles into the bush. Yatolema's weekly market day is Sunday. The women plan to buy whatever their heads can carry, then return to Kisangani to sell it. If they return with Mama Singa, and they may have little choice, they will pay extra for their cargo when the baskets are filled.

Meanwhile, Mama plans to pick up some cargo of her own in the villages—probably manioc, corn, or plantain, whatever looks profitable. A bunch of plantain worth $1 in the bush sells for about $3.50 in town. An 88-pound bag of manioc brings about $1.75 to the farmer who grew it and will be marked up to $7 to $10 in town. The market women in Kisangani who buy the bags from Mama at these markups will, of course, raise the prices still higher when they sell to their own customers by the cupful.

American farmers also complain of high retail markups. But U.S. markups include costly processing and long-distance hauling that allows New Yorkers and Bostonians to eat in January approximately as they do in August. The produce Mama Singa collects won't be processed or refrigerated. It will never reach the malnourished masses of Kinshasa, Lubumbashi, or Kananga—the three largest cities—or the hungry laborers in the big mining centers. There is no way to carry the food to these places. The price soars merely going back to Kisangani, because no one has invested in a transportational infrastructure for Zaire. The market belongs to the *commerçant*. When a *commerçant* comes along, the farmer doesn't know when he'll have another chance to sell his crop, or the consumer another chance to buy his food.

Mama's truck rolls treacherously over a narrow, mud-slickened wooden bridge over a raging brown stream maybe 40 feet across, then roars up a muddy hill out of Kisangani. The trip proceeds at about 10 miles an hour. Every 50 yards or so, if the road is dry, the truck slows even more, to navigate around craggy chasms a foot or two deep in the road, or to bounce slowly over them. Where there's water, the driver doesn't know if it's a shallow puddle or a deep pothole; trucks sometimes overturn when drivers guess wrong. In mud, the driver drops to first gear (he is rarely higher than second) and roars through, with everyone aboard praying silently that the truck won't stall. When it does, the driver, crew, and any recruitable roadside help, labor for an hour, shin-deep in slime, to shovel it out.

Every few miles is a village, where Mama stops to pick up more market women. Every few miles is a stream, where the driver stops to refill the badly leaking radiator. The clutch goes out again, and everything stops for an hour while it is fixed.

A roadblock. Four soldiers search the truck. Among the passengers they find a young soldier without papers permitting him to travel. He is forced down, shoved around, his luggage searched. The searchers see a few items they like, and keep them. The traveling soldier is allowed back on. The four searchers approach the cab and demand the driver's papers. Mama unwraps the pile of bills she has been collecting from the market women and hands a presorted fistful to the soldiers at the roadblock. "For beer," the driver mutters. He roars on.

Mama is also the mail. She occasionally stops in villages to drop off envelopes she has brought from town, or to pick up scrawled messages for passing on to the next village. Mama speaks only Lingala and Swahili, and not much of those, except to bawl people out and argue about the price of some dried fish she has brought to peddle along the way. She rarely smiles. For a transport operator, there isn't much to smile about. At rivers and streams, the truck must wait for ancient ferries. A ferry is eight or ten battered metal boats lashed together with planks on top. Work crews are rounded up from the bush and struggle to guide the truck onto the ferry, which almost tips over from the weight. A crossing takes an hour.

It is midnight when Mama reaches Yatolema and drops off the market women—58 miles in slightly over eleven hours, not counting the initial four-hour delay for the clutch breakdown. At 3 A.M. she reaches another village, where she and the crew sleep.

In three days of traveling, Mama encounters three other vehicles—a pickup jammed with people, a Land Rover driven by missionaries, and another big truck whose cargo is hidden. According to the authoritative Michelin map of Central Africa, this is the main national highway. It is the road you would take if you wanted to drive the 720 miles from Kisangani, Zaire's major northern and eastern city, to Kinshasa, the capital. But to do that, you would need a couple of months and much luck. After Opala, a town about half a day beyond where Mama turns back, the road is said to get much worse. Anything worse is hard to imagine.

Headed home, Mama's truck groans under a load of plantain. But villagers want to sell, and she keeps buying. Her offers are mostly nonnegotiable. One woman has lugged three huge bunches of plantain a mile or more from home. Mama pays her 3 Zaires, about $1, for one bunch, and 2 Zaires for another. The woman contends that the third bunch is also worth 3 Zaires, but Mama offers only $2.50. After much argument and wailing, the seller gives up, loads the third bunch back on her head and trudges home again. She still has her pride, but she also still has her plantain, which her family will have to eat.

Near Kisangani, the truck sinks into mud so deep that Mama herself has to get out and shovel. But on the fifth day she makes it home to market.

HASSAN NABHAN is an Egyptian working in Zaire with the U.N. Food and Agricultural Organization. He has spent most of his three years here successfully persuading about 9,000 of the 300,000 farmers in Eastern Kasai province that an expenditure of $100 a year for fertilizer more than pays for itself. He has raised demonstration fields of corn side by side, one fertilized, one not. The difference in productivity was certainly a shock.

To help the farmers finance the fertilizer payments, Nabhan gradually combined U.N. money and local farmers' contributions into a $1 million revolving fund. Farmers got fertilizer on credit from the fund, then paid off in installments as they sold their harvest.

In the week before New Year's Day, 1980, however, the plan was obliterated. At the insistence of the Western banking establishment, acting through the IMF, Mobutu imposed new restrictions on the national money supply. The Western press reported these restrictions in the most favorable language, and said that Zaire was "putting its financial house in order." Namwisi Ma Koyi boasted of the new restrictions in his speech at the St. Regis.

To insure that all the earnings from mineral sales were kept in the central bank, where they could be siezed by the big foreign creditors (or by the crooks who run the Zairian government), Zairians were prohibited from converting their money into solid foreign currency. When savers can't convert their money into dollars or francs, they can't buy things from abroad. Among these savers were Nabhan's farmers. When the decree was announced, they could no longer convert their farm income, or even their already-banked U.N. grants, into foreign currency. So they couldn't buy any more fertilizer. This was how the IMF, with the encouragement of the U.S. government, put Zaire's house in order.

Nabhan's farmers were mostly wiped out anyway, as were most other Zairian savers, by a second decree. The Western bankers wanted to coerce people into holding all their money in the government banking system. That way, the bank could control all substantial expenditures, and the Westerners could hoard the money themselves, which in their judgment would help strengthen Zairian currency as an international trading commodity. So the Western bankers had Mobutu invalidate all existing currency and make it exchangeable for a new, devalued currency. The plan gave people three days to visit a bank and exchange up to $1,000 of the old money for new. Anything over $1,000 was worthless, which punished people who kept their money outside the banking system.

This plan was hardly in keeping with the free economic market that the United States says it encourages throughout the world as the U.S. alternative to communism. In fact, if Cuba were to attempt such a program, the U.S. president might well denounce it on his next television appearance as an example of communist tyranny. Newspaper editorial writers would hang Fidel Castro from every masthead. (In truth, Cuba's economic restraints are considerably more humane than Zaire's, though ultimately no more respectful of individual freedom.)

The $1,000 currency exchange restriction in itself didn't bother most Zairians, because most Zairians didn't have $1,000. But communications and transportation are such that most people never got to a bank at all in the three days. Those who did found crushing lines, demands for bribes from banking officials, and sometimes an exhausted supply of new banknotes.

For example, the 4 million residents of Eastern Kasai province were served by exactly two banks, both in the provincial capital of Mbjui-Mayi, which is more than a three-days' journey for many residents by any practical means of conveyance. If the supposed legitimate purpose of the currency switch was to increase respect for the banking system as a repository of money, the effect was just the opposite.

Wealthy *commerçants*, both Zairian and Western, should have been wiped out by the plan. But they weren't. It is universally accepted that they cut the bankers and government officials in on the new money they got, and so were able to exchange all they wanted. As a teacher in Kinshasa described it, "There was a limit. But for the bosses there was no limit. For the poor people there was a limit."

There was a swift, dampening effect on daily life. A Peace Corps volunteer from the northern interior observed, "Some [people] lost 40 Zaires [about $13], some lost 400, some lost 4,000. But I can tell you there aren't going to be any weddings in this country for two years." An American missionary says his group, the Communité Presbytérienne du Zaire, lost more than $330,000 it had raised to run schools, hospitals, and rural dispensaries.

And so Hassan Nabhan, the agricultural advisor from Egypt, his fertilizer program in shambles, is discouraged. "If we had 1,500 millimeters of rainfall a year in Egypt, the whole land would be cultivated," Nabhan says. Fifteen hundred millimeters is about 60 inches—Zaire's annual soaking. Rain in Zaire is also more evenly spread through the year than in many African countries where half the months are dry, half rainy. This even rainfall allows Zaire a second harvest.

"Here they have the rain," Nabhan says. "If you just invested a little in imported fertilizer, worked on the attitude of the people to farm, you could easily double the production. If you put in a big investment in roads, transportation, and storage facilities, Zaire could support the Sahel countries [the famine-stricken lands on the fringe of the Sahara]."

He goes on: "In most countries you can only increase production horizontally, by increasing the amount of land. But in Zaire you can increase both vertically and horizontally, because you haven't reached maximum productivity. We proved in this local [demonstration] project you can get 4.5 tons of maize [corn] per hectare. Now they're getting 0.6 tons. It's just fertilizer, seeds, and a better method of cultivation."

Fertilizer could be produced domestically without any imported ingredients. Modern technology can suck enough nitrogen right out of the air to revitalize the soil. While many countries can't use this process because it requires a lot of electricity, Zaire, with its huge hydroelectric potential, could. Moreover, Nabhan and many other experts argue that if running water, electricity, schools, hospitals, and recreational activities were brought to farming villages, more people would farm. But little is left over in the way of development money after the Western corporations have their fill. Planners who do occasionally get some money to spend are themselves city dwellers. They are rewarded by politics, not economic productivity. Their investments tend to be urban.

The offspring of farmers flow out of the villages. Enormous shantytowns rise on the fringes of the cities. This happens in many countries throughout the Third World, as people are naturally attracted by the amenities and pleasures of modern life, which are concentrated in the cities. It happened in the United States, too, but usually as industry arose to occupy the new city dwellers, and machines arrived to replace farm workers and maintain food production. The marketplace was free to do its work. This is not the case in countries like Zaire.

MINGI is a twenty-one-year-old engineering student at the national university in Kinshasa. He shares a four-room mud house in Kinshasa with a sister, her baby, the baby's paternal grandmother, and five other people. They eat one meal a day, mostly manioc. Much of the time they go around feeling hungry.

There is no electricity or running water. The road outside is a scarcely navigable morass. In a field nearby, hundreds of buses sit idle, rusting, for lack of spare parts. Mingi takes an overcrowded bus to school. The round-trip fare is 33 cents. A paperback textbook is $10.

Mingi lives on a government allowance of $25 a month He can't supplement his allowance the way female students do, by selectively prostituting themselves from the age of fifteen. Mingi's intended bride is such a student.

He is bitter that he has to share her with two older, richer men. But they pay her $4 to $7 a night when she stays with them. In the summer of 1980, she becomes pregnant—with his baby, he says matter-of-factly, as if no other possibility exists.

That summer, Mingi and several thousand fellow students are on strike against the university, or say they are. Their chief demand is a higher living allowance, but the whole notion of free speech and democracy is at issue. Mobutu closed the campus as soon as the students took to the streets in April. Many students were beaten or imprisoned. So Mingi and his friends will talk only in private. They claim to be well organized, and they appear to be so at several meetings. But when the university reopens in October and they try to renew the strike, the police come out again. Mobutu threatens to put them all on planes and send them back to the farms. The student strike fails.

Not far from Mingi lives Remy, twenty-one, the son of a cabinet minister from the administration of Joseph Kasavubu, president of the republic in its early days. Now he is out of school and out of work. He sits on a battered metal folding chair on the dirt floor of an open gazebo made of cane and thatch, on the neatly swept compound of a mud house in Kinshasa. Half a dozen loaves of bread wait for sale on a stand outside.

One of Remy's earliest memories is of a night in 1964. He woke to find men at the door. They said Remy's father was needed. His father was taken away and never seen again.

Today, his mother runs a small store. It brings in about $6.50 a day, to support a family of five. They eat every afternoon: manioc flour, manioc leaves, and beans. Beans—the precious protein that keeps them alive—run between 33 and 45 cents a cupful, dry.

Remy says one meal isn't enough. His brothers (meaning cousins) have gone to France, where they wait tables, bag groceries, and clean streets. That's big money. "When they left here they were poor," he says. "When they come back they have cars." Remy wants to go, too.

Charles is nineteen. He used to make jewelry in a factory for $31 a month. Then, after IMF monetary controls were imposed, jewels and gold became too costly, and started flowing out of the country on the black market. The factory closed. Now Charles looks for necklaces and bracelets to repair. In the past six months he made maybe $80. He supports his father, who had to quit work because of illness, and his mother. He says they used to eat rice, but now can afford only manioc.

John is a teacher, a recent university graduate. He is bright, articulate, and a genius at navigating the red tape of Zairian bureaucracy. He is invaluable as guide and translator for an American reporter he met on a bus. Over beer, he bemoans the government. The reporter asks why John doesn't enter politics to try to right things.

"I don't like politics," he says. "You can lose your life unnecessarily. I am very important to my family. They cannot afford to have me go to jail.

With you whites it is different. I am a black, and the money I bring home isn't just for me. It is first for my mother and my sisters and my brothers." John says he wants to work in Europe as a laborer for a few years to earn money.

Now, John earns $93 a month when the government has the money to pay him. The government is several months behind on teachers' salaries. A Belgian expatriate of equivalent credentials, teaching at the same school, gets $1,333 a month living allowance plus $500 a month set aside in Belgium, and the money is paid on time.

DUSK falls in smokey hues of rose and gray over the vast, beige, open-pit mines outside Kolwezi. Their copper and cobalt—more than exists anywhere else on earth—have lent names to gayer colors, but those colors are not in evidence here.

Half a dozen mine workers find a patch of grass on the stony hillside and rest on their elbows. They wear tattered shorts of khaki or navy blue, frayed shirts and cheap sandals. These are the "clean" clothes they donned after bathing off the sweat of the day. They look out on the source of three-fourths of the foreign exchange that Zaire will use to hold its bankers at bay this year, and next, and probably for as long as the country is managed the way it is. Several of these men are ordinary miners, encountered at random. The rest are union leaders of low and middle rank, assembled by the others for a visiting reporter.

The Zairian government's well-paid public relations machine in Washington says Zaire is a big pro–labor union country. David A. Morse, Zaire's lawyer-lobbyist who whispered the answers at the St. Regis meeting, and who is a former U.S. secretary of labor himself, says, "The Zairian trade union movement is recognized as being one of the best, if not the best, in Africa." Morse says the Zairian trade union movement is "the most effective social instrument in the country for the delivery of medical assistance, development of cooperatives, development of clinics, leadership training programs, etcetera, and has built a labor college in the country." The labor movement Morse is talking about, however, is a Zairian government-approved organization funded by the U.S. government and the U.S. AFL-CIO. The organization was developed by people working with, and by some accounts directly for, the U.S. Central Intelligence Agency.*

In other words, the organization Morse talks about is a company union, and few Zairians who need a labor union know anything about it. It has absolutely nothing to do with these miners. The union in Kolwezi, like any other that complains about working conditions in Zaire, is illegal. If the

*For the many connections between the CIA and the AFL-CIO's international labor activities, see chapter 20.

government found out what these men are up to, they would be jailed, or worse. The mere existence of this union is secret.

The men do not tell their names. They do not tell what roles they played in the Shaba uprisings of 1977 and 1978, though they make clear their sympathies lay with the rebellion. They do tell of their salaries, spitting out facts in the same bitter tone one hears from many mining workers and family members around Kolwezi.

Veteran miners get $33 a month. The lowest menials get $13. Most support large families with this money—often the African extended family, which includes an assortment of orphaned or otherwise-uncared-for nephews, nieces, and cousins. The cheapest protein source, beans, costs 33 cents a pound in this part of the country. Beef is $3 a pound. Corn or manioc flour is about $20 for a 132-pound bag, or about 16 cents for a 6-ounce cupful. A month's charcoal cooking fuel is another $8 or $9. Wives often tend 2-acre farms to help fill tables, but it isn't enough. Malnutrition is rampant, especially among children.

For all that Zaire (and the West) owes to these 32,000 miners and their families, you'd think they would be well taken care of. But very little of the mineral export billions comes back to Kolwezi, and the miners know it. Nor have the huge Western loans secured by their work helped them. They blame "*les supérieurs de chez nous*"—"the leaders of our country." "The corruption is everything," said one worker. Another added bluntly, "The president of the republic puts it in his pocket."

The government of Zaire took control of the copper-cobalt mining monopoly from Société Général, the Belgian concern, in 1972. But it is still managed largely by Europeans, and Société Général still gets a big cut of the money through various contracts, the terms of which are secret. The framework of those contracts was negotiated back in 1967, obviously a momentous event for Zairian development.

So Mobutu hired a pretty good lawyer to hammer out a formula for protecting the rights of the Zairian people to their mineral wealth, against the predatory instincts of sophisticated Western cartels. The lawyer was Theodore Sorensen, who also happened to represent Maurice Tempelsman. Tempelsman was about to organize an international combine of American, Japanese, and European companies to develop and manage the world's richest undeveloped copper and cobalt lode, right there in Shaba. And he persuaded Mobutu to hire his own lawyer to represent Zaire as the pattern was set for franchised foreign management of Zairian minerals. The incredible thing is that when Sorensen was proposed as CIA director in 1976, the nomination was thrown back at President-elect Carter, mostly on the ground that Sorenson was a naive, mushy-headed liberal incapable of the hard-nosed pragmatism the CIA job required. What a slander on Sorensen!*

---

*Sorensen says (in an interview with the author) that no conflict of interest existed, because in the deal Tempelsman later made with Mobutu, the Zairian government got a

The Zairian government mining agency that eventually took over legal ownership from Société Général under the arrangement Sorensen helped construct is known as Gecamines.* By law, it turns its products from Kolwezi over to a state sales board known as Sozacom. Both Sozacom and Gecamines are controlled by Mobutu appointees. Société Général has shipping and selling affiliates that are believed to get a lot, if not all, of Sozacom's business. It also has European smelting operations that process Zairian ore. The Belgians haven't done badly.

After deducting freight costs and sales commissions, Sozacom is supposed to return an average of 45 percent of revenues to Gecamines for expenses and improvements in Kolwezi. This, of course, would include miners' salaries. Mobutu's administrators say that in an average month, Sozacom receives about $120 million from Kolwezi's minerals, nets about $102 million after sales expenses, and returns about $41 million to Gecamines.

But expatriates in Kolwezi say that only about $20 million a month comes back to Gecamines. They say the other $20 million plus is skimmed off in graft. John Castiaux, expatriate chief of Gecamines's computer operations in Lubumbashi (the Shaba capital), confirmed this, though he wouldn't explain further after he found out he was talking to a reporter. "It's politics," he said.

In any case, most of the $120 million-a-month stays with the central banking system, which is also pretty clearly a conduit for thievery by the privileged. And even that is only part of the picture. Someone apparently manages to send a lot of cobalt out of Zaire without its being included in the $120 million at all. The *Wall Street Journal* has quoted commodities market authorities in the U.S. as saying that strange fluctuations in world cobalt prices are probably due to big off-the-books sales from Zaire, which dominates the market.

MIBA, which has a franchise as the national diamond mining monopoly, operates in much the same way. MIBA's expatriate engineers estimate that nearly half as many diamonds are smuggled onto the black market as are sold officially. Most people in Mbuji-Mayi seem to think that the black market share is even bigger. They note that MIBA operates only in the eastern half of the diamond region, and that the province of Western Kasai is open to other, privately owned concessions.

One such concession is held by a company owned by Maurice Tempelsman. Many educated Zairians believe Tempelsman's organization, in partnership with Mobutu, is responsible for the small *comptoirs*, or private

---

minority interest in the copper-cobalt company. Therefore, he says, Tempelsman was never on the opposite side of the bargaining table from Zaire. "He was a participant in a consortium in which the government of Zaire was also a partner," Sorensen says. "The president [Mobutu] said he needed a Western lawyer. Tempelsman recommended me."

*The venture Tempelsman was organizing was separate and all new. For reasons explained in the previous chapter, it still hasn't been developed.

diamond buying offices in Western Kasai. Tempelsman insists that Mobutu doesn't have any interest in his company—in fact, he says they don't have any business partnerships and never have had. He also says that his company doesn't export any diamonds, it just looks for them.

Someone is exporting large amounts of diamonds outside the MIBA monopoly, however. The neighboring Republic of Congo, which has no known diamond deposits whatsoever, is ranked among the world's five leading diamond exporting countries.* That statistic is one of the most remarkable testimonials to corruption in world history.

Much of Zaire's coffee crop is smuggled out through Congo, too.

THE IMF team in Kinshasa admits it can't stop the outflow. In 1980, Belgian customs officials were sent to Kinshasa to supervise baggage checks at the bribery-riddled airport, but admitted they couldn't regulate the chaos. Graft is usually funneled through regional commissioners, about the rank of state governors in the U.S. The commissioners are appointed by Mobutu, and he always picks men from outside the region they are governing. Often they come from his own home region. Citizens complain about both practices.

David J. Gould, a University of Pittsburgh professor, did a field study of Zairian corruption in 1977. He says he interviewed big and small businessmen who reported paying bribes to the regional commissioner of Shaba province. Totaling up these reported bribes, Professor Gould says he accounted for $100,000 a month in graft. The commissioner's salary was $2,000 a month. Thus can the commissioners be expected to stay loyal to the regime. So, of course, can the army. With their roadside checkpoints, soldiers in Zaire are licensed to steal.

Still, despite poverty, misery, and injustice, the people of Zaire can be grateful to the people of the United States for one thing: we have kept their country from communism.

What is less widely considered, but equally true, however, is that we have also kept it from capitalism—or at least from anything that might remotely resemble a free market. And therein lies a key to many of the world's problems. The free market is demonstrably the most bountiful economic system on earth. And it has become the odd role of the United States of America to deny that system to hundreds of millions of people the world wide.

*Stated by diamond dealers and diplomats interviewed in Brazzaville. Back in the U.S., attempts to rank exporters with precise statistics failed, despite calls to the U.N., the U.S. Commerce Department and Census Bureau, spokesmen for DeBeers, and spokesmen for the European American Bank, which is active in the diamond business. One problem is that diamonds are divided into so many sub-categories, overall figures aren't kept.

CHAPTER FOUR
THE U.S. COMES TO AFRICA

TRY TO imagine 1960. Eisenhower's popular two-term presidency is ticking away. Americans are unaware that another such presidency will not soon follow. They don't know that in Vietnam they are already entering their first losing war. They believe that the people of most countries would welcome the arrival of American troops just about the same way the French did in 1944. After eight years in office, Eisenhower, the general who commanded those troops in 1944, surprises many supporters by worrying publicly about the growing uncontrollability of what he calls a "military-industrial complex" in the United States.

John F. Kennedy, the opposition candidate to succeed Eisenhower, complains instead of a "missile gap." (It later proves nonexistent.) He pledges to repair "our lost prestige, our shaky defenses, our lack of leadership." Over and over he charges that turmoil in Cuba and the Congo is proof of U.S. weakness. He campaigns to beef up the U.S. military to meet "the communist challenge" in such places. He declares the world "half slave and half free," and says it can't continue that way. He doesn't say which half he considers the Congo to be in—or to which half Fulgencio Batista, the deposed anticommunist Cuban dictator, belonged.

1960 sees new fleets of jet-powered Boeing 707's and Convair 880's begin to shrink the country and world. Runways are extended, propeller craft replaced, ocean liners mothballed. Europe, Asia, South America, and Africa swell up offshore, only hours away. These new planes, incidentally, create a need for a previously little-known metal that is vital to jet aviation: cobalt.

49

And in 1960, the giant central African land known as the Belgian Congo, later as Zaire, arrives on American television screens as something more than the backdrop for a Grade B jungle movie. It is big news. In the *New York Times* index for 1960, the Congo occupies sixteen pages of entries, more than any other country except the United States. By contrast, news of the Soviet Union occupies only six pages, and news of President Eisenhower only eleven.

That the Congo holds nearly 70 percent of the world's known cobalt ore, as well as other vital resources, is not often mentioned to viewers of popular newscasts and newspaper readers. They are thoroughly informed, however, about something else: the Congo, which is about to undergo the very American experience of independence from a European monarchy, has suddenly been threatened by Russians.

It is the current wisdom that the Soviet Union is using devious, illegal, and even violent means to take over that distant land. American journalists, schoolteachers, and elected officials perceive a Russian plot that will deprive the 14 million (1960 figure) innocent savages who live in the Congo of any link with the democratic West, of any hope that they may become a free society. The current wisdom also says that the Congo takeover is part of a Soviet design for world domination, and that if the design isn't stopped now, in Africa, it will become all the more irresistible as it closes in on Washington.

And so the U.S. government, a third of the way around the world, undertakes the burden of repelling this Soviet threat. Some of Washington's countermeasures are disclosed to the voters and taxpayers: U.S. diplomats speak out for a United Nations military force that can step between the Congolese factions. The U.S. government offers money, equipment, and administrators to create the U.N. force. But the government does not tell the American people that it is also arranging a bloody coup d'etat in the Congo, for which the U.N. force will provide a cover.

CONSIDERING the way the Congo was misrepresented to the U.S. public, it's conceivable that the coup, and perhaps even the attendant murders, might have been popularly approved of even if the government had confessed to planning them. Few government or journalistic opinion makers knew much about the leading characters in the Congo drama, or about the long-simmering tribal disputes that formed the context of Congolese political life. Pundits in the U.S. provided one main explanation for what went on—Soviet plotting. The explanation was wrong. Soviet manipulation would have been much easier to handle in the Congo than the problems that really presented themselves.

Editorial cartoonists loved to play with the Soviet theme. The talented and imaginative artist for the *Indianapolis Star* filled his space, frequently on the front page of the newspaper just below the banner headline, with caricatures of the portly, easily burlesqued, Soviet premier, Nikita Khrushchev, and the skeletal, big-lipped, loin-clothed, cannibal-suggestive black "natives" of the early Hollywood movie cartoons.

In one drawing, Khrushchev was shown cavorting with the natives in a jungle setting under the caption, which was the title of a popular 1940s song, "Bingo, Bango, Bongo, I Don't Want to Leave the Congo." In another, Khrushchev peered at the reader through tall grass, flanked by bone-in-the-nose types. The drawing was shown around the newspaper office with great glee under its original caption: "Ain't nobody here but us niggers." It was published under the caption, "Ain't nobody here but us natives."*

A documentary film on the life of President Kennedy, widely seen on U.S. television, contained only a single brief piece of footage on Africa. It was a scene of Congolese, rioting. Actually, on closer viewing, the film segment showed a couple of hundred African men running, all in the same direction. But the narrator assured the viewer that they were rioting, as Americans would expect Congolese to do.

This was the image that came to replace sixty years of mysteriousness since Conrad wrote *Heart of Darkness*. Perhaps the Congolese were still mysterious, but mainly, now, the Congolese were rioters. During the 1960s, "rioting" became to "Congolese" what "crisp" was to "five-dollar-bill" and "dull" was to "thud." The cliché was laid to rest only when the country changed its name to Zaire.

Time magazine depicted the colonial Belgians as heroes, whose occasional arrival in a village interrupted the sacrifice of innocent human victims in some savage rite. Under the headline "Freedom Yes, Civilization Maybe," *Time* reported that "once Belgian control ends, the self-rule everyone seemed to want will bring with it barbarism and strife."

The *New York Times* story about Congolese independence on June 30, 1960, did note in the second column of type that "the Kingdom of the Congo flourished from the fourteenth century and even exchanged envoys with Portugal, the Vatican, Brazil, and the Netherlands." But the *Times* said this was a "lost greatness," to be found again only with the coming of the Belgians, who "set out to substitute the carpenter's hammer for the tribal drum, introducing the twentieth century overnight to a primitive people divided into many warring tribes."

No doubt some Belgians did bring enlightenment. What the Belgians did mainly, however, was raise export crops, and mine copper and diamonds. (Cobalt didn't become valuable until high-technology uses were developed.) The Belgians laid roads and railroad track only as needed to haul products to the coast for shipping to Europe. Most of the huge colony, the part not of immediate use to the colonizers, was left to its own devices.

Like other colonizers, the Belgians encouraged missionaries to come,

*The author was serving a student internship at the paper at the time.

extending the colonial presence without cost to the colonial government. Many missionaries were dedicated humanitarians who carried literacy and healing where they were needed. Others were social misfits in convenient self-exile from their own countries. At best, missionary work was a haphazard way for a government to provide social services. Often it was an unfair and unacceptable way.

The best evidence for this assessment is the condition of the Congo after seventy-five years of Belgian rule. At independence, barely a dozen Congolese had graduated college. None of the prominent political figures was among them. Of doctors, lawyers, architects, or military officers there were none. Mobutu himself was just a sergeant until, of necessity and considerable desire, he made a fast rise to general. And in Yalifoka, there were still more drums than carpenters' hammers.

PIERRE Davister, a Belgian, ran a newspaper in the Congo in the 1950s and stayed on through the independence period as an advisor in various capacities both to Mobutu and to Patrice Lumumba, Mobutu's principal political rival. By some accounts, Davister was an undercover agent for the Belgian government. In an interview in his office at a magazine he now edits in Brussels, Davister just smiles at that notion, and says he's saving the details for his own memoirs, now in progress. A lot else, however, he shares.

"Each country there was trying to find a figure through which they could influence the Congo," he says. "Mobutu was taking [money] from Belgian State Security and giving information against Lumumba. Belgium was paying them all. They all needed pocket money. They all did it. Lumumba went to the Czech embassy to get money for information. Mobutu didn't go to the Czechs because he felt his future was more or less informing for the Belgians. But they all went to the American embassy."

Two influential players Davister remembers were Harry Oppenheimer, scion of the family that has controlled the DeBeers syndicate, and thus the world diamond business since early in this century, and Oppenheimer's U.S. business associate, Maurice Tempelsman. "Oppenheimer was clearly tied to the South African government," Davister says. "South Africa was supporting Mobutu because they wanted [to control the prices of] the diamonds. Tempelsman was tied to the American government. They were using these two men as a channel for money to keep the Congo on the Western side. Of course, Tempelsman didn't need *money* from the American government. He was there building his own empire. The same as with Belgium and Union Minière [the mining unit of Société Général du Belgique]."

Tempelsman had been shown around Africa by his father, Leon Tempelsman, a Belgian gem dealer. They came to the U.S. either during World War II or right after it, and started the firm Leon Tempelsman & Son in 1946 when Maurice was seventeen. Somehow they established intimacy both with the Oppenheimers and with various African rulers. Maurice Tempelsman carried the U.S. flag into the innermost councils of the chief of state not only in Zaire, but also in Gabon and Sierra Leone, and perhaps other countries as well. Mobutu eventually appointed Tempelsman Zaire's honorary consul in New York.

Davister remembers Mobutu walking into his newspaper office barefoot in 1954 to complain about conditions in the army. At the time, Mobutu was still on his rise up the ranks to sergeant, but eventually he left the army to work for Davister. Through the newspaper, Davister says, Mobutu first met Lumumba, Joseph Kasavubu, and other Congolese with ambitions to leadership. Davister even arranged a free trip to Brussels for Mobutu in 1959, under the auspices of a black education organization.

In February 1960, King Baudouin of Belgium invited eighty-one prominent Congolese to a conference in Brussels to chart a course for independence, which was scheduled for June 30. Kasavubu was in and out of the conference alternately boycotting it and trying to influence it. To allow Lumumba to attend, the king pardoned him after he served only three months of a six-month jail sentence passed upon him for inciting a crowd the previous October.

That twenty persons are supposed to have died in a riot after a speech Lumumba made may be some indication of his oratorical vigor, especially considering that he told the judge he had been advocating nonviolence. Lumumba, with professional experience as a postal clerk and beer salesman, had done a brief stretch in the colonial hoosegow a few years earlier for embezzling $2,500 from the post office; he claimed he spent the money on political activities. While working for the post office, he had been a president of a public employee union in the western province, the area around Stanleyville. According to the *Encyclopaedia Britannica's* biography of him (other sources don't mention it), Lumumba's Belgian political contacts were with the Liberal party, the most right wing of the major Belgian parties.

As Davister noted, Lumumba was basically taking money from any political interest that would pay him. But he was, in certain ways, oriented more toward the socialist-bloc countries than were his rivals. Or, at least, he was attempting to find some ballast against the force of the Western moneymen. Looking at the outsiders whom Lumumba chose to consult in times of trouble, it seems clear that his main socialist influence in terms of ideas (as opposed to money) wasn't from Eastern Europe at all, but from the more left-leaning of the new African heads of state, particularly Kwame Nkrumah of Ghana.

Nkrumah was still preaching his dream of a pan-African confederation operating under a hazily defined system called "African socialism." The dream was always described idealistically, but always featured Nkrumah as head of the confederation, of course. It was a dream that would impoverish Nkrumah's people and imprison many of them before they finally chased him out of Ghana one step ahead of a rope in 1966.* But as early as 1958, Lumumba was flown to Ghana (history is blank on the interesting point of who paid for it) to attend something called the All-African Peoples Conference.

THE preindependence Brussels conference of February 1960 settled on a parliamentary system of government for the Congo. Elections were held in mid-May. Elections then in a place like the Congo necessarily differed in some respects from the kind of thing Americans are used to. There was no television. Most people didn't have radios. They couldn't read, even a simple slogan. And even if they had had radios and could read, they used hundreds of different languages. There weren't telephones, and most Congolese lived several days' hard journey from the nearest airport. Most owed their principal political loyalty to their village chief and the tribal councils to which he reported. The chief's powers of persuasion over the ballots in his neighborhood surpassed those of even the most successful Jersey City ward boss. Moreover, where tribes brushed against one another in the same province (as provinces were drawn by the Belgians), violence broke out over who would be preeminent.

Nevertheless, despite these handicaps, elections were held. And they tended to be fair by comparison to other elections in recent African history—which is to say a lot fairer and more honestly contested than the one-party ratifications Mobutu staged in later years. At any rate, the supervising Belgians certified them. And when the ballots were counted, Lumumba's party got more votes than any other, winning 35 of the 137 seats in parliament.

Many factors contributed to this victory. That Lumumba came from a region that was particularly populous and yet not dominated by one strong tribal nation was perhaps most important. He was born to the Tetela tribe, one of many tribes in the east that wanted to keep power away from one of the potentially dominant tribes of the west and south. Lumumba probably also led the field of candidates in charisma. But as for the economic doctrines of Karl Marx or Milton Friedman—or even Kwame Nkrumah—it would be delusionary to think that the candidates themselves, let alone the voters, devoted much thought to them. There's a real question whether any of the scantily educated candidates was literate enough to *read* such philosophy.†

Nor did Lumumba's plurality constitute any kind of national movement. A lot of horse-trading went on before he could form a cabinet, with himself as prime minister, that parliament would vote into office. As part of the bargaining, Kasavubu was given a mostly ceremonial role as president and

*The author traveled extensively through Ghana in 1965 and 1966.

†Which wouldn't necessarily disqualify them as good leaders. Nkrumah was a highly praised student with a decade of successful university work in the U.S. and Britain, but he fell apart as a leader when he tried to apply abstract ideas to a country totally unprepared for them.

chief of state. All this occurred just a week before independence. Lumumba proclaimed a neutralist foreign policy, though any foreign policy at all was probably not an issue on the minds of his countrymen.

As the only system of national order that any living Congolese had ever known was yanked away, there still was no concept in the Congo of nationhood, let alone participatory democracy. Many Congolese apparently thought that independence would mean a quick role reversal with the Belgians. Workers in Leopoldville (now Kinshasa), the capital, demanded an immediate cash bonus. Some individuals assumed they were now free to murder white men and rape white women, and they did.

Congolese soldiers, barred by the Belgians from military leadership under colonialism, felt a far stronger loyalty to their own tribes than to their nation (as did most Africans), and behaved accordingly. Since soldiers from rival tribes were face-to-face in many provinces, a series of miniwars broke out. Within a week, under the guise of restoring peace, Belgian soldiers were back to killing Congolese in the Congo.

Lumumba, far from seizing power like a man possessed by some vision of utopia, wavered helplessly. To cap off the confusion, on July 11, Moise Tshombe, leader of the Lunda tribe in the Katanga mining province (later Shaba), declared his province an independent country. The Balunda had been largely shut out in the bargaining for national leadership, and since they were sitting on all the copper and cobalt, they decided to make their own deal with the Western buyers. These Western industrial interests had been egging Tshombe on toward succession, hoping to guarantee continued Western ownership of the mines. They promised to supply mercenaries to defend the province against whatever ragtag army Lumumba might assemble to reclaim it.

Lumumba, of course, opposed the secession. For one thing, his government needed income from the mines. For another, leaders of several other provinces were talking about secession, following Tshombe's lead, and if that kept up Lumumba wouldn't have a country left to be prime minister of. He conferred with Nkrumah, and then called for United Nations troops to establish the authority of his government. The troops were sent, under the administration of an American U.N. official, Ralph Bunche (a black, which became important as the situation worsened).

But the U.N. troops didn't have the effect Lumumba sought. The Belgian troops stayed, and while Belgium didn't formally recognize the Balunda secession in Katanga, its troops there seemed to be supporting the secession. These troops included an official army contingent as well as a growing assortment of mercenaries Tshombe recruited. Among the mercenaries, according to a CIA report from Elizabethville, January 17, 1961, were not only Belgian paratroopers but also "former members of German SS and former Italian Fascist soldiers."

In mid-July, after seeing that the Belgians wouldn't leave when the U.N.

force arrived, Lumumba and Kasavubu in a joint announcement asked the
U.S.S.R. to watch the situation and consider sending help if "certain Western
countries" didn't halt their "aggression." As tension mounted, there appeared
a clear split between Lumumba, who repeated the threat to call for Soviet
troops, and the parliamentary majority, which wanted neither Belgians nor
Soviets in the Congo, but only the U.N.

On July 21, the U.N. Security Council, with U.S. and Soviet support,
demanded Belgian withdrawal. Belgian troops did pull out around the capital,
though they stayed in Katanga. But within days, Lumumba dropped his threat
to seek Soviet aid. (U.S. Secretary of State Christian Herter called the threat
a "bluff" from the start, which was a good bet.) Lumumba reasserted his
neutrality, signed a big trade deal with U.S. businessmen and took off for
an official visit to Washington and an address to the U.N. in New York.

FOR an account of what really happened after that, as opposed to what the
American people were told at the time, we are indebted, first, to the 1975
report of the Senate Select Committee to Study Government Operations With
Respect to Intelligence Activities (the Church Committee), and, second, to
Madeleine G. Kalb, who, using the Freedom of Information Act, pried loose
copies of much of the secret cable traffic between Washington and its embassies in Leopoldville and Brussels. She recounted these secrets in her 1982
book, *The Congo Cables* (Macmillan).

The cables illustrate wonderfully two fundamental mistakes of U.S. foreign policy then and now. The first is provincialism. Accustomed to the
context of big-power diplomacy, no one in the policy-making chain of command could see the Congo for what it really was: a couple of hundred
mini-nations, whose people were consumed with the daily chore of warding
off hunger. These nations had long been occupied against their will by white
people and occasionally forced to do slave labor for whites. Suddenly, under
rules laid down by whites, they were proclaimed to be one "country," with
common leadership.

The official leaders were a handful of scarcely literate and totally inexperienced men who had little real authority and highly uncertain tenure. Few
Congolese trusted each other, and none had any reason to trust any white.
The leaders had no example to follow but that of Ghana, which had become
an independent country three years earlier and survived. They wouldn't have
another example until a large, more stable country like Nigeria (independent
in October 1960) or Ivory Coast (August 1960) or Tanzania (December 1961)
could emerge.

Apparently without exception, the U.S. officials involved in the cable
traffic failed to make the slightest effort toward a sympathetic understanding
of all this. They saw the Congo only in American terms, as a player in the
cold war with the U.S.S.R.

The second U.S. foreign policy failing, which rises from each batch of cables like a characteristic fume, is arrogance—an assumption that the U.S. knows what's best for other countries better than they do themselves, and therefore ought to impose its will wherever it finds the power to do so. The CIA people, from director Allen Dulles on down, thought that Lumumba threatened all Africa, even the world. They couldn't wait to bump him off. For blind arrogance, the most strident Leninists in the Kremlin couldn't take a backseat to these Washington policymakers. Richard Bissell, the CIA's deputy director for plans, recalled later, "The Agency had put top priority, probably, on a range of different methods of getting rid of Lumumba in the sense of either destroying him physically, incapacitating him, or eliminating his political influence."

At first, the U.S. embassy in Kinshasa (then Leopoldville) was a little more restrained. It reported to Washington when Lumumba visited the U.S. on July 26, 1960, "Lumumba is an opportunist and not a communist. His final decision as to which camp he will eventually belong will not be made by him but rather will be imposed upon him by outside forces." But by August 17, even Ambassador Claire Timberlake was recommending that the U.S. instigate a coup to remove Lumumba, though the ambassador didn't specifically recommend killing him.

As for the men who ran the U.S. government, Under Secretary of State C. Douglas Dillon told the Church Committee that the National Security Council, including President Eisenhower, believed that Lumumba was a "very difficult if not impossible person to deal with, and was dangerous to the peace and safety of the world." How far beyond the dreams of a barefoot jungle postal clerk in 1956, that in a few short years he would be *dangerous to the peace and safety of the world*! The perception seems insane, particularly coming from the National Security Council, which really does have the power to end all human life within hours.

With all the problems the Congo faced, the entire body of U.S. policymakers could focus only on the single problem that probably never occurred to Lumumba or any other Congolese: "to which camp he will eventually belong." Nor did it occur to the U.S. policymakers that if their question were asked openly, the honest reply of Lumumba and most of his countrymen would be, the *Congolese* camp.

The American inability to see events from an African perspective extended to the simplest cultural differences. Dillon, after meeting Lumumba, adjudged him an "irrational, almost psychotic personality," and cited as his first example that Lumumba "would never look you in the eye." Another U.S. diplomat made the same complaint about Kasavubu. In fact, many Africans are taught by tribal tradition that it is deferential to avoid eye contact; Lumumba and Kasavubu might have been fearful, polite, even repectful, rather than psychotic.

Dillon was annoyed that Lumumba, emerging from his meetings in the U.S., thanked and praised his hosts publicly, even though the Americans had resolutely turned down Lumumba's every request for direct (as opposed to U.N.) help. Dillon feared that Lumumba's public flattery might lead the Belgians to think that the U.S. had betrayed the Atlantic alliance and gone over to the Congolese. In fact, lavish public praise is also a common African custom, and anything less might have seemed impolite to Lumumba. It's also doubtful that Dillon and his colleagues would have been more favorably impressed if Lumumba had exited the State Department complaining to reporters about the lact of cooperation, instead of beaming to them about U.S.-Congolese friendship.

If the well-traveled folk of the National Security Council with their degrees from Wharton and the Johns Hopkins School for Advanced International Studies couldn't shed their parochialism, what could rightfully be expected of a displaced African villager? Lumumba certainly had been stupid to suggest bringing in Soviet troops, whether or not he was bluffing about it. But by what logic did anyone expect statesmanship of him? If he suspected that the U.S. would side in the end with the Belgian occupiers rather than the elected Congolese government, he was merely being perceptive. Secretly, the U.S. was doing exactly that. And since Lumumba faced the continued armed occupation of his country by one group of white men, it was not totally illogical of him to confront the problem by scouting around for other white men who were enemies of the occupier.

The Soviets, to be sure, had imperialist visions of their own and volunteered to provide Lumumba arms. A Soviet presence would have been bad news for the Congo, as it has been for other countries the U.S.S.R. has occupied. But Mobutu's two decades in power show that the U.S. presence also was bad news for the Congo. And we were the ones who intervened uninvited, facing no real danger to ourselves.

There was never the slightest indication that Lumumba wanted Soviet troops in the Congo, or wanted peaceful U.S. commercial interests evicted, unless perhaps that became the only way to prevent continued colonial military occupation. There was never the slightest indication that the Soviets would intervene uninvited. And in the unlikely event that Lumumba brought in Soviet troops, other African experience, such as that in Ghana, Guinea, and Egypt, suggest that the Soviets would eventually have been forced out. They never could have matched the staying power of the Belgian-French-U.S. forces, which were still around in the 1980s.

AN interesting example of this continuity is the career of Lawrence Devlin, the CIA station chief in the Congo in the early 1960s. After ensuring that a dictatorship of the U.S. government's liking was entrenched in the Congo, Devlin became manager of Maurice Tempelsman's business interests there. Tempelsman—the billionaire-class* escort of President Kennedy's widow,

*Tempelsman declines to disclose his worth, and because he has never sold stock in his companies to the public he doesn't have any legal obligation to do so. Dun & Bradstreet

as well as the employer of Kennedy's lawyer, Kennedy's son, and Kennedy's CIA station chief—was in the Congo during these years seeking and finding the inside track for future diamond and copper deals. Tempelsman says that's all he was doing. Pierre Davister, the Belgian journalist and reputed covert operator, says Tempelsman was involved in the U.S.'s political manipulations. Devlin, who could shed plenty of light on this, ducks reporters.

Devlin was full of words for Washington policymakers back in 1960, though. "Embassy and [CIA] station believe Congo experiencing classic communist effort takeover [of] government," he wired his headquarters from Leopoldville (now Kinshasa) August 18. "Whether or not Lumumba actually commie or just playing commie game to assist his solidifying power, anti-West forces rapidly increasing power Congo and there may be little time left in which take action avoid another Cuba," he declared. Devlin advised "replacing Lumumba with [a] pro-Western group."

At that time, by U.S. standards, the Congo was certainly in chaos. It was hard to tell who controlled the cities. A man with a gun might represent any of a variety of factions, or even just himself. Lumumba's allies, presumably on his orders, knocked on doors and arrested his enemies (an objectionable practice that the State Department learned to tolerate only later, when the U.S.-installed Mobutu began to door-knock). Congolese troops detained, threatened, and occasionally beat up U.N. personnel, including some Americans (though none was badly injured). No evidence was produced to indicate whether these acts were impulsive or done on orders, and if on orders, whose orders. But the events were making daily headlines.

Back in the hinterland, where Americans didn't go because the roads were too bad, millions of farmers hoed on, little concerned. Chaos in government is recognizable only to those who are used to getting some benefit from government. Very few Congolese fit that description.

But onto the Congo's pile of problems, the Americans heaped their own imported concerns and assumptions, all grim. Devlin certainly wasn't the only culprit. Ambassador Timberlake was convinced that Lumumba was trying to create an atmosphere of terror. "Objective seems clear," he cabled Washington. "Remove the bulk of Europeans and you eliminate effective Western influence. Once Europeans have gone, nationalize their property on simple theory that business and industry must run to keep Congolese em-

---

estimates the sales of Leon Tempelsman & Son at $70 million a year, and of Tempelsman's American Coldset Corporation, a Dallas-based manufacturer of diamond drill bits (the world's number two maker of diamond petroleum drilling bits, the company says), at $157 million a year. *Fortune* magazine says the companies pull in $100 million and $30 million respectively. But Tempelsman has many other companies in Europe, Africa, and the U.S. Although Tempelsman says he has no active mining ventures in Zaire, Dun & Bradstreet says he "has participating interests in mining ventures there," as well as in Mexico, though it says the participation is "principally confined to providing management consulting services." It also says his companies trade and broker "actively in a wide range of precious minerals and agricultural commodities."

ployed and if Europeans will not run them Congolese government must. Finally GOC [Government of the Congo] would invite commie bloc experts in to keep business and industry going."

While Lumumba's actions were consistent with that thesis, they were also consistent with the thesis that he was trying to rid his country of all foreign control and make it truly independent. Or that he wanted the Congo allied with other African powers and independent of non-African forces. Or that he didn't really know where he was headed. He may have been in it for the money. Africa has had more than its share of petty tyrants. In other words, Ambassador Timberlake attached a cerebral design to Lumumba's actions (or lack of them) that there's no reason to believe was present.

Even it one accepts the thesis that Lumumba was scheming with the Soviets, however, no one ever suggested that the Soviets were intervening in the Congo (at least to that point) by any means other than persuasive oratory, certainly a legitimate tactic. Lumumba was the elected leader of the Congo under a process devised and certified by the Belgians. The only charge that Washington could level against him was that he had made a policy choice that the State Department disapproved of, and that he was using subterfuge to carry out the policy because the Western powers prevented him from carrying it out openly.

Moreover, even if Timberlake was right in gauging Lumumba's machinations and designs, it still didn't mean that the interests of the U.S. people were threatened—the interests of Maurice Tempelsman and the Morrison-Knudsen Company, yes, but not the interests of the average American. Those interests were to be able to consume Congolese raw materials at a fair price and sell U.S. products in fair competition on the Congolese market. Unless the U.S. declared itself the military enemy of the Congolese government, there was no reason to believe that this basic trade would stop.

Timberlake said Lumumba was acting on the direction of "anti-white, pro-communist" Ghanaian advisors. But throughout Nkrumah's socialist rule of Ghana, the U.S. continued to buy cocoa at will and Ghana continued to import American products. In fact, the price of cocoa fell while the price of U.S. manufactured goods rose in the Nkrumah years, so that the time that a U.S. worker had to spend on the assembly line in order to earn enough money to buy his youngster a chocolate bar actually diminished.

In socializing their country, the Ghanaians certainly wrought inefficiency upon themselves. But this was the Ghanaians' problem, and they eventually reacted by dumping Nkrumah.* Under Mobutu, the Congo would suffer even

---

*A lot of people have speculated about the CIA's role in the coup that overthrew Nkrumah in 1966. The Church Committee would have learned about that, but didn't report on it. The most authoritative source available is probably John Stockwell, a veteran CIA officer in Africa, in his 1978 book, *In Search of Enemies* (W. W. Norton & Co.). Stockwell states that the CIA's civilian oversight board, the 40 Committee, rejected every

more stringent government controls and more inefficient production, but because of repeated intervention by the U.S. and its allies, Mobutu couldn't be dumped.

As for the possibility that the Congo would become a permanent Soviet satellite, the example of Ghana provides a good answer for that, too. Nkrumah's overthrow was no doubt mourned by the Soviets. But they didn't respond militarily. They probably weren't capable of doing so effectively. Nor would they have been in the Congo. The Soviet military and civilian advisors whom Nkrumah had invited to Ghana departed hastily, making their way to the airport through crowds of jeering Ghanaians eager to see them go. Eight Soviets were reported killed in the coup.

Back in 1960 (as today), many Third World ambassadors at the U.N. joined the Soviets in regular anti-American propaganda tirades. The apparent naiveté of many Third World countries toward communism could be attributed to their having been exposed to Western colonialism but not yet to Soviet colonialism. Though wrong, their views were understandable. The U.S., however, made no effort to understand. And in the end, the socialist rhetoric was self-defeating. The leftist propaganda only drowned out any voices of reason in the U.S. Hawkish tempers were inflamed.

The Soviets were indeed hypocritically selective in their support of self-determination for nations. They had shown no concern for self-determination when they trampled on the rights of Hungary a few years earlier. But in accusing the U.S. and other Western countries of violent, unprovoked intervention in the Congo, the Soviets were absolutely right. And in the end, for all the Soviet speechmaking, it was the U.S. that deceitfully manipulated the U.N. in the Congo.

IMMEDIATELY after Devlin's "classic communist takeover" cable arrived on August 18, Dulles relayed Devlin's thoughts to the National Security Council. Dulles declared that Lumumba was "in Soviet pay" (indeed, Lumumba apparently *was* in Soviet pay, as well as in U.S. pay and Belgian pay—as were his political rivals).

Eisenhower had just held a press conference in which he said that the U.N. was the chief hope for restoring stability to the Congo. It would appear

---

proposal for a U.S. action to oust Nkrumah. It encouraged the CIA station chief in Accra to keep close contact with Nkrumah's high-ranking potential enemies in order to gather intelligence, which, of course, is the CIA's job. The station chief did it well, and apparently had advance knowlege of the coup, which allowed the U.S. to recover some Soviet equipment. But Stockwell says, "CIA cables and dispatches infer that all contacts with the plotters were undertaken solely to obtain intelligence on what they were doing." That is a perfectly appropriate role for the CIA to play. The important thing is that the coup apparently was conceived, developed, and carried out independent of the U.S., and it certainly appeared, on the ground at the time, to have the overwhelming support of the Ghanaian people.

the president was lying to the voters. At the National Security Council, he responded to Dulles's announcement with an implicit or explicit order for Lumumba's forceful removal, by assassination if necessary. The exact words weren't recorded. Robert Johnson, NSC staff member from 1951 to 1962, testified before the Church Committee that Eisenhower's words "came across to me as an order for the assassination of Lumumba. . . . There was no discussion; the meeting simply moved on. I remember my sense of that moment quite clearly because the president's statement came as a great shock to me."

To us all, one would hope. What would the reaction be to news that Lumumba had ordered a member of his U.N. mission to kill Eisenhower? Lumumba had much more to fear from the U.S. than the U.S. had to fear from Lumumba. Yet there is no evidence that Lumumba sought to bring harm to a single American head. Nor is there evidence that the Soviets committed any violence during the crisis, or threatened to start any. (The Soviets certainly have initiated violence and employed assassination elsewhere—which is something the U.S. could marshal international outrage against much more effectively if our own hands were clean.)

Under Secretary of State Dillon, recalling that same August 18 National Security Council meeting, didn't remember that Eisenhower's assassination order was "clear cut," though he allowed that Eisenhower might have said, "We will have to do whatever is necessary to get rid of him [Lumumba]." Dillon also said that Dulles could have reasonably accepted such a remark from Eisenhower as an assassination order, "because he [Dulles] felt very strongly that we should not involve the president directly in things of this nature. And he was perfectly willing to take the responsibility personally."

Here we ascend to yet a scarier plateau. Dulles may have been acting on his own. To find in the U.S. Constitution authorization for the CIA director to "take the responsibility" for murdering other countries' prime ministers is even more difficult than to find authorization for the president himself to do so.

The day after Eisenhower talked to the National Security Council, CIA deputy director Richard Bissell cabled station chief Devlin to go ahead and replace by force the legally constituted government of the Congo—a nation with which the United States was not at war and had no cause to be.

RATHER than risk direct action, the U.S.'s representatives first sought to work through others. As they sold their program, they presented the Congo's neophyte leaders with a first lesson in the American philosophy of constitutional government. Ambassador Timberlake and his deputy, Frank Carlucci (who rose to a high CIA post under President Carter and became number two man in the Defense Department under President Reagan) visited Joseph Kasavubu, Lumumba's chief political rival. Kasavubu had accepted the role of president, or ceremonial head of state, in a preindependence compromise with Lumumba, who had beaten Kasavubu in the election.

Now Timberlake and Carlucci asked Kasavubu to stage a coup. He refused.* Then Devlin, the CIA man and thus more sneaky about it, met with President Kasavubu's Congolese allies, who approached Kasavubu and proposed that Kasavubu authorize *them* to kill Lumumba. The Church Committee didn't disclose who these allies were, though considering Devlin's close relationship with Mobutu, it's a good guess he was one of them.

By this time, Mobutu was out of journalism and back in the army as a colonel. The Church Committee report refers to Devlin's meeting "a key Congolese leader"—in her book Mrs. Kalb flatly identifies him as Mobutu—and says Devlin "urged arrest or other more permanent disposal" not just of Lumumba, but also of his allies, Deputy Prime Minister Antoine Gizenga and Minister of Education Pierre Mulele. This was no longer just an assassination; it was to be a full-scale bloodletting worthy of a Shakespearean curtainfall.

The fledgling Congolese leaders, so desperately needing an example to follow, were being instructed by the world's leading proponent of liberty and democracy on how a political system ought to work: you kill your legally elected rivals and seize power. The prospects of free society in Africa may have been crippled by those discussions as much as by any number of troop-laden aircraft. For awhile, Kasavubu stunningly refused the American entreaties to junk the Congo's six-week-old constitutional democracy, even though to agree would have allowed Kasavubu to take power under American protection.

"I confess I have not yet learned [the] secret of spurring Kasavubu to action," Timberlake moaned to Washington by cable on August 19.

---

*When I first called Carlucci to inquire about this, he asserted that asking Kasavubu to oust Lumumba was "very different from asking him to stage a coup. Kasavubu had the statutory authority to dismiss the prime minister" under the Congolese constitution, Carlucci said. A search of several libraries turned up only one set of excerpts from the original Congolese constitution, in a book edited by Jean-Paul Sartre, admittedly with a pro-Lumumba bias. A reading of the pertinent clauses reveals that while Article 22 did give the president the power to "appoint and dismiss the prime minister," Articles 17, 19, and 20 make pretty clear that this power was ceremonial, much as the power the queen of England has to perform similar chores. (Carlucci had compared it to the stronger power wielded by the president of France, but the words I found didn't bear him out.) Read the relevant clauses in a second phone call, Carlucci conceded that this had been "an issue at the time," and that it was "not without controversy. The State Department was comfortable in the interpretation that Kasavubu could dismiss Lumumba," he said. He cited an independent legal authority for this interpretation; the authority was a Belgian. All other accounts I have read, both from 1960 and more recently, justify the version I have presented. The Sartre book is *Lumumba Speaks*, published by Little, Brown & Company in 1972.

Lumumba soon revealed what it took to spur *him* to action. That happened when he sought U.N. assistance to oust the Belgians, and to establish his government's authority in the two secessionist provinces, Katanga (copper-cobalt) and Kasai (diamonds). The U.N. command refused. It said the U.N. troops were there to maintain peace, which seemed to mean the status quo, which seemed—to Lumumba at least—to mean secession. To put down the secession, Lumumba turned to the Soviets, who promised one hundred trucks and ten aircraft, with crews and weapons. Pending their arrival, Lumumba requisitioned five leftover Belgian civilian aircraft, and immediately dispatched an expedition to Kasai to restore authority over the independence-minded Baluba tribe. The expedition was then to move on to Katanga to rope in the Balunda. That was August 24, 1960.

Back in the U.S., where only a few college professors understood the difference between Baluba and Balunda, the secessionist movements came to dominate intellectual debate between liberals and conservatives. The liberals wanted the mining revenues to benefit all the Congolese people, and they misunderstood this to be the position of the Bakongo, Bangala, and Lulua tribes. The conservatives wanted to help local entrepreneurs avert socialization of their property, and they misunderstood this to be the position of the Balunda and Baluba tribes.

Thus, from his office in New York, William F. Buckley, Jr., looked at Katanga and saw the spirit of Edmund Burke in the eyes of the secessionist Balunda, while across town Eleanor Roosevelt favored the Bangala and Bakongo to move in. The situation in Kasai was less publicized, but in general, the followers of Mr. Buckley championed the Baluba while those of Mrs. Roosevelt sided with the Lulua. It was as if a production by the Topeka High School Thespian Society of a locally written drama were suddenly invaded by Edmund Wilson, Walter Kerr, and Rona Barrett, all arguing over the proper objectives of the theater and seizing one or another amateur actor by the collar, and shaking and haranguing the poor student to twist his performance to justify a particular theatrical philosophy. The pressure on men like Lumumba, Kasavubu, and Tshombe must have been enormous, if they weren't too bewildered to understand it.

Bewildering things happened. Lumumba one day demanded that the U.N. remove all white troops from its peacekeeping force, then a few days later withdrew the demand. He belatedly apologized for the beating up of eight Canadian U.N. workers by Congolese troops. He closed down a newspaper that had written unflatteringly of him. The Soviet Union delivered a shipload of wheat to Leopoldville, only to discover that no one had ever built a flour mill in the Congo. The embarrassed Russians had to reload the wheat and ship it out again. Far more serious, Lumumba's military expedition against the Baluba in Kasai turned into a massacre of hundreds, maybe thousands, of civilians.

And oh, if Mrs. Roosevelt had known what the U.S. was really up to! Even Buckley might have blanched. Dulles himself cabled Devlin (the CIA station chief who would soon become Tempelsman's mining and mineral agent) giving him almost carte blanche, and $100,000 of the taxpayers' money, to wreak havoc. Lumumba's "removal must be an urgent and prime objective," Dulles cabled. He authorized Devlin not only to stage a coup, but to take "even more aggressive action if it can remain covert. . . . We realize that targets of opportunity may present themselves to you," he said, and authorized Devlin to "carry out any crash programs on which you do not have the opportunity to consult HQS."

A CIA scientist, Dr. Sidney Gottlieb, was assigned to produce a poison that, in the words of his testimony to the Church Committee, "was supposed to produce a disease that was . . . indigenous to that area and that could be fatal . . . either kill the individual or incapacitate him so severely that he would be out of action." Then reports came that Lumumba, visiting an airport, had encountered some American U.N. workers who had been beaten up by Congolese soldiers, and had failed to aid them. Ambassador Timberlake cabled Washington that he hoped the incident "has removed any lingering trace of the fiction that we are dealing with a civilized people or a responsible government in the Congo."

In early September, something swung Kasavubu over to the U.S. idea of dumping the democracy. Maybe it was the arrival of the first Soviet planes and advisors, maybe the bloodletting in Kasai, maybe continued pressure from the U.S. But on September 5, he went on national radio and announced he was dismissing Lumumba as prime minister. He said he had asked Joseph Ileo, another politician the Americans had been talking to a lot, to form a new government.

Not only was this coup prompted by the U.S., it was openly assisted by the U.N. Before going on the air, Kasavubu had discussed his plans for at least two days with the highest ranking U.N. official in the Congo. By this time, Ralph Bunche had resigned in disgust, but he had been replaced by Andrew Cordier—another American. Moreover, the Kasavubu aide who had given Cordier full details about the coup in advance was A. A. J. van Bilsen— a Belgian!

After Kasavubu made his announcement, Cordier had U.N. troops seal off the radio station and all airports. The radio station and the airport are about the only physical manifestations that many Third World governments have, and seizure of them is often all it takes to carry out a coup. Cordier said the seizure of the radio station and airports in the Congo was a neutral act, but, in fact, it wasn't neutral. Kasavubu could and did cross the Congo River and use the radio in Brazzaville, the capital of the Congo Republic, which three weeks earlier had become independent from France and was still closely tied to Paris. Lumumba had no radio. Moreover, Lumumba's most loyal troops and political supporters were out-country, and with the airports closed, they couldn't reach Leopoldville. Leopoldville was Kasavubu's base, and was already filled with the troops most loyal to his government.

Still, Lumumba fired back. He declared that he was sacking Kasavubu—

something he was no more empowered to do than Kasavubu had been empowered to sack him. Then Lumumba went before both houses of parliament. Once more, to the consternation of the U.S. manipulators, the elected parliamentarians threw their overwhelming support to Lumumba as prime minister. But they also insisted on holding on to the constitutional democracy by refusing to recognize Lumumba's firing of Kasavubu. So it went for a week, confusingly, noisily, but peacefully.

Except that all during that week, Joseph Mobutu had been meeting intensely with Kasavubu at the president's house, as well as with Devlin and other Americans, and with Davister. On September 10, Cordier, the American U.N. official, produced $1 million in U.N. funds to meet the back pay owed to the garrison of Congolese troops in Leopoldville, and Mobutu and two generals personally passed it out. The loyalty of troops was bought with U.N. cash.

On September 12, Lumumba was arrested and held for three hours by troops loyal to Mobutu, then released. The next day, Kasavubu fired the army commander, who reportedly was responsible for Lumumba's release, and installed Mobutu in his place. On September 14, Mobutu announced that the army, now under *his* command, was taking over the government until January 1. Kasavubu, apparently neither surprised nor upset, cooperated by announcing that he was suspending parliament.

This obviously coordinated plot was almost certainly American in origin. Though Mrs. Kalb's cables contain no smoking-gun-type admissions of U.S. responsibility, she reports from other sources that the army takeover was financed by Western governments. Two State Department officials who worked intensely on Congo-Zaire policy have said* that the U.S. designed the September 14 coup and selected Mobutu for the job. The State Department's official document, "Analytical Chronology of the Congo Crises," tacitly admits this. The document refers to a plan "to bring about the overthrow of Lumumba and install a pro-Western government." Then it says, "operations under this plan were gradually put into effect by the CIA."†

Ambassador Timberlake was exuberant at the collapse of Congolese democracy. "Even the local clerks who worked for Lumumbavitch are being methodically arrested," he cabled Washington cheerily on September 16, as the Congolese finally learned the meaning of political freedom, U.S.-style. Timberlake described Mobutu—who after a decade of public service would credibly come to call himself the third-richest man in the world—as "completely honest." And he accurately forecast that the next day Mobutu would kick the Soviet and other East bloc embassies out of the Congo.

Then Mobutu, at Devlin's suggestion, tried to arrest Lumumba. But Ghan-

---

*In interviews with me, under a promise their names would not be disclosed.

†See Stephen R. Weissman, "The CIA Covert Action in Zaire and Angola," *Political Science Quarterly*, Summer 1979.

aian U.N. troops guarding the house where Lumumba was staying barred Mobutu's men. The U.S. and Belgium had lost command of the supposedly neutral U.N. mission. Rajeshwar Dayal, an Indian diplomat, who had taken over from Cordier as chief, declared that he was working on a compromise that might restore Lumumba to the government.

Washington jumped ten feet at the mere possibility. On September 19, agent Devlin received a cable announcing that Dr. Gottlieb, the poison specialist, would be there in a week, using the code name "Joe from Paris." Dulles sent a personal note saying, "We wish give every possible support in eliminating Lumumba from any possibility resuming governmental position." Washington had just supported a U.N. resolution banning anyone's sending soldiers or weapons to the Congo. The resolution passed. But apparently, in Washington's eyes, Gottlieb and his little vials didn't count.

Devlin told Mobutu to arrest and murder Deputy Premier Gizenga. Mobutu's troops hauled Gizenga in, but U.N. troops intervened and freed him. Lumumba was under effective house arrest, protected by a cordon of U.N. troops surrounding his quarters. Devlin tried to infiltrate the tight ring of associates who visited Lumumba, hoping to slip him the poison, but failed. One effort, the Church Committee learned, was to have someone inject the poison into Lumumba's toothpaste. Here again, the simplest knowledge of Africa might have saved the CIA some trouble; Africans commonly don't use a toothbrush or toothpaste, but clean their teeth with a piece of soft, aromatic wood known as a chew stick.

Devlin asked Washington for an additional CIA man to help the infiltration. In case it failed, he also requested that "HQS pouch soonest high powered foreign make rifle with telescopic scope and silencer. Hunting good here when lights right," he said.

With the appointment of Rajeshwar Dayal, a real neutralist, to replace Bunche and Cordier in running the U.N. operation, the U.N.'s active cooperation with U.S. policy stopped. Dayal recognized only Kasavubu as a legitimate Congolese authority. He refused to choose between Mobutu and Lumumba. In New York, the U.S. warned Secretary General Dag Hammarskjöld, Dayal's boss, that if the U.N. tried any compromise that would restore Lumumba to power, the U.S. would make "drastic revision" of its Congo policy, implying unilateral military action. The U.S. would not tolerate the return of Lumumba, the only man ever to hold office by legitimate vote of the Congolese people.

The U.S. State Department thought itself much more capable than the Congolese voters of choosing a suitable prime minister for that country, though there was debate about who it should be. The department's Charles Bohlen agreed with Hammarskjöld that Joseph Ileo was the man. Timberlake objected that Ileo didn't have the "necessary drive and flair," and proposed Cyrille Adoula. Adoula, who had come up through the CIA-connected labor unions, was another member of the small elite recognized by the whites as leaders. The department suggested yet a third choice, but Timberlake insisted on Adoula.

Timberlake also objected to the State Department's plan to reconvene parliament as a vehicle for legitimatizing its appointment. Timberlake was nervous that the parliamentarians might rebel against Washington's stooge. He pointed out that Lumumba "would have to be allowed to participate in session of parliament as a deputy. There is always danger that no matter how firm opposition line up, Lumumba oratory plus threats can turn it into victory for himself." In other words, if the Congolese were allowed even the least say in the matter of who would be their prime minister, they might once more, as always in the past, pick Lumumba instead of rubber-stamping Washington's candidate.

Then Timberlake added a wonderfully (if unintentionally) ironic obser-vation, that the Congolese lacked the "ability to produce anything resem-bling democratic government until they have been taught. . . . They obviously cannot practice something they do not understand. . . . Furthermore, I do not believe democracy can be imposed on any people over-night . . ."

Fortunately, a military dictatorship could be imposed, and Timberlake assured Washington that the "town was crawling with" Mobutu's troops. In mid-November, they did battle with U.N. forces, leaving four dead, in a successful effort to eject the Ghanaian ambassador. On the night of November 27, sensing that the stalemate was about to be resolved against him unless he acted, Lumumba had some friends sneak him past the troops who were guarding him. He took off for Stanleyville to try to regroup his political forces. His escape touched off a massive manhunt, and Devlin reported that he helped Mobutu's government set up roadblocks to catch the fugitive en route. Now that Lumumba was out of U.N. protection, Mobutu's men with Devlin's help could get their hands on him.

Lumumba was captured and returned to Leopoldville, where U.S. news agencies photographed him badly beaten and bloody. Ambassador Timber-lake voiced hope that the news agencies "could be prevailed upon to suppress" the film, but it was shown anyway. Timberlake continued to try to organize a civilian government around Adoula.

The African and Asian members of the U.N. had become more and more upset over Lumumba's treatment, and Timberlake suggested that "a govern-ment with more claim to legitimacy [than Mobutu's] would make it easier" for Washington to deal with this neutral bloc. Besides, there was now an opposite pole around which the socialist countries could cluster, because Lumumba's aide-de-camp, Antoine Gizenga, proclaimed that he was now running the Congo from a new capital in Stanleyville. A planeload of Soviet aid, some of it military, arrived there.

That Soviet planeload, however, was a doubtful match for the U.S.'s one-man reinforcement squad that had been sent in answer to Devlin's call for help. Code named WI/ROGUE, the new U.S. agent was described by the CIA as an "essentially stateless soldier of fortune, a forger and former bank-robber...a man with a rather unsavory reputation, who would try anything once, at least." Washington described him as "a general utility agent [assigned to] (a) organize and conduct a surveillance team; (b) intercept packages; (c) blow up bridges; and (d) execute other assignments requiring positive action. His utilization is not to be restricted to Leopoldville."

The CIA instructed Devlin that WI/ROGUE "is indeed aware of the pre-cepts of right and wrong, but if he is given an assignment which may be morally wrong in the eyes of the world, but necessary because his case officer ordered him to carry it out, then it is right, and he will dutifully undertake appropriate action for its execution without pangs of conscience. In a word, he can rationalize all actions." This is the man Washington sent to teach the Congolese about democratic government.

WI/ROGUE promptly went to Stanleyville and unwittingly tried to recruit another CIA operative, code named QJ/WIN, to join an "execution squad" for a salary of $300 a month. QJ/WIN didn't tell WI/ROGUE that he was already part of an execution squad, and working for the same government. Instead, QJ/WIN just declined the offer and reported it to Devlin. It is not known who else WI/ROGUE may have recruited or whom he may have executed.

Meanwhile, relations with the U.N. worsened as Mobutu began flexing his muscles and sabotaging the U.N. force's movements. Under U.N. and other international pressure, he still held Lumumba under relatively humane conditions. But on January 13, 1961, that changed. There were rumors of a pro-Lumumba mutiny in the army. President Kennedy was scheduled to take office in Washington, and Mobutu may have suspected that Kennedy would be less partial in Congolese politics than Eisenhower was. Mrs. Kalb reports that Kasavubu tried to strike a last-second deal with Lumumba, whereby Lumumba would have accepted a subordinate role in government; she says Lumumba turned it down.

At any rate, Lumumba never saw a Kennedy presidency. On January 17, Mobutu and Kasavubu did to Lumumba something just as bad as turning him over to WI/ROGUE, QJ/WIN, or Dr. Gottlieb. They packed Lumumba, and two aides who had been arrested with him, on a plane to Katanga. They sent along some goons who bruised the prisoners up pretty thoroughly en route. And they delivered the three men to Moise Tshombe, head of the Balunda, against whom Lumumba had recently sent an ill-disciplined and massacre-prone army.

The last reliable accounts of Lumumba alive came from Swedish U.N. troops at the Elisabethville airport that day. They reported seeing the prime minister being kicked and beaten by a group including Tshombe's soldiers and their Belgian advisors.

On February 13, Tshombe's government announced that Lumumba and

the two aides had escaped and been murdered by villagers. Tshombe declined
to identify the village—for fear of reprisals, he said. In November, a U.N.
commission reported that Lumumba and his aides were probably killed right
after they arrived in Elisabethville on January 17, probably in Tshombe's
presence, possibly by Belgians. It blamed Kasavubu for turning the three
men over to their enemies in the first place. Unaware of the unrelenting
pressure on Kasavubu and Mobutu, the commission didn't cite the role of
the United States.

‖CHAPTER FIVE

HOW THE AMERICAN TAXPAYER BROUGHT THE CUBAN CIVIL WAR TO LAKE TANGANYIKA

════════════════════════DR. GOTTLIEB's lethal virus, and the rest of Dr. Gottlieb's poison sampler, stayed locked in an envelope marked "Eyes Only" in Larry Devlin's office safe. In testimony before the Church Committee, Devlin and Dr. Gottlieb said that the poisons were eventually dumped into the Congo River. But each testified that he alone did this dumping, not the other. Dr. Gottlieb said he disposed of the poisons before leaving Zaire on October 5, 1960, and Devlin said he disposed of them many months later. Devlin allowed that he may well have held onto them until Lumumba was safely dispatched by other means. One only hopes that what was finally dumped was harmless after being diluted by the world's sixth-longest river, but the Church Committee report offers no assurance of that.

The U.S. role in the overthrow and murder of Patrice Lumumba stayed locked in the CIA's cellar of secrets for a full fifteen years, until the Church Committee negotiated its brief opening of the cellar door in 1975. Yet in all that time, while the cellar door stayed shut for the American people, there were few high school students in Africa who didn't "know" the Lumumba secret, at least to their satisfaction. As little else could have, Lumumba's death made the United States suspect to Africans. Lumumba attained true martyrdom. And the martyrdom wasn't just among leftist movements, which understandably played his death for all it was worth. Rather, in nations up and down the continent, even in basically capitalist countries like Nigeria and Kenya—most ironically, even in Zaire itself—one still finds Patrice Lumumba's name affixed to avenues, squares, parks, and schools.

Lumumba has become Africa's most widely recognized hero. People in cities and villages across Zaire say they look to Lumumba's sons to come back and govern their country someday. Most don't know how many sons he had, or where they are. In fact, an accurate count is hard to come by, although several sons have been reported living in Europe and North Africa. But for Zairians, they exist more as legend than fact.

Socialists, of course, claim Lumumba died for socialism. But there is little reason to believe he knew much about socialism. In fact, all through his brief career as a leader he had publicly pledged to respect private property and even foreign investment. He probably didn't know much about private property, either—no Congolese had much—so he may well have pledged to protect it only at Western urging. But it showed he was at least open-minded.

Lumumba had not even leveled claims against the foreign cartels that were toting away his country's minerals with scant compensation. One could fairly assume he would have insisted on changing the mineral deal after the situation had settled down. But that is hardly socialism. The main cartel operating at the time, the Union Minière unit of Société Général, was hardly a free enterprise, either—it was effectively an arm of the Belgian crown.

Lumumba might, of course, have created a Zairian government agency to take over the mineral business. This is what Mobutu did when he created Gecamines and Sozacom. This is socialism, although the U.S., having installed Mobutu to prevent such a thing, can't call it that. But if Lumumba would have differed from Mobutu on the issue of government ownership versus independent private ownership, it could only have been in the direction of more private ownership.

Nor did Lumumba ever threaten the multiparty political system, which Mobutu eventually outlawed. Maybe Lumumba would have outlawed it, too, but if he would have differed from Mobutu on this issue it could only have been in the direction of more political freedom.

Lumumba is a hero to Africans not because he promoted socialism, which he didn't, but because he resisted foreign intervention. He stood up to outsiders, if only by getting himself killed. Most Africans who think about such things at all would say that the principal outsider he stood up to was the United States. The facts seem to bear them out.

Lumumba may well have been a luckless victim of the U.S.'s growing frustration with Cuba. The U.S. government was determined never again to be fooled and betrayed by a Soviet ally posing as a nationalist, which is the way it perceived Fidel Castro. (After all, how could the United States ever not get its way, except that it was betrayed?) So one experience was overlaid on another, an ocean away, with typical inappropriateness.

Whatever one wants to guess about the secret intentions Castro harbored when he took over Cuba, and about whether Castro was ever open to dissuasion from at least initially adopting a socialist course, it is hard to argue that *Lumumba* had a prior ideological commitment. In their backgrounds, in the course of their rise to leadership, in their alliances, in their grip on the loyalties of their own peoples, the two men weren't comparable, despite the relentless determination of Allen Dulles and other U.S. policymakers to compare them.

Castro was an intellectual and a lawyer who spent a decade organizing and leading a successful popular revolution. Lumumba came relatively out of the woodwork.

Lumumba's association with socialism was largely involuntary and posthumous, the result of U.S. policy. Yet because of Lumumba's martyrdom, his association with socialism has become a successful slander against the cause of the free market in Africa. Lumumba's martyrdom identified socialism with independence, and, for Africans, endowed socialism with a luster that has been slow to fade. For many years, to some extent even today, the most logical actions of the free marketplace must sometimes be rationalized around the political need of African leaders to identify with "socialism" in the Lumumba tradition.

One can only guess what would have become of Lumumba's prime ministership had the U.S.-Soviet cold war, which didn't concern him, not intruded. Perhaps Nkrumah would have persuaded Lumumba to create a one-party socialist state and enroll it in Nkrumah's dreamed-of pan-African empire (built on socialist idealism, but with Nkrumah in charge, of course). Perhaps, like Mobutu, Lumumba would have created a one-party socialist state to achieve an empire of his own. Perhaps Lumumba would have been selfless enough to see that the interests of his people lay in dispersing control of the country's wealth widely among themselves, rather than in centralizing it. Perhaps he would have built a country with economic and political freedom. Perhaps, after a few years, he would have grown disenchanted with his first course, whatever it was, and tried another. Alas, the most likely answer is, none of the above.

Wiser, more calculating African leaders than he were swept off the pages of history within a year or two. Absent the big powers, the odds are that Lumumba's name would have been lost with the others. A couple of truckloads of soldiers could pull off a coup without firing a shot in the new states of black Africa. So remote were the governments from the people that few would even know of such a coup, except that music was interrupted on the radio for an announcement that one leader had been replaced by another, and there were some speeches until the music started again. (And as mentioned, in the Congo, most people didn't even have radios.) Unless one's own tribe were going from subordinacy to preeminence or vice versa, the change in government mattered little.

A personal note may illustrate: in December 1965, the author and some friends, all of us Peace Corps volunteers, were traveling up the West African coast on holiday. In Cotonou, Dahomey (now called the Republic of Benin), we visited the presidential palace as tourists one morning and noticed two open military trucks in the driveway, each with a single mounted gun and maybe two dozen soldiers in the back. We watched awhile, assuming it was some sort of ceremony. But nothing seemed to be happening, so we walked on to the market, where we browsed and chatted with people for hours.

That evening we rode a taxi to Lomé, the capital of neighboring Togo. After passing routinely through the immigration posts of both countries, we arrived at the Peace Corps hostel in Lomé, and were startled to be welcomed by several obviously relieved embassy and Peace Corps officials. They explained that a coup d'etat had occurred in Cotonou that morning, and that they were worried for the safety of Americans who might be trapped there. We had actually watched one of these coups take place and had not even known. In practical terms, nothing had happened. Talking with dozens of Dahomeyans that day, and being in every important public place in the country's main city, we had heard no mention of a coup until we met U.S. officials in a neighboring country.

Appropriately, the Dahomeyan president who had so peacefully lost his job that day was named Apithy.

SINCE 1965, governments throughout Africa and most of the Third World have noticeably increased their effect on daily life. A greater sense of nationhood has developed. But national governments continue to be a much more distant and shapeless factor in the lives of most people in most countries than the U.S. assumes. This remoteness of government would be dictated by poor communications and transportation, and by splintered ethnic loyalties, even if it weren't encouraged by other factors (such as the lack of an economy sophisticated enough to demand big government). The role of Washington in U.S. life is simply not analogous to the role of governments in the lives of people in most countries. Yet the State Department and the U.S. press corps often continue to act as if the mood of Upper Volta, or Indonesia, or wherever can be accurately gleaned from talks with a few government leaders.

Americans unfairly confuse the views and behavior of these leaders with the views and behavior of their people. Thus we discover that the government of Zaire, or Libya, or Panama is run by crooks, or irrational polemicists, and we deductively assign the sins of this leadership clique to the whole country. We want to vent our hostility on the general population. This is especially unfair considering that the leaders who are guilty of these affronts have sometimes been placed in power by U.S. government agents. It is also counterproductive, because hostile U.S. action can create genuine popular animosity toward the U.S., and toward our system, that didn't previously exist. It can rally popular support for the obnoxious leaders that they didn't previously have. If we don't interfere, these leadership cliques tend to come and go.

Occasionally, in the two decades or so of postcolonial African history, shots have been fired to bring down governments. More rarely, there were fair elections (but never, yet, a continuation of fair, multiparty elections from one administration to the next in the same country). Some rulers have died in disgrace, which was imposed on them by their successors, who then suffered the same fate after their own turn in office. Some rulers live out their days in obscurity, often in the former colonial capital in Europe, sometimes sheltered by some friendly potentate elsewhere in Africa. They typically reappear only once, in a two-paragraph obituary in the *New York Times*. This is the context in which Lamumba must be seen.

It is on the whole a pretty sorry record, though not exactly unpredictable, considering that native and colonial monarchies dominated previous African history. The democratic experiment had no example in Africa, and badly needed one. So perhaps the sorriest, and the most unnecessary, blight on the record of this new era, is that the precedent for it all, the very first coup in postcolonial African history, the very first political assassination, and the very first junking of a legally constituted democratic system, all took place in a major country, and *were all instigated by the United States of America*. It's a sad situation when people are left to learn their "democracy" from the Union of Soviet Socialist Republics.

IF the U.S.'s Congo policy worked against the interests of the African people, one might ask if the policy was at least necessary to protect the interests of the U.S. people. The answer may lie in the following: of the few African leaders from the 1960 era who survived long, at least two—Sékou Touré of Guinea and Julius Nyerere of Tanzania—were self-proclaimed socialists. Both decreed a one-party political system, and imposed an order on their people that would be unacceptable to Americans. (For example, Nyerere forced farm families to move out of their traditional villages and onto communes.)

Yet both Touré and Nyerere have maintained relatively good relations with the West. Neither is regarded as an enemy, even by the U.S. faction that rails against supposed Soviet puppet states in Africa. The U.S. courts Nyerere of Tanzania as a mediator in disputes, such as over the independence of Zimbabwe and Namibia. Much the same holds true in Zambia, where the venerable Kenneth Kaunda is completing his second decade of one-man rule, during which he nationalized practically everything in the name of his disease-ridden and ill-fed people. But he's friendly to us. Relations with Guinea were troubled in the early years when Touré was a follower of Nkrumah, but that's changed, and the U.S. and France have been Guinea's leading trade partners of late.

Despite their belief in the socialist ethic, these leaders could read the world's economic cards clearly enough to see that the deal offered by Western commerce was too valuable to pass up. In fact, Nyerere has successfully

soaked the West for all he could. His country is one of the world's leading
per capita beneficiaries of Western largess, with some $3 billion in aid gifts
to go with $1.5 billion in loans for 18 million people.

Those loans are in big trouble. Tanzania isn't making enough money to
repay them, and the U.S. taxpayer, through the IMF or some domestic
mechanism, may have to pick up much of the bill. But this is only because
U.S. bankers were allowed to use the taxpayer as a guarantor for the banks'
bad loans in the first place. Some taxpayers might grow to wish we had let
the Russians finance the communization of Tanzanian farming (except that
that might have driven us to invade the place, which would have cost even
more). Other than the bank loans, which were solely the result of our own
bad judgment, the U.S. people could scarcely have better relations with
Guinea or Tanzania. The unfortunate economic choices of those countries'
governments have hurt their people, but not ours (except in the abstract sense
that if Guineans and Tanzanians were wealthier, they would make better
trade partners). It would surely be nice to see more people enjoy more
freedom. But compared to the unfortunate choices made by most other governments on earth, the choices of Guinea's and Tanzania's are not really
below average.

THAT Lumumba could have survived in office very long, let alone as long
as Touré, Nyrere, or Kaunda, is doubtful. Because of its hugeness, its complex tribal makeup, and the presence of great potential wealth, the Congo
might have been more apt to follow the pattern of Nigeria, which has had
a long, alternating succession of civilian and military rulers.

For the fact that millions of people remember Lumumba, and respect him,
he shares much in common with Bartolomeo Vanzetti, the 1920s Massachusetts anarchist who publicly thanked his executioners for bringing the
ideas of "a simple fishmonger" to the world's attention by sending him to
the electric chair. Even Mobutu, the U.S.-supported dictator who effectively
pulled the switch on Lumumba, felt compelled to build his victim a martyr's
statue.

Today, the statue towers over the capital city of Kinshasa like the un-
payable foreign debt that helped finance it. The Lumumba memorial and the
foreign debt are, respectively, the city's most prominent physical and spiritual
landmarks. The American taxpayer hired the killers and then bought the
statue, too, like some Mafia boss supplying his victim with a first-rate funeral
and sending a carload of flowers to the widow.

And what did the American taxpayer get for it all? He got millions of
Africans who regularly encounter the name Lumumba, and who know not
only the fact, but the slightly exaggerated and oversimplified version of the
fact: Lumumba was a courageous African nationalist and the United States
of America killed him.

* * *

IF Lumumba's death was supposed to bring peace and order to the Congo, it certainly did no such thing. Congolese developments after Lumumba's passing had all the logic and neatness (though none of the humor) of a Marx Brothers movie. U.N. troops wound up on a bloody march against Katanga. When U.N. Secretary General Dag Hammarskjöld flew in for a peace talk, his plane crashed, killing him. His successor was U Thant, of Burma—a once-wealthy, now-poor country not noted for the wisdom of its own management in recent times. Thant publicly expressed the opinion that the Katangese leaders he was negotiating with were "a bunch of clowns."

Meanwhile, Kasavubu and Mobutu (in other words, the United States) were facing the same problem with Lumumba's lieutenant, Antoine Gizenga, that they had faced with Lumumba: namely, every time they held an election, Gizenga kept winning. In 1962, we tried to reorganize the Congo again under a new constitutional agreement. When parliament elected its own officers, it revealed a heavy pro-Gizenga plurality, if not an actual majority. So when it came time to vote for a new prime minister, Kasavubu undercut Gizenga's forces by announcing that he would nominate a "unity" candidate of his own. Mobutu then declared that if the "unity" candidate wasn't endorsed by parliament, the army would take over again.

Kasavubu's candidate turned out to be Ambassador Timberlake's favorite for the job, too—Cyrille Adoula. Adoula had long been on the CIA payroll, and had been a leader in CIA-supported "trade unions." These really weren't trade unions at all in the American sense of the term (you would not, for example, have gone to one of their meetings to propose a strike), but were agencies of government control.* The pro-Gizenga parliamentarians swallowed Adoula anyway, having been warned that if they didn't, they would all have to go back to their villages without their fancy titles and expense accounts.

Stephen Weissman, later of the House Foreign Affairs Committee staff, has reported being told by U.S. officials who had been in the Congo at the time that the CIA and even the U.N. were spreading secret bribe money around parliament during the balloting. He quotes a CIA memorandum saying that "The U.N. and the United States in closely coordinated activities played essential roles in this significant success over Gizenga." Gizenga himself protested, but to no avail, and finally agreed to take the title of "first vice-premier" (there were second and third vice-premiers to salve other egos as well).

Then the U.S.—which would have bellowed like crazy at much tamer Soviet interference in the affairs of other countries—set about trying to prop its man up. The State Department and CIA, according to the CIA memo-

*See chapter 20.

randum Weissman obtained, were "endeavoring to help Adoula improve his political base of support and enhance his domestic power and stature. This activity is in the areas of political organization with connected trade union and youth groups, public relations, and security apparatus." A U.S. agent, supposedly a public relations man, was stationed in Adoula's office.

But the voters, to the scarcely adequate extent that they had ever been consulted, had favored Gizenga. And Gizenga was understandably upset with the U.S. because it had been trying to kill him. (Devlin's execution plan in September 1960 was thwarted with minutes to spare only because of the chance intervention of some Moroccan U.N. troops.)

Actually, over the next few years almost everyone *but* Gizenga had a hand at being prime minister of the Congo at one time or another and failed, some more than once. Not only Timberlake's man, Adoula, but Charles Bohlen's man, Ileo, took a turn.

Most remarkable was Moise Tshombe, the secessionist Balunda chieftain who had captured the heart of the conservative movement in the United States, and who then (a) killed Lumumba and hid the body, (b) was arrested by Kasavubu and Mobutu a few months later when he showed up at a peace conference, (c) was charged with murder in the Lumumba case, although his accusers, Kasavubu and Mobutu, had planned the murder, (d) could not immediately be tried, because, as the *New York Times* noted, "the Congo has no high court, no judges, and only one attorney", (e) agreed from prison to end the Katangese secession, (f) was immediately set free by Kasavubu and Mobutu, (g) raced right home and seceded again, (h) fought against Congolese and U.N. troops for about two years using mostly white mercenaries, (i) lost, (j) went into hiding in Europe, (k) was begged by Kasavubu to come back and be prime minister of the whole Congo because nobody else could run the place, (l) did for about a year, (m) was fired and charged with treason by Kasavubu, (n) fled to Spain, (o) was sentenced to death in absentia, (p) wound up in Algeria thanks to an airplane hijacking in 1967, and (q) died there in jail, incommunicado, in 1969, while the Congo (by that time Zaire) was still trying to extradite him so it could hang him.

Meanwhile, Tshombe's Balunda army, those right-wing stooges for reactionary U.S.-Belgian neocolonialism, melted into the bush on both sides of the Angolan border and began changing costumes and makeup for their second act appearance as left-wing Cuban-backed communist guerrillas during the Shaba uprisings of 1977 and 1978.

Throughout this period of revolving prime ministers, Kasavubu and Mobutu stayed constantly close to power, and, one might say, held it. But a decision had been made, at U.S. urging, to maintain the facade of parliamentary democracy. Mobutu couldn't be prime minister because he had never been elected to parliament—or to anything else, for that matter (a condition that holds true even today, unless you count a few uncontested police-state referenda after he seized power).

* * *

MINERAL riches had focused the outside world's attention on the secessions in Katanga and Kasai. But after the U.N. force had ended those secessions, and had packed up and left, other rebellions remained. In 1964, the formal departure of the last U.N. forces was accompanied by a wave of rebel attacks on towns and missionary outposts throughout the Congo. Tshombe, then prime minister, blamed this, naturally enough, on China.

He said China was orchestrating the attacks through its embassy in a tiny but politically volatile country called Burundi, which borders the Congo on the east. In a move suspiciously reminiscent of a standard U.S. intelligence agency ploy, Tshombe produced what he said were some captured military documents, and a Chinese defector who announced that China was attempting to take over the Congo as part of a plot to conquer all of Africa.

Somehow, this determined threat from the world's largest country was beaten back rather easily, as soon as the U.S. fulfilled Tshombe's request for unilateral U.S. military aid: C-130 transport planes, C-47 transport planes, B-26 light bombers, T-48 fighters armed with rockets and machine guns, heavy-duty H-21 helicopters, technicians, mercenary pilots and crewmen, military ground vehicles, arms, ammunition, a contingent of U.S. troops (first only to guard the aircraft, then to protect "rescue" workers on missions), and, finally, help in recruiting and organizing a mercenary army.

The U.S. also agreed that the Belgians would send in up to 400 command officers for the mercenary army, which was composed largely of white South Africans and Rhodesians. The makeup of this army almost guaranteed popular opposition; no one outside black Africa can fully appreciate the depth of the hatred people there feel toward racist South Africa.

All this was a dramatic reversal of U.S. policy, and was accomplished over some congressional objection. Throughout the 1960 crisis, the corner-stone of the U.S. public position had been that all aid to the Congo should be channeled through the United Nations. It was on this ground that the U.S. condemned the Soviet Union for even talking about sending military supplies directly to Lumumba's Congolese government. It was on this ground that Secretary of State Herter and Under Secretary Dillon not only refused Lumumba's requests for aid during his trip to Washington, but fairly ridiculed him for even asking.

Suddenly, on the basis of some "captured documents" and a single defecting Chinese diplomat, the U.S. decided that channeling all aid to the Congo through the United Nations was no longer a fundamental moral principle of international relations. The jettisoning of that principle was to mean a lot to Mobutu in years to come.

ONE center of rebellion in 1964 was Kivu province in the far east of the Congo, bordering on Burundi. Kivu is really more attuned to open, touristy East Africa, with its large Arab and white populations, than it is to the teeming, jungly West Africa of Kinshasa, with its rich cultural traditions. Kivu is a whole continent apart, and there are no decent roads. Kivu's remoteness offered a sanctuary for old Lumumba troops, and some have held out as rebels even into the 1980s, persistently cutting off tourist access to some of the world's most spectacular mountain-and-lake scenery.

The Kivu rebels gained brief international attention in 1975 when they kidnapped three Stanford University wildlife students and a Dutch companion from a base in Tanzania where the students were observing primate behavior, just across Lake Tanganyika from Kivu. The students were looking for gorillas, and encountered guerrillas instead. After some chest-beating, however, the rebels released three captives, all in good health, and reduced their ransom demands from $500,000 and guns to $40,000 and no guns. Stanford arranged payment, under terms it still won't specify, and the remaining student was also released relatively unharmed.*

A far more serious problem were the remaining rebels in Lumumba's old stronghold of Stanleyville (later Kisangani, the place Mama Singa picked up her truck). The Stanleyville rebels were organized around Lumumba's lieutenant, Antoine Gizenga. Back in 1962, Kasavubu and Mobutu had lured Gizenga to Leopoldville, the capital (later Kinshasa), and talked him into ending his secession long enough for them to appoint a new government in Stanleyville that would be loyal to the Kinshasa regime. But Gizenga felt double-crossed by the way things had gone after that—the announcement by Kasavubu and Mobutu that Adoula had to be voted prime minister or parliament would be dissolved.

Gizenga announced the formation of a new political party with a strong anti-Western attitude, and he particularly accused the U.S. of having replaced the Belgians as colonialists. (It's not hard to figure out how he might have come to that conclusion; on top of everything else, the U.S. had tried and almost succeeded in killing *Gizenga*.)

Around Stanleyville, Gizenga held more respect than the appointed administrator, one of Mobutu's generals. There was fighting. In January 1963, the government charged Gizenga with carrying out secessionist activities, and Mobutu's troops surrounded his house. Gizenga was plucked out by the U.N. and flown to an island in the Congo River where he was held prisoner under U.N. protection.

*Relatively," in the sense that one is always harmed, in ways difficult to measure, by being held captive and put in fear for one's life. On the other hand, the suffering done by the average citizen in many places where hostages are taken—like Kivu, or Stanleyville, or Tehran—is worse. This is especially true with hindsight, now that we know there's a happy ending for those who get to fly back to a split-level in Palo Alto, but not those who must continue to live in fear and deprivation in Kivu, or Stanleyville, or Tehran. They have all suffered unjustly.

By 1964, his loyalists from the farming areas around Stanleyville—places like Yalifoka—were strong enough to set up a rebel government in Stanleyville itself. But Gizenga, who as a leader was already a cut below Lumumba, was held on his Elba, leaving operations in Stanleyville under the direction of associates who proved totally irresponsible. They started out under the guise of a left-wing "people's republic," but they called themselves the Simbas, or lions. No human being could be proud of the way they behaved.

In the fall of 1964, the rebels rounded up several hundred whites, including a renowned American missionary doctor, Paul E. Carlson, and held them hostage. They hoped the hostage-taking would forestall attacks by the U.S.-supplied mercenary army that had just begun a drive to end the rebellion. They also sought world recognition.

It is doubtful the rebels wanted or expected a violent resolution to a crisis they probably underestimated. They kept the hostages in the best hotel in Stanleyville. U.S. consular personnel were beaten, though apparently not seriously injured. There was emotional abuse. Two U.S. envoys had to chew on a U.S. flag. A mock trial was staged in front of screaming throngs who threatened to kill and eat the whites. Dr. Carlson's execution as a spy was threatened and postponed, threatened and postponed. But, at bottom, it was mainly talk until a U.S.-European military force was dispatched.

Assertedly, this force was on a humanitarian mission to rescue the hostages. But it was obviously timed to coincide with the arrival of the U.S.-supplied white mercenary army on the fringes of Stanleyville. Had the army entered the city without a plan to rescue the hostages first, the hostages might indeed have faced a massacre. Of course, if the U.S. hadn't formed and supplied the white mercenary army, the hostages probably never would have been taken. And if Lumumba hadn't been dumped from office and killed, the Simbas might never have rebelled.

For the rescue mission, the U.S. flew in 600 Belgian paratroopers. Even in its best light, the operation had a dual purpose. The Belgians intended all along that after shipping out the hostages who survived, they would stay on in Stanleyville for a week or so "mopping up." The *New York Times* reported in its multiple-story coverage atop page one, "The Western planners of the rescue excercise concluded that with the collapse of the rebels' Stanleyville 'government,' resistance elsewhere would probably crumble." The "rescuers" had come to conquer.

The rebels gathered all the whites in the area, more than 800 of them, and warned that they would be killed if the U.S.-Belgian force arrived. It arrived. On the day the crisis broke, shooting started as the white soldiers proceeded to town from the airport. The hostages were grouped together in front of the hotel. As the military mission approached, some of the hostages were shot by their captors, others started to flee, and the shooting became general. According to official figures, thirty white hostages were killed. Two were Americans, both missionaries; one was Dr. Carlson, who was shot while trying to escape over a brick wall. Thirty-seven other Americans were flown out safely, as were the great majority of white hostages. Fifty rebels died in the combat, none of the paratroopers, and one mercenary in the arriving "Congolese" army.

Many Third World countries protested at the U.N. what they contended was big-power intervention in a Third World civil war. Some revived speculation that the U.S. had planned Lumumba's murder. One U.N. ambassador said the Stanleyville raid had proved to him that a "white, if his name is Carlson, or if he is an American, a Belgian, or an Englishman, is worth thousands upon thousands of blacks."

The U.S. ambassador to the U.N., Adlai Stevenson, responded with righteous indignation. "I have served in the United Nations from the day of inception off and on for seven years," he said. "But never before have I heard such irrational, irresponsible, insulting, and repugnant language in these chambers; and language used, if you please, to contemptuously impugn and slander a gallant and successful effort to save human lives of many nationalities and colors.

"The United States took part in no operation with military purposes in the Congo," Ambassador Stevenson told the General Assembly in his big speech. "From the beginning, we have been opposed—and remain opposed—to foreign intervention in the internal affairs of the sovereign and independent State of the Congo."

Then Stevenson said, "Let us not be hypocritical. Either each government recognizes the right of other governments to exist and refrain from attempting to overthrow them, or we shall revert to a primitive state of anarchy in which each conspires against its neighbor. The golden rule is, do unto others as you would have them do unto you."

One thinks of how they must have smiled—Larry Devlin, Dr. Gottlieb, WI/ROGUE, QJ/WIN, Allen Dulles, Mobutu Sese Seko—when they picked up their newspapers and read Stevenson's lecture to other countries: "Let us not be hypocritical." As for Eisenhower, perhaps he wouldn't have understood the humor in it anymore than Stevenson did.

With all that Stevenson said, though, there was something he didn't say, which maybe people had a right to know. Before becoming U.N. ambassador, after leaving the Illiniois governorship in 1952, during the eight years in which he sought the presidency three times, Stevenson practiced law. And one of his larger clients was—Maurice Tempelsman.

Stevenson, a two-time Democratic presidential nominee, had toured Africa with Tempelsman in the late 1950s, meeting those Africans Tempelsman sought to woo.

Stevenson's U.N. speech was widely praised in the United States. The American people had not been advised by their government that the Congolese leaders who invited the Western intervention had been installed by a U.S.-

instigated coup. The people were not told that those leaders were unlocking a fortune for Stevenson's big law client. In a typical editorial, the *Wall Street Journal* compared Stevenson's remarks to the hallowed words of the country's first cold war secretary of state, Dean Acheson. The *Journal* said the West should stop "seeking moral justification [for its acts] in the proclamations of others," and start "looking for it in its own conscience. In its conscience the ultimate question must be not about tactics, but whether the policy is truly designed, as Secretary Acheson said, 'to preserve and foster an environment in which free societies may exist and flourish.' When the answer is yes, the West need not be ashamed of its policies, in the Congo or elsewhere."

THE U.S.-European military force secured Stanleyville and several other cities in the area. Then it pulled out, and the rebels poured back in from the bush. The real massacre began. For five years, the Simbas terrorized the whole northeast quadrant of the Congo. It would be impossible to estimate the number of people they killed. But you cannot find a family in the area that wasn't touched by their murderous gangs or forced to hide in the bush to avoid them. There was anarchy.

In a mad campaign to insure that traitors would never again allow rule by outsiders, the Simbas practiced prophylactic homicide against all educated people, anyone from the bureaucracy, anyone who appeared touched by foreign influence. Since there weren't any *truly* educated people, completion of primary school was the standard qualification for execution. Thousands of men, women, and children were chucked off a bridge that crosses a rocky, swift-flowing branch of the Congo River. Some were stuffed into burlap bags before chucking, others not. The river ran red for years.

On November 25, 1965, Mobutu kicked out Kasavubu and expunged any semblance of democratic government. He was then thirty-five years old. He stated, "The Congo's misery is rooted in a lack of discipline. The new government is going to change that and impose everywhere the spirit of discipline." No records have been released of what the CIA was doing at the time, but it is scarcely conceivable that Mobutu's seizure of power was a surprise to the U.S. or contrary to its desires.

Weissman, the congressional investigator, says he's obtained firsthand accounts of CIA involvement in this coup-to-end-all-coups. William Bader, recent staff director of the Senate Foreign Relations Committee and a former staffer on the intelligence committee, recalls testimony by a CIA officer that Mobutu once "whipped out a revolver and flung it on the desk" in front of the officer, saying that if the CIA didn't start supplying more financial support, the officer might as well "just shoot me on the spot."

Officially, by 1966, the Simba rebellion was over and Mobutu ran the Congo. Visas were issued for foreigners to travel to Stanleyville. But such travel was impossible, because the Simba violence in fact continued.* By 1970, the insurrection was indeed crushed, and visitors could at last travel through the area. It was a disaster. Whole towns were deserted. Life had returned to Stanleyville—foreigners said they had begun to come back in 1969—but government throughout the region was in the hands of appointed military officers, who ruled by discretion.

WHAT was going on in that secreted, closed-off quadrant of the Congo in the mid-1960s was perhaps the craziest episode of all, and perhaps the most bizarre civil war in history—not between Congolese and other Congolese, but between Cubans and other Cubans.

The U.S. and Belgium had infused the Congolese struggle from the beginning with mercenaries, many of whom were recruited through clandestine government channels, including the CIA. The CIA had long been looking for ways to employ the army of Cubans it had assembled for the unsuccessful 1961 invasion of Cuba at the Bay of Pigs. According to Church Committee evidence, the CIA began to bring anti-Castro Cuban pilots to the Congo early in 1964, to bomb railroads, bridges, and other targets in areas under rebel control or threatened by it. As the year wound on and the U.S. began to support a mercenary army for the Congo openly as well as covertly, more Cubans were brought in. According to Weissman,† a CIA force of Cubans was standing by near Stanleyville the day of the paratroop drop in case it failed.

Meanwhile, hearing Gizenga's call, Castro dispatched several hundred of *his* Cuban troops, under the personal command of Ernesto "Che" Guevara, Castro's closest friend and assistant. There is no sure public proof of which Cubans arrived in the Congo first, but the dates in evidence suggest ours did, and that Castro was impelled toward the fray by learning (as he inevitably would have) that the CIA's Cubans were already fighting on the other side. It's clear, though, that Guevara and his men also went to the Congo out of a genuine desire to help establish Gizenga's "people's republic"—to further the Simba rebellion. And when they did, the CIA responded with even greater numbers of its own Cubans.

So there, in the remotest corner of central Africa, 8,000 miles from the small Caribbean island where it started, the Cuban civil war resumed. At one point, according to veteran foreign service officers, U.S. taxpayers even launched a Cuban-manned navy, composed of several ships, on Lake Tanganyika, to clear the waters of Lumumba/Gizenga allies in Kivu province, and to stop any arms that Guevara's real Cubans might be bringing in from Burundi or elsewhere by water. Whether Cubans actually engaged in naval

---

*I was issued a visa, but was stranded in the jungle hundreds of miles from Stanleyville, on the fringes of an area no truck driver would agree to enter in 1967.

†Who published an account in *Political Science Quarterly*, Summer 1979.

combat with each other on Lake Tanganyika is unrecorded, but the mere possibility boggles the mind.

Castro finally pulled Guevara out, apparently in 1967. Little if anything was ever made public about the episode. In September 1981, a reporter for the *Wall Street Journal* (the author) suddenly raised the subject with Castro at a cocktail reception in Havana. Castro seemed shocked, took a step backward, and finally said, "Nothing has ever been published about that." The reporter pressed for an answer to the question of why Guevara left. Castro thought a moment, and said, "He went to help them with a revolution. He spent a short time there, and he succeeded, and he left."

The reporter asked how, with a ruthless, U.S.-allied dictator still in command, Guevara could have thought his mission had been accomplished. Castro paused again (noticeable because he responded to every other line of questioning with aplomb), and said, "He did not go there to conduct a revolution for them. He helped them. He did what he could, and Cuba needed him to come back."

The next year, the reporter filed Freedom of Information Act requests for CIA and State Department accounts of the episode. As this book goes to press, the requests are reported still being processed. Pending new information, however, one can make a pretty good guess why Guevara went home (or rather, unfortunately for him, to Bolivia, where the CIA finally caught up with him):

Castro had made the same mistake that his enemies in Washington had been making in the Congo since 1960—thinking that leftists were leftists, revolutions were revolutions, and that people in places like the Congo really cared about a global struggle between Left and Right, East and West, capitalism and communism.

Guevara and his men slipped into the Congo expecting to find a heroic, impassioned people fighting for the dignity and liberty of mankind—or at least some folks who could be dressed up and passed off that way. What he found instead was a barbaric rabble of starving farmers-turned-cutthroats, incapable of immediately being organized into anything that he or very many other people would want to be assoicated with. How many innocent souls Guevara helped them kill is something we probably can't know. His mistake, though, was eventually tempered in one way that Washington's was not: he left.

Trying to make sense of what seems almost definitional madness, there is one great overriding question behind these foreign intrusions. That is, to what extent would the mere survival of Lumumba, either in power or to his point of natural removal from it, have placated his followers and forestalled bloodshed. If the illusion of democratic order, civility, and law—which is what Lumumba represented when he took office—could have been maintained longer, would it have become the *reality* of democratic order, civility, and law? In the Congo, we forfeited our chance to ever find out.

CHAPTER SIX
WHERE THE MONEY GOES

======================IN 1980, reporters for a Belgian weekly, *Humo*, combed land and tax records in their country, and documented the long-standing rumors about the lavish European real estate holdings of Mobutu and his inner circle. The records they found,* not necessarily complete, show that Joseph Desiré Mobutu-Gbiatwa—address: Kinshasa; occupation: chief of state—owns two houses, a chateau, a park, a stables, and an undeveloped property, all in Belgium. *Humo* sent photographers out to get pictures of these places, and a couple of them truly look like the kind of thing a Vanderbilt or a Rockefeller would call home. One was a veritable castle, replete with spires and surrounded by a moat, some 25 miles outside Brussels. Mobutu's relatives and various government officials he appointed were also recorded as owners of apartment buildings and large tracts of land in Belgium.

Other secrets of Mobutu's reign were beginning to flow out of Kinshasa itself, as a few people began to talk. Mobutu had been tempered in his readiness to permanently silence the disloyal. He was pressured by the Carter administration's focus on human rights abuses by U.S. allies, and, perhaps even more, by the investigations of Amnesty International, the most respected independent human rights lobby. The Carter human rights crusade and Amnesty International have sometimes been laughed off as futile, or naive, but

*Examined by the author with the kind and much appreciated help of Dirk Van Der Sypen of *Humo*.

a lot of people are alive today because of them who otherwise wouldn't be, and some of those are Zairians.*

Former government officials dumped by Mobutu, instead of disappearing and never being heard from again, were occasionally moving to Brussels or Geneva and holding press conferences. Among them were Ngouza Karl-i-bond, the prime minister and former finance minister who had been scheduled to speak at the St. Regis Hotel meeting in September 1980, but didn't make it, and Bernardin Mungul-Diaka, another former cabinet minister, who had also served as executive secretary of Zaire's only political party (founded by Mobutu). Both men gave the Belgian press detailed accounts of corruption.

By draping Mobutu in scandal, Ngouza and Mungul-Diaka hoped to construct clean personal images, and perhaps attract a following as leaders-in-exile should Mobutu fall. But both were themselves living high off the hog, with no ostensible legitimate source of income. Asked the source of funds for his home and limo, Ngouza said, "This is my problem. A clever man would know that somebody who has been prime minister for all these years has not been throwing his money out of the window." Meaning that the reporter who asked the question must not have been very clever.

Mungul-Diaka, the former head of Mobutu's political apparatus, released an itemization of Mobutu's European holdings. His list valued Mobutu's Belgian real estate—the same holdings documented by official records—at about $100 million.† The list went on to cite a Swiss bank account of $143 million and a $5.4 million chateau at Cully, on Lake Geneva.

The list also included villas in Paris ($1.1 million) and Nice ($1.3 million), and châteaus in Spain, Italy, and Central African Republic. (Only the latter was valued, at $17.9 million; it was apparently part of a vast private hunting park set up in Central African Republic and given away to then French President Valery Giscard d'Estaing and his family and friends, including Mobutu.) In addition, Mobutu was listed as owner of hotels in Spain and Ivory Coast, tourist homes in Greece, and residences and properties in Senegal and Ivory Coast. If the end came at home, he would not be caught short of refuge.

Three pages were required to enumerate Mobutu's Zairian property. It took another page and a half to name companies in Zaire that were allegedly controlled by Mobutu but held in the names of two uncles and a friend, as intermediaries. Among the holdings that Mungul-Diaka listed (and reiterated in detail during a long interview) was a majority share in the diamond buying *comptoirs*, or agencies, in Western Kasai. That was where Maurice Tem-

---

*Amnesty exists on donations. Its U.S. office is at 304 West 58th Street, New York, N.Y. 10019.

†Values listed in francs have been converted by the author to U.S. dollars at prevailing exchange rates in December 1979, the date of most of the information Mungul-Diaka brought with him when he canoed to freedom across the Congo River on January 25.

pelsman's company had received from Mobutu a special government concession to explore for diamonds.

Any independent diamond holdings in Eastern or Western Kasai would seem to violate the monopolistic charter claimed by MIBA, the national diamond franchise that is owned jointly by Société Général du Belgique and the Zairian government. Tempelsman acknowledges that he was given a concession, but says it was just to explore, and he has repeatedly denied having any joint business investments with his friend and patron, Mobutu.

At any rate, Mobutu, the president, is obviously in a position to grant useful franchises and other conveniences to Mobutu, the businessman. If this seems untoward, it's only fair to note that Zaire's main model in modern government was Belgium, where the king is allowed all sorts of secret control over semimonopolistic private businesses, many of which owned the natural resources of Zaire throughout its colonial history. Société Général, for one, is still there. The United States government, with its own admirable restrictions on conflicts of interest, its belief in open government, and its dedication to fighting monopoly trusts, might have taught Zaire a better way to run a country. But the State Department and CIA preferred to teach the Zairians duplicity, bribery, and assassination instead.

ANOTHER source of information from Zaire was a secret group of dissidents in parliament, who, on November 1, 1980, anonymously published a fifty-page open letter to Mobutu. The letter politely but unmistakably accused him of suppressing his people's liberty and also welshing on his promise to improve their economic lot. The same parliamentarians are also suspected of being a source of other information, including a report issued jointly by two Belgian human rights groups* in February 1981.

The report challenged Mobutu's account of the July 1979 killing of civilian diamond scavengers just outside Mbuji-Mayi, the diamond center of Eastern Kasai province. Against Mobutu's assertion that only three people were killed when the army swooped down, the human rights groups identified by name ninety-seven persons they said died in the massacre. Not only that, they reported that another ten persons, also named, had been killed in a previously unreported massacre near Mbuji-Mayi two weeks earlier.

Shortly after the open letter to Mobutu was disseminated in Europe, thirteen parliamentarians were arrested and charged with writing it. Without much legal explanation, Mobutu had them flown to their homes, mostly in outlying parts of Zaire, and placed under house arrest for five years. Through secret couriers, some of the arrested parliamentarians continued to feed information to the outside world. Probably the most prominent of the group

*The Belgian League for the Rights of Man, affiliated with the International League for the Rights of Man, and the Zaire Committee, a political group with a leftist orientation.

was Tshisekedi wa Mulumba, from near Kisangani (Lumumba's area). Tshisekedi was among several Zairians—Ngouza was another—known to have been courted by U.S. diplomats, obviously with the idea in mind that Mobutu might some day need a replacement. On a visit to Brussels, Tshisekedi is known to have been a house guest of John Heimann, an important U.S. diplomat with expertise in Belgian-Zairian affairs.*

Tshisekedi and his twelve compatriots would have faced a much worse fate than house arrest—at least that is the opinion of their European contacts—had it not been for the Mbuji-Mayi massacre. When Amnesty International couldn't get into Zaire to investigate the massacre under terms it considered satisfactory, it launched a full-scale campaign against human rights violations throughout the country. In the glare of this campaign, Mobutu became much more cautious in his treatment of opponents.

In announcing the campaign in May 1980, Amnesty International said, "A twenty-page memorandum on political imprisonment, torture, and killing presented by Amnesty International to President Mobutu Sese Seko of Zaire in February has evoked no response. Instead, Mobutu claimed in a March 11 communiqué from Brussels that AI [Amnesty International] had 'congratulated' him on his government's human rights record.

"In fact, flagrant and gross violation of human rights has been common in Zaire for several years. In 1978, AI began a thorough study of those violations, which over the past two years have included:

"the detention without charge or trial of suspected opponents of the government for long periods.

"the imprisonment of political prisoners convicted at trials which did not conform with internationally recognized standards.

"the use of torture.

"the frequency of deaths in detention resulting from torture, ill-treatment, and harsh prison conditions.

"the use of the death penalty in both criminal and political cases and extrajudicial executions....

"There is no estimate of the number of untried political detainees currently in custody. Detention without trial occurs frequently, and it is used by authorities to suppress political opposition. Detainees frequently 'disappear' after their arrest. They are either transferred to another prison or they die in custody.... Most people killed for political reasons have...been summarily executed by members of the security forces without being given any sort of trial.... Prisoners are badly fed and have sometimes been starved to death. Medical facilities are grossly inadequate, and standards of hygiene and sanitation are extremely low."

In one year in one prison, Amnesty reported the loss, apparently from malnutrition and disease, of 2,309 prisoners—seventy-seven times the num-

*Heimann didn't respond to the author's written request for comment.

ber of whites killed in Stanleyville in 1964 during the episode that cemented U.S. support for Mobutu's rule.

Amnesty International issued this report four months before American businessmen and Zairian government officials gathered in September 1980 in the Versailles Room of the St. Regis Hotel in New York. But the report was never mentioned there. For all its effect on Mobutu, the report had received so little publicity in the U.S. that most people at the meeting may have been unaware of it.

Ironically, the report specifically condemned "the use of the charge of embezzlement" to camouflage arrests that are really made "on a political basis." Under the Belgians, embezzlement was the charge that first sent Patrice Lumumba to prison.

IN April 1982, Mungul-Diaka, the former political aide to Mobutu, issued a compilation of massacres in Zaire, attempting to show that the Mbuji-Mayi incident was part of a pattern. Among the fourteen incidents he cited were:

the hanging of four cabinet ministers, without the right of self-defense, in an alleged plot against Mobutu in 1966;

the killing of several thousand Katangese soldiers by burning or burying alive or jettisoning from helicopters in 1967;

the killing of several hundred peacefully demonstrating students at the national university in Kinshasa in 1969;

the massacre of more than 500 innocent people in several villages in May 1970, in reprisal for the killing of a soldier who had tried to steal a chicken;

the massacre of 2,000 to 2,500 religious sect members in Kitawala in January 1978;

the massacre of 150 people in Eastern Kasai on October 6, 1981, after some villagers challenged some army officers who were dealing illegally in ivory;

the alleged harassment during 1981 of Cardinal Joseph Albert Malula, archbishop of Kinshasa, for having criticized the government. (Mungul-Diaka said the archbishop slept in a different house very night because of the threats against him. Mobutu also held a grudge against the archbishop because when Pope John Paul II visited Zaire in 1980, Mobutu had wanted the Pope to marry him to a new wife, and the archbishop had been the one to inform Mobutu that the Pope wouldn't do it.)

Mungul-Diaka also reported the almost unexplained killing of thousands more people in other incidents.

AMONG the documents that reached the Belgian press were apparently accurate records from a committee of the Zairian parliament that was assigned to supervise the national bank. The records indicate that Mobutu was being a bit hypocritical back in December 1979, when he stunned his countrymen with the tough new financial restrictions designed to please the IMF. (Those were the restrictions that abolished people's right to spend their savings, or to convert Zairian money to foreign currency; it was the same crackdown that wiped out the $1 million fertilizer purchase fund that belonged to the farmers in Hassan Nabhan's U.N.-sponsored crop improvement program.) According to the records that turned up in Belgium, Mobutu himself withdrew 364.3 million Belgian francs from the Zairian national bank in 1979, the equivalent of more than $13 million. Members of his family withdrew $209,000 in various Western currencies.

The records show that from 1977 to 1979, the group withdrew $2.8 million in U.S. cash, $132.1 million in Belgian francs, $6.4 million in French francs, and $268,000 in Swiss francs, worth altogether some $141.6 million.* Mobutu also had access to the enormous funds that he could acquire in Europe from the European and U.S. businessmen willing to pay bribes, commissions or whatever you want to call them, for the favorable deals they received on their business in Zaire.

Everyone, from U.S. diplomats in Europe and Kinshasa to Western businessmen making money in Zaire, acknowledges that huge kickbacks are paid. Often they are paid by deposit in a bank in Europe or the U.S., before the money goes onto the books of the Bank of Zaire at all—and thus before hostile parliamentarians or the IMF can find out about it.

Even Tempelsman acknowledges that bribes are "probably" paid. He also argues, quite correctly, that Zaire is far from alone in this. U.S.-supported dictators around the world conduct business via kickbacks. This corruption can only rarely be cited in its particulars, because the culprits can cover their tracks in too many ways. Still, the Mobutus get their castles, and their overseas bank accounts.

Such thievery not only strips Third World countries of needed money, but more than that, it guarantees that the free market will not be able to determine where resources are to be applied. This, in turn, sabotages development. And the system, devised largely by Western governments, including the American, seems designed to tempt if not actually to encourage venality. We have seen this system at work in Zaire, and the chapters ahead will show instances elsewhere. At this point, an overview might be helpful.

The CIA, for one, actively strives to find up-and-coming foreign officials who are susceptible to bribery. People noticeably out to make a buck are approached and encouraged. The Economic Intelligence Committee in the CIA publishes a frequently updated Economic Alert List for each region of the world, telling U.S. spies what to watch for. Along with obvious queries on energy use and food supply, the lists stress a search for bribability. For example, the Economic Alert List for Africa for the period October 1981 to March 1982 gives the following priority instructions to spies:

Chad: "Continue reporting on corruption and graft in Chadian business

*Currency values converted by the author.

and government, especially names and positions of officials and groups, amounts siphoned abroad, and economic impact."

Kenya: "We are interested in attempts by any members of the government to gain personal economic advantages through their positions."

Liberia: "Report on any corrupt practices by the new leaders."

Zaire: "Reporting on military corruption has been exceptional; keep it flowing. Try to supplement the flow with more reporting on civilian corruption, including names and positions."

All four of these countries are considered friends and allies of the U.S., and the U.S. military has been brought in recently in at least three of them.

When time comes for the CIA to select which man it wants to push for higher office in some foreign government, bribeability is obviously considered an asset. Whatever other pressures might come to bear on a foreign ruler at a time of decision, the U.S. can be confident that if the contest is judged on graft, the CIA will be able to outbid any rival. And once someone starts taking money, there is always the threat of exposure to ensure his continued cooperation.

U.S. business offers a handy potential means of distributing this CIA bribe money. Corporations pay sales commissions to front men for the foreign rulers who purchase U.S. goods on behalf of their governments. If these payments are bribes, or kickbacks, they are illegal under U.S. law, even if they are made overseas. A 1975 Senate investigation into payoffs by multinational corporations uncovered a lot of apparently illegal money transfers. Some involved tens of million of dollars at a throw. It was originally assumed that these payments were simply a form of illegal commercial bribery.

But there's good reason to suspect that many payments, at least, weren't commercial bribes at all, but rather CIA payoffs channeled under corporate cover. For one thing, a disproportionate percentage of the payments were made by arms companies like Northrop and Lockheed, which must work closely with the CIA and Defense Department because of the technology they use. More intriguing, a disproportionate percentage of the payments, even by companies not in the military supply business, were made in countries around the perimeters of the Soviet Union and China, and in countries, like Italy and Japan, where communist parties were a strong political force. The money routinely went to political leaders, or their relatives, who were asserted anti-communists.

During the late 1970s, the Securities and Exchange Commission began efforts to expose violations of the Foreign Corrupt Practices Act, which prohibits commercial bribery by U.S. business overseas. A series of enforcement actions involving alleged illegal foreign payments by U.S. companies was announced, then withdrawn on the ground that to pursue them would endanger the national security. Although these cases involved millions and millions of dollars and companies whose stock is publicly traded, none of these cases has ever been explained. Attempts by several *Wall Street*

Journal reporters to clear up the mysteries failed to elicit a satisfying explanation for a single one of them. Requests under the Freedom of Information Act for documents from the SEC and State Department only brought more citations of "national security" as a ground for nondisclosure. The potential methods of subterfuge for making political payoffs through corporations are almost limitless.

In 1976, the Aluminum Company of America (Alcoa), the world's biggest aluminum company, disclosed that it had paid at least $25,000 to officials and political parties of an unnamed foreign country at the direction of the U.S. ambassador to that country. The statement was hidden in some forms that Alcoa was required to file with the SEC. No one would supply more information. There was no reason to believe that the instance was unique.

A new law requires fuller disclosure on questionable foreign payments, but contains a loophole whereby "national security" exemptions can be granted at the request of the CIA or other U.S. intelligence agencies. The number of companies that receive such exemptions, and the size of the payments they make, is secret. But the number has been rumored to run into the several dozens. And the mere existence of such an exemption is a tacit admission that the U.S. government uses private companies to bribe foreign nationals and influence the politics of foreign countries. This creates very unfair pressure on private U.S. companies to participate in adventures they can't control and may not approve of.

If the government wants to pass bribes, or to obtain cover for CIA operations overseas—for example, getting permission from companies for spies to pose as company officials—it can exercise considerable leverage over business executives. The government awards billions of dollars of domestic contracts each year, and despite bidding laws there are many ways to steer these contracts toward or away from a particular supplier. Government assistance can also be a powerful help in getting foreign contracts, as the Inga-Shaba episode in Zaire illustrates. And many laws important to business are enforced with discretion; for example, a massive Justice Department antitrust case against the major oil companies was dropped on White House orders while Big Oil worked with the State Department to support the shah of Iran in a crisis.*

Of necessity, the government controls almost *all* the work available for companies specializing in military or intelligence equipment. It isn't easy for these companies to turn down government requests for favors. The Pentagon and CIA are their only domestic customers, and they need government permission to export their deadly wares. Beyond that, such companies generally share with most of the military community a philosophical belief in an adventuristic, get-them-before-they-get-us foreign policy. Arms sellers

---

*Discussed in detail in chapters 10 and 11. Specific instances of questionable foreign payments can also be found elsewhere in this book.

make their money from it. So they might gladly agree without any pressure at all to let their overseas sales commissions serve as a cover for CIA payments to corrupt foreign rulers.

The discretionary exemption from SEC reporting requirements that may be gained by cooperating with government foreign policy adventurers could benefit a company in other important regulatory matters. If nothing else, the threat of exposing secrets could be used to hold Justice Department, or SEC, or Federal Trade Commission investigators at bay. Moreover, those companies that enjoy profiting from foreign intrigue, or that knuckle under to government pressure, gain an unfair advantage over other companies that prefer to mind their own business—whose owners don't want to get involved in bribery, kickbacks, and deception; whose owners may be ethical people. The corruption of foreigners cannot be accomplished without the corruption of Americans.

The obvious question raised by all this is what the best interest of the United States really is: to perpetually try to corrupt as many overseas governments as we can so that when a military crisis arises we may have some crook on the scene in our pocket? Or to try to encourage, by example and reward, a world of clean governments that are strong through their own popularity—governments that allow their peoples' free-market impulses to interact productively with our own peoples' free-market impulses, and which for all these reasons are unlikely to become involved in a military crisis at all?

ANOTHER enticement to corruption is the way the World Bank and most private Western lending institutions work. Their loans don't depend on the viability of the projects that the loans are allegedly financing. The projects often seem to be a mere excuse. Money is available, public money, and everyone dives for a quick share.

Proposals for projects to be funded by the World Bank are often prepared by the companies that will get the contracts (and thus the money), rather than by local citizens groups, or development workers, or the World Bank itself, or the governments that are supposedly receiving the loans. Instead of demand inspiring supply, the supplier is encouraged to write his own ticket. The company and the government then make their deal before anyone else considers the project. This opens the door for collusion and kickback arrangements, and forecloses any possibility that the bank could oversee fair competitive bidding on a project.

The people who decide whether to lend the World Bank's cash aren't bankers risking their own wealth, but rather bureaucrats, who are more or less on loan to the World Bank from their respective governments, and thus aren't even risking their careers. In fact, often the real decision makers are paid outside consultants who aren't risking anything, and who aren't meaningfully policed, either.

In 1978, the World Bank undertook a $9 million project to refurbish Zaire's palm oil plantations. Stated that way, it sounds like an appropriate enough investment. But the project proposal was prepared by Unilever and the two other companies, both Belgian, that, combined, control most of Zaire's palm oil industry. Unilever is a giant international agricultural growing, processing, shipping, and retailing firm. In Standard & Poor's stock guide, under the column that describes each stock-issuing company's principal business, the description of Unilever's is probably the most grandiose of any of the thousands of listings in the book; it just says, "Controls vast international enterprise."

Why should the World Bank spend taxpayer development money to beef up the balance sheet of one of the world's richest companies? The $7- to $13-a-month wages Unilever pays its local workers, from which it deducts rent money for the almost slavelike quarters it puts them in, certainly doesn't commend the company to the Zairians who are supposed to be benefiting from the development aid. One would think that if Unilever considered the palm oil project viable, it would invest its own money. It probably would— lots of people would—if Zaire had anything resembling an honest, popular, efficient government.

A Belgian company, Compagnie Sucrière, prepared an $80.4 million World Bank project in 1980 to improve its sugar plantation in Zaire and buy new processing equipment. The bank went along. (Compagnie Sucrière graciously agreed to put up one-third of the money itself to get the loan.) These two projects have been cited as examples here only because secret World Bank documents describing them happened to fall into the hands of sources friendly to the author. Many other examples would be available if the World Bank would allow U.S. taxpayers to see the documents that account for use of the taxpayers' generous credit and cash.

The World Bank and International Monetary Fund, sister organizations, don't disclose much about their operations. Helmut Hartmann, press spokesman for the IMF, says he won't answer a reporter's questions unless the answers are completely off the record—no fair sharing them with the reader.* Hartmann also declared that no one else at the IMF would be available to discuss things, either.

There has never been any evidence of kickbacks or other graft in connection with the Unilever or Compagnie Sucrière loans; there hasn't been much information of any kind available about them. We know only that both companies are very, very rich, and so is Mobutu, and they all use public funds in secret.

Beyond the question of individual enrichment is the question of whether our long-run best interest—a free, peaceful, productive world—is served by diverting Third World resources to Western businesses to build projects that will be controlled by unpopular governments. These governments are

*This reporter declined.

basically socialist, whether our momentary convenience is to call them left
wing, right wing, or moderate. That is, their money is spent by a dictator,
or by a central bureaucracy that has no personal stake in the ultimate economic
effectiveness of a project, and usually isn't even answerable to a free electorate.

One could envision some system the World Bank could adopt that would
promote fairly distributed local private ownership, with the project itself held
as mortgage collateral. If the project wasn't operated up to specification,
new local ownership would be found. This would foster real local capital in
exchange for the siphoned wealth, but it would do more. If the system
required that individuals, or small, freely formed cooperatives, not just governments, bid competitively with something of their own—even their pledges
of labor if money wasn't available—it might, through the free market, lead
to a better selection of projects.

Even private banks lending to Third World countries aren't concerned
with the viability of the projects they lend for, as they are when they lend
at home. To the extent that foreign loans don't depend on U.S. taxpayer
guarantees, they are secured by mineral wealth. Repayment doesn't depend
on the wealth to be produced by the project being funded. So even private
Western banks prefer to deal with governments, which control the mineral
wealth, rather than with individuals or cooperatives whose entrepreneurship
might yield better projects.

THE World Bank and IMF don't just operate in secrecy. They operate in
real deception. Sanguine press releases belie boardroom jitters. The World
Bank, for example, told the public that the deterioration in Zaire's economy
"was arrested" in 1980. The IMF reported 1.8 percent positive growth. *IMF
Survey*, the IMF's bimonthly public relations magazine, gave Zaire quite a
plug in the July 6, 1981, issue, announcing an extended credit agreement.
The announcement, as usual, blamed Zaire's problems on the downturn in
the copper market in 1975, and some "structural maladjustments that developed." It praised Mobutu's courageous action in wiping out all of his
countrymen's savings, which the announcement referred to only as "a com-
prehensive stabilization program." It said "significant progress was made
under the program in 1980, especially in slowing the high rate of inflation."

To read the *IMF Survey*, you would certainly never guess that Manoudou
Touré, the Senegalese economist who ran the IMF team in Zaire, had just
resigned, frustrated. In an interview in his office in the national bank building
in Kinshasa, right in the middle of 1980's "significant progress," Touré
moaned to a reporter that "I can't control" the illegal outflow of wealth from
the country. Nor, he said, could he tell how much Sozacom, the minerals
marketing agency, turned over to Gecamines, the mining agency that kept
getting shortchanged according to the expatriate professionals who help run
it.

"We are under the supervision of the Zairian authorities," Touré said. "I have to take for granted what they tell me. The people who are powerful here, the people who export coffee and diamonds and so forth, are very shrewd, very full of technical resources to bypass the law." What of the illegal withdrawals by government offcials and Mobutu relatives?—literally right out from under Touré's nose, since his office was on the top floor. "I cannot control that," he said. "When I want a clarification, I have to take for granted what they tell me."

Of course, the way the IMF crowd explained it to the *New York Times*, graft may be the only thing that can bail Zaire out. In reporting the news about an alleged 1.8 percent growth in the Zairian economy, the *Times* quoted an unnamed economist explaining, "The reason was that goods could be imported with black money, and the economy grew." Mobutu, it was explained, had decided to allow more smuggling so that the raw materials needed for expanded enterprise could be imported. Carried to its logical conclusion, this means that the IMF currency and exchange restrictions are the very thing that is *impeding* development in Zaire—which isn't surprising, except for an IMF economist's admission of it.

Of course, calculating Zairian "growth" down to such fine calibrations as 1.8 percent is absurd on its face. You can't measure the gross national product of a nation of subsistence farmers. By definition, all a subsistence farmer produces is himself and his family for one more year, and what is that worth?—and to whom? The progress of Zaire is measured by the health and prosperity one sees in little villages like Yalifoka, and in 1980, there was damn little of it.

WHILE all this was going on, you could pick up some leading overseas business publications and read that Mobutu had sold 200 tons of cobalt on the spot market in Switzerland and 10,000 tons of copper to South Africa—South Africa!—all off the books, without reporting it to his own bank or the IMF. The cobalt sale, at least, was said to be for the benefit of his countrymen, to pay for some French buses to get people to work. The old British ones were sitting, rusting, on the outskirts of Kinshasa, lame for lack of spare parts.

You could read similar stories in the World Bank's own memos—but only if you worked for the World Bank. According to a leaked memo dated October 5, 1979, and marked "Confidential," the World Bank knew very well that its public sanguinity was a lie. The memo complained not of the sub rosa sales in Switzerland and South Africa, but of another off-the-books 20,000 ton copper sale, to China, which was never generally reported in the press.

"A review of Gecamines's books indicated a number of special transactions undertaken since January 1979 which have reduced Gecamines's cash flow during the period by US $49.4 million," the secret memo said. Besides the

Chinese copper sale, the memo complained, Gecamines had handed out $5.3 million in foreign exchange, part of an overall plan to pay $59 million, for the improvement of a single farm. The memo didn't say so, but the farm sounded suspiciously like Mobutu's own, which was reported in the Belgian press to have received exactly one-half the entire national importation of fertilizer and two-thirds of a shipment of 125 jeeps sent by Belgium to spur Zairian development.

The secret World Bank memo also says that $25 million was drained from Gecamines for "two presidential centers," and notes that "A local construction firm involved with local political interests is attempting to secure the contracts without bidding at more than double the cost estimated by Gecamines."

For obvious reasons, Mobutu was not eager to discuss any of this. An endless series of requests for interviews both in Zaire and in the United States went without reply, and when a reporter* phoned or showed up at the palace, he was told that not only was the president unavailable, but that no one in authority was available to speak *for* the president, or would be, for weeks and weeks.

Another potential source of information wasn't talking much either, Société Général. Some 250 companies are under Société Général's wing, and the majority of the stock in most of them is owned by the others; they also own stock in the parent, which owns stock in them, a complicated arrangement that was banned as an illegal trust in the United States long ago. The units make money off each other by monopolizing the marketplace through their joint ownership. A mining company in Société Général will ship its goods by a Société Général shipping company to a Société Général smelting company, and all will insure with a Société Général insurance company. These deals are locked in by contract, so no new companies can try to compete, another thing that's illegal in the U.S. There are no consolidated financial statements, so it's hard to quantify how big the company is. But poor it is not.

Some 92 to 93 percent of Société Général's stock is held by the public, but the other 7 to 8 percent controls the company. Who owns it? Rumor is, it's the royal family, which obviously has influence over at least several seats on the board. Says a high corporate official, who would be identified only as a high corporate official, "It is natural for you to suppose so. But if you ask me if the royal family is a shareholder, the only answer I can give you is, 'Maybe.'"

Jean Dachy, director general of Société Général's main mineral subsidiary, will say his name, but not much else. How much did Société Général get when it sold its mining interests in Zaire to the Zairian government? "It wasn't for nothing, but that I cannot tell you." What does Société Général make now for supplying Zaire with expertise, customers, shipping, smelting,

*The author.

insurance, and who knows what else? "It's an agreement between two countries, and I don't think I can give you any information about that."

Is the price Zaire gets for its minerals at least fair? "A lot of people have very loose opinions about that, but they don't know anything," informs Mr. Dachy. "It's very dangerous to discuss this without understanding the whole arrangement. But I'm certainly not allowed to disclose that. We get something, they get something."

IN 1981, Mobutu broke his deal with the DeBeers syndicate to sell all of Zaire's diamonds through DeBeers (all, that is, except for the large percentage of diamonds Mobutu preferred to sell through someone else and not talk about so he could keep the money). In 1981, he contracted on Zaire's behalf with other buying companies, and happened to pick one represented by Herman DeCroo.

Before settling into private law practice, DeCroo had held several cabinet posts in Belgium. He was minister of telephone and telegraph while Zaire built up $1 billion in unpaid telephone bills to the Belgian government. The Belgian government still hasn't collected on this bill. Communications Minister DeCroo made trips to Zaire, and was close to Mobutu. After leaving public office, he continued to make trips to Zaire and be close to Mobutu.

"When I go, friends ask me some little services, the payment of some little bills," he says. "Sometimes my clients are Belgian. Small firms, which have some problem of payment." DeCroo gets payment for them. He should have done so well for the taxpayers.

Another recently retired cabinet minister in 1981 was Henri Simonet, longtime foreign minister and, like DeCroo, expected to come back to the cabinet some day when the right coalition comes to power. Simonet's wife did a booming business as a consultant, particularly while he was foreign minister. One client was Maurice Tempelsman. Others were arms traders seeking Belgian-manufactured military equipment; as foreign minister, Simonet held ultimate authority in granting export approvals for this equipment, though he has denied reports in the Belgian press suggesting that he ever personally handled cases involving businesses represented by his wife.

WHEN the Reagan administration took office, a "State Department official who has been intimately involved in U.S. policy toward Zaire" told the *Washington Post* that the administration wanted "to significantly increase military aid" to Mobutu. He told the *Post*, "It is one of the few tools we have to exercise any leverage with the Zairians to get them to reform their government."

A year later, an unreformed Mobutu visited the U.S. He traveled with eighty people, including twenty-one children, some his own, some nieces and nephews, and some just friends. They went first to Disney World in Florida, and then traveled for a week, ending up at New York's Waldorf Astoria. The *New York Times* reported, "The hotel's Presidential Suite, after years of serving as the New York headquarters for a succession of American presidents and a host of visiting heads of state, was finally getting a real workout."

The Mobutu party took over the entire thirty-fifth floor of the hotel. The children received all their meals in the Presidential Suite, served by three hotel waiters and three servants who came along from Kinshasa.

In November 1982, Vice-President George Bush visited Mobutu in Kinshasa. "I am pleased to announce that during my visit here the U.S.A. and Zaire have agreed to begin negotiations leading to a bilateral investment treaty," Bush declared. Reuters voiced the opinion that this signaled "an improvement of relations." The discussions took place aboard Mobutu's yacht.

WITHIN the corridors of the State Department, and in the newspaper columns of hard-nosed pundits who profess not to be disturbed by liberal or conservative ideology, the most commonly expressed reason given for the U.S.'s personal support of Mobutu is that there is no one available to take his place—as if, of course, this was the U.S.'s problem and not Zaire's.

One of the many who might take Mobutu's place, if the U.S. and its allies stopped supporting him, is an important regional administrator who was interviewed only on condition that he not be identified (for obvious reasons). What follows is what he said, in his own words, edited only slightly where bad grammar made the meaning unclear, and to delete redundancies. Some of it may seem naive, but all of it is real:

"If countries as large as the United States and France and other capitalist countries were more aware of what was really going on here, things might change. On the radio everybody hears that the U.S. just gave us a bunch of money, and nobody sees that money. I was born in 1952. Before independence, I was eight years old. And I've noticed that the changes and development in this country [since then] are nothing substantial.

"The financial assistance that enters this country never leaves Kinshasa. Skyscrapers and streetlights, you see those things in Kinshasa. It's the central government that receives it, and the central government that keeps everything. When people look at Zaire, they think of Zaire as a whole, and that it's all no good. People tell me that everything they have now is only what they have had from colonial days.

"The roads here are poorly kept up. The farmers want to sell their food to buy pants or soap or clothing. They always ask me, how do they ride into town? The first thing that should be developed is the road system. [Without it] nothing else can work. The second thing are the vehicles.

"We have foreign assistance, but we don't know how to use it properly. Why are things expensive? Because they are rare, because you can't transport goods to the marketplace. When someone asks you for a corruption [a bribe], it's because he has to eat. He asks you for a corruption so he can buy food for his family.

"Zaire takes a lot of money from international assistance. All the Western countries give money. But Zaire itself has everything it needs to exist. Where do the benefits of the diamond mining go? Gecamines, MIBA, Kilomotor [another big European company]. We're here, but we don't see any of the profits. Each company is here. If they didn't have a profit, they wouldn't be here. The profits go to the heads of the companies and the heads of the government. The MIBA company, for example, everybody knows they have a lot of profit. Why do children go to school in this town without shoes on? These aren't luxuries, these are necessities.

"There is nothing to lighten the load of life. I want the riches of the country to be equal, so everybody in the country can profit from it. The central government should give an order to MIBA, tell an organization like MIBA to build so many primary schools, so many secondary schools—to spread the benefits to the town that they're in. Now only a few can benefit.

"I don't think it's right that only the people who work at MIBA can use the dining room, shop at the stores. That the people in the central government should profit, and the people of the town not profit at all. The diamonds shouldn't only help those who work at MIBA. They pay taxes to the state, but are those taxes used for the general good of the state?

"The socialism. When I think of the individual unhappiness here, it makes me immediately want to embrace socialism. But when I think it through, I know that what we need is to take the system we have right now and make it better. [If] the distribution of political power is equal, everybody could be happy where he is.

"There should be a new constitution of federalism. The size of Zaire—regions are the size of whole states in the U.S., or whole countries in Africa. We adopt federalism, we stay as capitalism. The American system. Every state has its own government set-up. Now a man from Mbandaka [Mobutu's home district, far away] is commissioner [like a governor] of this region, appointed by the president. Kinshasa chooses and sends him. The commissioner may be here a couple of days and then leave. They help out the police. No one knows what they do.

"It's the opinion of everybody. Look at what just happened in Kinshasa with the students [this was at the time of the 1980 student strike]. I didn't go to Kinshasa and tell them these ideas. Everybody just has these ideas in their heads. If it hadn't been for the Amnesty International investigation, they would have killed the students. But because everybody's watching, they didn't.

"There's no group organized. Everybody is afraid to speak for their rights.

The people have seen people thrown in prison for speaking out. When the president gained his power, those who opposed him were killed. [He named several.] Those are people who wanted to revolt and were killed directly. People saw this. Other people were killed that nobody knows about. If I were to talk like this to reporters from this country, they would in turn report me to their superiors. They would give the reporters a pay raise and I would be caned. I wouldn't mind if you used my name, but I have to think of my family and my income.

"The central government can change if the president quits. It's you who are keeping him there. If the Americans put pressure on him to leave, he'd be gone today. They give him aid for this country, but the aid never reaches the country. Zaire is in a capitalist system, and who is the boss in the system but America? America should cut off all aid. Also the countries that are behind America—Belgium, France, and the other countries. If America set the pattern, they would follow. It would create a situation for the central government to think about. Until the president stepped down.

"Who [would take over]? There are many people. All the people in this government are hypocrites. When the president calls these people to work in this government, they can't refuse. But their hearts are not in it.

"Without doubt, we're going to vote. As soon as you [a reporter] get out of Zaire and go back with this story that's going to happen. Here in Zaire, there will not be violence. All the violent people are out of the country. Soldiers are unhappy here. They couldn't create a violence. Lawlessness? In isolated spots, but not a general situation. In Third World countries where there is change, there is [always] death.

"If the U.S. keeps on, we'll go back to how it was in the early days of independence. Lumumba took the hand of socialism. Without fault, we will most likely follow the path of Lumumba. There are groups of Lumumba's followers.

"It's clear the U.S. killed him. At that moment, Zairians were like children. We didn't have our political maturity. It was a political error [by the U.S.], and the Zairian people aren't against the American people. Followers of Lumumba don't hold it against America for that error because it was one man. But they do hold it against the Americans for the kind of system America has imposed on Zaire."

A room steward at a hotel in Kisangani was asked what he felt about the Mobutu government. He simply went to the beside stand, pulled out a Bible, turned quickly to the epistle of James, chapter 5, and read:

"Go to now, ye rich men, weep and howl for your miseries that shall come upon you. Your riches are corrupted and your garments are motheaten. Your gold and silver is cankered and the rust of them shall be a witness against you, and shall eat your flesh as it were fire. Ye have heaped treasure together for the last days. Behold, the hire of the laborers who have reaped down your fields, which is of you kept back by fraud, crieth; and the cries . . . are entered into the ears of the Lord."

CHAPTER SEVEN
ANOTHER WAY

SINCE WORLD War II, the earth has staggered through a gauntlet of crises over countries far too weak in themselves to threaten either of the major military powers, the United States or the Soviet Union. These current and former crisis points scatter the globe. The Congo—Zaire—is just one vivid case.

Each crisis claims the blood and relatively meager assets of the innocents who live at the scene, and risks anew the ultimate claim that nuclear war would make on American and Soviet citizens as well, and perhaps on all the world. Meanwhile, the lavish military and diplomatic (if that's exactly the word for people like Ambassador Timberlake) preparations for these crises impose enormous tax burdens on the earnings of almost everyone.

Some might argue that nothing new is going on here. Throughout history, powerful countries have marched their armies abroad to seize the wealth of those who can't resist, or to challenge rival powers on a neutral battleground in order to limit the stakes. But the U.S.-Soviet cold war *is* something new, at least in some respects. For one thing, jet engines, electronic cables, and satellite relays have shrunk today's world to where no country is so remote that we can ignore its humanity, or the conditions that breed these burdensome and threatening crises. Our economies interlock. We have news—accurate news, not the word of governments—which impels a reassessment of behavior. Other nations can't just be ciphers anymore. Moreover, these post–World War II crises are more dangerous than earlier military adventurism was. The global reach of the major powers has dissolved any concept of forward lines or protected areas. No country or individual can choose to sit out the game, even without nuclear chips on the table. And they are always on the table.

There is also a dangerous hypocrisy at work. Unlike the great imperial powers of the past, today's two great powers mostly shun nationalist rhetoric. They baldly deny that they are building empire. One hears little talk of the ethnic superiority claimed by other conquering peoples, like Rome's, or Germany's, or England's. Usually, the U.S. and U.S.S.R. even deny that they are acting to try to protect themselves from each other. Almost in unison, they proclaim an ideological motivation—and justification—for what they do. They argue that by enabling the rule abroad of those who proclaim an ideology similar to theirs, they are performing a selfless favor for other countries.

This is an ideological fervor maybe unmatched in history except by the Crusades, or by an occasional Moslem jihad. Moreover, it is a *blind* fervor, because few of the overseas rulers supported by either the U.S. or the U.S.S.R. actually follow the ideologies they purport to champion. Yet under the international ethic of the 1980s, the more a country aggrandizes, the more it claims to be sacrificing for the good of mankind.

Communism and capitalism are rarely at issue. Both sides say they are selling democracy, but looking out on their client states one sees mostly dictatorships—in Poland and the Philippines, Afghanistan and Zaire, Cuba and Indonesia. It is sad to note how similar are the tortured attempts of the State Department and the Kremlin each to justify its own brand of export tyranny.

One ought hardly to be stunned to learn that countries, now as always, don't plan their policies in a spirit of altruistic sacrifice, but from a perception of their own best interests. The question that needs asking is whether, out of ideological fervor or for some other reason, these perceptions have gone wildly astray of what any country's best interests really are.

THE U.S. won the war in the Congo. It took years of fighting, often in circumstances that would have been ludicrous had they not also been so tragic. It cost considerable American treasure, much of it hidden in the budget of the Central Intelligence Agency. Tens of thousands, maybe hundreds of thousands of people were slain in a series of local wars and police actions conducted by various groups, some of whom we supported and some of whom we opposed, but all of whom sought to snuff out opposition.

A far greater number of people no doubt died from starvation and other conditions suffered by civilians because of the fighting. Some of this strife obviously would have occurred even had outsiders not interfered; how much, no one will ever know.

But we won. The Russians, to the extent they had been there, were chased out, and all their surrogates and allies with them. What is left demolishes any ideological or sacrificial excuse for what we did.

One can encounter poverty and disease of the Zairian kind in other parts of Africa and the Third World. But there's a difference. In Upper Volta, the scrawny woman squatting before her bowl of gruel on a dusty crossroads, the baby with flies swarming around the open sores on his body clutching at her shriveled breast, seem more a part of the landscape—what nature produced, if not intended. That woman and her husband could hack all day at their barren crust of earth and extract little more.

Zaire, however, is the basket of nature's bounty. For such conditions to persist there after fifteen years of an American-French-Belgian-enforced peace, and after nearly a quarter century of U.S. domination, has required misfeasance and malfeasance of the worst sort. Untold billions of dollars roll in. The income is quite probably enough to meet the price of a better life not only for the people of Zaire but even for that poor woman and her baby in Upper Volta.

But the riches are quite literally untold—in the sense of unaccounted for. What figures are available for copper, cobalt, and diamond exports can't be trusted. The wealth is being stolen and squandered by a combination of American, European, and Zairian exploiters acting with neither the consent of the Zairian people nor their best interests in mind.

TO blame this tragic thievery on a particular economic ideology, such as capitalism, would be to miss the point. In many countries, capitalism produces increased bounty for all levels of society, while in many other countries working people are exploited under communist governments or governments largely independent of foreign influence. The point is that the government of Zaire is *not* communist or Soviet-influenced. Nor is it independent. It is one of ours. And the people who make U.S. foreign policy, and the people who elect them, cannot escape the moral or practical responsibility for what that policy does.

Since the basic tenet of our system is that government should be restrained to protect individual freedom, democracies lack the unbridled power of communist and other dictatorial governments to bully anyone at will. Western countries sometimes must commit their violence with a subterfuge that dictatorships can dispense with. But it is force nonetheless. Often this force is exercised by granting semimonopolies to private business interests, which can then act in collusion with local political factions without having to account to a democratic system. These business interests are greatly enriched completely outside the free market process, as a government-sanctioned reward for their corrupting influence on the leadership of such countries as Zaire.

The Zaire experience is in no way a test of our own domestic economic or political systems. In our handling of Zaire, great effort was made to suppress both democracy and free enterprise—in fact, to suppress almost everything we say we believe in. But the Zaire experience certainly *is* a fair test of our *foreign* policy. The measure of that policy is not alone, nor even primarily, in the condition of the Zairian people, poignant and compelling as their plight is. The test is in America's *own* plight. Nations do not operate as charities, and a nation unsuccessful in providing for its own people cannot be charitable at all.

At base, the test of our foreign policy in Zaire is this: after twenty-four years of manipulation, at great cost to the Zairian people and considerable cost to ourselves (not the least of which has been the jettisoning of constitutional standards), it can safely be reported that our future lifeline to the copper, cobalt, diamonds, and other potential resources that we need is less secure than it was in 1960. In fact, it has never been less secure than it is right now. The Zairian people are developing an urban class of students, low-paid workers, and unemployed who are bent on revolution.

It is hard to make a fair argument that they don't *need* a revolution. Even in the Zairian power structure, all but the most generously rewarded insiders tend to be discontented with the system. If Samuel Adams had been born thirty-five years ago in the Congo, he would today be in northern Angola with 5,000 loyal followers, trying to buy arms from anyone who would sell them to him.

The Zairian people are angry. Whether anything could have been done over the past twenty-four years to create a life that would not leave them angry is debatable. But things certainly could have been done that would not leave them angry at *us*.

So tenuous is our indirect line, through Mobutu Sese Seko, to Zaire's mineral wealth that it could snap at any time. Similar situations confront us around the globe. We have sought to accomplish so much that is beyond our ability to accomplish, that we have threatened our ability to accomplish the one thing we *need* to accomplish. Peaceful commerce is so natural, so universally beneficial, that real effort is required to sabotage it. Inadvertently, we have applied that effort.

The U.S. electorate seemed to sense such danger. The 1980 presidential election was influenced to an extraordinary degree by a foreign policy issue in peacetime. It was a legitimate issue, involving the loss of access to a vital resource, Iran's oil. As the electorate cast about for improved security, however, the only alternative was another administration dedicated to political confrontation and forceful intervention, the same tactics it unfairly accused its predecessors of shrinking from. They are the very tactics that cost the U.S. Iran's oil to begin with.*

The excuse for intervention, of course, is the notion that if we don't fight, Moscow will win by default. Yet as one travels the globe, from Indochina

*See chapters 10 through 12.

to Cuba to Angola, one finds that the Third World countries where the Soviets are alleged to hold the strongest influence are precisely those countries where we *have* fought. Meanwhile, in countries that weren't militarily threatened by the United States, where Soviet influence had a chance to flunk on its own merits, it has. In Egypt, in Ghana, in Algeria, in Somalia, in Nigeria, in Indonesia—except in occupied countries along the Soviets' own border, the Russians have been kicked out.

In fact, Indonesia, more recently a victim of U.S. intervention, has seen so much bad of both policies that it may become the first country to swing back to Soviet partisanship a second time after getting burned even worse by our side. The Soviet-backed nationalist movement of Sukarno merely screwed up the Indonesian economy. The United States helped his replacements plan a military repression that cost hundreds of thousands of civilian lives and still left the economy a mess.

Meanwhile, Japan, which avoids the hostile relationships and military expense engendered by confrontational policies, lures away our markets.

SOME lessons can be drawn from all this:

1. The legitimate international interests of any country are first, to be secure from external attack, and second, to be free to engage in peaceful commerce—to buy what it needs and sell what it makes at a fair price.

2. Each country and region has peculiar problems and sources of conflict to which cold war considerations are irrelevant.

3. Intervention by major outside powers in the affairs of smaller countries is usually based on a misunderstanding of what's going on.

4. Forceful intervention by a big power in a Third World country, no matter how well intentioned, is almost always dramatically harmful to the people who live in the country being intervened in.

5. Intervention by either major power, regardless of what the other is doing, usually tends to be counterproductive for the intervener.

6. Most of the world is in flux, current governments or economic models can't be assumed to be enduring, and stability in a bad situation is not only elusive but not particularly desirable.

7. Even when a big power marries a charismatic leader seemingly as strong as Kwame Nkrumah of Ghana or the shah of Iran, the marriage, as often as not, ends in divorce.

8. Force creates enmity. If it creates respect as well, that is less enduring.

9. Most countries not threatened by attack will tend to gravitate over time toward systems that by example provide the best lives for their people, and toward countries that make the best trading partners.

10. While forceful intervention tends to be wasteful and futile, real advantage lies in the peaceful intervention of good example, and in looking for ways to reduce the use of force in international relations in general.

11. So long as each big power can deliver nuclear weapons to the other, no significant military edge will be gained or lost through local conflicts, except as it might directly halt commerce in vital goods.

12. For purposes of foreign policy, all people share two basic traits: first, resistance to foreigners who try to apply a cosmic solution to local problems, and second, a desire for peaceful commerce, both in their personal lives and in the lives of their nations—a desire that develops a momentum of its own if let be.

13. The best way the United States can insure access to vital resources is to make itself a trading partner that any country seeking peaceful commerce would naturally want to deal with. This can be achieved in two ways: first, by maintaining a strong domestic economy, and second, by making sure that any leader who comes to power over foreign resources has never been shot at by an American gun.

14. A focus on peaceful commerce as the objective of foreign policy could save enough money from military expenditures, and divert it into the private market for goods and services, to strengthen the U.S. significantly as a commercial entity—and thus to *strengthen* it as an international power, while providing a substantially better life for the American people at the same time.

15. In short, while the U.S. needs an armed force capable of rebuffing attacks on our territory or our commerce, the loose application of that force only puts our truly vital interests more at risk.

CHAPTER EIGHT
SUCCESS BY NONINTERVENTION: NIGERIA

To UNDERSTAND the Congo crisis of 1960, or the Nigerian civil war (the Biafra war) of 1967–70, or the seemingly permanent Angolan civil war in which the United States intervened in the 1970s and threatened to intervene again in the 1980s—or to understand almost any other contemporary African crisis—it is necessary to go back to a series of conferences in Europe between 1885 and 1889. That is where the map of Africa as we know it was drawn. And not a single African-born person was present.

A bunch of white men from various European countries simply sat around a table and divvied up the continent. They were not, however, as they thought, drawing on a clean slate. There already was a map of Africa. None of the tribes, or nations, that occupied the map had explored far enough to know everything that was on it. None could have drawn a complete map, as the Europeans sought to do.

But it is important to understand that there was a map. The map that the Europeans drew was an overlay that ignored existing tribal kingdoms. Many of the kingdoms had been governing themselves for hundreds of years. The Congo (or Kongo) kingdom was only one. Thanks to oral history, young men in the Bini kingdom in what is now Nigeria can tell you as much about the oba, or king, of Benin in a given year in the sixteenth century as a British youth could tell you about the king of England in the same year.

The European kings in the 1880s rarely could erase the authority of an African king over his own people. But they did have power to overlay the local king's map and effectively erase his boundaries by enforcing new ones.

The colonial boundaries drawn on the map in Europe reflected the movements of a relatively few white explorers and troops. The lines on paper had little to do with the realities of African politics. Enemy tribes were lumped together in the same colony. Large, self-governing tribes were split, part going into one colony, part to another, part to a third. Fox example, if the Hausa-Fulani nation had been left intact, recognized for the loose confederation of a country that it was, it would cosntitute the largest country on the continent today. Instead, the Hausa-Fulani were split among Nigeria, Niger, Cameroon, Benin (formerly Dahomey), Togo, Ghana, Upper Volta, Senegal, Guinea, and Mali. In some countries, the Hausa-Fulani were a majority of the population (Niger), in some a plurality (Nigeria), and in some a minority (Togo).

To the European kings sitting around a table in Berlin in 1885, it meant no difference. It didn't matter that the Hausas in Niger were declared French, those in Nigeria English, and those in Togo German. The kings were playing Monopoly—not with Park Place, Marvin Gardens, and Boardwalk, but with the Congo, Kenya, and the Ivory Coast. The really big winners at the table got huge countries, Nigeria and the Congo, composed of literally hundreds of tribes, which couldn't talk to each other because they didn't speak the same language, and which had very different styles of life.

Western histories commonly refer to precolonial African nations as "warring tribes." They were indeed—as were the British, French, and Germans "warring tribes" during the same years. Colonial countries said they prevented bloodshed by policing Africa's disputants with superior power and suppressing intertribal wars. But they substituted wars of their own, on a scale far grander than anything the oba of Benin could have imagined.

Africans fought in World Wars I and II, both on and off the continent. African lives were continuously affected by hostilities among their foreign rulers. The net savings or cost for Africans in military casualties due to colonialism just isn't clear.

Colonial apologists say that economic advances in Africa justified colonialism. There's no doubt that exposure to European technology benefited Africans enormously. But this advantage was transmitted by example, not by power. Like anyone else, Africans, shown bicycles, preferred them to walking. Colonial *force* was something else.

The map drawn in Europe in the 1880s often didn't make good economic sense for Africans. Vertically shaped countries were created along the coast of West Africa, each governed by a different European power. So railroads were built with different-gauge track. Thus commerce between these artificial country-units was not facilitated but impeded. The Europeans didn't *want* their colonies trading with anyone but the mother country. British, French, and German border checkpoints and customs duties suddenly bisected traditional tribal trade roads and halted the passage of goods.

As for the alleged rescue of all those primitives from their barbarism, this also is a two-sided argument. Barbarism was certainly around in places. Alexander Mackay, an Anglican missionary in Uganda in 1879, wrote of the torture and burning to death of as many as 2,000 persons in a single day. "Every day," his journal noted, "there is a wanton slaughter going on of innocent victims. It is dark about 10 P.M. All is quiet, the last drum heard being the executioner's across the small valley, announcing that he has secured his victims for the day, and will spill their blood in the morning. Suddenly a sharp cry in the road outside our fence, then mingled voices; an agonizing yell again, followed by the horrid laugh of several men, and all is still as before. 'Do you hear?' says one of our lads; 'they have cut that fellow's throat—hee, hee, hee!" and he laughs too—the terrible Baganda grin of pleasure in cruelty."

The British did put a stop to such affairs for a good many years, but after their departure, the Baganda began to reveal such cruel traits again. The bloody reign of Idi Amin, and Uganda's continuing problems cannot be divorced from the fairly barbaric history of the country's largest tribe.

Other tribes were quite different, however. And so were other colonialists. There is a particularly graphic description of Belgian colonial work available from the pen of John Gunther. It accords with other accounts, but is especially convincing because Gunther generally accepted establishment foreign policy, and certainly never invited a reputation as a mushy-headed liberal.* In his 1955 book, *Inside Africa*, Gunther wrote:

"The appetite of [Belgian King] Leopold's agents for rubber and ivory grew steadily more voracious and insatiable. African workers were made to fill quotas, and if they failed to bring in the required amount of rubber and ivory they were mutilated or shot. 'Development?' Competent authorities say that the population of the Congo was about 20,000,000 in 1900; today it is 12,000,000. Leopold's regime is believed to have cost, in all, between five and eight *million* lives [Gunther's emphasis]. That is certainly 'development' of a peculiar sort.

"Most horrible was the practice of mutilation. If an African boy [Gunther's word, probably meaning "man"] did not satisfy his bosses, a hand or foot— sometimes both—were cut off. Photographs of such amputations are part of the record, and may be scrutinized today if anybody wants to rake through the old documents. Africans themselves in the Congo had never used mutilation as a form of punishment. It was purely a European invention. To prove their efficiency in this business, the bosses of labor gangs brought in to their superiors baskets full of human hands. The right hand was always

---

*Gunther's long series of *Inside* books, produced under difficult conditions in a different journalistic era, make a fascinating resource now.

favored. To preserve them in the humid climate, they were sometimes *smoked* [Gunther's emphasis]."

By all evidence, Belgian rule was harsher and less beneficial to African populations than was British, French, or German. So it may seem unfair to use this description of Belgian practice as a focal point for a brief discussion of colonialism.

But the Belgian heritage is precisely the one that United States power has been most active in maintaining in Africa. Fear of offending our Belgian allies in NATO was a major constraint that helped set U.S. policies in the Congo on their long-term course during the 1960 crisis. So the example is perfectly appropriate. Besides, this sort of experience to some degree characterized most Third World colonialism.

IRONICALLY, as the countries of black Africa became independent from 1957 to 1964, they decided not to go back to the old national boundaries. They determined to make the colonial boundaries drawn in Europe permanent and in fact inviolable. African leaders have consistently maintained this principle, even when they found that its practical consequences were ideologically distasteful. Temporary Soviet or U.S. alliances have never been strong enough to persuade African leaders to override this regional axiom.

Despite nearly three decades of talk by U.S. politicians about "Soviet puppet states," no African country has allowed Soviet support of any leftist rebel group to interfere with the principle of national integrity in Africa. The only times the principle has been violated at all were when four countries recognized Biafra in the 1967–70 Nigerian civil war, and when Somalia supported (as it still does) the right of the Ogaden region to break away from Ethiopia as the Ogaden people wish. Both these decisions were unrelated to East-West considerations. Julius Nyerere of Tanzania, a socialist, recognized Biafra although the primary weapons being used by the national government of Nigeria to fight Biafra were coming from the Soviet bloc. The positions of Somalia and Ethiopia on the Ogaden didn't change when the two countries switched sides in their East-West alignments.

There are several explanations for this devotion to preserving the boundaries that were set in Europe. The leaders who took over the black African countries in the transition from colonialism to independence understandably didn't want parts of their countries to be allowed to secede, because that would diminish their own power. They backed each other up on this point, against all other considerations, out of a mutuality of interest.

But there was also sincere idealism in their desire to overcome tribal rivalries and build modern states. As a practical matter, maintaining the larger units was to most peoples' economic advantage by now. Rightly or wrongly, commerce had developed to fit the colonial administrative mold. Realigning economic institutions and reestablishing old trade patterns would require a long transition of hardship. People generally preferred to just get on with nation-building.

In some cases, notably the Nigeria-Biafra war, one can fairly ask whether any principle or economic advantage is worth the cost in lives required to keep a country together. The word *idealism* becomes a parody of itself when million of people are killed in its service. On the other hand, if the redrawing of colonial boundaries began, there might be no end in our lifetime to the haggling and killing over where the new lines should lie.

THE Nigerian war is worth pausing a moment to recall. Its causes and resolution epitomize the problems bequeathed by colonialism and the agony inherent in overcoming them. And the war also illustrates the way a quiet U.S. stand on principle can produce a long-lasting diplomatic triumph for the American people that no amount of gunrunning could have matched. American restraint, and continued adherence to decent principles, even in the face of large-scale Soviet intervention, left the U.S. in position to become Nigeria's best overseas friend and trade partner—despite the fact that the Soviets intervened with pivotal help on the winning side of the war.

Nigeria is the most populous country on the continent, the home of one of every four* Africans. Its oil and gas make it the second-wealthiest African country (after South Africa), as well as the United States's second-leading foreign oil supplier (after Saudi Arabia). Of the thirty-nine independent black-run countries, it is by far the richest; $1 of every $3 of their income is Nigerian.

Nigeria also suffered one of history's most horrible civil wars.

No other African nation listened to the white man's line so devotedly as the Ibos, whose tribal homeland is in the southeast quarter of Nigeria. Ibos went enthusiastically to the white man's churches, schools, and workplaces. More than that, they accepted the fundamentals of the white man's philosophy, which was very different from the tradition of most African tribes: specifically, and partly because of their own unique tradition, Ibos accepted the notion that a person's position in life should be the product of his effort and accomplishment, not of his birth. The Ibos accepted universal education, equality of opportunity, job mobility, and reward by merit.

These precepts are hardly startling for Westerners. But most African tradition tends to teach that each person is born itno a certain station, and that as long as he doesn't abuse it, he shouldn't be dislodged from it. The capitalist syndrome of opportunity, accomplishment, and reward was a lump that hadn't passed the gullet of most Africans at independence, and remains unswallowed by many today. Personal ambition is not a valued trait.

No tribe held these traditional values more closely than the Hausa-Fulani,

---

*Or five, depending on whose statistics you use.

who inhabit the northern half of Nigeria. Numbering probably close to 30 million—five times the number of Ibos—they constituted a plurality of the country's population.* The Hausas held fast to the Moslem religion that had come to them centuries ago, and to the traditional tribal-religious hierarchy. They resisted any cultural inroads by the white colonizers. Western-style schooling was shunned by most people as a matter of principle. Groups of children (rarely boys and girls together) sat under a tree in the morning learning the Koran on slate boards, and that was considered all the education they needed. It was never expected that they would leave home.

At independence in 1960, the Moslem religious leader, the sultan of Sokoto (then Sir Ahmadu Bello) became the leading Hausa political leader, too. The Hausas were committed to traditionalism, male supremacy, and the economic rights of an aristocracy. Thus the colonial boundaries that threw the two divergent tribes together made some sort of Hausa-Ibo collision over the destiny of Nigeria almost inevitable.

For administrative ease, the British had divided their colony into three large regions, each dominated by one of the three main tribes in the country. In addition to the Ibos in the southeast and the Hausas in the north were the Yorubas, in the southwest quarter of the country. Of the two other tribes, the Yorubas most resembled the Ibos. There were 6 to 8 million Yorubas, compared to the more numerous Hausas. Both Yorubas and Ibos tended to be shorter and stockier and have more markedly negroid facial features than the tall, almost Aryan-looking Hausas. The southern tribes practiced rain forest agriculture, unlike the Hausas, who grazed their herds and farmed their crops on the northern savannah. And the southern tribes clung to African-rooted cultures and religion, which for the Hausas had long ago been supplanted by Islam.

Depite these Ibo-Yoruba similarities, however, when independence came, the Hausas began to court the Yorubas as allies against the Ibos. They succeeded.†

AS expatriates were replaced by Nigerians in bureaucratic and technical jobs throughout the country, the most qualified applicants to take over were usually Ibo. The Ibos' ranks included a grossly disproportionate number of college graduates and "been-to's" (people who had "been to" Britain, usually for advanced study). When Hausas left the country, it was usually to go to Mecca.

*Not only were the major tribes pitted against each other, but it's worth noting that in each region, many smaller tribes—Nigeria had 258 in all—were left unhappily under the domination of the one largest tribe.

　†All these numbers are approximate. There still has been no accurate census, and the leaders of all the tribes have tried to inflate their population figures to increase their influence in the central government.

Moreover, the Ibos, following the puritan ethic, weren't afraid to leave home to go where the work was. So they flooded the federal capital of Lagos, and particularly the north, where few of the native Hausas were prepared to step into expatriate jobs. Even to the Yoruba-dominated regions they came. The Ibos were the craftsmen who would rise earliest and work latest to earn money. They were the managers that foreign-owned retailing and service concerns wanted to hire to run local outlets. If the electricity went out on a Sunday and people needed candles, it was likely as not an Ibo who had kept his shop open to make the extra sales, while Ibo engineers worked on the power plant failure.

The white expatriates thought the Ibos were wonderful. The other Nigerians began to resent them bitterly. This was an old story. Back in 1959, residents of the colony of British Cameroon had stunned the British by voting in a plebiscite to become independent as part of Cameroon (a relatively poor, French-speaking colony) instead of Nigeria (a better-off colony with a familiar language); the only issue was the voters' desire to get away from the "pushy Ibos" who dominated the region of Nigeria that they would have been part of.

What sealed the Ibos' fate in Nigeria was the military coup d'etat of January 1966—which had seemed like a good idea at the time. The government that had taken over Nigeria at independence in 1960 was rife with corruption, even at the pettiest levels. The postal clerks and people behind the window where you paid your water and electric bills wanted a "dash," or bribe, for service. In business, it was even worse. Schools, hospitals, every public institution was corrupt.

Government was ineffective. Because the Hausa leader, the sultan of Sokoto, could not by tradition reside outside his Islamic administrative area, he became governor of the Hausa-dominated northern region. He sent a Caspar Milquetoast to Lagos as prime minister. Without leadership from a strong federal figure, bickering among the regions brought parliament to a standstill. Gross fraud in the Yoruba-area regional election in 1964 led to rioting.

So a group of well educated young army officers decided to junk the system, and make Nigeria work like a modern country. They hailed from many tribes, but, as in everything else, a disproportionate share was Ibo. There was no real strongman, and the military government was run by a council of officers representing all the major tribes and others. But the head of the council, the chief of state, was an Ibo. Worse, the coup was accomplished by the murder not only of the prime minister, but also of the sultan of Sokoto, which was something the Hausas could neither forget nor forgive.

Under the military government, though, for six months, Nigeria had the best government it or any country in Africa probably ever had, at least from the standpoint of fair laws fairly enforced. Much corruption was wiped out, and the rest had to go underground. School teachers (the author was one) suddenly noticed that the students with the best grades got their scholarships renewed (occasionally to their own amazement), and some chiefs' sons with poor grades failed for the first time to make the scholarship list.

Children were lined up to sing the previously little-sung national anthem each day before school, and absorb the meaning of its most ringing line, "though tribe and tongue may differ, in brotherhood we stand." The slogan "One Nigeria" was everywhere. Soldiers showed up at public buildings at the beginning of the work day and arrested civil servants as they straggled in customarily late. The tardy workers were marched to a public square, chastised by the military governor in front of laughing crowds, and warned of sterner punishment for repeat latecomers. Nigeria was being run under the puritan ethic.

Then, in July 1966, came the counter coup, from within the army. The Ibo leaders of the first coup were murdered. A northern-born army officer (though a minority tribesman, not by blood a Hausa) was installed as head of state. Anti-Ibo rioting began throughout the north, and finally turned into mass killing. Often led by Hausa members of the Nigerian army, crowds would organize in the night and go from house to house killing Ibos of all ages. With first light, crews went around to shovel up bodies from the streets.

The long caravan of big, open-backed trucks filled with fleeing Ibos, carrying chairs, tables, whatever they had, began to wend its way south. It flowed throughout the fall, as new massacres were reported in new towns. If you lived on the main road from the northwestern quadrant of Nigeria back to the Ibo homeland in the southeast (as the author did) you could wait at a service station (as the author did) and hear blood-curdling tales from refugees. Many had fled through back doors or windows with children, while other family members were being gunned down or hacked to death with machetes. Some had no idea what had happened to relatives, and hoped to reunite with them back home.

By late fall, it became obvious that the Yorubas, by their silence, were siding with the Hausas. Ibos from all over the country headed home, a diaspora melting back into what was already the most crowded part of Nigeria. Separation and war were only a matter of time.

Tens of thousands, maybe hundreds of thousands, of Ibos had been killed before the war started. But even more important historically was the shock to those who survived—the realization that tribal hatred was stronger than anyone's philosophy. The real problems of Africa were being written in blood over the platitudes and ideological cant that people had come to believe.

REUBEN was the best carpenter in Benin City, capital of the Bini tribe in the Yoruba-dominated southwest. As December 8, 1966, dawned clear and blue-skied, a typical Nigerian dry season day, Reuben was set to earn a hefty three pounds sterling from an expatriate who needed a shipping crate made right away. And the Nigerian Tobacco Company was scheduled to pick up—and pay for—a large order of display boxes he had just finished.

But that morning a commotion arose in the city's central roundabout, a few blocks from Reuben's shop. About a hundred men were parading down the middle of the main street shouting for the Ibos to go home to the Eastern Region.* Reuben was an Ibo. The crowd appeared rowdy, but not violent. When they reached the marketplace, police arrested a few in an effort to disperse the remainder. That move backfired, though, and a larger crowd marched to the police station and demanded—and won—release of the prisoners.

After that, the police walked behind the crowds, but didn't try to stop them. By midafternoon, crowds had been up and down the streets visiting all Ibo traders, carrying signs telling the Ibos to get out of Benin, and roughing up the Ibos' property—knocking over a pile of canned goods here, or (in Reuben's case) a stack of lumber there.

The expatriate who ordered the shipping crate reached Reuben's shop soon after the crowds had left. The pieces for the crate had been cut and planed, but not assembled. Reuben, a slight, short man, was alone in the shop, trembling, with tears in his eyes. The crowds had warned him he would not be safe in Benin another night. He was sure they would destroy or steal the wood in his shop. The Nigerian Tobacco Company order was still waiting and now might not be picked up until the next day.

Reuben had sent his family home to the east several months before, at the time of the biggest northern massacres of Ibos. Now he would have to join them—he was frightened for his life—but he needed the money from the tobacco company order. He also felt an obligation, despite the expatriate's protestations, to complete the promised crate.

Tearfully, he poured out his shock and his grief. Why did everyone hate the Ibos, Reuben asked. He had come to Benin years ago, only to work his trade and live quietly. He had brought no harm to the Bini tribe, or to any other local people. He had been well liked. But now even the people he knew as his friends were saying around town that the Ibos should pack and go.

He pounded away at the expatriate's crate. His assistants, also Ibos, had fled in fear of the mobs. They were already miles away, on the road home to the east. As he finished the crate, a line of fifteen or twenty blue Land Rover trucks packed with armed police rolled into town from the west, from Lagos. They were reinforcements to help snuff out the demonstrations before blood was spilled as it had been in the north. But the police wouldn't be there to protect Reuben forever. He finished the crate, collected from the tobacco company, and took off.

*   *   *

*The author witnessed the events of the day.

EUGENE earned an honors degree in physics at the University of Ibadan, the best in Nigeria. He set his sights on a teaching career, and won a scholarship to Oxford. He earned a postgraduate diploma in education there. A slight, soft-spoken, bookish young man who wore thick bifocals, he got a job teaching physics at Western Boys High School in Benin City. But he was an outsider, an Ibo.

Because his field was physics, Eugene could have sold his services in Nigeria even had he been a poor teacher. Probably more than any other subject, physics tended to be taught by Peace Corps volunteers and other expatriates. Trained Nigerians were scarce. Yet Eugene was generally regarded among expatriates as the best high school physics teacher in the city, and the best teacher on his school's staff, which included two expatriates.

When the 1965 school year ended, the principal left to take another job, and Eugene was appointed to fill his place. He moved into a modern apartment and drove a green Peugeot 404. He seemed on top of the world. But one evening over an orange soda—Eugene was one of very few Nigerians born without a taste for beer—he related the difficulties he was encountering trying to establish a system of admissions, grades, scholarships, and promotions unaffected by tribe and politics.

The school, like many in Africa, was owned and run by a proprietor as a money-making venture. While the proprietor sincerely tried to improve scholarship at the school, he felt pressures that don't exist at U.S. high schools. An important chieftancy in the Bini tribe had been bestowed on him by the council of tribal rulers, and he valued that. He also valued his seat in the regional legislature, which was assured him by the tribal chiefs' support. In return, the Bini power structure expected the proprietor to see to it that certain boys, perhaps the sons of chiefs, won admisson to the school and received grades high enough to maintain a government scholarship.

Eugene resisted stubbornly. Going to a high school at all, let alone a good one, was a luxury that few young people enjoyed. The stake was usually an office job for successful students, and a life of rubber-farming for those who failed. Eugene was making it as hard as he could for tribal aristocrats who were used to throwing their weight around, pulling strings for certain boys. If a competing applicant did better work, Eugene wanted that boy in school and the chief's son back on the farm. By and large the Ibos weren't fixers— with their abilities they didn't have to be—and that as much as any other single thing destroyed them.

With the riots of December 1966, Eugene remained in Benin City for a few breathless weeks, until all grades were turned in and the school year was over officially. Then he hired a lorry, packed his gear, and slunk back to the east, all in one day, telling no one.

Back home, he obtained a job as a school principal. Secession came, then war. Nobody outside Biafra could get in touch with him. He directed a refugee camp near Aba, the provincial center closest to his home village.

The camp's original inhabitants were refugees from the north, but later, as Nigerian troops gradually tightened the circle around landlocked Biafra, and the Russian and Czechoslovakian jet bombers and British long-range artillery took their toll on Biafran homes, new refugees flooded the camp.

Food arrived every week by truck from the airstrip at Uli. Catholic and Protestant charities—the people who had instructed the Ibos for years on the benefits of meritocracy—flew the food in. It was packed in bags marked, "Donated by the people of the United States of America." Whoever saw those words remembered them. Countless Ibos who had endured one refugee center or another mentioned it later to visiting Americans. Without the food, the people at the camps might have died, and they knew it.

But where was the U.S. recognition, and political help, they wanted to know. Where was American military aid to neutralize the Nigerians' overwhelming superiority of firepower, which was attributable largely to Soviet interference? Backed only by an occasional planeload of French small arms, the Biafrans could not hold out. Eugene and others still asked these questions long after the refugee camps, and Biafra, had fallen.

The Aba sector had collapsed first during the Nigerian army's fateful last push of December 1969. Eugene had retreated to his village, as Nigerian troops ordered. When word came that he could go to Owerri, another Ibo provincial capital, to seek a job in the reorganization of the region's schools, he took to the road with his armload of possessions—three cushions, to sleep on.

Soldiers stopped him on the road and threatened to relieve him of these. But he begged them not to, and they laughed and moved on. Once they threatened to break his glasses, which in a way symbolized Ibo superiority. A soldier threw the glasses to the ground and waved his boot over them. Eugene begged again, and the soldier laughed and moved on.

Eugene found the job he had been assigned, and a small room to share with two other men. Several months after the Biafran collapse, no money had been injected into the fallen region. No one was paid. Ibos had exchanged their Nigerian currency for Biafran, but now the government collected the Biafran money and gave nothing in return. Even if you found something to buy and had a shilling to buy it with, the seller wouldn't have enough pennies to make change. Ibo engineers had prepared plans to restore electricity and running water, but Lagos refused to fund these simple and relatively cheap projects.

Every evening a young boy brought Eugene a pail of water from the nearest creek, as he worked late under a small kerosene lantern. But Eugene's long labor accomplished little more than that of Sisyphus. The Biafran government had kept the schools open whenever the fortunes of battle permitted. Now, in preparation for reopening the schools, the occupation government had assigned Eugene to itemize the equipment that had existed in them prior to Biafran secession, but that was now missing.

The simple and obvious answer was that everything was missing—the Nigerian troops had systematically looted and destroyed schools as they went. They took every chair, blackboard, book, and doorknob. What they did not want to bring home, they burned. Had the government meant business, it would have reopened schools where the population had moved since the war—almost everyone in the region was a refugee by this time—and it would have distributed whatever equipment was available.

Nevertheless, Eugene compiled his lists dutifully for two months, and delivered them to the Ministry of Education in Enugu, the regional capital. The ministry officials, sent in from Lagos, didn't discuss the lists and in fact may never even have examined them. They merely informed Eugene that his appointment, and that of other workers in his office, had been illegal, and that all seven were being dismissed without ever having been paid.

That very night, an American visitor* slept in the open air on the roof of a government building with Eugene and hundreds of other men and women, presumably government employees who had no place else to go. On the hillsides around them they could see the fires of the families camped there under pieces of corrugated tin roofing that had been bombed off buildings during the war.

The visitor brought news: after having talked to the new principal and others at the school in Benin City, he felt sure that Eugene could have his old teaching job back. Eugene needed the money, and his family needed what money he could send home. Surely, the visitor said, enough talent was wasting away in the Ibo state, and the people would be better off if men who could find good jobs elsewhere would take them.

But Eugene would hear none of it. The spark extinguished so painfully could not be rekindled so easily. Someday Eugene might again venture out from the Ibo homeland to make his life, but the day would not come soon.

ON a trip to Nigeria in 1980, the same visitor couldn't locate Eugene. But he spoke with many others from among the millions who had endured similar experiences. Ten years had passed since the final, starving remnants of Biafra were overrun by well-supplied federal troops.

The Ibos still hadn't fully recovered economically. But the modern way of life they went down fighting for had become the country's official policy. And the political rearrangement the Ibos had sought had been accomplished by Nigeria's new constitution. The vast, Hausa-dominated north had been split into many equal states, so that the Hausas couldn't continue to dominate national politics by controlling the largest subunit.

With millions dead, it could hardly be called an Ibo victory. But the ideas were succeeding where the thinkers had failed. A Hausa elite of educated

*The author, who was present at much of what is recounted concerning Eugene.

young government administrators was even working with older tribal and
Islamic leaders to enforce the newly mandated ideas on their fellow Hausas.
Two-thirds of all Hausa boys and one-third of the girls were reported attending
modern (as opposed to Koranic) schools. While interviews suggested that
these figures were exaggerated, and they fell far short of compliance with
the new mandatory universal education law, they still represented a revolutionary improvement. A decade earlier fewer than 5 percent of Hausa
children went to modern school.

One of the young Hausa elite was Sani Ibrahim Tanko, minister of information in Zaria, an ancient Hausa slave-trading capital. "There are still
some tendencies to resist among the parents who aren't used to Western
ways," he said. "We go to the villages, and we campaign. We show films,
and in between we talk about the value of schools."

Boys were offered special classroom hours to allow them to continue their
Koranic schooling as well. Coeducation was rare, especially above the primary level. "For many parents, it goes against their grain, against their
religion," said Dahiru Kajuru, another government official pushing the program. "But the girls must be put into school till they want to get married.
You may not even choose a husband for the girl, and that's a big change,"
he said.

Only a small minority of northerners speak English, the national *lingua
franca* commonly used in the south. But even in tiny northern villages of
round, thatch-roofed huts, some farmers talked of sending their children to
school to learn scientific agriculture, which would require English. Many
parents had been taken to court and threatened with jail if they didn't send
their children to school. Most chose to obey.

The emir of Zaria, the traditional king of the Zaria region, had recently
been called on to judge the case of a girl from the tiny village of Zangon
Kataf who had run away to attend technical school and avoid an unwanted
marriage. The emir had surprised and impressed many people by ordering
her father to let her stay single and attend school.

Throughout Nigeria, ways were being found to soften the long-standing
contentiousness between civil authority and traditional rulers like the emir.
Local kings, or chiefs, were delicately left with certain powers that were
particularly important to them, always subject to overruling by political
authorities under the constitution.

Some Ibos had begun circulating around the country again, but they generally kept a lower profile than before. Their homeland, cleared of the rubble
of war, functioned normally, but was still behind other parts of the country
in road improvements and commercial construction. Ibos complained that
they were shortchanged on funds for schools and development (which the
government denied, of course). And Ibos bore the pain of seeing businesses
they once owned in other parts of the country, which were confiscated without
compensation, now being operated by new owners from other tribes.

For that and other reasons, the main tension in Nigeria seemed to be between the Ibos and the Yorubas, rather than between the Ibos and the Hausas. As Gunter Grass noted, writing about the end of World War II, betraying friends are often more vicious than acknowledged enemies. It was the Yorubas, the Ibos' southern rain forest neighbors, who inherited most of the technical, high-education jobs the Ibos formerly held, and took over many of their businesses.

Yorubas and Ibos constantly warned visitors to watch out for theft and violence when around members of the other tribe. "They are not like we are," each side would say. Yorubas and Ibos could often be observed taunting and being discourteous to each other. Ibo hotel operators sometimes refused accommodations to Yoruba visitors, and Yoruba transport operators sometimes refused to carry Ibos.

Ibos were even in a loose political alliance with Hausas, who just a decade earlier had slaughtered them. Nigeria's president, Shehu Shegari, a Hausa, ran on a ticket with an Ibo vice-president. Ibos claimed that the Yoruba political leader, Obafemi Awolowo, had devised the strategy of siege and starvation that eventually won the Biafran war at the cost of a million or more civilian lives. Awolowo narrowly lost the election to Shegari, and became the government's toughest critic (he had been elected governor of the Yoruba-dominated region from the time of independence, a veteran of the old-style corruption system).

ALSO in 1980, the United States, which had resisted appeals from both sides to intervene in the civil war, had become Nigeria's closest friend outside the continent. The U.S. Constitution had served as a model for the new Nigerian constitution, which in 1978 had brought the country back to democracy after thirteen years of military dictatorship. The reason for that is simple: the U.S. system had been more appropriate all along to Nigeria's basic problems than was the British system that had been thrust upon Nigeria in 1960.

The British parliamentary system was designed primarily to deal with class differences; but the differences between rich and poor weren't what tore Nigeria apart. People had never resisted dealing with chiefs. The problem was *which* chiefs. Like many African countries, Nigeria suffered from regional conflicts, which was precisely what the U.S. Constitution was aimed at resolving, with its two houses of legislature that gave regional equality equal weight with popular equality. Nigeria has gone beyond even that, with a clause requiring a president to obtain one-fourth the vote in at least two-thirds of the current nineteen states. This required the formation of national parties, campaigning nationally on national issues—an attempt to get away from tribe-oriented politics.

The problems aren't over. The system came within a whisker of collapsing at the outset when the leading presidential candidate, Shegari, collected the required minimum vote in only twelve states, just missing in a thirteenth. The supreme court (another contribution of the U.S. model) ruled in a rather convoluted way that since only two-thirds of the thirteenth state was necessary to constitute two-thirds of the total nineteen states, only two-thirds of 25 percent of the vote in that state was necessary to meet the requirement. Shegari had that, and was declared the winner. More important, the opposition accepted the rule of law and acknowledged his victory, averting a crisis.

Meanwhile, the Soviet Union, which played a critical if not decisive role in the civil war, is not nearly as close to the Nigerian government as the U.S. is. In the early stages of the war, in the summer of 1967, the Ibos of Biafra had been rolling toward Lagos for what appeared might be a forced political settlement or even the downfall of the national military government. A Biafran puppet government had been temporarily set up in Benin City to govern the Bini-controlled midwest region, and a Biafran column was rolling toward the crossroads town of Ore, halfway to Lagos.

It was at that point, with the U.S. refusing to get involved, that the Soviet Union and its Czechoslovakian agent brought in MIGs and turned the tide of battle. Biafra had no jet airpower—neither did the Nigerian army to speak of until the U.S.S.R. stepped in. The Biafrans were on the retreat from that moment.

Understandably, for awhile, Nigeria seemed to be growing closer to the Eastern bloc. It was giving them the tools to win their war. High Soviet officials came to Lagos and sweet talk was passed. With Soviet help, Yakubu Gowon, the colonel who had taken charge of government in the anti-Ibo coup of July 1966, consolidated his control alarmingly. Soldiers and students marched to a song, the lyrics of which were: "Holy holy, Holy holy, Another savior, Yakubu Gowon."

The United States clearly was going to need Nigerian oil in years to come. On the other hand, humanitarian and religious groups and former Peace Corps volunteers were pressuring Washington to do more for the Ibos than simply permit private groups to ship food and clothing to Biafra. This pressure increased as the Nigerian blockade of Biafra made starvation the major weapon of the war. The pathetic faces of dying Ibo kids were pictured everywhere.

But the U.S. did not intervene. It's hard to determine whether this is attributable to especially cool heads in one branch of the State Department or the coincidence of the Vietnam War's being in progress. State Department cables released under a Freedom of Information Act request reveal no tortured decision-making. Pleas for military help from the Nigerian government were appeased mostly with polite talk, once with an innocuous civilian-run driver education class for army truck operators. The U.S. refused Nigerian pleas that we interfere with humanitarian aid being delivered to Biafra by private agencies. Quite to the contrary, the U.S. government lent transport aircraft to those agencies to help them in their work. But, on the other hand, the U.S. refused entreaties by many of those humanitarian agencies to lend any political, let alone military, support to the cause of Biafran independence.

Within a few years of the Nigerian government's victory, the Soviets had lost their closeness to Lagos, and the U.S. was Nigeria's best trading partner. During the fuel shortage crisis, Nigeria sold the U.S. the oil we desperately needed, even offering breaks on price and quantity. A few years after that, the U.S. was Nigeria's constitutional model.

The reason for all this is simple. Nigeria had oil and needed money. The U.S. had money and needed oil. No Nigerian leader had ever been shot at with an American gun. No one who might conceivably become a Nigerian leader had been, either—not even an Ibo. If the U.S. hadn't helped Nigeria do its grisly work in Biafra, at least the U.S. had kept its hands off a Nigerian political matter, while maintaining our support for humanitarian relief. That was a position that *all* Nigerians could come to respect. Considering that the U.S. was a far better prospective trading partner than the Soviet Union, and considering that the U.S. had the constitutional system most worth emulating, there really wasn't any question what the Nigerians would do.

It was a wonderful, peaceful victory for U.S. foreign policy, exactly as Jefferson and Washington might have envisioned it.

CHAPTER NINE

FAILURE BY
INTERVENTION: ANGOLA

THE OCCASIONAL tribal conflicts that have followed independence in Africa are among the least surprising developments of recent times. What is really surprising is that full-scale civil war has broken out only where it has: Nigeria, Chad, Zaire, Angola, Ethiopia, Uganda, Rwanda, and Burundi.

Still more remarkable are the cases of progress, however tentative. Several were visible in the early 1980s. Nigeria with its new democracy was foremost. To be sure, oil wealth gave Nigeria a big advantage over other countries, but Nigeria's original problems ran deeper than most, too.

For a while, Kenya appeared to blossom with a new freedom and unity under President Daniel Arap Moi, after the death in 1978 of autocrat Jomo Kenyatta. Kenyatta had led the country at independence in 1964, and ruled it ever since, parceling out its dwindling resources among his family. The simplistic U.S. press treatment that designates countries as being on our side or their side—"pro-Western" or "leftist"—resulted in far too good a reputation for Kenyatta, who was adjudged to be on "our" side. His corrupt government's bias toward his own Kikuyu tribesmen, and even more toward his own family, was ignored over the years.

Even the Mau-Mau, which Kenyatta helped organize, was romanticized in retrospect into a legitimate independence movement. That the Mau-Mau killed hundreds of times more blacks than whites, that it spent most of its time in tribal purges, and that largely because of the Mau-Mau, Kenya's independence from England was delayed until more than a year after neighboring Tanzania's and Uganda's, all were ignored in the romanticization. The Kikuyu were a plurality of the country; Kenyatta's popularity among the non-Kikuyu majority was a public relations myth.

Because of an earlier gesture to minority tribes, Arap Moi, a non-Kikuyu, happened to be vice-president when Kenyatta died. He early on tried to display impartiality toward tribe, and to appeal for national unity. The non-Kikuyu majority was delighted, and the Kikuyu, still the most prosperous and holding on to the best land, accepted him. Originally expected to be a fill-in president, he stayed on. Everyone seemed to benefit.

1982, however, saw arrests and crackdowns by Arap Moi against political opponents and literary figures, raising questions of whether he was reverting to the repressive tactics of his predecessor. At least, so far, there were no murders of political rivals.

But the CIA has long had a hand in Kenyan politics, putting this candidate or that on the payroll. The best-known payee so far made public was Tom Mboya, who gained a reputation as a "liberal reformer" in the Kenyatta government until someone murdered him, presumably on orders from Kenyatta, who was getting plenty of U.S. taxpayer money himself. Now, in the early 1980s, the U.S. had an obvious growing interest in Kenya. With Afghanistan occupied by the U.S.S.R., and Iran in near-anarchy, the U.S. reached a deal with Kenya in 1980 to use bases on the Kenyan coast. This would allow the U.S. to maintain a naval presence near the Persian Gulf to protect U.S. shipping.

Considering the importance of the sea traffic, the volatility of the region, and the overt threats already made by such countries as Iran and Iraq, the U.S. desire for use of a port in this instance seems legitimate. And Kenya could benefit from the capital improvements, rent, and jobs. But, likewise considering the history of abuse of such installations, many Kenyans expressed concern over having a foreign military presence in their country. Some openly opposed it. One can only hope that the U.S. did not become so shortsighted as to bribe Arap Moi into client status and encourage him to suppress his political opponents, as we have encouraged other clients to do. The readiest example of the perils of such a course is Iran itself, where U.S. meddling created the very crisis that now sends us in search of a Kenyan port.

NEWLY democratic Zimbabwe, formerly Rhodesia, handled its first episodes of intertribal strife with restraint, if not aplomb. A large cache of Soviet-supplied guns and other weapons was found early in 1982 stored on a farm owned by Joshua Nkomo. Until 1980, Nkomo had led one of the two political movements whose guerrilla fighters were instrumental in winning majority rule and independence. The guerrillas defeated an army assembled by the white minority government of Prime Minister Ian Smith, which included thousands of mercenaries, many of them from the U.S.

But Nkomo had lost the first election for national leadership to Robert Mugabe, the leader of the other major black independence army. Mugabe's group found its basic support among the majority Shona tribe. Nkomo's group was mainly supported by the minority Ndebele tribe. Mugabe had appointed Nkomo minister of the interior in an effort to achieve national unity. But with guns as evidence of Nkomo's disloyalty, Mugabe ousted him from his cabinet post. Nkomo's loyalists did fight with Mugabe's government troops off and on in 1981 and 1982. The rebellion was suppressed; the fighting killed several hundred people, but never turned into a full-blown civil war.

What was encouraging was that Mugabe didn't inflate the episode with excessive repression. Nkomo denied knowing the guns were on his property, and renounced rebellion. He and Mugabe met to try to stop the fighting. The country seemed at least temporarily in equilibrium if not unity. Nor did Mugabe institute some sweeping Marxist design as the U.S. foreign policy establishment had predicted. Instead, he appeared to be sincerely seeking the fairest, least retributive way of undoing the economic imbalances caused by a history of racially discriminatory laws that had prevented blacks from acquiring property competitively with privileged whites.

Of course, it's still way too early to assume that Mugabe will go along with the democratic spirit and risk his power in a free debate or election. Nkomo complains that Mugabe is preparing to create a one-party state, as so many other African leaders have done. But the signs in Zimbabwe are still among the most hopeful in Africa, and Mugabe would have to lurch pretty dramatically to become more dictatorial than our socialist friends, say, Nyerere in Tanzania, or Kaunda in Zambia, let alone more dictatorial than Mobutu, or the white South Africans, or the king of Morocco—or any previous Zimbabwe–Rhodesian government.

The Zimbabwe story is especially instructive because the U.S. came within a hair's breadth of intervening against Mugabe. In fact, the U.S. shaved that hair many times, but never intervened quite so overtly that Mugabe can't ignore it, now that he, like most Third World leaders, wants commerce with the world's richest country.

For many years, despite official U.S. nonintervention, U.S. power seemed to weigh hypocritically in support of racist Rhodesia, and against the Zimbabwe revolution. The U.S. took no action when units of Mobil, Texaco, and Standard Oil of California shipped oil into Rhodesia in violation of U.N. sanctions against the white government, even though the U.S. had publicly pledged to uphold the sanctions.

The U.S. took no action when its citizens fought for the white government as mercenaries in apparent violation of the Neutrality Act. Many of these Americans were veterans of CIA covert operations in Southeast Asia, Zaire, or Angola, which gave some Africans the dangerous notion that the fighters were still employed by the U.S. government (and one of the sad things about the U.S. record of intervention abroad is that we can never be completely sure that they *weren't* employed by the U.S. government).

Of course, consistent legal action by the U.S. in such cases would have been difficult and of questionable efficiency. Oil and mercenaries are both fungible commodities, and to police the trading of them in distant lands through the welter of intermediary agencies employed to keep them secret would tax the resources of justice. Even prosecution of the cases that became obvious would have burdened a few hapless culprits, who were pursuing what seemed to them a fair commerce, with a political weight that more properly belonged on the shoulders of the whole U.S.

The real problem was that the United States would not lend its moral weight, its example, to the simple propositions that Zimbabwe, like any country, should be independent, and that its adult residents, regardless of race, should have an equal say in determining its leaders and its laws. The moral weight of the U.S. on this issue might have been decisive—simply making clear that the Ian Smith government had no major country it could turn to for support.

Instead, the U.S. continued to dangle the hope that if Smith could make cosmetic changes, could find a black front man, the U.S. would back him in his war against the Mugabe–Nkomo forces. And so for more than a year the world witnessed a charade, successful only in Washington and Salisbury, in which the white Smith claimed to be running Rhodesia in a triumvirate with two black stooges who, in the eventual real election against Mugabe and Nkomo, couldn't collect 10 percent of the vote between them. U.S. politicians, preoccupied by a fear that Mugabe and Nkomo were somehow Russians in disguise, cheered the charade on, while Zimbabweans seethed.

Throughout the fifteen-year struggle for majority rule in Zimbabwe, the U.S. would not assert in a believable way that it considered racist rule by the 5 percent white minority to be repugnant. The reason it would not do so is that it still sought to determine *by itself* who would rule Zimbabwe and how. We would be willing to see Zimbabwe independent of its entrenched white colonialists, all right, but never independent of *us*.

That is why the U.S. clung to the notion that racist rule in the reality was less objectionable than communist rule in the mere possibility. Not only was this notion generally unpopular throughout the world, but the whole concept of a communist scare on which it was based was largely phony. Once more, the U.S. was operating on a misunderstanding of the situation.

The U.S. refused to see that Mugabe was a popular leader of the Shona people who dreamt of leading a unified Zimbabwe. He had taken money and arms from communist bloc countries because they were the only ones offering such help, and he had been understandably grateful to them for it. But he could not have given Moscow a permanent lien on his country's independence even if he had wanted to, and there's no reason to believe he did.

Still, the U.S. government treated Mugabe as the agent of an international communist conspiracy that threatened Washington. It regarded Nkomo as much the same, though maybe as not quite so bad. Nkomo's army trained and hid out in Zambia, a neutralist country with stong commercial ties to the West, while the evil Mugabe camped his men in Mozambique, whose government was outspokenly leftist.

In fact, there was a most logical reason for the affinity between Mozambique and Mugabe (besides the simple justice of his campaign for majority rule). That reason was tribal, or national, loyalty. When the Portuguese and British drew the boundary between Mozambique and Rhodesia, they drew it neatly down the middle of Mugabe's Shona people. Half were put in one country, half in the other. U.S. policymakers feared that Mugabe's soldiers and the Mozambicans were *comrades*, but avoided the far simpler and less sinister explanation that they were *brothers*—which was quite literally true in the minds of Africans, who believe in extended families.

By 1982, Mugabe, now in power, was accusing Nkomo of plotting with the Soviets against his government. Apparently, Mugabe was not a friend of the Soviets at all, but, in their opinion, their enemy. He had emerged as a pragmatist who was trying to keep efficient white-run farms in operation while still providing fields for landless victims of racial discrimination. He was visiting Washington and trying to arrange the best economic deals for his people. Mugabe may yet emerge as a tyrant, as Smith was (more than 95 percent of his people were effectively disenfranchised), and as so many other African leaders are. But so far, by creating a popular, peaceful, pragmatic free-trading government, Mugabe has significantly advanced U.S. interests.

Through its inability to recognize what was happening, the U.S. almost lost this asset. It nearly delayed the victory of the revolution until, in desperation, Mugabe might have been forced to mortgage more and more of his future to the Soviets in order to continue fighting. Had that happened, the toll in blood would have gone far beyond the estimated 6,000 lives the Rhodesian war finally cost. It took the British to expedite the settlement by which Smith backed down and fair elections were arranged. This took place during difficult, protracted negotiations in London. The U.S. watched nervously, and acted as if it was doing the world a favor by not objecting.

The U.S. official most helpful in advancing this settlement, which would seem a solid U.S. foreign policy victory, was U.N. Ambassador Andrew Young. For his trouble, Young was laughed out of office, the foreign policy establishment unable to recognize his prescience in this and many other matters. Skillfully using a sympathetic press to spread its message that Young was unfit, the establishment seized upon Young's political artlessness in the face of impromptu questioning. Under the right circumstances, this artlessness could come off as charming, but in the wrong circumstances it was made to sound silly, and on a few too many occasions it actually was. (For example, Young's comments that Britain was racist, and that Cuban troops contributed a desirable stability in Angola, made sense only in the context of a complex intellectual discussion that wasn't nearly as portable as the comments themselves, which were rather jolting in isolation.) Still, Young was one of the few U.S. foreign policy officials in recent years who could consistently see foreign situations through the eyes of the people involved, rather than seeing them through the distorted lens of the cold war, and a few *mal mots* would seem a small price to pay for him.

As it turned out, the Zimbabwe settlement was successful even *in* a cold war context. Judging from their support of Nkomo, the Soviets obviously considered the Zimbabwe settlement a setback, though that is not the kind of thing that tends to get reported in the U.S. press. The European press reported that the Soviet clandestine services officer in charge of the African sphere was removed and demoted right after Mugabe's election, though this couldn't be confirmed.

Mugabe's triumph certainly wasn't a Soviet victory. What's relevant, though, is whether it was a Zimbabwean victory. The jury is still out on that, but the arrow is pointing up.

WITH a successful negotiation of the war in Zimbabwe, the logical next step was to settle a similar situation in Namibia, and then move on to the one truly explosive international issue in Africa, the single issue that the U.S. might not find duckable: majority rule in South Africa. Feelings about the current racist government in South Africa run so high throughout the continent that continuation of the present course could lead to large-scale war. Such a war would confront the U.S. with fundamental humanitarian issues in the midst of great loss of life, would disrupt access to important resources and markets in many countries (Nigeria and its oil, for example), and could even touch off a nuclear holocaust (South Africa apparently has nuclear bombs, and Nigeria, on the other side, has made noises about trying to build them).

So far, the U.S. won't even officially recognize the progress in Zimbabwe, much less capitalize on it by acknowledging the legitimacy of similar majority rule movements in Namibia and South Africa. Ironically, the person in all the world most capable of mediating these issues successfully would probably be Andrew Young, and not just because he is a black diplomat from the world's mightiest country. His value comes largely because what he tries to bring to issues is not the United States's raw power, but the correctness of the United States's fundamental beliefs, which include a decent tolerance for people doing things their own way.

In both Nigeria and Zimbabwe, the leaders and programs that have met this initial success were chosen by Africans—and were not imposed by the U.S.

* * *

POSTCOLONIAL African conflicts clearly are not manifestations of a cap-
italist-communist struggle for world domination. Yet the cold war view had
prevailed time after time, from the Congo in 1960 to the persistent conflict
in Angola. The view serves no one except professional soldiers and their
suppliers. It is not only ludicrous, it's dangerous.

"The Soviet intervention in Angola was probably the single most important
development in shifting U.S. foreign policy consensus [away] from support
of détente," says a 1979 book, *Implications of Soviet and Cuban Activities
in Africa for U.S. Policy*. The book was put out by the prestigious Georgetown
University Center for Strategic and International Studies, and its five coauthors include Chester A. Crocker, who was appointed assistant secretary
of state for African affairs in the Reagan administration, and Roger W.
Fontaine, who is also close to the Reagan team.

The book also says, "Few international developments in recent years have
been as disturbing to the United States as the new Soviet political and military
offensive in Africa. It is there that the U.S.S.R., for the first time, demonstrated to the world its ability and willingness to act as a decisive and
assertive global power."

If so, we have only our own interventionism to blame. In the case of
Angola, once again, the accepted wisdom that rationalizes our interventionism is cluttered with misunderstandings and deceits. The United States med-
dled early and deep in Angolan affairs, almost certainly earlier and deeper
than the Soviets did. If we had followed a noninterventionist policy while
openly offering friendship to those who shared our principles, such as national
independence and one-man, one-vote democracy, there is every reason to
believe we would have a friendly regime in Luanda, Cuban troops wouldn't
have come in, and the Soviet foot would be out of the door.

THE territory that was later called Angola may have been the first colony
in black Africa. Portuguese explorers reached it in the 1480s. They found
three tribal nations: the Kongo, whose kingdom stretched north through what
later became Zaire and the country of Congo (Brazzaville); the Mbundu along
the coast around what is now Luanda, who fought the Portuguese until nearly
the 1600s before succumbing; and the Ovimbundu, who lived inland to the
east and south, where the best farmland is, and who also rebelled frequently
against foreign rule.

These three tribal nations—the Kongo, the Mbundu, and the Ovimbundu—got along only a bit better than the British, French, and Spanish
did. That is to say there was a history of fighting, especially after the Mbundu
retreated inland onto Ovimbundu territory to escape Portuguese slavers. It
was not until the latter part of the twentieth century, however, that Dr. Henry
Kissinger and other political scientists discovered that the real reason the

Mbundu, the Ovimbundu, and the Kongo had been fighting off and on for the past 500 years was that the Mbundu were "Marxist" and the Ovimbundu and Kongo were "pro-Western." It was that discovery, constantly rereported in the press, that led the U.S. to intervene. Unfortunately, we jumped in on the side of the Kongo and Ovimbundu, at just the point in history when their rivals, the Mbundu, were geared to prevail.

The Portuguese, as colonizers, had been almost as bad as the Belgians. (The U.S. seems to pick the worst heritages to try to maintain, probably because these heritages understandably inspire the angriest, and therefore the most alarming, rebellions.) For a long time, the Portuguese saw Angola mainly as a slave farm. According to estimates accepted by George Houser in a history of Angola that he wrote as a pamphlet for the American Committee on Africa, a proindependence group, *3½ million* Angolans were shipped as slaves to work in the Portuguese colony of Brazil, another *3½ million* died in transit, and a million more were sent to North America. Even conservative estimates allow that 4 million Angolans may have been carted off. These are staggering figures.

When the Portuguese finally got around to developing Angola itself, they set up coffee plantations on which Angolans, mostly Ovimbundu, worked for a pittance. They also recruited 100,000 Angolans a year, many of them against their will, to work in South Africa's mines. For this work, South Africa paid Portugal a hefty fee, and the miners not much at all (from Mozambique, about 300,000 people a year were shipped off to these mines).*

While Angola is not quite the fountain of riches that Zaire is, it is well endowed with oil, iron ore, diamonds, manganese, and a few other minerals. It certainly has the potential to feed itself and still raise coffee and cotton as export crops. Its 7 million people (1980 estimate) could be well off.

After World War II, the Portuguese government, a dictatorship, discovered that its African colonies provided an ideal dumping ground for Portugal's own poor and unemployed. In Angola and Mozambique, these Portuguese ne'er-do-wells could live like kings, grabbing land and exploiting forced

*These figures are from *A History of Postwar Africa*, by John Hatch (Praeger Paperbacks). The Angolan history in this chapter comes from half a dozen books and scholarly articles, added to longtime personal observation and periodical-reading. Probably the most respected formal history of Angola is the two-volume work by John A. Marcum, *The Angolan Revolution* (MIT Press, 1969).

It is regrettable that so many secondary sources had to be referred to, but the author hasn't visited Angola. Beginning in 1966, with the Portuguese, and continuing through 1981, I have filed innumerable visa requests and been turned down on every one of them. I even accepted an invitation to be sneaked into territory held by Jonas Savimbi's UNITA guerrilla group without authorization from the Angolan government, but UNITA changed the arrangements unacceptably after I arrived in Kinshasa for the trip. An important rule in the news business is that you don't allow someone to keep you from writing about him simply by his refusing to talk to you. The same should go for countries.

African labor. And so, although Angolans weren't exported as slaves any more, they were treated much like slaves in their own country.

During the 1950s, thanks to the new Portuguese policy, the white population of the two major Portuguese colonies doubled, with Angola's reaching more than 170,000. The white populations doubled again in the next decade, and just before independence Angola's 6 to 7 million people included about 400,000 whites. Unlike the British and French colonies, where white workers were often the upper crust on temporary assignment overseas as a rite of passage toward top government jobs at home, Angola received settlers who were often cultural dregs in no position to educate Africans and with every inclination to mistreat them.

BY the time of independence, fewer than 10 percent of Angolans could read or write their simplest thoughts, and fewer than a third of the primary-school-age children were in school. Although Angola's Portuguese citizens, including a tiny handful of Africans, could vote in Portuguese elections, Angola was ruled from Europe without local institutions. Political organizing was illegal.

But it went on. And, as one might suppose, there were not *two* independence organizations, corresponding to the number of sides in the East-West conflict, but rather *three* independence organizations, corresponding to the number of major tribes in Angola.

The Kongo-based movement in the north underwent a series of name changes but eventually became the National Front for the Liberation of Angola, or FNLA. Its original goal in 1954 was to gain independence for the Kongo tribe as a unit; the group actually had been organized in Leopoldville, since more Bakongo lived in the Congo than in Angola. The group's first leader (Manuel Barros Necaca) died in 1961, passing control to his nephew, a globe-trotting, alias-using, slick-talking organizer named Holden Roberto.

Under Roberto, the group shifted its sights from Bakongo nationhood to the independence of Angola. The Congolese Bakongo had already been "liberated," if that's what you can call Mobutu's operation. Roberto is variously said to be a cousin, or in-law, or other distant relative of Mobutu; certainly the two men were close during Mobutu's consolidation of power in the early to middle 1960s, so that Roberto discarded the idea of a Bakongo separatist movement against the Congo. Roberto began drawing CIA pay, and his camps in the Congo were supported by CIA-sponsored "labor" organizations, at least as early as 1964. Roberto became what the CIA thought was its man in Angola, although when the CIA swung into action there in 1974, and relied on what Roberto said, his information turned out to have been self-serving and largely untrue.

*   *   *

A SECOND Angolan independence group, the Popular Movement for the Liberation of Angola, or MPLA, also was organized during the 1950s. Its base was among the Mbundi. This was the group that later came to run independent Angola with Cuban help. The MPLA included *mesticos*, or mixed Portuguese-African people, and some upper-class, intellectual types from minority tribes, as well as Mbundi. This mixture has been cited by leftist supporters as a sign of the MPLA's broadmindedness, but, more likely, minority groups were represented because the Mbundi area included Luanda, Angola's metropolitan center, where the *mesticos* and other educated classes most frequently lived. More of the MPLA's leadership elite thus had European exposure, which was obtained during the reign of the Portuguese dictator Antonio Salazar, who ruled from 1932 to 1968.

Considering the brutality of the Salazar administration in Africa, it's little wonder that Africans who went to Lisbon found they could get comfort and sympathy from underground anti-Salazar groups. These were mostly on the left, and included the Communist party. Among the Africans in Portugal was a young medical doctor (one of the few African politicians in this period who called himself "Doctor" and actually was one), and not a bad poet, either, named Agostinho Neto.

Neto was the son of a Methodist minister, and the church sent him to Portugal to get his medical degree, which he did in 1958 at age thirty-six. With only a couple of hundred doctors in Angola, he was one of a few who weren't white, and who would treat ordinary people. He was to become the MPLA's guiding light, and the first president of independent Angola.

Shortly after his return from Portugal, Neto underwent one of those experiences that can change the course of one's life. As related in many published accounts, he was arrested in his consulting room in June 1960, during a crackdown on political activists. He was flogged in front of his family, thrown in prison, and not allowed to sleep. When a thousand people from his home village went to protest, they were machine-gunned. Thirty were killed, 200 injured. The next day, Portuguese soldiers went to the villages and killed or arrested everyone there, and burned the buildings to the ground. Nothing was left. (When thirty whites were killed at Stanleyville four years later, it dominated world news for a week, threw the United Nations into turmoil, and justified an air and land invasion by the combined forces of the United States, Belgium, and the Cuban Bay of Pigs brigade.)

Galvanized by Portuguese brutality, the MPLA took to guerrilla tactics during the 1960s with several hundred soldiers. Most of them were trained in Algeria, before the 1965 overthrow of radical Soviet ally Ahmed Ben Bella. The Soviets also sent supplies to the MPLA, through Brazzaville, in the other Congo, across the river from Mobutu's; a coup had established a left-wing "peoples' republic" there in 1963. Before turning to communists, Neto had toured the U.S. looking for friends, in 1962. He had come away empty-handed.

* * *

THE third independence group (besides the FNLA and MPLA) was based among the Ovimbundu people, and was called the National Union for the Total Independence of Angola, or UNITA. Its founder was Jonas Savimbi, a former FNLA official, who calls himself "Dr." Savimbi although he never finished college. Savimbi joined Holden Roberto's group in 1961 after returning to Africa from an unsuccessful three-year attempt at education in Portugal and Switzerland.

A few years later he quit the FNLA and started UNITA, complaining that the FNLA was tribally oriented (it *was*, toward the Bakongo; so was UNITA, toward the Ovimbundu). Justifying his new movement ideologically, Savimbi adopted a leftist line. Referring to Roberto, he said, "No progressive action is possible with men who serve American interests . . . the notorious agents of imperialism." These were words that might have embarrassed Savimbi if they had been recalled when, in 1980, he went around successfully winning support from Ronald Reagan and the *Wall Street Journal* editorial page.

As previously noted, it is misleading to speak of sophisticated ideologies when talking about movements like these, composed of subsistence farmers who identify with the movement primarily because of tribal loyalty. Even discussing the ideologies of the leaders of these movements is a chancy affair. Their economic or political philosophy is rarely what qualified them for leadership. Generally, they are leaders because they held the right birth credentials, and displayed managerial ability and the charisma to excite a following.

All that said, however, Savimbi (and therefore UNITA) clearly had the most radical leftist ideology among the three movements in Angola. Neto of the MPLA accepted the orthodox Marxist doctrine of his Soviet benefactors, but always emphasized that his primary goal was Angolan independence. On the other hand, Savimbi's travels (traced by Professor Gerald J. Bender of the University of Southern California) took him to the most radical world-revolutionaries of the time: not just Egypt's Gamal Abdel Nasser and Algeria's Ben Bella, but also North Vietnam's Nguyen Giap, Cuba's Che Guevara, and China's Mao Zedong. Savimbi also visited North Korea, where the core of his army was trained. These people looked at Neto and his Moscow friends as right-wing revisionists.

No one could fault Savimbi's courage. He plunged into Angola itself with his band, raiding the Portuguese enemy, and hiding out in Ovimbundu villages. The two other guerrilla movements, FNLA and MPLA, operated from the relative safety of bases inside Zambia, Congo (Brazzaville), and Zaire. Seeking charisma, Savimbi gave himself a flamboyance that seemed imitative of Fidel Castro, even down to the battle fatigues and the beard. He made radical appeals that echoed the rhetoric of the radical and violent black power movement in the United States.

Strange, then, that in 1980 Savimbi and Ronald Reagan discovered their affinity. During that year's election campaign, each man saw the other as an opportunity to be seized. Reagan proved his readiness to fight communism by pledging to send arms to Savimbi. Savimbi hired a Washington publicity agent who churned out press releases saying, "UNITA is pro-capitalist, pro-West, wants a parliamentary democracy, and desires religious freedom for all its citizens."

But it was really Kissinger who started this confusion, when he redefined the sides in Angola back in 1974, and began listening favorably to Savimbi's appeals for arms (Ben Bella, Nasser, Guevara, Giap, and Mao being no longer available to supply them). Picking up on Kissinger's cue, the U.S. press to this day invariably refers to Savimbi's UNITA troops as "pro-Western guerrillas." One man's necessity, and another's ignorance, can be the parents of some awfully grievious misinformation.

THE dam of resistance to Angolan independence broke with the overthrow of the right-wing dictatorship in Portugal in April 1974. The new government immediately made a deal with the African colonies, including Angola, to bring quick independence. The scramble was on to see who would take over. Immediately, there was outside intervention, and it did not start with the Soviet Union or Cuba.

John Stockwell, the Congolese-born son of Texas missionaries who headed the CIA's Angola task force, has written a striking memoir of the U.S.'s attempt to install by force a government of its choice in Angola. His book, *In Search of Enemies* (W. W. Norton, 1978)*—the title alone is a wonderful commentary on U.S. foreign policy—has never been seriously challenged for accuracy. It gives this chronology: in May 1974, one month and four days after the coup in Portugal, 112 military advisors from China (which had resumed relations with the U.S. in 1972) led by a major general of the Chinese army arrived in Zaire and began training FNLA forces. China also supplied arms. Barely a month after that, in July 1974, the CIA upgraded its funding of the FNLA, beyond the steady income it had been paying Holden Roberto all along for his questionable intelligence reports.

The new CIA funding, according to Stockwell, was in "small amounts at first, but enough for word to get around that the CIA was dealing itself into the race." Moreover, Mobutu began supplying the FNLA build-up, and everyone knew where *his* guns came from. The operation had not been approved by the CIA's outside oversight body, the so-called 40 Committee, however. In January 1975, as payments built up, that committee was finally consulted.

According to Stockwell and the two best-known Angolan historians in the

*The account here is augmented by numerous interviews with Stockwell.

U.S.—John A. Marcum* and Professor Bender—the Soviets had sharply reduced military aid to Neto's anti-Portuguese guerrillas in 1972, and had suspended it entirely by the beginning of 1974. By those and Stockwell's accounts, new Soviet arms didn't begin trickling in to the MPLA until late 1974, long after the resurgence of the FNLA and the presence of Chinese advisors had become evident. Significant shipments of Soviet bloc arms to the MPLA didn't resume until March 1975. By that time, the Soviets were probably well aware of the CIA's activity.

At the least, this chain of events is entirely consistent with the thesis that the Soviets had sought to arm the MPLA against the Portuguese colonialists, but *not* to help the MPLA take power over other Angolans. On January 15, 1975, the three movements—the MPLA, the FNLA, and UNITA—agreed to a peace plan built around a triumvirate interim government in which they all would take part, with elections to be held in October. Portugal agreed, too.

The first known violation of the spirit of this agreement came one week later—in Washington. The 40 Committee approved $300,000† in aid to the already well-supplied FNLA, which then began attacking MPLA forces in Angola from the FNLA base in Zaire. Writes Stockwell, "In one instance in early March they [the FNLA forces] gunned down fifty unarmed MPLA activists. The fate of Angola was then sealed in blood. . . . Only in March 1975 did the Soviet Union begin significant arms shipments to the MPLA. Then, *in response to the Chinese and American programs, and the FNLA's successes*, it launched a massive airlift [emphasis added]." With the Soviet shipments in March came the first Cuban advisors. Marcum writes that the Russians came in because, "with independence promised and the Chinese in league with the FNLA, which had American connections as well, the Soviet Union faced the prospect of being shut out politically after years of diplomatic and material investment in the Angolan cause."

Nathaniel Davis, then the U.S. assistant secretary of state for African affairs, has written that the chronology doesn't necessarily prove that the U.S. provoked the Soviets into rearming the MPLA. Bending over backward for fairness, Davis noted in his account of the affair that the Soviet arms shipments *may* have been planned before the new U.S. aid was felt.‡ It is possible, he says, that the Soviets were provoked by the conspicuous Chinese intervention in 1974, or by the increased military initiatives Roberto was taking on his own with previously supplied weapons.

*Book previously footnoted.

†If this seems small, remember that soldiers will readily sign up for $20 a month in that part of the world, and rifles can be cheaply supplied.

‡*Foreign Affairs* magazine, Fall 1978. Davis also says that so far as he was told, U.S. support of the FNLA prior to July 1975, when he resigned in protest, was for "covert political" rather than military purposes. While this distinction may have helped one Washington official demark his act of conscience, Roberto clearly hadn't been spending all that loot on campaign literature.

Whatever one may guess about possible Soviet intentions, however, the sequence of events does seem to disprove the argument that Kissinger and other government officials offered in order to justify U.S. intervention. The notion that the U.S. intervened in Angola *in response to Soviet initiatives* there seems clearly and incontrovertibly wrong.

IN July 1975, the U.S. initiated the next big escalation. That was the Stockwell task force, which actually brought American men into the battle, and allowed Savimbi as well as Roberto to sup at the taxpayers' trough. That decision, to continue to try to put a government of our choosing in Angola by force, was made by Secretary of State Kissinger at a time when his chief assistant for Africa, Davis, still thought the issue could be satisfactorily resolved by negotiations; Davis resigned in protest.

As approved by the 40 Committee and President Ford himself, the new covert military program in Angola cost the taxpayers $32 million (which they weren't supposed to be told about). That amount didn't include the salaries of personnel already employed, or the cost of weapons previously shipped. It also didn't include about $100 million in arms and general aid quickly hustled to Zaire, which was fighting only one war at the time: against the MPLA.

Mobutu sent regular Zairian army troops with planes and armor along on forays against the MPLA deep in Angolan territory. This is an important point, considering all the hullabaloo Washington raised two years later when Zairian refugees living in Angola crossed over into Shaba province and touched off a rebellion against Mobutu. In 1975, Mobutu had not just harbored Angolan guerrillas, but had invaded Angola with his own troops to try to keep the MPLA out of government.

As the U.S.'s alleged allies, UNITA and the FNLA, began their build-up, they and the U.S. rejected or stalled several peace overtures, both from the MPLA and from Africans at the U.N. At one point, the CIA learned from a newspaper article that Savimbi himself had suggested a settlement with the MPLA. Stockwell reports that a CIA officer rushed to Angola from Kinshasa, and warned Savimbi that "we wanted no 'soft' allies in our war against the MPLA."

Then the CIA discovered that Savimbi had been receiving aid from South Africa—and, amazingly enough, the CIA was just delighted. CIA officials began joint planning with the South Africans. Angola-bound U.S. weapons were handed over to South African military transports at the Kinshasa airport, in apparent violation of the U.S. law prohibiting arms transfers to South Africa.

South Africa's white government was working on a long-range plan to protect itself from democratic currents. After World War I, the League of Nations had given South Africa administrative control over Southwest Africa, a former German territory sandwiched between Angola and South Africa.

The U.N. long ago ordered South Africa to leave the territory, whose occupants call it Namibia, because South Africa's white supremacy laws discriminate outrageously against the majority of Namibia's people. But South Africa has stayed on.

South Africa worries that if Angola becomes truly independent, it will provide a safe haven for Namibian revolutionaries. And if Namibia then wins independence, it might, in turn, open its borders to revolutionaries seeking the overthrow of the white minority government of South Africa itself. On the other hand, if South Africa could make a bargain with one Angolan faction, such as Savimbi's, and put that faction in power, a dam could be built against the southern flow of the movement toward independence and majority rule.

The issue of racist rule and apartheid in South Africa is the one common political concern that binds Africans, and it cannot be overestimated. When Savimbi told Stockwell about the South African contacts, Stockwell immediately realized that "once his [Savimbi's] acceptance of South African aid became known, he would be discredited as a black nationalist."

Worse, now the U.S. risked the same association. More than anything the Soviet Union could do, this voluntary association by the U.S. could cripple the important interest of American citizens in trading with the independent countries of Africa. One day South Africa itself would have a black government, and we would need to buy vital minerals from it. But Stockwell's superiors continued their military alliance with South Africa's white regime.

ANGOLA'S prospective triumvirate government had fallen apart over the summer of 1975, as the sides, busy fighting, stopped talking. Elections were obviously off. Independence was due November 11, but in October it was unclear who would be on hand to accept it. North of Luanda, MPLA troops with Cuban advisors fought a seesaw battle against the FNLA and units of the Zairian army with U.S. and South African advisors.

Then there were two swift, important developments. A big South African armored column crossed the border from Namibia and headed north, joining forces with UNITA and capturing every town in its path. South African leaders later said that though they didn't want to break confidences, it would be correct to assume that the U.S. encouraged them to invade.

Then came the Cubans. Cuba had gradually deployed 250 to 400 military advisors in Angola beginning in March (coinciding with the arrival of Soviet arms). Now, as the South African column crossed the border, Cuba introduced a shipload of about 700 actual combat troops. Then, as the column rolled relentlessly toward Luanda on independence day, a massive airlift of Cuban troops arrived to reinforce the MPLA.

With them came powerful rockets and big tanks that turned the tide of battle. (The nominally communist country of Congo, Brazzaville, had offered its territory as a staging area for Soviet bloc supplies to the MPLA, so weapons and men could be introduced quickly; the U.S. had the same arrangement in Zaire.) By this time, all possibility of an orderly settlement had vanished, and nobody was playing by any rules.

The Cubans—10,000 of them quickly and 20,000 eventually (plus another 10,000 or so civilian teachers, health workers, construction experts, and so forth)—won the day. They were present in numbers greater than the U.S. or South Africa would openly commit, and they were well supplied. They beat back the FNLA in the north and the South Africans and UNITA in the south. On November 11, the MPLA was in Luanda to proclaim itself the government, and so it remains.

TWO stories will serve to illustrate the kind of operation the U.S. was running in Angola, all secret from the taxpayers.

One is the case of Gary Acker:

After graduating from McClatchy High School in Sacramento, California, in 1972, Acker joined the marines. He became a corporal, but was released after three years for "psychological reasons." There had been constant arguments with officers, and with the enlisted men he was supervising, and an aimless four-month AWOL. Back home, trained only as a machine gunner, he failed in his efforts to find civilian work.

Then in the fall of 1975, at age twenty-one, he saw an article in the *Sacramento Bee* about a man named David Floyd Bufkin, who was hiring and training recruits to fight communism in Angola. Acker called Bufkin and signed up.

By Bufkin's own account, he was working for the CIA. He has recalled in an affidavit that he asked the CIA about work as a mercenary and was flown to Kinshasa, where he met some operatives at the FNLA compound. "I received orders from CIA agents to return to the United States and recruit American citizens to enlist as mercenaries with the FNLA in Angola," he said in the sworn statement. "I was given $20,000 in fresh $100 bills at this time by CIA agents to enable such mercenary recruitments and as compensation for my efforts."

Certainly Acker and the other people who signed to go to battle with Bufkin believed that they were working for the CIA, and told their friends and relatives that. Stockwell, who was running the operation, says Bufkin, a professional mercenary, was technically being paid not by the CIA but by Holden Roberto, with money supplied by the CIA. Other men recruited mercenaries for Roberto from Britain, Portugal, and France with CIA-supplied money.

Stockwell says he himself didn't meet people like Bufkin and Acker.* But he says, "We knew Bufkin was recruiting. We saw him on television

---

*In an interview, not in his book.

saying he was recruiting for the CIA. We never signed a piece of paper with him, but he received briefings as to what was happening, and what the missions were. He was flown into Angola in CIA planes. He stayed at one of our safe houses. He met with our chief of station in Kinshasa. He attended more than one meeting in CIA safe houses with CIA paramilitary managers of the Angola program. We were giving Holden Roberto big fistfuls of green, $5 million, and he used that for a lot of things, including hiring mercenaries, including Bufkin."

Acker's friends and lawyer say the recruits were misled by their CIA contacts about the support forces available to protect them. Stockwell—who quit the CIA in disgust after the Angolan mission was wound up—says the recruits were flat-out "lied to." Acker, three other Americans, and a Canadian, all hired by Bufkin, entered Angola on February 10, 1976, in a truck bought with CIA funds. They arrived from Kinshasa, Zaire, where Bufkin had stopped to check in with the CIA station.

Roberto's forces and the Zaire regulars were already in panicky retreat and, Stockwell says, "raping and pillaging. Into this we sent a ragtag bunch of ill-prepared mercenaries and we lied to them about help being on the way, [about] holding them [the MPLA] off until we could get a serious force in to contend with. The CIA and the U.S. government are definitely culpable in sending people out under false pretenses in an almost suicidal situation. They had very little chance of coming out. It wasn't someplace you would send your kid brother."

Just three days after they arrived, two of the Americans, Gustave Grillo, an immigrant from Argentina, and Daniel Gearhart, a father of four from Maryland, were captured while on patrol together. Grillo was wounded.

The next day, Valentine's Day, the remaining Bufkin recruits went looking for their missing comrades. One, George Bacon, a former CIA paramilitary officer, was killed. A second, Douglas Newby, the Canadian, was fatally wounded. Young Gary Acker was wounded and surrendered, apparently before he ever fired a shot. Bufkin had stayed safely behind, and returned to Zaire.

Acker was arrested by MPLA officers who emerged from behind a phalanx of Cuban armored troops. The three surviving American prisoners, and ten Britishers who apparently were also paid with the money Roberto was getting from the CIA, were tried in Luanda. Some international observers who were allowed to watch criticized the proceedings as unfair, though considering the circumstances of the men's capture, the gist of the charges against them would be hard to dispute. Four of the thirteen defendants were executed. Of the rest, Acker got the lightest sentence: sixteen years in prison.

Acker's parents say they tried to get the U.S. to supply legal counsel for the trial, but were refused. W. William Wilson, a St. Louis, Missouri, man who happened to be a friend of George Bacon's and who had just finished law school, agreed to defend Acker for expense money only.

To the elder Ackers' amazement, the U.S. government wouldn't have anything to do with their son. The State Department wouldn't talk about his case with reporters, nor would the Angolan mission to the U.N. The CIA insisted that it "neither paid nor authorized funds to Mr. Acker or other Americans engaged in armed combat in Angola," nor flew them in. Of course, this carefully worded statement didn't cover the actual situation because Bufkin was an independent operator rather than a full-time CIA employee, he never engaged in combat, and the men who did, and whom he paid, entered Angola by truck. But the CIA wouldn't elaborate.

Said Grillo's mother early in 1982, "For six years I go to Washington. The State Department tell me nothing. I don't want to hear anymore cause nobody does nothing about my son." Carl Acker, a retired fireman, and his wife got occasional letters from their son, but, as the elder Acker described it, "He just asks about the family and so forth, but he gives us no information."

The Ackers estimated that they spent nearly $20,000 unsuccessfully trying to free Gary. "They [the government] have not cooperated at all. They have not made any real effort to try to get him out," Mrs. Acker complained. The Ackers and Wilson, their lawyer, say they met in Washington in 1980 with Richard Moose, then assistant secretary of state for African affairs. They say they asked about efforts to free Gary, which they had been told were going on for years. But they say Moose and an aide just looked embarrassed, and said there hadn't been any. They say Moose told him he himself would be "very angry and upset" in their place.

Moose said later that during his talks with Angola he had been concentrating on nonmilitary cases that seemed more promising of success. He said that after the Ackers' visit he did talk to the Angolans about Gary, but was turned down. And he continued to insist that the government "hasn't accepted any responsibility for Acker as a U.S. government employee, or person to whom payment had been made. The CIA was involved in Angola, everybody knows that, but Bufkin is a link about which I know nothing." Moose now works for Lehman Brothers.

In November 1982, the Angolans released Acker, Grillo, and a U.S. pilot who was forced down in Angola in an unrelated case, in exchange for some Soviet prisoners taken by a South African patrol in Angola and other captives.

STORY number two:

In April 1976, with the Angola program obviously shot, the CIA expended the last $3.7 million or so left from its program budget, to pay debts— aircraft leases, boat crews, relocation of contract personnel, and so forth. Some $1.4 million was for Roberto and Savimbi—to pay their men, and to pay off other debts the guerrilla leaders had accumulated. The agency couldn't get the money directly to Savimbi, who was in Angola, and it didn't want to pay a lump sum to Roberto for fear he would abscond with it. Yet there was congressional pressure to end the operation quickly and have nothing more to do with the actors.

So the CIA decided to give the money to Mobutu, who could see that Savimbi got his share and that Roberto's share was parceled out to him over time. As Stockwell relates it, "It was only a matter of days before UNITA and FNLA leaders were hounding the Kinshasa [CIA] station, desperate, hungry, their debts still unpaid. Roberto wailed that thousands of displaced FNLA tribesmen in lower Zaire were starving. And Mobutu refused to receive anyone. He was pocketing their $1,376,700."

THE U.S. government and its policymakers reacted normally to the debacle. They lied.

When the press began to bear down on the story, the State Department and CIA flatly denied any U.S. involvement. "We have not been in the business of providing arms to the Angolan movements," the State Department said. "However, we have received reports that one of the movements, the MPLA, has for some time been receiving large shipments of weapons from the Soviet Union." Even Congress was given phony stories about the U.S. involvement; a State Department official denied the CIA was operating in Angola, or cooperating at all with South Africa, in congressional testimony as late as December 5, 1975,* and CIA officials had apparently misled Congress on the issue before that.

Stockwell says his superiors told him that Kissinger had been the prime cheerleader for the Angolan intervention from the beginning. In fact, the operation appears to have been pushed hard from the top down, against passivity or even resistance from the bottom up.

Stockwell reports that the head of the Angola desk at CIA headquarters, who had recently opened the CIA station in Luanda, scoffed at the whole idea of the intervention.† He says she believed that the MPLA was the best organized of the three independence groups, had the best educated leaders, and was most capable of running Angola. Moreover, this leading Angola

*The official was Edward Mulcahy, deputy assistant secretary of state for African affairs. He said in a 1983 interview that he gave false testimony inadvertently because he had been out of the country and didn't know the latest developments. Stockwell wrote that Mulcahy was "adhering to the ... line" of the State Department–CIA working group running the Angola program. Former Senator Dick Clark, Democrat of Iowa, who chaired the subcommittee Mulcahy was testifying before, says of Mulcahy's answers on CIA activity in Angola and cooperation with South Africa, "There was no question on my count that both of them were lies." He says he doesn't blame Mulcahy, but blames his boss, Kissinger, who had been asked to testify but sent Mulcahy in his stead. No charges were filed.

†Stockwell has scrupulously avoided naming CIA employees who weren't already known as such.

expert at the CIA believed that the MPLA wasn't hostile to the U.S.

The diplomatic chief of mission in Luanda, with the title consul general—the State Department's own professional foreign service representative on the scene—was considered so probably hostile to the program that it was kept secret from him as long as possible, until finally, in August 1975, the program had grown too big to hide. Even then, he was deceived about its purpose.* By this time, Kissinger's African specialist, Davis, had resigned over the program.

Kissinger justified the program to underlings on the ground that Angola was in a critical strategic location, and that a Soviet base there, in the southern Atlantic, could threaten U.S. shipping from the Persian Gulf. He said the same thing to the public to explain why he thought the Soviets wanted to take over Angola so badly. Kissinger's explanation, though, is so hard to reconcile with a map, and with simple logic, that one suspects he must have had a deeper motive.

The U.S.S.R. already has adequate force near the Persian Gulf to sink U.S. tankers. The U.S.S.R. also knows that if it did that, the attack would provoke a war in which a base in Angola would be a pretty small chip. Besides, in 1983, the MPLA after eight years of running Angola still hasn't allowed a Soviet base there, and presumably won't, because its constitution prohibits that.†

Stockwell says his boss, the deputy direction of the CIA's Africa Division, presented a different motive during the initial briefing for the task force job. Stockwell says he was told that Kissinger "saw the Angolan conflict solely in terms of global politics.... Uncomfortable with recent historic events, and frustrated by our humiliation in Vietnam, Kissinger was seeking opportunities to challenge the Soviets. Conspicuously, he had overruled his advisors and refused to seek diplomatic solutions in Angola." Stockwell also says that some advocates of the program within the agency realized that the MPLA would probably come out the victor, but argued in a policy paper that it would be enough if the U.S. could just prevent a "cheap Neto victory."

That argument made more sense than the one about tanker traffic. But it still ignored Angolan and African history. Instead of seeing ancient tribal rivalries readjusting to new national boundaries, the whole foreign policy

*This is according to Stockwell and Bender and isn't challenged by Davis. The official himself, Thomas F. Killoran, in a 1983 interview made the remarkable statement that he didn't remember whether he was deceived or not, though he said he might have been. The inference I drew was that he didn't want to talk about it. He also said that Stockwell's book was accurate in its account of things he knew about, and confirmed that he opposed intervention in Angola by the U.S. or any other outside power.

†The constitution has been interpreted liberally enough to allow "temporary" bases for Cuban troops who are propping up the MPLA government, and for independence fighters from Namibia. But the clause was aimed at superpower alignments, and the point is that the Soviet base Kissinger warned of has not materialized.

establishment from President Ford, Secretary of State Kissinger, and CIA Director Colby on down talked as if a European-style coconut curtain was descending across the free continent of Africa. Combined with their obfuscation of the U.S. role as the original intervener in Angola, it is hard to decide whether their position is characterized more by deceit or foolishness.

After a Kissinger press conference January 20, 1976, reporter Robert Keatley wrote in the *Wall Street Journal*, "Reporters traveling aboard Mr. Kissinger's plane were told diplomatic trouble could intensify if the Angolan problem isn't resolved soon. Indicating an apparent escalation of his worries, Mr. Kissinger is said to think Angola could complicate completion of SALT [Strategic Arms Limitation Treaty] negotiations and make difficult future Soviet-American political cooperation on other subjects, such as the Mideast.... Mr. Kissinger contends this Russian venture [in Angola] violates the kind of relationship the U.S. and U.S.S.R. profess to want. He fears that if Moscow gets away with this one, it will try again soon in some other area, spreading its influence while making the U.S. look weak to its friends and allies abroad."

Kissinger has since blamed the failure of his own venture in Angola on Congress's refusal in December 1975 to approve an additional $28 million for continuation of the program. Congress, having concluded it had been lied to, and now aware that a huge Cuban force would have to be met in kind to achieve victory, balked. Referring to that congressional decision three years later, Kissinger said, "We had them [the Soviets] defeated in Angola and then we defeated ourselves."

Back in that critical month of December 1975, however, he had told a press conference, "The United States favors a solution in which all of the parties in Angola can negotiate with each other free of outside interference and in which the problem of Angola is handled as an African issue."* That kind of hypocrisy reminds one of Adlai Stevenson in 1964, righteously defending the U.S.'s record of nonintervention in the internal affairs of the Congo. So do the words of Senator Daniel Patrick Moynihan, who, in 1978, still called the Angola episode a case of "openly flaunted Soviet aggression ... clearly meant to be a test of our will in the aftermath of our defeat in Vietnam."

Far more likely, Soviet premier Leonid Brezhnev saw the U.S. intervention in Angola as a test of whether *he* would stand up to the *U.S.* It was all the more a challenge to him because the U.S. and South Africa had been about to impose the most artificial of solutions in Angola. The factions the U.S. was backing were pretty clearly the ones most likely to *lose* if the matter had really been settled as Kissinger asked, "free of outside interference."

A pattern had already been established for turning colonies into countries

*Thanks to Professor Bender for collecting some of these quotes, and to Michael McCurry for helping in verification.

in Africa. Unfair as it may seem, the pattern gave disproportionate strength to the contending faction that had its support base in the capital city. (That had been one of Lumumba's big problems in the Congo—his support base was more than 500 miles from the capital.) In Angola, the MPLA grew out of the Mbundu tribe, which was centered around Luanda.

Had the capital of Angola been Huambo, a large interior city in the heart of Ovimbundu territory, Savimbi might have won. He would have started off as king-of-the-mountain, and the MPLA would have faced the uphill battle to dislodge him. The Ovimbundu are a bit more numerous than the Mbundu, Savimbi was a canny fellow, and he might then have become Angola's first president. But Huambo was not the capital, Luanda was, and that was MPLA territory.

Actually, if the three parties had been left on their own, with perhaps an offer of mediation, there was a very good chance that some kind of compromise settlement could have been negotiated, which is what the U.S. now professes to want—now that the MPLA has been solidly in power for eight years. Fair elections might have been held in 1975, as they were later in Zimbabwe. But back in 1974, the U.S. thought it could do better by political sabotage.

THROUGH 1983, Savimbi continued to hold out as a guerrilla. He claimed he had 15,000 soldiers, probably an exaggeration. They slogged endlessly through the vast and scantily populated southeastern quadrant of Angola. MPLA forces occasionally chased him. With South African arms, Savimbi would sometimes overcome a government outpost, or send a band out to blow up a railroad bridge. He pleaded for U.S. intervention, which President Reagan promised during his campaign, but then evidently thought better of.

Savimbi called himself pro-Western, but his main support was obviously tribal. This was not altogether unjustified. Long after taking over the government of Angola, the MPLA still shut the Ovimbundu, the country's largest tribe, out of any representation in the party's political bureau. It gave them only token representation in government.

Twice, the MPLA-Cuban forces, stretching the end of their supply lines, are said to have cornered Savimbi, but South African helicopters arrived on radio call to pull him and his men out of the trap. It was the South Africans, in fact, who were causing the major damage in the continuing war. Almost daily, their bombing and shelling in southern Angola indiscriminately hit civilian houses, schools, hospitals, and trucks, according to missionaries and other people who have been to the area. Several times, South African columns have plunged hundreds of miles into southern Angola from Namibia on the pretext of raiding Namibian guerrilla camps. The raids have killed many Angolan civilians, and destroyed much property.

Many of the weapons the South Africans have used are of U.S. manufacture. Some were transferred illegally to South Africa in a series of deals that have been uncovered and successfully prosecuted by the Justice Department. It has also been alleged, but never proven, that U.S. intelligence agents have helped arrange such illegal transfers. Either way, Angolans were being shot at with American guns.

Savimbi was sponsoring occasional journalistic tours, flying reporters in from Kinshasa via a devious route that skirts government radar. He marched newsmen for weeks through miles and miles of grass, brought them to village after village where he was greeted warmly, and thus "proved" to them that UNITA controls a third or so of Angola. Then he flew them out. Of course, the next day, the government forces could bring the same reporters through the same grass, to the same villages, and get the same warm reception, proving that the *government* controls that third of Angola.

It is, on the whole, the civilest of civil wars, neither side too eager for combat. But inertia is on the side of the government, which is running the country while Savimbi hikes around the hillsides. In the long run, the Ovimbundu, like most people, are more interested in farming than causes, and the MPLA government has not been particularly repressive or disruptive of farm life. In fact, largely thanks to all the trained Cuban medical workers and teachers around, the government is able to provide services the people have never enjoyed before.

That is a blemished blessing. Cuban education can be presumed to come, as it does in the Caribbean area, with a strong dose of politics. Communist ideology is taught with the same certainty as the laws of physics are taught, and there is allowed no more questioning of the ideology than of the correct answer to a long-division problem. This can produce, as it has in Central America, a legion of young revolutionaries who look and act like Sun Myung Moon followers and are devoid of any respect for individual worth or freedom. The Angolans would probably get better, less polluted services from the Peace Corps.

But that's not in the cards. The presence of so many Cubans in Angola is the direct result of United States policy, which pumped up a brief, third-rate skirmish into a major war that the U.S. never had any intention of fighting through—in fact, would have been crazy to fight through. Overt fighting would have compounded the losses already suffered in covert fighting, where there was never anything real to be gained anyway. Yet this is what Kissinger and Moynihan seem to be saying they wanted. In all respect to Kissinger, one really has to question the sanity of someone who looks at an ancient tribal dispute over control of distant coffee fields and sees in it a Soviet threat to the security of the United States.

As for Holden Roberto, the U.S.'s primary hope and beneficiary, it turned out that he had almost no support at all in Angola. His entire FNLA movement melted away. The Bakongo were simply never a dominant factor in Angolan politics—they live mostly outside Angola—and Roberto himself had nowhere near the kind of respect among the Angolan people that Neto or Savimbi had.

Roberto is now living in Europe. Apparently, no African country will accept him. Even Zaire threw him out, after Mobutu realized his own need to start dealing with the Angolan government over a series of practical concerns—for example, the lower Congo River occasionally changes its course so that ships must pass through Angolan territory to get to the main Zairian port of Matadi. Practical concerns led Mobutu to a formal reconciliation with Angola. What might they do for Washington?

STATEMENT: "There is an underlying mutual respect and trust which I believe is the key to understanding the productive relationship we have in Angola, productive for Angola as well as productive for [us]."

The speaker was not Leonid Brezhnev, nor was it Fidel Castro. The speaker was Melvin J. Hill, president of the Gulf Oil Exploration and Production Company, and he was testifying before the House Foreign Affairs Committee subcommittee on Africa, September 17, 1980. Shucking off the doomful of forecasts of three administrations in Washington, Hill was simply talking sense. "Gulf has not been unduly hampered by the socialist aspirations of the MPLA . . . government," he said. "In fact, Gulf has encountered no ideological or discriminatory problems of any significance." He went on: "On the basis of our business experiences, we can say that the government of Angola has proved to be a knowledgeable and understanding negotiator as well as a reliable partner. Moreover, Angola has not interfered, directly or indirectly, in the . . . production and . . . export of . . . crude oil."

He went on to say that the Angolan government all along had promised "a mixed economy in which there will be roles for domestic and foreign private investors alongside the state sector." He said that after the death of Agostinho Neto in September 1979, the new government of JoséEduardo dos Santos indicated it "must stimulate private investment in order to raise living standards, and specified several sectors as prime targets for private initiative."

Hill isn't alone in his satisfaction. Gene Bates, Texaco Inc.'s vice-president of production for Latin America and West Africa, told reporter Steve Mufson of the *Wall Street Journal*, "They [the Angolans] are pragmatic people. Althought they lean toward a Marxist-style government, their Marxist friends can't give them what they need, so they have turned to the West."

Agostinho Neto said it himself back in October 1976, when he defended his policy before disgruntled Marxist purists in his own party: "Can we solve this problem by simply issuing a decree? Can we solve it through an inflammatory editorial saying that the bosses will no longer be able to enrich themselves by means of the worker's sweat? Of course we can't. Cabinda's oil [Cabinda is the region where the oil is] is being extracted through an advanced technology. Have we got that technology at our disposal? No. Do those countries which are our friends, and which help us, possess this technology? No, they also don't. Well, then what are we to do?"

Gulf is now embarking on a natural gas development project in which Angola has a 51 percent interest. To obtain its necessary share of the capital, the Angolan government's oil and gas agency was approved for $85 million in credits by—now, get this—the U.S. Export-Import Bank, an agency of government. While Secretary of State-designate Alexander Haig was testifying before one congressional committee that inadequate U.S. support for UNITA "was the start of the slippery slope that brought about subsequent Soviet risk-taking in Ethiopia," John M. Duff, senior vice-president of the Ex-Im bank, was telling another committee that the Angolan gas project "will provide substantial jobs to American workers and also benefit the U.S. in terms of the output of that project."

Duff also said the Ex-Im bank had also offered to finance Boeing's sale of civilian aircraft to Angola, but that Angola had decided to buy only one plane and pay cash for it.

Who is talking about the best interests of the United Sates here, Haig or Duff?

One Gulf official told the *Wall Street Journal*'s Mufson, "What I want to know is, what have the Soviets gained in Angola for all their military and financial investment? Aside from fish [the Soviets have a fishing rights agreement with Angola], they haven't gotten anything. All the oil goes to the West. Even the coffee and diamonds go to the West. Perhaps they get a few votes at the U.N., but that isn't much to show."

THE Angolan government may be smart enough to turn a pragmatic face when dealing with foreigners, but it is still wedded to an ideology of domestic economy that is not very smart at all. The poverty of Angola is something that can't be explained by a lack of resources, or even entirely by the long years of fighting.

One of the few journalists from major publications who have been allowed to enter the country is David Lamb of the *Los Angeles Times*. In May 1980, he wrote, "The mosaic sidewalks have cracked and buckled and garbage fills the streets. . . . The odor of urine fills the corridors; rats scurry through the abandoned restaurants; torn and filthy awnings hang limply in the stifling afternoon heat. The parks are overgrown, the rusting frames of wrecked cars litter the streets. At 5:00 A.M., when the curfew ends, women start lining up for a loaf of bread or a can of powdered milk from Brazil.

"A visitor is struck by the eerie notion that he has entered a ghost town. Block after block of stores is closed, their windows broken and boarded up. Elevators don't work. Cargo stands rotting at the port. Neon signs flash above IBM, Sony, and Singer showrooms that have been empty for five years. At the airport there are no taxis to meet passengers arriving from Lisbon, Moscow, and Havana.

"The state removed virtually all economic incentives. The result is that the largely untrained, largely uneducated people care little about keeping a job. At Angola's only functioning cotton mill, Africa Textile, outside Benguela, so many workers were showing up three and four hours late that the company sold everyone a bicycle at cost and began rewarding punctual workers with cloth at reduced prices. Absenteeism still averages 30 percent.... Most factories are closed today."

Of course, Lamb seemed to talk mainly to Western expatriates and Angolan officials. He reported almost no conversations with farmers in a mostly agricultural country, or with villagers in a mostly rural country. One assumes the MPLA government is paying more attention to rural areas than to the urban sectors where the Portuguese colonialists used to live. But Lamb's is the best report around, and there's obviously a gist of the truth in it.

The economic misery Lamb painted was matched by a political situation not so much brutal as stultifying. There was socialism's usual lack of news, except for party propaganda organs, and of any forum for the expression of ideas outside the official doctrine. It is a Soviet-style system.

And there is only one reason the Soviets are present. For many years, even apparently to this day, the Soviets offered Angola its only hope of independence—independence from the Portuguese, independence from the United States, independence from South Africa. If the U.S. were ever to change its policy, to become the source of offers and not of threats, the Soviets might soon be invited out, and true freedom achieved.

CHAPTER TEN

UPSETTING THE BALANCE: IRAN AND AFGHANISTAN

THE SOUND broke your heart as it stunned your mind.

Allah Akhbar . . . Allah Akhbar. . . .

It was the sound not of one voice, or even a thousand voices, but the almost unbelievable sound of a whole city: the city of Herat, the major provincial capital of western Afghanistan.

Late in the night of December 27–28, 1979, the Union of Soviet Socialist Republics (estimated population 267 million, estimated gross national product $1.4 trillion), invaded Afghanistan (estimated population 16 million, estimated gross national produce $3.4 billion). For thirty-six hours, thousands of tanks and other heavy military vehicles, and trucks bearing some 100,000 soldiers, rumbled south in single column down each of the two main roads from Soviet central Asia, like two green iron snakes.

While their cargo of soldiers gazed out impassively, the mechanical snakes groaned on, and it seemed their tails would never come. One, on the eastern road, split apart to occupy the valleys around Kabul, Afghanistan's capital. The other, in the west, passed south through Herat toward the modern Soviet-built airport at Shindand, on the road to the major southern province of Kandahar. In these encampments, out of sight but not out of mind of the cities through which they had passed, the snakes coiled.

Row by row they lined up, trucks, tanks, and armored personnel carriers, in vast open fields by the roadside. The rows were so wide you could not see the end of them, so deep you could not see the back. Everyone knew the encampments were there, but only a relatively few Afghans passed by them, the few who traveled by bus along the country's one major road.

The road is shaped like a ∪ with its ends in the Soviet Union, and its bottom dipping down through Kabul to Kandahar and back up through Herat. Exit roads shoot out half-way up either side of the ∪, on the east to the Khyber Pass and Pakistan, on the West to Iran. When a busload of Afghans passed by the encampments, there was an audible gasp. Eyes widened, jaws dropped, and heads turned almost in unison to follow the awesome sight as the bus passed by. Despite much talk in the towns, no one who saw the encampments was prepared for the immensity of the occupation force.

Afghanistan is a ruggedly beautiful land of snow-covered mountains, lush valleys, and stony deserts—of camel caravans against distant horizons, and villages whose tan mud walls wind into labyrinthine mazes. Now the Soviets had determined to occupy it. As the grim parade of troops and armor had driven through the streets of Herat that first day and a half, 100,000 residents watched in awe from windows and doorways.

Every night afterward, for months, the people of Herat would climb to the rooftops of their homes, and stand in the cold, unlit winter darkness. The men, many with black beards, wore wool-stuffed indigo robes, or heavy, secondhand business suits from the West over floppy native shirts, and their heads were wound with flowing turbans. The women covered themselves head-to-toe in *chadri*, or veils, with only a small window of dark gauze to see through. The children were in rags.

And they would chant. The practice spread to communities throughout the surrounding countryside. For nearly two hours, from about 7:00 until well after the curfew of 8:30, the pathetic wailing of men, women, and children could be heard literally for miles: *Allah Akhbar . . . Allah Akhbar . . .* God is great . . . God is great. . . .

The Soviet-imposed government sent armored personnel carriers through the streets with loudspeakers urging the people to climb down from their roofs, assuring them that everything was all right. But the people knew better, and the chanting continued. In a sense, the whole country of Afghanistan was crying out its frustration against an alien communist government that seemed intent on trampling tradition and religion, while doing nothing that people believed was helping them.

Not quite two years before, in April 1978, a tiny band of Afghan communists, obviously acting on the promise of Soviet support, had killed the president of Afghanistan and toppled his government. As the new government tried to impose a communist system, the nation revolted. Officials and Communist party members who visited communities to enforce the new government's laws were attacked and killed.

For nearly two years, the unpopular new government wasted the Afghan countryside with sophisticated Soviet air and ground weapons, trying to suppress the revolt. Communities that resisted the government's will were shot up and bombed, apparently with napalm or other chemical weapons that were morbid as well as lethal. No one knows how many tens of thousands died; the world paid little attention.

But the Afghan army, under orders to kill its own people, shrank, from defections and sabotage. The ruling Communist party central committee literally shot it out among themselves to see who would lead. In September 1979, one tyrant replaced another in a gunfight. The revolt only intensified. Then, in December, the communists were riveted in power by the Soviet army itself. This was a force the Afghan people were ill-equipped to repel, short of a divine assistance that refused to materialize despite the nightly rooftop summons.

Thousands of market stalls closed in protest against the invasion, in Herat, Kandahar, Kabul, and villages all over Afghanistan. To stop the protest, soldiers visited storekeepers' homes, ordering them to open their shops or face Afghanistan's unmerciful penal system. So a new protest was made of the required reopening. The market men arranged to return to work on a day when the government had ordered all shops *shut* for a special holiday declared by the new puppet president Babrak Karmal. (Karmal, who had taken refuge in Czechoslovakia from political opponents in Afghanistan in 1978, had been kept on ice by the Russians and flown in on the night of the invasion.)

Secret resistance committees were organized in the marketplaces. Shopkeepers chipped in part of their profits, and solicited donations from customers—small amounts, whatever someone could afford. The money was smuggled outside the country, mostly to Pakistan, where arms and ammunition could be bought from ubiquitous village gunsmiths. Men and boys took to the Afghan hills with reconditioned rifles, mostly British one-shot models of World War I vintage. These *mujahadeen*, or religious fighters (sometimes called "green men" because green is the favored color of Islam), effectively prevented the Soviets or the puppet Afghan government from using the roads, except in heavily armed convoys. In fact, they prevented the government from functioning at all outside major cities.

In marketplaces, shoppers and shopkeepers attacked browsing Soviet soldiers and beat them to death with clubs. After at least a dozen such attacks around the country during the first few weeks of the occupation, the Soviets stopped visiting bazaars. They basically couldn't leave their encampments, except in heavily armed groups. What the Afghans put up was possibly the most heroic popular resistance movement of this century.

Comparison is frequently made to the U.S. experience in Vietnam. But in Vietnam, a substantial minority of the people had supported the U.S.-backed government, at least at first. Many others feared both sides, so it's doubtful whether a majority stood with the Vietcong. But in Afghanistan, the Soviets met a resistance that was almost universally supported.

Moreover, unlike the Vietnamese resistance, which got all the equipment it could use from the Soviets, the Afghans carried on their fight without major outside supplies of modern war material. And they were more effective than the underground French campaign against the Germans in World War II.

FOR understandable reasons, the Afghan resistance captured the imagination of the U.S. public. Our government cheer-led for the Afghans, and leaked stories about alleged CIA assistance to them, though it didn't seem to show up on the scene.* Mainly, Washington concentrated on the sea theory. The invasion of Afghanistan had brought the Soviet army just 375 miles from the Arabian Sea. Everyone knew that Russia had wanted a warm-water port for centuries. All that lay in the way now—assuming the Russians really controlled Afghanistan—was the Pakistani province of Baluchistan. And since Baluchistan had been rebelling against the Pakistani government for more than a decade, it appeared ripe for Soviet infiltration.

From the excellent and little-used port of Pasni in Baluchistan, it is only 400 miles to the Strait of Hormuz, the entrance to the Persian Gulf. Through the strait passes 60 percent of the oil used by the U.S. and its European and Japanese allies. The strait is only about 30 miles across, and the shipping channel is so narrow that one sunk supertanker would plug it.

If this progression of contingencies seems a little hard to follow, it is. But that was the theory. The invasion of Afghanistan threatened the oil supply of the Western world.

Of course, Soviet ships and planes had long had the power to sink tankers in the Strait of Hormuz, even without controlling Baluchistan—if the Kremlin really wanted to start a war with the United States. (If the U.S.S.R. wanted to provoke an attack on its people by a nuclear superpower, there are *lots* of things it could do.) But a map showing the closeness of the new Afghan bases to the Strait of Hormuz made a dramatic backdrop for President Carter's televised address to his constituents on what he called the gravest crisis since World War II. Never mind that the MPLA had taken power in Angola four years earlier, which, according to Henry Kissinger's warnings at the time, would *already have given* the Soviet navy control over the Persian

---

*In 1982, reports finally indicated that the guerrillas had an abundant supply of automatic rifles in a couple of eastern provinces bordering Pakistan, though not elsewhere. The fighters using them said these rifles had been brought over to the resistance by defectors from the Afghan army. Though there were tens of thousands of such defectors, some of the new guns may have been CIA-supplied. Still, the resistance fighters didn't have the hand-held antitank and antiaircraft missiles they needed to really damage the Soviets. The Afghans, through their spokesmen in Pakistan, were begging for such weapons, which are certainly in the U.S. arsenal. The arsenal door, if open at all, apparently wasn't open very wide. Moreover, some major publications reported that the CIA's harassment of Nicaragua in 1982 was the agency's biggest effort since at least the time of Angola, which, if true, would rule out much activity in the Afghan theater.

Gulf oil traffic. Only the most careful observers would detect such hypocrisy.

CIA reports surfaced suggesting that the U.S.S.R.'s rising oil use and declining production might force it to become a net oil importer in the 1980s. This estimate has since been radically changed (the CIA now says production *isn't* declining, and the U.S.S.R. continues to export oil to the West), but it fit the desired scenario at the time. If the Soviets became a competing market for Arab oil, a Soviet military thrust toward the oil region might intimidate our Arab friends. They might desert the dollar and sell our oil to the Russians. Friendly rulers might be overthrown.

Just the month before the Soviet invasion of Afghanistan, the U.S. had received two disturbing reminders of how transitory its Third World alliances were. On November 4, 1979, Iranian militants had seized the U.S. embassy in Tehran and taken American diplomats hostage. Then, on November 20, some young Moslem fundamentalists had seized the Grand Mosque in Mecca— the first open act of rebellion against the corrupt Saudi Arabian monarchy since the U.S. had begun stationing troops in Saudi Arabia in 1952.

As always, the State Department preferred to focus on how the Soviets might foment revolution by arming revolutionaries. The department generally prefers to ignore how the *U.S.* foments revolution by strengthening unjust governments and thus *creating* revolutionaries. Revolting against dictatorship is no longer in favor on the Potomac, and those who support revolts are our enemies. It's a good thing the Marquis de Lafayette's place in history was secure before Caspar W. Weinberger could express his disapproval.

STILL, the oil supplies were a truly vital interest, and the Afghans' plight was compelling. The Soviet army, not some ragtag guerrilla movement, was in action, and nobody knew for certain what the Russians had in mind. The Afghanistan crisis gave just cause for concern. And the U.S. reacted. The form this reaction took, however, didn't seem to impress the Russians much. It mainly levied its toll on the American people.

First, the Carter administration forbade American farmers and grain dealers to sell their wares to the Soviet Union. This transferred a $3 billion grain purchase bill from the Kremlin, which would have paid it, to the U.S. taxpayer. By coincidence, the 1980 presidential primary campaign had stopped off in Iowa, a grain state, at the time of the embargo announcement. Therefore, the embargo had to be arranged so that the grain market wouldn't suffer.

So Carter arranged for the U.S. taxpayer to guarantee the price of grain. This not only meant that the taxpayers paid the Soviets' grain bill; it meant they didn't even enjoy the compensating benefit of cheaper bread, because the domestic wheat glut brought about by the embargo wasn't allowed to reach the free market. The Soviets picked up their grain elsewhere. The futility of this policy was finally conceded when President Reagan, no softy toward Moscow, canceled the embargo.

Next, Carter announced that further Soviet military moves toward the Arabian Sea would bring a direct U.S. military response. A contingent of 1,800 marines was sent to the area to prove that the U.S. meant business— a gesture not only dangerous, but futile. All that the 1,800 marines could probably accomplish in the area of Afghanistan, even if joined by large numbers of their fellows, would be to get rolled over by a million Soviet soldiers and endless thousands of pieces of armor—not because the Soviets are generally stronger than we are, which they aren't, but because of geography.

The Soviets could invade Afghanistan as surely as the U.S. could invade the Baja Peninsula. The danger of a superpower fight in either place is that the inevitable loser, the visiting team, would be faced with a choice of being humiliated or going nuclear. Besides the probability of losing, there was an added disadvantage to the U.S.'s throwing its armed forces directly into the Afghan affair: outright intervention would have forfeited the political gift the Soviets had just delivered.

The Soviets had revealed themselves as self-centered bullies, and were doomed to face the wrath of Afghan patriots for the forseeable future. The whole Moslem world was upset. Even countries like Syria, Algeria, and Iraq, whose governments normally supported the Soviet Union in international arenas, expressed disapproval. They were obviously thinking twice about their long-term relationships with the Kremlin. Those relationships in fact softened in ensuing years (particularly in the case of Algeria and Iraq), and probably survived at all only because the Arabs needed support by a great power to compensate for the U.S.'s support of Israel.

If enough marines had been sent to Afghan theater to influence the Soviets' behavior, they would only have diluted the Soviets' disgrace. Yet Carter sent a token force—a stick to be knocked off his shoulder. Apparently, he believed that it would be an expression of weakness to admit there was a square inch of earth that U.S. troops couldn't take and hold.

The U.S. also led a boycott of the Moscow Olympics, which probably did shame the Russians, though at enormous cost to the National Broadcasting Company and its insurers; the network had paid $87 million for the television rights to the Olympics. Keeping the U.S. Olympic team home also permanently deprived talented U.S. athletes of earning the international recognition they had worked for and deserved.

Many athletes proposed instead a scaled-down appearance in Moscow, participating in the events but boycotting the ceremonies. This might have worked better than the total boycott, constantly reminding a watching world of Afghanistan's plight—the more so because the boycott of ceremonies would have represented the voluntary actions of individual American athletic champions, not the policy of the U.S. government. At the very least, it would have preserved the freedom of Americans to run, jump, or televise where they please. No one can say for sure whether the sacrifice of that freedom saved any Afghan lives, or brought home the message of Soviet imperialism more clearly to any third-party countries. Usually overlooked, though, is the positive value of showing the world an American system that requires a pretty dire threat to the national safety before the government can order its citizens around. The example of such a limited government would be appealing to many.

Finally, in response to the invasion of Afghanistan, the U.S. moved to support the dictatorships that ruled Pakistan and China. By doing so, it hoped to create some counterforce to Soviet might in the area. In both cases, military equipment was passed out that could some day wind up being used against U.S. interests—in China's case, maybe even against the U.S. itself.

But the Carter administration showed considerable restraint against attempts by both Pakistan and China to exploit the situation further. The U.S., in this one instance, refused requests to supply much greater military aid to regimes that, like the one in Afghanistan, haven't been ratified by the people they rule.

FOR all of Washington's flailing around in search of a meaningful reaction to the Soviet invasion of Afghanistan, however, one logical reaction was never considered. The long-standing U.S. policy of confrontation and intervention throughout the world was never questioned. In fact, analysts suggested, and the *New York Times* Hedrick Smith flat-out stated, that Carter's shock over the Afghanistan invasion was what led the president to move closer to the confrontational policies of his national security advisor, Zbigniew Brzezinski, during his last year in office. In doing so, Carter abandoned the more conciliatory policies of Secretary of State Cyrus R. Vance, which he had previously favored. Vance was soon out of his job altogether.

This response ignored the cause of the problem. One thing had made possible the easy Soviet move against Afghanistan. That was the establishment of a government in Iran that hated and feared the United States above all else. If Iran's government hadn't been preoccupied with undoing years of American domination, it would not have stood idly by while its Islamic neighbors were brutalized by the Soviets. If Iran's government could have cooperated with the U.S. and U.S.-allied governments in the region, the resources of the Afghan resistance would have more than doubled.

If Iran had a strongly nationalist government *just like the one the CIA overthrew there in* 1953, then a Soviet occupation of Afghanistan would have required so much greater a commitment of force that the Soviets might never have attempted it. The leader of the Iranian government in 1953, Mohammed Mossadegh, had chased the Russians out of his country, but also wanted to put some Iranian control on U.S. oil interests there. We wanted a government in Iran that we could cow; and we got one that was as easily cowed by the Soviets.

From the first weeks of Soviet occupation, the Afghan guerrilla resistance encountered a puzzling and frustrating refusal by Iran to cooperate. Resistance fighters filtered into Iran from western Afghanistan, just as they filtered into Pakistan from eastern Afghanistan. Yet the experience of Pakistan wasn't repeated. Instead of finding hospitality and returning with arms, Afghans found no support whatsoever in Iran.

This was especially puzzling, because Iran, far more than Pakistan, had a wealth of arms to supply. Largely thanks to the U.S., the Iranians were armed to the teeth. Moreover, their fierce Islamic militancy made them likelier comrades-at-arms for the Afghan fighters than were the less militant Pakistanis. But the Afghan guerrillas returned across the mountains from Iran disappointed and empty-handed.*

The closed door in Iran had the further effect of isolating Pakistan, and limiting Pakistan's own willingness to help. Without another country on the Afghan border cooperating, the full brunt of Soviet retaliation for any aid coming in to Afghanistan could be directed against Pakistan. The threat of a retaliatory air strike against Pakistani bases or industry was intimidating. (Maps show a tiny finger of shared border between Afghanistan and China. But this border is just uninhabited Himalayan mountain peaks, impassable even by yaks much of the year. As a supply route, it isn't worth much.)

With Iranian cooperation, modern weapons from Saudi Arabia, Egypt, and elsewhere would have flowed to the Afghan rebels without the U.S. as a primary instigator. A month after the invasion, an extraordinary assembly was called of the Islamic Conference, an organization of several dozen predominantly Moslem countries designed to keep religious values active in secular matters. Meeting in Islamabad, the capital of Pakistan, all thirty-six countries and various groups that were represented voted to condemn "the Soviet military aggression against the Afghan people."

It was an unprecedented stance for this or any Third World group. The delegations from Libya and the Palestine Liberation Organization were the only two that objected to naming the Soviet Union in the resolution, and when they were defeated on this issue they went along with the consensus. Saudi Arabia and Pakistan, two countries widely thought of as U.S. allies, were leading the charge against the Soviets and picked up full support from the whole raft of Moslem countries, even the likes of Iraq and Algeria. A speech by the charismatic Mossadegh, the man the CIA tossed out, might have welded the delegates into an anti-communist bloc.

But for the single fact of Iranian hatred for the U.S., and anything remotely connected to the U.S., this extraordinary moment could have produced a supply of modern weapons for the Afghan resistance fighters. The initiative

---

*The basic source for these statements is numerous interviews the author had with members of the Afghan resistance movement around Herat in January 1980, a month after the invasion. All available evidence since then suggests that the situation persists.

would have belonged entirely to the Afghans' Islamic neighbors, and the U.S. would have been no more than a cooperative trading partner.

A supply of modern missiles to the resistance fighters might eventually have sent the Soviets packing (or, more likely, the prospect would have deterred them from invading in the first place). But the one country most critical to organizing and carrying out this aid was clearly unwilling to do it. First, Iran dragged its heels on opening the conference, forcing a post-ponement. Then, whereas almost every other country sent its foreign minister, Iran sent a delegation of second-rate functionaries, declaring unabashedly that this reflected Iran's lukewarm support for the meeting. Although the Iranian delegation went along with the consensus resolution condemning the Soviets, it quarreled with the main supporters at every opportunity. It insisted on criticizng the U.S. at a meeting obviously aimed at the Soviets. It balked at a plan to let other Moslem nations mediate the hostage issue with the U.S., so that everyone could concentrate on the Afghan problem. In the end, the opportunity for Moslem military resistance to the Soviets was lost.

The U.S. had sabotaged its own cause—made itself so great an enemy of Iran that even the Soviet Union looked benign by comparison. With far greater efficiency and effect than the Soviets have so far shown in Afghan-istan, the U.S. violently repressed Iranian independence for twenty-six years. Every Iranian was aware of it. Yet despite the copious and unmistakable evidence, most Americans still have little conception of what happened. Nor did most Americans benefit from our Iranian intervention; in fact, they suf-fered from it, first at the gas pump, and now in their national security as well.

THE best record of how this repression of Iranian independence started comes from the pen of Kennett Love, who was the *New York Times* reporter in Iran in 1953. Love's detailed report of what happened that year was never provided to the readers of his newspaper, however. Nor has he chosen to publish it in the more than two decades since he left the newspaper. The report was submitted, rather, to Allen Dulles, who was the director of central intelligence and head of the CIA. And the report reveals something rather startling: that Love helped direct the revolutionary action while reporting on it for the nation's newspaper of record, never, of course, disclosing his activist role to his readers (or, according to the *Times*, to his editors).

Love has denied that he was ever actually employed by the CIA. Barring a truly astounding new disclosure, one can pretty well accept the *Times*'s word that it wasn't paying him on behalf of the CIA. (Many U.S. companies have provided such cover for agents, but the *Times* has stood four-square for a presidential decree against the use of any journalistic cover; it has in recent years provided its readers super-professionals in Tehran such as Yous-sef M. Ibrahim and John Kifner.) Kennett Love later explained, rather lamely perhaps, that he acted as he did because of "misguided patriotism."

Love's forty-one-page history of the affair was written in 1960, while he was enjoying a press fellowship on the Council on Foreign Relations—the most prestigious voice of the U.S. foreign policy establishment outside of government. Though Love never released the paper publicly, a copy was obtained from the late Mr. Dulles's papers, which are stored at Princeton University and are not open for public inspection.*

The background necessary to an understanding of Love's account is as follows: Iran was ruled for centuries by a series of dynasties, and was tussled over by British and Russian empires. In 1921, Reza Khan, an army officer unrelated to royalty, staged a coup and declared himself military dictator. Four years later, he decided to become first in a new line of hereditary kings, and had himself so crowned. He renamed himself Reza Shah Pahlevi.

In 1941, he abdicated in favor of his son, Mohammad Reza Pahlevi, who surrounded himself with ostentatious wealth and brutalized his opposition. Pahlevi was pushed into subservience to a constitutional civil government with an elected parliament during the early 1950s. Then he was reinstated to autocratic power by the United States, and finally was chased out for good in 1979.

The drive for constitutionalism in Iran dated back to 1906. The shah then in power had been threatened by a popular political movement. To make peace with his people, he agreed to accept an elected parliament, with a constitution to fix its power. The 1906 constitution stayed in place under the Pahlevi dynasty, though it wasn't until 1951 that parliament really began to take its power seriously.

It did so under the leadership of Mossadegh, head of a political movement called the National Front. Mossadegh had long been an ardent nationalist. Right after World War II, he campaigned successfully against lingering Soviet occupation of Northern Iran, and particularly against the Soviets' desire to pump oil from Iranian fields. Largely because of international pressure created by such appeals, the Soviets withdrew. Later assertions that Mossadegh was taking Iran into the Soviet camp usually ignored all this.

Mossadegh did appear eccentric to Western eyes. He concocted a Gandhi-like political image for himself, popular among his countrymen, as an old man, physically weak but morally strong. In public, he walked stooped and with a cane, but was at other times seen capable of running and jumping.

*The Dulles papers are administered by a panel, presided over by a former CIA general counsel. The panel opens the papers to certain people of its choosing. The *Wall Street Journal* has tried repeatedly to gain access to the papers, but has never succeeded because it wouldn't agree to a stipulation that any articles to be based even indirectly on material from the papers had to be presented to the panel for advance review; such a review would be contrary to *Journal* policy. The author obtained his copy of the Love paper without ever agreeing to such a stipulation. It was obtained with the help of John Kelly, editor of *CounterSpy* magazine. In an interview, Love acknowledged having written it.

He conducted business, and even met foreign dignitaries, from his bed, dressed in pajamas, much as Hugh Hefner would do later but for different reasons.

In connection with the leftist label the U.S. tried to pin on Mossadegh, it's interesting to note that Truman's secretary of state, Dean Acheson, described Mossadegh in his memoirs as "essentially a rich, reactionary, feudal-minded Persian inspired by a fanatical hatred of the British." As for the shah, Acheson wrote that "the plans, military and economic, that the shah unfolded were too ambitious for the means available" and noted that the impression the shah made on a visit to Washington was "a disappointment to all."

IN 1951, the Soviets gone from his country, Mossadegh turned his attention to the Anglo-Iranian Oil Company, which was not gone. It was operating on a sixty-year concession granted by a shah in 1901. The concession had been revised and renewed for another sixty years in 1933. The stock of Anglo-Iranian—which was later renamed British Petroleum—was held about half by the British government, a fourth by Shell Oil, and a fourth by individuals. But it had huge exclusive marketing commitments to Exxon and Mobil.

All these companies were working to prevent any independent oil dealers from breaking the monopoly that they and a few other major oil companies had on the great Middle Eastern sources of supply. The majors had gotten in on the ground floor, signing exclusive long-term agreements with well-greased autocrats decades earlier. They had then made agreements with each other, dividing the world into territories, and promising to restrict sales so they wouldn't compete with each other in various designated markets.

As stated in John M. Blair's landmark study, *The Control of Oil*,* "In addition to their natural desire to secure long-term substantial supplies, Exxon and Mobil shared with BP [British Petroleum] the common objective of preventing the inevitable increase in Iranian production from being funneled into world markets by companies less concerned in maintaining the stability of world prices." In other words, if independent companies were allowed to buy Iranian oil, either the U.S. consumer would get cheaper gasoline, or the people of Iran would get more money for their oil, or both. In any case, the cartel members' profit margins would shrink.

Largely because of this and other similar agreements, Exxon, Mobil, and the other major oil companies had antitrust problems with the U.S. government under President Truman. After several years of preliminary investigations, Truman, in June 1952, authorized full-scale legal proceedings designed

---

*Blair studied the oil industry for thirty-two years as leading economist for several government antitrust agencies.

to open the foreign and domestic oil business to free enterprise by all comers. A grand jury was convened, aimed at ending intercompany agreements that restricted foreign purchases and sales and domestic production.

But the major oil companies successfully resolved these problems when the Eisenhower administration forced the Justice Department to give up its case on August 6, 1953. That was exactly ten days before the CIA's planned coup against Mossadegh in Iran. (As it turned out, the actual coup took place three days later than planned, on August 19.)

The oil companies were represented in this vital antitrust process, and its successful negotiation, by the law firm of Sullivan & Cromwell. Both Eisenhower's CIA director, Allen Dulles, and Eisenhower's secretary of state, Allen Dulles's brother John Foster Dulles, were partners in Sullivan & Cromwell before their government service. Allen Dulles returned to the firm after government service (his brother became fatally ill in office). In other words, the CIA director *and* the secretary of state at the time of the Mossadegh coup were, in private life, well-paid lawyers for the major oil companies.

Voting control of both Exxon, the world's largest company, and Mobil, appeared to be held by Rockefeller family trusts. In *The Rich and the Super-Rich* (Lyle Stuart, 1969), Ferdinand Lundberg presents Senate figures from World War II putting Rockefeller control at an astounding 20.2 percent of Exxon, and 16.34 percent of Mobil. Because the shareholdings of such large companies are widely distributed, holdings of even a few percent of the stock can wield much power, and secure working control of management.* Rockefeller holdings in these companies have gradually declined as the family trusts have been diversified, but they remain substantial. Henry Kissinger, who figured in the Iran story greatly in the 1970s, came to power as a Rockefeller protégé, received large amounts of money from the family over the years, and showed in many ways that he never forgot it.

IN 1950, the parliament (called the *majlis*) appointed Mossadegh, a longtime member, to chair a committee to investigate the Anglo-Iranian contract. The committee came up with a plan under which Anglo-Iranian would pay Iran a 50 percent royalty on profits, identical to the arrangements Venezuela and Saudi Arabia had obtained from the big oil companies. But Anglo-Iranian insisted on a fixed royalty, which would inevitably come out to much less than 50 percent.

*This is an often misunderstood feature of U.S. corporate capitalism. Dissidents can, if they choose, mount a massive and costly proxy fight trying to rouse a majority of shareholders to vote out management. If ridiculously rich, they can buy enough shares to take control. This is rare, however, and hasn't happened at Exxon or Mobil. Usually, "corporate democracy" is exercised by selling one's shares in a company whose management one doesn't like, and buying shares in a company whose management one does, if such can be found.

Parliament refused the offer, in a session that a State Department observer reported was "marked by emotional excesses." Westerners just didn't understand how deeply Iranians resented the control by a foreign company of their country's biggest commercial asset. This foreign control had led them to hate the British as it would lead them to hate Americans.

In 1951, with negotiations at an impasse, Mossadegh persuaded parliament to nationalize Iran's oil. This proved so popular among Iranians that there were widespread demonstrations in support of Mossadegh. The shah succumbed to pressure and appointed him prime minister. But Iran alone couldn't make the oil flow. Before Anglo-Iranian would resume pumping and buying oil, it demanded compensation for the oil that was due under the concession, but which had been nationalized. Mossadegh said that on the contrary, the oil companies owed Iran back taxes. An agreement hung fire.

For two years, Mossadegh tried to peddle Iranian oil on the open market, but couldn't. Iran had fallen victim to a boycott. The major oil companies, in obvious collusion with each other, refused to buy Iranian oil pending a settlement. So pervasive was the power of the majors over oil supplies and marketing that no independent dared to break the boycott and risk its ability to buy oil from or sell oil to the big companies.

The Iranian economy foundered. The U.S. government responded by cutting off aid, tightening the noose further. This effectively underwrote the position of the oil companies. Truman may have authorized the Federal Trade Commission and the Justice Department to go after the oil monopoly, but the foreign policy establishment proved beyond reach of his or anyone's populist instincts.

At this point we can turn to the account of affairs that Kennett Love presented to Allen Dulles. It begins as *he* began it. All deletions are marked. All italicized phrases are emphasized for purposes of this book, and were not italicized in the original. Some spellings vary from those accepted for this book, but are phonetic from the Farsi, so it's guesswork anyway:

"What part did the United States play in the overthrow of Premier Mohammed Mossadegh and the restoration of the Shah in Iran in the summer of 1953? It is probable that the American role was decisive, that the Iranians who participated in the royalist coup could not have succeeded without American help. It is doubtful that the coup would have been attempted without American cooperation.

"The American activities on behalf of the Pahlevi monarchy were undertaken as the result of a belief by responsible diplomatic and government officials that Dr. Mossadegh's conduct was permitting Iran to fall under communist control. Washington's project to intervene with more than mere economic pressure probably became fixed within the month preceding the successful coup against Dr. Mossadeh [*sic*] on 19 August 1953. According to my observations at the time, operatives of the Central Intelligence Agency concerted plans for action with Major General Fazlollah Zahedi, retired, who was to lead the coup and assume the premiership. A number of active army officers were won over to the clandestine royalist organization. Bands of professional street-fighters from the slums of south Teheran were enlisted, evidently through the disbursement of large sums in U.S. currency, to carry out the tactics prepared by the CIA agents as a last resort. These bands played an essential part in controlling the streets when a resort to violence became necessary for the royalist cause on 19 August.

"Meanwhile, members of the U.S. embassy advised Mohammed Reza Shah Pahlevi and coordinated the Shah's course of action with the overall strategy of the movement. On a higher level, the U.S. government, having refused Dr. Mossadegh's request for economic aid, launched a massive emergency aid program for the royalist regime with a grant of $45 million shortly after the coup [and $850 million over the next six years]. At the same time, the CIA agents who had blue-printed the coup against Dr. Mossadegh continued to furnish technical assistance in quelling dissident movements that threatened the stability of the new regime. A year after the coup, American cryptographic and police experts and a CIA agent played an important part in rooting out an extensive conspiracy of army officers that was closely linked to the communist Tudeh party.

"The extent and variety of American operations in behalf of the Shah are widely known in outline in the Arab Middle East as well as in Iran. For example, Egyptians in London in 1956 immediately conjectured that Secretary of State Dulles' withdrawal of support for the Aswan High Dam was the opening move for an attempt to unseat President Gamal Abdel Nasser.... [An Egyptian diplomat] likened Mr. Dulles' move to President Eisenhower's refusal of aid to Dr. Mossadegh in June 1953.

"Iranian newspapers evinced awareness of American activities during the week preceding 19 August. Ever since then Middle Easterners have shown a greater appreciation than Westerners of the influence of the American contribution to the royalist cause both on the domestic scene in Iran and upon Iran's international alignment. Indeed, the American endeavors leading up to the coup have been largely ignored by Western accounts of the episode. Some versions [including Love's own in the *the New York Times*] treat the abrupt restoration of political power to the Shah as merely fortuitous for American policy, whereas, as we shall see, *it was a consciously planned accomplishment creditable to American Federal employees....*

"The Central Intelligence Agency, it is true, permitted a claim that it had contributed to the royalist coup to be made in a series of three articles published by the *Saturday Evening Post* in October and November 1954.

"The authors, R. and G. Harkness, stated that they had spent a year preparing the series in close contact with CIA officials in Washington. After attributing a role to the CIA in the Egyptian revolution of 1952 and the Guatemala revolt in June 1954, the authors wrote:

Another CIA influenced triumph was the successful overthrow in Iran in the summer of 1953, of old, dictatorial Premier Mohammed

Mossadegh and the return to power of this country's friend, Shah Mohammed Riza Pahlevi.

"The account spoke of the CIA's 'guiding premise' that indigenous freedom forces should be employed wherever feasible. It observed pointedly that, shortly before the August coup, U.S. Ambassador Loy Henderson, CIA Director Allen Dulles, and the Shah's twin sister, Princess Ashraf, were all in Switzerland at the same time. In the same manner, it noted that Colonel H. Norman Schwarzkopf, a former advisor to the Iranian gendarmerie, had visited Iran before the coup. For the rest, the article gave a summary of the developments of the crisis that were reported at the time in American newspapers without further reference to the crucial part played by American agents.

"The account given by the Harknesses is an exception in its assessment of the American initiative in rescuing the Pahlevi monarchy. It appears not to have influenced subsequent accounts and if later writers have quoted the Harknesses, I am unaware of it.

"The relevance of information on the American rescue of the Iranian throne to an understanding of American-Iranian relations would appear to be unarguable. The episode marked the entry of the United States as an interested party into Iranian politics. Previously, the U.S. had stood aloof from events in Iran, even during the existence of the Persian Gulf Command in World War II when thousands of American troops entered the country to maintain the Lend-Lease supply route to Russia. Deliberately or not, President Franklin D. Roosevelt carried the policy of aloofness to such an extent that he did not inform the Iranian government in advance of the American-British-Russian Teheran Conference and made only a perfunctory gesture of calling on the Shah while attending the conference.

"Individual Americans had rendered prominent service to Iran. Among them were Morgan Shuster, who was retained by the Iranian government as Treasurer General in 1911; Arthur C. Milispaugh, who headed two financial advisory missions to Iran in 1922 and 1943; and Colonel Schwarzkopf. *Iran sought the services of individual Americans precisely because the American government remained disinterested while Britain and Russia interfered in Iranian affairs and struggled for hegemony.*"

LOVE then relates some World War II history, and describes the beginning of the cold war with the Soviet Union and Washington's concentration on containing communism. This leads him to the intervention in Iran:*

*His discussion begins with a paragraph that seems contradictory of itself and of other opinions in his paper, so I have deleted it from the text. I include it here for fairness. It says, "It was the prospect of Soviet-controlled communism becoming dominant in Iran

"It was the dispute between Iran and the Anglo-Iranian Oil Company which drew the United States toward its major involvement in the Iranian scene. The United States came forward as a mediator with initiatives including the Harriman mission in 1951,* and only later became an associate with Britain in the fruitless bargaining. The Churchill-Truman proposals for a settlement of the dispute, presented in August 1952 and bettered in January and February 1953, were flamboyantly rejected by Premier Mossadegh. The experience prodded the United States toward its cloak-and-dagger Persian adventure by leading American statesmen toward pessimistic conclusions about Dr. Mossadegh's intransigence. . . .

"The final Anglo-American proposal in the oil dispute was made on 20 February 1953. Britain offered to submit for arbitration by the International Court of Justice at The Hague both her own claim for compensation for loss of profits in the 42 remaining years of the AIOC [Anglo-Iranian Oil Company] concession and Iran's counterclaims for back taxes and customs duties. . . .

"Dr. Mossadegh rejected the proposals in an intemperate radio broadcast on 20 March. He described the idea of compensation for lost profits as 'a form of plunder for which there is no precedent anywhere in the world.' He spoke of 'provocative activities of the cunning hirelings of foreigners' and called for the eradication of foreign influence. There were no further oil negotiations with Dr. Mossadegh.

"In truth, the premier may have wanted to shelve the oil dispute by taking an extreme position in order to deal with bitter divisions that had riven the domestic political scene. The sight of dissension within Iran, involving the first significant defections from the premier's National Front to the partisans of the Shah, may also have persuaded London and Washington to let the oil problem wait on the possibility of favorable shifts in Teheran.

"In Janaury 1953, the premier had overcome a surge of opposition in the Majlis [parliament] and obtained a year's extension of his plenary powers. He had obtained these powers in July 1952 after winning a showdown with the Shah on his demand for the War Ministry portfolio in addition to the premiership. Control of the army was the crucial issue. . . . The premier wanted United States support to enable him to hold office long enough to complete his overhaul of the army's top echelons and to legitimatize an interpretation of the 1906 constitution by a Majlis committee that would make the army responsible to the government instead of [to] the monarch. The Shah wanted United States help to dislodge Dr. Mossadegh before he could break the monarchy's traditional hold on the army. . . .

---

that prompted the United States to intervene. This was the threat held up by both the Shah's party and Dr. Mossadegh. Each of them wanted American support, each for his own reasons. The communist threat was definitely secondary, although both used it as bait."

*An unsuccessful negotiating mission led by Ambassador-at-large W. Averell Harriman, later governor of New York State.

"[A]t the end of February 1953, rumors that the Shah planned to leave the country indefinitely provoked wild rioting. A mob, elements of which were former Mossadegh supporters, stormed the premier's [Mossadegh's] house in Teheran after a colorful roughneck named Shaban 'Beemokh' ('the brainless one') Jafari had battered down the compound gate with a jeep. The premier then estimated to be at least 74 [birth date listed in reference works as 1880], leaped out of his famous bed and escaped with unexpected agility over the garden wall into the Point IV [U.S. aid] headquarters adjoining.

"The incident occurred eight days after the final Anglo-American oil proposal. It was believed in Teheran at the time that it [the rioting incident] influenced the unbridled xenophobia expressed in Dr. Mossadegh's reply to the proposal. In crises it is natural for politicians to try to outbid their rivals in nationalist extremism and to accuse their challengers of softness toward the foreign enemy. It happens in this country. . . .

"Thus far, Dr. Mossadegh had taken no positive steps to suggest to the United States that it had better help Iran or the country might turn to the communists. . . . *He had been anticommunist throughout his career*. During his first year in office the outlawed Tudeh [Communist] party fought him with the bitterness the communists usually reserved for Social Democrats. He was a bourgeois nationalist reformist diversionist rival in their eyes. . . .

"There was no real abatement of Dr. Mossadegh's anticommunism until after [the denial of] his appeal for aid to President Eisenhower . . . 28 May 1953. . . . [In this written appeal, Mossadegh pointed out to Eisenhower the economic hardship Iran was suffering due to the oil embargo. He then proposed, as Love summarizes it,] to concentrate on the development of resources other than oil if the United States could not see its way clear to overcoming the obstacles to the sale of Iran's nationalized oil. This prospect was mentioned with increasing frequency in Iranian nationalist circles in the spring and summer of 1953. An idea born of desperation, it indicated a belief by Dr. Mossadegh that he dared not compromise to achieve an oil settlement.

"President Eisenhower's reply was not dated until June 29. The President said he had delayed until he 'could have an opportunity to consult with Mr. Dulles (presumably John Foster, although the President probably conferred with Allen W. shortly afterward) and Ambassador Henderson.'"

HERE, Love appears to be absent some facts that have since been revealed. On June 22, a week before Eisenhower replied to Mossadegh's May 28 letter, Secretary of State Dulles called a meeting on Iran in his office. Present were his brother Allen, Ambassador Henderson, Defense Secretary Charles Wilson, and CIA operative Kermit Roosevelt.

Henderson had already written Eisenhower that "most Iranian politicians friendly to the West would welcome secret American intervention which would assist them in attaining their individual or group political ambitions.... Only those sympathetic to the Soviet Union and to international communism have reason to be pleased at what is taking place in Iran."

At the June 22 meeting, Secretary Dulles approved Kermit Roosevelt's plan to overthrow Mossadegh. Eisenhower must have been aware of the prospective coup when he replied the next week to Mossadegh's requests for help. Eisenhower told Mossadegh he would continue the existing small aid program, but wouldn't increase it, and more important, wouldn't help break the oil boycott. In fact, Eisenhower subtly suggested that Mossadegh could solve his economic problems by caving in on the oil dispute. After summarizing this reply, Love's account continues as follows:

"The letter was a blow to the Iranian premier. It was evidently designed as such....

"There are several theories as to why he [Mossadegh] did not resign.... The prevalent theory in the West is that he was power-mad. This view was also current among many Iranians at the time....

"Another hypothesis is that . . . he had a Messianic feeling that he alone could steer the country through the perils of the time.

"*Dr. Mossadegh may also have felt responsible for carrying to completion his campaign to make the Shah a truly constitutional monarch*, limited to reigning rather than ruling, as a matter of political principle. *He often stated this principle as well as his loyalty to the Shah.*"

LOVE says Mossadegh enjoyed "an improvement in relations with the new administration of Premier Georgi Malenkov in the Kremlin.... The prospect of receiving the eleven tons of gold and $8 million owed by the Soviets for wartime occupation charges was especially welcome in the absence of American aid [and, more important, the absence of American oil purchases under the boycott].

"Of far greater significance as far as Washington was concerned was the emergence of the Tudeh party in Teheran. Although the party had been outlawed since one of its members tried to assassinate the Shah in 1949 . . . the United States embassy estimated the party's membership in Teheran in June 1953 at 8,000 to 10,000 and its national membership, strategically concentrated in the cities, at 15,000 to 20,000 with perhaps two to five times that many reasonably dependable fellow-travellers. . . . The Tudeh had infiltrated many government ministries [a charge that was widely accepted about the U.S. Communist party in Washington in 1953].... *The Mossadegh regime was as vigorous as any in suppressing overt communist activities and in combatting the party in the streets until receipt of President Eisenhower's letter* [which came *after* Eisenhower and the Dulleses had ordered Mossadegh's overthrow]."

Love notes that when a judge and assistant prosecutor dropped charges against twenty-three members of Tudeh in the spring of 1953 (on the ground that the party wasn't communist), the Mossadegh government suspended the judge and prosecutor, and asserted the party was still illegal. But the Tudeh came out of the closet. In July it held a rally of more than 100,000 people right outside the parliament building. Love describes it:

"The multitude shouted anti-American slogans. . . . But the only American present, myself, was treated with respectful curiosity by the throng as he made his way across the square. I was received cordially at the speakers' platform by the Tudeh leaders. They were jubilant over the size of the demonstration they had organized and proud of its evident discipline. They were only too happy to give a newspaper man a grandstand view of it [though maybe they wouldn't have been if they had known he was getting ready to take an active, covert part in a CIA coup].

"The Tudeh leadership felt that the Nationalists, the disorganized remnant that remained nominally in control of government, would no longer be able to resist accepting Tudeh partnership in a Popular Front in which the Tudeh was certain to predominate. . . .

"I asked Dr. Mossadegh the following day, July 22, 1953, whether he planned to do anything about the resurgence of the communists. He replied that the activities of the communists were merely a symptom of Iran's condition and that it was more important to treat the condition than to attack the symptoms. . . .

"He said that in the absence of increased United States aid the situation in Iran was dangerous 'in every way,' militarily, economically, and politically, and that its outcome could not be foreseen. He also said Iran would have to seek 'economic ties with any government it can,' in reply to a question about whether he would seek aid from Moscow.

"I believe Washington made up its mind at this time to intervene in Iran. Dr. Mossadegh, in what was to prove his last interview, had certainly indicated that he might be letting the communist threat grow as a means of squeezing aid out of the United States [Love continually omits that aid wouldn't have been an issue if the big oil companies weren't boycotting Iranian oil, in collusion with the U.S. government and to the detriment of every U.S. gasoline, heating oil, and electricity consumer—in other words, the entire U.S. public]. . . .

"By the end of July [1953] the Shah's position in his struggle to retain control of the army was so desperate that he was willing to risk the onus of being restored by foreigners. . . . Dr. Mossadegh had been reshuffling the command echelons in the army to ensure his control over it. A commission . . . had forced the retirement of some 200 senior officers. And the premier had appointed his own nominee . . . as chief of staff. . . . Unless something could be done about it, Dr. Mossadegh would soon have every important command position filled by an officer owing his promotion to the premier rather than to the Shah."

* * *

LOVE goes on to describe tactical planning for the coup:

"The army was the key factor. Although the tribes had long been a fertile ground for foreign operations, they were unstrategically located far from the capital. The Qashqai, the strongest tribal group, favored Dr. Mossadegh rather than the Shah because of a family feud. . . .

"In order to use the army, the Americans had to find a leader who could persuade the bulk of the army to defy the new chief of staff and strike a blow to restore the Shah.

"General [Fazlollah] Zahedi had *all the requisites*. He had been Minister of Interior in Dr. Mossadegh's first cabinet in 1951. He had been interned by the British in Palestine during World War II because of *pro-Nazi activities* under Reza Shah. He had been twice accused of *plotting against the Mossadegh regime*, the first time in October 1952, when he escaped arrest because of his parliamentary immunity as a senator, and the second time in April 1953 in connection with the *murder* of General Afshartoos by a group of retired officers. . . . He possessed . . . *a reputation for decisive action without too many scruples*."

Love recounts that in his talks with U.S. embassy officials he learned that they apparently were consulting with the shah on plans to dismiss the premier. Love's account:

"The Shah went to Ramsar on the Caspian with Queen Soraya on 15 August 1953 leaving two firmans dated 13 August with General Zahedi. One served to dismiss Dr. Mossadegh and the other to name General Zahedi premier. General Zahedi was charged with seeing to the implementation of the royal decrees. The General delegated Colonel Nematollah Nasiri of the Imperial Palace Guard to arrest Dr. Mossadegh's cabinet ministers on the night of 15 August and to serve the dismissal firman on the premier. The plan was betrayed to Dr. Mossadegh [by another officer] and Colonel Nasiri was himself arrested."

The Mossadegh government spared Colonel Nasiri's life, an act of mercy that many Iranians would come to regret. After the shah was restored, Nasiri became the head of SAVAK, the torture-happy Iranian security organization that kept the shah in power over the next twenty-six years. In his memoirs, Kermit Roosevelt acknowledged that SAVAK was organized and trained by the CIA and Mossad—the Israeli intelligence service. When the 1979 Khomeini revolution kicked the shah out, Nasiri was one of the first persons executed. Love's account continues:

"The sleeping city was disturbed that night [August 15–16, 1953] by the movement of tanks through the streets. The curfew was strict, however, and the reason for the stir was not known until the government broadcast an account of an attempted royalist coup in a special bulletin at 7:00 A.M. on 16 August. The government's version of events ignored the issuance by the Shah of the two firmans. [This would seem to be evidence that Mossadegh *still* didn't want to break with the shah, *still* wanted the door open to compromise.]

"My first observation of the association of the United States with the royalist cause began with a telephone call to me at the Park Hotel from Joe Goodwin, a CIA man attached to the embassy as a political officer."

How did Love know Goodwin was CIA? Interesting question. The answer is not provided in the account being quoted. In a 1983 interview, Love said he didn't know that Goodwin was with the CIA at the time of the coup, but found out sometime during the seven years before he wrote the account. How? "I might have asked him," Love said. What occasioned the question? Love insisted upon repeated questioning that he couldn't remember. His account continues:

"Mr. Goodwin called shortly after the 7 A.M. news broadcast and asked if I wanted to meet General Zahedi to get the real version of what had happened. It was arranged for me to be taken at 11 A.M. to a rendezvous to meet General Zahedi, who was being hunted by the police. Don Schwind of the Associated Press, the only other American correspondent then in Iran, came too. We were driven to the residence of an American embassy official in Shimran. There we met Ardeshir Zahedi [the general's twenty-five-year-old son, who would later serve as the shah's ambassador to the U.S., right up to the time the shah was thrown out of office].... [Zahedi] told us that his father had decided on second thought that it was unsafe to be at any given place at any given time [and so wouldn't show up]. (The following day the government broadcast a price of 100,000 rials, equivalent then to about $1,200, on General Zahedi's head.) Ardeshir was waiting in the living room with the occupant of the house when I arrived. He greeted Joe Goodwin [the CIA man] without introduction [indicating they were previously acquainted] as we entered from French doors opening on the terrace and garden.

"Ardeshir told us about the Shah's issuance of the two firmans. He showed us the one appointing his father premier. Then he handed it to the occupant of the house [the U.S. embassy official, whom Love doesn't name] who took it into the adjoining dining room where there stood a large photoduplicating machine.... As Ardeshir talked, two operators made sheafs of copies of the firman. [Apparently these were U.S. government employees; our Iranian stooges couldn't even churn out their own propaganda.] Each of us took a handful back to town. I distributed mine at the Park Hotel [all in a day's work for a reporter], except for one copy, which I still have. Late in the afternoon came word that the Shah and Soraya [his wife] had flown to Baghdad, in the Shah's plane.

"Monday, 17 August, was a day of anxiety. The atmosphere at the American embassy was as grim and worried. Gordon Mattison, who had been chargé d'affaires since Ambassador Henderson's departure for consultations eleven weeks earlier, agreed with me that United States policy appeared to have suffered a major setback. During the day Ambassador Henderson was flown back from Beirut in a special United States Air Force plane. Only Joe Goodwin [the CIA man], who served as communications channel between

Mr. Schwind and myself on one hand and General Zahedi on the other, appeared unruffled. Mr. Goodwin, *who had been an A.P. correspondent himself in Iran some years before*, reported that General Zahedi had issued a declaration, not an appeal, ordering all Iranian officers to be prepared to sacrifice themselves for their king and religion when the command was given. General Zahedi proclaimed that Dr. Mossadegh's government had been in a state of illegal rebellion since Saturday night and that he, Zahedi, was the legal premier. Photostats of the declaration in General Zahedi's handwriting were circulated in the army.

"Tudeh-inspired mobs spent the day battering, hacksawing, and pulling down all the public statutes [*sic*] in Teheran of the Shah and his late father [obviously Love meant "statues"; it was the CIA that was pulling down the statutes]. I was nearly pulled from a taxicab by demonstrators who had just toppled a statue of Reza Shah at the railroad station. My life was saved by the driver, a card-carrying Tudeh member, who appeared to know a number of persons in the frenzied mob. . . .

"The press, especially *Shahbaz* and other Tudeh newspapers, published accusations that the United States and Mr. Henderson had been involved in the weekend attempt to unseat Dr. Mossadegh. [Thus the Tudeh papers gave their readers an accurate account; Love was giving his own U.S. readers an *in*accurate account that ignored what he knew about U.S. responsibility.]

"On Tuesday, 18 August, came the first resurgence of royalist sentiment. It was matched by an increase in the assertiveness of the Tudeh. The communists organized demonstrations at government cement factories, grain elevators, and textile mills demanding the release of 'political prisoners.' The Tudeh sacked the headquarters of the right-wing Pan-Iranist party. The Tudeh morning newspaper *Shojaat* demanded the expulsion of the 'interventionist' American diplomats [a not unreasonable demand, considering what was happening] and the ending of all United States missions except the embassy.

"But the morning had seen a small royalist demonstration and in the evening the tide began to turn. Soldiers, dispatched to quell fighting between the Tudeh and the Pan-Iranists, clubbed both factions impartially while shouting 'Long live the Shah, death to Mossadegh.' (*'Zindabad Shah, mordabad Mossadegh.'*) Carried away by excitement the soldiers swarmed into Lalezar Street and forced people emerging from movie theaters to repeat the same slogans on pain of getting a drubbing from a rifle butt or a jab from a bayonet. The soldiers were ordered back to their barracks as hastily as possible but the royalist tide had turned, as the morrow was to prove."

THE next morning, August 19, Love reports that as he taxied to an appointment at the embassy, he encountered a mob that said it was on its way "to attack Dr. Mossadegh's house."

He adds, "A few minutes later I related the incident to Ambassador Hen-

derson. He chuckled and turned to a couple of embassy officials whom he
had called into his office to hear my account. He said with obvious delight
something like: 'Well, do you suppose we will have to give the old boy
(Premier Mossadegh) asylum again? Where will we put him?'

"Mr. Henderson gave the impression that I was telling him something he
expected to hear. He seemed not in the least surprised. . . .

"On my way back to the hotel my taxi was stopped by an armed gang
which forced the driver to switch on his headlights and put a picture of the
Shah on his windshield. . . . All during the day similar gangs, armed with
clubs, knives, and stones, and occasionally a pistol or rifle, forced every
automobile driver in the streets to identify his car with headlights and picture
as belonging to a partisan of the Shah.

"This tactic smothered any possible Mossadeghist rally by preventing
anyone from moving in the streets who was not positively identified as a
partisan of the Shah. The opposition could not rally because they were
precluded from identifying each other.

"Credit for this tactic and for organizing its use by gangs to control the
streets was candidly claimed by a CIA agent named George Carroll, 6-foot-
4-inch 200 pounder who had arrived in Teheran from Korea, where, he said,
the CIA had been standing by while the United States was considering
organizing a popular uprising to oust Syngman Rhee. . . .

"I do not know at first hand through what channels Mr. Carroll approached
the south Teheran gangs that controlled the streets during the coup. [Love
says an embassy official, Richard Cottam, told him the gangs were organized
with the help of a friendly and influential Ayatollah.] Mr. Cottam also states
that Howard Stone, a political officer at the United State embassy, was active
in preparations for the royalist coup."

Baloney. Stone was no "political officer." He was a CIA agent—or
"master spy," as the *Wall Street Journal* labeled him in 1979, after reporter
David Ignatius got Stone to open up with war stories over beer and cigars
at Stone's basement poker table. Stone—known as "Rocky"—recalled even
"buttoning the uniform of General Fazlollah Zahedi on the day the general
was to announce over Radio Tehran that the shah had designated him the
new prime minister. General Zahedi, the CIA's key ally in Iran, was too
nervous to dress himself."

Ignatius also reported that Stone "remembers his young wife sitting in a
rocking chair at the Stones' home in Tehran, hiding a pistol under her knitting
as she guarded the life of Ardeshir Zahedi [the general's son, who later
became the shah's ambassador to the U.S.]."

AS to the role of the CIA agent George Carroll, Love reports being told by
an unidentified colleague, "in the days immediately following the overthrow
of Mossadegh, Ardeshir Zahedi came to see Carroll daily. Carroll had an
office that was obviously a temporary base with something of the atmosphere

of a field headquarters. He and Ardeshir would pour [*sic*] over the maps together for half an hour or so and then Ardeshir would go back downtown. Carroll was also a budddy of General Farhat Dadsetar, Zahedi's first military governor of Teheran. I believe Carroll worked with Dadsetar on preparations for the very efficient smothering of a potentially dangerous dissident movement emanating from the bazaar area and the Tudeh in the first two weeks of November 1953."

Love concludes that "there can be no dispute over the fact that Mr. Carroll made an important contribution to the royalist success before, during, and after the coup."

But what Love says next is even more telling. "It is conceivable," he says, "that the Tudeh could have turned the fortunes of the day against the royalists. But for some reason they remained completely aloof from the conflict. . . . As it turned out, Mr. Carroll's bands had the streets largely to themselves. Resistance was concentrated at government buildings. . . . *My own conjecture is that the Tudeh were restrained by the Soviet embassy because the Kremlin, in the first post-Stalin year, was not willing to take on such consequences as might have resulted from the establishment of a communist controlled regime in Teheran.*"

This last statement, unproven and questionable as it is, is remarkable. If the U.S. truly believed that the Soviets didn't *want* a communist government in Tehran, then the ostensible justification for a U.S. coup vanishes. We are left with no explanation for the coup except for one that might at first glance be rejected as a piece of Socialist Workers' party campaign rhetoric: a retrieval of the rights of two Rockefeller-controlled oil companies, whose lawyers were running the CIA and State Department, to monopolize Iranian oil in U.S. markets and thereby help fix gasoline prices for the American consumer. Can it be? If so, adding insult to injury, the same consumer was also being dunned for tax money to hire and outfit the U.S. agents who were carrying out the coup.

Of course, the U.S. consumer's suffering was nothing compared to that of the Iranians, who have been forced to live under brutal dictatorships ever since. The coup was the end of what Love himself admits was a movement toward popular, constitutional government in Iran. If Mossadegh had taken some steps away from popular government in his final months, it was by Love's own account reluctantly, and only after Iran had been put into an effective state of siege by the oil boycott.

NOW we get to the concluding scene of the coup, at Dr. Mossadegh's house, where Love says "a force of gendarmerie and soldiers aided by three tanks put up the longest and bitterest resistance of the day."

Admits Love with all modesty, "I myself was responsible, in an impromptu sort of way, for speeding the final victory of the royalists. After the radio station fell I went up there to obtain permission to broadcast a dispatch. All

commercial telegraphic and telephonic communications had been interrupted.... A half-dozen tanks swarming with cheering soldiers were parked
in front of the radio station. I told the tank commanders that a lot of people
were getting killed trying to storm Dr. Mossadegh's house and that they, the
tank commanders, ought to go down there where they would be of some use
instead of sitting idle at the radio station. They declared my suggestion to
be a splendid idea. They took their machines in a body to Kokh Avenue and
put the three tanks at Dr. Mossadegh's house out of action after a lively duel
with armor-piercing 75-millimeter shells."

And there we have it, folks—the Iranian correspondent for the *New York
Times* directing the successful tank attack on the home of the Iranian prime
minister, overthrowing the government, fixing one-man rule in Iran, and
setting off a chain of events that would include the loss of Iranian oil to U.S.
markets and the invasion of Afghanistan by the Soviet Union.

HOWARD "ROCKY" STONE, the CIA agent who did everything down to
buttoning General Zahedi's uniform, recalled for reporter David Ignatius the
victory party at the CIA station that night. General Zahedi, now prime
minister, accompanied by his son Ardeshir, went over to Stone and said,
"We're in.... We're in.... What do we do now?"

According to Love, this is what they did: they, and the street forces that
supported them, began converting into local currency the bribes the CIA had
paid them for their work—all U.S. taxpayer dollars, of course, and in such
abundance that they overwhelmed Tehran's not exactly unsophisticated marketplace.

Writes Love, "Large amounts of American currency began to flow into
the foreign exchange market immediately after the coup, reportedly coming
from sources in south Teheran. The United States currency entered the market
in such quantity as to depress the dollar in favor of the rial. On 23 August
I paid a dollar check to I. Finzi, a merchant, for an Isfahan rug, the transaction
being based on the assumption that the dollar had at least held its own at the
precoup rate of up to 128 rials. Mr. Finzi returned after an interval saying
that he did not know what had happened but that the rate for checks had
fallen below 80 rials to the dollar while dollar currency was selling for as
little as 50 rials.... I think it can be reasonably inferred that the glut of
dollars was coming from the *chaqu keshan* [street gangs] and that it represented their wages for the work of 19 August."

Love ends his account thus:

"The remainder of the story, Dr. Mossadegh's surrender and trial, the
dissipation of much of the Shah's esteem as a result of the excesses committed
by the police state developed by General Zahedi in place of the mob law
that evolved under Dr. Mossadegh, need be summarized no further here.

"What is significant is that Americans restored the Pahlevi monarchy when
it threatened to give way before a premier dependent on communist support

and that Iranians are well aware of the American role although the American public is not. *Thus it is that many Iranians hold the United States responsible for creating and supporting a regime that they believe has become an increasingly malign influence on the political, social, and economic life of the country.*"

All this, Love told Allen Dulles, while Dulles was director of all U.S. intelligence gathering. But as late as 1979, through Democratic and Republican administrations alike, the U.S. government was still going out of its way to identify itself with the shah, and acting amazed and even incensed that such a policy backfired with the Iranian people.

It wasn't the first time such warnings had been ignored. Back in 1950, before the nationalization of Iran's oil, the State Department's energy attaché, Richard Funkhouser, had informed the government presciently, "AIOC [Anglo-Iranian Oil Company] and the British are genuinely hated in Iran; approval of AIOC is treated as political suicide." Yet throughout the 1953 crisis, the U.S. had supported AIOC to the hilt.

HERE is how a standard U.S. university textbook reports the events described here:

"The fear had existed since the end of World War II that the Soviets, none too rich in oil, would move into the Middle East, whose hot sands covered the greatest known oil pool. This critical area threatened to erupt in 1951 when the Iranians, under their weeping Premier Mossadegh, nationalized the British oil refineries. If the British had resorted to strong-armed measures, as they were sorely tempted to do, the Russians probably would have invaded Iran in force, with calamitous consquences. Fortunately for peace, Mossadegh overplayed his hand, and following his internal overthrow, Washington used its good offices to achieve a peaceful settlement of the Anglo-Iranian controversy in 1954."*

Whew! Good thing the British didn't resort to strong-armed measures!

IN 1961, John Foster Dulles was dead. Allen Dulles had been reappointed to head the CIA as the very first decision announced by President-elect Kennedy. And President Eisenhower retired to a 576-acre farm near Gettysburg, Pennsylvania.

The farm, smaller then, had been bought by General and Mrs. Eisenhower

*The quote is from *A Diplomatic History of the American People* by Thomas A. Bailey, course text for a New York University history major (the author) in 1963. Bailey was and is a professor at Stanford University. In a 1983 interview, he said the book is still a standard text, and that he continues to update it with new chapters and to correct errors. But he said he hadn't heard about the CIA's role in the 1953 Iranian coup, and so hadn't corrected that. At the end of the interview, he said he would immediately report this news to his publisher, Prentice-Hall, and suggest a correction!

in 1950 for $24,000, but by 1960 it was worth about $1 million. Most of the difference represented the gifts of Texas oil executives connected to Rockefeller oil interests. The oilmen acquired surrounding land for Eisenhower under dummy names, filled it with livestock and big, modern barns, paid for extensive renovations to the Eisenhower house, and even wrote out checks to pay the hired help.*

These oil executives were associates of Sid Richardson and Clint Murchison, billionaire Texas oilmen who were working with Rockefeller interests on some Texas and Louisiana properties and on efforts to hold up the price of oil. From 1955 to 1963, the Richardson, Murchison, and Rockefeller interests (including Standard Oil Company of Indiana, which was 11.36 percent Rockefeller-held at the time of the Senate figures referred to earlier, and International Basic Economy Corporation, which was 100 percent Rockefeller-owned and of which Nelson Rockefeller was president) managed to give away a $900,000 slice of their Texas-Louisiana oil property to Robert B. Anderson, Eisenhower's secretary of the treasury.

In the Eisenhower cabinet, Anderson led the team that devised a system under which quotas were mandated by law on how much oil each company could bring into the U.S. from cheap foreign sources. This bonanza for entrenched power was enacted in 1958 and lasted fourteen years. Officially, it was done because of the "national interest" in preventing a reliance on foreign oil.

In effect, the import limits held U.S. oil prices artificially high, depleted domestic reserves, and reduced demand for oil overseas, thereby lowering foreign oil prices so that European and Japanese manufacturers could compete better with their U.S. rivals. It is difficult, of course, for a layman to understand how any of these things is in the national interest.

Meanwhile, President Kennedy turned the State Department over to Deak Rusk, who had held various high positions in the department under President Truman. For nine years—the entire Eisenhower interregnum for the Democrats and then some—Rusk had been occupied as president of the Rockefeller Foundation.

Has anybody stopped to think that from 1953 until 1977, the man in charge of U.S. foreign policy† had been on the Rockefeller family payroll? And that from 1961 until 1977, he (meaning Rusk and Kissinger) was beholden to the Rockefellers for his very *solvency*?

---

*Reported in detail by Drew Pearson and Jack Anderson throughout January 1961 and never substantially challenged.

†With all due respect to the nominal tenure of William P. Rogers as secretary of state during Nixon's first term, Kissinger better fills this description.

CHAPTER ELEVEN

REPRESSING THE MARKETPLACE: THE MIDDLE EAST

================================WE ARE taught that the opposite of communism is the free market. So one might imagine that the defeat of communism in Iran in 1953 would have brought a free market, at least as far as the U.S. was concerned. One might imagine that the U.S. government would have opened its information and its good offices to any taxpaying citizen who might have wanted to deal in Iranian oil, so that the marketplace could favor the most efficient, and provide the cheapest gasoline and fuel oil for the American public.

But of course not.

Almost before the Iranian street gangs could exchange their CIA bribe money for local currency, the State Department was at work deciding who was going to be allowed to buy or sell Iranian oil and at what price. It was all done, or so it was said, to help the U.S. cause in the cold war. But, as usual, the oil powers made out, the small-timers were closed out, and the public shelled out.

At least one voice in government did argue otherwise—the State Department petroleum attaché, Richard Funkhouser, who advised (as he later testified), "The U.S. government should promote the entry of new competition into the Middle East, particularly the competition of U.S. companies and particularly U.S. independent companies.... The control of Middle East resources by the major international companies is subject to serious criticism by both friendly and unfriendly states."

But instead, the State Department huddled with Exxon executives (according to the 1974 Senate testimony of Howard W. Page, vice-president of

Exxon) and sent them out to do some fast persuasion on King Ibn Saud of Saudi Arabia. That was the other major Middle Eastern supply source. Saud needed stroking because if Iran started selling oil again, The Saudis wouldn't be able to expand their own sales as fast as they wanted to. A restraint would be put on Saudi income. Yet the State Department wanted Iran to sell oil to strengthen the shah, whose government the U.S. had just installed. So Exxon, as the main U.S. buyer from both countries, went out to resolve the Saudi problem. Either Exxon had become an arm of the State Department, or vice versa.

Exxon told King Saud that it had been asked by the U.S. government to buy Iranian oil in order to promote Iranian political stability, Page testified. Exxon told the king "that we weren't doing this because we wanted more oil . . . because we had adequate oil in the Aramco concession [Saudi Arabia], but we were doing it as a political matter at the request of our government."

The king graciously agreed to give up expanding his oil sales for awhile, and to okay the forthcoming Iranian deal. After all, who knew when he might need the CIA to put *him* back on *his* throne. In the State Department's eyes, all the anti-communist governments would be strengthened, and never mind the American motorist. The oil output in the Arabian Gulf area would be coordinated by Big Oil.

Then the State Department sought to determine who else besides Exxon would be allowed to get the Iranian oil. As might be expected, it stuck with the majors that didn't really need the extra supply (by Exxon's own testimony, quoted above), and shut out the independents who thirsted for it. This was all done after consultation with Britain and France to make sure our allies also were spared the risks of a competitive market.

The U.S. government hired the accounting firm of Price Waterhouse & Company to study applications from the various free enterprises that were seeking government permission to buy Iranian oil. Watson Snyder, a petroleum specialist at the antitrust division of the Justice Department (whose case against the majors had just been surrendered on orders of President Eisenhower), immediately objected.

Snyder noted in a memo to superiors that Price Waterhouse was accountant for "most of the participants in the consortium. All through the documentary material delivered by the five defendants in the cartel [antitrust] case, you will find that Price Waterhouse & Company is the medium through which all the accounting is done for the participants in the various illegal arrangements. . . . Whenever either the domestic or foreign branches of the petroleum industry carry out any joint operations Price Waterhouse is chosen to do the accounting. . . . It would appear that the alleged activities of Price Waterhouse & Company in choosing additional American participants may well be in violation of the antitrust laws."*

*Thanks to John M. Blair, author of *Control of Oil* for gathering these quotes. I have verified them from the record, and found them a fair representation of evidence gathered at the Senate hearings.

Price Waterhouse approved eleven applicants who were not among the majors. These companies, though called independents, included Cities Service, Getty, and Standard Oil of Ohio (another Rockefeller offshoot). In other words, they were hardly mom-and-pop operations. Among them, they said they could handle 36 percent of Iran's oil. The State Department allowed them a combined total of 5 percent, on condition that they banded together as a newly formed combination called Iricon.

The rest of the oil went this way: British Petroleum got 40 percent, because, according to the testimony of Exxon vice-president Page, "as I understand it, the 40 percent for BP was the maximum that would be politically allowable within Iran." Shell, the other big shareholder in the original Anglo-Iranian company, got 14 percent. And 7 percent each went to Exxon and Mobil (the two Rockefeller offshoots that had held exclusive buying rights from Anglo-Iranian), and to Standard Oil of California (another Rockefeller offshoot), Texaco, and Gulf. These latter three were allowed in because they were part of the Saudi Arabian cartel. Since that cartel's output would be restricted, its members were allowed into Iran, partly to compensate them, but also, probably, to give them a stake in the effort to coordinate the oil flow. A French company got the remaining 6 percent of the new Iranian arrangement.

During World War II, the Senate committee investigating graft in military procurement, whose respected work boosted the career of its chairman, Harry Truman, had accused Exxon of what Truman called treasonable behavior. Since long before the war, Exxon had promised the German company of I. G. Farben that it wouldn't compete in rubber, and Farben had promised Exxon that it wouldn't compete in oil; they agreed to share information. This sharing continued after the German invasion of Europe. The Truman committee said Exxon had provided Hitler with valuable data on how to manufacture fuel, and deprived the U.S. of research into synthetic rubber.

Texaco had secretly delivered oil to Franco's forces during the Spanish Civil War, using devious routes through Belgium and Italy. President Roosevelt, finding out about it, condemned the shipments as a violation of the Neutrality Act (though Texaco wasn't prosecuted). Texaco also sent oil to Hitler after the invasion of Europe, skirting a British blockade. Later, units of Texaco (and Mobil, and California Standard) played a part in skirting the U.S. embargo on oil sales to the outlaw white-run government of Rhodesia.

The point is that the major oil companies did not appear to be particularly reliable as agents of U.S. government policy. To the contrary, the government seemed to be acting as the agent of oil company policy.

And so it was that the five major U.S. oil companies (Exxon, Mobil, Standard of California, Texaco, and Gulf) that had previously combined to monopolize oil from Iran, Saudi Arabia, and Kuwait, were specifically assigned by the State Department to do so again. Although competitors were restricted to a token 5 percent of Iran's oil output, a small fraction of what they wanted, the majors got a total of 35 percent, even though it was publicly admitted that they didn't need it.

Why? According to Page of Exxon, "They were selected by the State Department on the basis they were the five companies, and the only five American, that could provide [retail sales] outlets in the foreign area." Since this was not helping the U.S. consumer, apparently it was done to help the shah of Iran—and the big oil companies.

And why did the independents meekly settle for their assigned 5 percent? The State Department had orchestrated them wonderfully on behalf of the majors; Snyder, the Justice Department's antitrust man, said one independent had told him the secretary of state had promised the 5 percent only if "prior to the setting up of the consortium he would have no dealings with the Iranian government directly and... would not be a party to purchasing any Iranian oil whatsoever." In other words, anybody who tried to do any free market negotiating on his own would be shut out entirely from Iran by the secretary of state, John Foster Dulles, who was barely a year out of his private job as lawyer for the major oil companies.

Why did the State Department agree to let any independents in at all? Said Exxon's Page, "I don't know the reason for it but they had a feeling, well, 'Because people were always yacking about it we had better put some independents in there.'"

"Window dressing?" Senator Frank Church of Idaho asked him.

"That's right," Page said.

Not until more than a decade later did some independent companies crack the monoploy, thanks to burgeoning new fields in Libya. The Libyan king didn't want to be tied down to dealing with the major companies. The result—at least until the State Department got back involved—was price competition that lowered gasoline prices in the U.S. in the late 1960s, and cut profit margins of the major oil companies.

John Blair, in *Control of Oil*, comments, "The subsequent success of the independents in Libya demonstrated what must have been realized at the time [of the Iranian apportionment]: that an independent wholly lacking in established market positions can penetrate world markets very rapidly if it is willing to cut prices. An apprehension that with a greater share of Iranian output the independents might do just that seems implicit in [Exxon executive] Page's remark[s]."

On August 5, 1954, Iran signed a contract with the eight oil companies that the United States, Britain, and France had selected. The companies would operate the old Anglo-Iranian concession for twenty-five years, with a fifteen-year option after that. The contract did provide for a fifty-fifty profit split, which Anglo-Iranian had refused to agree to when Mossadegh had requested it. But the contract also provided that Anglo-Iranian would be paid $70 million in compensation.

IN 1979, another former CIA operative came out of the closet with his memoirs. He was Kermit Roosevelt, grandson of President Theodore Roo-

sevelt, and cousin of Theodore Roosevelt IV, the Lehman Brothers banker
who attended the Zaire meeting at the St. Regis Hotel. Kermit, the spook,
not only helped stage the 1953 coup in Iran, but stuck around to help run
the country later, working as a military aircraft salesman for Northrop Corporation.

His simultaneous ties with Northrop and the CIA were disclosed by the
1975 Senate investigation into illegal payments by multinational corporations.
Plenty of evidence was introduced that he still talked to the agency. *He* said
he had retired from it, but, as will be seen, the man lies a lot (in the service
of his country, of course). Quite possibly, Roosevelt had retired from the
CIA, but continued to do contract work for it, either in exchange for pay,
or with the understanding that the CIA would provide Roosevelt enough
information or government influence to guarantee that he would earn a good
income from Northrop.

When you're selling state-of-the-art weapons to foreign armies, you can
obviously benefit from CIA contacts. The CIA knows what the competition
is selling, and what foreign military plans are. In addition, U.S. government
aid and approval is often necessary for private arms deals. Documents released by the Senate investigating committee show that Roosevelt didn't let
Northrop, or the shah (whose restoration to power Roosevelt directed), forget
his CIA connections. The committee uncovered many questionable foreign
payments, too—including some by Northrop.

Whoever was responsible, private companies or the U.S. government,
plenty of money was passed out in Iran during the shah's time. The Senate
investigation flushed out news that Northrop had paid $2.1 million in "com-
missions" on sales of its F-5 aircraft, and Grumman had paid $24 million
on sales of its F-14s. The shah then made a show of having both companies
remit these amounts to the Iranian treasury (the commissions presumably
had been added to Iran's cost for the aircraft).

The curious thing about these particular commissions is that the sales were
made *through the U.S. government*, which bought the planes from Northrop
and Grumman, and sold them to the government of Iran. Why were commissions paid? No clear answer. There were still other deals in which Textron
Corporation paid $2.9 million and Northrop paid $6 million, much of it to
members of the Iranian armed forces and the royal family, for a telecommunications contract.

All these companies rely for their business on huge contracts with the
U.S. Defense Department. So it would obviously be easy for the government
to arrange to have corporate payments overseas underwritten by American
taxpayers. Domestic contracts that were otherwise legitimate could simply
be padded to contain the payoff money. But there's no proof of it, and the
deals are all shrouded in secrecy.

Lots of former U.S. officials besides Kermit Roosevelt were running
around Iran creating ways for the shah to spend the Iranian people's oil
money other than for the improvement of Iranian life. Admiral Thomas H.

Moorer, a few months after retiring as chairman of the Joint Chiefs of Staff, went to Iran as representative of a ship repair corporation (Stanwich International Corporation) with a large Iranian contract. Four-star general Hamilton Howze, father of the army's air mobility doctrine, signed on after retirement with Textron's Bell Helicopter unit, lecturing Iranian officers (as well as officers of other U.S. allies around the world) on military doctrine and Bell products.

Former members of the U.S. Military Assistance Advisory Group in Iran went to work as corporate salesmen after their retirement: major general Harvey Jablonsky to Northrop, air force major general Harold L. Price to Ford's aerospace subsidiary, and navy captain R. S. Harwood to TRACOR (a high-tech aircraft equipment manufacturer) and Rockwell International Corporation. Richard R. Hallock, who went to Iran representing the Defense Department, decided while there to sign a contract to advise the Iranian government instead, apparently for millions of dollars; he won't talk about it, but his friends say he did this with the blessing of defense secretary James R. Schlesinger. Schlesinger—himself at Lehman Brothers now—at first said Hallock "seems to have violated [my] trust"; later, told that witnesses said he had agreed to the deal, he declined to comment.

MOST of the information in the previous two paragraphs was reported by Barry Rubin, of the Georgetown University Center for Strategic and International Studies, in his book, *Paved With Good Intentions* (Oxford University Press, 1980).* Rubin's is probably the most highly regarded history of U.S.-Iranian relations yet written, and in many ways deservedly so, but it calls for some comment.

Ironically, the overriding flaw in Rubin's book is the way it discounts the role of business, and behind-the-scenes deals, in the formation and execution of U.S. foreign policy. Rubin seems to sincerely believe that foreign policy is the product of diplomats—the State Department bureaucracy. He thoroughly documents diplomatic dealings about Iran, both in Tehran and Washington, going back to the early 1900s. But he ignores other factors, leaving him with an exacting and enlightening view of the hind of the elephant, posing as the whole animal.

For example, Rubin recounts the Mossadegh coup in detail without mentioning a single major U.S. oil company (and only incidentally mentions one U.S. oil company at all). This is a history of U.S.-Iranian relations, and "Exxon" (or "Standard Oil") is not even in the index! Rubin doesn't mention Kermit Roosevelt's connection with Northrop. He presents his list of former U.S. officials doing business in Iran as if these men were obstacles with

*Of course, I have verified what appears here. Rubin did not report Hallock's side of the Schlesinger story.

whom State Department diplomats had to contend in setting U.S. policy. He apparently never considers that these men might *be* U.S. policy, and that to the truly powerful, it is the well-meaning diplomats who are the occasional obstacles.

All this is worth noting because it typifies an attitude common among academic writers and even journalists. The result is a picture of a U.S. foreign policy that is far more idealistic than the real thing. Foreign nationals often see through this veneer quicker than American taxpayers do.

NOW we come to Kermit Roosevelt's 1979 book of memoirs, *Countercoup*, in which he tried to justify the U.S. coup against an allegedly pro-Soviet Mossadegh. As it turned out, however, the book justified nothing, but increased suspicion of the CIA and its attempts to mislead the American taxpayers who foot its bills.

Two months after McGraw-Hill published Roosevelt's memoirs, it withdrew the book from stores because of protests from British Petroleum Company, which is 51 percent owned by the British government, and is the descendant of the old Anglo-Iranian oil consortium. The reason BP protested is that the book said, on page three, that "the original proposal for Ajax [the code name for the coup against Mossadegh] came from the Anglo-Iranian Oil Company." The book went on to say that the company had made the proposal to Roosevelt personally in November 1952, as he passed through London, and that the CIA had an important agent who worked for Anglo-Iranian, now BP.

Suddenly, after the book was recalled, Roosevelt announced that he really hadn't meant any of those things. The real instigator of the coup, he now said, was MI-6, a British intelligence agency so secret that it doesn't like to be talked about. He explained that he had attributed the idea for the coup to MI-6 in his original manuscript, but that he had submitted the manuscript to the CIA for its approval, and the CIA had ordered him to remove all reference to MI-6. So, according to the story Roosevelt was telling after the recall decision, he simply substituted British Petroleum for MI-6 all the way through the manuscript, apparently without asking BP.

Of course, with such a disregard for truth, there is no more reason for believing Roosevelt's later version than for believing his earlier one, or anything else he said, and the book didn't sell very well anyway. Nor can one feel confident about how much the CIA really had to do with the book, or what the book's purposes were.

In *Countercoup*, Roosevelt admitted (actually "boasted" would be a better word for it) that he lied to the shah. He said he made up a cable that President Eisenhower had supposedly sent to the shah in support of the coup, but hadn't. Interestingly, the cable Roosevelt concocted was not unflattering to Roosevelt himself. Among the words Roosevelt put in Eisenhower's mouth were these: "If the Pahlevis and the Roosevelts working together cannot solve this little problem, then there is no hope anywhere."

Roosevelt also told in his book of how he gave Ambassador Henderson a refresher course on how to do his own lying to the Iranian government. He wrote that on August 17, 1953, the day after the failed coup attempt, he told the allegedly confused Henderson to reassure Mossadegh that "Americans do not want to, and will not, get involved in the domestic politics of a foreign country." (How does one deal with such bald lies? The State Department *still* says things almost exactly like that today.)

Right after the successful coup of August 19, Roosevelt wrote that the shah summoned him. "The first words he said were spoken gravely, solemnly," Roosevelt recalled. "'I owe my throne to God, my people, my army—and to you!'" Not a bad introduction for Northrop Corporation—whose name, incidentally, didn't even appear in the index of Roosevelt's memoirs.

At one point, the book offered a photograph purporting to illustrate how the Iranian people felt about the coup. The photo showed a big crowd of banner-carrying demonstrators, and was captioned, "Crowds fill the streets in support of the shah." Under magnification, however, the banners translated into pro-Mossadegh slogans, like "Down with the shah." Some of the demonstrators in the photo were carrying pictures of Joseph Stalin.*

DOCUMENTS filed in federal court in Washington as part of the Securities and Exchange Commission's attempt to enforce the laws against overseas bribery, show that the shah's brother, Prince Abdul Reza, and cabinet ministers in charge of any relevant ministry, would routinely and blatantly shake down U.S. businessmen trying to sell things in Iran.

For example, International Systems & Control Corporation, an engineering and construction firm based in Houston, Texas, was accused by the SEC of making $23 million in "questionable" payments. Max Zier, an official of the firm, had visited Tehran in 1973. Afterward, he wrote his boss, A. M. Hurter, "There is another delicate situation.... Dr. [Max] Mossadeghi [the shah's director of planning and projects] invited me on Monday to his house for dinner, and on this occasion he told me that he is very disappointed about [a pulp and paper mill project] as he was promised by A. M. Hurter personally a payment if the project would be awarded.... I have never been told by A. M. Hurter that such a verbal promise was made."

Hurter shot back that he had indeed promised Mossadeghi $100,000. Not only that, the $100,000 turned out to be peanuts, compared to the $2.5 million paid to an associate of the shah's brother on the award of the same $82.5 million pulp and paper mill contract. A similar 3 percent "commission"

---

*First reported in the *Wall Street Journal* by David Ignatius.

to two Iranian government officials won a $142 million contract for construction of another pulp and paper mill, on which International System's winning bid was $17 million higher than that of a competing company.

Overall, "commissions" amounted to 8½ percent of the contracts for International Systems, documents showed.* The company was also charged with making illegal payoffs in Saudi Arabia, Nicaragua, the Ivory Coast, and Algeria. In a common SEC procedure, the company settled the case by promising never to pay bribes again, without admitting or denying that it had paid any to begin with.

The existence of bribery in Iran no doubt preceded the arrival of Americans. The U.S. can't be blamed for starting it. One can only speculate on whether the democratic changes that the deposed Prime Minister Mossadegh was gradually introducing would have extended to cleaning up the marketplace. But because the U.S. government replaced him, and installed and maintained a government that perfected corruption as an art form, the U.S. government acquired responsibility for the enormous sums being ripped off of U.S. shareholders and Iranian citizens.

In 1973, the U.S. sent an ambassador to Tehran—Richard Helms, just retired as head of the CIA—whose brother—Pearsall, a wealthy businessman living in Geneva—was a sales representative for Western business and negotiated contracts in Iran.† Iran, in turn, sent an ambassador to Washington—Ardeshir Zahedi, who, with his father, had carried out the CIA coup in 1953—who passed out millions of dollars in lavish gifts, from caviar to Persian rugs, to powerful Americans including congressmen and journalists.

With a budget of $25,000 a month just to lavish regular remembrances on journalists and other opinion makers, Zahedi had his chauffeur on the go, delivering $35 magnum bottles of Dom Perignon champagne and 300-gram tins of caviar worth $100 to $200 each. Katherine Koch, then a Washington journalist and now a Foreign Service officer, got hold of Zahedi's gift list, left behind in the embassy after the revolution, and published much of it in *Washington Journalism Review*.

Among those who confessed to Koch that they had accepted the gifts, were Walter Cronkite (cigars and caviar), Howard K. Smith (caviar and champagne), Joseph Kraft (champagne, caviar, perfume; Kraft wrote regularly on Iran), James Reston (caviar), John Chancellor (caviar; he called it

---

*First reported in the *Wall Street Journal* by William M. Carley.

†According to an unpublished interview with Pearsall Helms, done April 12, 1979, by my late *Wall Street Journal* colleague Jerry Landauer. I have called Helms's Geneva residence more than two dozen times to try to confirm Landauer's interview notes; the only two times someone answered, she acknowledged that Helms lived there, but said she did not know how to reach him and declined to take a message for him. Landauer's notes are detailed, and he was as accurate a reporter as ever worked the trade.

"super stuff"), David Brinkley (caviar and champagne), Mike Wallace (caviar, champagne, cigarette box), *60 Minutes* executive director Don Hewitt (caviar, an ashtray), Rowland Evans and Robert Novak (champagne, caviar), Carl Rowan (caviar, whiskey, table gifts), *Time* diplomatic correspondent Strobe Talbott who covered Iran (champagne), *Time* chief of correspondents Murray Gart (cigars, cigarette box), *Washington Star* social columnist Betty Beale (champagne, caviar, cigarette boxes), *Washington Post* editorial page editor Philip Geyelin (caviar, porcelain ashtray), and many others. *Washington Post* and *Newsweek* primary owner Katharine Graham conceded accepting caviar for a while, but said she finally told Zahedi to stop sending it. Barbara Walters reported returning a $6,000 diamond watch.

Some twenty-three reporters and news executives at CBS got gifts, twenty at NBC, eighteen at the *New York Times*, thirteen at ABC, twelve at Time Inc., ten at the *Washington Post*, seven at *Newsweek*, two from each of the major wire services, and many spread around to make a total of 284.

SOME $15 million was spent funding pro-shah demonstrations in the U.S., according to records found in the embassy after the 1979 revolution, and released by the new government. Demonstrators were flown to whatever city was selected for a demonstration, and kept in hotels. As in the case of South Korea and the famous "Koreagate" payoffs of the same time, records showed that much of the money that Zahedi's team was supposed to be distributing to influence people was in fact pocketed by insiders.

Zahedi oversaw an enormous Iranian campaign to influence U.S. opinion. For a gift of $750,000, Iran appeared to win over the prestigious Aspen Institute for Humanistic Studies, which lent its name to a variety of pro-Iran activities. Included was a 1975 conference in Iran of prominent persons from the U.S. and many other countries, all paid for by the shah. Accepting the free trip, though perhaps uninformed of who was really paying, were congressmen, leading academics and businessmen, including the Aspen Institute's chairman, Robert O. Anderson, board chairman and largest shareholder of the Atlantic Richfield Company.

From the proceedings came a book, paid for by Iran and distributed without caveat by the Aspen Institute. It sang the praises of the shah's well-publicized development projects, without revealing how the injection of Westerners and Western ways offended the Islamic traditions of Iranians. There was certainly no warning of the reaction that would explode in 1979. The book's opening was written by Daniel Yankelovich, the pollster, who gushed: "Among nations, human history records relatively few acts of creativity that bring forth a new model of the good society.... I feel we have had the rare privilege this week of catching a glimpse of such an act of creativity in the making."

Yankelovich had been contracted by the Iranian government to poll prominent Americans on their views of the shah. All this happened after the head of Amnesty International had declared that "no country in the world has a worse record in human rights than Iran," and the International Red Cross and other groups had voiced similar sentiments.*

The most blatant use of this kind of influence may have been the hiring of Marion Javits, wife of U.S. senator Jacob K. Javits of New York. Senator Javits was the ranking Republican on the Senate Foreign Relations Committee, and perhaps the leading spokesman in Congress on behalf of Israel and other Jewish issues. For a Moslem state and OPEC member to have put its hooks into him must have seemed a real coup.

Mrs. Javits's acceptance of a $67,500 "public relations" contract was disclosed in 1976 by the *Village Voice*, permitting one of the great page-one newspaper headlines of all time: "Sen. Javits Sleeps With Agent From Iran (See Page 6)." Mrs. Javits promptly resigned, after issuing huffy protestations that "The American public is not yet ready to accept the separate roles of a husband and wife in professional affairs." An associate said she had received only $33,750 of the money due her at the time.

Three years later, after the Iranian revolution, the new Iranian government gave *New York Times* reporter John Kifner, in Tehran, some documents it had uncovered in connection with the hiring of Mrs. Javits.† The documents made clear that her appointment as a public relations consultant was *not* because of her talented way of phrasing press releases.

Mrs. Javits had proposed her hiring in December 1974, and a month later, Prime Minister Amir Abbas Hoveida wrote an advisory to the shah, stating, "The existence of an Iran lobby in the American Congress seems useful.... At the same time, employing the services of a company in which Mrs. Javits has a share, taking into consideration the great influence and possibilities that Senator Javits and his wife have in New York City or Mr. Javits alone has in the American Senate may be a remarkable political opportunity."

The prime minister's aide, who handled the details, wrote, "I think the performance of this plan is advisable even if its only result will be to pour money in the pocket of Mrs. Javits." In another document he stated, "In discussions held with Mrs. Javits and company officials [officials of the public relations company, Ruder & Finn Inc., through which Mrs. Javits was paid] prior to the submission of the contract, the utmost necessity of keeping this cooperation confidential was stated over and over again as the primary condition." The contract was let by Iran Air, rather than the Iranian government, and it was let to Ruder & Finn, rather than to Mrs. Javits, "to have a cover justifying our mutual cooperation." An aide to the shah wrote

---

*Yankelovich, in a telephone interview, declined to comment.

†Kifner evidently satisfied himself of the documents' authenticity, and they weren't challenged on publication.

back that the shah "has stated that because they [the senator and his wife] are Jewish this should be kept confidential."*

Of course, we all know where the money came from to fund all this. During the 1970s, the price of oil went up. From the mid-1950s, the price of Middle Eastern oil had floated between $1.80 and $2.10 a barrel. By 1972, it was up to $2.59, and by 1973, $3.01. In October 1973, just as the oil producing countries were about to meet with the international oil companies to demand still higher prices, there came a war between Israel and two Arab states—Egypt and Syria—that aren't major oil producers.

Either in connection with that war, or with the attempt to increase prices, or, more likely, both, the Islamic oil producers embargoed shipments of oil to the U.S. Because production earlier in the year had far exceeded normal, there should not have been a severe shortage immediately. But there was. Across the United States, many gasoline stations closed, and long, infuriating lines appeared at others. Before supplies were restored, the Organization of Petroleum Exporting Countries (OPEC) decreed a price of $5.11 a barrel, and then, a few months later, $11.65 a barrel. Within a few years the price was around $30.

The embargo, the long gasoline lines that accompanied it, and the general sympathy of the American people toward Israel made it easy to affix blame. Americans concluded that oil prices were soaring because of greedy Arabs. Foreigners. Reinforcing this conclusion was the fact that it also was the more or less official position of the U.S. government's foreign policy apparatus, then under the control of Henry Kissinger.

Somehow the foreign policy establishment was able to have it both ways. Although we were supposed to blame "the Arabs," we were not supposed to blame Saudi Arabia or Iran, because they were important allies in Kissinger's anti-communist design. Never mind that they were the two major oil producers, between them accounting for two-thirds of all Middle Eastern oil. The impression was somehow created that Iran and Saudi Arabia weren't really at fault. They were said to be restraining influences on the really greedy Arabs. At any rate, this was the official, and generally accepted, story.

There were many skeptics, though, and they tended to fall into one of two camps. The theory of the common-man skeptics was that the oil companies were part of a "plot," and had arranged the price rise with the greedy Arabs to create more profits. The theory of the more intellectual skeptics was that the earth was running out of oil, and that the price increases were the product of scarcity.

There is another possible explanation for the price rises, however, which is not really incompatible with the notion of either oil company manipulation

_____

*A spokesman at Ruder & Finn declined to comment. Mrs. Javits's response appears in the text.

or petroleum scarcity. It does, though, shift at least some of the blame away from greedy Arabs, greedy capitalists, and a frugal Mother Nature, and bring the blame back to ourselves, and our government. From what we have seen of the U.S. government's predilection for involving itself in such affairs, one may fairly wonder if the State Department didn't play a greater role in the price explosion than has thus far been made public.

A strong, though not conclusive, case can be made that the oil price rise was a product of U.S. foreign policy. OPEC had been around since 1960, in the same sense that the Iranian constitution had been around since 1906; a long time passed before someone got it into his head to exploit their potential power. Whose idea was it to exploit OPEC? And why did the U.S. and other consuming countries, so determined over many decades to control Middle Eastern oil, suddenly cave in with so little resistance? Surely not because Kissinger was a softy.

Could the oil price explosion have resulted from a plan, conceived or agreed to by the U.S. government, to arm the Islamic oil countries? And to improve their economies, so that these countries—principally Iran and Saudi Arabia—would be strengthened as a bulwark against possible Soviet expansion southward later in the century?

If so, it would mean that foreign-policy makers decided they were so much wiser than the American people that they could make vital decisions and shield those decisions from the democratic process. It would mean that they took it upon themselves to substantially reduce the quality of life in the United States and throw hundreds of thousands of Americans out of work, in order to serve a chancy, almost hypothetical, geopolitical master plan for a region half a world away.

Nevertheless, such a decision would be no more foolish than other decisions that U.S. foreign strategists have made—just grander in scale. Henry Kissinger, who surely would have known of such a plot, or conceived it, denies through spokesmen that it ever was hatched. He may be right, though considering his loyal defense of other government secrets from public scrutiny, his word can hardly remove doubt. (The catalog of deceits presented in Seymour M. Hersh's book *The Price of Power* [Summit Books, 1983] is so thoroughly documented that one wonders how anyone could believe Kissinger about anything anymore.)

The loss of a U.S. citizen's ability to believe his own government officials on such matters is one of the saddest results of the whole anti-communist crusade. In some ways, it is sadder than the loss of life the crusade has cost, because officials who constantly lie for what they see as the greater good create more loss of life, through every war and covert action the country is sucked into. The soaring oil prices of the 1970s certainly cost lives—directly, of those who froze to death for lack of heating oil, and indirectly, in a hundred different ways, as billions of dollars were pulled out of the U.S. economy and shipped to the Middle East, much of it in the form of warplanes.

Oil prices soaked up the dividend that might have come to the U.S. people from the end of the Vietnam war. The ensuing inflation, the severe recession imposed on the country in the early 1980s to stop the inflation, the Reagan budget cuts—to at least some extent, we owe them to the explosion of oil prices.

THE strongest case that the State Department was responsible for the oil price shock was made in the April 15, 1976, issue of *Forbes* magazine. Drawing on extensive interviews and testimony, *Forbes* traced the price rise to a quick series of meetings in January 1971, between the shah of Iran and some State Department representatives. According to *Forbes*, these meetings fundamentally changed the price-setting mechanism for Middle East oil.

The meetings came about because of some price tinkering done a little more than a year earlier when Colonel Muammar al-Qaddafi overthrew Libya's King Idris, who, as previously noted, was a bit of an oil maverick. Libya had come relatively late to oil's big leagues; its discoveries weren't ready for exploitation until the 1960s. By then, the king had seen the power the oil majors had acquired in the other producing countries, and so he signed over 55 percent of the Libyan oil to independents. Qaddafi shared the king's preference for dealing with independent companies as well as with Big Oil, but he wanted to go even further.

As a revolutionary socialist, Qaddafi wanted to introduce price competition to reflect local market conditions. This, of course, shocked all the capitalist oil companies, which naturally believed that oil prices should be controlled at the same level for everyone. Until Qaddafi, the pricing mechanism didn't involve much bargaining. The oil majors just consulted with each other and set prices. When Premier Mossadegh in Iran raised his hand to disagree, we saw what happened.

Qaddafi, however, faced what anybody would have to call an unfair situation. He was locked into the same prices that the Persian Gulf countries were getting. Yet his oil was more valuable to the oil companies. Ever since the Suez Canal was closed in 1967 because of the continuing Israeli-Egyptian hostilities, it had been much cheaper and faster to transport oil to Europe across the Mediterranean from Libya than to transport it all the way around Africa from the Persian Gulf. So Qaddafi declared a 40-cent-a-barrel price increase on Libyan oil to reflect this difference in transportation costs.

At the time, his action seemed a lot less threatening to the major oil companies than Mossadegh's had earlier, for two reasons. First, it was a lot milder than nationalization without compensation. And second, it didn't hit mainly the major oil companies, but their *competition*—the independents. So when Qaddafi raised prices, the majors didn't scream. They may have figured he was actually helping them fight off newcomers in the marketplace. At least they reacted in a manner entirely consistent with this thesis.

Again, these independents, like Amerada Hess and Occidental Petroleum, weren't cottage industries. They could be called "small" only when measured against Exxon and Mobil. But their bigness may have been all the more reason that monopoly oil feared their competition more than it feared Libya's 40-cent price increase. Without the increase, the independents actually had a cost *advantage* over the majors because of shorter-haul transportation.

Independent gasoline chains, underpricing the majors by more than 10 percent a gallon, had been staking out an ever-increasing share of the U.S. market. The majors were forced to give away tableware and drinking glasses with every tankful, and to mount huge advertising campaigns. Said an Exxon document in 1968, "Libyan crude oil production is expected to increase dramatically in the next years." The document gave figures, then said, "This level is sufficient to make Libya the foremost producing country in the Eastern Hemisphere in 1971, displacing Iran to second place and Saudi Arabia to third. In contrast with historical ownership patterns in North Africa and the Middle East, the bulk of the new increments . . . will be produced by companies considered 'newcomers' to the international oil trade without established captive outlets and without a significant stake in the Middle East. Since Libyan oil is favorably situated with respect to the major European markets and has desirable low sulfur qualities, relatively little difficulty in capturing third-party markets is expected."*

The main Libyan independent was Occidental Petroleum, and it wanted to fight Qaddafi's 40-cent price increase. So Occidental went to Exxon and asked for this guarantee: if Occidental stood up to Qaddafi and refused to pay, Exxon would supply Occidental with Mideast oil from other sources at cost until the Libyan situation was resolved. But Exxon refused. So Occidental caved in and paid Qaddafi's price.

But Exxon apparently misjudged the reaction of the other oil countries. Libya was run by determined revolutionaries who were willing to sacrifice current oil income in order to redesign their country's economy. The shah of Iran, on the other hand, was not one inclined toward sacrifice. He always felt short of cash for some project or other, and now he wanted his own 40 cents a barrel. Much the same was true in Saudi Arabia.

At this point, the majors saw that they might get whipsawed as each country fought them for a steadily escalating price advantage. Now they decided they would have to negotiate a single price with all the oil producing countries. So they came to the U.S. government for the help they had always enjoyed in the past. Senior executives from Exxon and British Petroleum were going to Iran to negotiate, and the companies wanted a special envoy from President Nixon to visit the shah a few days before. The envoy would let the shah know that the U.S. government was behind the oil majors in seeking an all-Middle East contract that would prevent further price whipsawing. Nixon agreed to send an envoy.

But, according to *Forbes*, the companies were surprised when the envoy

*Blair, *Control of Oil*.

turned out to be John Irwin, a Wall Street lawyer with no oil experience, but who had served as an official with the Defense Department. And *Forbes* reported that the companies were even more surprised at what Irwin and the U.S. ambassador to Iran, Douglas MacArthur (the general's son), told the shah. As Irwin later testified, they said "that the U.S. government was not in the oil business and did not intend to become involved in the details of the producing countries' negotiations with the oil companies."*

Now *there* was a change in policy! And Irwin went on, "I stressed, *not* the negotiations, but the strategic and economic impact on the Free World— of which they [the Iranians] were a part—that a cut or halt in production would have."

That told the oil producing countries that they could get away with whipsawing and price increases, if they just kept the oil flowing. So the shah refused the Exxon-BP deal. Prices soared. The oil companies say they tried to hold the price down, but couldn't get the U.S. government to help.

Now, for the oil companies to seek lower prices would be another first. For years they had plotted to keep prices high. Certainly, the companies weren't *hurt* by the increase. Their main assets were vast underground pools of oil, whose value shot up tenfold in a few years. As the cost of oil for their refineries mounted, the companies simply raised the price of gasoline and heating oil to consumers.

Nevertheless, there *is* solid evidence that the State Department acted to raise prices independently of Big Oil. "Why?" asked *Forbes*. "Why did the U.S. so readily surrender to OPEC? . . . It is hard to avoid the conclusion that the State Department was, in effect, sacrificing economics to politics. This is not to say that . . . the State Department wanted to see oil go to $10 a barrel. But they [the policymakers] were quite prepared to have U.S. motorists and businessmen—and those of the rest of the world—pay a bit more for oil in order to help the shah of Iran and the Saudis. . . . The State Department realized full well that they could not persuade Congress to tax Americans for that purpose. So they did it by the back door."

IN fact, the U.S. had been doing exactly that for years, although on a much smaller scale. Since 1950, the major oil companies had been allowed a special gimmick on their federal income taxes. They could report their *royalty* payments to Middle Eastern governments—the fees they paid for the oil they pumped—as if the royalties were *tax* payments. The difference is that royalty payments are normally deducted from reportable income as a business expense (they are on oil pumped in the U.S., for example), while foreign tax payments count as a dollar-for-dollar offset, or credit, toward payment of

*U.S. Senate Foreign Relations Committee, Subcommittee on Multinational Corporations, 1975.

U.S. taxes. Thus the tax saving is effectively doubled, meaning that 50 percent of the royalties the oil companies were paying in the Middle East were coming out of the U.S. Treasury. In one sense, this was a gift to the oil companies. But the money was winding up in Iran and Saudi Arabia.

This was still peanuts, however—a mere $150 million or $200 million a year. The oil price jump of the early 1970s converted far more of the American workingman's cash into rials. It allowed our Persian Gulf friends to expand their military spending from under $800 million a year to more than $4 billion by 1975.

The gas price pill was sweetened somewhat, because most of these arms were bought from the U.S., and billions more petrodollars were spent with U.S. companies to work on modernization projects in the Middle East. The money, however, tended to flow to companies that hired U.S. operatives like Kermit Roosevelt, or string-pullers like David Morse.

In Saudia Arabia, one project alone, a whole new city, was worth $50 billion to Bechtel Corporation, which hired as its top corporate officers George P. Shultz, Nixon's director of the Office of Management and Budget and later Treasury secretary, and Caspar W. Weinberger, Nixon's secretary of health, education, and welfare. After a stint at Bechtel, they attained operating control of U.S. foreign policy as secretaries of state and defense in the Reagan administration. Under Reagan, it was widely reported, they swung U.S. policy away from Israel and toward the Arabs in the dispute over Palestine. But in all the news reports, it was rarely mentioned that every time an American fills his gas tank he makes a substantial indirect contribution to the Bechtel Corporation, a family-owned construction and engineering concern that girdles the globe from a base in San Francisco. The Bechtels are beginning to look like the Rockefellers of the 1980s.

For purposes of helping the overall U.S. economy, the petromoney was miserably spent. If the U.S. government was going to tax its citizens so much a gallon to stimulate U.S. industry, better that the blue-collar jobs go to Americans, not Saudis and Iranians. Better that the roads, schools, sewer plants, and new cities that resulted be available over here for our own use.

Perhaps it's fortunate enough that the guns, planes, and other military equipment the Saudis and Iranians bought haven't been used on Americans yet (though it isn't out of the question that they might be). The weapons haven't been used against the Soviet Union, either. They have been used, though—against the Iranian people, among others, both before and after the Khomeini revolution.

THE anti-American hostility of the Khomeini revolution really isn't so hard to understand. The U.S. struggled, really bent over backward, to create this anti-American hostility, right up to and through the hostage crisis that captured the attention of the U.S. public in 1979 and 1980, and maybe turned the presidential election that year. The presence of the shah in the United States after his people had thrown him out was an incredible slap in their faces—a defiant rejection of any remorse for what we'd done. David Rockefeller and Henry Kissinger, who had guided U.S. policy toward Iran for many years, were still messing up.

President Carter stated in his memoirs that he wasn't swayed by the continual pleadings of Rockefeller and Kissinger that the shah should be welcomed to the U.S. But the medical excuses Carter offers are lame. The United States's humanitarian obligations to help the shah with his cancer problem were questionable anyway—he had lied to the U.S. about the course of his disease, which contributed to our unpreparedness for his downfall. And under any circumstances, humanitarian obligations could have been met by shipping treatment machinery or medical expertise to his bedside, without intervening in Iranian affairs by harboring him.

Plenty of hospitality was offered to the shah by Egypt, Mexico, and other places, until the U.S. began to waver on his persistent requests to come here. In the long run, it probably would have been cheaper to have picked up the whole Sloan-Kettering cancer center (Laurence Rockefeller, chairman) right off East 68th Street and flown it to Cairo than to have touched off the ordeal that was caused by flying the shah to Sloan-Kettering in New York.

Most likely, despite protestations, the Kissinger entreaties affected Carter deeply. The president faced a reelection campaign the next year, and there was a growing likelihood that his opposition would come from Ronald Reagan, the farthest right of all the candidates. Carter simply couldn't afford to have a respected alleged moderate like Kissinger attacking him for deserting an ally. To rebuff an attack from further right, Carter had to usurp the kind of moderation that Kissinger represented. And so his whole administration turned to occupy the mainstream Republican position.

Two weeks after the hostages were taken, while their fate was still being determined day to day without a fixed scenario, the Chase Manhattan Bank (David Rockefeller, chairman) called in a $500 million loan to Iran. Chase asserted that Iran had defaulted on the interest. The reason for the default, though, was that Carter had frozen Iran's assets in the U.S. a week earlier. There is convincing evidence that Iran tried in good faith to pay the interest, but couldn't move the money.

But based on this, Chase and other banks foreclosed on all kinds of Iranian holdings in the U.S. and Europe. The governor of the Iranian Central Bank, Ali Nobari, launched a fusillade of public charges against Chase Manhattan, and, by implication, the U.S. Nobari said that Chase had moved the shah's billions out of Iran for him, and that it had swindled Iran on interest payments for many years. The truthfulness of these charges can't be weighed from evidence now available. But in calling the Iranian loan, Chase certainly worked squarely against the interest of the American people, which was to defuse the hostilities.

By all available accounts, the hostage-taking wasn't something planned by Khomeini, his authorities, or anyone else. It was, in fact, an unexpected tool of surprising potency, used by a more radical faction to take power from a more moderate faction. At the time of the hostage seizure, the Khomeini government had been moving rationally toward rapprochement with the U.S.

The original attack on the U.S. embassy, which had been the source of so many of Iran's ills, was made by radicals who opposed this rapprochement. They sought publicity, and they also wanted information from the incriminating documents they were sure must be inside (and were). Once the hostages were in hand, though, the radicals were simply too caught up in their own success to let go. All Iran suddenly loved them.

According to L. Bruce Laingen, the chargé d'affaires at the embassy at the time, "their action had so dramatically captured the support of the masses in the streets that their backers among the revolutionary clergy saw and effectively seized that opportunity to use the affair to achieve the restructuring of political power that had long been their purpose."

The faction that lost out was headed by Mehdi Bazargan, who had been Khomeini's choice for prime minister. Only a few days before the hostage seizure, Bazargan had met quietly with White House national security advisor Zbigniew Brzezinski. Tensions were easing. If we hadn't turned Iran into a nation of rabid anti-Americans, the whole course of the Iranian and Afghan revolutions might have been changed, and the U.S. (to say nothing of Iran and Afghanistan) would have been better off for it.

Iranian anti-Americanism was generated not only by the violent overthrow of the Iranian government and the brutalization of its people. It was generated also by the whole well-intentioned process of shoving Western goods and values into Iran faster than the people desired them. American planners never stopped to observe the effect of Islamic teachings.

Moslems haven't rationalized their religion the way most Christians have rationalized their Bible. For example, few U.S. policymakers who register themselves Christians really believe in responding to attack by turning the other cheek. Few believe in foregoing wealth because it would be easier for a camel to fit through the eye of a needle than for a rich man to enter the kingdom of heaven.

Islam, however, often means what it says about faith in the Koran being paramount. In many Moslem countries, five times a day, most people from all social strata stop whatever they are doing, no matter how inconvenient it is to themselves or others, to keep that faith. Laborers drop their shovels, drivers halt their taxis in midtrip, bankers clear their offices of borrowing businessmen. They wash their hands and feet (even in drought areas, they will sprinkle a few token drops of water on them), spread a prayer rug and repeatedly get down on their knees, bowing and scraping in a ritual lasting several minutes. The faith is kept. Whole busloads of Moslems will sit waiting for one empty seat to fill before leaving; if Allah did not send that last passenger, Allah did not intend the bus to go. (The Hausa-Fulani of West Africa tend to be the most observant, the Moslems of the Middle East and East Asia somewhat less, and the Moslems of North Africa least of all.)

All the construction crews and modernization programs that were sent to Iran struck the U.S. as the essence of progress. But the reaction against them in Iran was quite like the reaction that occurred in northern Nigeria against similar progress. Devout Moslems do not believe that progress comes from infidels. The infidel Ibos were slaughtered as if they had no human worth.

In Nigeria, at least, the United States stayed out, except to provide humanitarian relief to the starving and speak up for justice. In Iran, we confused the wants of a corrupt shah with the wishes of a people that never elected him, and we intervened in many violent ways on his behalf.

Today, in Saudi Arabia, with apparently less violence but no less single-mindedness, we are again acting as if the wants of a corrupt king are the same as the wishes of his people. Do we know?* If it is an assumption, it is a dangerous one to make in handling our last Middle Eastern oil card. It risks what needn't be risked. The only way we can lose access to Saudi oil is by creating enmity among people who would otherwise have no higher economic goal than to sell their oil to a customer like the United States.

EVIDENCE continues to surface that the U.S. government has conspired to inflate domestic fuel prices to support dubious anti-communist potentates overseas—in effect, robbing petrol-buyers to pay pols. By 1983, U.S. policy had perched itself so high on the scaffolding of this geopolitical design that getting down without falling appeared quite a challenge.

When the heads of OPEC met in Geneva in January 1983, Youssef M. Ibrahim brilliantly set forth for readers of the *Wall Street Journal* the ridiculous plight of U.S. policy. OPEC was finally on the ropes, where everyone thought the U.S. wanted it. The worldwide recession had caused an oil glut. Production had fallen from 31 million barrels a day a few years earlier to only 18 million barrels, and still there was too much oil for available customers. What a chance to bust the trust and get lower prices!

Except that the U.S. was encouraging just the opposite, and not because of any secret collusion this time. After the prices skyrocketed, the Western banks—and Chase Manhattan was only one of them—became flush with oil money and started making foreign loans. Many loans were to countries like Zaire, Brazil, and Costa Rica, which import oil, and would benefit from a decline in prices. But even bigger loans were made to countries like Mexico, Venezuela, Nigeria, and Indonesia, which looked forward to a building bonanza based on $34-a-barrel oil. If the price fell, these countries would be faced with default. This would not only cut off their credit and throw

*The author has not been there.

their economies into panic; it would also cause huge losses to the banks.

Enough to threaten their solvency? That hasn't been demonstrated. Nor do we know exactly what will happen if a few big banks do declare bankruptcy. Even many conservatives* argue that if a bank's stockholders and officers take a financial bath because of bad loans, they may have had it coming. But to the extent the bath spills over into the general economy, it could be a lot worse than gas lines.

Millions of Americans have accounts in these banks. They also have a compact with each other, through the Federal Deposit Insurance Corporation, to pay whatever taxes are necessary to protect the accounts. For purposes of this deposit insurance, the failure of one big bank might be the equivalent of a flood in one city. The bankruptcy of all the major banks might be the economic equivalent of a national nuclear attack. Almost everyone would be a casualty, and there would be no one to turn to for help. We'd all be broke and starting over.

There has been no demonstration that things could get that bad. But U.S. policy has permitted the threat. Much of the threat comes from the kind of lend-and-spend interventionism that occurred in Zaire and other African countries. And much of it comes from the oil policy. According to Ibrahim's report at the time of the January 1983 OPEC meeting, "Most bankers have lent money to countries on both sides of the situation [importers and exporters of oil], and, along with most nonbank economists, think that the international financial system would be ill-served by a drastic slide in prices."

The report quotes Gary Smeal, vice-president and economist at Chemical Bank in New York, the country's sixth largest, saying, "Given where we are today, I don't want to see a drop in oil prices. The benefits would be spread so thin that you probably wouldn't notice them right away. And the negative consequence would be immediate and real and put the financial system in a more precarious situation than it already is."

This has nothing to do with conservation. If oil needs to be conserved, then taxes and other incentives can be created to inspire the conservation, without turning billions of U.S. dollars over to foreign governments that rarely represent their own people.

For a mighty nation that imports oil to support higher oil prices as a matter of policy is definitional lunacy.

THE Iranian people were not the only ones to suffer under the armed might that the U.S. supplied to the shah. These weapons, and the Iranians whom the U.S. trained to fly them and fire them, were responsible for a very bloody war fought from 1973 to 1977 against the people of Baluchistan.

Now you remember Baluchistan. That is the Pakistani province that lies

*The *Wall Street Journal* editorial page, for example.

between Afghanistan and the Arabian Sea, near the Strait of Hormuz. Baluchistan is where the U.S. suddenly discovered it needed friends after the Soviets occupied Afghanistan in 1980. And what had the U.S. been doing to the Baluchs to earn their friendship? Killing them.

Of course, most people in the United States had never heard of Baluchistan, and meant the Baluchs no harm. Most Americans had no idea, and don't to this day, that they were paying extra on their federal income taxes and gasoline and heating oil bills in order to finance a high-tech air war that wiped out mountain villages and nomad caravans. But they were. The Baluchs' transgression was that they had resisted the rule of foreign dictators. And they knew very well that the war machine arrayed to suppress them wasn't put together in Karachi. It was American.

Baluchistan, the province, is not a natural political entity. Like the boundaries of many African countries, the boundaries between Afghanistan and Pakistan divide true nations rather than define them. This is because the nineteenth-century British armies that were sent out to conquer southwest Asia failed to complete their task. Boundaries fell at the line of their defeat.

So the Baluch people wound up part in Afghanistan, part in Pakistan, and part in southeastern Iran (which is one reason the shah wanted to help Pakistan suppress the Baluchs' drive for autonomy). The neighboring Pashtun people are part in Afghanistan, and part in the Pakistani North West Frontier Province (which they dominate). And in the province of Baluchistan, there are almost as many Pashtuns as there are Baluchs. Moreover, many Baluchs and Pashtuns travel around in tents and try to evade the efforts of governments to enforce any international boundaries at all.

At least twice since Pakistan became independent in 1947, the tribes have rebelled violently: once in 1962, and most recently from 1973 to 1977. The second rebellion stopped only after the overthrow of Pakistani president Zulfikar Ali Bhutto, who had replaced Baluchistan's elected government with his own appointees. Bhutto was overthrown, and executed, by the military government of General Zia ul-Haq. Zia promised to restore provincial autonomy and provide free elections for all of Pakistan. Six years later, at this writing, neither promise has been fulfilled.

The people of Baluchistan complain, with a justification that is obvious to any visitor, that Pakistan's development funds have been monopolized by the two more populous eastern provinces of Sindh and Punjab. The Baluchs complain that the army running Baluchistan under martial law is almost entirely from the Punjab. They say that not a single senior officer is Baluch. Baluchs are barred from teaching and most other prized jobs in government.

One articulate young man with a graduate degree in political science from the University of Karachi was running his father's farm because of the barrier against Baluchs in teaching. "I am on the provincial blacklist now just for walking with you," he told an American reporter. "They are watching. They will question me about this, but I can't get a government job anyway."

Indeed, for the reporter, entering Baluchistan was almost like entering Soviet-occupied Afghanistan. People he talked to were followed and constantly questioned and intimidated by authorities. Others were afraid to talk at all.

THERE'S no doubt the Soviets are interested in Baluchistan, though the Afghan resistance may have cooled their ardor. The interest was spelled out clearly by an Afghan Communist official in 1980. "It will take five years to give independence to those people in Pakistan who are trying for their self-determination," he declared. "They are struggling for their independence and it is very near. If the Iran revolution succeeds and our revolution succeeds in the next two years, then those people of Baluchistan and Pashtunistan will succeed. This border [with Pakistan], you cannot imagine that it is a border. It isn't a border."

The unintended but inevitable by-product of U.S. foreign policy over the previous decade—the 1970s—had been to soften natural resistance to this communist ambition.

Sher Mohammed Marri is a big man with a red mustache, a huge, bushy beard, and a turban like a bulging crown. He is number two chief among the Marri, probably the largest of about a dozen Baluch tribes. The number one chief is in London, purportedly getting prolonged medical care, but by general belief, just avoiding Pakistani jails.

"We are a colony," says Sher Mohammed. "We hear about freedom and Islam and democracy and Pakistan, and we don't know how to deal with it. This is our own country, and we are treated like a colony." Sher Mohammed sits in a courtyard in the village of Sibi, 100 bumpy miles through the Bolan Pass from Quetta, the provincial capital. "For thirty-two years I have been fighting for national identity," he says. "It used to be the crown versus Sher Mohammed Marri. Now it is the state versus Sher Mohammed Marri. That is the only difference. The crown has become the state."

Sher Mohammed's parents were sent to prison in India around the time of World War I for speaking out against the British. Sher Mohammed says he was born on a train taking them back to Pakistan. His father died soon afterward. Sher Mohammed himself spent five years in jail during the Baluch uprising of the 1970s. Many people say he went to school for awhile in the Soviet Union many years ago; he denies this, but says he "can't remember" where he did go to school.

If the U.S. gets into another antiguerrilla war in Baluchistan, Sher Mohammed will probably be the enemy again, as he was the last time. He talks a lot in Marxist terms, though they don't mean the same thing in Baluchistan. "In most of the area we have a primitive socialism, not a scientific socialism," he says of the Marri. "Seventy-five percent of the land belongs to the whole Marri tribe. Every male, regardless of age, even a small boy of two months, has a share, and when he dies his share goes to the whole tribe."

Now, he says, the government is "pushing us toward feudalism. They are trying to make this mineral wealth into feudal property [by putting it into private ownership]. If they can do that, then they can acquire it. Excuse me, but I think that your Carter and your Nixon and your Johnson, they are trying to buy the whole world and take it away from the people."

What does he think of the Russians in Afghanistan? "What did you do in Vietnam?" he replies. "What did you do in Cambodia?" He laughs. "Now the imperialist is the defender of the world."

As the hours go by, the scrutiny of the government becomes more obvious. Three different security agencies stop by to ask Sher Mohammed or a visiting reporter what is going on. The friend who owns the house is called to the police station for questioning. Bands of secret and not so secret police lurk outside the courtyard gates, and follow Sher Mohammed and the reporter wherever they go.

If Sher Mohammed were running Baluchistan, he says, his program would be, in order of priority: to install the Baluchi language in place of Urdu in the schools, to distribute all land and mineral wealth to the Baluch tribe communally, and to send all the Pashtuns back to the North West Frontier Province. "They have their own land, why they want to work here?" Sher Mohammed says. "I have my own land, why I work there? There would be four provinces in Pakistan and each would live in peace."

Whatever you call this philosophy, it isn't Marxism. Is it revolutionary? "For thirty-three years, what have I done to break up Pakistan?" says Sher Mohammed. "But if every government, they just beat and beat and beat on Baluchs, Baluchs will have to go to other friends or run away. They [the Pakistani government] do not know our people, they do not know our language, they do not know our customs."

The people around Sher Mohammed listen to him with respect. One of them offers his own opinion. "This revolution talk is for the money," he says. "They [the Pakistani government] want to get Saudi Arabian and American money."

AHMAD is a well-to-do young Baluch professional who, like many of his friends, served several years in prison during the 1970s uprising. "The jail is not over with," he says. "The martial law isn't just for us [in Baluchistan] now, but for all Pakistan. Political statements are banned. If we violate that we can be brought before a military court."

The last time Ahmad went to jail, he was bound by the hands and suspended from the ceiling for several days. Others, he says, were beaten, subjected to electric shock, and sometimes killed. Apparently, such tactics stopped after General Zia took over the government. Now house arrest is used where possible in political cases, although Ahmad says he knows ten people who are in jail for shouting political slogans.

Back in 1973, Ahmad was accused of "indulging in antigovernment activities." "They didn't say what activities," he says. "They never tried me. They just understood that if I am out of jail I would have convinced the majority of the masses to create certain troubles for them."

In fact, it was the arrest of Ahmad and other leaders of Baluchistan's political parties that touched off the rebellion, several months after the elected provincial government had been removed by the late President Bhutto. The rebellion began with guerrilla-style attacks on trucks and government soldiers, much as is happening in Afghanistan now. It finished with fiery attacks by fighter-bombers and helicopter gunships, much as is happening in Afghanistan now, except that these were U.S. aircraft flown by Iranian pilots.

"People are asking why [we rebelled]," Ahmad says. "Whether we were some sort of Marxist regime, some sort of independence movement. These are things I deny. It was only that the people voted for us, and this vote was dishonored. The only purpose was restoration of democracy here." He says Bhutto created the idea that the rebels were Marxist secessionists in order to get money and arms from Iran and the United States; it worked.

What do Ahmad and his friends really want? "We want development in this area. We want roads and schools and industrialization and literacy. There is marble mined here, but no carving; the marble is taken to Karachi for work. There's [natural] gas in Baluchistan. The pipeline takes it elsewhere and it comes back to Quetta [in Baluchistan] on a truck in cylinders. If there is literacy and economic development, then tribalism itself will vanish."

A university-educated Baluch who couldn't get a job in the government-dominated economy was helping a reporter check prices in a Baluchistan bazaar. There is no such thing as a free market here, although that is what the U.S. contends it is protecting when it arms Pakistan (and formerly Iran) to repress the Baluchs. The prices of staples throughout Pakistan are fixed by the military government, which means that important goods often aren't available except on the black market, at prices much higher than those the government decrees.

In one store, the reporter was ticking off goods that couldn't be purchased legally. Having covered sugar and flour, he asked what else wasn't available. The shopkeeper said something in Baluchi, and he and the interpreter broke out laughing. What was the joke?

"He said, 'Freedom,'" the interpreter explained. "Freedom to speak, freedom to act, freedom to earn."

BY what rationality did the United States help put down the Baluch revolution? By what rationality did it arm and train Iran and Pakistan, two nations that practice the antithesis not only of civil liberties but of *free enterprise*—everything the U.S. is supposed to stand for? How do we expect the Baluchs now to be a bulwark against the approaching Soviet army, which at least purports to offer them what they want—freedom, democracy, and independence—the very things that our own military power quite certainly has been denying them?

Of course, the U.S. didn't provide that might for the purpose of repressing Baluchs. But anyone who understood the situation—as opposed to the global geopolitical strategists who make policy—could have seen that repressing Baluchs, and other minority peoples, was the primary way the arms were going to be used. All those years we were working against the Baluchs' best interests, we were also working against our own.

CHAPTER TWELVE

TAR BABY WARS: THE RUSSIANS IN AFGHANISTAN

========================YOU LEAVE the two-lane tarmac somewhere in western Afghanistan, and slog several miles down a muddy, rutted dirt road toward the village of some newly made friends. You climb to the top of a 3-foot mud wall, and watch carefully where you jump on the other side— there are scattered piles of something you don't want to jump into. Like many such piles in Afghanistan, they were left by two-, as well as four-legged, animals.

According to the United Nations, there isn't a single sanitary sewerage system in the country, not even in the capital of Kabul, where open sewers follow the sidewalks, as they do in many African capitals.

In the village, two dozen farmers and some donkeys crowd around a reporter and his interpreter and the two villagers who brought them. Questions are asked and everyone shouts answers at once. Obviously, these farmers are filled with emotion and impatient to express it.

The mullah, the village preacher, steps forward and the others hush. He speaks for them. His black beard aquiver, he says it is by his command that the others have gone to their roofs every night since the Soviet invasion and chanted the name of Allah. Such is the teaching of his religion. Then he shouts, "I want to tell to the Russian people, they don't come to my house, they don't come to my mosque, they don't come to my country. If the Russian people don't come here, I have no business with them. If they do, I fight them to the last drop of blood."

*   *   *

AT a large and beautifully ornate tiled mosque in one of Afghanistan's large cities, another black-bearded mullah, a major religious leader, squats to talk with an American reporter and a British colleague who speaks Farsi. The mullah nervously eyes the Afghan military officers nearby, who are eyeing him. In the background, hundreds are filing into and out of the mosque for evening prayers.

What does the mullah think of the Russians? "Nobody likes the Russians," he whispers. The government? He mumbles. When the first communist regime took over in Afghanistan in April 1978, he says, he had asked the government whether it was closer to Islam or to the Russians. He says he is still waiting for an answer.

Is the city calm? "Not calm, still *shalugh*," he says, using a Farsi word meaning anything from unhappiness to open rioting.

Are the people prepared to fight? "Look at their faces. Can't you see?"

Then he borrows a pen and writes in Farsi on the pad: "Now isn't a good time for your questions."

Is he afraid? "Yes, I'm afraid," he says, returning the pen and pad.

As he draws away, however, he sends another man, more nondescript, over to talk to the reporters in his stead. This man, an airport technician, is rabidly antigovernment and anti-Soviet. He describes recent skirmishes in detail. "If they try to come to the bazaar, we will kill them," he says.

IN a small hotel room in Herat, Hassim sits on his bed. He examines three photographs of a man who wants to be smuggled across the border into Iran. He looks up at the go-between who brought them. He studies the pictures and the go-between some more. He accepts.

In three days, the man in the photographs, who is already on his way to Herat from Kabul, will join four other emigrés and an underground resistance fighter on a minibus to a town on the Afghan side of the border. Anyone else wishing to go to that town will be told that his particular bus is full.

The emigrés will stay in the town one night and all the next day. Then, in darkness, they will be walked to another town, on the Iranian side. Hassim charges 5,010 Afghanis per person (about $116.51 or 70 percent of the average person's annual income in good times). The fee is 5,000 Afghanis. The other 10-Afghani note will be torn in two. Hassim will keep one half. The emigré will keep the other, and send it back when he's in Iran. If the serial numbers match, Hassim will know everything is all right.

Hassim isn't greedy. If an emigré has only 3,000 or 4,000 afs, he'll take it. There are discounts for families. About half the fee goes to confederates in Iran to care for the emigré. Hassim acknowledges that many emigrés are leaving to get jobs in Iran because the living is better. But he likes to think most of them are leaving to join guerrilla bands, and will slip back into and out of Afghanistan, as quietly as they left, to fight the foe.

"I don't know why America, France, and Germany people don't help the Moslem people with tanks," Hassim says. "With just a gun it is very difficult fighting the Russian people."

THIS hostility was not expected by the soldiers who poured south out of the Soviet Union on December 27, 1979, in civilian trucks commandeered for the military so suddenly that you could still see the cotton lint sticking to their slatted sides (cotton is the main crop on the plains north of the Afghan border).

Russians tend to accept Moscow's propaganda as Americans tend to accept Washington's. Both sides raise willing armies of men who are convinced that they know, and can impose, the kind of government that some other country wants to have. The Russians apparently believed that Afghans would receive them as protectors and liberators. Soviet officers wandered into Afghan cities as their men did, in search of recreation, but found instead quick death or narrow escape.

Even after the popular hostility became so evident that the Soviets had to retreat to camp and hunker down, they continued to delude themselves. Who can accept being hated by everybody? Who can accept that everything his leaders have said is wrong? They rationalized that the opposition was coming from a minority of Afghans, who were merely extraordinarily active. The U.S. Army had the same delusion in Vietnam.

The tiny band of native Afghan communists had kept their own, similar delusion alive even long after their coup d'etat of April 1978 had fallen under widening-siege. In reality, the Afghan communists were like the Diem family that ruled Vietnam in the Eisenhower–Kennedy years, or like any number of other U.S. clients overseas: heroes to the blind foreign giant that put them in power, and enemies of their own people.

IN 1970, Gholan Dustagher, age eleven, had a teacher in his village of Ghaarkali, near Kandahar, who was a member of the Khalq—the Afghan Communist party. At the time, Afghanistan was a monarchy. Since World War II, Afghan governments had tried to walk a narrow neutral path between the superpowers, taking aid from whoever offered it.

The teacher didn't like young Gholan's name, which meant "slave of the phophet." So the teacher began calling him Meerwise, or "commander," the name of an old Afghan hero. Other members of the class were similarly renamed.

Now, a decade later, the teacher is a senior party official in Kabul, and a candidate for the ruling central committee. His swift rise wasn't due to good fortune or exceptional skill; there are just very few communists to go around. Back in Kandahar, Meerwise calls himself a student. But he works for the party, and for the government, which the party controls. He is the personal message-bearer and errand-runner for the provincial governor. He doesn't like to acknowledge his original name. "It will not be good for me," he says. "Our fathers give us religious names. When we become conscious, we don't like it."

The governor summons Meerwise to this office and asks him to guide a visiting American reporter around in a chauffeur-driven car to see how good things are.* It quickly becomes apparent that the governor has few people he can trust with such chores.

Anytime the reporter asks to stray from the assigned tour, Meerwise refuses. He says it is too dangerous for the reporter to leave main roads, or stop at unscheduled spots, because the people don't understand foreigners. "Villages are very dangerous," he says. "The people are uneducated. They are poor. They do not know what is going on. They have been given the impression that every person for the revolution is a *kafir* [nonbeliever]." What Meerwise means, of course, is that it is dangerous for *him* to travel away from a few well-guarded spots. A visiting American is welcome anywhere.

Shanawaz† Shanwany is the governor of Kandahar province, who assigned Meerwise to escort the reporter around. At thirty-eight years of age, Shanawaz is the highest-ranking government official in the south of the country. He was appointed by the party's central committee in Kabul, a week after the Soviet invasion. Before that he had been governor of Kabul province for six months, and before that governor of Konar, a less-populated province in the northeast. Before that, he had been an army officer. There's a very fast track for the rare reliable communist.

Shanawaz proved his reliability on April 20, 1979, eight months before the Soviet invasion, at Kerala, a village of about 4,000 people in Konar province. Shanawaz arrived on the outskirts of Kerala accompanied by Afghan troops, tanks, and Soviet advisors.

They were chasing some *mujahadeen* guerrillas who had run into the village for protection. Refugees interviewed by Australian journalist Philip Cornford said that a door-to-door search was made, and all male occupants

---

*It is a commentary on communications in Afghanistan that at the time this happened, none of us knew that my presence there was illegal, all Western reporters having been banned from the country. I traveled around for another week, well-marked with American flags and messages in Farsi that I was an American journalist, to keep from being mistaken for a Russian. Finally, chance led me to have lunch in a teahouse also being patronized by a police official who was aware of the ban on U.S. journalists, and of a mind to enforce it. Only then was I arrested and after two days marched out of the country at gunpoint.

†Also translatable as "Shah Nawaz."

were ordered to assemble at a bridge on the road into town to be talked to by Governor Shanawaz. From his perch on a jeep, Shanawaz is said to have waved a pistol at the assemblage and yelled, "Where are your American and Chinese friends now?" Then, it's said, he laughed, went to the side of a Soviet colonel, and together they ordered a junior Afghan officer to have his troops shoot every man and boy in the village.

Cornford was told that 1,200 people died. Such figures are usually much exaggerated in Afghanistan, but from other hearsay stories the toll apparently was well into the hundreds. The junior officer who carried out the order was later appointed to a high defense ministry job. According to those who escaped, the shooting was done by Soviet advisors as well as Afghan troops, and the Soviets were barking orders. After the shooting, a bulldozer buried the victims, many of whom were still writhing.

Shanawaz says he was born and raised in a village near Farah, about 235 miles west of Kandahar. He says he was appointed governor because he is "a specialist in this culture," meaning that of Kandahar. Asked what the population of Kandahar is, even roughly, he says he doesn't know.

Asked how many people in the province were affected by the communists' land reform program, or how many were ordered to leave their traditional homes in the provinces to take land assigned to them in other regions of the country, he says he also doesn't know. And he is unable to find anyone who *does* know. Asked the major items of trade between his province and the bordering province of Baluchistan in Pakistan, he says he doesn't have any idea. But he's sure the trade is continuing as normal. (It obviously isn't.)

"Now every member of Afghanistan is very happy," he says. "We have not seen any person around the city or around our villages who is against the government."

How many Soviets are in Kandahar province? "As a governor, I have never seen any Russians here," Shanawaz says.

AJIBNUR lives in a village between Kabul and Kandahar. Most young men from the village left after it was bombed and strafed by MIGs and helicopter gunships in May 1979. Many were killed in the attacks. Scores climbed into the mountains to become guerrillas. In November, when the snows came, they went to refugee camps in Pakistan. With spring, Ajibnur is sure, they will return to Afghanistan, freshly equipped, to mount a new campaign. Ajibnur would like to fight now, but says he hasn't got a gun; the government confiscated it. On the other hand, government guns are being made available by deserting soldiers, with whole outposts sometimes quitting and joining the rebellion in unison.

Every Afghan male must enter the army for two years at about age twenty-two. The government intentionally stations soldiers in sections of the country far from their homes, so they will have minimal understanding of local dialects, customs, and grievances. Many citizens seem to hold nothing against the soldiers, and chat in friendly fashion. But hostility frequently erupts, and soldiers obviously are under great pressure from the civilian population and their own consciences, as evidenced by the 50 percent-or-more desertion rates.

Soldiers frequently sit alone in restaurants, ostracized. On a bus from Kabul to Kandahar, a soldier tries to bum a free ride, offering to protect the other passengers. He is hooted off, and several people call out, "Go back to your Russian friends." Many who stay in the army are merely playing out a role, afraid of the consequences to themselves or their families if they desert, but in no way loyal to the government they serve.

The Soviets don't help their cause with the Afghan soldiers. They treat them and other Afghans with the same haughty colonialist disdain that generally characterizes the Soviet presence abroad, which has alienated potential allies from Cuba to Indonesia. A jeep-like vehicle carrying two Soviet officers veers around a Kabul streetcorner, sideswiping a car carrying five Afghan soldiers, and sending it to the curb. The Russians drive on, not even looking back at the dented car and its disgusted-looking occupants.

AN easily discernible Quisling class arose quickly after the communist takeover—young men in Western dress who occupy senior positions in the communist government and support it. Mouths close when they are around. They are resented and joked about. Some are encountered in hotels and government ministries. On a bus, passengers whisper that the driver, who fits the description of this group, is a government spy.

In Jallalabad, a large city east of Kabul, the bank manager is just such a young man. He announces that business couldn't be better, and jokingly tries to talk an American reporter into taking out a loan. During an hour-long interview in midmorning, the only customers who come into the bank are exchanging currency, mostly Pakistani rupees. (Both Pakistan and Afghanistan tightly restrict the amount of money that can leave their countries.)

The road between Jallalabad and Kabul has just been cut off by a massive guerrilla ambush of some Soviet troop trucks. The bank manager displays easy telephone access to provincial government officials, and repeatedly asserts that nothing is wrong, that civilian traffic was just delayed so the military could move some big equipment. As soon as he leaves the room, though, some men who came in to change money and have been sitting around stiffly, suddenly loosen up and begin discussing the attack on Soviet troops. They obviously do not disapprove.

Merchants from the bazaar sit on rugs and cushions in their mud homes, drinking tea and complaining that business is bad, that all the money has dried up. They tune their radios to Farsi broadcasts of Voice of America or the British Broadcasting Corporation, though the Soviets often jam those frequencies. They contribute substantial portions of their income to a secret committee that smuggles the money to Pakistan for arms. Asked what kind of government they would like to have in Afghanistan, they say the kind the Ayatollah Khomeini has installed in Iran. The world is certainly not as simple as Americans would like to have it.

Guerrillas attack convoys along the highways. In forested areas they set up roadblocks with felled trees, and open fire on Soviet soldiers who get out of their armored cars to clear the way. They also stop civilian vehicles. Bus passengers are checked, and government officials or Communist party members removed and shot. Others are allowed on. Some Robin Hooding occurs if substantial money is found, but the loot is obviously used for revolutionary purposes.

Those who want to rationalize what is going on in Afghanistan now say that it's simple banditry—that Afghans have a centuries-old predisposition for stealing. You can hear that from leftists, and you can hear it from some of the more cynical of the journalists who travel the international crisis circuit. Yet throughout Afghanistan, bicycles are parked unlocked by the dozen outside stores and offices, and though most Afghans are dirt poor no one takes them. Waiters and taxi drivers will chase after you to refund any overpayment, even money that was intended as a tip. Before the reaction to the April 1978 revolution, you could hitchhike safely all over the country, and not be molested, robbed, or put in fear.*

Another theory you can hear is that Afghans have always reacted unpleasantly to foreigners. This is said to account for the fierceness of their attacks on Soviets. But an American reporter traveling outside Kabul in 1980 couldn't ride a bus without being offered oranges, candy, bread, or whatever else was handy, by fellow passengers. He couldn't walk down a street without shopkeepers bidding him in for pots of tea. Strangers constantly offered friendly greetings.

The Afghans' reputation for hostility probably derives from the frequency with which foreigners have invaded their land, shot their officials, and taken over their government—and the success with which Afghans have resisted these intrusions. The Russians are just getting what the British got a hundred years ago in Afghanistan. It's the same way the Iranians felt about us.

THE per capita gross national product in Afghanistan is recorded as $168 a year, which has to be a wild guess since most people are subsistence farmers. To say this places Afghanistan among the poorest countries in the world is misleadingly sanguine. In most other poor countries, the weather is warm and people can live comfortably on less money.

Health conditions are a human low. In the countryside, almost anywhere you look, you are apt to see people squatting and spreading their robes. The results may make good fertilizer, but feces also gets into the drinking water.

*The author did so in 1967.

Everywhere, people of all ages are wheezing and coughing up phlegm. Much of the year it is simply too cold to bathe, and few do. Half the children die before they reach the age of five—worse even than in Zaire, where there is less to eat, but more concern with cleanliness.

"I know a family and they had eleven kids and they all died," says a Western-educated doctor. "They were all respiratory and gastrointestinal infections. They all could have been cured or prevented. You need a dependable clean water supply that the people will use and rely on. Seal the wells with concrete so the manure doesn't fall into them."

It is utterly incredible how little was accomplished here when for thirty years the two superpowers supposedly tried to outdo each other in impressing Afghanistan with their aid capabilities. The most visible results are that one good U-shaped road, and the airports (some American, some Soviet), which have now become a mechanism for the invasion and conquest of the country.

Where Western-style toilets have been installed, many Afghans simply climb up on the seat and squat, spewing feces in all the wrong places. The resulting conditions are less sanitary than the ones previously existing.

The literacy rate in Afghanistan is estimated at 20 percent, perhaps the world's lowest—and we're talking about the ability to read a simple signboard, not the works of Kierkegaard. At a conservative minimum, 80 percent of the people live off the food they grow and the animals they raise.

This appalling poverty and ill health is the excuse, if there could be one, for the brutal upheaval the communists have caused. Yet the communists themselves aren't addressing the problems; most won't admit there are any. Fateh Mohammed Tarin, deputy minister of planning since the April 1978 coup (and designated by the government to describe its program for a reporter), acknowledges that public health, water projects, schools, and family guidance programs aren't among the party's priorities. Tarin associates such things with Western aid.

He insists that development can't begin until there's a basic change in the social system. So the party's ten-year program is silent on the country's desperate health needs. The program frees farmers from all mortgages and other debts to what Tarin calls "the feudals and big farmers." It declares equal rights for women (the most talked about practical effect of this is abolition of the bride price, by which fathers "sell" their daughters to husbands-to-be). And it also decrees land reform. Holdings are legally limited to about 5 to 60 acres, depending on the kind of land. The land confiscated from people who had more than the maximum was to be distributed in lots of about 5 acres each (less for good land, more for bad) to tenant farmers. Ironically, in light of decree number seven (sexual equality), decree number eight awarded land only to *males* over eighteen.

Tarin says land was actually distributed under this plan to 300,000 households; Shanawaz says 248,000 households. Yet one could travel two weeks in the Afghan countryside and never encounter a single person farming land acquired under this program.

A large but uncertain number of land grants called upon the recipients to move to other regions of the country, as much as 500 miles from traditional homelands. Much of the fiercest rebel activity has been in areas affected by the relocation plan, indicating either that the plan was a major irritant to the people, or that the government designed the plan with the ulterior motive of breaking up known guerrilla strongholds.

At any rate, these three major decrees were hardly carried out as planned. The problem wasn't so much that the decrees attempted to change long-established national policies. The problem was that they attempted to *establish* national policies—and strange ones at that—for the first time among peoples accustomed to self-rule.

THE land that is Afghanistan has long been inhabited by many tribes that jealously guard their independence. In past centuries, whole tribes have been slaughtered or forcefully relocated, but they have never been peacefully persuaded. Two attempts by England in the nineteenth century to conquer the land that is now Afghanistan collapsed in complete routs of the British army.

What today passes for a nation was largely the creation of one chieftain, Abdur Rahman Khan. Before his death in 1901, Abdur Rahman managed to defeat enough rivals in battle that Russia on one frontier and Britain on the other agreed to recognize his territory as a loosely defined buffer zone between their own expansionist-minded empires.

Abdur Rahman's eldest son peacefully succeeded him as head of state in 1901. *It was the last peaceful succession in Afghan history*. The son, Habibullah, was shot to death, as have been most of his successors. A few have fled. So Babrak Karmal, the man the Soviets flew in from Czechoslovakia in December 1979 to be president of Afghanistan, may have had the most dangerous job on earth. His three predecessors had all been shot to death within the previous 20 months.

THE communists, with their social reform decrees, received an obstinate, violent reception. But it was the same reception accorded to every other emissary from Kabul who had ever tried to tell folks in the countryside what to do.

The bride price remained accepted practice. (The mullahs and laymen who support it even offer a modern rationalization: the bride's father normally holds the money as a kind of prepaid alimony to care for his daughter if her husband ever runs off.) Women are being equalized only very slowly, at about the same rate they have been for many years. Almost all still wear the traditional veil, or *chadri*, and most don't venture out of their houses into public.

In villages, tenants still split their crops with the landlord 50-50. But landlord holdings are only about about 50 acres each, unchanged from before the revolution. Afghanistan wasn't a country of large, Latin American-style plantations run by an ostentatiously wealthy upper class. Afghan landlords tend to hold recognized places in the tribal or religious structure. Many are mullahs. That may be why tenants in Afghanistan are angrier at the government than they are at the landlords.

One predictable result of the land reform program has been a substantial shortfall in wheat production. The main staple of most Afghan diets is a thin, brown wheat bread called *nan*, baked in the shape of a snowshoe. Noncommunist diplomats in Kabul estimated that the 1979 Afghan wheat crop was down by at least 20 percent from the crop of 1978. Filling bellies required big imports from the Soviet Union, which itself was importing wheat from the United States.

Five-acre plots are less efficient than larger ones. So the government tried to increase plot sizes by encouraging cooperatives, offering them discount prices for seed and fertilizer. But seed and fertilizer often weren't available at any price.

Two other changes decreed by the original communist government were also evaporating in nonenforcement. One was the confiscation of houses, trucks, and other property from middle-class businessmen. Many refugees in Pakistan complained bitterly about the early confiscations. Apparently, after the Soviets invaded, the confiscations stopped.

A second decree ordered all foreign trade to be monopolized by state-run import-export corporations. This created an enormous black market. It also shifted economic reliance to camels, which can sneak anything—up to the size of a refrigerator—through unmonitored mountain passes to Pakistan, and away from trucks, which have to pass through monitored checkpoints. After the Soviet invasion, the decree was changed so that only basic staples were controlled. But by that time, the government was generally helpless to enforce anything it said, except by on-the-spot deployment of troops.

ALL this points to the notion that the Soviets invaded Afghanistan not to create a communist revolution, but to end one—or at least postpone it for many years.

The critical decision for the Soviets really came with the original communist coup of April 1978, when they suddenly encouraged their communist allies south of the border to end more than thirty years of carefully balanced Afghan neutrality. Why they did that is a wonderful question, still without certain answer. Selig S. Harrison, a former *Washington Post* correspondent now with the Carnegie Endowment for International Peace, has compiled an impressive case that the Soviets did *not* make the first move to tip that careful balance, but, rather, that our side did.

The Carnegie Endowment is a think tank that tends to attract State Department types from the Democratic party mainstream. It certainly is no hotbed of radicalism. Harrison, a specialist in West Asia and frequent visitor to the region, first argued his case in a *Washington Post* "Outlook" article on May 13, 1979—*before* the Soviets actually invaded.

He argued that the U.S.—or its ally-at-the-time, Iran—made the first move against the neutralist tradition by trying to swing the Afghan government toward an anti-Soviet alliance. That suggests that the Soviets reacted defensively. Harrison calls the 1978 communist coup in Kabul "one of the more disastrous legacies of the shah's ambitious effort . . . encouraged by the United States . . . to roll back Soviet influence in surrounding countries and create a modern version of the ancient Persian empire."

Harrison relates* discussions he had with Iranian foreign ministry officials from 1974 to 1977 in which they told him of their plans to bring Iran and Afghanistan closer together. This would begin with a $2 billion aid program through which Iran would supersede the Soviet Union as Afghanistan's major benefactor. An Iranian-funded rail and highway network would open Afghanistan to the Persian Gulf and the Arabian Sea, supplanting Soviet trade routes.

In return, Iran was exercising considerable influence over the Afghan government. Harrison says he was told that the SAVAK (Iranian secret police) office in Kabul was as strong as the KGB office, and was helping Prime Minister Mohammed Daud identify and eliminate communists with high government or military jobs. Daud had maintained good relations with the local communists, but at Iran's urging he broke off this liaison. In 1975, at Iran's urging, forty Soviet-trained officers were removed from senior army posts, and replaced with officers trained under new agreements with Egypt, India, and Pakistan.

Harrison says Daud told him that Afghanistan "must adapt to the new realities" of Iran's oil wealth and desire to dominate the region with U.S. weapons. In March 1978, encouraged by the shah, Daud signed a treaty with Pakistan in which he guaranteed not to help the Baluch or Pashtun separatist movements. Daud then visited Egypt and Saudi Arabia, invited the shah to Kabul in June, and accepted an invitation to visit President Carter in Washington in September. This was not a schedule evincing a carefully balanced neutrality.

On April 17, 1978, Mir Akbar Khaiber, an Afghan communist leader, was murdered. Harrison suggests that Daud's interior minister arranged the murder. A week later, seven top communist leaders were arrested. Two days after that, April 26, a purge swept hundreds of perceived communist sympathizers out of government jobs. And two days after that came the coup, now hyperbolized as the "Saur [April] Revolution," in which Daud was murdered, and Noor Mohammed Taraki, the communist leader, took over.

*In the article and in an interview.

It is hard to believe he did so without assurance of Soviet backing; in any event he quickly got such backing.

Conceivably, the Kremlin had grown alarmed over the threat of a string of Islamic states with U.S. military alliances all along the Soviets' southern border. The string, from Turkey to Pakistan, linked up to the Chinese enemy on the east. That is the picture Harrison draws, and rather compellingly. On the other hand, how much of a true threat little Afghanistan could ever be to the Soviet Union is a fair question.

But one way or another, the Soviets in 1978 made the same mistake Washington had made so often. They surrendered to temptation and took a poke at the tar baby, never realizing what they were getting themselves into. Less than two years later, Afghanistan was in turmoil. If Moslem rebels overthrew the Soviet puppet government, they might produce a militant anti-Soviet state, just as Iran had become a militant anti-American state by fighting and defeating a U.S. puppet. And Afghanistan is on the Soviets' own border. So the Soviets swung the other fist at the tar baby.

THE map of the world that is commonly used in Europe and its former colonies in the Eastern Hemisphere is one that Americans are unaccustomed to seeing. The "world" consists of Europe and Asia, with northern Africa and Australia thrown in, but the Western Hemisphere excluded, as if it didn't exist. On a map that could be seen on many Afghan walls, each country was a different color. The Soviet Union was purple.

From 15 feet away, the world appeared to be one big purple blob, surrounded by little dots of yellow, pink, orange, and green. China, in red, had a definite presence, as, to a lesser degree, did Saudi Arabia in yellow. The only other country on that huge land mass that looked like anything at all worth bothering about was India, which was also purple.

How must events look to one who lives in the middle of that huge purple Soviet blob that stands in the middle of the whole world? What was Afghanistan? Was it one of the little yellow dots, or little red ones, or little pink ones? What was Italy? Switzerland? Pakistan? Thailand? Japan? If one of those little dots started to cause trouble, wouldn't the easiest thing be to just color it purple, too?

But the paint wouldn't stick, and the Soviets couldn't get it back in the tube. Almost nobody in Afghanistan wanted communism. They rebelled. And the more they were repressed, the *more* they rebelled. The Soviets invested tremendous armed power in the hands of Afghan soldiers with Soviet advisors. But this force on loan didn't work. So the Soviet army came down— not to heat things up, as it appeared to Americans, but to try to cool things off.

The land reform program was immediately declared a success—and cancelled, or at least "phase one" of it, the redistribution, was. "Phase two," the allotment of seed and fertilizer, was promised. The confiscation of private property was stopped, and compensation was promised for property already confiscated. Promises were immediately made that the import-export business would be returned to private hands, except for a few staples. "In the next ten years, the private sector will have a more important role," an official declared. "We won't make everything public."

All attempts to go out to the villages, where at least 80 percent of the people lived, were called off. The villages were visited only by helicopter gunships and dive bombers, which were in no position to inquire into the enforcement of female equality laws. The new president, Karmal, was from the Parcham, or "flag" wing of the Communist party, as opposed to the Khalq, or "people's" wing, which had produced the other two communist presidents. The Parcham was traditionally more moderate. Obviously, the whole revolution was being called off.

The Soviets had all kinds of plans to industrialize Afghanistan. The main exports had been natural gas (which went to the Soviet Union in exchange for cheap, refined gasoline) and agricultural products, mostly fruit and nuts. What little industry Afghanistan had—metal work, cement, plastic shoes, and textiles—was for local use. (Sadly, some of the industries were owned by Uzbeks from Soviet Central Asia, who had fled south to Afghanistan to escape Soviet rule in the 1920s; after fifty years it caught up with them.) The Soviets planned to revive the economy with fertilizer factories, factories to process cotton into exportable textiles and cottonseed oil, and even a petroleum refinery.

But it was too late for all that. The Soviet intervention in 1978 had touched off a revolution that was only going to get worse as the Soviets intervened more. Tight Soviet information control prevented anyone from fairly reporting on how the war was going and how high Soviet casualties had risen, but certainly they were well up in the thousands. Probably no one in the Kremlin had guessed how big a commitment it would take to subdue this little country, if indeed it could be subdued at all. With another can of worms open in Poland, the whole Soviet military apparatus was in danger of being tied down. From all evidence, it had been a giant miscalculation.

THE United States had an opportunity to make its own miscalculation in 1980, but apparently avoided it. In the months after the invasion, when the situation was still a front-page "crisis," Pakistani president Zia ul-Haq made a pitch for enormous U.S. military aid. What he proposed, in essence, was that he replace the now-deposed shah of Iran as America's "main man" in western Asia, on a scale no smaller than the shah's. The U.S. wisely turned him down.

The U.S. did offer $400 million in aid, plus help in recruiting Saudi Arabia and West Germany to supply additional aid. That would seem pretty significant. But General Zia called it "peanuts." He wanted to at least double the size and strength of his 450,000-man army.

Zia's spokesmen made clear that his first order of business would be to tighten his grip on Baluchistan by deploying far more forces there and buying a lot of high-tech radar and communications gear. Even the civilian aid in the package he wanted was to build roads, airports, and other infrastructure in Baluchistan. To the extent these were nonmilitary, they would have been a good thing. But in context, the improvements were clearly part of a military program.

As for Pakistan's planned military buildup, of course, it wasn't the Russians who were worried, but the Baluchs, the Indians, and the Pakistanis. Things hadn't been going well domestically under Zia, the American ally. Only Saudi Arabian aid had prevented Pakistan from defaulting on its foreign debt. Prices of commonly used goods were controlled, so a black market dominated commerce, and merchants were shaken down by soldiers demanding "protection" money to avoid prosecution under the myriad trade restrictions.

Meanwhile, the wife of former president Zulfikar Ali Bhutto, who herself probably would have won an election for president simply because her husband had fallen martyr to Zia, was held under house arrest. Even though cancer was diagnosed, she continued to be held there for many months without treatment until finally she was allowed to fly to Europe, perhaps too late to contain the malignancy. A prominent journalist, his newspaper banned, was also held in solitary confinement in jail while a series of severe illnesses progressed untreated until they threatened his life.

Doing nothing is a thankless way for a national leader to win political popularity or even historical recognition. It gets no publicity. Most people are never aware of what it is the leader hasn't done. Yet it is often the correct course to follow in international affairs. Brezhnev may have gone to his grave wishing he had followed it in Afghanistan. Certainly it was the correct course when Jimmy Carter refused to bestow on Zia ul-Haq, as he had on Shah Mohammed Reza Pahlevi, all the benefits of membership in the "free" world.

CHAPTER THIRTEEN

MAKING OUR BED
IN CENTRAL AMERICA:
PART I

For almost a century now, the sight of a United Brands Company (until 1970, United Fruit Company) ship in a Caribbean harbor has been pretty common. But the two United Brands freighters that lurked off Cuba's Playa Giron on April 17, 1961, weren't there for the usual load of bananas. In fact, their mission was so extraordinary that it remained a classified military secret until Thomas McCann, a retired corporate vice-president for public affairs at United Brands, published his memoirs in 1976. Neither the government nor the company has challenged his account of how the freighters became warships that day.

Playa Giron—Giron beach—lies on a body of water called the Bahia de Cochinos—the Bay of Pigs. There, from April 17 to April 20, 1961, Cuba won what most Cubans regard as the most heroic military victory in their history—maybe in all of Latin America's history. The little island nation of about 6 million people (today around 10 million) overwhelmed and wiped out an invasion force sent by the world's mightiest country.

On that beach at Giron (pronounced "here-own"), the leadership of Fidel Castro was ratified, and his popularity insured. The Latinos had finally put it to the gringos. Whatever economic hardship Castro's inefficient socialist system would bring to Cuba in ensuing decades, Castro would continue to breathe strength and life from the glory of that triumph. Twenty years after the fact, it remained the most popular subject in Cuba for slogans on signboards and T-shirts. More often than you saw "Coca-Cola" in the United

States, you saw "Giron" in Cuba. And it was always displayed with pride. The U.S. had delivered Castro a power he never could have bought—a legitimacy he could have won no other way.

Actually, there were only about 1,500 invaders at the Bay of Pigs, and they were all Cubans. But they were recruited, organized, maintained for a year, trained, thoroughly armed (even with an air force), transported, and directed by the U.S. Central Intelligence Agency. When squabbling broke out at the training camps between supporters and opponents of the former dictator, Fulgencio Batista, the CIA imposed order. Cubans seeking power could only vie for influence with the CIA command.

Since U.S. taxpayers supported the operation so generously, one might wonder why the invasion relied on transport ships that were on loan from United Brands, a private, profit-making enterprise. But when you think about it, this arrangement was only fair. The whole CIA had been on loan to United Brands for years. The loan of a couple of company ships in return was the least the taxpayers could have expected after paying for United Brands' coup d'etat style of trade.

To this day, United Brands is part of a business lobby opposing improved relations with Cuba until Cuba pays the claims of 979 U.S. companies whose property was seized by the Cuban government. United Brands is third on the list, with a claim of $85.1 million.

Of course, the military use of United Brands' freighters wasn't known to the taxpayers at the time of the Bay of Pigs invasion. Nor was the extent to which the company disgraced the U.S. flag it carried throughout Latin America. United Brands had a shiny, cheerful public face, in the person of its ubiquitous trademark, Chiquita Banana, a banana-shaped, miniskirted Latino cutie who sang and danced on radio and television. Kids played with Chiquita Banana dolls, and the first nutrition lesson most Americans learned, as conveyed in the last line of Chiquita's song, was "never put bananas in the refrigerator."

What a comedown, then, to learn that back in 1954, for example, the CIA had accepted and carried out a proposal from Chiquita to overthrow the Guatemalan government, which was the only democratically elected government Guatemala had ever had. Chiquita and the CIA replaced that government with thirty years (and still counting) of bloodshed under a series of almost barbaric right-wing dictators. The U.S. taxpayers continue to fund these regimes under the recurrent threat that if they do not, the Guatemalan people will fall prey to the evils of communism. That was the same line United Brands sold the country back in 1954.

THE elected government we overthrew then was run by Jacobo Arbenz. As a captain in the army a decade earlier, in 1944, Arbenz had helped lead a coup that toppled the long-standing right-wing dictator, General Jorge Ubico.

Arbenz and the other junior officers who took over looked about for a new leader, and settled on a college professor, Juan José Arevalo, who had been living in exile in Argentina for fourteen years.

Under Professor Arevalo's rule, political parties were formed and contested elections were held. In 1945, Professor Arevalo was inaugurated as Guatemala's first popularly chosen leader. He proceeded to fashion a welfare state along the lines advocated by his hero, Franklin Roosevelt. Roosevelt, he said, "taught us that there is no need to cancel the concept of freedom in the democratic system in order to breathe into it a socialist spirit."

At the time of the 1944 coup, Guatemala's economy was almost entirely agricultural. A mere 2 percent of the landowners owned 72 percent of the land. Ninety percent of the landowners were confined to 15 percent of the land. Peasants paid taxes by putting in 150 days of labor. Illiteracy was 75 percent among the general population and 95 percent among Indians. Life expectancy was fifty years for whites, forty for Indians.* United Brands made a lot of money.

Professor Arevalo moved to adopt a social security system like Roosevelt's, and a labor law modeled after the Wagner Act. Unions were authorized, child and female labor was regulated, and minimum wages were established. Credit and other help was offered to small farmers. Arevalo proclaimed himself a socialist, but at the same time an anti-communist. Communism, he said, "is a socialism which gives food with the left hand while with the right it mutilates the moral and civic values of man."

Nice talk, but you can still imagine what United Brands thought of all this. It was by far the biggest employer (40,000 jobs in a country with fewer than a million working-age men, most of them subsistence farmers). United Brands ran the only railroad, the only major port, and the telephone and telegraph service, and was a big influence on the U.S.-owned electric utility. United Brands thus was at the throttle of every significant enterprise, foreign or domestic, in Guatemala. It must have seemed unfair to the company to have come so far south to build an empire, and then suddenly discover that the unions and minimum wage laws had followed it. United Brands began to complain to its friends in Washington that Guatemala was going communist.

To the contrary. When Professor Arevalo's elected term expired in 1950, he performed the noblest and most uncommunistic of political deeds. He retired voluntarily—one of the few heads of a foreign state who ever emulated the stunning example that George Washington set back in 1796. Arevalo believed, as did Washington, that a country was better off with periodic fresh

*These statistics and some quotes and history about the coups of 1944 and 1954 are taken from Stephen Schlesinger and Stephen Kinzer's thoroughly documented and highly praised book, *Bitter Fruit: The Untold Story of the American Coup in Guatemala* (Doubleday, 1982).

leadership. To replace him, an election campaign shaped up between his major critic, a political conservative, and the professor's enthusiastic supporter, Jacobo Arbenz. The campaign was aborted when men loyal to Arbenz shot and killed the critic.

Arbenz was challenged by a new candidate from the right, but still won, with 65 percent of the vote. He immediately moved to advance Professor Arevalo's plan, which was to give Guatemalans equal rights in their own country with the executives of United Brands. Arbenz sought to build a port that would be an alternative to United Brands' port, a highway that would be an alternative to United Brands' railroad, and an electric company that would be an alternative to the U.S.-owned electric company.

To eliminate the concentration of wealth, he seized the largest landholdings, all with full compensation in the form of twenty-five-year, interest-bearing bonds that would give the wealthy holders a stake in the successful running of the country. He did not communize farming, but rather distributed the 1.5 million acres he seized to 100,000 families. He even confiscated his own family's landholdings, probably the *next* noblest gesture a politician can make, other than retiring from office.

The land reform of Jacobo Arbenz fell perfectly within the guidelines that would be recommended by the U.S. State Department a mere seven years later, as part of President Kennedy's Alliance for Progress program.* Arbenz's program was positively *tame* compared to the land reform program in El Salvador in the 1980s, which the United States not only conceived but enforced, with the full vigor of its munitions makers and military advisors. Arbenz, however, jumped the gun by a few years. And for that, he was decreed a communist and a menace to U.S. national security. Or, maybe his problem wasn't just timing. Maybe his problem was that *his* program adversely affected an American company as the biggest landholder.

OF course, when large landholdings came to be confiscated, United Brands was involved. And some tables were unexpectedly turned on the company. Over the years, United Brands had won itself a number of fancy tax breaks in Guatemala, with many of its operations excused from paying any taxes at all. To hold down real estate levies, it had undervalued its landholdings. General Ubico and other dictators had agreed to this, in exchange for United Brands' support. Now, under the confiscation law, these low valuations didn't look so good (although even at top dollar United Brands probably wouldn't have wanted to give up its land).

*See *The Alliance that Lost Its Way*, by Jerome Levinson and Juan de Onis, a Twentieth Century Fund study. The U.S. wanted expropriation compensated with local currency. A program calling for payment in twenty-five-year bonds just like Arbenz's was launched by Chilean President Eduardo Frei, who was not overthrown but *supported* by a CIA covert action program.

So the company threw its Washington lobbying campaign into high gear. Back in 1947, at the first stirrings of Professor Arevalo's welfare state, United Brands had hired a high-powered lawyer and all-purpose Mr. Fixit in the person of Thomas G. Corcoran, a former Roosevelt brain truster. Among Corcoran's friends was General Walter Bedell Smith, who ran the CIA under Truman and moved over to be number two man at the State Department under Eisenhower.

Smith, known as "Beadle," had attended the small meeting in John Foster Dulles's office at which Kermit Roosevelt presented his plan for taking over Iran in 1953. Smith was part of the unanimous vote to authorize the plan. In fact, the CIA–State Department apparatus was feeling euphoric and all-powerful after its "success" in Tehran. Now Corcoran besieged Smith with news of how Guatemala's communist government was endangering the stability of Central America, and, incidentally, of the awful way it was treating poor United Brands.

Stunningly, Under Secretary of State Smith replied with his own news— that he had always wanted to be president of United Brands! As Corcoran recalled it,* Smith "told me he always liked to watch those pretty sailing ships on the Atlantic—the Great White Fleet." This is as close to a bald-faced bribe solicitation as the annals of Washington lobbying are likely to turn up. Corcoran says he took the proposal back to his client, United Brands, advocating it. "You have to have people who can tell you what's going on. He's had a great background with his CIA association," Corcoran said.

"He doesn't know anything about the banana business," was the reply from United Brands.

"For Chrissakes," Corcoran told the company, "your problem is not bananas. . . . You've got to handle your political problem."

While his business career struggled to be born, Smith brought Corcoran's idea for a CIA overthrow of Arbenz to his own boss, Secretary of State John Foster Dulles. The attentive reader will not need prompting at this point when asked to guess which law firm had been garnering the fees from United Brands' big acquisition of its Guatemalan and other Central American railroads. That would be Sullivan & Cromwell, whose partners included both John Foster Dulles and his brother Allen, now, in 1953, the CIA director. In fact, Foster Dulles had handled the railroad deal personally.

IT might be useful here to digress on the meaning of these constantly recurring business relationships. When the sums involved are large, they allow gentlemen to take payoffs that could never be accepted as outright cash bribes.

---

*In an interview with Schlesinger and Kinzer for *Bitter Fruit.* Both Corcoran and Smith had died before this author could confirm the conversation. Corcoran's son, also a Washington lawyer, says it sounds consistent with what he knew, and Schlesinger says it is confirmed in part by what he was told by McCann and others.

But these relationships also operate when the cash profit alone seems far too small to sway the important decisions of a public official.

There is a form of old-boy networking involved in all this that can be just as insidious as outright bribery in steering vital public decisions against the public interest. Early in a career, a sense of where the money comes from— and the power, and the esteem—can lock a prospective public official into his course. For Dulles to have defended what Arbenz was doing in Guatemala in 1954 might have required him to contradict laboriously drawn positions he had been paid to advocate as a lawyer for twenty-five years. For him to have double-crossed Exxon in Iran would have jeopardized more than just his own hypothetical (and probably replaceable) future income from Big Oil's fees to Sullivan & Cromwell. Even the possible loss of income to other Sullivan & Cromwell partners, many of whom were no doubt his close friends, is not the heart of the issue. Double-crossing Exxon would have threatened the oil company executives with whom they all worked, and probably played. It would have required Dulles to renounce his circle.

While this black hat of conflict-of-interest may seem to fit most neatly on the head of a Wall Street–Republican administration, in fact it knows no party or ideological bounds. Corcoran was a Democrat. And Maurice Tempelsman's lawyer, Adlai Stevenson, who argued so eloquently in support of the invasion of Zaire by U.S. forces, was a *liberal* Democrat. Indeed, the spectrum of past political positions represented today among the partners at Lehman Brothers Kuhn Loeb is so broad that only their mutual love of profit and power could possibly hold them together, as they influence the course of world politics more than they ever could have influenced it back when they were toiling in the State, Defense, and Commerce departments' bureaucracies.

UNITED BRANDS used its clout to influence men in positions of public trust, not necessarily more than other companies have, but probably more baldly. If the double-play combination of Tommy Corcoran to Beadle Smith to the Dulles brothers wasn't enough, United Brands also hired John Clementz. Clementz, while taking money as a part time publicist for United Brands and other companies, was employed full time as an executive of the Hearst newspaper chain (which today says that he is dead and that it doesn't have any record of his outside activities). Clementz was concerned in part with Hearst's International News Service subsidiary, then one of the three major U.S. wire services (it has since merged with United Press to form United Press International).

The reach of the plotters also extended to the *New York Times*. It was feared that Sydney Gruson, the *Times*'s Central American correspondent, was too liberal and might report things he shouldn't when the overthrow took place. So Allen Dulles used his friendship with the *Times*'s business manager to pass a message to Arthur Hays Sulzberger, the publisher, to keep Gruson out of Guatemala until after Arbenz was deposed. Sulzberger obliged, and replaced Gruson until after the coup.*

Foster Dulles's assistant secretary of state for Latin American affairs, John Moors Cabot, helped launch the attack against Arbenz by accusing him of "openly playing the communist game." Cabot's brother, Thomas Cabot, was a recent president of United Brands, and the Cabot family still held stock in the company. It was a member of that family, U. N. ambassador Henry Cabot Lodge, who fended off Guatemala's efforts to get U.N. protection. And President Eisenhower's personal secretary, Anne Whitman, was the wife of United Brands' public relations director, Edmund Whitman.†

The poor bastards in Guatemala never had a chance.

CIA officers actually went around with United Brands executives to prospective Guatemalan leaders, scouting for a suitable replacement for Arbenz—a Guatemalan Zahedi. (Kermit Roosevelt wrote in his memoirs that right after his triumphant return from Tehran, Allen Dulles had offered him the Guatemalan job. But Roosevelt said he turned it down because he sensed too much support of Arbenz among the Guatemalan people.)

Of course, the CIA and United Brands weren't willing just to *give* the presidency of Guatemala away. Their rather stiff requirements were spelled out by one of the first men they approached, General Miguel Ydigoras Fuentes. In his 1963 memoirs, *My War With Communism* (Prentice-Hall), Ydigoras Fuentes recalled: "A former executive of United Fruit Company, now retired, Mr. Walter Turnbull, came to see me with two gentlemen whom he introduced as agents of the CIA. They said that I was a popular figure in Guatemala and that they wanted to lend their assistance to overthrow Arbenz. When I asked their conditions for the assistance, I found them unacceptable. Among other things, I was to promise to favor the United Fruit Company and the International Railways of Central America [which United Fruit owned]; to destroy the railroad workers' labor union; to suspend claims against Great Britain for the Belize territory [an old border dispute involving a former British colony]; [and] to establish a strong-arm government, on the style of [General] Ubico." Ydigoras Fuentes wrote that he told the men he wanted

---

*Recounting the incident in *Without Fear or Favor* (Times Books, 1980), his book about the *Times*, Harrison E. Salisbury says it "left a bad taste in Sulzberger's mouth," furthering his resolve to make the *Times* independent in the future.

†The information in this paragraph is from the Schlesinger-Kinzer book. Schlesinger says its original source was Thomas McCann, the retired corporate vice-president at United Brands, who in turn verified it for me. Henry Cabot Lodge says he didn't personally own stock in the company, and doesn't know whether his family did. United Brands says no one was around who can recall such details, or can locate the Whitmans.

to revise the terms, because they "seemed to me to be unfavorable to Guatemala. [To say the least!] They withdrew, promising to return; I never saw them again."

The United Brands–CIA search team had moved on. They finally settled on a candidate, a man originally proposed by United Brands, a lawyer named Cordova Cerna—who just happened to be United Brands' longtime local counsel! But Cerna soon contracted throat cancer, and had to be replaced. Cerna suggested that his patrons turn to Colonel Carlos Castillo Armas. They did, and set Castillo Armas up just across the border in Honduras, training an army of U.S.-supplied mercenaries.

At this point, Ydigoras Fuentes picks up the story again in his memoirs: "I was soon informed [he discreetly avoids saying by whom] that Colonel Castillo Armas had been chosen. . . . My job was to inform all of my supporters in Guatemala that Castillo Armas and I were in complete agreement, that he was to lead an armed invasion to overthrow the Arbenz government and immediately convoke free elections. I was to urge the fullest support, strategic and financial, to the movement. This I did and this was the extent of my participation in the movement. However, it was important. Carlos Castillo Armas had no political following in Guatemala. He was hardly known."

Oh, but that didn't matter. The U.S. gave him a full complement of Guatemalan exiles, American recruits, and others of the type the CIA rounds up in times of need. Of course, they were all paid, armed, and flown to Honduras for training, by the American taxpayer. As for Ydigoras Fuentes, his initial recalcitrance was forgiven and his eventual loyalty rewarded; he was allowed to serve his own term as president of Guatemala from 1958 to 1963.

Meanwhile, President Arbenz was becoming understandably upset about the army being raised over his border, led by the right-wing Castillo Armas, whose hostility toward the new welfare state had long been manifest. Naively unaware of who was arming Castillo Armas, Arbenz asked the U.S. for arms to defend Guatemala. He was, of course, refused. Now on the U.S.'s blacklist, he did no better elsewhere.

Desperate, Arbenz arranged to buy a $1 million boatload of small arms and artillery from Czechoslovakia. Of course, the CIA tracked the ship from the day it left port in Szczecin, Poland, where an agent was in place. (Sleep well tonight, America, your spies are alert in Szczecin.) The arms' arrival in Guatemala was quickly exposed, and provided a splendid excuse for the overthrow that had long been planned anyway.

"The Reds are in control," Eisenhower declared to congressional leaders, "and they are trying to spread their influence to San Salvador as a first step to breaking out of Guatemala to other South American countries." Never mind that Guatemala isn't even in South America. Thirty years later, Ronald Reagan is still making the "spread their influence" speech, about the same exploited, pathetically poor fruit and coffee farmers, who probably have never considered themselves very influential.

So Castillo Armas moved into Guatemala. Surprisingly, his U.S.-operated mercenary army failed to roll over the resistance forces as fast as expected, and for a while his victory was in doubt. But U.S. planes, flown by U.S. pilots, bombed and strafed and eventually took their toll. Once again a U.S. ambassador, this time John Peurifoy instead of Loy Henderson, brazenly conned a patriotic Third World leader who had tried to obtain minimal justice for his people. As Henderson had lied to Mossadegh about the U.S. role throughout the coup in Iran, so Peurifoy lied to Arbenz as the noose tightened around him. But finally, the last democratically elected president of Guatemala (to this writing) resigned and went to Mexico.

Eisenhower received the responsible CIA operatives at the White House and thanked them, saying, "You've averted a Soviet beachhead in our hemisphere." Then, as had become the custom in these affairs, the secretary of state ordered the U.S. ambassador to take care of business. Peurifoy was to instruct the government the U.S. had just installed in Guatemala to issue a fat contract favoring United Brands, a supposedly competitive private enterprise. When United Brands itself told Dulles it had doubts about the timing of the contract—which returned all its land, among other things—Ambassador Peurifoy cabled Dulles that there was nothing to worry about, and that United Brands should proceed with the deal.

Keeping another custom, U.S. newsmen were brought to Arbenz's home and shown stacks of Soviet textbooks and other evidence of Arbenz's alleged communist stooge role. But even Paul Kennedy, the *New York Times* reporter who apparently had passed CIA inspection after Sydney Gruson failed, decided the evidence was planted. He wrote in his memoirs, *The Middle Beat* (Teachers College Press, Columbia University, 1971) that it was "suspicious enough that some of us held off on the story." Others—notably *Time* magazine—reported it.

BUT some justice was done. For all his trouble, old Beadle Smith never got the presidency of United Brands. He settled for a seat on the board of directors.

And United Brands itself fell prey to the Justice Department, which is consistently more independent of corporate political pressure than the foreign policy apparatus is. With the same devil-be-damned spirit it demonstrated in the oil monopoly case, the antitrust division at Justice accused United Brands of monopolizing the banana business—which, about as certainly as night follows day, it had.

There is a bit of irony in the suit that the Justice Department filed, of course. It said that the banana business the U.S. had just gone to war to protect was illegally cheating the American public out of the right to buy

competitively priced bananas. Just as with Exxon and its Iranian oil, the
citizens were losing on both ends. They were paying exorbitant taxes and
committing heinous moral crimes in order to protect an anticompetitive private monopoly, which then overcharged them for its goods. In both cases,
Americans would have been better off *losing* the war they were financing,
so that the resultant free market could bring them cheaper oil and bananas.
At least that's true if you accept the Justice Department's argument.

In 1958, United Brands itself surrendered to that argument. It settled the
Justice Department's antitrust case by agreeing to sell, over time, all of its
Guatemalan banana fields. This might seen the final irony to the story—that
the whole effort, raising an army, overthrowing a government, was for
nothing. But that would be a hasty conclusion. A good circumstantial case
has been made that the State Department again subverted Justice (as it did
with the oil monopoly, and with the overseas bribery cases). The sale of
United Brands' Guatemalan banana fields was delayed fourteen years, and
when Del Monte Corporation finally bought the fields in 1972, some aspects
of the sale may not have been strictly as the Justice Department intended.

There had been no shortage of potential buyers for the properties. But
Del Monte, a big fruit grower in Hawaii and California, seemed to have a
special track. A close relationship had developed between the companies in
1968, in the aftermath of an attempt by United Brands to buy out Del Monte.
Del Monte's management had sensed the danger and cleverly dodged the
takeover plot by acquiring a Florida banana property. The 1958 antitrust
settlement clearly precluded United Brands from buying another banana-
growing company, so if Del Monte started growing bananas, United Brands
couldn't take it over. As Del Monte management saved itself, however, it
fell into intimate discussions with its attacker.

In 1970, the two companies announced that Del Monte would buy the
United Brands Guatemalan banana properties for a sum exceeding $10 mil-
lion. (The price was later disclosed to be $20.5 million.) The announcement
sent up howls from some Guatemalan businessmen who wanted to buy the
properties themselves. At least two of these Guatemalan bidders were in
association on the deal with an independent American investor. There were
allegations of unfair collusion to keep the banana fields under the control of
big U.S. agribusinesses that might, as the oil companies did, work together
to block true competition.

The Guatemalan government announced it wouldn't allow the sale to Del
Monte. Castillo Armas, the U.S. stooge, had by this time been shot and
killed by an assassin, and in 1960, his replacement, the emboldened Ydigoras
Fuentes, had called in U.S. arms, planes, and pilots to put down a rebellion.
Over the next decade the country had dissolved into the Guatemala that we
know today, a revolving order of rightist dictators inflicting massive blood-
shed on a discontented population. But in 1970, one of them said no to the
United Brands-Del Monte deal.

The U.S. Justice Department also objected to the sale. It argued that United Brands should open up its operating data to allow fair competitive bidding for the property. As it turned out, the critical conflict in the banana affair was this clash between the two great arms of the U.S. government. On one side, the Justice Department stood for the rights of Americans to buy, sell, grow, or eat bananas in a free market (and of United Brands shareholders to get the best available price for their banana fields). On the other side, the State Department stood for halting the communist menace.

The Justice Department was beseeched by United Brands' lawyers to stop interfering with the Del Monte sale. United Brands argued that if the sale wasn't made quickly, and with U.S. government support, Guatemala might confiscate the properties. If that happened, United said, other Central American governments might start confiscating properties of other U.S. corporations. The Justice Department believed otherwise, and on February 7, 1972, Bruce B. Wilson, the deputy assistant attorney general running the antitrust division at Justice, stated his argument in a letter to John R. Breen of the State Department Office of Central American Affairs.

Wilson wrote, "We believe it might be prejudicial to U.S. interests... to refuse to give Guatemalan nationals an opportunity to bid for the properties.... We believe that a successful purchase by Guatemalans at fair market value would show that expropriation is unnecessary as a means to further nationalistic economic development. We recognize United's concern that detailed data concerning its Guatemalan operations will become known to the Guatemala government and [employee] union.... There seems no way in which potential purchasers can make informed bids on the property unless they have access to such operating data."

THE State Department, however, may have known much better than the Justice Department exactly what data United Brands wanted to hide. And, like General Smith on the board of directors, it may not have had anything to do with the banana end of the business. At any rate, the U.S. ambassador to Guatemala, Nathaniel Davis, coached United Brands and Del Monte on how to change the mind of the Guatemalan government, and persuade it to okay the transfer. Davis's advice, according to cable traffic that has since been declassified and obtained, was to see "a local consultant."* After trying unsuccessfully to go it alone, Del Monte did see a "local consultant," whereupon Guatemala suddenly reversed its opposition and approved the transfer.

On July 14, 1975, the *Wall Street Journal* published a page-one story by reporters Jerry Landauer and Kenneth H. Bacon disclosing that Del Monte had paid an influential consultant $500,000, hidden in the books of Pana-

---

*Davis—the same man who resigned over the Angolan escalation in 1975—said in a 1983 interview that he had not referred Del Monte to any *particular* consultant.

manian shipping companies, entirely contingent on the consultant's ability
to turn the Guatemalan government around. The story provoked a flurry of
official investigation and press activity. Within a couple of weeks it was
known that the consultant was Domingo Alejandro Moreira Martinez, a
Cuban who had fled to Guatemala after Castro overthrew Batista. Moreira
now had close ties to Guatemalan leaders. By some accounts, he was involved
in an oil deal with the president of Guatemala.

Then State Department cables disclosed that more than $1 million may
have been paid in connection with the banana property approval. The SEC
learned that a $300,000 tax on the land transfer had apparently been avoided,
and that currency export controls had been lifted to allow United Brands to
remove from Guatemala the $20.5 million that Del Monte paid for the prop-
erty. After two years of steadfastly maintaining that none of its corporate
cash ever went to any government officials, on May 5, 1977, Del Monte
quietly filed a disclosure statement with the SEC acknowledging that "in
some cases consultant's bills, to the knowledge of the company, included
funds to be transmitted to government officials or others." No more was
said.

The government of Costa Rica charged that United Brands, Del Monte,
and another company, Castle & Cooke Inc., had a joint $5 million slush
fund to pay off Central American officials to keep them from raising export
taxes on bananas. The three companies denied it.

But the dam had long since broken. The *Wall Street Journal* had reported,
again on page one, in a story by Kenneth Bacon and Mary Bralove, that
United Brands had paid a $1.25 million bribe to the president of Honduras,
which persuaded him to reduce an announced increase in the banana export
tax. Eventually, United Brands was indicted and convicted in U.S. District
Court, New York, on six felony counts for the Honduras bribe. Judge William
Conner responded by slapping United Brands with the maximum fine allowed
by law: $15,000. Almost as a footnote to that case, it came out that the SEC
had also learned of a $750,000 payoff United Brands had made—in another
matter altogether—to officials of the Italian government.

Then it was learned that United Brands had been bribing a top officer of
the International Longshoreman's Union, Fred H. Field, Jr., who was indicted and convicted in federal court, New York. In connection with that
case, prosecutors discovered a big slush fund kept by United Brands. Its
purpose wasn't fully disclosed. Field was sentenced to one year in jail and
fined $50,000—the fine alone being more than three times as much as the
piddling penalty levied against United Brands. No charges were brought
against United Brands' executives, which aptly illustrates the favored treatment businessmen get under U.S. criminal law.

But one United Brands executive did choose to fall on his sword. In
February 1975, in the early stages of the investigation, Eli Black, the chairman of United Brands, jumped to his death from the forty-fourth floor of

the Pam Am building in New York, rather than answer to his part in the scandal.

Then came Thomas McCann's memoirs, in which he explained why United Brands had chosen to settle the antitrust case by selling its Guatemalan banana fields. The company also could have satisfied the law, he pointed out, by selling its plantations in Panama. But, said McCann, "I felt the reasons we went back to Guatemala to satisfy the conditions of the consent decree were the same reasons we had gone there in the first place: it had a weak, permissive, and corrupt government, and the company's social responsibility to the country was not likely to be made the issue that it had been in Panama. It worked; the company's Guatemalan operations were soon sold to Del Monte, following, I was told, the promise of a bribe."

The news was certainly out by now. What should have been plain for the past fifty years to anyone who read the newspapers was now inarguable: Chiquita Banana was a whore.

IF Chiquita could say anything at all to her formerly adoring fans by way of a defense, it could only be that she was no ordinary whore, but rather something of a modern-day Mata Hari—a spy who slept around.

And that was exactly the explanation offered by Herbert Berkson, a business consultant and investor from Boston who had been associated with two Guatemalan businessmen in an effort to buy the United Brands banana property. In 1974, Berkson filed suit in state court, Massachusetts, charging that United Brands and Del Monte had gypped him out of a fair chance to buy the property. The suit was dismissed in state court in December 1978, and reinstituted in federal court, Boston, in June 1979. At this writing in 1983, it is still in contention, with hundreds of pages of briefs and interrogatories floating back and forth among the parties.

Berkson has claimed that United Brands and Del Monte held "secret meetings" to exchange plans, fix prices, and falsify actual costs to evade taxes. He has accused the companies of pressuring his chief Guatemalan business partner, a big banana planter, into backing out of the bidding. Berkson says the companies threatened to boycott the planter's bananas. Through interrogatories, Berkson had elicited the information that United Brands gave the planter a $250,000 loan just before selling out to Del Monte. The companies deny any collusion, and say the planter later paid the loan back.

The obvious question, though, is why United Brands was so determined to sell to Del Monte. Berkson's answer lies in a series of allegations he keeps serving up in the form of court interrogatories, questions in the sense that he is asking for comments on his statements:

"That United Fruit provided a deep intelligence cover for the Central Intelligence Agency in Guatemala and other countries in Central America.

"That [officials of United Fruit] allowed the radio wires of its subsidiary, Tropical Radio, to be monitored clandestinely by a Central Intelligence Agency member without the knowledge of United Fruit stockholders.

"That the Securities and Exchange Commission has been influenced by the Central Intelligence Agency *not* to prosecute... for illegal bribes in Guatemala because of United States foreign policy and American national interests.

"[That] Del Monte and United Brands have been afforded select and preferential treatment by United States investigatory agencies because of past favors tendered by United Fruit to these agencies, and the delicate geopolitical considerations being dealt with in Central America at the present time."

United Brands has denied that it or Del Monte got preferential treatment because of past favors done for the U.S. government. United Brands also said that it "made reasonable inquiry" about whether the CIA had intervened in the case and hadn't been able to learn enough "to admit or deny same." As to its relations with the CIA, it refused to comment on the ground the answers weren't relevant to Berkson's lawsuit. The SEC didn't respond to requests to comment for this book on whether the CIA had interfered in the Guatemalan investigation.

The allegation about United Brands' little-known Tropical Radio Telegraph Company subsidiary (later known as TRT Telecommunications Corporation) is particularly interesting. Beginning in the 1920s, Tropical Radio provided the communications system not only within Guatemala, but in Nicaragua, Belize, Honduras, Costa Rica, Colombia, and other Central and South American countries. In 1972, the Federal Communications Commission (FCC) expanded Tropical Radio's authority over most of the world, and the company quickly began handling Telex, telephone, and satellite communications with Italy, Britain, Germany, and Switzerland.

Years ago in Boston, Berkson became friendly with a man named Frank C. Bibbs. Bibbs showed a personal knowledge of United Brands' top management, whom Berkson also knew as a result of an earlier business deal. According to Berkson, Bibbs eventually disclosed that he was a government agent (presumably CIA) who was allowed by United Brands to monitor Tropical Radio. Now, to monitor Tropical Radio would be the equivalent of wiretapping every phone and Telex in Guatemala, and much of the calling in many other countries.

Bibbs is now dead. His widow stated in an interview that he worked for Tropical Radio, but said she didn't know if he monitored it for the CIA. How could she not have known? "Well, if he worked for the CIA, I wouldn't know what he was doing," she said. "I really can't talk about it," she declared in response to other questions, and hung up. But a friend, Frank Ferrando— owner of the Charles Restaurant in Boston, where Bibbs liked to hang out— remembers quite clearly "that he worked for the government. People said the CIA. He never said what he did for the government, but he traveled a lot."

* * *

IN 1979, the Inter-American Development Bank, a kind of regional World Bank, surveyed land ownership in Guatemala. The figures it came up with were almost identical to those of 1944—a concentration of wealth that inspired a revolt then, and has continued to inspire each new generation of revolutionaries. Ninety percent of the farmers shared 16.2 percent of the land, while 2 percent of the farmers held 65.4 percent of the land.

A swell of revolution in 1966 brought a full-scale U.S. counterinsurgency program to Guatemala—arms, advisors, and even Green Berets. A 1980 State Department study analyzed the program: "To eliminate a few hundred guerrillas, the government killed perhaps 10,000 Guatemalan peasants," it said.*

In 1974, elections were held. Though both leading candidates were right-wing generals, one appeared to be more accommodating to the poor. Opponents of the regime in power agreed to participate in the election and back him. He won. But the regime prevented him from taking power, and gave the victory to his opponent. The U.S. said nothing. The election was widely recognized as a fraud, and the majority opposition was understandably disillusioned about democracy.

Still, each new administration that comes along in Washington is purportedly unable to understand why people who are not communists, and not Soviet allies, might still resort to violence. An almost identical episode had occurred in El Salvador in 1973, where elections were accepted, the most centrist candidate won, and the oligarchs refused to allow him to take office.

Not only did the poor have the least land, they had the worst land. And with the discovery of oil on Indian land in Guatemala in the late 1970s, it was necessary to clear the poor even off what land they did have, so that senior military officers could take it over in anticipation of the oil profits. In the town of Panzos, in north central Guatemala, about 700 Indians who had complained about the loss of their land were invited by the government to meet officials in the town square on May 29, 1978. Without warning, soldiers opened fire on the Indians, killing about 100, including women and children, and burying them in a predug grave. That kind of thing certainly discourages protests—and encourages a movement of people away from productive farming toward city slum life.

In 1979, Stephen Kinzer reported in the *Boston Globe* on a U.S. AID project to try to develop 125,000 acres near the oil land for use by peasant

---

*This quote comes from an article in *Foreign Policy* magazine by Marlise Simons, a reporter for the *New York Times* with much experience in Central America. In telephone interviews, she verified the existence of the study and the accuracy of the quote, but said she couldn't locate her copy to send to the author. Without specifics, the State Department couldn't locate it either. I trust her reporting, but include this caveat.

farmers. After roads, hydroelectric dams, and other modernizations made the area liveable, AID planned to distribute the land in 25-acre plots. Sound noble? Kinzer also reported that General Romeo Lucas, then the president of Guatemala, had reserved for himself an additional 130,000 acres, which will also be opened up—courtesy of U.S. taxpayers.

Amnesty International reported in 1982 that in the village of San Juan Comalapa, "more than thirty bodies were pulled out of the gorge" after a visit by the Guatemalan army. "Most had been strangled with a gar-rotte.... No recognition or explanation of the murders has ever been made by the government of Guatemala," the report said.

One escaped political prisoner told Amnesty International investigators, "Before my very eyes they [the army] killed three people. They strangled them. The way they killed them was with a piece of rope, a kind of noose, which they put round the neck and then used a stick to tighten it like a tourniquet from behind—handcuffed, and with their heads held down in the trough. Then they came out, their eyes were open; they'd already turned purple. It took at most three minutes in the water.... They just showed me the other six bodies and said the same thing would happen to me if I tried to lie to them."

Amnesty International interviewed a former soldier:

Q: Did you have permission to kill anyone?

A: Anyone who was a suspicious character.

Q: The soldiers can kill people without orders, just because someone is a suspicious character?

A: Yes, certainly.... We have got the right to kill him, and even more so if we have been given strict orders to.

According to a 1981 report by J. Michael Luhan, a former Peace Corps volunteer in Guatemala writing in the *New Republic* (which is almost Reaganistically anti-communist on foreign policy matters), twenty-seven directors of the Guatemalan National Workers Confederation were kidnapped from a meeting of the organization. They were hauled off by plainclothes cops in June 1980, and not seen again. Nine members of the Coca-Cola workers' union were assassinated during the year.

Luhan wrote that in May, the army established a camp in Comalapa, a town that had not had a single homicide in more than forty years. After the soldiers came, fifty villagers were dragged from homes, sidewalks, and buses, and were tortured and killed. When the family of one slain youth went to the army to complain, the army sent them home. That evening as they prepared dinner, two carloads of armed men arrived, broke down the door, and murdered all seven, five of them women and girls.

Things got so bad in 1982 that Father Ronald Hennessy, a Maryknoll priest, decided to go public and allowed his sisters, two Maryknoll nuns, to publish some of his letters in the *Des Moines Register*. This brought the wrath of the Church down on him, and he was ordered to keep quiet after that. But his pleas to persuade his fellow Americans to stop aiding the

Guatemalan government in carrying out this slaughter make poignant reading. The following is quoted from copies of his letters, not from the *Register*.

"General [Efrain] Rios Montt, president of Guatemala, thanked the U.S. in his address to the nation last evening for the $11 million granted to Guatemala," Father Hennessy wrote on July 27, 1982. "I'm wondering if the U.S. knows what is going on here. On the spot I cannot tell if Rios Montt [a self-styled, born-again Christian] is truly a mystic elevated beyond the cruel reality imposed on the people by his subordinate military officers, or if he is really a genocidist. . . . Let me give you a few of the happenings of just this month in just this parish and let you decide for yourselves:

"July 2: The military came to San Mateo and read off a list of forty people (only one woman) 'selected for leaders of the newly constituted Civil Defense.' The people were somewhat skeptical, but these people for the most part were the leaders, so ten men presented themselves. The military told them that they would have to come to the base in Barillas for special training. As they neared Barillas the soldiers tied their hands behind their backs, cut their throats, and tossed them off the cliff.

"July 9: The soldiers hung Diego Mario Mateo head downward from the light pole at the corner of the town square. They applied their boots to his face, shot him, and left him to hang for twenty-four hours before ordering his body thrown into the river. His two companions who were supposedly runners for the guerrillas were taken away by the soldiers supposedly to 'entertain' the people of two other towns in a similar way.

"July 10: Guerrillas shot Juan Bautista, health promoter in the *aldea* of Canaj.

"July 11: Four tortured bodies were dumped on the road above the *aldea* of Ixbajau. At least one, Sister Francisca's nephew, was definitely anti-guerrilla, as his father and brother were killed by them a year ago. He had been taken a week before by the army and tortured for days at the soldiers' base. . . .

"July 13: Soldiers with a defected guerrilla selected seven people in the *aldea* of Yolcultac and forced the people to beat him to death with clubs. They shot a thirteen-year-old boy there as he ran as they approached, making eight dead.

"July 14: The local military commander sent word for all of the people of the *aldea* of Petenac to be assembled for his 11:00 A.M. arrival. . . . At 4:00 P.M. all of the men, with hands tied behind their backs, were escorted by the soldiers to one house, shot, stabbed, piled one on top of the other, and covered with burnable items of the very house, which were sprinkled with gasoline and set on fire. The women were treated the same as the men, differing only in that some had live babies on their backs when they were stacked for burning. The other children were tied, one to another, and pulled alive into the flames of a third house by the soldiers. The two houses of the women and children were completely gutted; the fire designed to consume the men went out without burning the house or even the ropes binding their hands. Since the soldiers had left, they were unaware that one of their three pyres was ill-prepared. . . ."

Julia Preston, reporting in the *Columbia* [University] *Journalism Review*, said the number of violent deaths had increased so rapidly (50 percent higher each month than the last) that in September 1981 an association of Guatemalan coroners complained that they couldn't keep up with the demand for autopsies.

Still, the attitude of the U.S. government could be summed up by this verbatim report from the *New York Times*, December 19, 1982, datelined Guatemala: "Loopholes in congressional restrictions on aid to Guatemala have made it possible for the United States to continue to provide some military parts, instruction, and informal advice to this country's armed forces, according to Western officials here.

"Officially, United States military aid to Guatemala has been cut off since 1977, when the government here refused assistance after the Carter administration issued a report highly critical of the Guatemalans' performance on human rights. Congress then followed by imposing restrictions on military aid, citing the human rights situation.

"Now military aid appears increasingly likely to be restored at the request of President Reagan, following reports that the violence in the countryside has eased after strong government actions to control a guerrilla insurgency there."

THE direction Reagan would take in Guatemala was predictable long before he took office, not so much because of anything he said as by the actions of his close advisor, Michael Deaver. In the year of Reagan's election campaign, 1980, Deaver's public relations firm, Deaver & Hannaford, took on various right-wing Central and South American landowners and businessmen as clients. Among them was a group of Guatemalans.

It certainly doesn't require extraordinary imagination to figure out what "public" these Guatemalans wanted to improve their "relations" with. They got what they paid for. When Reagan took over, Deaver moved into the White House. By consensus accounts, he was one of the three men closest to the president (with Edwin Meese and James Baker).

Deaver's partner, Peter Hannaford, not only continued their public relations business, but also bought out the consulting business of Richard V. Allen, Reagan's national security advisor. Allen's clients also tended to be foreign nationals whose interests Allen would be tending after taking office.

IN May 1981, General Vernon Walters visited Guatemala. An intelligence specialist since World War II and former deputy director of the CIA, Walters, representing the president of the United States, made top-secret travels around the globe on national security matters. He was a kind of covert secretary of state. At the time of his visit to Guatemala, Amnesty International had already reported that "some 3,000 people described by government representatives as 'subversives' and 'criminals' were either shot on the spot in political assassinations or seized and murdered later."

But that didn't faze Walters. According to the *Washington Post*, he "said the United States hopes to help that [the Guatemalan] government defend 'peace and liberty' and 'the constitutional institutions of this country against the ideologies that want to finish off those institutions.'" Added Walters, "There will be human rights problems in the year 3,000 with the governments of Mars and the moon. There are some problems that are never resolved. One has to find a solution that respects a being's right to live without fear. But as I see it, the best way to do that is *not to impose the ideas of one nation on top of another*. [emphasis added]."

Try *that* for hypocrisy. Anyway, full aid was restored, as the *New York Times* had predicted. Guatemala's help was needed in the fight against the guerrilla insurgency in El Salvador, where similar conditions prevail.

Things don't change. Back in 1960 and 1961, our Guatemalan preserve was where the CIA chose to organize and train the invasion force for the Bay of Pigs. The property used was a plantation owned by Roberto Alejos, a conservative businessman who had formerly worked for the CIA—and for United Brands.

CHAPTER FOURTEEN

MAKING OUR BED IN CENTRAL AMERICA: PART II

==============================THE LANDSCAPES of Guatemala, El Salvador, Nicaragua, and Honduras have long been reddened by the blood of their citizens. People there and elsewhere in Central and South America dwell in poverty, illiteracy, and disease, sometimes in the shadow of a wealthy few. There may be nothing the United States can do that would quickly or dramatically change all this, which is sad. If these conditions *could* be eliminated, not only the Latins would benefit. The people of the U.S. would get a rich new marketplace. Prosperity and peace breed good trading partners.

For the past quarter century, the United States has fretted and fumed, and applied great resources trying to change conditions in Latin America. Yet the condition the U.S. has concentrated on changing has not been bloodshed, poverty, illiteracy, or disease. The U.S. effort has been directed toward changing the government of Cuba, where all these evils exist *less* than almost anywhere else in Latin America. And the U.S. has punished any nation that tried, even slightly, to emulate Cuba.

By almost any standard statistic for measuring minimum human economic needs—life expectancy, infant mortality, number of doctors or hospital beds or deaths per 1,000 population, calories consumed, literacy, number of television sets and radios in use relative to population—Cuba ranks high. It ranks ahead of Guatemala, El Salvador, and Honduras, where the U.S. has intervened recently to preserve established governments. It ranks ahead of Brazil, Chile, the Dominican Republic, and Guyana, where the United States intervened to help install governments that are now in power. It ranks ahead of most other countries in the region, and right up with the wealthiest states of Latin America, Argentina and Mexico.

And Cuba is certainly as safe and peaceful a place as you can find— when the U.S. isn't invading it. To be sure, Cuba uses police state tactics to insure this peace and safety. But governments that the U.S. supports and protects also use police state tactics, and often to promote violence. Terror, torture, and mayhem simply aren't part of Cuban life, even in prisons.

The truth is that the average Cuban lives very well these days by Third World standards. He appears much happier than his counterparts living under regimes that the U.S. supports or imposed. He endorses his government's foreign and domestic policies much more enthusiastically than his counterparts endorse the policies of their governments.

While some South American countries have much higher per capita incomes than Cuba does, the difference is diverted to the upper classes. Thus Cuba is well down on the statistical list in such items as the number of private cars. But it has put a high floor (or in President Reagan's term, safety net) under the laborers and farmers.

Money flows freely. Most families are well-fed and decently dressed. They are decently housed, though sometimes crowded and unable to move where they want because of an apartment shortage. Increasingly, they are enjoying home television and nights on the town. Big new hotels can't keep up with all the family vacationers. The average Cuban can go to a fancy restaurant and order the pick of the menu.

Much about Cuban life would certainly be unacceptable to Americans, and isn't particularly liked by Cubans. Local busybodies are parked on every residential street, watching who comes, who goes, who's friends with whom, and what people spend their money on. Anything out of the ordinary is reported, and will be questioned; people realize that if they ignore warnings and become known as troublemakers, they can lose job advancements, new housing assignments, or travel privileges. Ultimately, even jail is possible for political or social strays. Despite the Cuban government's assertion that these neighborhood watchdogs are democratically selected and uniformly respected, a lot of Cubans don't like having them around.

And Cuba is still a poor country by Western standards. Not only luxuries but many routine items are scarce. Decent clothing doesn't always translate into desirable fashion. One may accumulate conveniences only as government planners budget to put them on shelves. Because of the U.S. boycott on sales to Cuba, many goods aren't available even if the government wanted resources to be spent on them; other goods are available only as produced by the Soviet bloc, which almost everyone acknowledges makes inferior products.

The *libretta*, or ration book, limits citizens to one pair of pants and shoes, one shirt, and four sets of underwear a year, though all are available at prices well below those in the U.S. Most Cubans can afford more, and so a growing number of ration-free clothing stores are springing up; prices are higher there, however, and selection unpredictable. In addition, uniforms are provided free at schools and many workplaces, so daily apparel is often taken care of by the government.

Staples are rationed at food stores, and rations are too small for a healthy diet (each person is entitled to three quarters of a pound of meat every nine days, and one and one quarter pounds of beans and five pounds of rice a month). So, under the inevitable anomalies of a socialist economy, families often go to restaurants, order big meals, and then instead of eating the food, bag it and bring it home, where it lasts several days. That is sometimes easier and cheaper than buying the uncooked ingredients in a store.*

Most people eat at least one meal a day at work or school, or at ubiquitous lunch counters and cafeterias, where variety is limited but nutritious food is cheap, plentiful, and ration-free. In fact, there seems to be an organized effort to coerce people into eating food prepared at mass kitchens, where a national diet, well-balanced nutritionally, can be imposed. The sight of Cubans carrying doggie bags home from such informal restaurants is common.

---

*Perhaps my most startling experience in Cuba came at the graceful old Spanish mansion that is now La Verja, the most elegant restaurant in the port city of Cienfuegos. The dinner line formed in the mansion courtyard half an hour before the restaurant opened. After one or two squabbles over who had arrived first, the doors swung wide and dozens of Cubans—workers from the city docks, from the new cement and fertilizer factories, and from various government offices, along with their wives, children, and often elderly parents—were formally escorted by the tuxedoed maître d' to white-linened tables. A three-piece combo began dinner music.

Suddenly, without benefit of menus or conversation, waiters burst from the kitchen with trays of food. The meals coming off the trays were identical—huge, meaty ham hocks, a delicacy known in Cuba as *lacon naturale*. Just as quickly, out from the patrons' pockets and purses came plastic bags. Waiters assisted parents, grandparents, and kids in shoveling the ham hocks off the white East German china and into the baggies. And people got up to leave.

The soiled hand of a workingman, who obviously hadn't been home to change clothes since pulling his nine-to-five, reached over from the next table and thrust before me a five peso note, valued at $6. "Will you buy a *lacon naturale* for me in addition to whatever you're having for dinner?" he asked in Spanish. It seemed the limit was one to a customer, and he had already bagged his.

Within minutes, two-thirds of the restaurant had emptied out, the combo resumed playing and the rest of us, plus other diners who strolled in, were politely offered daiquiris and menus. It was a ridiculous way to distribute goods, all right. But working people had money in their pockets, and they had access to pleasures that working people find in few other Third World countries. By the same token, you can see hordes of children pouring out of schools at 3:00 P.M., and ambling over in their neat little shorts and shirts to soda shops with change in their pockets to buy ice cream or fruit juice, just as they might in the U.S. or France.

Since 1980, Cubans have been able to patronize "free markets," where pork, beans, and other commodities are sold unrationed by farmers who produce a surplus after fulfilling their government crop quotas. Free market prices are, of course, much higher than the 1960s-level prices enforced at restaurants and government markets.

For all its inconveniences, life is better than in most comparable countries. Abject poverty seems to have been abolished—an extraordinary accomplishment for a Third World country that relies on a single volatile crop, sugar cane, for 80 percent of its foreign exchange. Even a Yankee must be impressed with how the removal of all traces of destitution improves the quality of life for everyone in a society. In neither the cities nor the countryside of Cuba does one encounter the pitiful shoeless, shirtless urchins who populate much of the globe.

Nor is there evidence of idle people of any age, or of malnutrition, hunger, or begging. Everyone gets a free education, although it's obstructed by the absence of such items as ballpoint pens, which are unavailable, and by a shortage of schools, which means that half the children have to drop out before finishing ninth grade.

No one dies from easily preventable or curable diseases. Cubans frequently volunteer to tell a visitor how well their latest malady was treated at the free clinics. One occasionally encounters people with plaster casts, or modern wheelchairs or crutches; in most countries, such care is available only to the very rich. Cuban infant mortality has been knocked down to the lowest in Latin America, and life expectancy has risen to approximately U.S. levels, both great improvements over the days before the revolution.

Most Cubans believe their lives are getting better, and will continue to get better. They expect their children will find jobs based on ability, not birth station. They argue that despite the Orwellian government snooping, real restrictions on their lives are less now than under previous right-wing dictatorships. On the whole, as a place to live, it beats hell out of Guatemala.

WHATEVER success the Cuban economy has enjoyed isn't the kind that many other countries could easily emulate. The success depends on the Soviet bloc's pumping about $4 billion a year* into Cuba by buying most of the sugar crop for several times the world price and selling oil to Cuba at well below the world price. This is equivalent to about one-third of Cuba's gross

*Another slippery statistic. The Cubans and Soviets, the only ones who might know for sure, won't say. The CIA released figures in 1981, supposedly valid up to 1979, placing the aid and subsidies at $3.11 billion a year, though the CIA tends to underestimate the strength of the Cuban economy, and there are other reasons to believe the amount has increased since 1979. I settled on the $4 billion estimate after long talks with Cuban finance officials, and governmental and nongovernmental authorities in the U.S.

national product. If Fidel Castro hadn't swung his deal with the Soviet Union, the safety net wouldn't be nearly as high as it is, and Cubans wouldn't be nearly as happy as they are.

But he *did* swing the deal, and he deserves credit for it. At home, he gets that credit. He sold his country's political and logistical support to the Soviets and got top dollar. Cuba is held under no force. It can ask the Soviets to go anytime it wants to give up the $4 billion a year and Soviet military protection against a U.S. invasion. But why should it?

Probably no other Third World country has struck such a profitable bargain with a major power. What allowed Castro to do all this? What has kept his people so solidly behind him through all the hardships of an inefficient, luxury-less socialist economy, and all the indignities of a Big Brother police state?

We did. We have.

The animosity of the United States is the mortar that binds the bricks of the Cuban revolution. Cubans were long accustomed to their country's being a little guy. But now they have watched Goliath attack and get beat. Now Cuba isn't just *any* little guy; it's David, victorious, and the people love it. It has galvanized them as nothing else could have.

As long as the U.S. continues to attack, it will likely continue to galvanize them. Cubans are cheerfully willing to work harder, to suffer more adversity, and to complain less. The United States, by playing a mean, boastful, bungling Hertz, has allowed Cuba to play Avis. The Cubans don't have to be number one to feel like winners. All they have to do is hang in there, and they have.

THE Senate Intelligence Committee in 1975 reported finding "concrete evidence of at least eight plots involving the CIA to assassinate" Castro, and another to kill his brother Raul. The plots, the Senate report said, involved devices "which strain the imagination," including Mafia hit men, poisoned cigars, and a diving suit contaminated with disease-causing organisms (the diving suit was to be delivered as a gift by a negotiator on a humanitarian mission to get prisoners released, but the negotiator chose to give Castro a different diving suit).

In addition, the CIA acknowledged nine other assassination attempts against Castro by persons with "operational relationships" with the CIA though "not for the purpose of assassination." In other words, we hired them and sent them to Cuba to spy, or blow up power plants, or some such thing, and we were surprised when they took a shot at the premier.

Senate hearings showed that the CIA tried to drug Castro so he'd talk silly in public, drug the sugar cane workers so the crop would rot, and drug the sugar itself so that it would taste bad. Saboteurs were sent in to blow up industrial installations. The Senate report wasn't news to the Cubans, of course. They had uncovered many of these plots in thwarting them. The Cuban government had howled about this covert war for years, while the U.S. government denied it was taking place.

Much else was discovered outside the Senate's public hearings, by various reporters.* Among other things, it was learned that:

—CIA agents in Cuba regularly set fire to sugar cane fields. National Security Council staffers remember long discussions on manipulating the world sugar market, and how to persuade Japan and Western Europe not to buy Cuban sugar. (They also remember President Nixon, unhappily receiving a State Department presentation on how to relax tensions with Cuba, then reassuring the NSC, "Never mind, as long as I'm president it won't happen.")

—The CIA tried to cut off the supply of baseballs to Cuba. Agents persuaded suppliers in other countries not to ship them. (U.S. baseballs were already banned by the trade embargo the U.S. had declared.) Some balls got in from Japan, and Cubans continued to play baseball, but the supply was so limited that the government had to ask fans to throw foul balls and home runs back onto the field for continued play.

—In 1964, a shipload of British Leyland buses destined for Cuba was dumped into the Thames River and ruined after the East German freighter carrying them was rammed by a Japanese cargo ship. According to Jack Anderson and his colleague, Joseph Spear, relying on sources at both the CIA and the National Security Agency, the sinking of the buses was arranged by the CIA.

—CIA frogmen blew up boats in Cuban harbors, much as someone did back in 1898 to the battleship *Maine*. (Remember?)

—A CIA team entered a warehouse in Vera Cruz, Mexico, in 1966 and sabotaged a mechanical sugar cane harvester on its way to Cuba. The $45,000 machine, which could do the work of 300 men, had been built in Thibodaux, Louisiana. A man bought it there for shipment to Mexico, not revealing that he was a Cuban agent, or that the machine would be transshipped to Cuba to evade the U.S. trade embargo. The CIA learned of the deal, and intimidated the Thibodaux factory manager into letting operatives take apart an identical machine and copy the operating manuals.

With what they learned in Thibodaux, the CIA team was able to go to Vera Cruz, reverse all the gears on the machine, and substitute forged operating manuals for the real ones, to insure that any attempts to get the machine to work would be futile. When the machine reached Cuba, the Cubans—unable to buy machines in the U.S.—sent it as a prototype to the

*Their information came from interviews with former CIA officers, State Department officials, and other persons who participated in the goings-on. Sufficient of these sources have been located and reinterviewed by this author to confirm what's printed here. One outstanding journalist from that era, who, because of his present job, asked not to be named here, graciously gave me entree to many of his original sources.

Soviet Union, where twenty-six copies were reproduced, and shipped back to Cuba; none of them worked. All this infuriated Edward Lamb, of Toledo, Ohio, who owned the Thibodaux factory. A believer in free trade, Lamb figured the embargo had just cost $2 million in sales of his harvester. He traveled to Cuba and the Soviet Union to piece together the above story.

A RUMOR-MONGERING operation was set up in Cuba by General Edward Lansdale, a specialist in such covert actions.* President Kennedy had personally asked Lansdale to run the secret war against Cuba after the Bay of Pigs invasion failed. Lansdale had perfected his rumor-mongering technique while running covert operations in the Philippines during the 1950s, and later in Vietnam.

CIA agents in Cuba were usually Cubans, often with relatives in the U.S. Recruits were promised that their own transportation to the U.S. would be arranged in time, and that money would be waiting for them when they arrived. They were particularly instructed to spread rumors of shortages of various goods. The intention was to start people complaining while waiting in lines, and to make rationing more difficult to administer.

Lansdale also ordered a campaign to sabotage Cuba's lubricating oil. This was another skill Lansdale had picked up in Vietnam—interestingly enough, back in 1954, when the U.S. supposedly wasn't a combatant in Southeast Asia. Lansdale's secret war was being waged long *before* North Vietnam was accused of having violated the Indochina peace arrangements, justifying overt U.S. military assistance to South Vietnam.

Just as the French were being thrown out, Lansdale sent a team to sabotage the Hanoi bus and rail systems, which the victorious Viet Minh were about to take over. His postaction report said, "The team had a bad moment when contaminating the oil. Fumes from the contaminant came close to knocking them out. Dizzy and weak-kneed, they masked their faces with handkerchiefs and completed the job." By the time of the anti-Cuban campaign, the CIA had determined to come up with a better contaminant.

EDWARD OWEN BENNETT, a professor of biology at the University of Houston, Texas, was and is perhaps the country's leading expert on biodeterioration of petroleum products. He remembers when a CIA officer, flashing a badge, recruited him in 1959. That first approach came in the lobby of the

---

*In a reinterview in 1983, Lansdale didn't remember particular incidents of rumor-mongering in Cuba that he had mentioned in an interview ten years ago with a very reliable reporter, although Lansdale said it was possible these incidents had taken place and he had forgotten them. He did confirm completely the rest of the episodes recounted here.

old Commodore Hotel in New York City, where Bennett was presenting a paper on lubricants at a scientific conference. "It was a little bit on the weird side, sort of cops and robbers," Bennett recalls. "They said, in essence, 'We have been watching your work and would like to help support it because it may have some applications we're interested in.' That's essentially what they did."

His assignment was to prepare a substance that would contaminate lubricants. He wasn't told at first that Cuba was the target, but he knew that sabotage was the intent. Then, as now, however, Bennett regarded his work as research into how to *improve* lubricants. "We had to understand what makes oil deteriorate in order to make it last longer," he explains. "Once we know the basic mechanisms by which petroleum is broken down, it is not too difficult to control it, or take it the other way."

Eventually, he says, he was able to make a product for sabotage that would make oil "deteriorate 100 times faster than it normally would." When the oil lost its lubricating ability ahead of schedule, of course, the engine or machine that it was lubricating would also deteriorate. "It would destroy the engine," Bennett says. And that was the whole idea.

Bennett says the CIA was great to work for. "They were excellent scientists. The money was generous. There was a minimum of red tape. Many grants, you have to spend half the time filling out papers. They weren't that way. The techniques we worked out, they took to American companies that were cooperating with them and tested them under field conditions to confirm they did indeed do what I said." Only two people at his main place of employment, the Univeristy of Houston, knew the CIA was paying Bennett on the side. But he says that when the payments were revealed in congressional hearings in 1977, only one professor objected.

"I have no apologies for doing my work," Bennett says. "I'm sorry they used it against Cuba. I have mixed emotions about that. Any scientist—say he's developing a nerve gas. He may develop the gas so he can better understand the nervous system. He may not like the idea it can be used in nasty ways. But I am not greatly grieved. If I hadn't done it, someone else would have. I would imagine it's still going on. It was always humorous to me that I had students working on this work who to this day don't know that CIA supported a lot of them."

Though Bennett didn't find out about it until later, his product was dumped into Cuban-bound lubricating oil as it passed through the French port of Marseille. Teams of four and five Cubans were slipped into France to doctor the oil shipments, and were slipped out again. The French government wasn't told. Since right after World War II, the CIA, on its own, had infiltrated the corrupt gangs that control the Marseille docks. The U.S. government had secretly decided that it was America's responsibility to make sure that the French dockside unions remained under the domination of hoodlums, and that they didn't fall into the hands of left-wing labor organizers.

Now this capability was employed in the anti-Cuban campaign. One CIA career officer who helped put the oil sabotage operation together in the U.S., and has since retired, says his bosses were terrified that a team might get caught, which is why the missions were restricted to the CIA's Cuban agents. Discovery by French authorities that U.S. paramilitary forces had sneaked onto French soil to sabotage the legitimate commerical transactions of a French oil company might have damaged relations with our purported ally.

According to Bennett, his substance was also applied by agents in Cuba to sabotage oil already in machines. That is "more insidious," he says, because the adulteration then becomes impossible to detect by sight or smell.

Bennett refuses to say whether he is still working for the CIA. He does say he traveled to South Africa in the late 1970s and early 1980s to help the South African government devise ways of preventing the deterioration of oil in long-term storage. (South Africa is stocking up for a possible cut-off by its Islamic suppliers in event of a war over majority rule.)

As for the Cuban campaign, after the oil and sugar had been sabotaged as well as possible, Lansdale was reduced to ruminating sadly on the limitations of his craft. "Anthracite coal and cement, there's not too much you can do against it," he once said. "How you sabotage anthracite coal, I've never figured out."

EVEN CIA operatives involved in the secret war against Cuba concede they really didn't think they could make the Castro government fall. They say they wanted "to raise the price for the Russians" of keeping a Cuban ally. Of course, they also raised the price for Americans; they estimate that the campaign cost the taxpayers more than $1 billion.

But whatever the dollar cost, it was pale compared to the stain on America's moral fiber. Professors weren't the only professionals called away from their proper pursuits. Nor were Edward Bennett's students the only subordinates who were led unwittingly into working on behalf of a secret, possibly unconstitutional, sabotage campaign.

Attorney General Robert Kennedy's declared war on the national crime syndicate was compromised by the employment of Mafia underbosses to help in the undeclared, but obviously higher-priority, war against Fidel Castro. The president of the United States wound up sleeping with a woman—Judith Exner—who at the same time was sleeping with a Mafia gangster who was working on a hit contract awarded by the U.S. government.

The Cuban immigrants secretly hired and trained by the CIA went wildly out of control, perpetrating shootings, bombings, and vigilante law wherever they went, from Miami to New York. During the 1960s, they received special protection from prosecution, which outraged dedicated law enforcement authorities. When the government tried to pull the reins on these terrorist thugs in the 1970s, it was often too late.

Donald Skelton, recalling his distinguished career with the Dade County, Florida, police, clearly remembers both his first disillusioning episode, and also his last, sixteen years later. "When I was just a rookie, back in 1962," he says, "I stopped Orlando Bosch with a whole truckload of machine guns." Bosch, one of the most violence-prone of the CIA-trained anti-Castro activists, would later lead an explosion-happy group called Acción Cubana. Among other things, in 1976, Bosch's group helped plant the car bomb in Washington, D.C., that killed Orlando Letelier, leader of the exile opposition to the government of Chile; it also killed Letelier's American assistant.

Skelton wanted to lock Bosch up and throw the book at him that night in 1962. Had he been allowed to do so, he might have saved scores of innocent lives in the U.S. and elsewhere. Skelton had found Bosch's gun-laden car in a high-price residential area late at night. "When I reported in the tag number, the CIA was all over my ass in seconds," he recalls. "Several carloads of men in casual clothes" arrived on the scene and took over. Skelton's supervisors explained to him that the CIA was working with Bosch, and others like him. No charges were filed.

Skelton would go on to command the Dade County Department of Public Safety's vigorous war against narcotics trafficking and the crime syndicate. But he quit in 1978, after the CIA again squelched a major case. Skelton had commanded the local half of the investigation into the World Finance Company,* a money-moving network with offices around the world, and with connections to narcotics, fraud, and espionage. It was based in Miami and run by Cuban-exile CIA veterans.

World Finance is the company (discussed in chapter 2) founded with the help of Walter Sterling Surrey, the former U.S. intelligence officer who is now a high-powered Washington lawyer-lobbyist. Surrey's partner, David A. Morse, the former U.S. secretary of labor, orchestrated the St. Regis Hotel meeting on Zaire. Their firm, Surrey & Morse, has obvious influence with government. Until 1976, the year Skelton's investigation started, Surrey was listed as a shareholder and director of World Finance. (He has denied knowing of any illegal activity there.)

Since federal law was apparently being violated, the U.S. Justice Department took control of the World Finance investigation from Skelton's local team. Dozens of FBI and Internal Revenue Service investigators from all over the country were assembled in Miami to handle the case. Then, in 1978, despite what attorneys on the scene considered an overwhelming amount of criminal evidence, the federal government scotched the World Finance investigation.† The big investigative team was called off and sent home right

*Formally restyled WFC Corporation.

†One tax indictment related to World Finance was handed up in 1981, but it ignores most of the issues raised by the investigation.

after the CIA asserted a protective interest in a dozen prime suspects. One, Richard Fincher, was a prominent Florida politician.* Another, a Cuban named Guillermo Hernandez-Cartaya, was the chief executive at World Finance. The CIA had paid $50,000 to get him out of a Cuban jail after he was captured at the Bay of Pigs.† During that time, several government investigators say, he went on hunting and fishing trips with Vice-President Nelson Rockefeller.

Says Skelton now, "It worked fine up to a point where somebody said, 'Hey, this goes all the way up to the White House. We better pull the plug on it.' Then all the boys went home." Skelton himself gave up on the Miami dope wars, and took a job as police chief in a safe, prosperous Atlanta, Georgia, suburb.

The secret war against Cuba still haunts the colleagues he left behind, as they continue to try to pacify Miami. Officer Skip Renganeschi, who worked under Skelton and has stayed on with the Dade County police, complained in 1982, "Cubans kill and bomb and go to jail thinking that the CIA is going to get them out. [They think] they're doing it for their country. There are bombings going on here all the time."

THE backfire from the secret war on Cuba was felt even in the Watergate affair. President Nixon commented in his tape-recorded White House conversations right after the break-in at Democratic headquarters in the Watergate Hotel in 1972, "The problem is, it tracks back to the Bay of Pigs." One of the burglars, Eugenio Martinez, an enthusiastic soldier in the secret war against Castro, was still on the CIA payroll, regularly reporting to an agency higher-up, when he was arrested at the Watergate.

At sentencing, Judge John Sirica asked Martinez why he had broken into the Watergate. Martinez replied, "It pertained toward the Cuban situation. When it comes to Cuba and when it comes to communist conspiracies involving the United States, I will do anything to protect this country against any communist conspiracy."

Potentially the most important backfire by far from the Cuban attacks was the confrontation between the U.S. and U.S.S.R. in October 1962—the Cuban missile crisis. It was the most frightening time yet in the nuclear era, and Americans generally placed the blame for it on a warmongering, adventuring Soviet premier Nikita Khrushchev. Khrushchev later contended in his memoirs that his "main" reason for placing the missiles in Cuba was "to

---

*Of at least fifteen calls to Fincher's listed telephone, day and evening over several months, only one was ever answered—by a woman who said Mr. Fincher wasn't there and that she knew of no number where he could be reached.

† According to law enforcement and published sources. Hernandez-Cartaya is reported by former associates to be living in Brownsville, Texas, but there is no listed telephone for him in Brownsville, and all efforts to reach him failed.

restrain the United States from precipitous military action against Castro's government." It sounded like propaganda at the time. But Khrushchev and Castro knew what the U.S. public didn't know: Cuba really *was* being invaded. Khrushchev was coming to the defense of an ally under direct foreign attack—a motive that the United States has used to justify more than one war.

Once more, U.S. diplomacy was out of the hands of diplomats. The work done at the State Department sometimes seems like a mammoth (and costly) charade. The real U.S. policymakers, in the White House and at CIA head-quarters in Langley, Virginia, apparently made no effort to coordinate their secret war with the officials who bore public responsibility for U.S.-Cuban relations. The three men who served as assistant secretary of state for Latin American affairs from the Johnson years until the secret war supposedly was called off in the early 1970s (Lincoln Gordon, Covey Oliver, and Charles Meyer) all say they were never informed the war was going on—even though their job was to supervise U.S. policy toward Cuba.

IN recent years, the U.S. government has disavowed the acts of the Cubans it hired in the 1960s. But for obvious reasons, Cuba continues to take what they do very seriously. In 1977, a congressional study mission visited Cuba to explore the possibility of improving relations under President Carter. The mission found that Cubans all over the island were profoundly concerned with the October 1976 in-flight bombing of a Cuban airliner. The plane exploded shortly after it took off from Barbados, killing all seventy-three persons on board, including Cuba's Olympic fencing team.

The crash got little publicity in the U.S., and when Castro gave a funeral oration blaming the CIA for the explosion, his remarks were passed off as the usual communist propaganda. Kissinger's denial of responsibility was perfunctory. But the Cuban people were irate. One Cuban told visiting representative Jonathan Bingham (a Democrat from New York), as Bingham's report summed it up, "When eleven [Israeli] athletes were killed by terrorists at the Olympic games in Munich, there was an outpouring of sympathy and outrage from the entire world. But when fifty-seven innocent Cubans were killed by terrorists in Barbados, including Cuba's Olympic fencing team, there was little reaction in the press or from other governments."

The explosion occurred on the second leg of a flight that had begun in Trinidad. Riding the plane from Trinidad to Barbados, and getting off there minutes before the fatal blast, was Hernan Ricardo, a current or former—who knows?—CIA operative who was traveling under a false passport. Ricardo immediately headed back to Trinidad. From there, he telephoned an associate in Caracas, Venezuela, and used euphemistic words to indicate that a mission had been accomplished. The conversation was overheard by authorities.

Not long before he traveled on the doomed plane, Hernan Ricardo had met in the Dominican Republic with Orlando Bosch—the same terrorist leader whom police officer Donald Skelton had wanted to arrest back in 1962, when Bosch was instantly able to summon protection from the CIA. After his meetings in the Dominican Republic with Ricardo and others, Bosch had promised that international acts of terrorism against Cuba would be forthcoming. In fact, groups related to his group specifically mentioned airliner bombings. Ricardo, Bosch, and an associate were captured in Venezuela and jailed for the Barbados tragedy.

Were Ricardo and Bosch killing people on behalf of the CIA in 1976? Probably not. But how can anyone, particularly the Cubans, know that? Ricardo and Bosch apparently *were* killing people with weapons just like the ones the CIA had given them, and trained them how to use. They apparently were killing people in the same spirit the CIA had encouraged as patriotic less than a decade earlier. In his speech that charged the CIA with the airliner bombing, Castro also read off a laundry list of smaller terrorist attacks, some fatal to Cubans, carried out by persons who had been paid, trained, and housed on U.S. soil by the CIA.

Anti-Castro saboteurs still train at bases in Florida. The U.S. government says it is powerless to stop them, though it howls at the Palestine Liberation Organization and other groups, including the Cubans themselves, who harbor terrorist training bases. Boatloads of anti-Castro terrorists are still captured, from time to time, trying to enter Cuba, direct from their Florida camps.

BUT the Cuban revolution has survived. Through Cuba's role as a stalwart, successful underdog, Cubans have won respect and honor throughout the Third World. It is a reverence that constantly irritates the United States foreign policy apparatus, which makes it all the more enjoyable to the Cubans. In 1979, Castro was chosen leader of the large group of "nonaligned" nations, and Cuba, which is hardly "nonaligned," hosted their conferences.

The U.S. government was able to comprehend this tribute only as a naive misunderstanding of communism by the majority of nations of the world. In fact, the general respect for Cuba isn't a tribute to communism at all, but to the ability of one small nation to stand up to a powerful and threatening neighbor. It is the same respect that most Third World countries have tried to show to the less-well-organized Afghan resisters. It is the same respect they would probably also show to Lech Walesa if Poland is ever fortunate enough to gain the same freedom from the Soviet Union that Cuba has gained from the United States.

The two men, Castro and Walesa, really have much in common. Both have faith in utopian socialism. Both have sworn a commitment to bring their peoples independence, despite a history of domination by an overwhelmingly powerful neighbor. And Castro and Walesa also share a staggering physical and moral courage, which allows each of them to wake up every day staring at death and spitting at it in defense of principle.

Yet one man, and his followers, we idolize. And the other, and his followers, we have waged war on for twenty-five years.

CHAPTER FIFTEEN

THE CHOSEN ENEMY: THE CUBANS

WHO ARE these Cubans we have sacrificed so much to try to "liberate"? How many are followers of Castro? How many really want to get in a boat and go to Miami—and what motivates the ones who do? If we as a nation are going to expend so much of our foreign energy on Cuba, and on preventing "other Cubas," we had better be sure we have the right answers to these questions.

Recently, the U.S. mission in Havana (called an "interests section" rather than an embassy because the U.S. government doesn't recognize the Cuban government) was sitting on 50,000 applications from Cubans to emigrate to the U.S. Though most Americans presume otherwise, it is the United States's reluctance to admit more Cubans, not Castro's reluctance to let them go, that impedes the "liberation" of these people.

U.S. diplomats in Havana have estimated that 10 percent of the island's remaining population, about one million people, would like to join the one million who have already exited to the U.S. since the Cuban revolution. But a reporter who traveled the length and breadth of Cuba by bus, train, and taxi, talking with hundreds of Cubans from all walks of life, in their homes and in public places, using an American interpreter and mostly unaccompanied by any Cuban official, failed to find this army of malcontents.

The only Cubans who expressed serious interest in leaving were a few young men just out of school, who talked about their desire for rock music, cars, and the good life, and some lonely looking retirees who say they have family ties in the U.S. and also miss a free-market society. Considering that throughout the Third World there are endless millions of people who at least *think* they would like to emigrate to the land of two-car families with a Sony in every bedroom, and that the U.S. now faces big immigration problems from the so-called "free" nations of the Caribbean basin, the number of people wanting to leave Cuba today is not extraordinary. If you were to open a port in El Salvador and provide boats and U.S. visas, you would see a yacht race at least the equal of any flotilla that ever left a Cuban port.

Cuba has had its émigrés. It was clear from the moment Castro rode into Havana in January 1959 that a lot of Cubans would be better off elsewhere. No small number had attained privileged status by selling out their countrymen's freedom to the Yankees. Still more, though, were honest, upper middle class victims of Castro's decision to reorient the country's economy toward the service of the millions who had been powerless. Many hard-working Cuban business and professional people and their families chose, years ago, to flee to places like the U.S. where markets had long been relatively free, and thus where no such sudden leveling need occur.

But Cuba started over. More typical of today's Cubans are these:

═══════════════════════THE DOMINO PLAYERS

After a working day, hundreds of Cienfuegos men gather at social clubs for dominoes and conversation. Sitting at a table picked at random, one finds Andrew, who left school a year ago at age seventeen to work on a shrimp boat. His base pay is 192 pesos, about $233, a month. But most of his earnings come from bonuses paid for exceeding his quota. When he and the other five men on his boat haul in more than 8,000 kilos (17,600 pounds) of shrimp a month, which they have done a couple of times, they earn about 1,100 pesos each—a staggering $1,320.

Andrew's friend, Elario, twenty-two, jokes that Andrew works too hard for this money, often night and day, and risks his life on rough seas. "He is hardly ever here to live," Elario says. He says he's happier working as a hauler on the docks, earning $196 a month base pay and up to $360 more a month in bonuses for extra work.

A third friend, Ernesto, thirty-eight, says he earns $186 a month assembling large industrial refrigerators, and averages another $240 to $360 in productivity bonuses. Almost every worker and farmer interviewed in Cuba was making well over the $114.36-a-month government guaranteed bottom wage. What is the one message that Andrew, Elario, and Ernesto would like to send to the U.S. people? "How good the work is paid here," each responds.

THE MECHANIC

Roger Rojas, thirty-two, is chief mechanic of the Talleres Provinciale, a busy, five-man automobile repair shop in Santiago, Cuba's second-largest city. He is one of the small army of wizards who keep Cuba's fleet of 1940s and 1950s U.S. cars running despite the embargo on parts. Though an increasing number of Soviet bloc and Argentine cars have arrived in recent years, Cuba still relies on relics from Detroit's tail-finned heyday—so much so that an American visitor sometimes feels he's walked into a time warp.

Some cars are still privately owned, and the owners pick up extra money by operating their cars as taxis. The government encourages them, though, to turn their cars over to the state in exchange for guaranteed jobs as drivers.

How do they keep these old flivvers chugging? "Sometimes we put a Soviet piston in them," Rojas says. "We bore out the cylinder to make the piston fit. We adapt Soviet carburetors to American cars. Transmissions also. For us, it's nothing abnormal. You've got to do it or the car just stops."

Today, he is installing a new Soviet-made four-cylinder Volga engine into a 1952 Willys station wagon. "The original engine was just getting too old and we were putting in too much work on it," he says. His black face drips with perspiration. Even though he has found an engine of matching horsepower, he is having trouble adapting it to the original U.S.-made transmission, which may also have to be replaced with Soviet parts.

Rojas was born about 50 miles north of Santiago, one of seven children of a sugar cane inspector. He wanted to leave school to fight at the Bay of Pigs in 1961, "but they wouldn't let me. I was too young." A year later, on finishing seventh grade, he was allowed to join the army. He drove heavy equipment, near Havana. In 1968, he left the army to do the same work on civilian road crews. Two years later, he moved back to Santiago to marry a teacher he had fallen in love with. He got a job as a chauffeur for a government official, then, when he learned a mechanic was needed at the repair shop where he took the official's car, and which was close to his home, he took it. He started at $196 a month and now makes $305, a big jump in real earnings because most Cuban prices haven't risen as U.S. prices have.

Cuban salaries also understate real income in other ways, because much of the cost of living is subsidized. Medical care and education are free. Rent is no more than 10 percent of the income of the head of the household, and most households have more than one income earner. Subsidized lunches are served to 3.1 million Cubans daily at work or school. Working women are offered free child care.

In 1978, Rojas volunteered for the army reserve, and applied to join Cuban forces in Angola. So far, he says, there hasn't been a place for him. "There are a lot of us that want to go," he says. Though the trip might cost him his job, separate him from his family, and expose him to danger, he wants it. "We've had a great experience with all the help our revolution has received from the Soviet Union," he says. "All Cubans have a debt to other countries that want their freedom."

These words were volunteered privately, out of earshot of other Cubans. They were typical of those heard from many young men. Rojas was interviewed without prearrangement; a reporter simply asked at random on the town square where to get a car repaired, went straight there, and started asking questions. Also typically, after most of the interview had taken place, a government official dashed in, allegedly to get his car fixed, and insisted on taking over the bulk of the conversation from Rojas. The official left as soon as the reporter did.

THE VIGILANTES

Juan Denysiuk, about seventy, son of a Ukrainian immigrant, is a retired airport worker and the elected president of his local Committee for the Defense of the Revolution (CDR) in a Havana suburb. CDRs are in every neighborhood, whether it covers a city block or a country mile. Officially, the CDRs are a grass roots way to give people control of their revolution. Often, though, it's obviously the other way around.

Denysiuk and his wife, Mercedes Fortes, who is the "political orientator" for their CDR, live on a narrow street lined by one- and two-story houses. From their door, they can—and do—watch everything. Their house is clearly marked, as it has been for most of the past twenty years, as CDR headquarters. She is past president of the CDR, as he was before her. They take turns at it. They are thin, gaunt, cheerless replicas of the couple in the painting *American Gothic*, but without the pitchfork.

Their assigned neighborhood has eighty residents over the CDR minimum membership age of fourteen. Of the eighty, seventy-two have joined the committee. Eight have chosen not to. Two other neighbors who weren't members quit the country for the U.S. a year earlier, when Castro opened a port for anyone who wanted to leave. These ratios appear typical.

One of the nonmember neighbors is actually an African witch doctor, who performs pagan rituals with chickens and various vegetables. People with problems, usually concerning love or money, come from all over the metropolitan area to see him. They pay what he asks, and he performs his witchcraft. He is a seemingly free entrepreneur, although he makes what he says are "large donations" to the state. Says Denysiuk, "There's never been any problem."

According to Ms. Fortes, who does most of the couple's talking, the CDRs have three assigned functions: "The first job is to be vigilant—to see that no one does anything against the revolution. Then comes ideological education... that they understand the plight of other people in the world and the friendship with the Soviet Union and other peoples of the Americas, including the workers [as opposed to the government] of North America [the official euphemism for the U.S.]." Finally, she says, comes "social work... to help the children who don't study, old persons who live alone," and others who need help.

But she seems most interested in the vigilance. Daytimes, she and her husband handle it. At night, they and other volunteers take turns guarding the street, wearing arm bands but not weapons. Strangers are questioned, packages searched. It is a legacy from the Bay of Pigs and other U.S. attacks, although obviously it serves other purposes.

Denysiuk and Fortes are helping organize elections for local parliaments known as People Power, which in turn elect national figures. Street windows display posters that contain the candidates' résumés, sometimes their pictures, but never their positions on issues. Midway through the interview, a girl of eight or ten bursts through the open door and asks if her costume is ready for an upcoming pageant. Fortes says the costumes will be ready in a few days. The girl leaves. The pageant is to celebrate the twentieth anniversary of the CDRs.

=================THE OLD WOMAN

She is seventy-seven, lives alone in a one-room Havana apartment, and every day goes out for a nice restaurant lunch, alone. Before—in Cuba, "before" means 1958 or earlier, before the revolution—she earned $300 a month working in the office of an American steamship company. The husband of her only child was an aviator, and his father a general, in the army of Fulgencio Batista, the U.S.-backed dictator.

At 1:00 A.M., January 1, 1959, she recalls, Batista called the two men in for a New Year's drink. When they arrived, he told them the revolutionary army was nearing Havana and that they had better collect their wives and fly to the U.S. before daylight or they might be killed. They did, and that was the last that the old woman saw of her family.

A few weeks later a new boss arrived in her office. He told her she would have to leave because she had family ties to the old regime. She refused. She was, she recalls, taken to a mental hospital. "They told me I would be there a month for observation because they thought by then I would be driven crazy," she says. "But the doctor wasn't a revolutionary. He was a Catholic. He said he'd sign that I wasn't crazy, just to stay [at the hospital] and take it easy." She stayed the month, then went back to work.

Four years later she completed twenty-five years in the office and qualified for a pension. "They didn't want me to retire, they needed me," she says.

But she retired. Her pension is $106 a month. She also has $27,000 in the bank, including proceeds from the sale of her jewelry. The government lets her withdraw what she wants, but doesn't pay interest. She says all she has to spend it on are the lunches, the movies, and the gifts she likes to give to people.

She had a large apartment, but five years ago the ticket seller at the movie theater mentioned that she and her husband were expecting a child and were desperate to get out of their one-room quarters. The old woman figured one room was all she needed, so she agreed to swap. Finding someone to swap with is about the only way people can move in Cuba because of the housing shortage.

"I'd like to go to the U.S.," the old woman says, "but I'm too old now to start over. I made a mistake not going before." If she left, she couldn't take her money. She also complains about her CDR. "Everybody in my apartment house is watched," she says. "When you go out you have to say where. They clock you out and in. They want to know everybody's business. If I buy something, they know. If I bring a guest back, they observe. If it's a man, I have to leave the door open." (Not all CDRs are so nosy. Rules seem to vary from neighborhood to neighborhood.)

THE FARMERS

In a stucco and wood farmhouse on a hill a few miles outside the little village of Sibonicu, Andre, a thirty-four-year-old veterinarian, talks about the surrounding farm where he grew up. It is still owned by his father and grandfather, and he helps them run it. In rural Camaguey province, around Sibonicu, horseback is the major means of transportation. People wear big straw hats and real spurs on their cowboy boots. It's been called Montana with palm trees.

Andre says the family sold off eighty cows this year, almost double the rate in past years, because the government increased beef prices more than it increased milk prices. Because of the sale, the farm has produced 20 percent less milk. (Inquiries in Havana produced no sure explanation for these price changes. It's not even certain that there *is* a reason, or that the incentive to shift from milk production to beef was intended.)

Andre's family installed its own electric generator six years ago, "with a little old motor I bought." The government supplied subsidized fuel to run it. But the electric lights haven't been turned on for several months. Andre says the motor is broken, and that no one has had time to fix it. The family has its own outdoor water well. Another family, across the road, with only fifteen cows, doesn't have a generator and goes to a neighbor's well for water.

Andre's family sells through a cooperative that the government organized right after the revolution. "You give them 2 percent, they give you wire, rope, hammers, all kinds of things. They bring two empty milk cans every day to replace what you had," Andre says. A government truck comes around every morning to pick up the full ones and leave the empties.

Like many private businessmen in Cuba or the U.S., Andre is edgy about disclosing finances. But with prices running about $360 for a cow and 48 cents for a liter of milk, the farm would seem to have grossed about $42,500 for the first nine months of this year, with many expenses covered by the government.

The cooperative's twenty-six members are all private farmers. They have approved a plan to increase the cooperative's sales of beef and milk to the state by about 15 percent this year. But the co-op intends to increase pork production by almost twice as much, because pork can be sold on the free market; beef and milk can't be. The government says it has to keep greater control over cows because they reproduce slower than pigs.

One day, Andre thinks, he won't be on the farm, though under Cuban law he would have the right to inherit it. "When the old people can no longer work," he says, "perhaps it will be good to turn it over to the state." Six miles down that dirt road is a state-owned co-op where the farmers have new housing, TV sets, and electricity that they don't have to generate themselves. It seems to Andre a more efficient way to operate.

Unlike many Third World countries, Cuba is trying to keep rural incomes and amenities moving apace with those in industry and the bureaucracy. This encourages people to stay on the land and grow food.

THE COMPETITORS

The afternoon sun is broiling the sweat-drenched throng at the Matanzas market. They lined up on the west side of the market stall this morning, because it was in the shade. Now, after eight hours of waiting, they aren't in the shade anymore. Still, they wait, fanning themselves, because beans are on sale in 25-pound bags for 72 cents a pound without regard to ration coupons, which normally allow only 20 ounces of beans per person a month.

Inside the small cinderblock market stall, Jorge Diaz supervises a crew of several men who are shoveling beans and weighing sacks. Diaz is the accountant for the government cooperative that is holding the sale. "It's our gift to the people," he explains. "The harvest was good, and there was a surplus." He says he earns only $205.20 a month, much less than the farmers who grew the beans.

At another market stall about 50 yards away, the supervisor is not nearly so happy. His crew has little to do. They are from a 100-man private co-operative that also sells beans without regard to ration coupons. But they charge $2.40 a pound. The government sale is driving them out of business.

"Those are leftover beans, broken beans," he scowls. But all the customers remain at the government stall.

The members of the private co-op are sugar cane farmers, who took to planting beans on some spare land in the hope of exploiting the new free market. They pay the government $24 a year to rent the stall, and they must sell 30 percent of their beans to the state at low official prices. Then they are free to sell the rest for whatever they can get. But now their own low-price beans may be coming back to haunt them as the government offers a sale of its own.

THE DIVORCÉE

She gets off the bus in a little town west of Matanzas, enters the cafeteria, and buys lunch. Her husband just left her to move in with his girlfriend in Santiago. So she is moving from Matanzas to Havana where there are lots of men. She just arranged to swap apartments with a Havana woman whose husband just left *her*, and who wants to move back to Matanzas, where her family is. "Everything here is done for love," she says.

Separation and divorce are frequent and casual in Cuba. "If he stopped loving me, why do I want him?" the woman off the bus says. The main problem is finding a new place to live. Once housing is arranged, the state employment office will always come up with a decent job, the woman off the bus says. Now she works in an office. In Havana, they'll find her another.

Her brother, on the other hand, fled the country for Boston last year, with his wife, children, and father-in-law, a former Batista military officer who served two years in jail after the revolution. She says her brother wanted cars, stereos, and other goods unavailable in Cuba. She condemns this as "youthful clownery." She wants to keep in touch with him, and even exchange visits, but never to leave Cuba for good. "I'm a revolutionary," she says.

THE ENTREPRENEUR

While working for the revolution as a college student, Eugenio Balari spent three months in a Batista prison. Soldiers who raided his home had found revolutionary propaganda and several revolvers. An uncle, an official under Batista, pulled strings to get him free. Since then, Balari has been an editor, a municipal politician, a fruit-farm operator, a dress designer, a pollster, an economist, and a publisher.

But his big innovation was bringing classified advertising to revolutionary Cuba in 1979. Restless running the economic research institute he had founded, Balari plowed part of his institute's budget from the government into starting a monthly tabloid called *Opina*. With features, jokes, and even cheesecake showgirl photos instead of the usual official announcements, *Opina* comes as close to irreverence as a communist newspaper is likely to get. But its most controversial facet is a pullout middle section carrying such items as:

> OFFERED: House Miramar [a Havana suburb], 3 bedrooms, porch, garage, patio terrace, telephone 79–1442 after 6 P.M.

> NEEDED: House or apartment Vedado [another suburb], 2½ or 3 bedrooms.

Until *Opina*, people found a place to move, if at all, by word of mouth, bulletin board, and a not-highly-thought-of government housing office. Balari boasts that he has almost put the housing office out of business. *Opina* sells more than 500,000 copies a month, one for every twenty Cubans. People use it not only to swap housing, but to buy and sell TV sets, pianos—almost anything.

Opina was almost shut down by the bureaucracy, and Balari put in hot water. "At first, there were some people in official circles who didn't understand," he says. "But the population understood."

Now, with his research institute spending $2.4 million a year and his magazine turning a $300,000-a-year profit (he says it's rebated to the state), Balari has won approval to take over a textile factory with 200 employees to produce blue jeans and high-fashion sports clothes. He says the minister of light industry was very upset about this, because he wanted to use the factory to turn out school uniforms.

Balari concedes that much of his success is due to an influential old friend—Fidel Castro—who personally approved the fashion idea. Balari says he convinced Castro at a get-together one evening that "if fashionable clothing isn't available, young people will be disaffected and it will cause political problems."

Balari says he still lives in the house he grew up in, and that his $500-a-month salary hasn't changed since before *Opina*. His institute's budget does now include a sporty new Soviet car he tools around in. Told that with his ingenuity he might fast become a millionaire in the U.S., he laughs, and says, "There are some things more important than money. What is the value of a smile? People here are happy."

THE MUSICIAN

He'd love to be a famous recording star, but at age twenty, he is content to be a class B guitarist with the Ministry of Culture, earning $240 a month. The salary affords him such essentials as the two bottles of imported Czechoslovakian beer he consumes while breakfasting daily at a pleasant rooftop restaurant in Camaguey. If the government "norm setter" ever classifies him a class A guitarist, which apparently is a very unscientific determination, he'll get $420 a month; class C gets $180. (The government has norm setters to classify almost all workers A, B, or C.)

He went to work for the Ministry of Culture right out of music school. It placed him in a rock band with five other musicians, most of whom he hadn't met before. The ministry assigns the group to various dances and affairs. Sometimes he hires himself out freelance to earn extra cash. If a club or organization wants to select its own musicians and pay them, rather than rely on what the ministry sends over cheap, it can.

There are no starving musicians in Cuba. "The government wouldn't allow someone to try to work full time as a freelance musician," he says, smiling at the notion. "If you refused to look for work, the government would assign you to an office or factory or wherever. If you didn't do it, you'd go to jail."

There are musicians working at office or factory jobs, he says, who occasionally scrounge up freelance gigs performing. And if he finally does get to cut a record, he will be paid on a scale according to how many copies the record sells. Meantime, he says, "girls are easy to come by after dances." What with the housing shortage, though, he still lives at home with his mother.

THE JOB COUNSELOR

Felix de Valois Mejias is chief of the labor-resources department at the Ministry of Work for Santiago. He has been a job counselor in Cuba's eastern provinces for fourteen of his thirty-seven years. As head of the Santiago office for the past four years, he still sees individual job applicants, as well as supervising a staff of other counselors.

Never in these fourteen years, he says, has he had an applicant for whom there was no job. The reason is obvious: in every administrative zone, the government always has some big project under way that can absorb anybody. Officials acknowledge that this leads to inefficiency in whatever project is involved. But the inefficiency is factored into the project's budget, and the guarantee of jobs is considered worth the price.

Today, for example, de Valois says he has sixty-eight *empresas*, or "work centers," that have notified him they have job openings for which no suitable applicant has applied on his own. The *empresas* include the tourist office and the railway station. But the big fallback project that can hire anyone is the construction of a textile factory that will become Cuba's biggest when it comes on line in a year or two. Santiago was chosen for the factory precisely to fill its employment needs, de Valois says.

The first applicant today is an eighteen-year-old who wants any kind of job he can get while he studies for the university entrance examinations. De Valois sends the young man to Construction Empresa No. 11, which is building the textile factory. Because the work is construction, the pay is higher than for other work even though it is staffed with surplus labor. The applicant will receive $144 a month, $30 over the minimum wage for "service worker," which is the lowest classification. The pay could go over $240 a month depending on the danger, the difficulty, and the skill shown.

The next applicant is a thirty-two-year-old class B solderer. He, too, was sent to the textile factory. Explains de Valois, "All I had in hand was a document saying he had dropped out of his previous job about a week ago because it was too far from his home and he had to get up really early. When we advised him that there was work in the textile factory, nearer his home, you can imagine how glad he was." Class B solderers get $291.72 a month. De Valois himself, who picked up a university degree a year ago by studying part time, gets $300 a month.

When you get a new job classification, the Ministry of Work registers it on page twenty-two of your identity papers. If you are just entering the job market, or if you have a job you aren't satisfied with and you want to look for a better one during off hours, you must first check in with the Ministry of Work. It will note on page twenty-two of your identity papers that you're on the market. If you don't have a job, the papers say you are in the "labor reserves."

Efforts are made to satisfy an applicant's preference. No one has to take the first job offered, or even the second, right on the day it's offered. But ultimately, everyone must go to work. Cubans fortunate enough to be in the 3.5 percent of all students who get to attend a university are also *un*fortunate enough to have the least say where they work. Government planners have jobs waiting for each graduate. The graduate must stay three years, and most stay longer. The government tries to keep husbands and wives together, but admits it sometimes fails.

Despite the government's stance for female equality, sex discrimination is clear. "We don't send women to work in construction," de Valois says. "It's not good for the women. We have specific jobs for women: administrative work [which pays $145 a month], service work [the lowest paid at $114 a month], technical work [$150 a month]. We're always looking to replace a man who's in an easy job with a woman, and to put men in a job only a man can do." The male jobs, of course, pay more.

Women you see in Cuba are generally secretaries, receptionists, office clerks, sewing machine operators, and tobacco sorters—jobs almost exclusively for women. On the other hand, women *can* leap to the highest levels of the bureaucracy. De Valois's boss, the provincial director of Work and Social Security, is female.

THE CHRISTIANS

Roman Catholic clergy either refused to talk to a reporter, or couldn't be located in repeated visits to padlocked churches. Reports say membership is way down, composed mostly of older people who have held their faith since before the revolution. Protestants have fared similarly. One pastor in central Cuba says his church has forty-five members, down from 200 before the revolution. Most of the lost membership fled to the U.S., he says, including his predecessor as pastor.

Proselytizing is a problem. "Before, we could go to the park, and we could sing. Young people could go out and visit people in their homes, but now we can't do that," the pastor says, speaking gingerly in obvious fear of saying the wrong thing. Some of his church's members have gone to jail. Preachers say the government doesn't interfere with activities inside the four walls of the church. But when a Baptist rally overflowed the church in 1981, one preacher was jailed for four months, and another for three, for sponsoring an illegal assembly.

Says a Methodist minister, "They are Marxists and we are believers. They believe in evolution and we believe in God as the creator. But in many things they do, we also believe. They build hospitals. When a man retires, they see to it that he has money to live his life. And while the quantity of our membership may have gone down, the quality has gone up. They come now because they really want to."

THE CIGAR MAKER

"At age eleven, I had to leave school to learn to roll cigars, to help my parents," Rene Perez says. "I am the grandson of a tobacco worker and the son of a tobacco worker." But now Perez is director of the Francisco Perez German Tobacco Factory, renamed in honor of a worker who was tortured to death for revolutionary activities under Batista. Before the revolution, the factory was known as Partagas, and many of its cigars are still exported under that label.

Partagas was one of four principal Cuban cigar brands, all of which are still being produced. The others are H. Upmann, Montecristo, and Romeo Y Julieta. None can legally be imported into the U.S. (except by visitors to Cuba carrying them back for personal use). Recently, the U.S. cigar market has been invaded by ersatz brands, grown elsewhere, with the identical names and logos as the Cuban. The Cubans consider this infringement of their trademark to be a great affront.

The men who owned the big four tobacco companies (and eleven others that are still producing cigars in Cuba) aren't around anymore. Presumably they fled to the U.S. "That the owners left made no difference to us," Perez says. "We knew the work." Everyone insists the quality of the cigars has been maintained.

"What we wanted to change [in the revolution], we changed. Not the tobacco. Not the rum," says Carolos Rosada, leader of the workers' union at the plant (which in a communist system is tantamount to management). Some supervisors from the prerevolutionary management are still on the job. "Those who desired to leave, left," says Rosada. "And of those who stayed, those who maintained the proper socialist attitude continued in their work here."

Cuba now exports more cigars, with more market receptivity, than it ever did. "When the U.S. broke relations, it affected us," says Perez. "But we found new markets. We export now to forty-four countries. Spain, England, France, Switzerland, the Soviet Union. Right now, if the U.S. asked us to begin selling, well, we cannot meet the requests we have for tobacco already."

THE tougher and more threatening the U.S. gets, the more resolute the Cubans become. People waiting in long lines to buy scarce goods commonly blame the lines on the U.S. trade embargo, which is known in Cuba as "the blockade." Obviously, the embargo isn't responsible for all of Cuba's economic shortcomings. But the accusation is partly true, and subject to easy exaggeration by the government information monopoly.

The embargo was intended to make Cubans resent their own government and attract them to ours. It has done exactly the opposite. Cubans resent the U.S. for making life difficult. In Santiago, women defiantly insisted that they didn't mind waiting in line for an hour to buy fancy $17 scarves that had just arrived from Europe. When a reporter expressed doubts about this, they answered with calls of "Long live Cuba." Because of the scarf sale, their supervisors had given them time off from routine jobs that paid them $200 a month.

In a long line outside a Camaguey store where deodorant and talcum powder had made their first appearance in four months, there was similar cheerfulness, as well as agreement with a woman who said proudly, "With the force of all the people, things will get better."

This patriotism seemed spontaneous and genuine. When a long army train carrying tanks, armored personnel carriers, and trucks (all looking pretty worn and old) rolled through Camaguey one evening, dozens of surprised people waiting in the station for passenger trains moved to the platform to cheer enthusiastically, and exchange smiles and waves with soldiers riding on the equipment.

A room in the national museum features photographs of the throng that filled Havana's streets in 1980 to demonstrate support for the government. The occasion was the decision by thousands of other Cubans to emigrate to the U.S. through the suddenly opened port of Mariel. The emigrés were augmented by thousands of criminals, homosexuals, and others who were considered undesirable. Castro took them out of captivity and dumped them on his enemy to the north, an idea that many Cubans found appealing.

ACHIEVING unity at home by exhorting against a foreign threat is, of course, a trick common to politicians of all continents and all ideologies. But with American help, Castro has needed no magic to make the trick work in Cuba. When Secretary of State Alexander Haig repeatedly threatened that the Reagan administration would take the war in El Salvador to what he considered "the source," meaning Cuba, he merely fanned the same flames that the Bay of Pigs invaders had fanned before him.

His remarks got big play in Cuban newspapers, and were generally reported straight; they didn't need the usual propagandistic embellishment to be effective. Cubans knew that the source of the rebellion in El Salvador was a lousy government in El Salvador. This was just one more affront to their own revolution.

Similar remarks, and the Reagan administration's bellicosity, had the same effect on Nicaragua. The Somoza family had been placed in charge of Nicaragua under Franklin Roosevelt, after a seven-year occupation by U.S. Marines. The Somoza government was supported by every U.S. administration including Jimmy Carter's, right up to the moment it was overthrown in 1979 by overwhelming nationalist opposition. Then, within a year or two, the Sandinista revolutionaries who replaced Somoza were carrying Nicaragua closer to a Cuban-style police state than many of Somoza's opponents had intended.

The U.S. might have strengthened the position of freedom-loving Nicaraguans by showing, through hands-off behavior, that Nicaragua could achieve its nationalist ends without creating a police state. If a Latin American country could obtain independence from Washington without going the Cuban route, it might set an example throughout the hemisphere, and the Cuban route might lose its appeal.

The main concrete interest Americans have in Nicaragua, besides promoting peaceful commerce by encouraging Nicaraguan prosperity, is in keeping out a Soviet military force that might endanger the U.S. homeland. The only reason a Soviet force is remotely in prospect is that the U.S. threatens Nicaraguan independence, just as we have long stifled popular government and free markets in the surrounding countries. Nicaragua's long-range interests don't lie with the Soviet Union, half a world away, any more than Cuba's do. In fact, the Sandinistas had been shocked from the start by their discovery that the Soviet budget doesn't include $4 billion a year for them and every Latin American country that wants to go independent. Nicaraguan requests for Soviet aid were being politely rejected, which would inevitably have turned Sandinista heads northward, where their logical economic ties lay.

But the Reagan administration would not let the Sandinista revolutionary flames cool down for lack of fuel. Instead, the administration sprayed gasoline on the flames by threatening—and then waging—war. The administration funded various right-wing groups, including even the hated remnants of Somoza's army and aristocracy, in carrying out armed harassment against Nicaragua. This support was covert to the U.S. voters who paid for it, but hardly a secret to the Nicaraguans who suffered under it. It was a replay of the disastrous secret war against Cuba.

Washington publicly tried to embrace some Nicaraguans who were resisting the more radical Sandinista leaders. By doing so, the administration threatened to contaminate those very leaders it wanted to support, and make them an anathema to the main body of Nicaraguan nationalism. One of the moderates who begged not to be kissed in public, Alfonso Robelo Callejas (head of the Nicaraguan Democratic Movement and coordinator of the front representing the conservative opposition), actually said, "I wish the United States would keep quiet for awhile. Every time Haig opens his mouth, he strengthens the Sandinistas by justifying their arms buildup and stimulating the nationalism of the people."

YOU soon get the idea that if the U.S. wasn't galvanizing Latin nationalism in this way, supporters of Cuban-style police states in Latin America would have to plumb their imaginations to create a threat. In fact, during slack periods, that happens. The U.S. record is now so bad that the country can believably be blamed for almost anything.

In the summer of 1981, for example, Castro began spreading the word that U.S. germ warfare was responsible for a severe outbreak of dengue fever that hit Cuba. Hundreds of thousands of Cubans were incapacitated for up to a week by the epidemic, and at least 130 died, mostly children. Officials from the Cuban mission to the United Nations tried to get play in the U.S. press by offering reporters evidence to support Castro's charges. The evidence included newspaper clippings, excerpts from U.S. congressional hearings, and medical reports.

But interviews with leading international medical authorities, including those suggested by the Cubans themselves, make it seem highly probable that the epidemic was a natural occurrence, and that dengue fever would be an unlikely choice for biological warfare. Castro's evidence, though accurate, was incomplete and one-sided. Still, Castro repeated the charges, even reading some congressional hearings verbatim, in a speech in Havana before a gathering of legislators from some eighty countries. The speech was televised across Cuba. Afterward, everywhere on the island, people cited the dengue outbreak as an example of U.S. agression—one more reason to remain doggedly loyal.

The dengue fever charges appear to be false propaganda. But it would be a mistake to see them as nothing more. Nor is it fair to assume that the Cubans who spread the story, including Castro himself, knew it was false. They may well have believed it was true, for the same reason that the Cuban people readily believed it: so many similar stories in the past really *had* been true.

If Cubans have become suspicious by now that U.S. intrigue lurks behind every misfortune, you can hardly blame them. As for Castro, how would *anyone* feel if agents of the world's greatest military power had tried to kill him at least seventeen times and were still coming?

PERHAPS the saddest result of all this is the widespread notion in Cuba, and in many Latin American opposition movements, that independence from the U.S. can be obtained only at the price of civil liberties. To millions of people, political repression appears necessary to prevent the return to Cuba of military rule, a U.S.-dominated oligarchy, and the Mafia (which ran the casinos and other vice rackets in Havana before the revolution). The record of attempted U.S. subversion is the excuse constantly raised by Cubans to justify their Committees for the Defense of the Revolution.

The record of U.S. attacks is the history that is drilled into the many students who come to Cuba from Nicaragua, El Salvador, Mali, Angola, Palestinian exile camps, and elsewhere. These students, the future leaders of their countries, are taught that political surveillance and repression of dissent are essential for the survival of even the most popular independent government.

They are constantly reminded of the U.S.'s role in crushing the democratically elected Chilean government of Salvador Allende. Allende's death in a military coup in 1973 left his country in the hands of a U.S.-sponsored junta that has brought simultaneous political repression and economic disaster. This is repeatedly cited as evidence that Allende tolerated too much freedom. The lesson is that if nationalists like Allende in Chile and Arbenz in Guatemala had discarded the free political institutions they inherited—which both of them refused to do—the U.S. might not have been able to destroy their presidencies.

The intellectual disregard that these Third World students express for individual liberty is absolutely chilling. Their attitude is probably a far more dangerous Cuban export than the elusive arms deals the State Department has worked so hard to try to prove. The worst features of the Cuban revolution—its intolerance of political dissent, and its ruthless disregard for personal privacy in seeking to eliminate all deviation from prescribed norms—have become their model.

Yet these students, and people all over Cuba, are fond of pointing out that the Committees for Defense of the Revolution weren't started until five months *after* the Bay of Pigs; that Cuba didn't expropriate U.S.-owned oil refineries until *after* the refinery owners refused to handle oil that Cuba bought from the U.S.S.R. at bargain rates; that Cuba didn't tie its sugar sales to Soviet purchases until *after* the U.S. cut its import quota in reprisal against Cuban policies; and that the U.S. broke relations with Cuba, not the other way around.

None of this, of course, proves that Cuba's revolutionary course wasn't precharted by Castro—that he wouldn't have headed toward repression and the Soviet bloc regardless of what the U.S. did. It does suggest, however, that every anti-Cuban action the U.S. has taken has backfired. The Cuban revolution has been strengthened, not weakened, by U.S. belligerence, both in the eyes of the Cubans and in the eyes of people who seek to overthrow right-wing dictatorships elsewhere.

In U.S. politics, the question is usually phrased thus: did Castro intend to take Cuba toward a Marxist dictatorship and the Soviet camp, or did the U.S. drive him to it? That question, of course, cannot be answered satisfactorily. But the answer doesn't matter. Even if we grant, for argument's sake, that Castro *did* intend from the start to steer Cuba toward Moscow— and there is substantial evidence that he did—there is no reason to believe that Cuba would have stayed on that course for a quarter century. Ghana didn't, Guinea didn't, Egypt didn't, Somalia didn't.

And geography argues more strongly in Cuba's case than in the case of any of these others that Cuba would have drifted back toward a U.S. commercial orientation if it hadn't felt its independence was threatened. Castro himself might never have survived his economic failures of the 1960s, before the Soviets raised his allowance. Indeed, it is entirely consistent with all the known facts that Castro cleverly, consciously, and successfully suckered the United States into providing the bellicose antagonism he needed in order to coerce Moscow and cajole his domestic constituency all these years. He may have known very well that if he couldn't rouse the U.S. into grabbing for the black hat, his own hero act might not have been able to stay on stage.

FIDEL CASTRO's government preaches and practices much that is repugnant to the principle that men and nations should be free to choose their own course. But the U.S., in its dealings with Cuba, shredded that principle also. It can't even be said that the U.S. answered Cuban transgressions in kind. The U.S. has tried to *anticipate* such transgressions, and thereby, in many eyes, has justified them.

There is still a great natural reservoir of goodwill toward the U.S. in Cuba, if the U.S. government were to seek to exploit it. For all the gratitude the Cubans feel toward the Soviet Union in an intellectual sense, they, like most other Third World peoples, don't really *like* the Russians close up. Where individual Americans abroad tend to be regarded as sociable, the Soviets are cold and graceless. What is probably a fear among traveling Soviets of somehow offending their own repressive police state, translates abroad into an image of arrogance.

The 12,000 to 14,000 Soviet civilians and 3,000 Soviet soldiers in Cuba (U.S. estimates) keep mostly to themselves. Even Soviet civilian advisors live in segregated quarters. A reporter traveling around Cuba encountered them only at a beach resort, where they arrived together on chartered buses from Havana, and stayed together as a group.

When attacking U.S. policy, Castro goes out of his way to exclude the U.S. people, whom he describes as decent, hard-working, and admirable. But the biggest attraction the U.S. has is still the stereo sets, cars, and other items that socialism finds it so hard to provide. The Cuban people—*no* people—will ever be seriously convinced that these luxuries are really creations of the devil, as Castro sometimes tries to assert by way of justifying his shortcomings.

People *want* nice things. Many Cubans in the U.S. send packages of clothes and other items to relatives on the island (which can be received as long as they aren't sold). Everyone admires their quality.

Almost everyone you meet in Cuba seems to have family in the United States. This often causes confused feelings. On the one hand, the government characterizes those who flee Cuba as "scum." But when a boy, about ten, repeated such a remark in a restaurant line, apparently something he learned in school, his mother gestured as if to slap him. "Shhh," she said. "You're talking about your grandmother."

As a reporter waited in an anteroom to see a provincial official, the official's secretary burst into tears. She explained that her son had left for the U.S. the year before after being let out of jail, where he had gone for a robbery she insisted he didn't commit. She had heard from him once in Wisconsin, then lost touch. She said she still didn't understand why he left. "I never had any other children," she sobbed. "It hurts me very much. I am a revolutionary." Then she composed herself and asked that nothing of this be mentioned to her boss.

These scenes are particularly graphic; the confused feelings they represent are widespread. Yet instead of playing to this ambivalence by emphasizing the genuine attraction of American ideals and prosperity, the U.S. government has opted to affront the Cuban national pride—and bunglingly at that (you'd think that in seventeen tries on a man's life, the CIA could find somebody who could at least *wound* him!).

William Bader, former staff chief of the Senate Foreign Relations Committee and now a Washington consultant, may have put it best: "Whether it's in revolutionary France, revolutionary Iran, or revolutionary Cuba, you need an external enemy. And in Cuba the U.S. has gladly and enthusiastically fulfilled that role."

CHAPTER SIXTEEN

DOMINOES: EAST ASIA

AN AMERICAN takes his daughters, nine and ten, to China. The night before they are to enter Beijing, they stop at a hotel nestled in verdant hills outside Tokyo. The hotel patio is adorned with grass huts, and luau music is being piped in, to simulate the atmosphere of the South Pacific islands where World War II was fought. One wonders how many people know or even care what is on those islands now—except for the ghosts of the best young men that the United States and Japan had to offer.

It occurs to the father to explain to his daughters that their country was once at war with these people they have been talking to all day, and who are now serving them drinks. That was the war their grandfather went to. The idea seems so strange to the ten-year-old that she responds only with a quizzical look.

She has often expressed a naive misunderstanding of war, as if it were some single ongoing event that moves from place to place, like a scary carnival. She has seen war on the television news, usually, each day, in a country different from the one that had been shot up the day before. And she knows that her father reported on war in Afghanistan for his newspaper. "Will the war ever come here?" she sometimes asks. She is genuinely afraid.

Feeling committed now to amplify his original statement, the father says that the United States once dropped terrible bombs on Japan. Then, in fairness, he has to add that the Japanese had started it all by dropping bombs on Hawaii. This only elicits more quizzical looks. Why would anybody want to bomb Hawaii? People *live* there. You go *swimming* there.

How, then, to explain that twice in her father's lifetime—once even in the brief span of hers—the United States has sent its young men to Asia to fight the Chinese (or, in Vietnam, a threat that was perceived to be Chinese)? Fourteen-and-a-half million U.S. servicemen went to Korea and Vietnam to fight China; 112,901 died, another 258,703 were wounded. And the other side lost more.

How can a couple of American kids now go to China on their summer vacation—unarmed? Why have the Chinese been so friendly in extending an invitation? Why is the U.S. government now selling high-tech equipment of potential military use to China? Unlike Japan, China never surrendered, or turned over its government to the U.S. for redesign. The U.S. and China do have a common antagonist in the Soviet Union, but that was true the whole time U.S. troops were fighting in Vietnam. So what has changed so quickly, and so dramatically, as to warrant this reversal of attitude toward China? Them? Us?

"ASIAN Communism," or the new "Yellow Peril" (racial mystery made it appear more potent), was a misperception rooted in a time of unexpected fear. Sociologists, psychologists, and historians could probably find all sorts of explanations for this misperception, but certainly one explanation was the need for a scapegoat. Barely past the euphoria of winning World War II, we suddenly found ourselves, as never before in U.S. history, exposed to a danger we could not escape or control: Soviet nuclear power. After all the sacrifice and victory, we were worse off than before. We were just minutes from death. So frightening and unjust was this situation that great irrationality was inspired.

In panic, we sought ways to distill the danger into something containable— one evil, small enough that we could grasp it and snuff it out. We could have chosen nuclear weapons themselves to be the evil essence. We might then have restrained the production of those weapons, maybe not altogether, but at least to quantities and sizes that are small enough to hide, and therefore too small to destroy whole continents.

Of course, given the propensity of the U.S. and U.S.S.R. to meddle in the affairs of other countries, the absence of nuclear arms might have led to a conventional war between the two, which the nuclear danger has so far prevented. Because of the nuclear danger, the major powers have battled only indirectly, mostly in the Third World, where bystanders shed most of the blood.

Skirmishes mount up, though. With each Korea and Vietnam, the U.S. nickels and dimes its way toward the enormous casualty figure that a Soviet-American conventional war might have brought all at once. And we make these Third World sacrifices without achieving a weakening of the Soviet adversary. The nuclear terror has brought us a pretty hollow peace. If the U.S. had striven for a spirit of cooperation to forestall that terror, we might just as easily have escaped without major casualties, and without any more concessions to Soviet tyranny than we've had to make anyway.

At any rate, the U.S. did not choose nuclear weapons for its scapegoat. The U.S. got hysterical about communism. We had never much liked communism, and for good reason. But in the past, we had been able to deal, when necessary, with people who advocated it. Communism hadn't stopped us from allying with the Soviet Union to defeat Germany. A lot of the left-wing liaisons that cost people their jobs in the U.S. during the 1950s had been perfectly tolerable in the 1930s when the liaisons took place, back when the enemy was poverty and the Great Depression.

We had faith that communism, like other forms of dictatorship, would not take hold in the U.S. because the U.S. had a superior system and most people would see that. Obviously this faith was justified, and the United States is in no more danger of succumbing to communism now than it was in 1950.

When communism became a scapegoat, however, it was no longer an evil among evils. It was a unique evil—so insidious that it could override all cross-cultural barriers and all known norms of human behavior. Thus the Chinese revolution could never be seen as an ordinary civil war, the coming of yet another dynasty to China. One side called itself communist. That side must, by our perception, consist of brainwashed hordes, manipulated by a handful of satanic agents. It was inconceivable that they were rational human beings pursuing what looked to them, rightly or wrongly, to be the most advantageous course.

Even though all the participants were Chinese (and not a single truckload of arms from Cuba was reported), it was still not a civil war in our eyes. It was an invasion—if not of foreign men, then of this evil foreign *thing*, communism. Long after the victory of Mao Zedong was sealed, the U.S. refused to recognize his government. Instead, it recognized Chiang Kai-shek's government on Taiwan as the true government of China, and not just by way of formality, but with a vengeance.

More important, the U.S. rejected overtures from Mao *during* the Chinese civil war, when good-faith discussions might have substantially modified his future course. Instead, the U.S. actively supported Chiang, up to and well beyond the moment he fled from the mainland. The CIA's Civil Air Transport, the airline flying Chiang's logistical support, simply pulled up roots in Shanghai and Nanking and opened an expanded headquarters in Taipei. Then it gradually evolved into Air America in time to join our Indochina campaign.

IN the first few years after World War II, Soviet-organized armies tested our World War II truce lines. Defending these lines required no bloodshed in Berlin, and should have required relatively little in Korea. Just three months and one week after the North Korean invasion of South Korea in June 1950, the U.S. had secured South Korea, occupied much of North Korea, and broken the North Korean army's capacity to wage war. At this point, U.S. casualties stood at 3,614 dead, 4,260 missing or captured, and 16,289 wounded.

Then U.S. action widened the war to include China. U.S. troops drove to the Chinese border in North Korea, while the U.S. military established bases in the Chinese province of Taiwan, in hostility to the Chinese revolution. General Douglas MacArthur, the supreme commander in Korea, visited Taiwan to coordinate his war effort with the continuing attempts of Chiang Kai-shek to recapture the Chinese mainland. The CIA's Civil Air Transport carried on a secret war against China; it dropped commando teams onto Chinese territory and supplied remnants of Chiang's army that had based themselves in Burma and repeatedly invaded the Yunnan province of China. MacArthur publicized his beliefs that he and Chiang were fighting the same war, and that it should be taken to the mainland.

The Chinese had tacitly accepted the U.S. defense of Taiwan, biding time until they could negotiate or inveigle a change. But they wouldn't tolerate the U.S. Army, a self-declared enemy, fronting against mainland territory. The Chinese didn't leave their intentions to guesswork or speculation. They announced precisely what they would do to prevent the North Korean buffer state from being overrun, and when the U.S. wouldn't listen, they did it. Their entry into the Korean War—only after U.S. troops and planes were at the Chinese border—extended the war tenfold to thirty-seven months, and increased the U.S. casualties by about tenfold to 54,246 dead and 103,284 wounded.

The North Korean army that originally invaded South Korea was built and trained *not* by the Chinese, but by the Soviets, who occupied North Korea from 1945 until the very end of 1948. The Korean invasion was a last-gasp Soviet effort to see if they could pick up some free turf along the World War II truce lines. The effort was fairly easily rebuffed. But the U.S. turned that last Soviet gasp into a vision of the first breath of power of the new Asian Communism.

THE U.S. then saw its task as keeping this evil *thing* from spreading to still other countries. Invasion routes were imagined in arcs running from China to Indochina, Thailand, Burma, East Pakistan (now Bangladesh), and on to India in the west; through Malaysia, Singapore, Indonesia, Australia, and New Zealand to the south; and the Philippines, Taiwan, Korea, and Japan to the east and north.

President Eisenhower told a press conference, "You have a row of dominoes set up. You knock over the first one, and what will happen to the last one is that it will go over very quickly. So you have a beginning of a disintegration that would have the most profound influences." He also told Winston Churchill, "If... Indochina passes into the hands of the Communists, the ultimate effect on our and your global strategic position... could be disastrous."

As Eisenhower pursued this belief, it was the U.S.—not at first the North Vietnamese—who violated the accords that settled Indochina's war of independence from France. Ngo Dinh Diem was taken out of a Catholic seminary in New York State (where he chose to spend the years of his country's fight for colonial independence), and was posted as our man in Vietnam.

The administration Diem headed in Saigon was not even a government as such under the peace settlement. It was a caretaker administration, pending national elections in 1956. When 1956 came, however, Diem—not the Viet Minh administration in the north—declared that there would be no elections. Eisenhower later conceded what everyone involved believed: that Diem would probably have lost an election, and that Ho Chi Minh, the Viet Minh leader who was both a nationalist and an avowed communist, would probably have won it.

General Edward Lansdale and his team of commandos had already headed into the northern half of Vietnam, which was officially one country, very temporarily partitioned. Lansdale and his men were contaminating the oil supply, and spreading antigovernment rumors—techniques that Lansdale would use in his later campaign against Cuba. Historians have treated Lansdale favorably, for the same reasons that presidents liked him. He concentrated on trying to convert, rather than slay, the enemy. And he continually challenged the overoptimistic status reports that more conventional commanders were supplying to Washington. Thus he was a modern, realistic, intellectual-style warrior.

But he still advocated, as well as led, intervention in Vietnam and Cuba, two actions that brought disastrous defeats to the United States. And, unlike most Americans who were called upon to express opinions on these issues at the polls, he knew the truth. He knew the State Department was lying when it told the American public that North Vietnam and Cuba had initiated the violent conflicts. He knew that the U.S. had begun the violence, because he, as much as any military man, was responsible for it.

Lansdale recalls one rumor as being particularly effective when dropped around a Vietnamese marketplace. If he wanted to isolate a certain village because its work for the communist cause was successful, his agents would falsely suggest that the village was receiving aid from the Chinese. Lansdale and his men had learned that Mao's Chinese were strongly disliked, even by followers of Ho Chi Minh. That should have been a tip-off right there that a basic assumption of U.S. Asian strategy was way off the mark. But the assumption survived.

*   *   *

THERE were plenty of other tip-offs. Ralph McGehee, a former Notre Dame football star who served as a CIA officer in southeast Asia throughout this period, mentioned some in his memoirs, *Deadly Deceits* (Sheridan Square Publications, 1983). McGehee recalled numerous pieces of intelligence he tried to submit to superiors, all of which suggested that the substance of U.S. policy was in error, or that the tactics being employed to carry it out were malfunctioning. The reports weren't circulated. Among them was an intelligence coup that passed through McGehee's hands while he was working at CIA headquarters in Langley, Virginia.

Someone had obtained an internal Chinese government document for use by Chinese diplomats that outlined China's policy goals toward many countries. The forty-page document indicated that China's intentions toward these countries were not nearly so hostile or conspiratorial as Washington imagined. The document included considerable detail, and it all ran counter to the U.S. government's image of China's aggressive intentions.

McGehee stressed its importance to superiors, but later found out that they had refused to pass the information up the ladder, even though the document's authenticity was never doubted. One reason was that it wasn't what the agency and the White House wanted to hear. Another, McGehee wrote, was that "case officers developed a very personal interest in keeping China as one of the primary enemies of the United States. Promotions, foreign travel, and assignments abroad all depended on maintaining that concept."

Washington continued to insist that North Vietnam was just an extension of the spreading evil known as Communist China (as distinguished from the real China, which wasn't *in* China anymore). So the U.S. government increased its aid to, and reliance on, the South Vietnamese government of Ngo Dinh Diem.

Diem's Roman Catholicism didn't inspire the loyalty of his Vietnamese constituents. The great majority of them had not been so captivated by Western missionaries, and still clung to various forms of Buddhism. But Diem's Catholicism helped him greatly in Washington. Much of the expert advice that the U.S. government and people were getting came from Catholic missionaries, such as Thomas A. Dooley, a physician and best-selling author. Dooley's sympathetic accounts of refugees flowing south from newly communized North Vietnam were presented in the context of drumming up support for Diem.

Some important people had befriended Diem at the New York seminary where he stayed. They began to champion his vision of a non-French, non-communist Vietnam. One was the politically influential Francis Cardinal Spellman, a militant anti-communist, and Church leader for all the Catholic voters around New York City. Another was young Senator John F. Kennedy.

While known as a liberal, Kennedy was also concerned with avoiding any of the "soft-on-communism" taint being passed around by his still respectable

Irish Catholic colleague, Joseph R. McCarthy (for whose committee Senator Kennedy's brother Robert worked). John Kennedy became a charter member of a Diem-related organization called the American Friends of Vietnam.

Kennedy's commitment to maintaining an independent, anti-communist South Vietnam was not nearly so hesitant as some of his supporters, and Lyndon Johnson's detractors, later wished it. In 1956, he said that Vietnam was "the cornerstone of the free world in Southeast Asia, the keystone to the arch, the finger in the dike. . . . Burma, Thailand, India, Japan, the Philippines . . . are among those whose security would be threatened if the red tide of communism overflowed into Vietnam. . . . The fundamental tenets of this nation's foreign policy . . . depend in considerable measure upon a strong and free Vietnamese nation."*

In the closest thing we have to a Kennedy memoir—"my substitute for the book he was going to write"—his most intimate aide and speechwriter, Theodore C. Sorensen (later, Maurice Tempelsman's lawyer) described the extent of Kennedy's commitment. The beginning of Sorensen's discussion of China (or as his topic heading labeled it, "Red China") was truly remarkable. It said (emphasis added):

"Behind both the Laotian and Vietnamese crises loomed the larger menace of Communist China. That nation's unconcealed, unswerving ambition to impose upon the Asian continent a system bitterly hostile to *our* fundamental values and interests imposed in turn upon John Kennedy an obligation not to desert *any independent government desiring our protection.*"

By this dictum, any tyrant who might grab control of some spare spit of Asian real estate, whoever he was, whatever he did, could always write out a check against China, and as long as Jack Kennedy was there, the American taxpayer would honor it. Or, turn the passage upside down, put it in the mouth of a Chinese historian, and see how it comes out:

"Behind both the Laotian and Vietnamese crises loomed the larger menace of the United States. That nation's unconcealed, unswerving ambition to impose upon the Asian continent a system bitterly hostile to our fundamental values and interests imposed in turn upon Chairman Mao an obligation not to desert any independent government desiring our protection." That would cover North Korea and North Vietnam. It would also cover any left-wing Indonesian general who fired a pistol at his right-wing rival, grabbed a microphone, and announced that he was in charge and wanted the Chinese army to keep him that way. There would be one mitigating difference, however, if this presumptuousness had come from a Chinese: at least they live in the neighborhood.

*   *   *

*Thanks for this quote to Frances FitzGerald in her monumental book on Vietnam, *Fire in the Lake* (Atlantic Monthly Press, 1972).

THIS warlike U.S. attitude continued right up to the threshold of our rapprochement with China in 1972. On October 12, 1967, for example, our fundamental purpose was questioned and defined, very directly, at a State Department press conference. The unequivocal pronouncement came from the government's chief foreign policy spokesman, Secretary of State Dean Rusk:

"Q: Mr. Secretary, one of the questions—basic questions—that seems to be emerging in this Senate debate is whether our national security is really at stake in Vietnam, and whether Vietnam represents an integral part of our defense perimeter in the Pacific.... I think it would help in this debate if you would perhaps elaborate and explain why you think our security is at stake in Vietnam."

"A: Within the next decade or two, there will be a billion Chinese on the mainland, armed with nuclear weapons, with no certainty about what their attitude toward the rest of Asia will be. Now the free nations of Asia will make up at least a billion people. They don't want China to overrun them on the basis of a doctrine of the world revolution. The militancy of China has isolated China, even within the communist world, but they have not drawn back from it.... Now we believe that the free nations of Asia must brace themselves, get themselves set, with secure, progressive, stable institutions of their own, with cooperation among the free nations of Asia.... Now from a strategic point of view, it is not very attractive to think of the world cut in two by Asian communism, reaching out through southeast Asia and Indonesia, which we know has been their objective, and that these hundreds of millions of people in the free nations of Asia should be under the deadly and constant pressure of the authorities in Peking, so that their future is circumscribed by fear. Now these are vitally important matters to us, who are both a Pacific and an Atlantic power. After all, World War II hit us from the Pacific, and Asia is where two-thirds of the world's people live. So we have a tremendous stake in the ability of the free nations of Asia to live in peace and to turn the interests of people in mainland China to the pragmatic requirements of their own people, and away from a doctrinaire and ideological adventurism abroad."

It must be remembered that Rusk had spent nine years as president of the Rockefeller Foundation before moving over to the State Department. So he naturally tended to overstate the stake that Americans not on the Rockefeller payroll had in the political problems of distant peoples with strange cultures. Also, words like "free" translate poorly when trying to describe, say, the Philippines.

But in general, everything worked out just the way Rusk said it had to. In fact, it worked out even better than his most optimistic forecast allowed. It worked out that way the minute the U.S. *lost* in Vietnam, brought its troops home, and resumed a primarily commercial rather than military relationship with the nations of the area.

Instead of falling like dominoes, Thailand, Malaysia, Singapore, and Taiwan blossomed. Generally, the whole region did. Southeast Asia was identified by the World Bank in the late 1970s as the world's premier economic growth area. Instead of left-wing guerrilla insurgencies' flourishing, they died down. (Robert Shaplen has reported in the *New Yorker* that the rulers of Indonesia and South Korea, believing their U.S. tutors, braced themselves for trouble right after the fall of Saigon, and were surprised when nothing happened.)

The region's problems aren't resolved, of course, even to the extent they could be. Only a fool would be surprised by new upheavals in the Philippines or Indonesia. Radical-left governments could emerge. But that will be controlled by conditions within those countries. They are certainly not "under the deadly and constant pressure of the authorities in Peking." To the extent that "their future is circumscribed by fear" of any outside force, it is fear of the United States that haunts them.

TAKE the case of the country Rusk singled out as needing protection from China: Indonesia, the fifth-largest country on earth, with about 150 million people. Indonesia became an independent country under the leadership of Sukarno (like many Indonesians, he went by only one name). He was a lifelong independence fighter who was (and still is, in memory) generally respected and beloved by his people. Spiritually, he did much to help them. He gave Indonesians a sense of national identity, and a national language.

Typical of the problems he faced, and how he solved them, Sukarno picked a minority tongue from East Sumatra to be the Indonesian language because of its simplicity. Even though Javanese was spoken by 60 percent of the people, Sukarno decided that Javanese was too difficult grammatically; it also grated against his democratic ideals, because it was structured on a caste system that required different words to be used depending on whom one was addressing. Indonesians now almost universally applaud Sukarno's choice of the Sumatran dialect, and use it.

But, like so many postcolonial leaders, Sukarno had fallen into the trap of judging the capitalist economic system by the way the system worked in the colonies. Just as the U.S. today defends monopolistic, non-free market economies, the European colonial countries generally did not export a free market system as an example to their foreign wards. Rather, they sent abroad a form of feudalism.

Thus to Sukarno, capitalism was an economic system under which the Dutch owned everything. This system worked fine in Holland, where everybody was Dutch, but in Indonesia it seemed grossly unfair. So Sukarno adopted socialism. The Indonesian economy, potentially one of great wealth, was mismanaged. Inflation ran rampant, discouraging trade. Natural resources weren't properly exploited. The political environment discouraged Western investment, and nothing took its place.

Available funds were wasted on grandiose spectacles, while badly needed rural development went unattended to. The crowded central island of Java, where the government sat, became more crowded, while Sumatra, a vast green expanse of fertile land, valuable mineral deposits, and potential tourist sites, languished. People were discouraged from the pursuits of simple farming, by which they had always lived, but weren't offered a more sophisticated alternative. While Sukarno still held the gratitude and affection of millions, the economic situation had engendered some strong political opposition, particularly on Sumatra.

The U.S. didn't wait for that opposition to wax or wane in its natural course. It invaded.

The U.S. action to overthrow Sukarno in 1958—really, bald-faced aggression—attracted little public attention in the U.S. Although similar to the Bay of Pigs invasion, and far grander in scale, it was so far away that most Americans aren't even aware of the disaster. But L. Fletcher Prouty, the liaison officer between the CIA and the air force, and a longtime military intelligence official with experience in Asia, has written a detailed account.*

The CIA trained large numbers of Indonesian dissidents and mercenaries at bases in the Philippines, and returned them to Sumatra, where they recruited other rebels. Prouty puts the number of trainees at 42,000, based on the number of rifles the CIA asked the marines to supply (it was so many rifles, Prouty writes, that the marines had to go to the army for 14,000 of them, which puzzled army brass because they hadn't been informed of the operation).

Meanwhile, the U.S. Air Force, from a base in Taiwan, supplied a fleet of old B-26 bombers, refitted with a new machine gun package that greatly enhanced their firepower. Former U.S. military officers, working as CIA

*Gallery magazine, August 1976. Large parts have been confirmed from other sources. Ralph McGehee, the retired CIA officer, has referred to the 1958 Indonesian operation in two manuscripts, though CIA censorship deleted big chunks. The actual number of men taken out of Indonesia, trained, and returned has been impossible to learn.

It seems outrageous that the U.S. government can still hide its role in the 1958 invasion of Indonesia, or in the 1965 coup there. The voters and taxpayers who employ the government need to know what has gone on in countries like Indonesia in order to exercise control over U.S. policies today, or even to understand what those policies may be. It seems impossible that information on events twenty or twenty-five years old, where no nuclear technology was involved, could include legitimate military secrets—that is, could threaten life or U.S. security today. Little if any of the 1958 material could even involve people in power in Indonesia today.

Obviously, the material is being kept secret because it is embarrassing to those in the U.S. government who advocate continuing the same policies. If the U.S. government did things it's ashamed of, it shouldn't have done them—and the voters and taxpayers have a right, and a duty, to pass judgment.

mercenaries, flew the planes. The U.S. Navy landed many of the rebel troops on Sumatra by submarine, while others were parachuted in from the Philippines. Sumatra was where several U.S. oil companies were pumping, including a unit of Standard Oil of California. A rebel government was established and lasted several months.

Of course, the U.S. press, and history books, recorded the whole episode as a native rebellion. Sukarno was, to say the least, suspicious. At the height of the invasion, Howard P. Jones, the U.S. ambassador, answered Sukarno's suspicions by denying any U.S. involvement. He declared that Washington had no intention of interfering in the internal affairs of Indonesia. Reporting Jones's statement from Djakarta for the *New York Times*, Bernard Kalb noted, "Communist propaganda linking the United States with the rebels has been getting wide publicity here."

Premier Viliana Siroky of Czechoslovakia, visiting Djakarta, correctly accused the U.S. of supporting the rebellion. It seems likely that he did so in order that Sukarno, who himself had been trying to buy arms from the U.S., could maintain a diplomatic pose. Kalb wrote in the *Times*, "Some Western diplomatic sources said tonight that Mr. Siroky had committed a grave breach of diplomatic protocol by making accusations during a state visit against nations with which Indonesia has diplomatic relations."

Although such one-sided pronouncements were reported, apparently there was no attempt—by *any* newspaper—to find out if the charges were true. (Kalb failed to return several phone messages, although a secretary said he had received them.) Even after a U.S. pilot was shot down and captured, the evidence wasn't considered impressive; the pilot's company hadn't yet been exposed as a CIA front.

After Sukarno was turned down by the U.S., he bought small arms and military jets from Yugoslavia, Poland, and Czechoslovakia to help repel the invasion. The State Department condemned him for it. Secretary of State Dulles said the U.S. wouldn't arm either side. "We intend to conform scrupulously to the principles of international law," he intoned.

At a press conference, he was specifically asked, "Mr. Secretary, have we received a request for arms from the Indonesian rebels in Sumatra?"

And he replied, "No, we have not."

"And while he was publishing that falsehood," Prouty writes, "the United States furnished and piloted B-26 bombers, and these were bombing shipping in the Makassar Strait. Some had even flown as far south as the Java Sea. Almost immediately all insurance rates on shipping to and from Indonesia went on a wartime scale and costs became so prohibitive that most shipping actually ceased," which certainly didn't help the struggling economy Sukarno was trying to sustain. The effective embargo on Indonesian exports also didn't help U.S. motorists in the market for a new set of tires or a tank of gasoline.

Politically, the CIA-sponsored rebellion achieved exactly the opposite of what it supposedly intended for Indonesia. When Sukarno's army crushed the rebels after a few months, he immediately tightened security by abolishing the existing democratic framework. In 1960, he abolished parliament, and in 1963 he had himself named president for life.

Then, in 1965, a strange and terrible series of events occurred in Indonesia, that has never been satisfactorily explained. The standard published version is that leftists in the government staged a coup to wrest complete control, either of the government or of the army, and began by killing six army officials; the army, led by General Suharto (another one-namer), then staged a retaliatory coup against the left, reduced Sukarno to a figurehead, and called in massive U.S. military and civilian assistance. This doesn't make complete sense, because Sukarno was already in power and hardly needed to stage a coup against himself, though perhaps it's conceivable he wanted to snuff out some independent voices, or that the communists wanted more influence over him.

At any rate, we know these things for certain: U.S. military, intelligence, economic, and administrative experts immediately flocked to Indonesia and began reorganizing things. The generals, with the advice of U.S. government agents but hardly against their own inclinations, had the army begin a massive elimination of communist sympathizers throughout Indonesia. Estimates of the number killed have ranged from a low of 300,000 to a high of one million.

From *Time* magazine:

"Backlands army units are reported to have executed thousands of communists after interrogation in remote rural jails.... Armed with wide-blade knives called *parangs*, Moslem bands crept at night into the homes of communists, killing entire families and burying the bodies in shallow graves.... The murder campaign became so brazen in parts of rural East Java that Moslem bands placed the heads of victims on poles and paraded them through the villages. The killings have been on such a scale that the disposal of the corpses has created a serious sanitation problem in East Java and Northern Sumatra, where the humid air bears the reek of decaying flesh. Travelers from these areas tell of small rivers and streams that have been literally clogged with bodies; river transportation has at places been impeded."

TRAVELING through Indonesia more recently, one notices a particularly cruel and unfriendly streak in people. That's especially true in contrast to the Indonesians' neighbors to the north, the Filipinos, who have borne their bad government with a saintlike grace, warmth, and generosity. In Indonesia, you constantly see kids throwings stones at dogs or goats, or at each other, and sometimes even at you. People on the street often snarl or sneer when asked for help or simple directions.

But no history of unfriendliness can explain the scale of human slaughter that occurred in Indonesia in 1965–66. Teams of U.S. advisors were on the job through all of it. Exactly how big a role they played—suggesting the killings, or merely congratulating the killers—can't be said for sure. Nor is there evidence that the U.S. advisors knew how far the killing would go once it started, though they did watch as it unraveled.

Ralph McGehee, the former CIA officer who couldn't get superiors to listen to him about China and Vietnam, was also involved with Indonesia. Much of what he wanted to write about the 1965 coup was censored by the CIA. This much was published: "The Agency seized upon this opportunity [General Suharto's coup] and set out to destroy the PKI [Indonesian Communist party]."

McGehee wrote of a CIA-planned campaign to spread false and incendiary propaganda. It began right after Suharto took over, when photographs of the badly decomposed bodies of the six army officials murdered by leftist plotters appeared in newspapers and on television. Wrote McGehee, "Stories accompanying the pictures falsely claimed that the generals had been castrated and their eyes gouged out by communist women. . . . This cynically manufactured campaign was designed to foment public anger against the communists and set the stage for a massacre."

The U.S. presence left the United States indelibly associated with that time in the minds of Indonesians. Sukarno was removed from office in 1966 and kept under house arrest until his death in 1970. The generals created a system of indirect elections, sometimes reported in the Western press as if they were real. The elections allow Indonesians to vote only for candidates from approved parties, and only for a minority of the members of an assembly that in turn elects the president (Suharto) and vice-president. There is no meaningful democracy.

AND, of course, under U.S. advice, General Suharto built an economy based on a much more ruthless brand of socialism than Sukarno had ever dreamed of. Perhaps the best description of this system was provided by reporter Barry Newman to readers of the *Wall Street Journal* in 1980: "Through a maze of cooperatives, foundations, and private holdings, the armed services . . . have a dominant interest in hundreds of companies. . . . The military-dominated companies run banks, bus lines, and movie theaters. Foreign investors and influential local Chinese have taken them on as partners (in return for their contacts, not their cash) in dozens of ventures from logging to insurance.

"Admiral Lines, a shipping company, is widely recognized as being owned by the navy," Newman wrote. "The military elite, along with its bureaucratic and business associates, gets many of the choice concessions, contracts, and licenses. Projects opposed by the country's development experts are often approved anyway, and at least partly as a result, the gap between rich and poor is widening. Perhaps more important, the system has frustrated the ambitions of small enterpreneurs who don't have pull."

A secret World Bank report in 1981 found essentially the same thing Newman had. "A study of ownership patterns in Indonesian industry," it said, "shows that several hundred of the largest industrial concerns are partially owned by high-level military or government officials or their immediate families." In other words, foreign investors were coerced into giving away part of their companies to Indonesian government officials.

Optimists might hope that private ownership, even if unfairly and monopolistically distributed, could inspire the new Indonesian owners to sharpen up their industrial management skills and develop their country's economy. But the World Bank report discounted this possibility. The incentive, the bank said, was for wealthy power-brokers to concentrate their time "developing their connections and maximizing their returns as front men." In other words, there was more money to be made by increasing the number of up-front cash rake-offs than by developing the businesses afterward.

Sukarno's government had been corrupt, but Indonesians—at least in retrospect—tend to forgive this, or to describe it as a kind of foible. Certainly it pales against the multibillion-dollar graft that developed under Suharto, when Western businessmen arrived and found that control of both government and commerce was in the hands of the same small circle of generals. When the price of oil then shot up, the generals and businessmen acted like kids who had picked the lock on the candy store.

All of Sukarno's graft and waste stood on end couldn't reach the kneecaps of the corruption at just one of Suharto's state-owned enterprises—Pertamina, the oil company Suharto created in 1968. It had sole rights to Indonesia's oil and gas, and all related ventures. And Suharto placed it in the hands of a general, Ibnu Sutowo. With the OPEC price increases, Indonesia's oil export revenue soared from $232 million in 1966 to $5.2 billion in 1974. Western firms lined up to get the money. They were selling telecommunications systems, steel mills, tanker fleets, anything that might strike an Indonesian general's fancy.

Of course, that also included weapons. There were squadrons of U.S. Skyhawk jets, a single $112 million squadron of F-5 fighters, landing ships, tanks, submarines, patrol boats, plus new vehicles, rifles, and uniforms for sixty combat battalions. (It's an irony worth noting that the only country that ever invaded independent Indonesia was the United States.)

So that the generals could spend even more than $5.2 billion a year, the banks scrambled to lend Indonesia money, secured by oil that wouldn't be pumped for years. A former senior executive at one of the five largest U.S. banks says that Indonesia became his bank's most profitable country of operation for a while in the 1970s, more profitable even than the U.S. These profits, he explains, were largely built on the discrepancy between heavy loan demand and the lack of an investment market. On the one hand, the Indonesian government was gobbling up loans so that it could buy things to be paid for with future oil revenue. On the other hand, many people were developing sizeable incomes and had no convenient place to put their money.

The economy that had been created by U.S. advisors and was being run by U.S.-trained Indonesian "technocrats" was centrally controlled. It offered little opportunity to invest locally, and the controls forbade the export of cash (unless you were a general, and could sneak it abroad). So a spread of 9 percentage points developed between the low interest rate that the bank paid to its Indonesian depositors and the high interest rate it charged the Indonesian government on loans backed by the full faith and credit of the country. This spread was pure profit.

THOSE profits are considered legitimate. Now we get to the corruption, which is just as impressive. For example, the government rice-purchasing and trading agency has been hit by recurrent scandals. One time, the agency, known as Bulog, or the National Logistics Board, was found to be taking money designated for buying rice from farmers, and putting it instead into a bank controlled by the army. Later, the head of just one provincial office of Bulog was arrested in a two-year, $18 million swindle of farmers and others in the rice industry.

And, of course, Western firms clamoring to do business had to see somebody first. For example, in one case exposed by the SEC, Katy Industries Inc., of Elgin, Illinois, wanted an oil concession from Pertamina. So, the SEC said, Katy slipped $316,000 in secret funds to Indonesia, part or all of which would up in the pocket of Indonesian vice-president Adam Malik. (Malik wouldn't talk to U.S. reporters about it, but denied all in the Indonesian press.)

Katy said it didn't knowingly pay money to Malik, but did pay fees to a consultant knowing that he "intended to reward some Indonesian officials for their help." And who was the consultant? He was I. Irving Davidson, a Washington wheeler-dealer who was a close friend of Malik, as well as of the Teamsters' Union crowd, with whom he arranged deals involving the scandal-ridden union pension funds they controlled.

In one of the baldest shakedowns in history, General Sutowo sent out letters on Pertamina letterhead soliciting "investments" in the Ramayana restaurant, a big New York eatery he was opening. The solicitations went only to companies the SEC said were "either doing business with, or negotiating to establish business relationships with... Pertamina." A company called Indonesian Enterprises Inc., which owns the restaurant, raised $1.1 million through this method; Indonesian Enterprises turned out to be located in Pertamina's New York office, and General Sutowo, the head of Pertamina, turned out to be its chairman.

The companies that found his solicitation to be an offer they couldn't refuse included Mobil Corporation, Atlantic Richfield Company, Armco

Steel Corporation, Continental Oil Company, Monsanto Company, Phillips Petroleum Company, Dresser Industries Inc., and others. It also came out that Sutowo had pocketed at least $2.5 million from a tanker deal Pertamina entered.

All this money that has been siphoned off on the side is part of the price that foreign companies are willing to pay for Indonesian oil, based on what oil costs elsewhere, and on how much they can get American customers to pay for gasoline. It is money coming right out of the pockets of Indonesian and American citizens.

PERTAMINA eventually collapsed in scandal, $10 billion in debt and unable to pay. The money is still owed by the 150 million citizens of Indonesia, who have also learned that their oil reserves are a lot smaller than originally thought, and that their oil exporting days might be all over within a decade. Even *with* the oil exports, and the big boom years that were brought to them courtesy of Western investors, two-thirds of Indonesia's rural population and almost half the urban population (according to U.S. AID) lived at or below the subsistence level in 1982.

Indonesians eat only about 75 percent of the minimum daily calories they require. They are mostly without electricity or decent water. Most of the kids aren't in school, and have nothing else to do. Health statistics are miserable and the life expectancy is forty-seven years.

And we all know what happened next. The International Monetary Fund came along and demanded that food and fuel subsidies be wiped out. These were the price breaks that the government gave to Indonesian citizens, so they could buy the essentials of life for less money than the government would get selling the goods for export. By eliminating the subsidies, under the IMF plan, the government would sell all its goods at the higher prices, and raise more money to pay the foreign debt. And bills for essential items for Indonesians would rise by 90 percent. The Indonesian government, like so many other governments, bowed to the IMF.

And the *Wall Street Journal* had this to say in its "Foreign Insight" column when reporting the forced price increases for food and fuel in Indonesia: "There's little doubt...that by biting the bullet now, the government has chosen the responsible road to long-term economic well-being. After a period of economic dislocation and price adjustments, Indonesia's economy, the experts say, is likely to emerge stronger and healthier."

If Indonesians can't afford food to chew on, "the experts" will let them bite bullets.

How grateful the Indonesian people must be that 58,655 American soldiers gave their lives in Vietnam to protect Indonesia, one of "the free nations of Asia," from "the deadly and constant pressure of the authorities in Peking."

CHAPTER SEVENTEEN
THE CHINA SYNDROME

VERY LITTLE has been known about what was really going on inside China all those years. The U.S. would not recognize China, and so couldn't establish diplomatic or journalistic listening posts. Without diplomatic entrée, even covert intelligence gathering was restricted. Much of the information the U.S. relied on came from biased sources among the anti-communist Chinese who reentered China for their own purposes.

What was *thought* about the Chinese then is so untrue today that one wonders how true it ever could have been. For a quarter century, encompassing the Korean and Vietnam wars, available books and articles and snatches of television film footage showed us a billion brainwashed automatons. Any Chinese, plucked from the crowd, halted on his bicycle, would faithfully parrot the current opinions of his leaders. He would not only accept, but extol the government's design for his life. As for his own preferences, he denied he had any.

The Chinese we saw all worked and played with industrious, single-minded devotion to their revolution. City or village, they were all skilled at rice growing, factory working, and, above all, soldiering. They were prepared to march—even run screaming in suicidal charges—at any enemy their leaders pointed out. They had no feelings, no independent reason, and no human specialness. They loved Big Brother—and nobody else.

We were shown Nazi-like schools where individuality was methodically snuffed out of the kids. Row upon row of scrubbed, beaming, youngsters chanted and exercised in unison, as if they had been stamped out by some great oriental cookie-cutter. Asian fortunes appeared bleak.

From the stories one hears Chinese tell now about the years of the Cultural Revolution, and from what Westerners who visited China during those years say, this image seems built around a grain of truth, but only a grain. The zeal with which the Chinese supposedly did the crazy things they were told to do was always largely fiction. Now, even the grain of truth is gone from the automaton image. The Chinese communists achieved a Stalinist control of bodies, but not an Orwellian control of minds.

The Cultural Revolution lasted from 1965 until it tapered off in the mid-1970s. In other words, it coincided almost precisely with the expansion in U.S. force on China's southern border. It came with the U.S. combat troops, and wound down as the troops were pulled out and the South Vietnamese government fell.

Obviously the U.S. intervention wasn't the sole cause of the Cultural Revolution. You could even argue that the corresponding dates are a coincidence. Strange bees had always had a propensity for getting into Mao's bonnet—witness the ludicrously unsuccessful Hundred Flowers and Great Leap Forward campaigns earlier. But to the extent that the exercise of U.S. power had any inlfuence at all on Chinese policy (and surely it had some), we can say this: the more the U.S. applied military force, the more China behaved the opposite of the way we wished; and as the military force was withdrawn, the more China began behaving the way we wished. With the Yankees licked, and their national pride no longer threatened, the Chinese began to think of the U.S. in terms of the marketplace and their self-interest. Suddenly we were valuable, to be catered to.

Today the myth of the Yellow Peril stands exposed. China really does invade Vietnam—feeling threatened by a country it perceives as a Soviet ally—and gets *beat*. It tries to help guerrillas in Cambodia and gets beat again by Vietnam. Apparently China has even less success controlling its southern neighbor than the U.S. has controlling Cuba.

And while the Chinese people are still afraid to speak out directly against their government, they say enough to establish their hatred for the Cultural Revolution and their unhappiness with many policies of the current leaders. In fact, what they approve most about the government of Deng Xiaoping and Zhao Ziyang are its tentative steps toward restoring a marketplace economy.

OF all countries, China invites comparison most to Cuba. They are the two successful communist revolutions of our era that have had a chance to show what they can do. Whatever the similarity in the original rhetoric of those revolutions, the tone and mood of the two countries are now worlds apart.

With China, the United States has made its accommodation. With Cuba, it hasn't. Yet if most Americans could travel through them, see what life is like, and learn all the rules, the preference would clearly be the other way around. Neither China nor Cuba would strike most Americans today as a desirable place to live. But if forced to choose one or the other as a home, most would find the choice easy.

A comparison could be stated thus: In the United States, people can do almost anything they would normally want to do without asking permission of the government. In Cuba, they would have to ask permission, but the government would usually say yes. In China, they needn't bother asking, because the government would almost always say no, and then denounce them for thinking of it.

What follows is a look at the China we went to war against, and what happened there when we lost.

SHEN MINGHE wanted to be an architect. When he qualified to go to college, the government put him in a political science course. Upon his graduation, it told him, to his complete surprise, that he would be working for the *People's Daily*, a newspaper. That was almost twenty years ago. He is still at *People's Daily*, in a job roughly comparable to deputy foreign editor on a major U.S. newspaper. But he is obviously being groomed for advancement, next, perhaps, a job covering the U.N. in New York.

In 1968, a few years after being surprised by his assignment to *People's Daily*, Shen got an even bigger surprise. He and the other editors were given a week to pack a small box of belongings, and were shipped out to cadre school in Yan'an, in Shaanxi province near Inner Mongolia. Shen's wife and small son stayed home in Beijing, about 420 miles east of Yan'an.

Over the next three years, Shen was part of the Cultural Revolution. He saw his family twice, for three or four days each time. He worked in the fields of Shaanxi, planting vegetables. All the other "intellectuals" on the *People's Daily* were also shipped out around the country to plant vegetables, or perform similar labor. The newspaper was run by university students.

Shen says he doesn't know how well the students did at his job, because he was forbidden to read, or even listen to the radio. This was Mao's idea of seeing how the other half lived. Shen plainly preferred his own half. Twice, he was caught listening to a radio in bed at night. He unabashedly admits he preferred the programs of Voice of America and the British Broadcasting Corporation to anything Chinese. He was reported and scolded in public, but not punished further, he says.

Three years doesn't seem like an oppressively long time in retrospect— compared to fifteen or twenty years in the Gulag Archipelago, for example. But in the madness that must have been China then, no one, least of all Shen in his remote cadre school, knew when, if ever, normality would be restored. Finally, the cabinet minister who controlled the *People's Daily* "fell"—was fired—and just as suddenly as they had left, everyone was invited back to his old job, with a month's vacation to boot.

Shen still won't try to explain these reversals of policy. The government hasn't yet determined the official history of that period, and so the people of China must wait to see how roundly they can condemn the Cultural Revolution or reject Mao's thoughts. It's clear, though, that Shen would be hard-pressed to endorse or defend what happened. He was miserable, and who can blame him?

You hear similar stories all over China. Most statues of Mao have been taken down, and visits to his mausoleum have been restricted to a few odd hours a week.

CONSTRUCTION on the Sichuan Number One Textile and Dye Factory began in 1958. In 1959, amid the confusion of the Great Leap Forward, when everyone was supposed to go smelt steel in his backyard, construction stopped. In 1961, The Great Leap having fallen flat on its face, construction started again. In 1962, it stopped again, for reasons no one can recall, but, in 1964, it started again.

In 1966, the textile part of the plant finally opened for business. A few months later, in December of that year, it closed because of a dispute between two groups of workers. According to Wu Xinming, the administrative assistant to the director of the plant, who is the highest authority you can get to, the dispute was this:

"Both [factions] considered themselves as being leftist. One was really rightist. One faction [the real leftists] considered that although the leaders may have made some mistakes, they were still good cadres. The other faction, the rightists, suffered the influence of Lin Piao [former defense minister, very close to Mao]. They said that all the leaders of the plant were capitalist roaders. This group made a lot of excuses. They tried to deceive workers in the plant to follow them."

Finally, in May 1967, everyone managed to get the plant started again. But this was "the tense period of struggles between the two factions." Wu says there was no substantive issue relating to pay, work rules, or manufacturing procedures. "The only thing they wanted was to get power," he says. "They sabotaged the production of the plant to win the support of the Central Committee [by making it look like management was doing a bad job]."

In July 1968, the rebels—the radical rightists who were only pretending to be radical leftists—took over. Production declined. "They ordered people to stop working whenever they wanted, to use the workers' time to carry out the mass movement to criticize the capitalist roaders," Wu says. "To those who worked very hard, they said, 'You only know how to work, you don't know the direction.' They said cadres who increased production were hurting the revolution. High producers were following the capitalist solution, they were not revolutionaries."

In 1974, the plant was closed again for five months, because it was considered necessary to take time out to criticize Lin Piao (who died in 1971) and Confucious (who died in 479 B.C.). In 1976, the plant was closed for two months to allow time to criticize Deng Xiaoping, who is still alive, and in fact one year later, in 1977, bounced back from his criticism to become head of the Chinese government. The 1976 work stoppage proved to be the swan song for the rebel managers, however. Soon afterward, the Gang of Four fell, which obviously required new management at the textile and dye factory.

According to Wu, about $55 million of production was lost during the three work stoppages caused by the Cultural Revolution. Finally, in 1977, the plant for the first time surpassed $40 million in production, which was the annual production rate when it opened.

It took the Chinese eight years to build the plant, and nineteen years to get it into full production, during which time Chiang Kai-shek and Son had turned Taiwan—formerly China's poorest province—into one of the world's leading textile producers. Taiwan's per capita income (1978) is $1,300; China's (1979) is $232. Statistics can be misleading, but anyone who travels through can see that the standard of living on Taiwan is much higher in every visible respect, at every level of society. Of course, it's common knowledge that China has had a tougher time of it than Taiwan, because China is more overcrowded. But common knowledge is wrong. Taiwan has about two-tenths of an acre of arable land for every person. China has about three-tenths of an acre.

Wu's explanation for this discrepancy is stunning. "Taiwan relied on international investment from the United States and Japan," he says. That, of course, begs the question. China could have had all the Western and Japanese investment it wanted, but chose to reject that and go its own way. For the Chinese to say now that Taiwan outstripped them because it dealt with the West is an enormous concession.

China's government has pulled back the ideological bolt that barred it from the world marketplace, and has even opened the door the tiniest of cracks. It is filling the airwaves with English lessons (sometimes they are the only programs on television).

In many ways, China's history is a cycle of openings and closings to the outside. There is always the lure of material advances, followed by the threat of internal disruption, and then the clampdown. How do you let in things and keep out thoughts? The emperors never learned. The current government is searching for a way to admit technological ideas while filtering out other ideas.

But much of the very technology China wants to bring in involves communications advances that make the other ideas harder to keep out. If the door ever really opens, the U.S. will have won with its economy a victory far more significant than the one that keeps eluding the U.S. military on Asian battlefields. As an investment, money is cheaper and more productive than blood.

* * *

MEANWHILE, Sichuan Number One Textile and Dye Factory seems to be on a straighter track. Its production rose steadily to about $130 million worth of cloth in 1981. Of course, those are management's figures, and since this management accuses prior management of falsifying its figures, and the prior management accused the one before it, we can't take anything for granted.

Whatever the output, though, 11,700 workers are required to achieve it, which Wu readily admits is "a terribly low production rate." Most of the equipment was built in China in the 1950s, and is, Wu says, "very backward." In addition, he says, "We have a lot of youngsters working here to solve the unemployment problem of China." The staff continues to grow. Once a worker starts at a factory, he doesn't quit. In July 1980, the plant began giving workers two days off, instead of one, after every six days worked.

The workers earn an average of $25.40 a month base pay, plus an average of $5.40 in bonuses if they exceed quotas. They also get housing for only $2.70 a month, including utilities, and free medical care and schooling. But housing is so overcrowded as to make Cuba's look capacious by comparison. (The Chinese language doesn't even have a word for *privacy*; in Beijing, a university-trained engineer lives with his wife and two children in one 12-by-15-foot room, the same one he has occupied for seventeen years.) And medical and preschool care frequently appear to be perfunctory, nowhere near the equivalent of Cuba's.

China's reputation for strange and wonderful medical advancements appears to be yet another myth—acupuncture notwithstanding—at least as far as delivery to the average person is concerned. At one communal clinic not meant for foreigners to see, there are dirty floors, peeling paint, a shabby tile ceiling that is coming apart, stagnant pools of water in the yard, and flies everywhere. There is one dentist for more than 10,000 people in the commune. "It's not like in your country where you go to see dentists two times a year," the dentist says. There are said to be four doctors and a paramedic, but only one doctor seems to be available on the day of a visit.

SICHUAN Number One Textile and Dye Factory is a model workplace, the best of several dozen in Sichuan province. That is why foreigners are allowed—in fact, encouraged—to see it. The other factories admittedly don't approach it for size, modernity, or efficiency. Yet only about 10 percent of the workers are wearing masks in rooms swirling with cotton lint. Asked about byssinosis, or brown-lung disease—a big issue at U.S. textile plants— Wu says, "Chinese people don't get that." Pressed, he explains that the Chinese have invented a medicine, made of pig's blood, that clears the lungs of cotton dust. Every worker takes it twice a week, he says.

The first worker a reporter approaches says she doesn't take any such medicine. She talks as if she never heard of it. Wu comes over and is told she doesn't take the medicine. The worker gets a frightened look on her face, and begins insisting that she takes the medicine every day. A second worker is approached in another area, and exactly the same thing happens. Management must have some concern, because no one is allowed to work in the lint-filled part of the plant past age forty.

Cotton cloth is rationed in China, along with rice and a lot of other things. There is a shortage.

YOU get up a couple of hours before your guides so you can lose them. You hop a bus headed to some distant town that contains a tourist attraction foreigners are authorized to visit (that way, there are fewer questions from the ticket-seller). About halfway to the destination, you get off at a random stop out in the country, where foreigners aren't expected to go. You ride a horse-cart as far as 25 cents will take you, slog more than an hour through rice paddies stepping around water buffalo and ruining shoes, and finally come upon what appears, after a half dozen similar excursions, to be a typical village.*

The houses, from prerevolutionary days, are of mud blocks. They have dirt floors and thatched roofs, but compounds are spacious. A lot of brick

---

*Always taking along an American interpreter fluent in Mandarin. If anyone from the Chinese government is around, even an interpreter, you have given the game away before starting. I am indebted to Laurie Cohen, then a journalism student at Columbia University and now a reporter for the *Wall Street Journal*, not only for her interpreting, but for the benefit of her considerable Chinese scholarship and reportorial instinct.

The government's rules about talking to foreigners aren't clear and are obviously in flux. There is no strict rule that people can't talk to foreigners, and foreigners are certainly told they are free to talk to people. But authorities constantly disrupt such conversations on one pretext or another, and the Chinese involved are quickly in trouble over it.

So in big cities and other areas frequented by foreigners, people are on their guard. Those eager to practice English will chat innocently, even initiate the chat, but will quickly grow wary if the conversation turns controversial. In areas foreigners don't visit, however, this wariness is less developed. There is still a vague sense of caution, but often it's forgotten in the excitement of the unexpected, or in normal human byplay. Truths lie closer to the surface. Government agents have come around to places they later learn were visited by foreign reporters; so it's unsafe to name a village.

Most foreign travelers see an artificial China that has been created for them. It is kind of like Disneyland, a series of glossy fictions pretending to be reality. The difference is that while all the fictions in Disneyland are gathered in one place and labeled fantasy, China's Disneyland is dismembered and distributed around the country. At each stop on a trip, a visitor can be taken to half a dozen different phony scenes—factories, child care centers, clinics—each posing as a real thing.

It won't matter whether the foreigner is a tourist, a businessman, or a journalist planning to write a story. The model commune he is taken to see has approximately the relationship to a real commune as Main Street USA in Disneyland has to the Bowery. The Chinese he will be introduced to have approximately the relationship to any real Chinese as the strolling Mickey Mouse does to the average American.

and concrete housing is under construction around the Chinese countryside, but people in this village (or, as it's called in China now, "production team") say they aren't jealous. They say the old style is cooler and roomier (and it is).

Everyone has electricity (the hot wires and wet rice paddies lead to occasional accidental electrocutions). Everyone has a radio and a bicycle. A few privately owned television sets have appeared in the area, but most people rely on the TV set in the communal building. (In one village, a reporter approached several men busily spading the earth at the edge of a vegetable patch, and asked what they were planting. It turned out they were planting a large new TV antenna.)

Water must be carried by bucket from a central spigot a few hundred yards down a dirt path. But the spigot works round-the-clock (in some villages, water is available only three hours a day). The Chinese long ago figured out what to do about plumbing; every bowel movement is carefully saved, mixed in equal proportions with compost, and used as fertilizer.

A small crowd gathers, maybe two dozen including children, to meet the foreigners. They all farm the communal rice paddies that lie in every direction. They also farm private vegetable gardens on small plots the government gives to each family. The communal work pays them about one Chinese yuan—worth 53 U.S. cents—a day. This varies with the number of hours worked; most production teams employ two or three persons as auditors to keep track of when workers come and go.

"We set our own work time," says a woman of about twenty. Most set six-hour days during planting and harvesting. When there's no work to be done, or on rainy days, people don't work at all. Married women work less than others, devoting time to household chores. Consequently, they get paid less.

Sloth is certainly contrary to the U.S. image of gung-ho, revolutionary China. Throughout the rest of Asia, and in North America, persons of Chinese descent are known for their industriousness. But inactivity is the most observable characteristic of Chinese workers in China. The notion that everyone in China is up doing calisthenics at cock's crow is just false. Old photographs suggest that it may once have been a national habit, under orders, during the Cultural Revolution, and you can still see groups of a dozen or two Chinese exercising in the public squares of cities in the morning. But if the practice was ever widespread, it has withered.

China may be the only country in the world where farmers sleep late. If you arrive on a Chinese farm in the gray light of dawn, when almost anywhere in Africa (or Iowa for that matter), people are starting to churn the earth, you will find no Chinese. Farmers sleep till about 7:30, and, what with breakfast and puttering, may not be in the fields until 9:00. The national *xiuxi*, or lunch and nap period, runs officially from noon to 2:00. But most people begin knocking off at about 11:00 or 11:30, and don't return in the afternoon until 2:30. Five P.M. often comes early, too.

These hours apply not only on farms, but at almost every job site in China. The laziness of industrial and office workers often infuriates Western businessmen and diplomats who come to China to get something done. For example, at Qinhuangdao, the country's third-largest port, the berths are full. Ships are lined up for an average wait of three or four days in the harbor before a dock is available. But most dockworkers sit or stand idly. A few slowly unload cargoes of Canadian wheat and U.S. lumber. (China ought to be able to produce wheat and lumber in abundance.)

The slow pace even carries over to the Public Security Bureau, which is certainly an aid to foreign reporters trying to elude their official tails. During the *xiuxi* period, nobody watches anybody, and you can slip away where you will.

By 8:00 or 9:00 P.M. (when Cubans are uncorking some rum and heading for a dance hall) China is turning in. City streets and village roads are deserted. Only foreign visitors can find a public place to eat or drink after that hour, and only in their segregated hotels, even in Beijing. If you arrive during the night, even in a large provincial capital, you will find the streets deserted and the hotel doors locked.

BACK at the farm village, the young woman who described her work hours begins telling of her education—or lack of it. After high school, she had to work in the rice paddies. "Everybody wants to go to college, but we can't get in," she says. Those around her volunteer that the entrance exams are biased toward city students. They say rural schools don't teach well enough for students to have a chance, and that the exam results may even be rigged so that the government can deny advancement to farm people and keep them working the rice paddies.

"Our development has been very uneven," one woman says. "First we had the Great Leap Forward, then we had the Cultural Revolution, then we had the Gang of Four. Lin Piao." She ticks the faults off on her hands and stops complaining only when she runs out of fingers.

What reason is there to think the new regime is better? "Given what we had before, anything that came after was better," she says. Everybody around seems to agree with her. Where are the brainwashed automatons?

"If I get married, I can go and live someplace else," the first young woman says. If her husband farms, she could move to wherever her husband's family is from. If he is established in his lifetime city job, she could move to that city.

Where would she like that to be? An old woman calls out, "I would like to live in America." Everybody laughs. They ask questions about life in the U.S., indicating that they haven't been allowed to read or hear much about the outside world. They have almost no idea how U.S. life is different from theirs, except for an abstract sense that Americans have more money. They can't imagine what we buy with all that money. They are surprised to hear that the government allows us to choose our own jobs and spouses. Shown a U.S. dollar bill, people ask if the man in the picture is Nixon.

What many people would really like to do is move to the provincial capital, the way farmers all over the world have gravitated to more industrialized jobs and city life.

"We would like it, but there's no way to leave. The government won't allow it," a young man says.

Why? "We're peasants," an old woman answers. "If I could move, I would," she says.

A married woman, thirtyish, says, "We can't move anyplace because we can't rent houses, and we can't get anything to eat, and we can't get work." What she means is that the government controls all these things, and provides them only to people who do what they're told.

CHINA'S nearly 900 million or so peasant farmers are the largest captive labor force in the world. They are almost literally chained to their plows by government edict. By keeping them that way, the government has undoubtedly protected China's food production from the disasters that have befallen other Third World countries where farmers are free to migrate to town.

Moreover, the government has guaranteed the farmers a higher standard of living than most of them would have if they moved to the city, at least at first. Even in the mountains of relatively poor Yunnan province, villagers said there had been no shortages of food since the early 1960s. Though rice and other items are rationed, there is no malnutrition.

But this security, guaranteed by the Chinese government, is no different from the security that is constantly offered and rejected in freer societies. By the millions, Africans and Southeast Asians have moved from the relative comfort and abundance of village farming to joblessness in wretched shantytowns on the edge of cities. However difficult it is for an affluent American to understand, people are willing to give up a lot just to be in sight of cars, bars, running water, the easy life—to smell the possibility, however remote, that they could make the transition to real wealth. Tennesseans once followed the same trail; Detroit was more ready for them.

"I would like to marry a rich man," the first young woman says.

"Do you have a friend you can introduce her to?" asks the old woman who had said she wanted to move to the U.S. They are laughing, but there's a hard edge of seriousness to what's being said, and the thoughts didn't come from the Little Red Book.

People recall the Cultural Revolution. When city workers were shipped out to the rice paddies, an occasional farm girl bagged one, and later went off to live with her new husband's parents in the city. No local men were so fortunate.

*   *   *

IN the cities and among the better educated, the state often splits up young lovers by intentionally assigning one of them a job in a distant city. This is part of the government's effort to restrain population. Sometimes lovers hastily marry before their job assignments come through. But they usually are separated anyway, and are cynically told to stay in touch with each other by annual visits. Because many jobs don't come with vacations, the annual visit may be limited to a few days.

Ordinarily, the state discourages people from marrying before their late twenties, when their lifetime jobs have been set. Persuading the lovelorn to go along with the state's wishes is one of the major functions of the "neighborhood committees," China's equivalent of Cuba's Committees for the Defense of the Revolution (though the Chinese committees are less significant in the overall scheme of things). The committees provide counseling for couples who fall in love against the desires or convenience of the state.

The state places little value on the family. Vacation schedules aren't coordinated, so couples don't travel together. Work is paramount, and often vacations are organized through the workplace. Most people openly say they don't like these policies. The policy limiting families to one child is also unpopular—a sudden, radical change from tradition. But it is being strictly enforced. Officially, the sanctions for having a second child are financial, but in practice second babies have been taken from mothers at birth, with no more ever being said.

People give only the most grudging defense of the state's job-control policies—something along the lines of the following, from a dye mixer at a chemical factory in Shanghai: "It doesn't matter whether you like your job or don't like it. It's the system. That's where the state needs us. You grow up thinking like that from when you were very, very young, and you don't know how to think any other way."

Next to the pride and defiance of Cubans defending their revolution, that is pretty pallid stuff. Supposedly, it was stronger years ago, back when the Chinese had Yankee attackers of their own to roil and bellow about. Today, the careers they mention are the ones they would *like* to have had if they had been permitted: Shen, the journalist, talking wistfully about architecture; an engineer wishing he could have been a musician; and a woman who wants to be a teacher as both her parents were, but instead is assigned as a translator for an import-export house. It's hard to find anybody who asserts that he really wanted to do whatever it is that he is doing. Maybe that's why people keep such short hours, and why a lot of work doesn't get done.

NONE of these genuine problems that the Chinese face is discussed at meetings of the rural work brigades, or the urban neighborhood committees. These are supposed to be the grass roots organizations of the revolution, but no one outside government asserts that the grass roots has any control. Average people are even confused about how the leadership for these organizations is chosen. Before every meeting with farmers or workers, the leaders meet with party officials and are told what should be said and done.

A big problem seems to be getting people to attend the meetings at all. Often only a minority shows up, even after the district committee sends around trucks with loudspeakers to try to rouse an audience. If people do attend, they talk or laugh throughout. Some sleep.

The idea that Chinese are tightly disciplined is a joke. True, for people with official power there is almost paranoid rule-following. But for the average Chinese, there is no discipline at all. Kids run loose around villages, totally ignoring the rare attempts of adults to curtail their boisterousness. In an urban day care center, not intended for visitation by foreigners, a tired-looking woman sits glassy-eyed in one corner of a dirty room, ignoring her flock. Children of various ages, their noses running, some with unattended open sores on their faces or bodies, are scrambling wildly over dangerous-looking pieces of broken wooden and metal furniture.

Nine-year-old children are allowed to wander about big cities alone, un-attended, even at night. In one sense, there is the overriding order of knowing that each person has been assigned his lot in life, and probably can never escape it. But within that framework, there is shockingly little sense that anyone has direction or dedication.

The government is a fence, there to restrain people who would violate its major dictums: not to leave the assigned home and job, not to have more than one child, not to mix with foreigners, not to spit in public. But within that fenced-in space, the government doesn't seem to be around. Completely contrary to the Cuban experience, people don't seem to feel any sense of participation. They are mostly bored stiff and purposeless, which, given their circumstances, is perfectly understandable.

A few run away, but they usually get caught. If they do make it to the city, they find that the best jobs are often controlled by nepotism, and living conditions are incredibly crowded. Derelicts sleep against building walls, bathing on sidewalks, defecating in gutters. At what government guidebooks say is the best restaurant in Chengdu, the capital of Sichuan province, beggars come in asking for food. Such things could never happen in Cuba today—not just because of more efficient policing, but because no one is that neglected.

The land of the billion brainwashed automatons, relentlessly determined to communize Asia, turns out instead to be just one more poor Third World country. And, as in so many other such countries, the purportedly socialist leaders have no interest in being part of the egalitarian society they proclaim.

While 80 percent of China's youth are permanently chained to the plow by a rigged education and employment system, about half the members of the Central Committee of the Communist party, the country's ruling body, have children studying in the United States. The son *and* daughter-in-law of Deng Xiaoping are studying physics at the University of Rochester, in New York, and the son got a summer job with RCA. The son of foreign minister Hua Guofeng went to Harvard.

IN most rural areas, living conditions have clearly been improving since Deng Xiaoping replaced the Gang of Four in 1976–77 (right after the U.S. pulled out and Saigon fell). A year later, the private plot system and some other free-market incentives were introduced. The government supplies cheap materials to people willing to work on their own houses. With neighbors laboring for each other, a lot of new houses are getting built. The people who live in them tend to say they've saved for many years to build them, but that the bulk of the money came in since private plots were started.

It's hard to tell exactly how much land is given over to these plots. The provincial and communal leaders don't want to say. Apparently the plots occupy much less land than is occupied by communal farms, but the private land is much more productive.

Traders risk their own money to buy vegetables from farmers, then sell at the free markets for whatever the traffic will bear—within upper and lower limits set by the government. Before the new rules of Deng Xiaoping in 1978, all markets were run by the government. Before that also, people say, the vegetables weren't as fresh and the meat was so expensive they could afford to eat it only several times a week. Now they eat at least some meat or fish every day.

People find the new system hard to reconcile with what they've always been taught. All they know is that they like it. "This is not capitalism," someone from the market says when the question is raised. "Capitalism is on a larger scale." Most onlookers seem satisfied with this explanation. A farmer in another commune insists that China isn't copying Western capitalism so much as it is copying Western decentralization. "In your country, you have small companies producing things," he says. "In this country we have only recently turned to smaller organizations." Of course, the Great Leap Forward was predicated on small-scale production. But admitting that there's a movement toward capitalistic incentives is a huge pill to swallow after thirty years of Maoist rhetoric. "Capitalism," says the farmer, "is when it costs you $1 to produce something and you sell it for $2."

Still, messages on television encourage individuals to open their own small businesses. Explaining this poses problems even for senior public officials, like Guo Wei, secretary-general of the *People's Daily*. (As the government official in charge of the main national newspaper, he occupies a lofty post in the scheme of things.) At first, Guo says that small businesses aren't capitalism "because they don't exploit people." What precisely is the exploitation they avoid? "No one is hired. Only the people running the business work there," he says. But on questioning, it turns out that people *are* hired—staffs of up to ten or fifteen employees. What it gets down to is that right now, the government limits the size of private businesses, and the kind of ventures they can engage in. As businesses become more successful, however, they may well be allowed to expand.

THERE'S an all-night train from the farmlands in northeastern Yunnan province, to Kunming, the capital. It has no seats. The cars are boxcars, and the passengers consist almost entirely of farmers, carrying big baskets or burlap bags of eggplant, cabbage, peppers, onions, and watermelons. The farmers perch on wooden slats around the sides of the cars. It is miserably uncomfortable, and the train makes interminable slow stops, picking up more farmers.

None of these men and women is commercing on behalf of his work team or commune. They are private farmers, bringing the goods from their private plots to market. The ride is only about 55 cents a person. The problem is the tax on the vegetables. This is where the government tries to get its cut from private enterprise, and the process is different only in sophistication, not contentiousness, from that process anywhere.

Everyone is supposed to have his goods weighed and taxes paid before getting on the train. The tax collector thinks there has been cheating. A woman with three big bundles can produce only two receipts. She insists that the third basket, mushrooms, is to give to her relatives, not to sell. "I don't need a receipt," she is yelling.

The tax collector points an angry finger, and hollers back, "You're going to get more than 30 yuan [about $16.20] for that basket."

"All right, I'll sell it to you for fifteen," she screams. She is close to tears, or a good actress. He still charges her, but only half a yuan, about 27 cents.

Similar words are repeated over and over, with almost every farmer. A man with watermelons loses his fight, and complains the whole rest of the way. He has been charged a tax of 8 yuan, or $4.32. He complains that 8 yuan is all he can get for the melons, and runs through calculations for the tax collector predicated on a melon price of 10 mao per jin (approximately a pound), which he says is the going price in Kunming.

In Kunming, however, it turns out that similar melons are selling on the street for 60 mao a jin. Who says the free-enterprise spirit is dead in China!

ANOTHER old man, in another commune, doesn't like the new trend. He and his three sons work hard on their private plot; the young men pull the plow by hand with enormous effort. "The people are stronger than animals," the old man says. "Even if there was enough money, we would not have an animal. There are a lot of people and so little land." But even after all that effort, he won't sell on the private market. What they don't eat, he says, he will give away.

"Some people are willing to make money, I am not," he says. "I don't think those things are important. The attitude most people have is asking for more and more. I think people should take only what they need to live on. The state must have economic planning, or else there will be trouble. My asking for more things would hurt the country."

On his wall is a poster, a picture of some Viet Cong, and the slogan, "The Vietnamese People Must Be Victorious." It is from 1965. It is the only such poster seen on a trip throughout China. Visitors point out that it's out of date. The last country the Vietnamese were victorious over was China. The old man laughs.

"I don't think most people feel the way I feel," he says. "I have children who make money. Chinese thought is getting narrower."

CHAPTER EIGHTEEN

THE ZAIRE OF ASIA: THE PHILIPPINES

=For all of America's frustrations with its recent overt wars in Asia, there is one Asian country where we have engaged in *covert* political activity, and sometimes fighting, and where things have gone pretty much our way. Every antiguerrilla campaign has been victorious, and every election, real or rigged, has produced the winner the U.S. government desired. But our victories in the Philippines very closely parallel our victories in Zaire: they have only hurt us.

In the first years after World War II, probably no country in the Third World harbored a greater reserve of popular goodwill toward the United States than did that lovely archipelago. Twice, U.S. military power rescued the Philippines from hated occupiers, first the Spanish, then the Japanese.

The intervening four decades of U.S. colonial rule were often misguided, but our excesses were noticeably less than those of other colonizers, and came mostly at the beginning. The U.S. demonstrated democracy, and granted considerable self-government—enough to leave Filipinos with an abiding respect for the democratic system. Americans tended to be friendlier than European colonizers, and less condescending in the way they went about things. The relatively egalitarian system that worked in the U.S. was admired and gradually imitated. And, with a planned and orderly* transition beginning

*Except for time out to beat the Japanese.

in 1935, well before European colonizers were pushed into surrendering their colonies, the U.S. voluntarily delivered to the Philippines the independence that was promised. Or so it seemed.

The resultant Philippine friendship was an asset to be cherished, not only for Philippine resources and markets, but also because the Filipinos willingly provided military bases. These bases play a valid and important part in protecting free commerce in the Western Pacific and East Asia, and (though less so as technology has improved) in maintaining a credible deterrent to the Soviet Union.

But Philippine friendship was squandered in the hysteria over Chinese communism. As a result, the Philippines may now fit the leftist definition of a prerevolutionary state more neatly than any other country on earth.

As Ferdinand Marcos, our man in Manila, nears the end of his second decade as president, his regime is morally bankrupt. And, despite bountiful resources, the country is headed down the World Bank–IMF road to financial bankruptcy as well. Most Filipinos who think about such things—and there are many, thanks to the American-style school system the U.S. established— will tell you that the Marcos family's personal accounts overseas could buy far more gold than could be bought by the Philippine treasury. Marcos, who began life on one of the lower rungs of the upper class, has become the richest man in his country, and one of the richest in Asia.

Instead of stealing this money from the great faceless mass of citizens via the treasury, as Mobutu stole his, Marcos took much of his wealth directly from the people who earned it—businessmen large and small, whose assets have been effectively expropriated. They are the very people one might expect to support an authoritarian U.S. ally. Yet they oppose him.

Marcos says he takes from the rich to help the poor. But more than 90 percent of the Philippines' 50-or-so million people are estimated to live on incomes of less than $55 a month. Most farmers don't have their own farms. They work as farm laborers for $1.50 to $1.85 a day, despite announced minimum wages of about $2.50 a day. Even so, they find work only half the time. When work comes, at planting or harvest, wives and young children are often sent to the fields to earn extra money.

Manila is pock-marked by shantytowns—temporary hovels covered by corrugated tin or cloth and filled with skinny children just off the farms. These slums are as bad as any in the world. The men of Manila consider themselves lucky to find office or dock work for $45 a month during the day, and to pick up another $32 a month moonlighting in other menial work. Streets and bars teem with educated young women from good families offering their bodies for $20 a night or almost anything men will pay.

Living costs are low, too, but not that low. In 1982, a 5½-pound bag of rice cost 93 cents, and meat cost about $1.40 a pound. Families of eight or ten children are common. In fact, the annual birthrate in this mostly devoutly Roman Catholic land is 41 per 1,000 people, one of the highest in the world (in the U.S. it's about 16 per 1,000; in India, 34), and there seems to be little effort to cut it down.*

Prices of imports rise as the peso loses ground against foreign currency by 10 percent a year. Foreign debt, much of it originating in loans to enterprises owned by Marcos and his family and cronies, has reached $16 billion. In 1982, the big new export became talent. Newspapers don't offer much local work, but there are plenty of ads for engineers and other skilled people to work in Saudi Arabia and Kuwait. The government encourages this outflow of skill because it keeps 70 percent of the workers' foreign earnings, to pay the Western debt, and compensates the workers by giving them newly printed pesos.

Even the tiny middle class lives in slum conditions in Manila, with open ditches serving for sewers and dead rats rotting along the rutted pavement. Neelo, for example, is a business college graduate who can't find an office job, and so works in his family's overstaffed luncheonette in the Manila business district. His wife sells canned goods through the window of a store in the front room of their three-room apartment.

They live with their five children and a servant, a young girl from one of the out-islands (the Philippines consists of more than 7,000 islands). Neelo and his wife sleep on a bed in the middle room, opposite the TV and the record player. The five youngsters sleep on the floor of that room, and cry at night when the rats brush against them. The servant sleeps on the kitchen table.

Neelo and his wife scrimp to send their children to private school. Like many parents in the Philippines, they think the public schools today send more children home with bloody noses than with good educations. Despite a constitutional mandate requiring free primary education for all, money problems now keep most kids from making it through seventh grade.

YET, ironically, the citizens who seem to have lost the most in the past decade live a few miles from Neelo, in the ghettos for the rich. Private guards inspect cars or pedestrians wishing to enter these fortresslike suburbs. Inside, the houses hide behind concrete walls whose tops are imbedded with jagged glass. Huge German shepherd dogs pace behind the iron gates, growling at strangers.

The residents of these elegantly furnished, fortified homes sit around complaining about Marcos. They used to do it over tumblers of Chivas Regal; now that the corrupt foreign loans have provoked stricter exchange controls,

---

*In 1970, I traveled to the Philippines with my wife of two years. The people of many Third World countries were incredulous that she still hadn't become pregnant. But the Philippines was the only place where men insisted on pulling me aside and making sure I knew how it could be accomplished.

there is no more Chivas Regal; the complaining is done over local rum. The intricately woven rugs and fine upholstery are allowed to fray, unreplaced. The rich are as angry as the poor, and more articulate.

Some wealthy families live in the countryside, though fewer now than in former years. Their homes are less and less separated from the envious poor by the dogs, the fences, and the jagged glass. Agriculture isn't so profitable anymore. City and countryside alike, Marcos has made himself such an implacable enemy of business that the relatively wealthy classes are already aiding a budding guerrilla revolution, although they know very well they may lose control of it.

The Marcos government itself has fundamentally stifled free enterprise. Using the power of the state, it has in effect nationalized many large and medium-sized businesses that in other countries live in fear of communism. From the richest to the poorest, Filipinos make clear that they believe this couldn't have happened without the full, active support of the United States.

Marcos was elected in 1965—fairly, by most accounts. He was reelected in 1969 in balloting that many Filipinos assert was rigged. According to official returns, he swept the election by 2 million of the 9 million votes cast, but a year later Filipinos were still complaining that he "won" in districts where almost everyone opposed him. The government committee that administered the elections reported "rampant overspending, fraud, and terrorism." The committee listed seventy-two political murders during the campaign, although unofficial estimates put the death toll as high as a thousand. *Time* reported that just before the election, Marcos's government paid out $50 million in "local development funds" to thousands of village leaders, in $500 packets. In interviews* with about fifty Filipinos from half a dozen provinces and various walks of life, only one, an international tobacco dealer, said he voted for Marcos. Most of the others completely disbelieved the official election results in their districts.

The constitution prohibited a third term for Marcos in 1973. There was speculation he might run his wife, Imelda, a former Miss Universe contestant who in personality has been variously compared to Lady Macbeth and the cartoon character the Dragon Lady. Instead, though, Marcos did something even more cynical. He seized power under martial law in 1972, ending twenty-six years of Philippine democracy. He lifted martial law in 1981, but only after changing the constitution to allow rule by decree if he has trouble with the national assembly, which opponents say is controlled through rigged elections anyway.

From the beginning, Marcos has received U.S. political, economic, and military support. He did everything he could to ally the Philippines with the U.S. in the Vietnam War (reversing a campaign pledge to stay out), and thereby gained support from the Johnson and Nixon administrations for even his most antidemocratic and anti-free market policies. So long as he stays

*With the author, in 1970.

in power with U.S. support, he guarantees the U.S. permission to operate
the air and naval bases that the Pentagon considers vital. The trouble is, as
Marcos's policies drag his country down further, and the U.S. remains inex-
orably identified with those policies, both Marcos and U.S. interests could
be cast off in a single blow.

President Lyndon Johnson helped glamorize the Marcoses early in their
tenure. Pictures of the two first couples dancing with each other were widely
circulated. That kind of thing was still going on in 1981, when Vice-President
George Bush visited Manila and went out of his way to toast Marcos in
public. Said the U.S. vice-president, "We stand with you, sir.... We love
your adherence to democratic principle and to the democratic processes. And
we will not leave you in isolation." President Reagan was almost as enthusiastic when Marcos visited the U.S. in the fall of 1982.

How big a commitment it would take to keep Marcos from isolation isn't
clear. He continues to outlive persistent rumors that he is suffering from
various fatal illnesses. "Huk" guerrillas continue their so-far-futile thirty-
year fight against him. But lately another, much more widely accepted guerrilla group has sprung up, the New People's Army, or NPA. The U.S.
embassy in Manila spreads word to visitors that Soviet submarines have
deposited arms on the coast for the NPA. The embassy won't comment
officially.

Prodemocratic Filipino businessmen have begun to talk of guerrilla suc-
cesses as the main hope for persuading the U.S. to accept a compromise
substitute for Marcos. Most people in the Philippines, however, must wonder
why the U.S. should have a say in the matter at all.

IN 1981, Marcos decided to hold local elections and permit a carefully
restrained opposition. Under the rules Marcos dictated, his candidates were
guaranteed to win most contests. But the opposition got a toehold. Its constituency so far is mainly entrepreneurs and executives frustrated by Marcos's
exploitative clampdown on the free marketplace. Under the rules, the opposition was splintered into an array of small groups. But early in 1982,
representatives from many of these groups met and elected a single leader,
Salvador "Doy" Laurel, scion of one of the old-line ruling families.

At the time, the election might have had mostly symbolic importance,
because the most popular opposition politician, former senator Benigno
Aquino, wasn't around. Fearful for his life, he was living in exile in the
United States. But Aquino decided to return in August 1983, to take up true
leadership of the opposition. He was murdered a few seconds after leaving
the plane in Manila in custody of a Philippine military guard, pretty clearly
with their complicity. That left Laurel with more than just a title.

A lawyer with a reputation as a rich playboy, Laurel appears able to get
away with saying things about Marcos for which other men have paid with
their lives. One reason for Laurel's freedom is his late father, a former

Philippine president under Japanese occupation (who narrowly escaped being tried as a traitor after the war). Back in the 1930s, Marcos, still a student, was caught red-handed in a gunshot murder. The victim was a political opponent of Marcos's father, a provincial politician. Laurel's father, then a justice of the supreme court, arranged for the murder charge to be dropped. Later, during the war, the elder Laurel once again saved young Marcos's life by warning him of an impending Japanese raid.* There obviously is a debt, and young Laurel is testing it.

In speeches, Laurel sometimes tells supporters that he opposes the mining industry. He reassures them that he has nothing against digging out the Philippines' rich deposits of coal, iron, silver, gold, chromite, manganese, nickel, and copper. What he opposes, he says, is the mining done by President and Mrs. Marcos, and their family and friends. "They are always saying, 'This is mine, this is mine, this is mine'—soon they will own everything," Laurel says.

Few Filipinos would miss the joke. Marcos's family and cronies have effectively expropriated almost everyone's business to one degree or another. As far back as 1970, a visitor to the Philippines could be stunned by frequent chance encounters with entrepreneurs who said they had been forced to give up as much as 50 percent ownership in their operations to a relative of the president's. One night, a traveler stayed with a husband and wife who started and ran a small lumberyard in northern Luzon. The traveler was told that the lumberyard had just been bought by Marcos. The next night he visited a hotel, one of a small chain, and was told by the mom-and-pop operators that a year earlier it had been acquired by a syndicate fronting for Marcos.

A few nights later, in one of the walled Manila suburbs, an executive of a major import and wholesale firm who also dabbled in resort motels sat down with the same traveler. Devaluation of the peso had confounded the firm's international business deals, and the more pesos you had in the bank the more you lost. The executive and his wife, talking contemptuously, accused Marcos of ordering the murder of a prominent politician whose gunshot slaying in a church monopolized local headlines that week.

Even government officials said they thought Marcos's behavior—especially his schemes for self-enrichment—had grown intolerable. All this came at a time when the U.S. press still seemed mesmerized by the glamorous Marcoses. Nowadays the glamor, if not the power, is gone. Only the White House and State Department seem mesmerized, but as long as they continue to provide the money and arms, the Marcoses keep going. The industry "centralization" policy, as the Marcos takeovers are sometimes politely referred to, has spread throughout the economy.

---

*The first story has been widely told and printed. The second story, like the first, was related to the author by Laurel himself in an interview and was confirmed by several people who know either Marcos or Laurel.

* * *

THE Philippines' two biggest cash industries, coconut products and sugar, have effectively been nationalized. This has infuriated millions of people who depend on these industries for their living. The anger is consistent, from the mass of tenant farmers and illegally low-paid $1.88-a-day farm laborers, to the middle class mill operators, and right on up to wealthy plantation owners.

When, in 1982, government forces shot four teenagers to death in the town of San Juan Batangas in the heart of the coconut region on suspicion of being members of the New People's Army, it was not just the poor who mourned them; Horacio Marasigan, the heir of the biggest landholding family in the area, assailed the shootings as "a massacre."

The 62,000 people of San Juan Batangas stand mostly united, rich and poor, against Marcos and his patron—us, the American people; it is not their opposition to freedom that drives them to sympathize with the rebellious youth, but rather their opposition to socialism. Of course, socialism isn't the name they give to the Marcos system, and socialism is certainly not the name the U.S. embassy gives to it; but socialism is a fairly apt term for what Marcos has done to Philippine industry.

The coconut industry has effectively been declared public property and turned over to an old friend and political ally of Marcos, Eduardo Cojuangco (pronounced KoWHANKo), who manages it under a long-term contract from an organization called the Coconut Federation, or Cocofed. Marcos started this organization back in the 1970s, and required all coconut planters to join.

The organization was formed in good times, when the world price of copra (copra is everything in a coconut that yields oil) had soared. Planters were making much more money because of the higher prices, but the rising price of coconut cooking oil in the home market was hurting Filipino families, who traditionally consumed half the national output. Marcos's original proposal was to impose a tax on coconut planters, taking part of their increased incomes to create a fund that would subsidize domestic coconut oil sales.

Of course, as so often happens with taxes, when the original motivator disappeared—when coconut prices fell back to previously low levels—new rationales were found for collecting the money. The coconut tax, it was now declared, would fund scholarships, insurance, and other social benefits for people engaged in the coconut business, from planters down to common farmers. The tax ran from 25 percent to 30 percent of the export price of copra, enough to pay for plenty of benefits. But people in the industry complained that they weren't getting any such benefits.

The hundreds of millions of dollars in coconut taxes go into a special bank created to hold this money, the United Coconut Planters Bank, or Cocobank. The coconut planters have been told that they collectively own

70 percent of the stock of the bank; they paid for this stock through additional taxes. But the holders of the remaining 30 percent of the stock actually control the bank, and they, of course, are Cojuangco and a few other Marcos insiders who were given directorships in the Cocobank at the outset. These insiders were allowed to buy shares in the bank for only 5 percent of the per-share price charged (via taxes) to the planters.

Marcos arranged for defense minister Juan Ponce Enrile, another member of the ruling clique, to be chairman of Cocobank and honorary chairman of Cocofed. Cojuangco became president of the bank, while still managing Cocofed, which imposes the tax that supplies the bank its money. Because Cocobank is supposedly owned by the planters, it doesn't pay interest on the tax funds it receives from them; but it charges market rates when it lends the money back out, and the same planters are often the borrowers.

The Cocobank and Cocofed don't account publicly for the money they get. (Cojuangco, Enrile, and their colleagues avoided strenuous attempts to interview them.) But the money is known to have financed the development and distribution of hybrid coconut tree seedlings by a company privately owned by Cojuangco. Still other funds have been spent hoarding oil, in an unsuccessful experiment to control the world market. (The U.S. Justice Department has charged some related companies based in America with price fixing in connection with this.)

Perhaps most galling of all, proceeds from the levy—the farmers' own funds—were used to buy up almost all of the country's coconut processing mills. This has created a purchasing monopoly, run by Cojuangco's organization. In the style of purchasing monopolies everywhere, the Cojuangco mills began paying lower prices to farmers for their copra. The farmers were deprived of their traditional option to shop around for more generous markets.

The farmers say they now get only about two thirds as much money for their copra as they used to (figured as a percentage of the world market price), while, on the other hand, the mills in the Cojuangco monopoly appear to be earning several times more money than coconut mills used to earn. One could argue that with world coconut prices falling recently, Philippine farmers would hurt anyway. But the farmers say they are willing to take their chances with the market. Horacio Marasigan, the big landowner of San Juan Batangas, put it this way: "We feel that if there was no monopoly, and free enterprise was allowed to work, the price [to the farmers] would be much higher."

Marcos's original plan, at least as he announced it, was to squeeze the landowners a little so that the poor would benefit. But while the landowners have been squeezed a lot, the poor do not seem to have benefited at all; certainly in their eyes, they have suffered.

MUCH the same happened with the sugar industry. In 1974, the world sugar price soared, which should have been a boon to Filipinos. But Marcos responded by creating the Philippine Sugar Commission—Philsucom. Farmers could no longer take their sugar to the mill of their choice, get a receipt for it, and then sell the receipt to whichever of the many competitive sugar brokers was paying the highest price.

Just as with the minerals of Zaire under Mobutu Sese Seko, Philippine sugar under Philsucom became owned by the state. The farmer still gets a receipt for his sugar when he turns it in at the mill, but the receipt entitles him only to wait until the government decides, much later, what to pay him for it. A lot of farmers no longer think the prices are fair. With copious charts and calculations, they are willing to illustrate for a reporter that the price paid to farmers is now much lower than it used to be, figured as a percentage of the world price of sugar.

The announced aim of Philsucom was to level the fluctuations in world sugar prices, in order to make planning easier for the farmer. But Philsucom arrived just in time to "level" downward the high prices the farmer would have received when sugar hit all-time peaks in 1974. The low-end prices in ensuing years didn't get leveled upward similarly. The reason, the government announced, was that Philsucom had hoarded sugar as prices soured, part of what it thought was a clever plan to sell at price peaks. But Philsucom misjudged the peaks, got less than it could have for the farmers' sugar, and took a bath.

In 1979, prices rose again. But then it was announced that the farmers owed Philsucom $350 million for the losses incurred when prices were down. So a fourth of the money that farmers are to be paid for their sugar nowadays, even by Philsucom's stingy reckoning, is held back to pay off the $350 million debt.

It turns out that the farmers owe this money to the government-owned Philippine National Bank, to a consortium of private Western and Japanese banks, to the IMF, and to two private Philippine banks. These private banks are largely owned and run by the same man who is chairman of Philsucom—Robert Benedicto, a schoolmate and lifelong friend of Marcos. Benedicto is also reported to have interests in the export and shipping of sugar, as well as in television and other businesses. He won't make himself available for questioning. But his two banks lend money not only to Philsucom, the agency he runs, but also to individual sugar farmers. These loans, at high interest rates, are to tide the farmers over between delivery of their sugar and the belated payments made for it by Philsucom—which, of course, is run by Benedicto.

Just as with the coconut industry, the sugar industry has been united against Marcos top to bottom. Wilson P. Gamboa, who audits the books for many of the wealthiest planters on Negros, the main sugar island, says the farmers "have never been in debt before. Now they are paying 21 percent interest on restructured loans. They are losing patience." As he speaks to a reporter, he is surrounded by big sugar planters. One used to be political party chairman for Marcos on Negros. Another used to be a good friend of Benedicto's. Today, they have given the reporter a tour of the island's capital, pointing out ubiquitous wall posters and graffiti, which say things like, "Revolution, not Election" and "Long Live the NPA (New People's Army)."

"We only want free enterprise," says one planter. "If the price of the world market is low, we accept it, what can you do? But if the price is high, why can't we take advantage of that?"

He says the reason they can't is that the U.S. has pledged to stand behind a crooked, anti-democratic, anti-free market autocrat.

IT would be hard to find a family that has experienced a stranger political transformation than have the Lopezes. Since Marcos declared martial law in 1972, the Lopezes have gone from ruling aristocracy to alleged radical-leftist bomb terrorists.

The Lopezes may have lost more than any other family in the Marcos nationalizations. In fact, they used to own so much that U.S. law, too, would have forced them to divest a lot of property for anti-monopoly reasons. They owned twenty-one radio and television stations with two thirds of the national audience, the country's only energy pipeline company and lubricating oil refinery, the biggest sugar refinery, some prominent newspapers, and considerable real estate, from cane fields to high-rise office complexes.

One Lopez, Fernando, was elected vice-president on a ticket with Marcos in 1965 and again in 1969. At about 3:00 A.M. on September 21, 1972, however, he received a phone call from the palace announcing that martial law had been declared, and that the Philippines no longer needed a vice-president. He says he never even went back to clean out his desk.

Fernando's nephew, Oscar, then president of Philippine Electric Corporation, says he also was rousted from bed at about 3:00 A.M.—by a call telling him not to come to work that morning. He says he tried anyway, but found that "the entire building was sealed by the army." The building, Lopez-owned, also housed the *Manila Chronicle*, Lopez-owned. The government had shut down all newspapers and broadcast outlets, and only those specially approved by Marcos could reopen.

Two weeks later, Oscar Lopez says, a *Chronicle* editor reported that he had been approached by Benjamin "Kokoy" Romualdez, the brother of Imelda Marcos, the president's wife. "Kokoy wanted to start a newspaper," Lopez says. "He said, 'If you would lease us the [*Chronicle*] building, we could start up.'" Apparently, Kokoy had faith that he could obtain his brother-in-law's permission to publish. The lease was signed, and Romualdez effectively took over the Lopez's newspaper. "We had no choice," Oscar Lopez says.

Since then, Romualdez has acquired holdings in many industries and has been appointed governor of a large province. He wouldn't talk to a reporter.

The Lopezes owned two of Manila's seven TV channels including the most popular. The only channel immediately relicensed after martial law was a smaller one owned by Roberto Benedicto—the same Marcos crony who runs the sugar industry and who was also in the meat business with government financing. A few months later a second channel, owned by an American, Robert Stewart, also was relicensed—after Stewart gave part ownership of the station to what Mr. Stewart's son and partner, Leslie Stewart, calls "some people from the government." (He notes that these people were acting privately, not as public servants.)

In 1973, Benedicto's broadcast center burned down. Oscar Lopez says he was approached to lease his old, delicensed facilities to Benedicto, and agreed. Thus Benedicto effectively took over Lopez's broadcasting network. By this time, Oscar's older brother, Eugenio Lopez, Jr., had been jailed on charges of conspiring to kill Marcos. (No actual attempt was alleged.) The Lopez family considered Eugenio, Jr., a hostage.

So they also signed over their electric company—not only because Eugenio, Jr., son of the head of the company, was a captive, but also because a prolonged refusal by Marcos to grant a rate increase had caused an evaporation of profits.

In 1977, Eugenio, Jr., escaped (some people say he was let out by Marcos as part of a deal; the Lopezes deny that). He went to San Francisco, where his sister Pressy and her husband, Steven Psinakis, had helped start an anti-Marcos movement among Philippine-Americans. For years, the Philippine and U.S. branches of the Lopez family had feuded. The Psinakises disapproved of efforts by the Philippine Lopezes to placate the Marcos government and hold onto the family sugar lands.

But the family joined ranks after the U.S. Justice Department began harassing the Psinakises. (It was after an FBI raid on the Psinakis house in San Francisco that Oscar Lopez agreed to give a reporter the interview quoted above.) Psinakis came under U.S. pressure after his name was given to Philippine authorities by an acquaintance who was captured in a bombing incident in Manila in 1980. The acquaintance told Philippine police that Psinakis had put him up to the bombing; later, on arriving in the U.S., the acquaintance withdrew that statement and said it had been forced from him in Manila.

Just before dawn on December 17, 1981, a stranger carried away the Psinakis family's garbage from the front of their home on a pleasant San Francisco suburban street. Psinakis says witnesses identified the man as a Filipino. Later that day, the FBI says, an unnamable, confidential informant gave them the garbage, which then contained detonating cords, empty packets of explosives, parts of clocks, and other bomb-making equipment.

Despite the improbability that anyone actually making bombs would leave the remnants of a do-it-yourself bomb-making kit on top of the garbage in front of his house, that night about twenty FBI agents raided the home where the Psinakises live with their three youngest children. The FBI found nothing relating to bombs, but seized letters and files from the dissident movement.

Psinakis says that two dozen Filipinos who had been in touch with him were quickly jailed or otherwise harassed, indicating that the FBI had turned his files over to Philippine authorities. He also says he has sources in the Philippine government who told him the files were turned over. (He declined to give a Manila-bound reporter a list of names for verification, explaining that to do so might further compromise the safety of his correspondents.) Psinakis has renounced terrorism, and claims the bomb material was planted in his garbage as a ruse to get a search warrant for the raid on his files.

Documents from the U.S. Defense Intelligence Agency and other material that became public in 1983 make clear that U.S. authorities have long known Philippine agents were active in this country, and have cooperated with them in suppressing the liberty of expatriate Filipinos. So far, Steven Psinakis hasn't been charged with a crime in the U.S. Whatever the truth about the bomb material, the Lopez family has come a long way in a decade.

THE Marcoses wouldn't discuss these issues, or provide a spokesman who would. There are some Marcos defenders around Manila (most seem to have plush government jobs). They acknowledge that industry has been excessively centralized, but deny that corruption had anything to do with it. They say Marcos wanted to create a Japanese-model economy, built around a few private conglomerates, run by people he could trust to operate them in the national interest. Be that as it may, most Filipinos, and businessmen throughout Asia, say Marcos is mainly lining his own pockets, and those of his family and friends.

Corruption and the unequal treatment of citizens has characterized Philippine administration since Spanish colonial times. In precolonial Philippine society, when fewer than a million people lived on the islands, land was usually owned by the community. Anyone could farm unoccupied plots, of which there were plenty. Came more people, there remained the same amount of land.

The Spanish granted large tracts to the Church, to Spanish nobles, and to favored members of the local aristocracy. Tenant farming began. Corruption in government hiring also started under the Spanish, who literally advertised jobs for sale. In 1732, the post of secretary to the municipal board of Manila was offered for 14,000 pesos.

The first U.S. administration wanted to return land to the people, but wasn't willing to annoy the aristocracy. William Howard Taft, the first colonial governor, actually went to Rome and bought nearly 400,000 acres of productive farmland from the pope for $7.5 million. The colonial administration then sold the land in small plots to 60,000 tenant farmers. But powerful landlords living on the islands kept their holdings.

The U.S. granted substantial self-government, but the aristocracy domi-nated the ruling party. It thwarted U.S. efforts to spread landholdings and insure minimum rights for tenant farmers, and the U.S. let the aristocracy have its way. Tenancy actually increased during the U.S. administration, and quickened its rate of increase after independence. With more tenants, the plots shrank. Now, in many areas, a direct turnover of land to the farmers would result in a plethora of tiny, impractical farms.

Early in his presidency, Marcos preached land redistribution. But he never funded the government agencies that were supposed to finance it. The pro-gram fizzled. As he did with the Lopezes, Marcos busted up some of the semimonopolistic empires by which the aristocracy controlled the economy, but he merely replaced them with his own monopolies.

A COUPLE of observations unique to the Philippines ought to be added to any discussion of the nation's prospects, especially considering the tendency of U.S. policymakers to ignore local uniqueness. Although the gulf between rich and poor is wider in the Philippines than in other Asian countries—wider than in most other countries altogether—the Philippine esteem for graciousness infects even the common man. A deep regard for the national tradition of hospitality, geniality, and warmth binds this economically dis-parate society.

Perhaps even more important, many Filipinos, particularly older ones, have studied U.S. history and government with an emphasis on idealism. To a degree much greater than in other Third World countries, the Philippine people understand the principles of democracy—not in Marxist rhetoric, but in the Jeffersonian-Madisonian spirit. They realize, with considerable so-phistication, the falseness of the current government.

The Philippine press was among the freest in the Third World until Marcos subdued it with his overnight decrees. While tempered somewhat by pub-lishers who were rich politicians, the newspapers had usually managed to get the facts to the people in a lively way; there were enough rich political publishers that they exposed each other, and left the system open to criticism as well.

Perhaps the most poignant complaint heard during a trip to the Philippines in 1982 was that of a middle-aged career journalist, the mother of several children, who used to work for vigorous newspapers and now writes for a soppy life-style magazine. She observed that her youngest children had gone through school learning from new textbooks that praised martial law and condemned dissent. She lamented the whole generation that is being brought up this way. "They don't even know that there's something wrong with what's happening," she said.

Filipinos value the election process in a way that, say, the inexperienced

Congolese might not. Most postcolonial peoples talk about elections as a foreign idea, a means to the end of setting up a modern state. Filipinos talk about the democratic process more as Americans would, as an end in itself.

Back in 1970, for example, the Philippines was preoccupied with an election for delegates to a constitutional convention. The country's original constitution, adopted under U.S. tutelege in 1935, required a review of itself by a new convention in thirty-six years. Filipinos from all economic stations talked about this convention as the last great hope for emerging from the autocratic centralization Marcos was imposing. Marcos saw the convention as a means of obtaining permission to run for a third term in office. Debate over the views of the candidates surged through the islands.

The convention didn't grant Marcos the new powers he wanted. It preserved democracy. So—clearly with U.S. approval if not actual U.S. instigation—Marcos kicked the constitution out the window and took over with the army.

CHAPTER NINETEEN

THE UNPREDICTABLE RESULTS OF COVERT ACTION

IN MARCH 1917, the German general staff executed what may still be the most important covert-action dirty trick in history. Hoping to monkeywrench the Russian effort in World War I, the Germans made a deal with what looked to be a bunch of kookie left-wing radicals in Switzerland. These radicals included Swiss socialists and some exiled Russian revolutionaries calling themselves Bolsheviks. They wanted to get their hero, Vladimir Ilyich Lenin, back into Russia.

Lenin had left Russia in 1900, after completing a thirteen-year stretch in Siberia for propagandizing on the streets of St. Petersburg. Since then, for seventeen years, he had been hopping harmlessly around Western Europe, writing tracts and getting into arguments with other radicals. He had returned to Russia briefly during the constitutional changes of 1905–1907, but left again in fear that the impending counterrevolutionary repression might land him back in Siberia.

As late as January 1917, Lenin had cautioned some young followers in Geneva, Switzerland, that his generation wouldn't live to see the revolution. His only hope was that theirs might. But a month later, thousands of hungry Russians in line outside empty food shops accomplished his revolution for him. As the mobs swelled, police proved unable and then unwilling to restore order. In barely a week, the tsar was shoved aside and a provisional civilian government set up in his place.

Lenin longed to return and see if he could get anywhere in the power struggle. But because of the war, and his own bad reputation, passage couldn't be arranged. Britain and France flatly refused to let him out of Switzerland on the side their forces controlled, and the Germans were his deadly enemies. According to Edmund Wilson's history, *To the Finland Station*, Lenin actually "thought seriously about going in an airplane, but in the morning he knew he couldn't manage it." Lenin might have been trapped in Switzerland for years.

But the German high command knew of Lenin, and his antiwar writings. It decided that if it injected him into the volatile Russian political picture, he might create just that touch of added turmoil necessary to close the eastern front and remove Russia as a threat to Germany. At least it was worth a shot. So the Germans arranged the famous "sealed" railway car for Lenin's voyage to Sweden. From there, he could make his way home and reenter politics.

As we all know now, the plan worked perfectly—except for one thing.

The lessons never seem to sink in. The history of meddling by one country in the affairs of others, no matter who does it or why, is littered with backfired actions like the Lenin caper. Governments often misjudge what their own people will do; so how can even the most learned and advanced of rulers safely make assumptions about other societies, and other cultures? The manipulators never stop to consider what their dioxin might kill besides the weeds.

Wilbur Crane Eveland, a former CIA undercover operative, published his memoirs, *Ropes of Sand*, in 1980, and in reviewing it, former CIA officer Victor Marchetti told this story from their combined experiences:*

"Eveland recounts how he helped to fix parliamentary elections in Lebanon in 1957, and was planning also to fix the presidential election, scheduled for the following year, on behalf of President Camille Chamoun. But in the 1957 election, the CIA had helped elect so many pro-American candidates that the established Arab nationalist politicians were furious, realizing that the cheating was eroding their power base. Partially as a result of this, the feud that had been brewing between Arab nationalists and the pro-Western Christians erupted into civil war. President Eisenhower sent in the marines; they were withdrawn after a few months, but what had been perhaps the most stable state in the Middle East was on the road to total polarization and eventual disintegration."

Barely two years after Marchetti wrote those words, the marines were back in Lebanon.

*   *   *

*Eveland's book published by W.W. Norton. The review appeared in *Inquiry* magazine, November 10, 1980.

MACBETH had some good advice about covert-action dirty tricks. Like occasional well-intentioned presidents who can't say "no" to their foreign policy experts, Macbeth was just too weak to follow his own counsel. Shortly before he went ahead and killed the king anyway, he said, "We but teach bloody instructions, which, being taught, return to plague the inventor. This evenhanded justice commends the ingredients of our poisoned chalice to our own lips."

Suppose Castro really *was* behind the assassination of John Kennedy. (The bulk of the evidence opposes this thesis, but it's plausible, and sexy, and so it persists.) Would Kennedy and the people of the United States have a just complaint, considering what we tried seventeen times to do to Castro? We started the shooting contest; all you could say about Castro would be that he found a surer marksman. What if Castro started a campaign of industrial sabotage against the U.S., or tried to contaminate some city's water supply?— all variations on a theme we started.

Nowhere does Macbeth's advice apply more strongly than to the export of arms. And yet the United States, under the constant encouragement of the government foreign policy elite, has turned more and more of its economy toward that lethal business. We not only pass the poisoned chalice that will return, we make it one of our chief exports, all in the name of fighting communism.

In the decade of the 1970s, annual international arms transfers, world wide, more than doubled, from $9.1 billion to about $20 billion. Meanwhile, U.S. arms sales rose from $1.1 billion in 1970 to about $16 billion in 1980. While the statistics aren't precisely comparable, the U.S. was clearly leading the way in the arming of humanity.*

It wasn't just the amounts that were scary. The weapons we were exporting became ever more sophisticated, too. And although the U.S. has tried to create legal devices to control who can use these weapons and how, the controls are largely fictitious. For example, the airplanes that the U.S. supplied to Iran in the mid-1970s—really, multifaceted, rocket-equipped, computer-guided airborne mass killing machines—were covered by written limitations on their use. Supposedly, Iran could employ them only to resist attack (presumably by the Soviet Union, or the Soviets' perceived ally, Iraq). But, as we have seen, the main known use of all this equipment during the

*These figures come from a recognized authority on the subject, Andrew J. Pierre, and his book *The Global Politics of Arms Sales* (Princeton University Press, 1981). In an interview, Pierre said he was able to obtain only transfer figures for the world, and sales figures from the U.S. Since sales precede deliveries, sales figures would run ahead of actual transfers. Pierre said he wasn't able to obtain comparable figures, and the author, in phone calls to the U.S. Arms Control and Disarmament Agency, couldn't do better. It's also worth noting that one can't be confident about any precise figures for something like arms deals, which many of the participants are trying to keep secret. But the point here is *relative* growth, which can be sensed even if the figures are imprecise.

U.S.-Iran alliance was to put down a movement for equal rights and self-rule in Baluchistan. These attacks on Baluchistan, besides being basically inhumane, later turned out to have worked against the U.S.'s desire for a Baluchi bulwark against Soviet aggression in Afghanistan.

The weapons *were* finally used against Iraq, in the Iran-Iraq war that began in 1980. But by this time, the U.S. and Iran had become enemies, the Soviet-Iraqi alliance had broken down, and the State Department was *rooting for Iraqi victories*. In this new war, still going on in 1983, our Saudi allies were aiding Iraq. They feared that Iran's superior U.S.-made military equipment would tip the Iran-Iraq power balance, which other countries in the area found handy.

ONCE the U.S. delivers weapons to an ally, usually along with a big contingent of technicians to help the buyer use them effectively, a publicly perceived military alliance is formed. The U.S. is in no position to criticize its ally publicly for violating the terms of the sales agreement. The weapons are used only during crises—their use *creates* crises—when our insistence on legalities would appear to be a sign of betrayal. For instance, over the years, Israel has repeatedly violated the restrictions that the U.S. placed on the weapons it delivered—Israel's use of cluster bombs in the 1982 invasion of Lebanon is one example.

Cluster bombs go off in two waves; the first bomb explosion merely scatters many smaller bombs over a wide area, and then each of those other bombs explodes. This means there is no place to hide, so such bombs are especially sinister when used in populated areas. In Israel's 1967 war with its Arab neighbors, our ally even used U.S.-made weapons to attack a U.S. electronic spy ship, killing thirty American sailors. We kept our mouths shut and stayed loyal, like some Mafia member who just watched his friend be rubbed out for the good of the organization.

Sometimes, it appears, the men who run foreign policy for the U.S. executive branch make under-the-table deals with arms recipients, in order to circumvent the official restrictions. These restrictions have been imposed by Congress to reflect what the U.S. electorate apparently wants, and is told it is getting. The foreign policy experts think they know better.

At times, the intention of the recipient country to use the weapons for offensive purposes is so obvious that signed statements to the contrary seem nothing but a charade, to get around the law. The Reagan administration's arming of various Latin groups trying to overthrow the government of Nicaragua in 1982 and 1983 would seem to be one example of this illegal subterfuge. By law, the groups were being armed merely to intercept shipments of weapons leaving Nicaragua for El Salvador. Despite a lot of combat activity, however, no gun shipments were being intercepted, and anyone could see the real purpose of these groups.

Congress has tried to limit the use of U.S. arms in other ways, such as by requiring purchaser countries to pay at least some respect to human rights. In the case of El Salvador, however, an "embassy official" who declined to be identified practically admitted to the *New York Times* that Reagan routinely lied his way around this law. "It forces the president to overstate things in order to get the aid that must be sent. What choice did he have?" the official complained.* Apparently telling the truth wasn't even under consideration.

IN the case of Central America, however, the proximity of the fighting, and the fact that public attention had been focused on the region for a long time, allowed the situation to be exposed so Congress and the public could wrestle with the issue. The long, U.S.-supported war against the desert peoples of the Western Sahara is another matter. Few Americans even know that anybody lives on the Sahara Desert, let alone that Saharans have their own country (or want to), or that since 1975 U.S. high-technology weapons have targeted them. We have killed thousands of these people and made most of the rest refugees.

The Western Sahara is hardly a threat to anyone—a hunk of sand and gravel about the size of Colorado, which probably would have fewer than a million inhabitants even if all the refugees came back home. Other than the basic interest we have everywhere in quietly encouraging self-determination, civil liberties, prosperity, and free markets, our only interest in the Western Sahara would seem to be having access to the territory's phosphate deposits.

When things are normal, the Western Sahara is the world's second-largest supplier of phosphate. The largest supplier is Morocco. And Morocco is the U.S. ally that is using our arms and advisors to fight the Saharan independence movement; the Moroccan monarchy declares that it has an ancient claim on Saharan territory. If Morocco wins, it will control the Saharan mines as well as its own, and thus have a lock on more than half the world's phosphate. In fact, just by continuing the fight, Morocco has shut down the Saharan mines, and thus eliminated its main competition. (If either side tried to operate the mines now, attacks by the other would close the mines down again.)

So helping the Moroccans in their Saharan war would seem to be contrary to the interests of phosphate consumers—for example, the American public. On the other hand, if the Saharan people were allowed their independence, consumers would have two major independent African sources of phosphate, competing for sales.

Not only does the arming of Morocco alienate the Saharans, who could wind up controlling the phosphate, it also alienates neighboring Algeria, an important supplier of oil and natural gas. Algeria is afraid of Moroccan strength, and for good reason: the king of Morocco not only claims

*February 26, 1982; the reporter was Raymond Bonner.

that his ancestors endowed him with sovereignty over the Western Sahara, he claims they endowed him with sovereignty over much of Algeria, too. If he gets the Sahara, who knows where his army will stop?

Algeria, therefore, has been the main source of support for the Saharans. Algeria had to fight a bitter war with France to gain its own independence, and it spent the first couple of decades of that independence living under socialism. It was sympathetic to the Soviet Union on most international matters. But in recent years, Algeria has manifested an understandable desire to edge away from that, and to entertain trade and friendship with Western countries. In fact, Algeria helped negotiate the freeing of the U.S. hostages from Iran in 1980, and when the hostages stopped in Algeria on their way home, they were widely reported as having landed on "free soil."

One would imagine that the United States would want to encourage this trend by refraining from belligerent actions like arming Morocco, a country that Algeria legitimately fears. Thus every realistic inducement seems to be toward nonintervention in the Saharan dispute, with benevolent feelings toward Saharan independence. Yet all these inducements have been ignored, for the standard geopolitical reasons. We continue to cast all international disputes in the mold of our own dispute with the Soviet Union. So, unbeknownst to most Americans, their tax money has been staked on Morocco.

From the looks of the war so far, though, the Moroccans can't win. Nor should they. They can come down to the Sahara in modern uniforms, with the best guns, tanks, planes, and helicopters that the U.S. can provide. But they wind up being evacuated, leaving their dead behind. The soldiers of Polisario,* the Saharan political organization, have the run of the land.

Dressed in turbans and robes and driving Land Rovers, they have repeatedly demonstrated their ability to take U.S. observers all over the Western Sahara, from the Algerian border to the Atlantic Ocean, even within sight of the few fortified cities the Moroccans hole up in. The Polisario display captured weapons, all of U.S. manufacture, including ground radar, cluster bombs, air-to-surface guided missiles, mines, various kinds of artillery, and downed F-5 jets. On the squares of towns long since deserted by their civilian populations, the Saharans display the bodies of dozens of Moroccan soldiers, lined up side by side looking like a flagstone footpath.

The Saharans can't stay in any one place for long. Given a sitting target, the Moroccans could call in air power and strike relentlessly with electronic guidance systems. So the population lives as refugees. Most have moved voluntarily to areas under Polisario control, including semi-autonomous refugee camps in Algeria. Very few Saharans fled to the several Saharan coastal cities under Moroccan control. The overall size of those cities has dwindled by 25 percent since before the war, and most of those

---

*An acronym for the Popular Front for the Liberation of the Saguia el Hamra and Rio de Oro, two former territories linked by the Spanish colonialists.

who live there now may not be Saharan. The one American reporter* who has talked to and written about the townspeople says most are transplanted Moroccans sent down to Moroccanize the country.

There is abundant evidence that most Saharans think the Moroccans are alien invaders. A U.N. mission was dispatched to the area in 1975, composed of representatives from Iran (then a U.S. ally), the Ivory Coast (a government closely tied to France and the West), and Cuba. The mission unanimously reported "an overwhelming consensus among the Saharans within the territory in favor of independence and opposing integration with any neighboring country." The commission said the Polisario had "considerable support among all sections of the population."

Our war against them stayed secret until 1979, when the Polisario displayed its captured U.S. equipment for Representative Stephen Solarz, a Brooklyn Democrat who chaired the House subcommittee on Africa. In authorizing arms for Morocco, Congress had specified that they could be used only for defense, and thus not in the Saharan war. The U.S. government had insisted all along that this restriction was being enforced.

But when Solarz and a few others howled that the law was being violated, the Carter administration just asked Congress to reverse the ban on U.S. intervention. Moroccan press agentry has long sought to woo U.S. support for its Saharan campaign by falsely painting the Polisario as lackeys of Moscow. This idea plays to the proclivity of the U.S. press to categorize everyone in the same us-or-them reference that the U.S. government uses. On November 23, 1979, the *Wall Street Journal* printed a page-one story, stating in its lead, "Cubans may be fighting on the guerrillas' side."

No other report of Cubans in the Saharan war has appeared, before or since, but the story quoted "military sources" as saying that "some guerrillas killed in recent battles were uncircumcised outsiders who 'looked Cuban.'" The story conceded that no Cuban prisoners had been taken, but suggested that this was because the Moroccans killed most of their prisoners.

The story ran under the headline, "Stakes Are Substantial as Guerrillas Step Up War Against Morocco," implying that the guerrillas were aiming to overthrow the government of Morocco, rather than to establish a government of their own in what had been a separate colony since the nineteenth century. The story said that the U.S. side wanted a referendum on independence, but that the guerrillas "oppose any such vote," which is the exact opposite of the truth. The story said the Sahara had a "long history as part of Morocco"—untrue—and that "it is likely that Morocco would win any referendum" because most "tribesmen" were loyal to Morocco's King Hassan.

The story, presented as a straight news account, was probably the most prominent write-up the Saharan war has had in the U.S. press. It warned

*Tami Hultman of *Africa News*, who has also written about the Saharan war for the *Washington Post*.

that if King Hassan, "a friend of the United States," didn't maintain control of the Sahara (which he never had), "Morocco's free-enterprise government could be weakened," and "leftists could gain another African foothold. If American aid proves ineffective, the U.S. could appear to the world as a weak and indecisive ally that waited too long to help a friend in a showdown," the story said. Briefer accounts that appeared in back pages of other papers reported the same situation.

In fact, the Soviet Union had studiously avoided aiding the Polisario, perhaps because of its strong trade ties to Morocco. The Soviets, too, need Moroccan phosphate, and the Soviets are Morocco's biggest customer for citrus fruit. Morocco—not Algeria, not Guinea, not Angola, not Mozambique, but Morocco—is, in fact, the U.S.S.R.'s largest trade partner in Africa.

Morocco's small pro-Soviet political group ardently supports King Hassan's war effort. No Eastern bloc country recognized the Polisario government-in-exile. On the other hand, the Organization of African Unity, the main regional organization of African governments, voted thirty-three to two with eight abstentions to endorse the Polisario's call for independence and free elections in the Western Sahara.

Washington has long thought of King Hassan as being a pro-Western voice in the Moslem group of nations, where, at least until the Soviet invasion of Afghanistan, the West had been short of friends. Hassan declined to join other Moslem countries in condemning the Camp David peace settlement between Egypt and Israel, and pro-Israeli groups in the U.S. still see him as soft on the Israeli issue.

These groups make up an abnormally large part of the Brooklyn constituency of Representative Solarz. After returning from Western Sahara, Solarz had said, "I came away from my trip persuaded that the proposed sale of offensive arms to Morocco for use in the Western Sahara would have significantly negative consequences for U.S. foreign policy, and that the advantages cited in behalf of such action are either minimal or nonexistent."

But 1980 was an election year, so Solarz, chairman of the House subcommittee on Africa, caved in to the pressure from the pro-Israeli groups in his district. In Congress, he actually supported the sale of high-tech air weapons to Morocco. Deadly cluster bombs were supplied. So were heavy transport helicopters—needed because the Polisario controls all the roads in the Sahara making it impossible for the Moroccans to use any surface transportation bwtween cities or military bases.

The result was predictable. The Polisario didn't give up. It just went out and got more sophisticated weapons of its own, probably from Algeria or Libya, or someone else who got them from the Soviet Union years ago. The Soviets probably didn't know their weapons were going to be used to fight Morocco, any more than we originally knew that U.S. weapons were going to be used to fight the Polisario.

But in for a dime, in for a dollar, and now the Polisario acquired portable, heat-seeking surface-to-air missiles, among the scariest nonnuclear weapons on earth. They can knock the Moroccan helicopters out of the sky, and they can just as well bring down a Pan Am 747. Fortunately, the Polisario have thus far *not* turned out to be as irresponsible as Moroccan propaganda would have predicted.

There is an ironic similarity between the Polisario soldiers and the Afghan guerrillas who have become the object of much sympathy in the U.S. If you were to stand a Polisario fighter side-by-side with a *mujahadeen* (Afghan guerrilla), you probably couldn't tell them apart. Their dress is almost identical from the turban on down, except that the Afghan stuffs wool into his robes in winter. Both would be devout Moslems, most likely of the Sunni sect. Both would likely be carrying Soviet-style AK-47 automatic rifles that were originally supplied by the Soviet bloc for use by others.

Their responses to a series of ideological questions might be hard to distinguish. On economic policy, they would share a fundamental conviction that their goats ought to be able to graze the same turf their fathers' goats grazed. Yet one, the Afghan, is looked upon as a courageous freedom fighter, an *anti-communist*, while the other, the Polisario guerrilla, is bombed, strafed, and rocketed by U.S.-supplied planes for being a *communist*. Actually, for all our sympathy, any military aid the Afghans have received from the U.S. wouldn't last them ten minutes against the kind of firepower we have supplied to King Hassan of Morocco to use against the Polisario.

The Polisario guerrillas are, if anything, more in line with American ideals than is the king of Morocco, or, for that matter, the governments of many other U.S. allies. "All we want is a plebiscite," says Magid Abdouallah, the Polisario's observer at the U.N. "The United Nations has called for a plebiscite, the OAU has called for a plebiscite, and only Morocco will not go along." Of course, a plebiscite—a free election—is something King Hassan hasn't offered to try in his own country. Yet the U.S. has staked its reputation, and the blood of the Saharans, on Hassan.

Historically, the kingdom of Morocco never had sovereignty over Western Sahara. It did have some trading concessions, but in the nineteenth century Morocco was colonized by France, while the Sahara became Spanish. Morocco was among the first colonial nations to gain independence; that was in 1956. Spanish Sahara was one of the last. A dying Francisco Franco gave it up in 1975, and didn't lift a finger to stop the Moroccan army from marching in when his own army left.

Africa News, a weekly digest published in Durham, North Carolina, and probably the most consistently reliable source of information about Africa,*

---

*The staff monitors African shortwave radio broadcasts and African newspapers, and has contacts that must make the CIA envious. It also operates on a shoestring and appreciates donations. Address: P.O. Box 3851, Durham, N.C. 27702.

has published evidence that the U.S. may even have helped ignite the Saharan war, by covertly trying to engineer what Henry Kissinger thought would be an easy Moroccan takeover. As Franco lay dying, Kissinger sent General Vernon Walters, then deputy head of the CIA, on a secret mission to the Mediterranean, to tighten the U.S. hold on Morocco by doing a favor for King Hassan. According to the testimony of Spanish military officials before the Spanish Chamber of Deputies, quoted by *Africa News*, Walters persuaded Franco not to interfere with Morocco's plan to annex the Sahara.*

Walters wouldn't comment on the story, but his stated reason for not commenting certainly doesn't cast doubt on it: "It would look like the king of Morocco and the king of Spain [sic] are pawns of the United States, and that wouldn't be in anyone's interest," he told *Africa News*.†

It is unlikely that the Saharan war would still be going on if not for a steady—and until 1980 illegal—flow of weapons from the U.S. Our arms sales to Morocco, which had been running less than $10 million a year, soared to $296 million in 1975, and stayed high. Foreign military credits from the U.S. government to Morocco also rose more than tenfold, from $3.6 million in 1974 to $45 million in 1978. In 1980, Saudi Arabia agreed to pay $232.5 million for F-5E and other jet fighters and helicopters destined for Morocco. Some sixteen F-5A fighters were transferred from Iran and Jordan to Morocco.

In 1977, Westinghouse was authorized to sell Morocco a $200 million air defense system, which brought U.S. technicians into the Western Sahara. There followed more than $100 million worth of helicopter gunships. Morocco faced no new outside threats. Clearly all this gadgetry was intended for the Saharan war, where it could not legally be used.

In Algeria, an estimated 50,000 to 100,000 Saharan refugees live in tents and govern themselves through a system of indirect elections without Algerian or other outside supervision. Each camp has committees for health, education, handicraft (including tent making), food distribution, and the administration of law. There are clinics and schools. Almost everyone is said to be involved in some part of the self-governing process.

The *Wall Street Journal* article on the war reported—from the Moroccan side—that "most of" the refugees in the Algerian camps were "victims of the recent droughts in the Sahara," for whom "war is considered something of a diversion." It said the refugees also included Moroccans who were

---

*Terms of the alleged deal weren't spelled out, but Morocco lets the U.S. use military air facilities there (though these are hardly irreplaceable; Morocco is no better positioned strategically than many nearby NATO countries). Morocco also consented to deploy its troops as African window-dressing to the international "peace" force in Zaire's Shaba province after the 1978 U.S.-French-Belgian intervention there.

†The author tried many times over several months to reach Walters about this. His office said he was traveling and unreachable by phone, and when the day of his promised return finally arrived, the office said he had already left on another trip.

"involved in attempts to overthrow King Hassan and fled Morocco during ensuing purges...."

But George Houser, who was helping distribute U.S. charity in the camps on behalf of the Africa Fund in New York,* says, "I have visited many refugee camps in Africa over many years, but I have never seen a group of people who are as self-reliant and as well-organized as are these Saharawi [Saharan] people.... I had the feeling, as others have, that in visiting these camps I was seeing something of what the nation of the Western Sahara would be like under the independent control of Polisario. I had a feeling that in visiting these camps I was visiting a nation in exile."

Women and children predominate in the camps. Most men are back in the Sahara, fighting. They have on occasion taken the battle into southern Morocco itself. There is a danger that such incidents could spark a full-scale war between Morocco and Algeria. That could cause terrible carnage, and set back economic progress for the whole region. Ironically, it could also bring down the Moroccan monarchy, which the American republic is, for some reason, shedding enormous blood (all of it other people's) trying to preserve.

What Lenin might reach his Finland station in such confusion?

IN the Saharan war, the uncontrolled and illegal use of U.S. weapons appears to have been the conscious, though secret, intention of a few foreign policy manipulators. In other cases, though, it is the intention of no one. CIA, army, and State Department officials all acknowledge that they don't keep close tabs on American weapons shipped overseas. Despite the law that says they must, they can't.

The law not only limits the occasions of the use of these weapons; it bans the recipient country from reselling them without U.S. permission. Sometimes, recipient countries can pressure the U.S. into letting them spread armaments in ways that might be contrary to U.S. interests. In 1981, for example, Israel, arguing that it needed foreign exchange, persuaded the Reagan administration to approve its sale of jet fighters to Ecuador; the Carter administration had vetoed that sale.

Most Americans know why we arm Israel with jet fighters. But how many Americans know anything about Ecuador, or who its enemies are? Its main enemy is Peru, with whom it fights intermittent shooting wars over the ownership of certain tracts in the Amazon. Peru, in 1981, was just pulling back from twelve years of socialism and military dictatorship, and effecting plans for democracy and private enterprise. Did we really want to threaten Peru just then? A few months after the jet sale was announced, terrorists bombed the U.S. embassy in Lima.

Do we want sophisticated, high-tech weapons in that part of South America

*Address: 198 Broadway, New York, N.Y. 10038.

at all, or are we better off keeping the wars small? The Argentine navy that invaded the Falkland Islands and fought England in 1982 relied on ships and planes obtained from the United States. That firepower, which we supplied Argentina, not only killed Englishmen, it also put the U.S. in a terrible diplomatic quandary. We wound up alienating much of Latin America by supporting Britain, which immediately weakened our negotiating position in the Central American crisis.

AT least Israel asked U.S. permission before selling its U.S.-made arms, as the law requires. Other recipients don't always bother. U.S. intelligence usually can keep track of something as big as a squadron of jet fighters. But watching smaller arms—including many kinds of powerful missiles and automatic weapons—is impossible. There is plenty of evidence that recipients all over the world have disregarded resale restrictions.

As a result of our various adventures in fighting communism, and the Soviets' in promoting it, the world is awash in arms that are lightweight, lethal, low-cost, and easy to use. Getting them poses no serious impediment to any group of revolutionaries, vigilantes, or just plain nuts who are willing to spend a little time looking.

The word *terrorist* has become politically contentious in recent years, with persons on both the left and right ends of the political spectrum applying it to the other end's heroes. But almost all the people who have worn the terrorist label, willingly or unwillingly, do have one thing in common: they are using weapons that were produced for another purpose.

The U.S. screams about a truckload of American-made M-16s that had been sent to Vietnam and is later found with leftists in Honduras. Afghan rebels rely on Soviet-made AK-47s they looted from the communist government. Most of the guerrillas in the world today may be fighting with arms intended to defend the very kind of government they are being used to attack.

There are interesting parallels on the larger arms scene, too. Possibly the most valuable bases the Soviet Union and the United States have in the Third World, from the standpoint of both modern facilities and strategic location, were provided for each by the other. The United States, thinking it had an ally in southeast Asia that would be a bastion of anti-communism, built a wonderful naval and air facility at Cam Ranh Bay, Vietnam. In 1975, the Soviets took it over, giving them their only modern military outpost on China's other flank and allowing them a presence in the Indian Ocean.

Meanwhile, the Soviets, thinking they had a real ally in the horn of Africa, built a marvelous new naval and air facility at Berbera, in Somalia. This allowed them a military presence near both the Persian Gulf and the potential turmoil spots of Africa. To their surprise, however, in 1977, Somalia's dictator, Siyad Barre, kicked the Russians out and sought aid from the West. Lo, without overthrowing a single government, the U.S. was offered, and accepted, this spiffy Russian-built base, providing the only mililtary thing we legitimately needed and didn't have: a means of protecting our commerce with Persian Gulf ports.

The United States and the Soviet Union bear about equal responsibility for letting the arms traffic get out of control. Sophisticated new weapons designed to put increased firepower into the hands of individual soldiers are rolling off assembly lines in both countries, and are being shipped to third parties all over the globe, after which no real accounting is kept. The arms often wind up on the black market.

From a shelf in almost any library you can pull down a volume of *Jane's Infantry Weapons* and find advertisements for mayhem. An antipersonnel grenade maker guarantees "uniform dispersion of fragments in every case." A firm called Euromissile proclaims, "A mere infantry soldier now has the means of killing enemy tanks anywhere within a 6,500-foot range . . . minimum training required." Euromissile lists addresses in France and Germany that you can write to. If you can destroy a tank, think what you could do to a speaker's platform. Besides the ads, *Jane's* features detailed and fully illustrated instructions on how to assemble and operate almost every known small arm from the Thompson submachine gun to the M-11 and the Strella.

The M-11 is the perfect assassination weapon. It is a machine gun held in one hand, like a pistol. It fires bullets by gas propulsion, without sound, flash, or smoke. It can empty its 32-round clip in 1.7 seconds. It comes in two pieces, each 9 inches long, and weighs about 7 pounds. Some 14,000 of the M-11, and a similar M-10, were made in Georgia in the 1970s, priced at about $80 each—though when the manufacturer went out of business, leftover M-10s were sold at auction for $5.

"They're all over the world now," says Geoffrey WerBell of Powder Springs, Georgia, whose father helped design the guns. "Thailand, Philippines, Malaysia, Venezuela, different countries in South America. The Israelis bought the initial production." The WerBell family has done work for the U.S. government for many years. They don't like to discuss every detail, but rumor has it they design such things as explosive pens and cigarette packs for the CIA.

The WerBells are particularly adept at silencers for guns. Explains Geoffrey WerBell, using a silencer "doesn't imply anything, it simply implies that if you're going to use it you don't want everybody else to get excited and cause great pandemonium." Says another U.S. gun merchant, discussing the capabilities of the M-11, "I could kill a hundred people in the next room and you'd never hear it." The WerBells have been involved in many private international arms deals.

The Strella is a Soviet-made, heat-seeking, precision guided missile. You can tote one comfortably on your back, yet it will knock a jetliner out of the sky. It is the weapon the Polisario obtained after the U.S. improved the quantity and quality of aircraft firepower it was delivering to Morocco. You can get tips on exactly how to use the Strella by reading *Jane's Infantry Weapons*, which also lists some countries that have them: People's Yemen, Egypt (which got them while it was still a Soviet ally), North Korea, and India.

In 1973, Italian police burst in on five Arab terrorists setting up Strellas in a rented apartment 4 miles from the Leonardo da Vinci Airport near Rome, directly under the traffic pattern for the north-south runway. Italian authorities speculated that the weapons came from a Soviet consignment to Egypt, which then sold them to Libya, which has become an equal opportunity deployer for the guerrilla industry.

Libya is one of two main arms supply sources for the Irish Republican Army, the other being the United States. At least two arms shipments from Libya to the IRA have been intercepted—one by boat on a tip from intelligence sources, the other when a box of weapons marked "machine parts" was accidentally broken open by a clumsy British airport worker. Libya has plenty to offer. The U.S.S.R. has supplied it with large quantities of, among other things, RPG-7 rockets, which weigh less than 10 pounds and will destroy a tank, let alone a limousine or speaker's platform. The IRA has used RPG-7s against armored British military vehicles and police stations.

From the U.S., the IRA gets rifles. The most popular are the AR-15, made by Colt Industries, and the AR-180, made by Armalite Inc. Both may be bought legally in the U.S. by almost anyone. Both are versions of the M-16, the principal U.S. military rifle, which was developed by Armalite (the WerBells say they helped design the noise moderator). Colt bought manufacturing rights to the M-16. *Jane's Infantry Weapons* prices the M-16 at $85, though the AR-15 and AR-180 commonly retail for about twice that much.

Federal law prohibits the sale to civilians of fully automatic weapons like the M-16; "automatic" means that a squeeze of the trigger causes repeat firing until either the trigger is released or the magazine is empty. Fully automatic rifles are the same as machine guns. The law against selling them to civilians appears to be why the AR-15 and AR-180 were designed. They are different from the M-16 in that they are semiautomatic; that is, they produce one shot for each pull of the trigger—so they're legal.

But a few hours of tinkering can undoctor the AR-15 and AR-180 so they, too, will be fully automatic. Many IRA weapons the British have recovered have been converted in this way. The AR-180 also has a folding stock, so it can be easily concealed. Still, by U.S. law, it and the AR-15 are "sporting" weapons. Guns found on IRA members have been traced by their serial numbers to U.S. buyers, but without further evidence the buyers can't be prosecuted.

That's because the State Department doesn't require the registration of serial numbers of weapons shipped overseas. A federal court in Philadelphia, Pennsylvania, reversed the convictions of five men acccused of shipping more than a hundred AR-180s to the IRA. Despite traced serial numbers showing that the men bought the guns, the court ruled that there was no way to prove they didn't sell the guns to some third party who then transferred the guns to the IRA.

The defense in the Philadelphia case argued successfully that the machine guns could have entered Ireland from anywhere. A half-million firearms a year are legally exported from the U.S., not including the three firearms everyone is allowed to take with him out of the country without a special export license. In addition, many U.S. firearms, including M-16s, and AR-180s that can be converted into M-16s, are made overseas by agreement with U.S. companies.

Clearly, there are far more military-type guns than there are soldiers in the world, as evidenced by the tremendous stores held by private arms dealers. The biggest of these is generally thought to be Samuel Cummings, who was set up in business while working for the CIA; supposedly, Cummings's formal tie with the CIA has been cut, although obviously they still interact.

According to Cummings himself, and others, his warehouses bulge with more than half a million light arms and more than 100 million rounds of ammunition, enough to equip an active-duty army the size of those of the U.S and U.S.S.R. From his base in Monaco, Cummings controls agents around the world, and maintains connections with East bloc, West bloc, and Third World governments. He says he can buy surplus machine guns for as little as $5 to $25 each. Both the Costa Rican civil war of the 1950s and the Bay of Pigs invasion, and possibly other wars, were fought with weapons that *both sides* had bought from Sam Cummings.

Whatever his connection with the CIA now, Cummings clearly wouldn't be in business without the contacts that were bought for him by the U.S. taxpayer. He learned the gun trade in the army in the 1940s and joined the CIA right afterward. His private firm laundered weapons for the CIA in the 1950s. Though he apparently sells now only to governments, those governments often deliver arms to the black market, either by design, corruption, or carelessness. The Soviet bloc is believed to have its own private arms distributor, a Czech trading company that operates through a purportedly independent arms merchant in Amsterdam.

Those who don't want to pay the prices of private arms dealers have equipped themselves through theft from the many U.S. military depots all over the world. A House Armed Services subcommittee has reported that many tens of thousands of U.S. military weapons have been lost or stolen from storage, that records were "haphazard" and that "losses of sizeable quantities of weapons and munitions were frequently written off as inventory errors without any investigation."

Many weapons are distributed through the aid and training that the U.S. gives to Third World police forces, particularly in Latin America. Police are shipped potent U.S. military weapons, then pass them out to private right-wing terror groups representing businessmen and big landowners. Latin exiles in the U.S. make convincing cases that such weapons handouts have occurred in Chile, Argentina, Brazil, Bolivia, and Uruguay, as well as in Central America.

The rightist groups set about to provide the kind of ruthless vigilantism that has decimated the populations of El Salvador, Guatemala, and other countries. But often their nonprofessionalism lands the guns in the hands of guerrillas, either through capture in a fight, or through theft from poorly guarded storehouses.

MUCH of the vigilante violence the U.S. spawns abroad has returned to create terror in our own country. The investigation into the killing of Orlando Letelier, the Chilean exile leader living in the U.S., and his American assistant, uncovered a sickening chain of connections. CIA operatives had cooperated extensively with counterpart agencies in both Chile and South Africa that showed no respect for U.S. peace or justice.

Chilean agents with whom the CIA worked had hired Americans to help in their hit jobs against Letelier and others in the U.S. They worked also with anti-Castro Cuban exiles living in the U.S. to project terror onto the Cuban exile community here. As recently as 1978, four Cubans were acquitted of weapons charges in federal court, Miami, on defense claims that they were working on behalf of the U.S. government, even though the Justice Department, on behalf of the government, denied it. The men were arrested with a 20-millimeter cannon, a 50-caliber machine gun, a 30-caliber machine gun, and five AR-15 rifles.

The Justice Department made a sincere—in fact, extraordinarily diligent—attempt to prosecute the Letelier and other killings. But most of the culprits escaped because the Chilean government, which owes its existence in large part to U.S. covert action, refused to turn over murderers and witnesses. By some accounts, Chilean officials threatened and intimidated witnesses in the U.S. The U.S. government leveled no meaningful sanctions on the Chilean government for this behavior.

DINA, the Chilean secret police, which the CIA helped organize, plotted to kill U.S. citizens and visitors to the country on the streets of Washington, D.C.—Macbeth's cup of poison, returned again. All during the plot, DINA was dealing with active and retired CIA personnel. Among the retired agents were Edwin Wilson and Frank Terpil. Wilson and Terpil used their CIA connections to sell high-tech weapons and explosives all over the world. Their main client, though, was Muammar al-Qaddafi in Libya, who hired them to arrange the murder of a Libyan opponent of his in Colorado.

Former CIA men regularly go into business working privately for countries where they had once represented the U.S. government. The pattern begins at the top—former CIA directors Richard Helms and William Colby do a big business consulting for foreign countries—and reaches all the way down to people like Daniel Arnold, former CIA station chief in Thailand, who now gets $50,000 a year as the Washington representative of the same Thai government that the CIA used to practically run.

THE two main organizations funneling heroin into the United States over the past quarter century both started in business with a nest egg provided by American taxpayers through our anti-communist intelligence agencies. One was the remnant band of soldiers from Chiang Kai-shek's Kuomintang army, who kept invading Yunnan province, China, from a base in Burma during the early days of Mao Zedong's revolutionary government.

When the KMT (as the Kuomintang was called) soldiers were finally driven out of Yunnan, many did not go to Taiwan. Instead, they stayed in the jungly, mountainous Golden Triangle, where Burma, Thailand, and Laos meet, near China. They spent most of their time in a region of Burma that has carried on a prolonged rebellion against the Burmese government, and is beyond control of that government except for occasional armed incursions.

The one efficient crop in that region is the opium poppy, and the KMT army took control of collecting and buying opium from local farmers, converting it into heroin in local laboratories, transporting it south out of the jungle, and, finally, selling it. The CIA had supported the KMT when Chiang's men were still an active thorn in China's side. The agency's responsibility for the resultant KMT heroin network might be considered unwitting had its role stopped there.

But Civil Air Transport, and its successor CIA airline, Air America, continued servicing the KMT at remote airstrips. And when the Vietnam war came along, the CIA's support service for dope dealers increased. Montagnard (or Hmong, or Meo) tribesmen, whom the CIA organized to fight the various communist guerrilla groups in the region, made their living growing opium poppies. And Air America often flew the product out to Saigon or other Asian capitals for transshipment to the U.S., although there has never been conclusive proof that CIA headquarters in Virginia directed this activity.*

The other big heroin operation the CIA helped get off the ground worked out of the Mediterranean, particularly the port of Marseilles. The racketeers

*The best published documentation of all this may be found in *The Politics of Heroin in Southeast Asia* by Alfred W. McCoy (Harper & Row, 1972). Other sources for the author include numerous interviews with U.S. officials and others in southeast Asia and the U.S., and viewing some truly remarkable films that British television crews made inside the Golden Triangle. For contacts that led to these films and many of the interviews, I owe a great debt to Joseph Nellis, Washington lawyer and former chief counsel to various congressional anticrime committees, and to an outstanding Thai journalist who must remain anonymous.

there were put on the CIA payroll right after World War II to buy their help
in keeping the dock unions out of leftist hands. They worked with the Sicilian
Mafia, which struck its bargain with the Office of Strategic Services (OSS),
the CIA's predecessor, during World War II.

Charles "Lucky" Luciano, perhaps the most powerful Mafia boss who
ever lived, arranged for the Mafia to aid the allied invasion of Sicily. In
exchange for this, he was freed from prison in the U.S. in 1946, and allowed
to leave the country for Sicily. From his base there, he continued to direct
racketeering in the U.S. until his death in 1962. For a while, he even took
up residence in Cuba, where the Mafia ran casinos and laundered money
that was smuggled in from its Las Vegas and other U.S. operations.

Luciano's lieutenant, who took over formal leadership of his U.S. crime
family when Luciano was deported, was Vito Genovese. Under arrangements
Luciano set up, Genovese was translator for top U.S. Army officials, as Italy
was captured and the Fascist government replaced.

In the 1970s, much of the U.S. heroin traffic started coming from Latin
America, which also supplied the increasingly popular drug, cocaine. Many
of the traffickers were known to the CIA, But the agency kept their identities
and their businesses secret, in exchange for intelligence about leftist organizations, which the CIA obviously considered a greater threat. Whether the
average American voter and taxpayer would have agreed that nipping revolutionary movements in the bud in various banana republics was more
important than keeping heroin off the streets of American cities is debatable.
But they never had a chance to debate it.

The CIA valued the intelligence that drug dealers could collect. This trade-
off also gave them leverage over important politicians from all political
factions in Latin America. Politicians, regardless of their ideology, seemed
unable to resist the lure of heroin money. Many knew that the CIA had
information that could ruin them—although they also knew that such blackmail was a two-way street, and that they could sabotage or expose CIA
operations.

The CIA's attitude in all this was summed up by Joseph Nellis, former
chief counsel to the House of Representatives' Select Committee on Narcotics
and now a Washington lawyer. While with the committee, Nellis made a
daring trip into the Golden Triangle to meet the major heroin warlords and
hear their offers to sell their product to the U.S. government, which could
then destroy it.

Says Nellis, "The CIA did help bring some very powerful, cheap heroin
into Vietnam, out of the Shan states, the northern states of Burma, [in
exchange] for radio communications intelligence. In return for that intelligence, the CIA winked at what went in its airplanes." Officials in the Drug
Enforcement Administration also confirm this.

Dope shipment plans and military information were often discussed in the
same private radio transmissions, because intelligence agents and goverment

officials were involved in the drug trade. Today, in Latin America, the same thing goes on, Nellis says.

"Drug traffickers employ very sophisticated means of communications," Nellis says. "Let's assume the CIA has infiltrated a drug smuggling ring [in Latin America] and it is using a very high-powered radio. Maybe the radio involved in the drug smuggling operation is also transmitting defense secrets in code. I was an intelligence operative in World War II, and I can tell you that the ways of the intelligence community are devious. If a message were passed to a Latin American government, the CIA would know about it within twenty-four hours."

Why let the Latin smugglers get away with dope trafficking? "It's important for the CIA to know which members of the cabinet can be bought," Nellis says. "If CIA deals with a cabinet minister, they have to know whether he's honest or not. *Mordida* [the payoff] is a way of life down there." So the U.S. Drug Enforcement Administration's hands are often tied by anti-communist considerations.

"If the DEA runs across a high-powered radio, it has no way of knowing [whether] the CIA is running it," Nellis says, "[If] it tells the friendly government [about the dope ring], the CIA loses a listening post. The DEA would be told to stay away from it because the defense implications are more important than the narcotics implications. These decisions are made in the National Security Council, where they should be made. And none of us ever knows all the reasons."

Probably the most vivid example on record of this kind of thing occurred June 22, 1972, in the office of Panama's dictatorial chief of state, General Omar Torrijos. John Ingersoll, director of the Justice Department's Bureau of Narcotics and Dangerous Drugs (precursor of the DEA) came to Torrijos in person, almost on his knees, with an astonishing disclosure.

The U.S. Customs Service had uncovered, and brought to the BNDD's attention, a giant smuggling ring. One courier alone was stopped at John F. Kennedy International Airport in New York with 175 *pounds* of heroin in his luggage. The investigation, still secret, had found General Torrijos's brother Moises, Panama's ambassador to Spain, at the center of the dope ring. It wasn't the first occasion when high Panamanian officials had been found in such a position. But apparently the upper echelons of the U.S. government were most concerned with maintaining General Torrijos's cooperation in spying on and thwarting left-wing groups.

Our foreign policy experts were terrified of offending the leader of this den of dope purveyors. They were also terrified that the citizens of the United States—who had not been told any of this—might find out and demand a halt to support for Torrijos. So Director Ingersoll—obviously not acting on his own—traveled to Panama and laid out for the dictator all the evidence about the ring, involving Moises Torrijos and other prominent Panamanians. Then, according to the official BNDD minutes of the meeting, he said:

"Recently a grand jury in New York City has indicted Moises Torrijos on a charge of conspiring to smuggle heroin into the United States. This indictment is sealed, in the hands of the court, and has not been released. [The reason such indictments are kept secret is so the persons named in them will continue to move about in public until they can be arrested.]

"If Ambassador Torrijos enters the United States," Ingersoll went on, "he will be arrested and prosecuted. This information is limited to a few individuals in the United States government, and we hope General Torrijos will be able to deal with the matter before it becomes public knowledge. I am passing it on in the hope you will investigate the matter further, recall your brother, and persuade him to remove himself from the illicit drug business."

General Torrijos's response was equally remarkable. "The general stated that he would recall Ambassador Torrijos and investigate the matter," the BNDD notes read. "If his brother was guilty, he would go to jail. However, he could not have his brother in prison while his mother was living. He . . . felt that he would find that his brother was duped. . . . He described his brother as an intellectual idiot who does not understand the difficulties of life and how to survive."

Despite the general's promises, and his assessment of his brother's competence, he kept his brother on as ambassador to Spain for another six years, during which the brother steered clear of U.S. soil. The U.S. government did nothing, and the public remained unaware. The heroin may well have kept flowing. The general removed his brother the smuggler from office only when this embarrassing episode was uncovered. That happened quite by chance, as Congress investigated the treaty for turning over the Panama Canal. How many similar episodes have taken place—or are taking place today—is anybody's guess.

CHAPTER TWENTY

THE CORRUPTION OF DOMESTIC ORGANIZATIONS: THE AFL-CIO

AT THE height of the cold war, as Russian tanks smashed into Czechoslovakia, a silk manufacturer from Milan named Pietro Ruffini flew across the Atlantic for hush-hush meetings in New York with American bankers and industrialists. Ostensibly, Ruffini came on business. But in fact, he carried credentials from the "highest responsible authorities" in Italy. He stayed at the Hotel New Weston at Madison Avenue and Fiftieth Street. With the help of intermediaries selected by the U.S. State Department, he began soliciting contributions from corporations to fight communism in Europe.

Ruffini's trip was a success. The cash he collected went into a special account for transfer through a Vatican bank to anti-communist political parties in Italy. But his mission deserves special notice for another reason: it is the earliest documented example of collaboration between government and business to achieve American foreign policy objectives through the use of corporate payments abroad.

In recent years, continuing disclosures of payments overseas have given American business a lasting black eye. It is not entirely undeserved. Payoffs encouraged an atmosphere of corruption that helped erode the authority of pro-American regimes such as the shah's in Iran. Many corporate payments clearly were bribes intended solely to promote business purposes. But many American businessmen got into the habit of making foreign payments at the instigation of the State Department, as part of a cooperative arrangement with the U.S. government.

In fact, corporate payments instigated, approved, or condoned by the State Department or the Central Intelligence Agency were—and to some extent still are—a critical tool of U.S. foreign policy. They serve to prop up friendly foreign governments, buy the temporary loyalty of foreign politicians, and acquire intelligence. "In lots of places the people in power don't distinguish between a direct payment from the CIA or, let's say, a sales commission from a big American company," one U.S. official explains. "To them it's all the same. It came from America."

"This era of cooperation between business and government was common all over the world," says John J. McCloy, who served the oil companies and other legal clients in between various high government foreign policy jobs.

In fact, Pietro Ruffini's cash collecting trip was actually organized by the U.S. embassy in Rome. A 1948 State Department cable marked "top secret" says, "His plan, as outlined to a member of the embassy, is to form a small committee in New York of industrialists and bankers with European interests who might be willing to contribute to the Democratic Christian party, which is leading the fight against communism in Italy. No publicity whatsoever will be given to his activities."*

So started an unusual form of corporate taxation to pay for covert foreign aid, a kind of under-the-table Marshall Plan that became permanent. But many leaders of the political parties that the U.S. wanted to support overseas were also businessmen. So after a while, there was natural confusion over where politics stopped and business started. One could well raise the question of who was using whom for a cover.

For example, Lockheed Corporation admitted to the SEC that between 1970 and 1978 it paid $30 million to $38 million in improper foreign payments to influence aircraft sales in fifteen foreign countries. The SEC wanted to go after Carl Kotchiam, who was Lockheed's president part of this time. But Kotchian's lawyer, Mitchell Rogovin, warded off any bribery charges. He told the Justice Department that if Kotchian was charged criminally, Rogovin would "demonstrate at trial the reasonableness of our client's belief that the government knew foreign payoffs were being made." He said that not only did the State Department and CIA know that such payoffs were commonplace, it knew Lockheed was among the companies making them. Kotchian wasn't charged, and the public never got to find out what really happened.

---

*This chapter, to this point, with only minor editing, was the beginning of a news story being prepared by Jerry Landauer of the *Wall Street Journal*, an irreplaceably good reporter and friend, at the time of his death in February 1981 at age forty-nine. The draft ended there, and was found in a folder with some State Department documents on which it was obviously based. The identification of McCloy is mine.

The same problem arose time and again. Philip Heymann, head of the Criminal Division at the Justice Department in the Carter administration, speaking about the situation generally, acknowledged, "If there was extensive acquiescence by federal officials, it could be a very troublesome objection to our prosecution." And he said if the government "actually encouraged the wrongdoing," it couldn't prosecute at all. A series of prospective SEC bribery cases was never taken to court; details weren't disclosed, for obvious reasons.

IN the beginning, of course, in Western Europe, the CIA's cause was much more noble than it was to become later in places like Zaire, the Philippines, Indonesia, Cuba, Guatemala, Iran, and Chile. It would be hard to argue that France and Italy, for example, aren't much better off for history's turning out the way it did. Those who worked for the U.S. cause in those countries might assert that the Soviets started the sabotage of the democratic system, and the U.S. had to fight fire with fire to keep them from taking over.

But this is the same argument made for covert intervention everywhere. Much of the time it's clear that the Soviets *didn't* start the cheating. And when they do misbehave, one may fairly ask why the response must be secret. If we learn that covert Eastern bloc aid is being poured into the communist parties of Western Europe, why not say so, offer our proof, and announce that we are prepared to balance the scales? If the majority of the people in those countries wanted to resist the left-wing advances, as they surely did in 1948, they would welcome the aid. If they didn't, better to find out quickly and readjust the policy.

The Marshall Plan was no secret, and was a great success for every country that participated. The Berlin Airlift was not carried out by mysterious Cuban mercenaries with forged IDs flying planes with painted-out serial numbers. The Battle of Midway wasn't subcontracted to the Mafia. If what we're doing is right, why hide it? Why set in motion all sorts of secret alliances that can't be monitored later?

THE same year Ruffini made his trip to New York, 1948, the CIA also began turning private U.S. citizens into spies. While U.S. schoolchildren were told that Soviet schoolchildren had to report on the loyalty of their parents—stories all too often true—U.S. businessmen were assigned to perform the same function on their business associates. There was an important difference: the U.S. businessmen who were asked to become spies were free to say "no." But a lot said "yes," and although the deal may have been fair for them, it wasn't fair for colleagues, clients, and employees here and abroad who might have trusted these men with information that they did not particularly wish to be conveyed to the government.

Of course, law enforcement has always relied on the cooperation of public-spirited citizens who pass on information about their associates' misbehavior. But again, there is an important difference. Law enforcement officers must eventually play their hand in open court. They are allowed to collect information only if they have reasonable ground to believe that a crime has been committed, and even then the information collected must be related to the crime.

Intelligence officers, on the other hand, work secretively to know everything about everything. Blackmail is not outside their rules. Their ultimate goal usually is to influence political decisions covertly, outside the normal democratic process. Unlike the criminally accused, the victims of intelligence operations may never know what hit them. The victims include not just Americans, who have many legal protections, but also foreigners who are subject to arbitrary political imprisonment or execution.

According to a classified State Department report dated September 3, 1948, "During the past year, the Central Intelligence Agency has established throughout the United States a number of regional offices for the purpose of obtaining, on the highest possible level, foreign intelligence information which is available to bankers, commercial firms, corporations, and institutions of various kinds. The arrangements for obtaining this information are made with the senior executives of the institutions and corporations concerned and, in most cases, a maximum of only four or five senior officials know that reports and information coming to their organization from their foreign agents and connections are being made available to the intelligence organization of the government. The information obtained through this means is disseminated by CIA on a pink report form entitled 'Information Report' bearing in the right-hand upper corner a serial number beginning 'oo-B.'"

So some high company officials secretly agreed to open their companies' internal and external correspondence to the government. From there, it wasn't much of a jump for the government to obtain agreements from the same companies to provide "cover" for full-time spies. This means that the guy at the next desk might not be who you think he is. This was an even more threatening situation in years past than it is today, because the U.S. was less tolerant then of minority viewpoints on politics, social life, religion, and sex than it is now. And that tolerance could someday recede once again.

What companies were—are—involved? It's been published, and not really denied, that Exxon, Chase Manhattan, Lockheed, Moore McCormack (steamship lines), and Control Data were at one time or another doing chores for the CIA. Ashland Oil admitted it was.

During the 1970s, some of the domestic spying was toned down. Journalists uncovered many inroads that the CIA had made into American life. Seymour Hersh of the *New York Times* more than any other person was responsible for curtailing these invasions of privacy and liberty. The CIA began to rely more on putting its spies in foreign embassies, under diplomatic cover. It also created its own phony businesses to serve as commercial cover; that way, everyone working for the businesses could be a knowing and willing spy, and so only selected targets would be spied on, not innocent bystanders. Obviously, though, many of the old practices continued.

Then, in 1981, the Reagan administration announced it would purposefully make more use of "nonofficial" cover for its clandestine operations around the world. Reagan and his CIA director William Casey declared a renewed emphasis on infiltrating U.S. business, trade, and educational concerns with overseas operations.

If the nation were truly in peril of losing its freedom to foreign invaders, of course, one would hope that plenty of citizens would line up to carry on the tradition of Nathan Hale. But in light of the U.S. government's record since World War II, one must ask where the greater peril lies.

U.S. business was not alone in being enlisted as a covert political agency, secret from shareholders and customers. Organized labor has worked hand-in-glove with the CIA, and has lied to its members about it.

Take Irving Brown. Few men in the history of the U.S. labor movement have been more extolled than Brown, who for many years has been a top international representative of the AFL-CIO (and continues so at this writing). Brown was considered the most vocal anti-communist in the U.S. delegation that walked indignantly out of the International Labor Organization in 1977 to protest the ILO's increasingly leftist slant.

The ILO, part of the United Nations, was intended to bring together management and labor from many countries to promote the general goals of fair labor standards—regulating wages, hours, job safety, and so forth. Like other U.N. bodies, the ILO got more and more frustrating for the U.S. as the U.N. came to be dominated by governments without traditions of democracy, and without industrial economies—where capitalist distinctions like independent management and labor were out of context. As in the case of other U.N. bodies, the ILO drifted toward the concerns of its new majority.

In 1977, partly at Brown's behest, the U.S. decided to counterattack. The U.S. delegation stalked out of the ILO, claiming that communist and Third World delegates were not really independent employer-employee representatives as the ILO constitution intended, but were really political operatives of their governments. Brown accused Third World governments of sabotaging the ILO with their mostly political concerns. In 1980, after President Carter decided that the ILO was halting this "politicization" (which had culminated in a call for seating the Palestine Liberation Organization), Brown was in the forefront as the U.S. delegation returned to Geneva.

The AFL-CIO's international magazine, the *Free Trade Union News*, lavished praise on the veteran unionist. It described how he defeated "the Soviet bloc–Arab alliance" in crucial votes, and "pressed the ILO to move in a direction that serves the needs and interests of the workers rather than the political aims of governments."

What lies and hypocrisy!

At least five former U.S. intelligence officers say that while overseas Brown has done undercover work for the CIA—this was when he was ostensibly championing the cause of independent trade unionism. In fact, Brown has been an important factor in three AFL-CIO international organizations that operate in seventy-five countries throughout the world, funded mostly by U.S. tax dollars. And various former intelligence officers and others say that all three organizations have been used to do CIA work. Yet Brown and the AFL-CIO continue to scorn other countries' trade unions on the ground that they are government-influenced.

Brown's secret connections go back many years.

On February 24, 1948, while Pietro Ruffini was passing his hat at the Hotel New Weston, the U.S. ambassador to France, Jefferson Caffery, wrote a "top secret" letter to Under Secretary of State Robert A. Lovett: "The noncommunist French leadership in the labor field has suffered two rather serious setbacks as a result of trade union elections in which both the printers and miners voted in favor of remaining within the communist CGT," the letter said. The CGT was a left-wing confederation of trade unions that was opposed by the International Confederation of Free Trade Unions, which Brown helped start, and which was run with CIA money.

The ambassador's letter went on: "According to our information, a major factor in these unfortunate elections was the lack of organization on the part of the non-communists which, in turn, is attributable in good part to their lack of funds. I have just heard that certain important American business interests in France recently sent representatives to Washington with an offer to donate certain sums for the battle which we are waging. I understand that they spoke to Admiral Hillenkoetter who informed them that the government should and would shoulder this burden. I am entirely in accord with this position in principle, but as pointed out in my previous letter, time is of the essence and it seems to me that if there is to be any appreciable delay in providing funds through government sources, it would seem desirable to reconsider this offer from private sources. . . .

"I am enclosing a rough outline of a concrete plan for work among the port workers, which heretofore has been the stronghold of the communists, and I think that this project should be pushed as rapidly as possible. On this we are in close touch with Irving Brown, European representative of the A F of L, who is working out the details, including the choice of competent militants."

The ambassador's rough outline included an expense estimate, alloting 1.5 million francs (about $7,000) for eight organizers, plus "propaganda material, typewriters, etc." The money would cover just four months of organizing in various ports around France. The estimate noted that the corporations had better be prepared to pay much more money later, because "this phase of trade union work, which is largely clandestine under existing conditions, is relatively inexpensive as compared with the latter phase which involves setting up and running trade union organizations on a local, departmental, and national level."

So that's how it worked. Irving Brown, purported servant of the American working man, selected candidates for leadership of the French trade unions. Then he reported back to the U.S. government and various multinational corporations, which put up the money for these men to run for union office. The sponsoring corporations employed not only the French workers who were members of the unions, but also American workers who were members of the AFL-CIO and paid Brown's salary. None of the workers in either country was clued in on what was being done with their dues and good name.

Next stop, Italy.

On March 12, 1948, the U.S. embassy in Rome cabled "top secret" to Secretary of State George Marshall: "Norris Chipman [not identified] tells me that Secretary Harriman was of great assistance in obtaining contributions for Irving Brown from U.S. industrialists with large stakes in France. Could he not be of assistance to us. Following companies have large interests in Italy: Standard Oil of New Jersey [now Exxon], Vacuum Oil [now Mobil], General Electric, Singer Sewing, American Radiator and Standard Sanitary, National Cash Register, Great Lakes Carbon, American Viscose Company, Otis Elevator. Would you speak to him about this matter."

It was an official shakedown list. Jimmy Hoffa went to *jail* for arranging less egregious sweetheart contracts.

MORE recently, the AFL-CIO has carried out its patriotic work on behalf of American industry through three international organizations, all of which have enjoyed the talents of Irving Brown at one time or another. They are the African American Labor Council (AALC), the Asian American Free Labor Institute (AAFLI, pronounced "aff-lee"), and the American Institute for Free Labor Development (AIFLD, pronounced"a-field"), which operates throughout Latin America.

At least the first of the institutes, AIFLD, was started not by an act of labor, but by an act of government, according to the "confidential" minutes of the Labor Advisory Committee on Foreign Policy, a group President Kennedy set in motion under Secretary of Labor Arthur Goldberg. AFL-CIO president George Meany was a member of the committee, which voted to establish AIFLD early in 1962, according to the minutes of the meeting. A second decision at that meeting was to give AIFLD $350,000 in taxpayer money "in order to facilitate securing contributions from private foundations, organizations, and companies." And finally, it was agreed that Goldberg would bring Secretary of State Dean Rusk and CIA director John McCone to the next meeting, March 12, 1962.

The three institutes over the years have received about $120 million from the U.S. Agency for International Development (AID). The funds are designated for organizing and promoting "free labor unions." The State Department says unions foster economic development, and therefore labor organizations qualify for federal funds just as many religious and charitable organizations do when they distribute food and medical relief abroad.

Currently, the ever-growing organizations are gobbling up about $20 million a year of AID money, plus $500,000 or so in AFL-CIO funds, and other cash from "special funds" allotted by the State Department to U.S. embassies. There have also been substantial contributions from private corporations with big interests in the Third World, including ITT, Kennecott and Anaconda copper companies, Pan American World Airways, and, of course, the Rockefeller family. Until May 1981, these interests were represented on the board of directors of what is supposed to be an AFL-CIO labor organization.

By contrast to these three big-spending institutes, the AFL-CIO says its entire domestic budget is $31 million a year, of which only about $10 million goes for organizing and field services for workers in the United States.

The institutes clearly engage in some educational and humanitarian projects for Third World workers. They provide typewriters and business equipment for union offices, and send teams out to dig wells. But they consistently get involved in contentious activities in political hot spots. In El Salvador, AIFLD has spent at least $7.7 million of AID money to promote a land reform program that was designed by U.S. government "experts" and supported by a U.S.-maintained military junta, until the voters of El Salvador got a chance to throw the junta out of office and vote in an opponent of land reform.

U.S. policymakers concerned with El Salvador had tended to think of the junta as a centrist government, implying that it represented the bulk of the population with only fringe elements on either side. That seems to have been another miscalculation. Judging from the election of March 1982, the junta government represented a fringe element in the middle, which was outnumbered by opponents on both sides.

The new right-wing government (left-wing candidates couldn't run) effectively called off the land reform program, which by most accounts wasn't working very well anyway. The stated intent of the program was to redress a distribution problem; 2 percent of the population controlled more than half the fertile land. But many landless farmers trying to claim the new plots they were entitled to had been machine-gunned to death by the long-standing owners. This discouraged other farmers from claiming anything. And where small farmers did obtain land, production declined, either because the cooperatives AIFLD set up were inefficient, or because the war interfered, or both.

One gauge of the sincerity of this program to help the poor of El Salvador is that it was suddenly thrown into operation in March 1980, just as Americans were getting interested in the war. Salvadorans both rich and poor understandably perceived the program to be a device to justify U.S. military support for the junta. Two AIFLD land reform workers and a Salvadoran colleague were machine-gunned to death in the Sheraton Hotel coffee shop in San Salvador in 1981, a crime still not satisfactorily explained.

While all this was going on, the other two AFL-CIO institutes were having their own problems. An African American Labor Council official was thrown out of the West African country of Sierra Leone in a dispute over a general strike against the government there. And an AAFLI official was held hostage by laborers in a South Korean garment factory, whose union the AAFLI man was advising. The laborers were complaining, not without cause, that AAFLI was helping the government of strongman Chun Doo Hwan repress labor rights. South Korea being a police state, the factory's union was approved by the U.S.-supported government, but not necessarily by the workers it represented. Police stormed the factory, freed the AAFLI official, and arrested two dozen underpaid garment workers. Another victory for organized labor.

In the past, AIFLD has been active in Brazil, Chile, the Dominican Republic, and Guyana at the time of U.S.-supported government overthrows. And AAFLI sponsored a huge project ostensibly to organize the workers of war-torn Vietnam.

AID and foreign service professionals often resent the labor institutes, which seem to have privileged access to funds. "The State Department more or less directs us to fund these people," says an AID official in Washington. In El Salvador, where AIFLD has put some 250 Salvadoran organizers on its payroll, a U.S. official says, "They aren't unifying the *campesinos* [farmers]. They are dividing them. The people regard them as gringos, possibly CIA, and if it weren't for the current political situation, the El Salvador government would have them out overnight. I don't like the idea of someone using an agricultural organization to gather intelligence. I'd like to keep it as far from my office as possible."

IN 1964, a House Banking Committee investigation into tax-free foundations accidentally stumbled onto some that were fronts for the CIA. Through these foundations, the CIA secretly passed taxpayer money to various political, cultural, and labor organizations without specific appropriation by Congress or accountability to the voters. Clearly, the purpose was not mainly intelligence gathering, but the manipulation of private institutions and the democratic process.* Although this might seem reason enough for an investigation,

---

*Even where intelligence gathering was involved, the tactic was to say the least questionable. One group secretly working on the CIA payroll was the U.S. National Student Association. In the summer of 1962, the author led an NSA student tour group to the Soviet Union and Eastern and Western Europe. The group leaders, students ourselves, handled liaison with student leaders in the countries we visited, who were our

the committee backed off at the CIA's request, and confined its inquiry to the tax concerns of private foundations.

But newspapers and magazines, tracing records of gifts from foundations that the committee had exposed as CIA fronts, revealed payments to a number of labor groups associated with the AFL-CIO. Among them were the Retail Clerks International Association, the International Federation of Petroleum and Chemical Workers (which was involved with organizing oil field workers in Iran), the Communications Workers of America (the phone company workers, here and abroad—consider the possibilities), the clothing and Textile Workers' unions, and several others.

AFL-CIO president George Meany put on a wonderful show of outrage, insisting that he had been unaware the payments had orginated with the CIA. "I think the CIA has a job to do, but it can do it without using or subsidizing the labor movement," he said. But right after the scandal broke in the press, and President Johnson ordered the CIA financing stopped, a replacement plan was filed by Meany's brother-in-law, Ernest S. Lee, then the assistant director of the AFL-CIO's international department and now its director. Without publicity, Lee obtained AID financing for some of the same organizations, with the money channeled though the three institutes, AIFLD, AAFLI, and the African American Labor Council. Though CIA money has been hidden in other AID grants, and could be in these, Lee and other AFL-CIO officials have consistently denied that the institutes have ever received CIA money or policy direction.

Irving Brown—a close confidant of his boss, Meany—helped start the African American Institute in 1964. He ran it for four years, then went to AAFLI, which was started in 1968 to organize Vietnamese labor unions and land reform as part of the Vietnam war effort. Brown is also close to AIFLD, whose president, William C. Doherty, Jr., says, "He [Brown] is a very dear personal friend of mine and most people who work for this organization."

Brown, interviewed by phone from his Paris office, staunchly denied ever having contact with the CIA. But former CIA officer John Stockwell says, "Irving Brown was 'Mr. CIA' in the labor movement." Former CIA officer Paul Sakwa* says that he served as Brown's case officer, or control, in the CIA for several years.

And former CIA officer Thomas W. Braden says that he personally delivered $15,000 in CIA cash to Brown "to pay off his [Brown's] strong-arm

---

guides. We were assigned to write reports of what we saw and heard. I was granted a refund of part of the tour price as a reward for the adjudged excellence of the reports I filed, which I thought were for the use of the NSA in setting policy (it took stands on political issues) and arranging future tours. Apparently, I was really working as an unwitting CIA agent. I later resented being duped, and if this is evidence of personal prejudice on this particular issue, I confess it.

*In 1982, Sakwa, broke and with an alcohol problem, living in a one-room Washington apartment stacked with old newspapers, was indicted in a conspiracy to sell some em-

squads in Mediterranean ports so that American supplies could be unloaded against the opposition of communist dockworkers." Braden, a writer and former syndicated columnist, served as Allen Dulles's assistant in the 1950s. He says Brown used the pseudonym Norris A. Grambo for undercover work, while serving under his own name as AFL-CIO representative in Europe.

Stockwell, Sakwa, and Braden were interviewed separately and without each other's knowledge. Though Stockwell and Sakwa now regret many things they did with the CIA, Braden is unabashedly proud. He says that the $15,000 was one of many regular CIA payments to AFL-CIO officials, that he assumes such payments have continued, and that he thinks they are a good idea.

Brown at first denied ever meeting Braden, but then conceded, "I could have met him because I think he was in Paris for a while." But he denied taking any money from Braden.

Sakwa says that as Brown's case officer from 1952 to 1954, he approved— and sometimes reduced—Brown's CIA budget of from $150,000 to $300,000 a year. He says Brown picked up the money from CIA undercover officers at the U.S. embassy in Paris and spent it paying off French labor organizers and on his personal travel expenses. One former CIA employee Sakwa named, reached at his current job at a major U.S. bank office in Europe, confirmed that he worked at the Paris embassy in the 1950s in intelligence, and that Brown and several other AFL-CIO officials were getting CIA money. (He agreed to be interviewed only on condition he and his bank not be named.)

After Sakwa's Washington work as a case officer, he served the CIA from 1955 to 1958 undercover as assistant labor attaché in the U.S. embassy in Brussels. He says he continued to be aware that Brown and other AFL-CIO officials received money. He says Brown carried CIA cash to Tom Mboya, who, until his murder in 1969, was a leading politician in Kenya. Under Brown's leadership, the African American Labor Council set up training programs for union leaders in Kenya that continue today.

Brown also was involved in the purported organizing of Zaire's working men and women. When David Morse, Mobutu's high-powered Washington laywer and advisor, touted the Zairian trade union movement as "one of the best, if not the best, in Africa,"* he went on to say, "All of this work is being done with the support of the American-African Labor Institute [sic]

---

bargoed technical equipment to the Soviet Union. He had been trying to scrape up work as a business consultant. Sakwa was eased out of the CIA in 1962 after protesting, within channels, against assassinations and other covert action he was assigned to carry out in Vietnam. He had been rebuffed in long efforts to get a government pension or be rehired. His interviews for this book were conducted prior to his legal problem. They were corroborated in many respects by other people and by documents, and were totally convincing. In 1983, he pleaded guilty to the export charges and was sentenced to one year of probation and 300 hours of community service.

*See chapter 3.

with headquarters in Washington, D.C., which, in turn is supported by the AFL-CIO and is financed by the U.S. AID program.... The leader of the mission ... described to me in detail the magnificent job being done in Zaire by the labor movement in its effort to improve the social conditions of the people."

Obviously, the medical clinics, cooperatives, and leadership training programs Morse talked about are well camouflaged. Morse's statement is absurd on its face. Zairian workers, many of whose children literally starve to death for lack of money to buy food, aren't allowed to join legitimate unions. One American who can attest to that is Meyer Bernstein, a former United Mineworkers' and Steelworkers' official who worked for the AFL-CIO institutes in Zaire and in Latin America off and on until 1974. He is now with the Labor Department.

Bernstein recalls being sent to Zaire to train "union leaders," and being stunned to learn that they "couldn't strike, couldn't criticize the government, couldn't negotiate wages. We had to walk on eggshells to keep from being thrown out, because it is a dictatorship." He also complains that Irving Brown and two other AFL-CIO officials were taking money from the CIA, which he thought was "foolish." (Bernstein emphasizes that the labor groups did perform some valuable humanitarian work.)

Brown did organize at least one group in Zaire, however: the National Front for the Liberation of Angola, the CIA's star-crossed army, which tried to put Holden Roberto in power in Angola in 1975–76. George Houser of the American Committee on Africa recalls visiting the Roberto group many times in its camp in southern Zaire, most recently in 1974. He found Brown's union a strange one, mostly without employees—or employers for them to bargain with.

"They were mostly refugees who may have had various odd jobs," Houser says. "You can't liken it to a trade union as they are here. It was political, just an excuse to get money to Roberto." Brown himself doesn't deny that very few of the men had jobs, but says his union was "an attempt to train people for trade union activities when they went back [to Angola]."

John Stockwell, the CIA officer who supervised aid to the Roberto military campaign in Angola in 1975 and later wrote a book about it, recalls a 1966 conference of African labor leaders that Brown was supposed to organize in Ivory Coast. Stockwell says he was flown in to attend. "It was a colossal flop of a conference," he says. "In a hall that could have seated several hundred, there were eight people. And I knew that five were CIA. Brown was one of the five."

ANOTHER labor official whom Sakwa and Braden remember parceling out cash to foreign union leaders is William C. Doherty, Sr., the longtime president of the National Association of Letter Carriers. Sakwa says Doherty's personal expenses were paid by the CIA. Doherty's son, William C.

Doherty, Jr., is the current president of AIFLD, and a strong defender of its efforts in El Salvador and elsewhere.

Reached by phone at the Letter Carriers' Florida retirement town, Doherty, Sr., acknowledged that he "worked with" Brown and Braden "very closely up till the time I retired in 1962, and I look on both men in a very favorable light." About suggestions that he had funneled CIA money overseas, he would only say that he had "never been on a CIA payroll," and that he "never supplied any money to anybody except on behalf of the organization I represented" (neither statement contradicts what Braden and Sakwa said). Doherty went on to urge "widespread support for our Central Intelligence Agency," and said that "those who criticize our CIA the most tend to be dissidents who tend to flee to other countries and be identified with the KGB."

His son, the current head of AIFLD, frequently refers to critics as "communists," or "right-wing oligarchs." Large, ruddy, gray-bearded, and talking so fast as to almost preclude questions, Doherty, Jr. describes his road to union power. Long and arduous it wasn't. He received a philosophy degree from Catholic University in 1949, immediately got a job helping administer the Marshall Plan, and within one year was voted by fellow workers to be the president of the American Federation of Government Employees, "one of the largest public employee unions in the country."

After two years of that, he left for Europe to work for the International Confederation of Free Trade Unions (the organization Brown and the AFL-CIO helped form to use CIA money to combat a rival organization of leftist unions). Then Doherty went to South America to work for the Post, Telegraph, and Telephone Workers International (PTTI), which received CIA money through a CIA-controlled foundation. After the foundation was exposed, PTTI was one of the labor organizations that began getting replacement money indirectly from AID, via a grant to AIFLD.

Former CIA officer Philip Agee, in his book *Inside the Company* (Stonehill, 1975), said PTTI was "used by the CIA in labor operations." He said Brown and Doherty, Jr., were CIA agents. Although Agee has been widely denounced as unpatriotic, and although in recent years he has issued some false information,* his first book has stood up in every detail. An internal analysis of *Inside the Company*, done by the CIA and made public under the Freedom of Information Act, calls Agee's reporting "complete" and "accurate." The many complaints about Agee's treachery only underscore the CIA report's acknowledgment that the book is reliable. The book says that AIFLD, where Doherty, Jr., went to work in 1962, is a "CIA-controlled labor center financed through AID."

Doherty vehemently denies Agee's assertions. But others give accounts that tend to corroborate them.

Ironically, one such piece of evidence about AIFLD's ties to the CIA

---

*Particularly the assertion that your obedient servant is a plagiarist of Agee's work.

surfaced at the U.S. Supreme Court hearing in 1981 over Agee's appeal of the government's decision to revoke his passport. It was the job of U.S. Solicitor General Wade H. McCree, Jr., to plead the government's case against Agee. As the court fired questions at him, McCree tried to convince the questioning justices that Agee used his passport to publicize important secrets, such as the identities of CIA men abroad, which endangered their lives. Suddenly, in the passion of his argument, McCree seemed to let slip an important secret of his own. "Just recently," he blurted out, "two Americans have been killed in Salvador. Apparently they were some kind of undercover persons, working under the cover of a labor organization." Afterward, McCree tried to explain to reporters that he really didn't mean anything by this. But later, when the official transcript of his remarks became available, he confessed "it doesn't sound so well."

McCree obviously had been referring to Michael Hammer and Mark Pearlman, the two AIFLD officials working on the El Salvador land reform program who had been shot dead in the Sheraton Hotel in San Salvador just the week before. Hammer, much the senior of the two, was given a rare (for a person without a military record) hero's burial in Arlington National Cemetery on special authorization of President Carter. Hammer had joined the AFL-CIO through AIFLD seventeen years earlier, while still completing work at the Georgetown University School of Foreign Service. The Georgetown school has long been a favorite recruiting ground for the CIA.

RICHARD MARTINEZ was a telegraphers' union official in Albuquerque, New Mexico, in 1962, when Thomas Robles, a state AFL-CIO leader, recruited him for a job with AIFLD in Brazil. Martinez says* he met Doherty, Jr., and other AIFLD and PTTI officials both in Brazil and Washington. He says he organized telephone and telegraph employees at ITT Corporation in Brazil so effectively that he was returned to Washington and given special training by the CIA.

Martinez says he was warned about being too aggressive with ITT, and that he was sent back to Brazil with instructions to organize local labor leaders and mobilize workers for a new purpose: to harass and eventually to topple the government of President Joao Goulart. Goulart had been elected

---

*Martinez first told his story on film for a Public Broadcasting Service documentary produced by Allan Francovich. He repeated the story for me, answered questions consistently, and showed corroborating photographs and documents. By "corroborating," I mean this: he can generally prove he was where he says he was and talking with whom he says he was, though he can't prove exactly what was said. His story is entirely consistent with known events, whereas the denials of the people he talks about are disprovable at points.

in 1960* by the largest margin in Brazilian history, but he was a populist and a bit of a demagogue, and had earned the journalistic tag "left-leaning."

On the day Goulart was overthrown by a military junta in 1964, Martinez says he was running a large-scale operation of anti-Goulart workers seizing various important buildings. Goulart was Brazil's last popularly elected president. The U.S. has criticized succeeding military regimes for, among other things, suppressing free trade unions.

But it hasn't overthrown those regimes. To the contrary, it has poured in loans, until Brazil is the IMF's biggest scare case, with $90 billion in foreign debts and uncertain means to pay. The press is censored, and reports of political arrest and torture persist.

In 1982, the Brazilian Institute of Economic and Social Analysis, a private research group, reported that the 33 million people in Brazil's massive and fertile northeastern region lived "in a state of extreme poverty," and that many suffered from chonic malnutrition. It blamed this on an imbalance of land ownership. In a separate report, the National Conference of Brazilian Bishops said 87 percent of the productive land in the area was held by about twenty large landowners. An archbishop called the situation "shameful."† Meanwhile, the Brazilian government and business community was moving toward resuming trade with Cuba against the entreaties of the United States government to maintain a boycott. This was the kind of government produced by the overthrow of Goulart.

Right after the Goulart overthrow, Doherty boasted in a radio interview that AIFLD trainees were "intimately involved" in planning and executing it. Interviewed recently, he said this didn't mean that AIFLD plotted the overthrow. He said Martinez and every other former operative cited here was "lying—they're all lying." He called a Public Broadcasting Service documentary covering Martinez's work "a bunch of Communist propaganda."

AFTER the 1964 Brazilian coup, Martinez says, he quit his PTTI job and returned home. But he says he was called back to do similar work in the Dominican Republic in 1965, right after U.S. Marines landed. They were there to halt a civil uprising that promised to restore to power an elected president, Juan Bosch, who had been ousted in a coup in 1963. Bosch had fathered a new constitution, which limited the foreign acquisition of Dominican land. It provided profit sharing for agricultural workers, and required owners of land in excess of certain broad limits to sell the excess or distribute

---

*He was elected vice-president with a president who resigned unexpectedly after seven months, leaving him the job. In 1963, on his own, Goulart won a constitutional plebiscite confirming his authority in the unexpired term.

†Thanks to Interlink Press Service for gathering these quotes.

it to landless farmers. The coup, of course, deposed the constitution as well as Bosch.

The big crop in the Dominican Republic is sugar cane. After Cuban land was mostly nationalized, the largest U.S. sugar holdings were those of the South Puerto Rico Sugar Company, which held upwards of 10 percent of the arable land in the Dominican Republic—80 percent in one large sugar-growing province, 60 percent in another. It also owned a large mill. These were the holdings that Bosch and his supporters threatened. How the South Puerto Rico Sugar Company obtained this land is remarkable. It happened while the U.S. Marines occupied the Dominican republic, 1916–24. Adolph Berle, Jr., a Roosevelt confidant, New Frontiersman, and sugar executive, told about it in a memoir, *Navigating the Rapids* (Harcourt Brace, 1973).* A Harvard Law School graduate, Berle had a rare experience after joining the Signal Corps in World War I:

"The equivalent of the War Production Board of that period was seeking to increase production of sugar. Accordingly, in February 1918, Mr. Ralph Rounds, a New York attorney whose firm represented the South Puerto Rico Sugar Company . . . requested to the War Department to place me on 'inactive duty' for the purpose of going to Santo Domingo in connection with land titles and the movement of the sugar crop in the island.

"In March 1918, I landed in Santo Domingo City and went to work on clearing the land titles for the South Puerto Rico Sugar Company," Berle recalls, then adding, "and any other company that would produce more sugar and export it to the United States." He doesn't name any others. Berle notes that he "was working with a first-rate Dominican lawyer, Francisco Peinado [later spelled "Paynado"]. Eventually, we worked out a theory of land titles and a land court which would clear title to land and permit immediate sugar production."

There go the good old free-enterprising Americans again. Just give them an army of marines and their pick of U.S. government lawyers to cow the local officials, and our fearless enterpreneurs will show you how to win out in the marketplace every time. In the 1930s, Francisco Paynado's son Jacinto became the puppet president of the Dominican Republic under the U.S.-trained military dictator Rafael Trujillo. (Trujillo lasted until his assassination in 1961.)

Federico Paynado, a member of the family, in the 1970s was legal counsel to Gulf & Western Industries Inc., which acquired control of the South Puerto Rico Sugar Company in 1966, a year after the latest marine invasion saved the company fields. Jacinto Paynado's law partner, Polibio A. Diez, was chief counsel and closest friend and advisor to President Joaquin Balaguer, a former appointed president under Trujillo. In 1966, Balaguer was "elected" president under the U.S. military occupation.

*Assembled from his diaries and other papers by his widow, Beatrice Bishop Berle, two years after his death.

The usual litany of statistics showing poor health, low wages, and hunger can be recited. The U.S. Department of Health, Education, and Welfare reported in the mid-1970s that malnutrition was "endemic in the population," and that "only 15 percent have fully adequate diets." According to the Interfaith Center on Corporate Responsibility, wages in the Gulf & Western fields rose only 16.4 percent from 1964 to 1979, to $2.13 a day for standard production. Meanwhile, living costs rose 113 percent, leaving the workers with a net loss. The *Wall Street Journal* reported in 1971 that one of every four Dominicans subsisted on U.S. food charity. Considering the low wages that Gulf & Western gets by with, the food aid could be seen as a U.S. taxpayer subsidy to the *company*, not to the people of the Dominican Republic.

When Paramount Pictures was looking for a filming locale for the scenes of *The Godfather, Part II* set in prerevolutionary Cuba, it picked the Dominican Republic. Paramount is a subsidiary of Gulf & Western. Some Dominicans think their government often acts like one, too.

MEANWHILE, George Meany, his successor Lane Kirkland (then AFL-CIO secretary-treasurer), and several other AFL-CIO officials and their labor mediator friends reaped their own rewards. A decent interval after AIFLD had helped secure the Balaguer government, they established a semiprivate resort and tobacco plantation along a gorgeous stretch of white beach in eastern Dominican Republic, not far from the biggest Gulf & Western sugar fields (actually, not much in the Dominican Republic is far from a big Gulf & Western sugar field).

To create room for the resort, hundreds of Dominican peasant farmers had to be chased off their land, for this was a region of small, private farms until the AFL-CIO came along. The chasing seems to have been done pretty deviously. In 1968, a man named Carlos Manuel Rodriguez Valeras—about whom nothing more is known—walked into the Superior Land Court in Santo Domingo. According to court records, he announced that he owned the 15,000 acres that is now the AFL-CIO resort, but that he had lost his deed and wanted a new one.

On December 13, 1968, the classified advertising section of the newspaper *El Caribe* carried a small notice advising that anyone who cared to challenge Valeras's right to the property should come forward immediately. After three days, not one farmer or fisherman had traveled the 140 miles by road to Santo Domingo, across the jungle, to file his claim. So on December 16, the court gave a fresh deed to Valeras. One year and two days later he sold it for $115,000 to a corporation of which Kirkland and several other labor leaders were principals.

The residents were stunned to learn they would have to vacate to make room for the resort and plantation. They were offered token payments of $50 to $70 a family, but many considered that inadequate, especially since they didn't want to leave their homes anyway. President Balaguer's soldiers chased them out.

Some fifteen men were jailed over the next few years for cutting through George Meany's and Lane Kirkland's barbed wire to plant some crops on their old land. A half dozen others, who used to have their own tobacco farms on the land, went to work for Meany and Kirkland and their group. The AFL-CIO bosses paid them $60 a month.*

RICHARD MARTINEZ says he became disgusted after a few months in the Dominican Republic, quit, and went back to Albuquerque to work in industry.

Thomas Robles, now area director of the Equal Employment Opportunity Commission in Albuquerque, confirms that he recruited Martinez to work for AIFLD in Brazil, but says he doesn't know about the CIA. The PTTI official Martinez says was his supervisor denies that the CIA was involved in the union; he also says Martinez was just a bookkeeper, never an organizer, although documents and photographs clearly show Martinez *was* an organizer.

Edna Fowler, Doherty's assistant, confirms Martinez was an active organizer who worked with many Latin American union leaders, including some in the Dominican Republic, though she says she doesn't know anythng about the CIA. A former CIA officer active in Latin America says he didn't know Martinez, but that Martinez's story fits all the known facts, and that the CIA did pay "in whole or part" for AIFLD's training programs.

These training programs—supposedly run independently by the AFL-CIO—have long constituted the major part of AIFLD's work. More than 350,000 persons from thirty-three Latin American countries have been through the programs. Thousands of Latins have been brought to the U.S. for intensive training at AIFLD schools near Washington. AIFLD pays them salaries while they study, and afterward awards them AIFLD "internship" jobs in their home countries. The salaries are high by Latin standards—Martinez says they were three times a worker's normal pay at home. AIFLD denies this and says that recently it has cut down on internships.)

SEVERAL retired officials from organized labor and the intelligence community say that the CIA used U.S. labor officials to instigate a series of mass strikes in Guyana from 1962 to 1964, which eventually brought down socialist president Cheddi Jagan. Jagan had been popularly elected three times, but was finally defeated for reelection in 1964, largely because of the economic turmoil.

Doherty's response to these charges is, "I was there [in Guyana] many

*All based on personal interviews and documentary research in the Dominican Republic by the author in 1975.

times and had dear friends there, but I had nothing to do with the CIA." As in other cases, including Chile in 1973, Brazil in 1964, and the Dominican Republic in 1965, he said AIFLD trainees may have taken part in the upheavals, but he denied that this made AIFLD responsible.

President Nixon's order to the CIA after the election of Salvador Allende in Chile was to "make the economy scream." That was the clean and supposedly civilized way of bringing down a foreign government: force deprivation by covertly sabotaging the economy, until the public grew disenchanted with the leaders. Whip up strikes, interrupt the importation of vital goods.

The overthrow of Goulart in Brazil and Jagan in Guyana followed this pattern. What more wonderful tool could the CIA have than to put foreign labor unions under the influence of its covert operatives? And if it needed to subvert the U.S. labor movement to do that, the American workers would never know, anymore than would Chile's or Brazil's. In fact, unlike Chile's or Brazil's, America's workers were probably too trusting even to suspect.

THE labor institutes have been kept functioning around the world by the American working man, his dues, and, mainly, his reputation for independence and integrity. He is the front, the come-on, for what seems to be an international fraud. The question naturally arises as to how much he has ever known about the institutes. Apparently the answer is very little. Its direction has been primarily conservative Republican and OSS-CIA.

AIFLD's first director was Serafino Remauldi; Doherty, his deputy, took over at Remauldi's death in 1968. Remauldi had been recruited into the OSS in World War II by Nelson Rockefeller, whose family fortune helped fund AIFLD, and whose family employees helped direct it. Rockefeller, then a State Department Latin American official, had been introduced to Remauldi by New York labor leaders. Remauldi was an Italian immigrant with labor organizing experience. Rockefeller sent him on covert missions to Latin America to search for possible efforts by the axis powers to infiltrate labor unions there. In his memoirs, Remauldi proudly refers to himself in those days as an "American spy." Then he went to work for the AFL-CIO.

Until corporate ties were ended in 1981, AIFLD's chairman was J. Peter Grace, an outspoken political conservative and president and chief executive of W. R. Grace & Company, a chemical and diversified concern with operations throughout Latin America. The company was founded by his grandfather.

Meyer Bernstein, the former unionist now with the Labor Department, says he was always suspicious about Remauldi, who, he says, often turned his back on workers' difficulties. "Remauldi wasn't a union man," Bernstein says. "I went to Remauldi a couple of times with problems and the attitude he took was so antiunion, I said the hell with him. He was just a power broker."

Victor Reuther, semiretired advisor to the United Auto Workers, has been particularly upset at the land reform program in El Salvador. "That's an incredible budget for a very small country that has little or no trade-union movement," he says. "How does one explain that, except that it's purely supportive of military activities? A trade-union organization in the U.S. that virtually has to be dragged kicking and screaming into supporting farm workers in California suddenly becomes an expert in El Salvador land reform."

Ironically, Reuther and his brother, the late UAW president Walter Reuther, two of the labor institutes' biggest critics, themselves had what Victor Reuther now calls "an unfortunate involvement with the agency [the CIA]." In the early 1950s—a story confirmed by both Reuther and his former CIA contact, Thomas Braden—the Reuthers funneled $50,000 of CIA cash to "democratic" French and Italian trade-union leaders who needed organizing money. Later, however, when U.S. funds were aimed at Latin American groups whose democratic standards the Reuthers questioned, they balked. Several former UAW officials, including Reuther, say that the CIA's perceived relationship with the three AFL-CIO institutes was a significant factor in the UAW's decision to leave the AFL-CIO in 1968.

Another major union official who has worked with AIFLD complains that the institutes have allowed government to buy excessive influence over the policies of organized labor. "You're a bureaucracy and you want more money," he says. "Somebody comes along and says, 'We have money. You work on the El Salvador land reform program and we'll give you an extra couple of million bucks.' It's bound to have some parallel relation to what the U.S. government wants. If you don't do what they want, they don't give you the money."

Yet another official, William Winpisinger, president of the International Association of Machinists, among the AFL-CIO's five largest unions, says, "I don't think we ought to be doing the bidding of the government by taking their money. I don't think it's the mission of the American labor movement to prosecute the interests of corporate America."

Government budget-watchers aren't happy with the three institutes, either. A 1980 government audit of them complained that they bypass normal AID budgetary procedures. The audit said that budgets for the institutes were "dictated by fund availabilities" in Washington rather than by "need" determined "in the field."

In other words, the White House is ramming the money down the throat of a reluctant and suspicious bureaucracy with directions to give it to the institutes and not ask questions. The audit also said the institutes' work tends to be seen as "political in nature rather than for developmental purposes."

Apparently, to the U.S. government, politicizing international labor organizations is wrong only when other countries do it.

CHAPTER TWENTY-ONE

LIES: THE GOVERNMENT AND THE PRESS

===============================ON FEBRUARY 6, 1981, as the newly elected Reagan administration calculated how to schedule and win a quick confrontation with communism, an exclusive, leaked story appeared at the top of page one of the *New York Times*. Datelined Washington, it said:

"Indications that the Soviet Union and Cuba agreed last year to deliver tons of weapons to Marxist-led guerrillas in El Salvador are contained in secret documents reportedly captured from the insurgents by Salvadoran security forces.

"The documents, which are considered authentic by United States intelligence agencies, say that the weapons were to come from stockpiles of American arms seized in Vietnam and Ethiopia.

"Copies of the documents obtained by the *New York Times* include a report on a trip by a senior Salvadoran guerrilla to the Soviet Union, Vietnam, Ethiopia, and Eastern European capitals where party officials apparently agreed to provide arms, uniforms, and other military equipment for up to 10,000 guerrillas. . . .

"The documents reported captured in El Salvador by security forces last month describe how the highest levels of the Communist leadership in Eastern Europe and Vietnam approved collaboration with the Salvadoran guerrillas.

"In one document, which appears to have been written in Havana, the Salvadoran emissary reports to his comrades in El Salvador on a visit to Hanoi from June 9 to 15 last year during which he was received by Le Duan,

355

secretary general of the Vietnamese Communist party; Xuan Thuy, vice-president of the National Assembly; and Lieutenant General Tran Van Quang, deputy minister of National Defense.

"The guerrilla, who is believed to be Shafik Handal, secretary general of the Salvadoran Communist party, reported that the Vietnamese agreed to supply 60 tons of arms and ammunition.... The list included 1,620 M-16 automatic rifles, 162 M-30 and 36 M-60 machine guns, 48 mortars, 12 antitank rocket launchers, 1.5 million rounds of ammunition, and 11,000 mortar rounds.

"On a visit to Ethiopia from July 3 to 6, the report said, the guerrilla met with Lieutenant Colonel Haile Mariam Mengistu, president of the ruling Marxist Revolutionary Council, and was promised 150 Thompson submachine guns, 1,500 M-1 rifles, 1,000 M-14 rifles, and over 600,000 rounds of ammunition."

The story continues in a similar vein, with other stops on the guerrilla's trip. Information is all carefully attributed to sources or documents, but the sources aren't named and the story doesn't say what kind of person supplied the documents, or what his motive might have been for doing so. The story shows no sign that the writer tried to verify the information independently, or to balance it with comment from Handal or his revolutionary colleagues.

The Democratic Revolutionary Front, of which Handal's group was a part, had a public office in Mexico City, and its representatives have been quoted regularly by the *Times* and other newspapers. In addition, revolutionary sympathizers maintained information offices in New York and Washington, and scholars at several major universities closely followed events in El Salvador and regularly commented on them. The *Times* story doesn't indicate that the documents it obtained were shown to anyone who could be expected to look at them skeptically. Nor could the *Times*, in the space available, print enough detail to allow skeptical readers to make their own analysis.

Yet the story was picked up by other newspapers and broadcasters. "The *New York Times* reported today that...."

This is the way leaks are normally handled—the way leakers expect them to be handled. Were it not so, the history of U.S. foreign policy might be different. Other administrations and other newspapers have played by the same rules. Governments want to fix their version of a story in print before opponents can get a crack at it. Newspapers want to be the first to report what the government is going to do next—to make sure the reader hasn't seen it somewhere else first. A bargain is struck.*

---

*A major factor in the author's thirteen-year romance with the *Wall Street Journal* is my conviction that pressure for this kind of story at the *Journal* is less than at any other major newspaper. Despite occasional slips, *Journal* editors have always tried to respect the philosophy that it is better to lose the "beat" on a story than to turn out later to have had a part in misleading the reader.

Domestic news is handled differently. The "other side" is usually consulted, because the other side is usually easier to find, and a reporter can be fairly sure he will hear from them later if he doesn't check with them first. When a Reagan budget plan is reported, Speaker of the House Tip O'Neill's opinion of it can be counted on to appear on the same page. Accusations of domestic wrongdoing are handled still more carefully. Even the president of the Teamsters' Union can force a retraction, or file a libel suit, if a newspaper prints a falsehood about him. A Shafik Handal or a Yasir Arafat is powerless to fight back. They might belong in jail, just as the president of the Teamsters' Union might (at this writing, he is under sentence). But in his case, newspapers are still held accountable for every word they say about him, and in their cases, newspapers are not. Yet the spread of misinformation about people like Handal, or Arafat, or Ho Chi Minh, can lead to enormous national mistakes.

It's often said that truth is the first casualty of war.* Plenty of false and slanted stories were written during previous wars. Much was written about the German and Japanese people during World War II that would not read comfortably now. But previous wars usually had a finite beginning and end, maybe a few years apart. The war against communism has been with us nearly four decades.

It's one thing to put an embargo on the truth until all the ships are back safely. It's another for generations of leaders to come and go forgetting what the truth is. The great iconoclastic journalist I. F. Stone once said, "Every government is run by liars and nothing they say should be believed." Until the time of Lyndon Johnson, near the end of the second decade of the anticommunist war, that would have sounded shockingly cynical. Now a lot of people feel compelled to believe it; based on the evidence, it's certainly a wise operating rule for newspapers.

Obviously, the lying started well before Johnson's time. But not until 1964 did government lies affect public safety so profoundly. It took at least three years for the truth to start coming out about the Gulf of Tonkin incident, which opened the door for full-scale U.S. involvement in Vietnam. The whole truth isn't available yet, and the facts that *are* available aren't generally known. Most Americans who know what the Gulf of Tonkin incident is, probably retain the impression left by the initial reporting of it in 1964. Much more ink and air time was given to the lie than to the correction.

The Tonkin incident, a supposed unprovoked attack by North Vietnam on two U.S. ships, was used to rile the public. Reports of the attack then persuaded Congress to give Johnson what he considered his marching order,

---

*In his book, *Truth Is the First Casualty* (Rand McNally, 1969), Joseph C. Goulden credits the quote to U Thant. In *his* book, *The First Casualty* (Harcourt Brace, 1975), Phillip Knightley credits it to Senator Hiram Johnson. Of course, since both authors were writing about war, maybe neither was being truthful.

the Gulf of Tonkin Resolution—which Attorney General Nicholas Katzenbach determined under oath to be the "functional equivalent" of a congressional declaration of war. But the incident never happened, at least in any way like the government announced it. Two U.S. ships were *not* the victims of a willful, unprovoked attack by North Vietnam while on routine patrol in international waters.

One ship, the destroyer *Maddox*, did take fire on August 2, 1964, though there were neither casualties nor major damage. But we know now that the *Maddox* was deliberately ordered into a zone where in recent days similar-sized ships attached to the South Vietnamese navy had been attacking North Vietnamese islands and even attempting an invasion. The North Vietnamese had every reason to judge that the *Maddox* was part of these operations. The *Maddox* sailed within 4 to 6 miles of the North Vietnam coast; the U.S. adhered to a 3-mile territorial limit, but most communist countries, including North Vietnam, declared their belief in a 12-mile limit.

From ship's logs, communications records, and eyewitness testimony, all finally made available during Senate hearings in 1968, chaired by J. William Fulbright, we know that the *Maddox* had advance warning that it would be attacked if it persisted in the battle area (the *Maddox* was listening to radio messages among North Vietnamese officers—it was an electronic spy ship). We know it proceeded anyway (against the inclination of its commander who radioed back to his superiors at the Seventh Fleet that he thought the location was too dangerous). Then, as revealed by ship's logs, the *Maddox* fired *first*, while North Vietnamese patrol boats were nearly 6 miles away. It fired repeatedly at the North Vietnamese boats before they launched torpedoes, all of which missed or misfired.

Planes from a U.S. aircraft carrier rescued the *Maddox*, whose commander then once again suggested getting out of the battle zone. But Admiral Ulysses Grant Sharp, Jr., commander of U.S. Pacific Forces, ordered the *Maddox* to be joined by another destroyer, the *Turner Joy*, and to stay in the zone. Not only was Sharp aware that South Vietnamese boats were going to launch an attack against the North Vietnamese mainland on August 4, 1964—two days after the first incident—but his orders specifically noted that the *Maddox* and *Turner Joy* might act as a decoy to North Vietnamese forces, thus assisting the South Vietnamese attack.

So a second attack, on August 4, was actually *invited*. Still, there was no sure evidence that it ever took place. The crews of the two ships testified that original reports of torpedoes fired at them, all at night, might have been in error. At one point, things were so confused that the *Maddox* mistook the *Turner Joy* for a North Vietnamese ship and a gunner was ordered to fire at her point blank—which would have sunk her—but he illegally refused the order pending an identity check. That was the closest that a U.S. ship came to being hit that night. Nevertheless, the incident was reported as an unprovoked attack on two U.S. ships minding their own business, and in the resultant public furor, Congress was induced to pass the broadly interpreted Gulf of Tonkin Resolution.

We also know now that a draft of the resolution, authorizing "all necessary measures to repel any armed attack against the forces of the United States and to prevent further aggression"—supposedly submitted to Congress in outrage over the incident—was in fact prepared three months earlier by William Bundy, then assistant secretary of state (he later became editor of *Foreign Affairs* magazine, the official publication of the Council on Foreign Relations).

What we know is entirely consistent with the possibility that the Tonkin gulf incident was a put-up job, designed to sucker the North Vietnamese into providing justification for a planned U.S. expansion of the war. We don't know that's what happened, but we know it's a possibility. At the very least, the North Vietnamese had every reason to believe they were under attack before they approached a U.S. ship, and they certainly *were* under attack before they fired a shot.

The press was lied to, and so misinformed the public. We were all lied to.*

ON February 23, 1981, shortly after the leak to the *New York Times* of the captured-documents-from-El-Salvador story, the government released an eight-page "White Paper" entitled "Communist Interference in El Salvador." Thus the government gained a second round of publicity from the same material. A lot of people think the White Paper included the supporting documentation; in fact, it didn't.

Copies of the documentation were harder to come by. Few got a chance to analyze it, and reporters and commentators who did could do so only after the initial rash of stories was published. Those stories were generally based only on the contents of the White Paper itself, and statements made at a press conference at which the paper was released.

The White Paper would have done Johnson proud. For all its casual twisting of the truth, it was perfectly sincere—meant for our own good. Central America seemed doubly important to Reagan. For one thing, he had been elected on a promise to restructure U.S. foreign policy so that never again would we be pushed around. The cornerstone of this new toughness would be a quick victory that would make our resolve clear to all. In El Salvador, Reagan saw a chance to deal the needed bloody nose to the Soviet

---

*The best source on the Tonkin affair is Goulden's *Truth Is the First Casualty*. But additional valuable material and perspectives appear in *The President's War* by Anthony Austin (Times Books, 1971), *Tonkin Gulf* by Eugene G. Windchy (Doubleday, 1971), and *The War Conspiracy* by Peter Dale Scott (Bobbs-Merrill, 1972).

Union and teach the Ayatollah Khomeini his lesson. We would do this by fighting a mere 5,000 guerrillas in our backyard—much easier than, say, trying to set tanks ashore in Baluchistan.

Second, Reagan accepted the superhuman bogeyman theory about the communist menace and its domino effects—the same theory that U.S. policy had been based on since 1946. The idea that the Invasion of the Bodysnatchers might now have reached the foothills of Mexico was unacceptable. And if communism was really what Reagan thought it was, and the El Salvador guerrillas were really its agents, the situation *would* have been unacceptable.

The White Paper served as a perfect launching pad for the Reagan offensive. Its authors, who saw themselves rising stars in the State Department under the new administration, displayed no false modesty in their introduction:

"This special report presents definitive evidence of the clandestine military support given by the Soviet Union, Cuba, and their Communist allies to Marxist-Leninist guerrillas now fighting to overthrow the established government of El Salvador. The evidence, drawn from captured guerrilla documents and war material and corroborated by intelligence reports, underscores the central role played by Cuba and other Communist countries beginning in 1979 in the political unification, military direction, and arming of insurgent forces in El Salvador.

"From the documents it is possible to reconstruct chronologically the key stages in the growth of the Communist involvement:

- "The direct tutelary role played by Fidel Castro and the Cuban government in late 1979 and early 1980 in bringing the diverse Salvadoran guerrilla factions into a unified front;
- "The assistance and advice given the guerrillas in planning their military operations;
- "The series of contacts between Salvadoran Communist leaders and key officials of several Communist states that resulted in commitments to supply the insurgents nearly 800 tons of the most modern weapons and equipment;
- "The covert delivery to El Salvador of nearly 200 tons of those arms, mostly through Cuba and Nicaragua, in preparation for the guerrillas' failed 'general offensive' of January 1981;
- "The major Communist effort to 'cover' their involvement by providing mostly arms of Western manufacture.

"It is clear that over the past years the insurgency in El Salvador has been progressively transformed into another case . . . a textbook case . . . of indirect armed aggression against a small Third World country by Communist powers acting through Cuba.

"The United States considers it of great importance that the American people and the world community be aware of the gravity of the actions of Cuba, the Soviet Union, and other Communist states who are carrying out what is clearly shown to be a well-coordinated, covert effort to bring about the overthrow of El Salvador's established government and to impose in its place a Communist regime with no popular support."

THE White Paper's findings were generally accepted as fact by the press, and there were numerous follow-up stories with Washington datelines quoting administration spokesmen on their plans for countering the allegedly growing military power of the Salvador guerrillas. Within days, it was announced that the National Security Council had approved plans to supply the tiny Central American country with $25 million of additional military aid and $40 million of economic assistance.

Immediately upon the issuance of the White Paper, Reagan's special envoy, Lawrence Eagleburger (a former Kissinger aide) was dispatched to visit the capitals of Western Europe, where he presented copies of the findings and collected statements of support from France, Belgium, and West Germany.

To help personalize the achievement and allow for some dramatic coverage, the State Department put forward young Jon D. Glassman as a hero. As recently as the month before, in January 1981, Glassman, thirty-seven, was still deputy chief of the political section of the American embassy in Mexico City. Then, according to the story he told at the press conference and elsewhere, the department sent him to El Salvador, because of the guerrilla offensive that month, to see if there might be any captured documents (one batch of documents had been reported found the previous November).

As the story went on, Glassman discovered some captured documents at the National Police office, cracked the guerrilla code, and revealed the underlying international conspiracy behind the Salvadoran uprising. Glassman got to tour Europe with Eagleburger, telling war stories to potentates. Then he was promoted to the State Department policy planning staff, with a big new office on the seventh floor, just one floor below the secretary of state's.

The *Washington Post* wrote him up on page one under the headline, "Sleuth of the Salvador Papers." It said, "His role is described as more that of one of Smiley's people than of James Bond—the man who does the drudge work of international intrigue, who burns the midnight oil over superficially meaningless documents, and painstakingly puts together the pieces after the G-men have given up and moved on to more adventurous pursuits.... It was Glassman, according to U.S. officials and diplomats...a relatively unknown, thirty-seven-year-old foreign service officer...who discovered and pored over '18 pounds' of guerrilla documents captured by Salvadoran soldiers who had blithely stacked them on an unused desk, assuming they were useless."

The *Post*'s story was sprinkled with a few grains of skepticism for careful readers, and eventually *Post* staffer Robert Kaiser analyzed the supporting documents thoroughly and wrote a long takeout tending to discredit the White Paper. The White Paper deserved it.

* * *

JUST to look at the copies of the original papers—not the State Department's English language reconstruction of them, but the original documents themselves—would have raised most people's eyebrows. Only about 200 pages were ever released, many with very little on them. The word *document* seems far too dignified for most of them. Though some typewritten or handwritten reports were included, a lot of what was in these was sophomoric. And many "documents" were just scratchings—the kind of thing you might find wadded up next to the cigar butts after an afternoon of gin rummy. True, that doesn't mean they might not be important evidence, but they didn't suggest any grand conclusions on their own, and there didn't seem to be much else to support them.

For months after the White Paper was issued, reporters who specialized in Central America privately voiced serious doubts about the truth of it— even reporters from newspapers whose front pages seemed to accept the White Paper on faith. Eventually, when the dust had settled, and Glassman and others at State could be interviewed in detail about the White Paper's sweeping conclusions, the whole story began to unravel.*

For one thing, 18 pounds wasn't the weight of the evidence, it was the weight of Glassman's entire suitcase coming home from El Salvador, including all his other gear. For another thing, William G. Bowdler, who ran the Latin American affairs section of the State Department under Carter, and Luigi Einaudi, the policy planning official who supervised the analysis of the documents, recalled different beginnings to the trip. They said that Glassman, rather than discovering the second batch of documents on his own, was sent to El Salvador to examine a second batch of documents already known to exist. Glassman, told this, stuck fast to his original story—a strange contradiction.

The first batch of documents had been found the previous November during a raid on an art gallery owned by the brother of Shafik Handal, head of the small Communist Party in El Salvador. These documents had been sent to Washington, analyzed, and shipped out to relevant embassies. Glassman had already seen them, with Washington's analysis, at the Mexico City embassy where he worked.

Among these earlier documents was the report on the trip by an unnamed guerrilla, identified as Handal, to various communist capitals the previous summer—by far the most relied on of all the White Paper documents. In other words, the most sensational document had already been passed around. It was interesting, but no big deal had been made of it, because in fact it didn't say quite what the new interpretation of it said it said.

*His explanations here come from a three-hour interview with me in his office in May 1981.

What was new was as much interpretation as documentation, and in a three-hour talk in his office, Glassman acknowledged that the White Paper's interpretation included "mistakes" and "guessing," and that some of what the State Department handed out may have been "misleading" and "over-embellished." As amazing as those concessions were, considering the importance given to the White Paper, Glassman was understating the case.

Basically, three "documents" were critical to the White Paper: the type-written trip report, a typewritten list of arms, and some handwritten notes that were purported to be minutes of a guerrilla meeting. All three documents were attributed by the State Department to guerrilla leaders who, it was eventually admitted, didn't write them. And no one at the State Department knows who *did* write them, or how authoritative they are.

The two most widely reported figures from the White Paper—"800 tons of the most modern weapons and equipment" promised by foreign communist governments, and "the covert delivery to El Salvador of nearly 200 tons of those arms, mostly through Cuba and Nicaragua"—do not appear anywhere in the documents. They were extrapolated, and in questionable ways. Much important information in the White Paper doesn't have any reference point at all in the documents.

Glassman and other State Department officials continued to defend the White Paper's conclusions, and even to indulge in hyperbole. ("We possibly never again will have such an intimate insight into the development of a guerrilla movement and its gathering of financial and military support," Glassman said.) But the White Paper had stated that the evidence was "drawn from captured guerrilla documents and war material," and was only "cor-roborated" and "verified" by "other intelligence sources." Now Glassman and others were reduced to saying that much of the White Paper didn't come from the documents, but came from secret sources, and had to be taken on faith. Which is fine, if you have faith.

GLASSMAN acknowledges that problems arose almost immediately after the White Paper and its documents were distributed. A message came from the El Salvador government itself, saying, as Glassman recalls it, "You guys have made some mistakes." Among the mistakes cited was the misidenti-fication of an alleged guerrilla leader whose code name Glassman thought he had broken.

This guerrilla figured prominently in two of the three critical documents, including as the alleged author of the weapons list. The weapons list was signed "Ana Maria." Glassman somehow determined that "Ana Maria" was Ana Guadalupe Martinez, a reputed leader of the ERP guerrilla group. The list was said to prove what weapons and other equipment were coming from Vietnam, Ethiopia, Bulgaria, Czechoslovakia, Hungary, and East Germany. It was the only document actually pictured in the White Paper; a full page of it was reproduced as an illustration. The data on the list provided the only chart used to illustrate the White Paper.

But the alleged author, Ana Guadalupe Martinez, didn't write it. After several months, Glassman admitted that not only didn't he or the Salvadorans know who did write it, they weren't even sure which guerrilla group it came from. "Ana Maria" could be somebody's real first name, and not a code at all. What it all comes down to, then, is that the document is merely a list of weapons, a list of uncertain origin or meaning, and that there is no reason to believe the weapons were necessarily ever shipped or received.

"We completely screwed it up," Glassman concedes.

IF there is clear evidence of willful deception in the White Paper, it is in the identification of Handal as author of the main document, the report about the arms shopping trip. The report of the trip identifies the traveler only as "the comrade." From the context, Glassman concedes, the writer of the report clearly was in Cuba, and "the comrade" had just as clearly left Cuba. So the writer could not have been the same person who made the trip, though the White Paper identified him as such. Interestingly, this same mistake was also carried over to the advance story that appeared in the *Times*.

Glassman says that the main Salvadoran communist representative in Cuba couldn't have written the trip report because of the way she is referred to in the text. Moreover, the report refers to "our embassy" in Ethiopia, and "our ships." Glassman now speculates that "embassy" might refer to a Salvadoran communist representative permanently stationed in Addis Ababa, though no such representative is mentioned in the section of the report describing Ethiopia.

Whoever wrote the report, though, the most interesting point in reference to the Soviet Union isn't cooperation, but lack of it. The Vietnamese and Ethiopians had offered surplus armaments—which both countries had because the U.S. taxpayers bestowed it on them. But what the Salvadorans still needed was transportation. "The comrade" repeatedly knocked on doors in Moscow seeking logistical help to get the arms to El Salvador. The Soviet reception was barely cordial, and was provided by lower-ranking officials than those "the comrade" had expected to see.

Russian flunkies kept telling him that senior authorities hadn't yet gotten around to approving the transportaiton arrangements, until finally "the comrade" had to go home. In addition, he had asked the Soviets to provide military training in the U.S.S.R. for thirty Salvadorans, but the Soviets told him that there wasn't space in Soviet military training programs for them. This was hardly a sign that the Soviets were goading the Salvadorans into war. The U.S., on the other hand, was bringing hundreds of the Salvadoran government's soldiers to North Carolina for training, and U.S. officers were training thousands more in El Salvador.

The White Paper doesn't report any of "the comrade's" turndowns. It says, "Before leaving Moscow, Handal received assurances that the Soviets agree in principle to transport the Vietnamese arms." In context, though, the agreement in principle appears to be a cop-out, and "the comrade" keeps complaining that he can't get a commitment out of the Russians, which is what he keeps asking for.

Describing a final meeting, the document says, "The comrade again requested weapons, and transportation of [weapons] that Vietnam provided, expressing the conviction that the CPSU [Communist Party of the Soviet Union] is capable of resolving these problems, as well as insisting upon the training of the group of thirty comrades. After this meeting," the document continues, "the comrade made known through other channels his disagreement with the absence of the meeting at the proper level and lack of decision concerning the requests for assistance."

So "the comrade," frustrated and angry, returned to Cuba empty-handed. Eventually he got a telegram there, in which the Soviets agreed to take the thirty trainees, but still wouldn't commit themselves on supplying or transporting weapons. The document ends at this point, with the comrade left "expressing concern." This is the kind of Soviet aggression the Afghans would dearly like to see. The only actual aid reported in the documents as being received by the Salvadorans was an airplane ticket to Hanoi for one guerrilla, presumably, but not assuredly, Handal.

THE White Paper also identifies Handal as the author of certain opinions that turn out to be contained in Document C, two pages of handwritten notes. The notes, however, don't include Handal's name or any date or other identification. The White Paper says they are notes "taken during an April 28, 1980, meeting of the Salvadoran Communist party." Glassman now says the identification of the notes came from other sources—which can't be revealed.

Next problem: the notes also appear to be written in at least two different handwritings. Glassman acknowledges that this makes it difficult to ascribe the work to one author. "They change people writing on them," he admits, although in four places the White Paper quotes the words as Handal's own.

Based on these notes, supposedly taken by Handal himself, the White Paper says, "In reference to a unification of the armed movement, he asserts that 'the idea of involving everyone in the area has already been suggested to Fidel himself.' Handal alludes to the concept of unification and notes, 'Fidel thought well of the idea.'"

Glassman now concedes "that could be a misleading statement." *And how!* In the context of the document—in all its various handwritings—the idea that had been suggested to "Fidel" was getting various communist parties in Latin America to cooperate, apparently about labor unions. The discussion is about union organizing, not "the armed movement."

At another point, the White Paper says Salvadoran guerrilla leaders formed a unified front "as a precondition for large-scale Cuban aid." Glassman acknowledges that there's nothing to that effect in the documents, either. He says it was true in Nicaragua, though, so the White Paper carried the idea over to El Salvador. Apparently it was nothing but an assumption.

The White Paper also says that on July 22, 1980, Yasir Arafat, the PLO leader, met Salvadoran guerrilla leaders in Managua and gave "promises [of] military equipment, including arms and aircraft." But the only mention of Arafat in the documents is an aside, in parentheses, in one document, which says, "(. . . on the 22nd there was a meeting with Arafat.)." Nor does such a meeting have the sinister connotation one might suppose; they were all in Managua for the anniversary commemoration of the Nicaraguan revolution, and it's perfectly natural that they might have said hello. There is no indication the subject of arms ever came up.

Again, as with the report of the trip to Moscow, the document that refers fleetingly to Arafat indicates on the whole a lack of cooperation more than cooperation. It is an unsigned report that the State Department labeled Document G. It is full of complaints that the Salvadoran delegation was cold-shouldered and otherwise insulted on its visit to Nicaragua. The delegates were kept locked in a hotel room for a week, until they finally threatened "that if they [the Nicaraguans] did not attend to us either we would go to H. [apparently Havana, not Hell] or return to the country [apparently El Salvador], since we were wasting our time."

The Nicaraguans eventually agreed to a meeting. After much squabbling and mutual criticism, the document says, the Nicaraguans promised to supply rifles—"hunting weapons" are mentioned—and ammunition, but not in the quantities the Salvadorans expected. And the Nicaraguans refused to send any guns unless the Salvadorans agreed to certain unspecified "political conditions" that the Salvadorans strongly objected to. There is no indication in the documents whether this dispute was ever resolved, or whether the guns were ever sent.

Salvadorans living in Managua complained to the visiting Salvadoran delegation that "there was not a relationship of mutual respect" with the Nicaraguans, "but rather one of imposition." None of the squabbling is mentioned in the White Paper, which is intent on proving conspiracy.

Glassman explains that the White Paper's mention of Arafat's role came from other, secret intelligence. The White Paper doesn't say so, but Israel, Arafat's nemesis, was the major arms supplier to the El Salvador government until the U.S. became directly involved in 1979 and 1980.

The White Paper says that the Communist party of El Salvador "has become increasingly committed since 1976 to a military solution." Actually, the communists had supported the government that took over El Salvador in a coup in October 1979—the very government that the U.S. then maintained in power until the 1982 elections. The communists pulled out of that government two months after the coup, in December 1979, and joined the armed opposition because, in Glassman's own words, the government was "still arresting them, still shooting them"—which isn't an illogical reason for revolting, when you get right down to it.

GLASSMAN also says the figure of 200 tons of arms allegedly smuggled into El Salvador through the network of communist countries "comes from intelligence based on the air traffic, based on the truck traffic. In other words, it does not come from the documents."

The White Paper, however, specifically states that it does come "from the documents."

Glassman says part of the estimate of the truck shipments into El Salvador was based on extrapolating the cargo-hauling potential of several trucks that are listed in one document, Document N. The document, an undated, unsigned, barely legible hand-scrawled sheet, lists four trucks, three of which apparently are still to be bought or built. Alongside the trucks are the initials of four guerrilla groups, and some tonnage numbers totaling 21 tons, under the headings, "sea," "air," and "road."

The other commonly quoted figure from the white paper, 800 tons of promised weapons, was, says Glassman, extrapolated from a single comment made in Document I. This document is a typewritten report identified as minutes of a meeting of three men said to be the "guerrilla joint general staff." The State Department translation of the document includes a date at the top. September 26, 1980, which isn't on the actual document (but would be more than two months after the meeting in Nicaragua at which guns were promised but held up because of political conditions).

Although the three men in Document I call themselves a "general staff," and refer to having been in Cuba, they are identified only as Companero Ramon, Companero Vladimir, and Companero Jonas. As in other documents, the words seem so amateurish that they could have been set down by three teenagers with delusions of grandeur. The information is interesting, but hardly definitive.

Most of the "minutes" are taken up by quibbles over where to meet— they start out in a coffee shop and wind up at somebody's house—and by the minute-taker's complaints that nothing is being planned very well. Only at the end is there a quibble over how arms should be distributed. At this point, the minute-taker says, "It contradicts military reality to discuss percentages of arms when hardly 4 tons of the 130 warehoused in Lagos [believed to be a code word for Nicaragua] have been brought into the country. These 4 tons have been in intermittent supply and the material now in Lagos is only equivalent to one-sixth of all the material obtained that the DRU [a group of revolutionary organizations] will have eventually concentrated in Lagos."

Glassman says he multiplied 130 by 6 to get 800. But from the document, these numbers could be a pipe dream. Even if the 4-ton figure is correct, considering that one M-16 without magazine or bayonet weighs 7 pounds, and a week's supply of ammunition weighs 42 pounds, 4 tons wouldn't make much of a revolution.*

A common highway truck in the U.S. carries about 20 tons. Steel armaments are so dense, however, that 20 tons of weapons would probably occupy much less space. The guerrillas wanted not just light combat rifles, but mortars, shells, and rockets. Measurements of arms by tons is unusual. But even 800 tons is not enough to equip a large guerrilla army for very long, and such a supply would be dwarfed by the amount of arms the U.S. has sent to the El Salvador government.

MOST of the documents distributed along with the White Paper were said to have been found in a Salvadoran grocery store in early January. As Glassman tells it, the Salvadoran police "had captured a Venezuelan correspondent, a journalist who was bringing in money for ERP [a guerrilla group], and by following him were able to capture the ERP propaganda commission as a whole, meeting in a house." The owner of the house denied involvement, Glassman says, but was persuaded to tell police of other locations he had heard people on the propaganda commission talk about.

One such location was a grocery store owned by a known leftist. There police found a false wall, behind which were a mortar and some shells, and documents, which were in a plastic bag and a suitcase. Glassman says he thinks the documents were kept there because the guerrilla coalition consists of four groups, "none of which fully trusts the others," so that records must be maintained.

Hearing this story, Robert White, who was the U.S. ambassador to El Salvador at the time, is incredulous. "All of this is news to me," he says. "It strikes me as unlikely that I would not have heard this story before—this business about following a Venezuelan and finding this wall and breaking it down." He also denies the statements by Assistant Secretary of State Bowdler and analyst Einaudi that he had asked for anyone—let alone Glassman—to be sent down to help analyze captured documents. He says the White Paper is "bizarre, tendentious, [and] tries to prove more than the evidence warrants."

Yet *Time* magazine reported as fact the story about the hollow wall and about Glassman's heroic analysis of documents that "were mostly in code." This last, at least, was absolutely untrue; the only "code" words were some place names, on which Glassman has so far been given the benefit of the

---

*Figures courtesy of Captain Farrar of the Pentagon press office, based on his estimate that a soldier should carry 15 to 20 one-pound magazines of ammunition for three days of combat.

doubt, and some personal nicknames or pseudonyms, which Glassman concedes he got *wrong*, at least in assigning authorship of the most important documents.

Time also reported, "The grocery-store papers represented over 70 percent of the material that Washington used to draw up last month's White Paper documenting Soviet and Cuban arms aid to El Salvador's insurgency." This was also untrue; on analysis, little that is in the text of the White Paper can be nailed down by anything that is in that group of documents.

THE Salvadoran government has a history of press manipulation. Anne Nelson, who has covered the Salvadoran war for many publications, has reported witnessing Salvadoran forces placing guns in the hands of murdered civilians so they would look like guerrillas when photographers arrived; she and others wrote of the flaws in the Salvadoran government's story that a team of Dutch journalists died when caught in a crossfire, whereas apparently they were deliberately ambushed for meeting with guerrillas.

So, understandably, there has been speculation that the White Paper documents were concocted and planted, either by the CIA, or by Salvadoran authorities, or both. Former Ambassador White says, "The only thing that ever made me think that these documents were genuine was that they proved so little."

Assuming their genuineness, what *do* they prove? Barely even the obvious.

Considering the history of U.S.-supported right-wing repression in Central America, and considering the propaganda schools that Castro has created to teach Marxism as the only workable alternative to U.S. repression, it only makes sense that revolutionaries in El Salvador would seek aid from Marxist governments.

Few would doubt that Marxist governments would encourage the revolutionaries, coach them when they asked for it, and sneak them weapons if that could be done under the table (although this material aid could never match what the U.S. has supplied to the Salvadoran government; it probably hasn't even approached what the Salvadoran guerrillas have obtained from other sources).

But the White Paper says more than that. It says that a unified, Soviet-run international communist network took over the El Salvador rebellion to such an extent that the uprising constitutes a foreign, armed aggression rather than a legitimate civil war. In fact, so far as we can rely on the documents at all, they show the opposite: a disorganized, ragtag rebellion. Some of its participants have gone around begging for help from the most likely sources, and have been consistently stalled off and sent home empty-handed, or with much less than they asked for. Not only do the documents not prove the thesis, the thesis simply isn't true.

*   *   *

IF a couple of newspapers hadn't published prominently displayed, skeptical analyses of the White Paper in June 1981, there would have been more. The State Department was already leaking stories, preparing the way for another White Paper. This one would have libeled some major charities, in a manner that truly deserved the overused characterization, McCarthyism.

Glassman was saying in speeches that other captured documents, not yet released, showed that relief funds raised by several charities were subject to diversion to the communist war effort in El Salvador, perhaps even with the charities' knowledge. Needless to say, this upset the charities, which included Catholic Relief Services, Oxfam America, and the World Council of Churches, all of which denied the accusation.

All the charities said they had investigated the charges, and found them false, after learning of them in leaked newspaper accounts. This time, the leakee was United Press International. UPI assured its readers of "extensive" documentation for the charges, and didn't even bother to report the charities' denials. (Reporting denials might offend the leaker, who then couldn't be counted on for the next leak. Like every administration, Reagan's railed against unauthorized leaks to the press, and like every administration, it operated by leaking things to the press any time it could control the news by doing so.)

The purportedly incriminating documents were alleged plans to merge two Salvadoran relief agencies into a single agency, known as CESAH. CESAH would be secretly controlled by communist revolutionaries and its money would be used to buy arms, among other things. In fact, the charities said, the two agencies *did* merge into one organization, called ASESAH, which the charities continued to support.

Monsignor Robert J. Coll, assistant executive director of Catholic Relief Services in New York, said he visited El Salvador to check with church and political leaders about the charges. Monsignor Coll said he got endorsements for ASESAH's work from two rather impressive sources. One was the Salvadoran president, José Napoleón Duarte, whom U.S. forces were supporting. The other was Bishop Rivera y Damas, head of the Catholic church in El Salvador. The bishop told the monsignor he had "the best priest in his diocese committed to it [the charity]," the monsignor says.

A spokesman for the World Council of Churches denounced the allegations. "There are thousands of people, chiefly widows and children, for whom this money is responsible for their daily food," she said. Lawrence Simon, an official of Oxfam—a worldwide food assistance organization founded at Oxford University in England*—expressed fear that the stories would affect a lot more than just fund-raising.

*Which does wonderful grass roots work in many countries, not only distributing food gifts, but, more important, helping increase local food production. The author has seen

"We're more worried about the Latin American newspapers getting this information," he said. "Saying someone is connected to the Communist party of El Salvador is tantamount to signing someone's death warrant down there. We're concerned about the danger this has placed our field staff in."

After all this was reported in the press, the second white paper, publicly promised, was never issued.

ON March 10, 1982, The *Washington Post*, one of the three premier newspapers in the United States, published a stunning story on its front page, above the fold. One of the story's coauthors was no less than Bob Woodward, who had rightfully earned his place as a hero in American history during Watergate. The story unequivocally reported that President Reagan had approved a $19 million plan to establish a covert paramilitary force in Central America. The object of the force was to bring down the government of Nicaragua, a nation with whom the United States was not legally at war.

The story was based on the word of anonymous administration officials. It said the paramilitary force of 500 men would try to destabilize the Nicaraguan government by attacking vital economic installations such as dams and power stations. No one who said the plan was approved was ever identified to the reader. Yet the plan was reported authoritatively.

One day later, on March 11, 1982, the *New York Times*, another of the three premier newspapers, published a story on page one, above the fold, reporting authoritatively that Woodward and Patrick Tyler, the *Post* reporter who shared the byline on the earlier story, were wrong. Of course, the *Times* didn't say exactly that, but there was no other possibility open. The *Times*'s story said, "Mr. Reagan and his top national security advisors *rejected* a proposal to finance and support the creation of a paramilitary force in Central America [emphasis added]." It said the administration was aware that several South American countries were establishing a force in the area, but had "declined to provide financial or military support." Of course, the story was attributed to "senior administration officials," who were never identified to the reader.

Three days later, the *Times* struck again, on page one, above the fold. The story was by Leslie Gelb, a *Times* reporter who had been a State Department official in the Carter administration and who joined the *Times* as national security reporter after Reagan's election. (Gelb took the place of Richard Burt, who left to become a State Department official in the Reagan administration—prompting press critic Alexander Cockburn to twit that the *Times* should hold public hearings before filling its national security beat.)

Now, Gelb, for all intents and purposes, reported that not only were

Oxfam at work, donates regularly himself, and encourages the reader to do so. (Oxfam America, 115 Broadway, Boston, Mass. 02116.)

Woodward and Tyler wrong, but the *Times* had been wrong, too. Contrary to what the *Times* had said previously, there really *was* a plan for a paramilitary force. But the plan wasn't what the *Post* said it was, either. "According to interviews and documents obtained by the *New York Times*," Gelb wrote, "the plan approved by Mr. Reagan calls for using the paramilitary unit to attack what the administration says are Cuban arms supply lines in Central America." The plan "seeks to focus attention on the Cuban presence in Nicaragua," he wrote. It's hardly necessary to say that his sources weren't identified.

The same week that the *Post* and *Times* ran these stories, *The Nation*, a weekly political magazine (and practically an institution on the American left), ran as its lead story a report that a paramilitary operation against Nicaragua—run by the CIA—was not only approved but actually in operation. *The Nation* said that Assistant Secretary of State Thomas O. Enders had informed the relevant congressional committees of this back in December.* *The Nation*'s report was authoritative and unequivocal, and, of course, its sources were anonymous.

Here were four stories in three major national publications, all the same week, all displayed with top prominence, all dealing with the most vital of subjects—whether or not the United States was at war—and all claiming to be completely authoritative on the answer. And after reading all four stories, the only thing you knew for sure was that three of them were wrong. Maybe all four.

Somebody in government was lying to the public—a lot of people in government were lying to the public—and using reporters to do it. They weren't using just any reporters, but in the case of the *Times* and *Post*, several of the best reporters in the country. Not one of the reporters admitted in his story to the possibility that his sources might be sandbagging him. Not one gave weight to sources with an opposite point of view, just to let the reader know there might be something else to say on the subject.

None of the reporters indicated that he had asked his sources how the information could be verified independently. None told the reader why, if the story was true, it *couldn't* be verified independently. All the stories were written from Washington, none of them from Honduras or Nicaragua, where the facts supposedly lay. None of the stories suggested what self-serving motive the source might have for saying what he was saying.

THE Sunday after all these stories ran, there was a hint about what really may have been going on. The lead story in the *New York Times* was headlined, "High Aide Says U.S. Seeks Soviet Talks on Salvador Issue." The story said

---

*Members of these committees flatly denied this in interviews with me, some off the record, some on.

that the U.S. government believed that the Central American situation should be negotiated and resolved on a global basis.

Aha! A peace offensive!

First you let the other side discover that you're about to launch a war against them, then you let them know that they can get out of it by coming to certain terms—not a unique diplomatic ploy, if that's what happened. Officials weren't sending out phony messages for nothing. Washington and Moscow bluff and parry each other a lot through the front pages of newspapers. But how is the public supposed to arrive at foreign policy opinions if reporters are busy carrying diplomatic feelers for politicians, who are fighting a war in which truth was that first casualty, so long ago?

The story reporting the peace offensive was, of course, attributed to an anonymous "senior administration official." The story gained its authority by what appeared to be its exclusivity. The impression one is left with, after reading the story, is that the *Times* diplomatic correspondent had spent all week chasing the conflicting rumors, and finally pinned down a source who would explain the administration's *real* policy, but only on condition he not be named:

"'We have to talk to the Russians,' the official said. 'There are discussions that must be held, there are steps that must be taken in political, economic, and security areas which tend to influence calculi in Moscow, in Havana, in Nicaragua, and in the regional context.'" Finally, the press had dug out a source who could explain the government's behavior. And everyone understood that the press couldn't mention this cooperative official's name, because his honesty might cost him his *job* (as if his syntax didn't give him away).

Is that what happened? No. Two days later, a small item appeared on the "Washington Talk" page of the *Times*, a more informal, gossipy place in the newspaper. It said, in its entirety:

"On Saturday morning in Washington, Secretary of State Alexander M. Haig, Jr., held a meeting with a group of reporters and spoke at length about his conviction that the problem in El Salvador could not be solved in El Salvador alone, but on a 'global' basis in which the Soviet Union, Cuba, Nicaragua, and other Latin American countries had to be involved.

"Mr. Haig, in that session, spoke on condition he be identified only as a 'senior administration official.'

"When President Reagan returned to the White House yesterday from a weekend at Camp David, he was asked by reporters about articles attributed to the 'senior administration official.' He responded. 'I always have trouble about wondering who those senior officials are. I haven't met any of them yet.'

"This led to questioning aboard Air Force One yesterday in which Larry Speakes, the deputy press secretary, was asked if Mr. Reagan was actually unaware of Mr. Haig's 'backgrounder' on Saturday. Mr. Speakes said that Mr. Reagan was talking 'in jest.'" End of story.

So a secret source can be disclosed at will in an amusing item in the back pages, but cannot be disclosed at the top right of page one when the reader is relying on the source to say whether the country is going to war or not. This is the way the game is played. The *Times* is used as an example here not because it is the worst newspaper at foreign reporting, but because it has always been the *best*. This wasn't a mistake, this was the system at work, and that is what is wrong.

All these stories, from Woodward's first news break in the *Post* to the peace offensive story in the *Times*, got their authority by a single device: they were all written as if the reporter had dug out an exclusive source who knew all the answers, and had coaxed that source into revealing the truth. Perhaps with Woodward's story, that is what actually happened, and all the other stories were wrong. Perhaps with Gelb's. We don't know.

But it is clear what happened with the peace offensive story. The secretary of state called a big press conference to put across the official line. To make it believable, he demanded anonymity. What incredible gall! It seems a blight on journalism that the press corps didn't arise in unison and walk out of the room, much less that under the rules reporters don't even clue their readers in on the process at work. Surely one of the things the public has a "right to know" is that what is being said isn't necessarily the truth, but maybe just what the government wants the Russians and Nicaraguans to hear, for reasons of its own.

What really happened? Did Haig leak the first story to the *Post* in order to scare the bejesus out of the Nicaraguans? Did Philip Taubman, the excellent *Times* reporter who wrote that paper's first story, then begin to sniff out that it was a plant? Did Haig then pick up Taubman's story and say, "My God, just when I had the Nicaraguans where I want them, the *Times* says it isn't true," and so proceed to call up Gelb and give him a more credible story, which then allowed Haig to launch the peace offensive as planned?

We'll probably never know.

A year later, it had become clear that a U.S.-run paramilitary program was in operation on the Nicaraguan border. Many in Congress suspected that the program was designed to overthrow the Nicaraguan government—as the Nicaraguans themselves contended at every opportunity—although the administration continued to insist that the purpose of the program was to interdict arms headed for El Salvador. Was this the program that the *Post*, or one of the other publications, had reported? Or was it a newer program, launched *after* Haig's peace offensive had failed, perhaps intended to make good on the original threat, which had never had much practical hope of success anyway?

We may never know the answer to that, either.*

---

*The right of the press to protect the confidentiality of its sources is vital to the function of the press in a democratic society—otherwise, many persons with valuable information would never come forward, for fear of losing their jobs, or in some cases their lives.

* * *

ON May 27, 1981, the *New York Times* reported on its front page that the citizens of Libya were getting fed up with Muammar Al-Qaddafi, and that a resistance movement was growing on the Sahara. A legitimate story perhaps—one could think of a lot of reasons for becoming disaffected with Qaddafi. The story reported authoritatively on conditions inside Libya. ("There are shortages of food and other necessities. Libya is short of skilled administrators.") But the story was datelined Washington. It was based entirely on anonymous sources, mostly, apparently, from the U.S. State Department.

One "Arab diplomat" was also quoted as confirming the stories. Who? A Saudi, perhaps? Saudi Arabia's own government is worried about a Qaddafi-style revolution, and it has to cater to the State Department for permission to buy high-tech military equipment from the U.S. Such factors might have colored the Arab diplomat's comments. We are never told.

At about the same time, the *Washington Post* sent out a story, also datelined Washington, quoting "senior U.S. and allied intelligence sources" as saying that "the Soviet Union has been effectively building in Libya a potential military threat to southern Europe and to U.S. forces in the Mediterranean." The story ran as the lead item, covering all eight columns at the top of page one of the *International Herald Tribune*.

Usually, if what those sources tell the reporter is true, the information can be verified elsewhere. The confidential source is thus not relied on as to truth—he is just indispensable in pointing the reporter in the right direction.

In such cases, when the courts or the executive branch want to learn the identity of the source, they simply want to punish the bearer of bad tidings; for the purpose of discovering truth, the facts stand or fall independently. Sometimes, as in the case, say, of an exposé of the Teamsters' Union's exploitation of its members, all sources for certain information are confidential, but there are hundreds or thousands of such sources. Confirmation can be obtained by interviewing more teamsters at random.

What is being talked about here is the use of this confidentiality by government officials to mislead the public. The officials involved are not blowing the whistle on wrongdoing by the system; they don't need confidentiality to protect themselves. Rather, these officials are speaking *for* the system, but saying things that the system doesn't want to be responsible for, possibly because they will turn out not to be true.

It is especially outrageous for a senior government official like Haig to invoke this privilege of confidentiality (the protection is for the source, not for the reporter). While such officials routinely ask reporters to pledge not to identify them as sources, they turn around and argue in court, sometimes successfully, that reporters should be jailed for keeping just such confidences with regard to *other* persons who have provided information *contrary* to the official line. Haig's old boss Kissinger, who constantly invoked the privilege of confidentiality when speaking with reporters, turned around and *wiretapped* some of the same reporters to learn their other sources. Haig's more recent boss, President Reagan, wants lie detector tests to do that job.

It quoted "sources recently in Libya" as saying that East Germans now staffed Qaddafi's bodyguard. Without any attribution, it reported that "a small contingent of North Korean air force personnel . . . now operates in Libya." Doing various military and civilian chores, the story said, were between 1,000 and 2,000 Soviets, between 600 and 1,000 Cubans, and from 1,500 to 2,000 East Germans. This information wasn't attributed to anyone.

Contrary to what those two stories might have led readers to expect, in the two years that followed there were neither rebellions against Qaddafi within Libya (that we know of) or Libyan attacks on southern Europe or the U.S. forces in the Mediterranean. What there has been, instead, is thoroughly documented evidence from Seymour Hersh of the *New York Times* that the most frightening source of Libyan terrorist power came from former CIA agents on the make—Edwin Wilson and Frank Terpil and their colleagues— and greedy U.S. munitions suppliers.

When Qaddafi wanted to put his military machine into action against Chad, he turned to U.S. mercenaries supplied by Wilson and Terpil to make his air force work. When he wanted to assassinate a political opponent, it wasn't East Germans or North Koreans he turned to, but the retired CIA operatives. (Wilson has since been convicted of supplying deadly munitions to Libya; Terpil is a fugitive from justice.)

Western journalists have been allowed into Libya, where one might get a better sense of the conditions there than one could get attending a State Department briefing in Washington. Why was there a spate of leaks to Washington reporters in the spring of 1981? Maybe to scare Qaddafi so the U.S. might gain an edge in some secret negotiation or maneuver? Maybe to justify some CIA overthrow attempt that never came off? Maybe just to paint the Carter legacy in such dark hues that the Republicans would get credit for doing a good job when nothing awful happened?

Or, maybe the stories were absolutely accurate. But they offered no in- dependent confirmation, and they offered no explanation of why there couldn't be such confirmation.

Even reporters who actually go to the countries they write about tend to get far too much of their information from the U.S. embassy, or other official sources in the capital. Then they return to the standard surroundings of a world-class hotel and file their stories. How many stories about what is "really going on" in Libya, or any of a hundred other countries, are written by reporters who have never slept a night in a Libyan home, or eaten a meal at a Libyan family's table or relaxed with a Libyan worker after work? And how tuned in are the sources who are informing the State Department itself?

A personal note:
Early in 1980, just after the Soviet invasion of Afghanistan, the author was in a conference room in the U.S. embassy in Kabul. The event was a

secret, confidential, not-for-attribution briefing for the entire press corps—more than a dozen people. The instructions were to attribute what was said to "Western diplomatic sources."

The purpose of this briefing was for the military attaché to announce to the press that Soviet troops were concentrating near the Iranian border, rather than spreading out around Afghanistan. The unmistakable implication was that the real purpose of the Soviet invasion might be to march into Iran.*

The attaché seemed knowledgeable and articulate, so I went up to him privately, after the meeting was over, and told him my plans to take off around the countryside. Though I knew the country a bit from a previous visit as a backpacker, I wanted advice on what to look for, and asked him where he would recommend I try to go. The attaché basically admitted that he was operating on very little information. He wasn't allowed outside Kabul. He said that the news he had just told the press conference had come from Washington, not from anything gathered at the embassy. He did give me a list of things he had been wondering about, mainly, what the Russian troops were really up to.

He seemed to know so little that I decided his briefing wasn't worth a story, and besides, I was naive enough then to assume that if the information had come from Washington, my newspaper's Washington bureau would already have it, and would have filed it. I didn't realize that the State Department had deliberately sent its latest propaganda line halfway around the world to Kabul, Afghanistan, to be released to reporters there, presumably because after the news wended its way back home again, it would seem more credible to readers if it had a Kabul dateline on it.

So I went out in Afghanistan and saw the Soviet encampments the attaché had been talking about. They were near Iran, all right. But the encampments seemed logically placed there to interdict a main route of guerrilla activity, to protect the main military airfield used for air strikes against Afghan villagers, and to have a convenient highway link to Russia and all parts of Afghanistan. Since there was no invasion of Iran, my judgment has since seemed vindicated.

I was amazed to get back to the U.S. more than a month later and see the press coverage while I was gone. The day after the press conference I had attended, papers all across the country screamed with headlines like the one atop a New York tabloid, "Russ Troops Mass on Iran Border." The reports were said to have originated in Afghanistan. The newsmagazines featured the story, too.

The import of this story just wasn't true, and I felt the frustration of being perhaps the only one around who knew it.

*I came in late and missed the instructions on attribution, and so feel no reluctance to say now what happened.

* * *

ON March 1, 1981, the *New York Times* (and the same reporter who wrote
the original White Paper leak story) reported:

"President Reagan stressed that he had 'no intention' of involving the
United States in another Vietnam, and, indeed, it appeared the administration
had decided to intervene in El Salvador precisely because the situation there
was so different from Vietnam. Defeating a small Marxist-led insurgency in
the United States's backyard seemed an easily 'winnable' test of the administration's determination to, in Mr. [Edwin] Meese's words, 'stop the expansion of communism throughout the world.'"

Two years later, on April 22, 1983, the *Times* reported, "A range of
administration officials say the United States must make a sustained, increased effort in El Salvador or lose the war to the guerrillas. Even with
such an effort, the officials believe, it will take *from two to seven years*
before significant progress can be made toward bringing the situation there
under control [emphasis added]."

And the story went on to say that two years earlier—about the time the
first story was printed—"Senior United States military commanders concluded . . . that even with increased military assistance from the United States
the Salvadoran military as then constituted could not defeat opposition guerrilla forces, according to Reagan administration officials."

According to the *Times*'s 1983 account of the 1981 military study, the
problem was not Shafik Handal and the Soviet-Vietnamese-Cuban-Nicara-
guan connection. Instead, the *Times* said, "The report, officially known as
a Defense Requirement Survey, concluded that in the long term only a
dramatic restructuring of the Salvadoran military, including the removal of
many senior officers, a crackdown on corruption, and the adoption of more
aggressive tactics, could turn it into an effective fighting force."

A month earlier, in March 1983, the *Times* had reported, "American
military officials in El Salvador . . . recently said that they had seen little
evidence that guerrillas were using arms provided by the Soviet Union and
Cuba. . . . Intelligence officials said there was evidence that some weapons
the United States has sent to friendly nations in Central America, including
Honduras and El Salvador, have been sold by officials in those countries to
guerrilla forces in El Salvador." Fortunately, the intelligence sources said,
the number of such weapons was not significant so far.

CHAPTER TWENTY-TWO

ON CAPITALISM, COMMUNISM, AND FREEDOM

═══════════════════════THERE IS A verse common in English folksongs that usually, as singers say, goes something like this:

> *The men of the forest, they once asked of me,*
> *"How many blackberries grow in the blue sea?"*
> *And I answered them back with a tear in my eye,*
> *"How many tall ships in the forest?"*

The misunderstanding and inappropriateness captured in this quatrain characterizes the long, bloody experience of the United States as a global power since the end of World War II. It characterizes Soviet foreign policy as well, but that is beyond our direct control, and does us no direct harm.

The image of a tall ship in the forest describes the U.S. adventure abroad particularly well. The Soviets' political and economic system is a rusty battlewagon that leaks even in the familiar harbors of Leningrad and Kiev. Our ship, on the other hand, is a majestic and heroic instrument. It was crafted and launched with genius and love. It is just out of place.

The crew are fishermen, not expeditionaries—artisans and architects and farmers and machine designers, not gunners. The men at the bridge have steered them far off course. The ship lies beached in jungles from Vietnam to El Salvador. The foreigners who see it don't understand that it behaves

differently in these surroundings than it does in the free and productive society
that set it sail.

The ship doesn't represent us well. Its cannon blaze until the powder runs
out, and then the people of the forest emerge, and bury their dead comrades.
In a rage, they strip the ship plank by plank. With the lethal booty they
savage first the crew and then each other.

A lighter metaphor for the U.S. experience abroad can be found in the old
joke about the city-slicker salesman in his stylish new car, who loses his
way as the interstate gradually becomes a highway, the highway a road, and
the road, finally, some dirt tire tracks. In the end, the salesman comes to a
wretched farmhouse on whose ramshackle front porch sits a farmer in tattered
coveralls, chewing tobacco and strumming an ancient banjo.

The two men run through an exasperating series of questions and answers
as the salesman tries futilely to get directions. ("Can I take this road to Fort
Mudge?" he asks at one point. "Yup," says the farmer, then adds, "Won't
do you no good, though. They already got one.") At last, the salesman flings
his new hat in the mud and screams at the farmer, "You know, you're pretty
goddamn stupid, you know that?"

"Yup," says the farmer, spitting out a long swill of tobacco juice. "But
I ain't lost."

WE reduce the world's problems to simplicities: the efficiency of marketplace
incentives versus the efficiency of central control, the efficiency of pluralistic
politics versus the efficiency of a one-party state. How easy foreign relations
would be if that were all there was to it! On those terms, we could not lose.
Our basic values are fine.

Back in the 1960s, President Kennedy invited skeptics to come to Berlin
to see the difference between the Western and Soviet systems. The comparison was a touch spurious, because the Soviets had deliberately restrained
East German recovery for reasons of vengeance, while the U.S. had helped
capitalize a boom in its sector of Germany. But the economic and political
contrast between the two Berlins was stunning and undeniable. And the
Soviets' instinct for malevolence, and America's for industrious cooperation,
were legitimate factors for emerging Third World countries to consider when
choosing the models they would follow.

In the decades since then, the Third World itself has offered many equally
stunning examples of similar countries that chose different roads. In every
case, the more market-oriented and the more pluralistic the road chosen, the
more successful the country has been in meeting the needs of its people:

Morocco versus Algeria, Malaysia versus Indonesia, Thailand versus
Burma, Kenya versus Tanzania, the two Koreas, and—still instructive despite a certain obvious unfairness in exact comparison—Taiwan versus main-

land China. These pairs of countries are roughly similar in mineral wealth, agricultural potential, and racial makeup.* Most of the pairs are similarly sized, too.

There are differences. Kenya is populated by the industrious Kikuyu tribe, while Tanzania's indigenous tribes were slaved out, so that its present occupants are mostly descendants of wanderers. Indonesia has ten times as many people as Malaysia and only five times as much arable land. But Nyerere of Tanzania and Sukarno of Indonesia specifically invited comparison of their development results with those of Kenya and Malaysia, which they knew were following different, more free-market, policies. That was back when Nyerere was optimistic, and Sukarno claimed to have all the answers.

To measure the contrasts between countries most fairly, one must compare them percentile against percentile—that is, the top one percent of one country against the top one percent of the other, the tenth percentile against the tenth percentile, the fortieth against the fortieth, and so on down to the lowest percentile. The more successful country will have made a better life for a majority of percentiles without inhumanely repressing any of them.

The percentile-against-percentile comparison eliminates the skewering effects caused by philosophical choices. Some countries, for example, can run a high per capita income without benefiting most of the population, because the extra income is confined to the top percentiles. Other countries can improve the lot of most people while leaving a substantial minority frustrated and angry. (Cuba, the lone communist success in the Third World because of its windfall Soviet aid, is an example.)

One could cite many statistics describing the various pairs of countries listed above, showing that freer markets produce more goods for more people. Probably the most astounding fact is that Burma, the world's number one exporter of rice before the socialists got hold of it, was importing rice in the 1970s. (By the 1980s, using new seed strains, it returned to a slight surplus, though nothing like before.) Indonesia, which also could produce food in abundance, began importing it during Sukarno's time and still does.

But to appreciate what these statistics mean, for the population of the countries, you have to be there, walk the fields, and visit the homes. Kennedy said, "Let them come to Berlin." By like measure, we could now invite anyone to visit these sets of countries and choose which he would rather live in, at any given percentile.

THE Malay resident of the peninsula's lesser-developed east coast is apt to live in a decent house, eat well, have a free school for his children and access to running water, electricity, and paved roads. The roughly 45 percent of

*Taiwan is a special case. If you don't want to call it a country, you don't have to, but it's been acting like one.

Malaysia's population that bears Chinese or Indian blood lives mostly on the west coast, and in European style. Many own cars. The countryside is abuzz with motorcycles.

Although Malaysia is the world's largest producer of rubber and tin, Indonesia has the resources to produce more rubber than Malaysia, as well as substantial amounts of tin and petroleum, making Indonesia potentially the richer of the two countries. Yet conditions in Indonesia appeared miserably backward after the fifteen years of government by Sukarno, who adhered closely to the left-wing socialist prescription for nation-building (and to some degree, created it). Conditions continue to be backward under the socialism, hidden in anti-communist rhetoric, of the U.S.-supported generals.

Sukarno was so busy campaigning to save the whole Third World from European-American imperialism that he lacked time to devote to Indonesia. He squandered many of his country's resources trying unsuccessfully to conquer Borneo, a part of Malaysia. He railed against Malaysia's trade orientation with the West.

Meanwhile, the rupiah (Indonesia's currency) became wildly inflated, discouraging investment by Indonesians as well as foreigners. Sumatra, an agricultural gold mine that produces most of Indonesia's wealth even though its potential has barely been scratched, had a road system right down with Zaire's (and only those who have survived the overland journey to Kisangani can quite imagine what that means). A four-wheel-drive vehicle could average no better than 10 miles an hour over some main roads in dry weather.

Schools and teachers were few, and children seldom bothered to attend class even if a class was available. Curable illness was everywhere—pus dripping from children's eyes, ringworm eating away their hair, skin infections—things you didn't see in Malaysia.*

Sukarno spent a fortune on useless public showplaces in Djakarta—a skyscraper modern department store that did little business, numerous monuments (one topped with a small mountain of solid gold, supposedly in the shape of a flame but actually more resembling a human hand with the middle finger upraised), and the shell of a mammoth national mosque that he never completed.

Sukarno also established a police state. Every group of living units in Djakarta was assigned a block captain to keep track of the comings and goings of each resident. (After U.S. intervention, when General Suharto made Indonesia part of the free world again, these regulations were relaxed; residents were required to report to their block captains only if they did something unusual, like invite a guest over, or travel.)

---

*These observations were made in 1970, well after Sukarno's death, yet they were by all accounts valid for Sukarno's time. They certainly applied to the Suharto government, then in power, thanks to U.S. advisors and weapons. By 1970, we had kept Suharto in power five years and he had improved nothing, except to make peace with Malaysia and partially stabilize the rupiah.

Malaysia did have a couple of advantages over Indonesia unrelated to their forms of government. For one thing, British colonialism had given Malaysia much more in the way of public services—like roads, electric power, and schools—than Dutch colonialism gave Indonesia. For another, Malaysia was helped over the years by a large, gradual influx of Chinese, whose instinct for productive enterprise has made them a success in every country in Asia (except their own).

But neither of these excuses—the relative benefits of British colonialism, or the success-prone stock of Chinese settlers—is available to Marxist apologists for Indonesia, because Marxists don't recognize that colonial contributions or racial differences exist. Indonesia, which followed socialist notions, failed.

THAILAND wasn't colonized by anyone, and the Chinese aren't a big part of its economy. It succeeded, relatively speaking, because of the degree of free choice its people were allowed. Western-quality goods have appeared in towns throughout Thailand and have worked their way into the lives of the people. Even in farming areas, Thais are well-dressed, live in clean wooden houses often of two stories, and make meat or fish part of their daily diet. Television is common and radios, phonographs, and wristwatches almost universal.

In early morning and midafternoon the sidewalks fill with children in freshly ironed school uniforms and toting satchels of books. Not many kids are seen outside of school during school hours. Roads range from good to excellent by Third World standards, and are heavily used by trucks, modern buses, private passenger cars, and the ever-present motorcycles.

From across the border in socialist Burma, Thailand looks like paradise.* Thailand is the source of Burma's "luxuries"—everything from underwear to hair tonic. They are smuggled across the northern border to Mandalay and travel down to Rangoon. This black market, possibly the biggest in the world in terms of the percentage of national commerce it accounts for, makes the grim life in Burma bearable for those who aspire to more than the annual change of clothes that government rationing permits them, and who can pay the stiff mark-ups.

Army officers are best able to afford these luxuries, partly because they collect heavy bribes from the black marketeers. Army officers also have the most highly paid government job classifications in an economy in which the

---

*Although the author has traveled in Thailand as recently as 1982, my only journey through the two countries in sequence, for comparison, was in 1970. But the Burmese government then in power—ruled by General Ne Win—stayed in power until late in 1981, and its policies didn't change. Recent accounts suggest that this portrait remains accurate, and at any rate, conditions in 1970 reflect fairly on twenty years of socialism.

government is almost the sole employer. The piles of Burmese-produced dry goods available on the streets at night without rationing testify to enormous pilferage from textile plants. Workers often earn more stealing the products of their factories for resale through the black market than they receive in wages.

Civilian wages, low as they are, are paid in kyats (pronounced "chats") whose value on the black market is only one-third the official exchange rate declared by the government.* In an economy so heavily dependent on illegal trade, the citizens hurt most are farmers. Burma is 80 percent rural. The farmers are "the people" in whose name and for whose benefit the government allegedly communized commerce. But most farmers lack any access to the black market economy.

The streets of even major cities like Rangoon and Mandalay seem deserted by comparison with those of an average Thai town. The shops are relatively empty of goods, and except for some buses and a few cars in Rangoon, motorized transport is rare. The main means of getting about in Rangoon is the bicycle ricksha; in Mandalay it's a horse-drawn cart with passenger seats. Most vehicles on Burmese streets would be in museums in Thailand. In 1970, one could travel the 300-odd miles from Rangoon to Mandalay—Burma's main highway—and see only a few ancient trucks chugging along at 30 miles an hour, and not a single passenger car.

Construction, perhaps the most important bellweather of prosperity in any country, and certainly one of Thailand's most flourishing industries, seems moribund in Burma. Multistory buildings are few, steel and concrete scarce. The whole country gives a visitor the appearance of having gone out of business.

Though the government extols itself through its newspapers, and doesn't allow anyone to publish anything different, "the Burmese way to socialism" is a joke to the population. Ne Win and his associates made themselves one of the most despised governments in the world. When Westerners were allowed into the country in 1970 for the first time in many years (other than for a one-day layover in Rangoon), people either poured out their hostility against the regime or cautioned that discussions about politics weren't allowed. It was next to impossible to elicit a favorable comment about the government, even from the army officers who were supposed to be running it.

BY the late 1970s, the economic discrepancy between mostly free market Kenya and socialist Tanzania became so great that Tanzanian president Julius

---

*In 1970, the highest civilian wages, even for university graduates, were only about $15 a month. In 1983, some wages were reported nearing $100 a month, but, of course, much of the increase was due to inflation.

Nyerere felt compelled to close the border between the two countries. He explained that he didn't want his people contaminated by the "immoral" ideas they might get if they saw that other Africans owned cars, television sets, and wristwatches, while Tanzanians waited in line for bread.

Nyerere is an almost perfect example of the point at issue, because his failure can be blamed so singly and clearly on his ideology. Other than his belief in the one-party socialist development model, he has all the virtues that an Episcopalian missionary could have wished on him. He is bright, well-educated, hard-working, honest as the day is long, and, for a politician, he is almost humble—certainly not given to the kind of megalomania that destroyed Kwame Nkrumah in Ghana. The leftist prescription for nationhood could not have been pursued with greater rectitude than it was by Tanzania.

Nor could Tanzania complain, as Cuba could, for example, that U.S. embargoes and other hostile acts interfered with its economic growth. The U.S. and other Western countries *lavished* aid on Tanzania—food, construction projects, Peace Corps volunteers, and big bucks. The U.S., the U.S.S.R., China, Western Europe, and even Israel queued up to supply Nyerere with roads, railroads, ports, and machinery. Per capita, Tanzania has been one of the largest recipients of foreign aid in the world.

But the companies were nationalized, the banks were nationalized, and, most important in a chiefly agricultural country, the farms were nationalized. Hundreds of thousands of Tanzanians were resettled out of their traditional villages and onto government communes. Ironically, the process resembled nothing so much as the colonial practice of moving villagers into low-wage jobs as virtual slaves on foreign-owned plantations.

Under colonialism, the plantation system accomplished its purpose, which was to feed the colonizer, not the farmers. It wasn't fair, but it was efficient. Europeans who were making good money could enforce ruthless discipline to maintain high production of export crops. Afterward, the farmers or their families could go dig private gardens as necessary to ward off starvation.

As a method of central development planning, however, this system didn't work at all. Without colonial force, and with no incentives other than an occasional compliment from Nyerere, production slid. And since the communes were supposedly organized for feeding the people as well as for export, private plots weren't considered necessary, and there was often no practical way for plantation workers to have them. Essentially, people could increase neither their incomes nor their caloric intake by working harder. So they didn't.

Sudan is another centrally planned state, although instead of pursuing neutrality as Nyerere has, Sudan's socialist leaders have allied themselves militarily with the U.S. As an experiment, in 1982, Sudan's largest farm (owned by the government, of course) began to pay farmers on delivery for each bale of cotton produced, instead of waiting until the end of the season and paying each farmer an equal share of the commune's total receipts.

Under the new incentive system, production was reported up one-third in the first year, and growing by one-third more than that in the second.

Meanwhile, directly between Tanzania and Sudan, Kenyans have lived largely by market incentives since independence. Obviously, they have a better life at every percentile. Corruption among the leadership gives some an unfair advantage, but even without benefit of graft, a typical extended family in Kenya has its 20 acres or so (an extended family might include three or four grown brothers with wives and children and maybe a retired parent or two). Several members of the family also are likely to have jobs in town that contribute an average $100 a month per job, in addition to the farm income. The basics of life are assured to most people, and in Africa today that's a lot.

Some problems have yet to be faced in Kenya. Women continue to bear an average of eight children each. With modern health care delivered more widely, most of the children now grow up, and adults live longer. Annual population growth has risen to 4 percent, perhaps the world's largest. Suddenly, Kenya has become one of the few places in Africa where land is scarce, and the same 20 acres is going to have to support a lot more people in the future unless something is done.

The hunt for land threatens the animal herds, which are important not only as a heritage of mankind, but also because they help make tourism Kenya's third-largest industry. Tourist income is needed because the price of oil imports going up has already passed the price of coffee exports going down, leading to the new phenomena of trade deficits in the 1980s.

The years 1982 and 1983 also saw the reversal of the political liberalization that followed the death of national founder Jomo Kenyatta in 1978. Kenyatta had become a corrupt dicatator who biased national development toward members of his own Kikuyu tribe. His successor, Daniel Arap Moi, a non-Kikuyu, began by preaching national unity and freeing political prisoners. But eventually, he clamped down on dissent, and moved to straightjacket what had been one of the most vibrant free presses in the Third World.

For all their problems, though, Kenyans seemed to have learned from their Tanzanian neighbors that Marxism doesn't hold the answers. Says a sociology professor at the University of Nairobi, Kenya, "They [the Tanzanians] condemn our systems and say we are exploited, but they come begging to us for food. They come here to shop. They are just mismanaged." Now that the Kenyan-Tanzanian border is closed, Tanzanians must sneak into Kenya through Uganda in order to buy and sell in a productive economy. They do it.

Uganda has its own problems. In 1978, Nyerere's army helped rid Uganda of Idi Amin, a lunatic terrorist of a dictator. Amin had overthrown the elected government of Milton Obote in a coup in 1971. But with Amin gone, Nyerere simply reinstalled his old friend, Obote. While certainly an improvement over Amin, Obote still subscribed to Nyerere's original concept of the one-party socialist state as a road to Third World development.

Philip C. Githongo, a Kenyan who works at Union Carbide's Eveready battery plant in Kenya, says, "Nyerere and Obote tell Kenyans they are downtrodden masses and being exploited. It's the Tanzanians and Ugandans who suffer, under a system that produces nothing. They make people work in communes and nothing comes out."

PERHAPS the most influential thinker in the transfer of Marxist ideas to the Third World was Frantz Fanon, an Algerian whose works are not nearly so widely read today as they were in the 1960s—perhaps because history has proved them so wrong. Fanon tried to adapt Marxism to the Third World as Lenin's prerevolutionary writing had adapted it to twentieth century Europe. He became a darling of the New Left.

Fanon's most famous work was *The Wretched of the Earth*, in which he spoke of "the necessity for a planned economy, the outlawing of profiteers." He wrote, "In a colonial economy, the intermediary [retail] sector is by far the most important. If you want to progress, you must decide in the first few hours to nationalize this sector.... Nationalizing the intermediary sector means organizing wholesale and retail cooperatives on a democratic basis."

A few years after Fanon wrote those words, the West African country of Mali put them into practice. In every town, one or two government stores were established. Lines quickly stretched the length of a city block. After waiting up to two hours, the shopper reached the clerk, who stood between a wooden counter and the few shelves of sample articles. One could choose from among ten to fifteen items, usually no more than one brand of each: tinned tomato paste and sardines; bulk rice, onions, peppers, salt, and garlic; packaged soap and dry noodles; bottled oil and kerosene. And every store offered the same two toys, and only two: a sparking machine gun and a wind-up train, both imported from China. And that was it.

Yet in those same towns were stores, suddenly closed by government decree, where the traditional wide range of trading goods had been set out, where customers had been able to walk in and buy what they wanted, choosing from a variety of brands, sizes, and prices. Item for item the cost of shopping had been no more than what the government stores were charging, maybe a bit less.

The private stores were mostly owned by French expatriates. But they were almost all men and women committed to making Mali their home. Months after they were forced to shut their doors, they still sat, lonely and betrayed, in what had been their shops. Unsold merchandise, not available in government outlets, just gathering dust on shelves around them.

French expatriates had gained an unfair advantage during colonization, and the Malian government understandably might have wanted to help other citizens overcome this advantage. But if this had been the government's purpose, more reasonable programs could have been attempted. For example, the government might have opened a chain of franchised stores with local citizens applying or bidding for rights to the franchises.

Franchisees might then have bought their stores by making scheduled payments to the government from profits. No profits, no franchise—thus assuring that if a manager didn't compete successfully in the marketplace, someone else would get a crack at running his store. Meanwhile, the franchisees would have competed with existing stores, and the competition might have helped to weed out whatever inefficiency or unfairness was present in the existing ownership system.

But by banning all private stores—the so-called profiteers—the government worsened living conditions for everyone. It reduced its citizens' freedom of choice. It put direction of retail merchandising—the power to judge quality and price—into the hands of distant bureaucrats who had no means of testing customer preferences and no reason to respond to those preferences anyway.

Parallels existed elsewhere. There was the half-empty government department store in Djakarta, Indonesia—what a contrast to the bustling, competitive shops of Kuala Lumpur, Lagos, and Singapore! There were the ludicrous nationalized nightclubs in Baghdad, once boisterous belly-dancing salons, where now a handful of mirthless customers rattled around, invariably outnumbered by machine gun-toting army guards.

The issue is not simply public versus private. The productive economies of Malaysia, Taiwan, and Singapore have benefited from considerable government participation. On Taiwan, especially, the government intervened to make sure that much of the economy's profit was spread to the poorest parts of the countryside via large public works—hydroelectric projects and good schools, for example. This intervention helped keep production high, by maintaining morale among farmers who might not otherwise have participated in the industrial boom.

Government intervention under Marxist socialism is obviously very different. The problem with these radical governments is that instead of attacking poverty, they invariably wind up attacking only wealth. Some government intervention is generally necessary in order to attack poverty, especially after decades or centuries of feudal accumulations of wealth. Monopolies must be restrained and competition encouraged. Industrious individuals need access to land or other means of production to show what they can turn out. Marxism, though, has almost invariably brought about the vengeful destruction of productive power, not the thoughtful redistribution of it.

The limitations of Marxism are felt in its Soviet heartland, not just in Third World countries. The poor quality of Soviet production is renowned, and anyone traveling through the Soviet Union can see it. The respected publication *Africa Confidential** reported in 1979:

*Though *Africa Confidential* articles are unsigned, I was by chance able to authenticate this passage with its author; while discussing socialism at a restaurant in San Salvador

"Several African states have complained that the U.S.S.R. unloads inferior quality goods in exchange for its raw material imports. Others have entered into bitter business quarrels. For example, Sékou Touré [longtime socialist president of Guinea] was dismayed by the low prices for bauxite paid by the Russians—$6 a ton compared with $23 per ton from American companies. Guinea-Bissau [a neighboring country, also socialist, created from a Portuguese colony] has three times angrily demanded a renegotiation of its fishing agreement with Moscow. Mauritania has repeatedly protested against overfishing by Soviet fleets in its waters. So, more recently, has Mozambique. Since the overthrow of Francisco Macias Nguema in Equatorial Guinea, the new authorities in Malabo have sharply denounced Soviet application of the fishing regulations agreed between the two countries. Statements by the new government have been virulently anti-Russian. 'They leave us with only a few sardines,' now says the fishing ministry."

Cubans, both government officials and average families, readily acknowledge the inferior quality of Soviet imports. While people are glad to have stereo sets, or washing machines, the availability of only one rather tacky-looking model, and its propensity to break down, take the edge off the pleasure. Much of our enjoyment of material goods springs from choice and spontaneity, which the Marxist system shuts off.

When *New York Times* columnist Anthony Lewis went to Mozambique in 1982, he was besieged with pleas for more trade with the United States. "There is no doubt here about the capacity and efficiency of American companies," one official told him. "And there is no ideological obstacle. We want [to explore for] oil not for its own sake, but to develop the country and especially to increase trade with the United States."

In May 1983, Mozambican president Samora M. Machel, a big supporter of socialism when he was fighting the Portuguese for independence, and in the years immediately afterward, made some stunning admissions. "We have erroneously developed a hostile attitude to private enterprise that must be changed," he announced. "Our country must undertake a profound reorganization starting with the government itself"—whereupon he slashed the government payroll in urban areas, and sent workers out to the countryside. His intention was to encourage private enterprise farming.

THERE is only one reason why a country would want to adopt Marxist-socialism today. Unfortunately, it is often a valid reason. Marxism-socialism is often the only way a country can avoid American imperialism. Joining the Soviet arms network is often the only way to have a national government

---

in 1983, I recalled the passage to Susan Morgan, my dinner companion and then a reporter for *Newsweek*, who revealed that she had written it while working in Africa a few years earlier.

that is independent of CIA manipulation, and that stands a chance of bargaining at arm's length with multinational corporations.

A great irony is at work. The philosophers of both systems have generally preached that Marxism seeks economic improvement for the majority, while the free market is concerned with such noble ideas as human dignity and the worth of the individual. In the debate, the fact of a billion empty bellies is normally juxtaposed against the principles contained in the U.S. Declaration of Independence and Bill of Rights. Marxists contend that political liberty is a luxury that only the rich can use, and only by exploiting the poor. The democracies insist that man cannot live by bread alone.

Yet out in the world, the exact opposite applies. It is the U.S. that offers pure materialism. The alleged economic benefits of socialism are a joke to practically everybody. The only attraction the Soviets have is the offer of national dignity and independence. Of course, this offer is ultimately phony, and the Soviets seek to impose their control just as we seek to impose ours.

But for a couple of reasons, the Soviet threat often seems less frightening. For one thing, it is an unknown threat. So it may seem worth accepting, as a price for protection against the known reality of U.S. intervention. For another, the Soviets have shown themselves far less efficient at imposing and maintaining control than the U.S. has.

Except in areas contiguous to Soviet borders, where the might of Soviet ground forces can be brought to bear, Soviet personnel have generally given up and gone home when a nationalist or U.S.-imposed government has asked them to. Doubtless this is more the result of military incapability than of political good faith. But either way, it stacks up as less threatening than the U.S. record. As we have seen in country after country, the U.S. has rarely been tolerant of any sentiments contrary to its own. The first scent of national divergence has quickly evoked repression by covert or overt U.S. military action, even in a country like Iran, on the Soviet border.

The need for protection from U.S. intervention is what has given the Soviet Union the world influence we complain about. Just go down the list of countries that are constantly described as being "in the Soviet orbit." Many, of course, are Eastern European countries that were conquered by the Soviet army in World War II; that is a tragedy one hopes can some day be redressed, but the situation has not proven itself a continuing threat to other countries. North Korea was another World War II conquest. Then there is Afghanistan, on the Soviets' southern border, which has been overtly invaded and is resisting.

Beyond that, it is hard to find any Soviet "orbiters" that didn't get that way voluntarily, for nationalistic reasons, and that wouldn't leave the Soviet sphere if these nationalistic problems could be resolved. They are countries seeking protection for themselves or their close brethren, either from the U.S. directly, or from the real or perceived U.S. presence in Israel and South Africa.

Angola and Mozambique started off Marxist for one reason only: the U.S.

was supplying weapons to its NATO ally, Portugal, which was killing and enslaving the Angolans and Mozambicans. The Soviet Union offered an unarmed and unsophisticated people weapons to fight for their independence, and an ideology that purported to explain their colonial oppression.

Meanwhile, the United States turned its back on its own history, and tried to rationalize this oppression. When the Portuguese gave up, the U.S. tried to replace them, at least in Angola, with a longtime CIA operative who had almost no support among the people. What was any right-thinking patriot in these countries supposed to do?

And now there is pressure on the Angolan and Mozambican governments to stay nominally Marxist for the same kind of nationalistic reasons. The movement toward majority rule in South Africa is precious to blacks throughout Africa, probably the single foreign issue most of them are much aware of. Angola and Mozambique are naturally in the forefront of African support for this cause, both by geography and by the recentness of their own violent struggle for nationhood.

Because of this, South Africa has both countries under violent attack. Neither Angola nor Mozambique has any reason to hope the U.S. will provide protection or support, even moral. There is, in fact, much reason to believe that the U.S. is already intervening *against* them, and against the movement toward majority rule in South Africa—a movement that is not only inevitable, but that is in accord with the principles the United States has enunciated since the day of its founding.

U.S. intervention against this movement not only makes a Soviet alliance attractive to Angola and Mozambique, but it invites a Soviet liaison with the inevitable black government of South Africa itself. South Africa is the richest country and most promising trading partner on the continent. The only way we can lose it is by voluntarily making ourselves the enemy of its future leaders, whoever they turn out to be. The most likely leaders are being shot at with American guns today.

Beyond such practical considerations, it is hard to believe that the American people would knowingly choose to support a government run by a tiny minority of the population, a minority that brutally forces the nonwhite majority to live in segregated, second-class housing in undesirable areas, to send their children to grossly inferior schools, to forego the most desirable jobs regardless of their qualifications, and to be paid much less than whites for the jobs they *can* have, regardless of their productivity. This isn't our kind of government, but the Henry Kissingers of the world have got us defending it.

If the understandable nationalistic ambitions of southern Africans could be pursued without U.S. opposition, the Soviets would have little to offer and would soon be gone. Genuine U.S. diplomatic cooperation with South African blacks in trying to achieve these just ambitions peacefully would probably create more friends for us than shiploads of Soviet arms could create for the U.S.S.R. Certainly such cooperation would do most to encourage the development of free institutions in South Africa, something sorely lacking for 85 percent of its people today.

United States policy, with its intervention for and against mislabeled causes, has convinced millions of South Africans that they are living under capitalism, and that only socialism will liberate them. The truth is they are suffering under a state-controlled—state socialist—economy, and the very things they seek are the gifts of a free market. If the United States doesn't show it to them, who will?

FOR many years, Ethiopia and Somalia have traded off the U.S. and U.S.S.R. as patrons in their long war against each other, over the disputed border territories of Eritrea and Ogaden. Ethiopians have the greater grudge against the U.S., because of long decades of American military support for their brutal and corrupt dictator, Haile Selassie.

Selassie gained an undeserved good reputation in the U.S., thanks to the historical accident that Ethiopia was invaded by Italy in 1935. Somehow, the image of Selassie as an underdog fighting off giants stuck with him, even after he in fact became a giant fighting off underdogs. When Selassie was overthrown in 1974, the U.S. was tossed out of Ethiopia as part of his baggage. This is what Henry Kissinger called Soviet-Cuban encroachment in the "Horn of Africa."

Selassie's replacements had been forced to resort to the Soviet Union for arms and ideas all during their long struggle against him. They weren't about to switch patrons as they redirected their struggle against Somalia, and an Eritrean independence movement. The Ethiopian government's new link with the Soviets, of course, forced the Somalians to kick the Soviets out, and to seek a *U.S.* alliance. What does this have to do with Marxism, or a Soviet military threat to the West? Very little, except that the Soviets built a good naval base in Berbera, Somalia, and now we're using it to protect our Middle Eastern oil shipping.

ALGERIA had to fight for independence against a U.S. ally (France). Iraq's longtime antagonist, Iran, was armed and supported by the U.S. Both Algeria and Iraq were thus driven into Soviet attachments. Both show signs of wanting to shed those attachments now, but there remains the problem of their Islamic allegiance to Palestinian nationalism (and for Algeria, the problem of U.S. military support for its expansionist neighbor, Morocco).

The Palestinian nationalists were also driven into the "Soviet orbit," by U.S. support for their perceived enemy, Israel. Yasir Arafat is clearly a one-issue politician. With a Palestinian-Israeli settlement, Palestinian nationalists wouldn't need the Soviets anymore. Syria wouldn't, either. Without a settlement, a Soviet liaison remains, but it is geographically limited, and results from the U.S. choice to underwrite Israel.*

All these Soviet friendships lack fundamental support in the sense of shared values, or long-term mutual interests; they are based on local exigencies. They don't necessarily threaten the U.S. at all. Turmoil is a cause for concern, but if the U.S. would focus on protecting its legitimate trading interests in these areas, instead of imagining a global conspiracy aimed at the White House, the problems seem happily manageable. The level of violence might even be reduced to the benefit of everyone. And U.S. values—free politics and free markets—would be more respected by all, and perhaps even emulated by some.

READERS of Latin American history should have no trouble understanding why countries like Nicaragua would fear the U.S., and seek protection from the Soviets. Despite many attempts, the only government in the area to raise the least exception to U.S. domination and survive the inevitable onslaught has been Cuba's.

Back in Jimmy Carter's time, when the U.S. maintained a bit more perspective on the Latin front, Jamaica was allowed its flirtation with socialism, and eventually rejected it. Without belligerence from Washington, the socialist experiment never became chained to the buoy of Jamaican nationalist pride, and, therefore, sank.

Cuba would be a tougher nut to crack, because of the billions of dollars it receives in Soviet aid. In Asia, Vietnam would be a tougher nut still. The craters of U.S. bombs are only recently dug into Vietnamese soil. Moreover, Vietnam perceives a need to counterbalance the Chinese giant on its northern border, and thus wants arms, which the Soviet Union supplies.

Still, in the long run, the world's biggest economy, the U.S., is 90 miles off Cuba's shore, whereas the Soviet Union is half a world away and can't even take care of its own people. It's hard to believe that the natural economic relationship between the U.S. and Cuba wouldn't redevelop if Cuba could stop fearing for its independence. And the Vietnamese have hinted that they, too, want to move toward normal commercial relations with the U.S.— although their belligerence in taking over all of Indochina, and their brutality in running it, doesn't particularly recommend Vietnam as a trading partner if alternative suppliers and markets are available.

Among the Soviet "orbiters," then, that leaves only Muammar Qaddafi as much of a soulmate. And the Russians can have him. (Would *you* want to depend on Qaddafi?) For the time being, Qaddafi is willing to—in fact,

---

*There are strong cultural and moral reasons for making this choice, and the purpose of this book isn't served by getting into the merits or demerits of those reasons. The important point is that the decision, with its consequences, was and is a U.S. choice.

needs to—sell the West his oil, which is the main U.S. concern with Libya. Some day, in the process of shooting himself in the foot, Qaddafi will probably wound himself fatally, and another leader might bring Libya into a more rational policy.

The U.S. seems to have excellent intelligence out of Libya, which allows it to intercept arms shipments and departing terrorist squads pretty routinely. At least, after a decade of Qaddafi, the known damage seems relatively minuscule, and if it worsened, then overt rather than covert action might be widely accepted, perhaps even with broad international sanction.

Washington, of course, insists on seeing Libya as a threat to all Africa. So far, Libya's only invasion has been of Chad. To undertake this, Qaddafi had to hire the layoff list from the CIA, and even then, he failed. If you can't even conquer Chad, a barren stretch of scrub whose defenders are mostly on horseback and preoccupied with looking for the next waterhole, what kind of conquerer are you?

IT should not be surprising that needless U.S. intervention leads to popular resentment of the U.S. And this, of course, can be marshaled into support for local leaders, sincere or demagogic, who choose to exploit it. The hostility the U.S. sometimes finds overseas isn't hostility toward the U.S. *system*, or toward the U.S. people as they exist at home. It is hostility toward U.S. *foreign policy*, which usually has nothing to do with the U.S. system.

What we send abroad with our covert and overt military intervention doesn't resemble democracy or free markets in the slightest. No organization can be more socialistic and antidemocratic than an army, even the American one, and even if it dresses in civvies like the CIA. When our forces intervene, local people don't see the flag of individual liberty; they see one more meddlesome government bureaucracy, and it's not even theirs.

Often our main economic contribution to a country is the sale of weapons. These sales are encumbered by all sorts of government regulation and involvement (mostly for good reason, of course—weapons are dangerous) that is uncharacteristic of a free economy. Our concentration on the sale of weapons, and even of major civil development projects, is a concentration on goods bought by governments. Therefore, the sales enhance the socialist part of the purchasing country's economy, which is counterproductive to our supposed goal.

We continue to press not our system, which encourages free choice, but some convoluted notion of our system, which imposes *our* choice. We insist on imposing solutions to particular problems involving foreign people. They are asked to live by our choices, when they often don't want or even understand them. Nor do American voters understand, or necessarily want, the kind of administration that our colonial bureaucrats bring to the countries we take over.

The government of El Salvador that started dragging the U.S. into its civil war in 1980 had, since taking power in a coup in October 1979, seized control of the country's banks, and nationalized exports of coffee, cotton, and sugar. When an organization of wealthy businessmen, mostly from the oligarchy, protested in July 1981 that these "structural reforms" were wreaking havoc with the economy, the U.S.-backed government granted the businessmen a request: it froze the wages of Salvadoran workers. At the same time, however, it continued controls on rents; school tuition; fees charged by doctors, ophthalmologists, and dentists, and for hospital services; and the prices of rice, corn, sugar, and beans.*

Boy, the Marxist guerrillas would sure have to put on their thinking caps to top all that!

As the war ground on, American liberals made a hero of the former U.S. ambassador to El Salvador, Robert White, who spoke out for continuing the land redistribution and other U.S.-designed reforms; this was after the Salvadoran voters, who weren't allowed to vote for anyone on the left, defeated the "moderate" candidates Reagan was pushing, and chose instead a far-right constituent assembly. This assembly was proceeding to undo the reforms, which White and other Americans had created.

So Reagan switched, and backed the election winners. He probably never considered the possibility that the reason the right wing won was that it presented the only opportunity for local voters to express their disagreement with having the U.S. run their country. So now the U.S. was supporting a dismantling of the "reforms" it had coerced the previous Salvadoran government into enacting. And White and other liberals called for coercing the new government into reinstituting the reforms.

White's reforms certainly were kinder to most Salvadorans than some of the bloodthirsty alternatives being offered. But at bottom, White was still taking the same position that his adversaries were—namely, that the United States could run El Salvador better than El Salvador could.

If that sounds like a reasonable proposition, consider Chile. After the U.S. played a large, but not precisely known, role in dumping the socialist government of Salvador Allende, the U.S. brought in the University of Chicago economics department to run the place. The most eloquent description of what happened after that comes from Everett G. Martin of the *Wall Street Journal*.

Reporter Martin had been in the forefront of chronicling the economic damage done under Allende's socialist policies (much of the damage, we now know, was caused by CIA sabotage). He had even entered a long-running editorial debate with Allende's mourners, insisting that the shortcomings of the overthrown government not be forgotten. In other words, Martin is no apologist for the Left, and, in fact, gave the new Pinochet junta

---

*Story by Raymond Bonner in the *New York Times*, July 2, 1981.

the most favorable send-off it could have had from an objective press.

But on January 18, 1982, Martin wrote from Santiago:

"This country's plunge into a free-market economy is in serious trouble, the worst since the experiment began eight years ago. Almost daily, more factories go bankrupt, copper mines and construction projects close, and farms go on the auction block. Some smaller cities have been left without a single industry. Bankers struggle to deal with mountains of bad debts; the government had to act in November to save eight financial institutions from collapse.

"Unemployment climbs sharply.... The seventy-four-year-old head of Chile's Roman Catholic church, Cardinal Raul Silva Henriquez, who receives reports from Church parishes all over the country, tells an interviewer, 'I could be wrong, but never in my long life have I seen such a disastrous economic situation.'" That lifetime obviously encompassed the elected socialist, Allende, who was operating under the handicap of President Nixon's order to the CIA to "make the [Chilean] economy scream"; now, Pinochet had the U.S.'s earnest help. In fact, Martin wrote in the *Journal*:

"The critics' prime target is the reclusive finance minister, Sergio de Castro, fifty-one. He heads an economic team called the Chicago boys because so many of its members trained at the University of Chicago under Milton Friedman, the Nobel Prize-winning economist who champions free enterprise."

We rescued Chile from the socialists, all right. Then we did even worse to it ourselves.

WHEN it comes to foreign affairs, the U.S. is no kinder to itself than to others—witness the policy (discussed earlier) of attacking the Russians, after their Afghanistan invasion, by clobbering the U.S. grain market (and making the taxpayers pay). U.S. industry next felt the sting of our anti-Soviet wrath when President Reagan decided we shouldn't help build a natural gas pipeline that our European allies desperately wanted (the pipeline would allow them to buy Soviet natural gas as an alternative to Arab oil).

Reagan ordered American companies to cancel the contracts they had won to help supply the pipeline project. The supposed justification for this was that the Soviets were using compulsory labor to work on the pipeline. This was a remarkable discovery—communists use "slave labor." It was as if no one had noticed that this is the way communism operates.

Even Cuba, which makes extraordinary efforts (for a communist state) to accommodate individual preferences, requires some people to work at jobs they don't want to do; the Soviet Union has never been known for going out of its way to accommodate individual idiosyncrasies. The worst offender of all is probably China, and the U.S. was sending the Chinese equipment with direct military application.

But on the discovery that Soviet pipeline workers were being exploited, the U.S. government robbed the Caterpillar Tractor Company of a contract to get $90 million of Russian money, and General Electric Company of a contract to get $175 million of Russian money (this in the middle of a recession). The government also got into fights with our French and Italian allies by trying to pressure *them* into turning back Russian money for products made in Europe with U.S. parts.

On the other hand, the government of Guatemala, not exactly a model of decorum, received from the U.S. a $135 million guarantee in taxpayer funds for a project Texaco was embarking on there. In 1981, two Democratic congressmen threatened that unless the Guatemalan government stopped murdering its citizens, they would start a congressional debate over the guarantee. Texaco promptly announced that it was dropping its application for the guarantee, in order to stop the embarrassment to itself and to the Guatemalan government.

In this case, Texaco said it would go ahead with the project on its own— a bald admission that the guarantee wasn't necessary in the first place. It was just a needless taxpayer subsidy, voted for on the ground that it would help Guatemala fight communism, when obviously it was mainly helping Texaco avoid the kind of risk that smaller capitalists have to take when investing their money.

Despite the well-grounded opinion of some congressmen that it was too brutal, the Guatemalan dictatorship continued to receive U.S. government support, financial and military. Costa Rica, though, which was behaving the way we say we *want* countries to behave, was getting hell from us. In 1981, T. D. Allman, writing in *Harper's* magazine, made the wonderful point that there were only two countries in Central America where a citizen could feel safe walking the streets and going about his business. They were Belize and Costa Rica—the only two countries in Central America that had no armies.

Costa Rica dissolved its army thirty years ago. It is a democracy that has chosen leaders who roughly adhere to U.S. ideals of civil liberties and human rights, at least more than other countries in the region. But instead of trying to keep it independent and peaceful, the U.S. has seemed bent on bringing Costa Rica into the turmoil that has enveloped its neighbors.

With U.S. aid, Nicaraguan exiles who were fighting to overthrow the Sandinista government in Nicaragua began operating from Costa Rican soil. The Costa Rican bases may have been handy, logistically, but they made Costa Rica part of the war, and opened it to retaliation. To counter the expected dose of regional violence, Jeane Kirkpatrick, the U.S. delegate to the United Nations and a favorite foreign policy advisor of the president's, suggested having the U.S. beef up Costa Rica's security by providing military training to its police. Leaders of both the Costa Rican government and the opposition angrily rejected that idea. A more heavily armed police, they said, would simply have increased Costa Rica's involvement, and therefore *weakened* its security.

Meanwhile, Americans helped undermine Costa Rican stability further by springing the IMF debt trap on the country. The world recession had battered the prices of Costa Rica's major export crops—coffee, bananas, sugar, and meat. Meanwhile, oil import costs had risen to $220 million a year. The Costa Rican government needed a $60 million loan from the IMF in 1982, to meet payments, already in arrears, on the country's $2.7 billion foreign debt (mostly owed to Western banks). To get the loan, the government was required to halt subsidies on in-country sales of exportable food. So Costa Rican grocery bills shot up.

The IMF offered a few hundred million more—which would mostly wind up right back in the pockets of the Western bankers, of course—if the government would double water, electricity, and telephone rates, and increase fuel prices by 70 percent and interest rates by 40 percent.*

As a result, the overall inflation rate in Costa Rica rose to 40 percent, and unemployment doubled, exceeding 10 percent. Small businesses were collapsing in bankruptcy. The *New York Times* quoted "a foreign diplomat" marveling at how docile the people remained through all this. "There haven't even been protest marches about the cost of living," the diplomat said. "Everyone is just waiting for the next government to solve the crisis."

Still trusting in democracy, are they? We'll show them. And if they finally do rebel, the State Department will blame it on Cuba.

OUR intervention via international financial institutions like the IMF and World Bank is much like our intervention through covert and overt military operations. Both kinds of "aid" strengthen central governments overseas without necessarily improving the *quality* of those governments. Both kinds of "aid" tend to concentrate power in existing leaders, and suck away what little power has been left in the hands of individuals, and in small businesses and living units.

We misunderstand our own message to the world. We misunderstand the source of our strength, our prosperity, and our freedom. The distinction between private and state enterprise is not what is fundamental to American achievement. Our achievement is based on a division of power.

We divide power throughout our society. The powers of government are divided among federal, state, and local units. At each level, power is divided among the executive, the legislature, and courts. Even so, government doesn't play nearly so great a role in the U.S. as we encourage it to play overseas. Most decisions here are barred to government. Many decisions are reserved to each individual to make for himself. Others are relegated to professionally competent authorities: within broad social guidelines that are politically or-

---

*Figures from Interlink Press Service. Judging from other published material, they are at least in the ballpark. The IMF doesn't disclose loan terms.

dained, doctors guide the day-to-day functioning of their own profession, as do accountants, plumbers, English literature professors, and (there's a hair in every pudding) lawyers.

In the business field, what has distinguished American society has been not only its Rockefellers, but its ability to *restrain* its Rockefellers, and to preserve open competition. What has distinguished us is not only our Standard Oils, but our ability to *break up* our Standard Oils. Monopolistic controls have been allowed to persist mostly in foreign dealings, through influence over the State Department, not the Justice Department.

The open chance for small business to grow, for the eccentric with a gift to become an entrepreneur, for the individual farmer to figure out a better way of planting or marketing, has been a lifeblood of our system. Equally so has been the power of consumers, individually or banded voluntarily together, to contain the excesses of large and small business.

The strength of American ingenuity is not just that it invented so much, but that when some of its products turned out to be dioxin and leaky nuclear power plants, concerned groups arose and quickly obtained enough influence to thwart the spread of the suspect products. As evidence has mounted that existing regulatory structures are inadequate, both industry and consumer groups have produced heavy hitters to debate the creation of new ones. Every General Motors has its Ralph Nader, and vice-versa, and the public can judge who happens to be talking the most sense at any given moment.

Yet overseas such dissent isn't possible. The drugs and insecticides we ban from the marketplace as unsafe are quickly shipped to Africa, Asia, and Latin America for sale there on the street. Boys on the streets of Lagos, Nigeria, carry trays on their heads bearing cans of bug spray with the labels of major U.S. oil companies on them, and no listing of ingredients. When the U.S. Food and Drug Administration outlawed cyclamate as a potential cancer-causer, a million and a half cases of Bristol-Myers Company and Carnation Company products containing cyclamate were shipped to Africa.

Like so many other things we do in the Third World, this "dumping" of dangerous products seems at first glance to be someone else's problem. But, in fact, it returns to be ours. The carcinogenic insecticides we send abroad come back to us in our coffee, and other imported food products. The counterbalancing powers that protect us at home don't exist in most countries.

The importers overseas who make money from what the U.S. sends abroad frequently operate with monopolistic authority granted by nondemocratic governments. Bribes may have been paid to secure the operating authority. There is no vehicle for complaint. There is no competition. Overseas, we allow no small shoots to flower. We will not recognize healthy tensions. We distinguish only two great camps. We help Ferdinand Marcos eliminate any challenge to his absolute authority. On Fidel Castro, we train our rifle sights.

* * *

FOR more than 650 miles, the Congo River and its tributary, the Ubangi, divide two African countries of great contrasts. On the northwestern bank is the People's Republic of Congo, which in 1963 proclaimed itself the first Marxist-Leninist state in Africa. It still flaunts that label. Across the river to the southeast is Zaire, a drumbeating Western ally.

It isn't surprising, therefore, that people constantly cross the river seeking economic freedom. For example, a Belgian, who wishes to be identified only as "Jimmy," crossed the river to avoid a state takeover of his paint business, which he has reestablished on the opposite bank. (He imports chemicals from Western Europe and mixes and sells paints locally.)

And a wealthy Bakongo tribesman, who doesn't wish to be identified at all, crosses the river every couple of weeks with hankies full of diamonds, so he can sell them on the competitive market instead of to a state-controlled monopoly.

What the American foreign policy establishment might find hard to understand, however, is the *direction* in which these people, and many others, cross the river. They are leaving the purportedly free capitalist country of Zaire, which is, in fact, a totalitarian state that seeks to control all economic activity above the subsistence level. And they are coming to the purportedly communist country of Congo, which, in fact, has discovered the benefits of the free market.

The Congo isn't, of course, a democratic or laissez-faire country. Like Zaire, it is a one-party state with a controlled press, and regional administrators who are appointed by the central government. A corporation that started to become a dominant force would soon find the government getting involved. But both economically and politically, the Congo is much freer than Zaire. Zairian political exiles make homes in the Congo and dream of one day returning to "liberate" their own country. For now, American firepower stalls those dreams. It is the same firepower that established the Mobutu dictatorship to start with.

The contrast between the Congo and Zaire reflects a worldwide disparity between big-power perceptions and local actualities. As local politicians have sought foreign patrons, and the U.S.S.R. and United States have sought local clients, labels have been stuck all over the globe that are quite inappropriate to the countries that bear them.

The long American misperception of Iran as a Western-style country, when in fact it never was one, led to a tragic breakdown of relations between two nations that basically need each other, both for economic health and for protection against the Soviets. Now the same kind of mislabeling threatens to create new Irans in Zaire and other places, which, like Iran, have vital mineral resources.

Despite its pro-Western label, the Zairian government spurns Western values. Government boards claim monopoly rights to all mineral resources. Marketing constraints discourage agricultural production. The controls can be beaten, if at all, only by those rich enough to bribe their way through. The Zairian form of government was described by one Peace Corps volunteer there as a "kleptocracy."

By contrast, the Congo allows considerable free commerce. "Here there is no trouble," says Jimmy, who has been in the paint business in Africa for thirty-eight years. "The government encourages investment. Here I am a socialist and a communist and a capitalist. The people are"—and up goes his thumb. He is so happy in the Congo, he says, that he recently bought a bar and restaurant in the capital city of Brazzaville, and has encouraged his son, just finishing school in Europe, to settle in Brazzaville and run it.

True, over the years the Congo has cooperated with the U.S.S.R. It funneled arms to the MPLA movement, later the government, in Angola (which has its own questionable pro-Soviet label). But Congolese citizens don't look furtively about for secret police when they speak, the way Zairians do. As Nicole Brenier, economic officer at the U.S. embassy, puts it, "They are Marxists, but not living like Marxists. Nothing is Marxist in the culture here. They are living like capitalists." Adds John Archibald, another U.S. diplomat in the Congo, "It's like day and night with Zaire. The economy here is working. The people are happy. The policy is very pragmatic. They're not dumb. Who needs enemies?"

From the moment one passes cordially through customs, one senses that the Congo is largely free of the corruption and routine restriction that plague Zaire. No one has his hand out to the Zairian traders who have bribed their own officials for permission to cross the river. They travel by ferry from Kinshasa, or by boat in the remote jungles upriver. Whole bargeloads of Zairian coffee reach the open Congolese market.

The hard currency from this trade is lost to the Zairian nation and its Western creditors. The IMF watchdog team, with its copious financial regulations, merely encourages illegal trading. Many Zairian smugglers keep their money in Brazzaville, to avoid the exchange controls at home.

Persons who enter Zaire with foreign cash are given accounting forms, and must register every conversion at a bank. Anyone who dares the law by converting on the black market can obtain about twice as many Zaires for the dollar as Mobutu's banks will pay. In the Congo, currency exchange is free. The local currency, the CFA, is tied to the French franc. It is so solid that most people prefer it to dollars, and merchants generally offer an exchange rate slightly *less* than is available in banks, on the theory that they are performing a service by taking foreign money.

At the insistence of Western creditors, cobalt must now be airlifted from Zairian mines to Europe at great cost. When cobalt was shipped by river, too much was offloaded illegally in the Congo, where Western and Soviet dealers are allowed to bid competitively for it. Diamonds are too small to control, so they still flow. "We do quite a big business," says the branch manager of Brazzaville Diamonds, one of the competing European-based companies that operate in the Congo (which has no known diamond deposits of its own). "Obviously, we have to keep a very low profile, but it's all quite legitimate [with the Congo government]," he says.

While Zaire receives financial aid from U.S. taxpayers, the Congo doesn't, and not just because of its "communist" label. With a per capita gross national product exceeding $500, the Congolese are simply too *rich* to qualify for U.S. aid. In Zaire, which is potentially much wealthier, per capita GNP hangs around $150.

One quick gauge of an economy is the restaurant trade. Zaire, where malnutrition is a leading cause of death, has strikingly few public eating places. Of course, it has European-style restaurants with New York-level prices for foreigners and the very wealthy. But ordinary people just can't afford the extra 25 cents or so that it would cost to consume their manioc and beer in convivial surroundings with someone to serve it, instead of at home. When you do find a local restaurant, $1 or $1.50 will get you only a watery soup with one or two scraps of meat to flavor your manioc.

Many people dine out in the Congo, where small restaurants abound, and where approximately the same $1.50 will buy a thick stew with six or eight pieces of meat big enough to cut with a knife, or a whole quarter of a chicken. In such restaurants, one finds people like Jerome, an auto mechanic who earns about $340 a month working for a local car dealership; or Joseph, a freelance welder who pulls in about $85 a month; or tailors, teachers, and others with salaries in the hundreds of dollars. Rarely do salaries in Zaire, even for college graduates, exceed $80 a month, and most people can't find salaried work. Congolese university students get a monthly living allowance of $140 a month; Zairian students, $25.

Moreover, prices in the Congo are substantially lower. A bolt of print cloth from a local textile factory goes for about $18 in the Brazzaville market; in Kinshasa, identical cloth, which has to be imported from Europe, runs $75 or $80. The price of shirts and dresses runs accordingly. A cup of beans that goes for 27 cents in a Congolese market costs 34 cents in Zaire.

The people of the Congo are clearly benefiting from open competition, and from the encouragement of private investment with guarantees of no government interference. Congolese president Denis Sassou-N'Guesso has issued a standing call for private investment in such practical activities as agricultural exportation, animal raising, forestry, mining, small industry, hotel and restaurant construction, and tourism. His Zairian counterpart, Mobutu, has devoted his much more lavish Western investment money on public sector showcases of questionable utility—a $233 million assembly hall known as the People's Palace, a national satellite and microwave communications system that's more or less permanently on the fritz, and a $1 billion-plus power line across the country to places where local souces of hydroelectric power are untapped.

If the men who make U.S. foreign policy were forced to walk through those countries and talk to the people in them, and then were forced to choose one of the two countries to live in—live as the citizens of those countries live at any given percentile—they would quickly see that the "communist" Congo offers a better life in almost every regard, mainly because it is no more communist than Zaire is free.*

We constantly overlook the distinction between what a country's government says, and what the people of the country do. Newspapers report that "Brazil believes . . .," and what the newspapers mean is that a relative handful of Brazilian generals and rich businessmen believe. *Brazil*—a consensus of its 125 million people—may well believe that those generals and businessmen should be lined up against a wall and shot. But only the government's views get reported, until suddenly, to everyone's surprise but the Brazilians', a rebellion starts.

By viewing the world as a chessboard, on which all pieces are either black or white, either our friend or the Soviets', our leaders are ignoring the principles of which genuine friendships, and partnerships, are made.

Only out of such principles can come true national security.

THE question inevitably arises: whom should we support in El Salvador, in Lebanon, in Chile, in South Africa? The answer is not to think in terms of *whom* we should support, but in terms of *what* we should support. Basic principles are easier to discern than personalities are, if we focus on them. We support free and democratic politics, free and prosperous markets, free and lively culture, equal and improved opportunity, individual rights, open and equal justice, and a fair distribution of public resources. We oppose violence, and outside intervention in the rights of nations to govern their own affairs.

We will find few leaders or factions around the world that fully subscribe to those principles. We will often have to do business with leaders and factions that subscribe to them hardly at all. Thomas Jefferson, our first secretary of state, set a policy of recognizing (that is, conducting civil relations with) *de facto* governments, even though we might not regard them as *de jure*, or proper, governments. The policy served us well until hysteria over communism confused the issue.

Nonintervention is not isolationism. More than ever, with communications shrinking the globe, we have some interest in what happens everywhere. Interests derive both from our membership in the human brotherhood, and from our very real commercial needs. Yet to become worldly wise does not

---

*To be sure, there are reasons why the two countries don't lend themselves to exact comparison. The Congo has fewer than 2 million citizens while Zaire has between 25 and 30 million, and is seven times bigger. The Congo is nicely endowed with resources, but isn't, like Zaire, a prime source of vital materials. These differences, however, should operate to Zaire's advantage.

mean to become an enforcer of worldwide dogma. It means, on the contrary, to understand the differences and complexities of each country and region, and to understand the limits of our ability to change them.

Nonintervention is not neutrality, either. We don't approve of the kind of governments that run the Soviet Union, Poland, Afghanistan—and El Salvador—and a lot of other places, and there is no reason to be shy about saying so any time anybody asks us. We sympathize with the subjugated, often terrorized people of those countries, and want to help them, however we can, within our principles.

We care about our principles, and nobody should doubt it. Inevitably, in supporting those principles we will sometimes appear to prefer one faction over another in specific disputes. But the preference is for the principle, not the faction, and our support should never become permanently attached to one faction by joining it in violence against its compatriot rivals. Rather, we should encourage all factions toward our principles, by making clear that we will adhere to those principles ourselves, and prosper by them.

And nonintervention is certainly not pacifism. There are potential violent threats to our safety and our commercial rights, and we should be prepared to defend against them. Guaranteeing our trade with the Middle East requires a strong navy—which we seem to have, because our merchant ships aren't being sunk. Guaranteeing our trade with the Middle East does *not*, however, require controlling the government of Angola, and every other country that may be blessed with a little beachfront.

Because we care about our principles, and aren't pacifists, our wishes go out to people elsewhere who fight for their freedom and independence. Our willingness to arm them, however, must be constrained. We must consider the ease with which arms get out of hand, and we must consider the likelihood that the principles of most other peoples, especially in the Third World, will at some point diverge from ours.

In an extreme case like that of Afghanistan, where virtually the entire population is united with us on the paramount issue that they have a right to be independent of Soviet occupation, and where other countries of the region are wihout exception in accord, it would seem a shame not to add our superior resources to some genuine cooperative effort to kick the Soviets out. But the arms we supply, and our contact with Afghans, must be governed by the knowledge that when the issue of Soviet occupation is resolved, other, local issues will continue to divide the Afghans, both within the country and in relations with their neighbors. We must not be lured into a continuing dispute that would ally us against new and so far undreamed-of enemies.

It should be the clear policy of the United States that we will not tolerate Soviet or any other foreign military presence in our own neighborhood if it seems to pose a serious new threat to our ability to defend our borders. We showed that policy in the Cuban missile episode in 1962. And if faced with a similar threat in Cuba, or Nicaragua, today, we should be prepared if necessary to obliterate the threat with a quick strike, or naval blockade, using the minimal, but still adequate force necessary. We should maintain satellite and other intelligence capabilities—including a reliable human spy network—necessary to warn us of such danger.

But we also ought to recognize that the only reason such a danger is even thinkable is that our government has threatened the sovereignty of these countries. The Soviets put (and were invited to put) missiles in Cuba in direct response to our invasion of Cuba and our scarcely veiled plots to repeat it. In 1982, we organized an invasion force to try to overthrow the government of Nicaragua, much along the pattern by which we successfully overthrew the government of its neighbor, Guatemala, not so many years ago. And then, when that invasion force began to act, and the Nicaraguans turned for military aid to the only place that would give it to them, the Eastern bloc, we howled about the menace.

The U.S. government contended that Nicaragua had been arming to invade its neighbors. But the armaments cited were puny, and the only foreign national soldiers "invading" the surrounding countries were American. Nicaragua was arming only as needed to defend its independence, and maybe not well enough to do that.

Surely a large, well-supplied Soviet military presence in Nicaragua would be an intolerable threat to the U.S. But it would be a threat we created. By returning to those principles we value, we can extinguish the threat without hiring an extra soldier or building an extra warship.

LET'S make an analogy between foreign policy and our personal lives.

Suppose that every few months we took a walk down the block, knocking on every door. At one house, we would announce to our neighbor, "I like you, I approve of you," and reach down into our pocket and hand him $1,000. At the next house, perhaps the same thing would happen. Then, at the third house, we would tell the neighbor, "I don't like you, I don't approve of you," and we would reach under our coat, pull out a sawed-off, 12-gauge shotgun, and blow him away, along with his entire family. And so we would go, down the block, making a decision at each house: the $1,000 or the shotgun blast.

Obviously, this sort of behavior wouldn't work in our daily lives. There aren't many friends on the block so close that we'd want to help support them. And while there are plenty of people on the block with whom we may have disagreements about fundamental matters such as politics and religion and property, and whose habits we may not approve of, and whose wit we find tasteless, we do not seek to destroy them. We exchange greetings on the street, we shop in their stores, and once a year we may visit them or welcome them into our home. None of this amounts to a compromising of our beliefs, or an endorsement of theirs. It just means it is in our own interest to maintain a code of civility that protects us as well as others. Regardless of the justness of our complaint, we don't invade and harass our neighbors, because we don't want to live behind barricades in our own homes. We do business with them because their commerce helps ours.

The analogy isn't exact because in our neighborhoods, in the grossest cases of misconduct, we can call in the police. The international bodies that we can appeal to as a nation have standards way too low—we need to work steadily to raise them—and they can levy mainly moral sanctions, which aren't always adequate. Still the fact remains that no nation has the power to police the world all by itself.

The lack of an international police force we can trust does impose military burdens on us as a nation that we don't have in our personal lives. As a nation, we must maintain sufficient force to defend ourselves, and use it when, in our judgment, we are under physical attack at home or in the international marketplace. But we were under no such attack from Angola, or even Cuba, when our forces invaded those countries. We judged them basically by our dislike for them, and for the crowd they hung out with.

In foreign policy, as in the neighborhood door-knocking situation, reacting to others according to whether we like or dislike them doesn't result in just police work. Our record of foreign intervention does not neatly align with the grossness of other countries' transgressions. For every Angola, where we intervened, there is a worse government—for example, Emperor Bokassa's in Central African Republic—where we did not. Bokassa passed our liking test because he was a friend, at least for a while, of our friend France.

More important, using force according to the standard we have used for the past nearly forty years simply hasn't given us a successful foreign policy. What it has given us is anti-aircraft batteries and concrete road barriers around the White House. Our embassies overseas and even many federal courthouses at home are designed like military fortresses. We have not produced a friendly world, or even a mostly friendly world, to do business in. We have produced enemies, in endless supply.

But if we can learn, as General Omar Bradley advised, to "steer by the stars, not by the lights of each passing ship," we will find that those enemies become fewer, and much more manageable, than we now think possible.

POSTSCRIPT

==================================DURING THE long months of editing and production work that followed completion of this book, in August 1983, two events occurred that seem to bear on the theme. The first was the U.S.-led invasion of Grenada in October 1983, and the second was the military coup that overthrew the democratically elected government of Nigeria in January 1984.

This book has tried to show that much of what we hear about such episodes when they happen is illusion, and that the truth doesn't begin to seep out until months and usually years later; summing up so soon, then, presents a problem. Important facts almost certainly remain secret. Still, some comments may be in order.

Over the weekend of October 21–24, 1983, the United States secretly negotiated a pact with the governments of six tiny Caribbean island-nations. On Tuesday, October 25, they all—which is to say mainly the United States— invaded an even tinier Caribbean island-nation, Grenada. The result was unique in the recent history of American intervention: our troops were genuinely welcomed by the local citizens, and, even more amazing, we won. If all foreign intervention turned out the way the Grenadan invasion appears to have turned out, the policy would be tough to argue against, even on moral grounds. So it is important to emphasize that Grenada *was* unique, and to understand *why* it was unique. This is especially so because even now it's clear that the American people were broadly misled by their government

407

about Grenada, in ways that might create the false impression that the Grenadan experience is transferrable to other situations.

Some necessary background: For five years after it gained independence from England in 1974, Grenada was run by a man named Eric Gairy, an autocrat, witchcraft practitioner, and flying-saucer buff, who was commonly thought to be crazy (in the clinical sense). His government was overthrown in 1979, in a coup costing one life, by Maurice Bishop, leader of the long-standing opposition. Bishop espoused socialism and was a close personal friend of Fidel Castro. Bishop's group governed until the third week of October 1983, when, over several days, it was overthrown by a group ultimately led by General Hudson Austin, in fighting that apparently cost about 17 dead and 50 wounded. (These figures originated with the Austin government, but were roughly verified—"plus or minus ten or fifteen"—by the staff of the American medical school in Grenada based on hospital checks. During the U.S. invasion, Washington said hundreds had been killed in the coup against Bishop, but in its official printed chronology the U.S. later slashed that to a hedged estimate of "50 casualties.") Finally, the last week of October, at a cost of 88 dead and 533 wounded (U.S. Defense Department figures), we succeeded in overthrowing the Austin government.

The most important point here is that the government that the U.S. forces overthrew was not the one most Americans *thought* they overthrew. For nearly three years, ever since the Reagan administration took office in January 1981, the American public had been hearing nasty things about a *different* Grenadan government, the one that took over in 1979 and was run by Maurice Bishop.

The Reagan team, as it took office in 1981, was determined to take an aggressive stance toward Cuba and its friends, and win a quick victory that Reagan thought would change the course of foreign relations. Targeting Grenada as an enemy, the administration immediately found a way to stall Bishop's development program. The U.S. reversed the Carter administration's approval of an International Monetary Fund loan that was in the works for Grenada. We effectively vetoed the loan, apparently believing that if we "got tough," the "other side" would give up socialism.

Bishop had wanted the loan to allow construction of a new airport that Grenada badly needed if it was to attract tourists.* The Reagan administration contended from the beginning that the airport was designed mainly for military use, part of a Soviet-Cuban plot to make Grenada a staging base for spreading revolution throughout Latin America. The airport was to be ap-

---

*Technically, as has already been explained, IMF money can't be used for development projects, and the U.S. can't veto a loan; but money is a fungible commodity and the U.S. is the cornerstone of the IMF, so what is stated here is what, in effect, happened, and I have taken shortcuts to keep it simple. In fact, Grenada got a loan, but the U.S. drastically reduced the amount and the terms, curtailing its usefulness.

proximately the same size as the tourist airports on neighboring islands—smaller than some—and was to replace a badly outmoded mountain airstrip on Grenada that can't accommodate modern passenger jets, and that is nearly an hour's rough ride from town and the beaches.

With Western money restricted, construction on the new airport proceeded slowly. Bishop's friend Castro provided about 700 skilled construction workers and equipment. Most of the construction crew, like most Cubans, had military training; Cubans abroad had been attacked too often for Castro to send out workers unprepared to defend themselves. But as events ultimately showed, these workers were on Grenada primarily to build an airport, not to fight. The airport was scheduled to open in the spring of 1984, three years after IMF financing had been denied.

Reagan continued to argue that Grenada wanted its new airport only to serve as a Soviet military base, but there are several reasons to doubt this. First, it is hard to understand how, if the Soviets really thought a Grenadan air facility was militarily important, they could not have built even one runway on Grenada in less than three years. Twenty years ago, Khrushchev showed that the Soviets could construct a whole nuclear missile base in Cuba in a matter of a few weeks. The sleepy pace of Grenadan airport construction seems strong evidence that the Reagan administration was wrong in its projections.

Second, the spot picked for the airport is right in view of prime tourist areas and actually next to housing for an American medical school. From a map, it is hard to see how such an airport would offer the Soviets a significant strategic advantage over more clandestine bases that are already available on Cuba. After the U.S. invasion, President Reagan went on television with stories of warehouses on Grenada packed "almost to the ceiling" with modern terrorist weapons; in fact, when journalists and other independent observers were finally allowed on the island to examine the evidence, the warehouses were found to be only half full, and many of the weapons antiquated; in type and amount, the arsenal was quite consistent with the claim that it was there for the defense of Grenada (a task for which it was obviously inadequate).*

There is a third and better reason to doubt the U.S. assertion that Grenada needed an airport only to serve as a Soviet military base: when the U.S. took over Grenada, we announced plans to complete the airport ourselves.

The most critical point, though, is that the Bishop government that had supposedly laid these deadly plans with the Cubans and Soviets was no longer in power when the U.S. invaded. Washington tried to present the replacement Austin government as just another Cuban stooge regime, a continuation and perhaps a hardening of the Bishop government. But it just

---

*For a good account of discrepancies between the administration's original statements and what reporters actually saw when they were allowed onto the island, see Stuart Taylor Jr.'s account in the *New York Times*, November 6, 1983.

wasn't so. Bishop had been a very popular man in Grenada—even the official
U.S. history of the affair concedes that. Like leaders everywhere, he saw
his popularity wane somewhat after a few years in office, as he failed to
accomplish miracles. In response, he stifled outspoken opposition, and jailed
scores of people for political reasons. Nevertheless, there was speculation
that Bishop might allow elections as he had promised in 1984, because, in
the judgment of many, he probably would have won.

In contrast, few Grenadans appeared to be in favor of the bloody and
hard-to-explain events that removed Bishop from office during the third week
of October 1983. While Bishop was traveling in Eastern Europe and Cuba,
some members of his cabinet, led by Deputy Prime Minister Bernard Coard,
who by all accounts was not liked very much, plotted Bishop's overthrow.
Their reasons have not yet been satisfactorily explained. On the night of
October 13–14, shortly after his return to Grenada, Bishop was put under
house arrest and Coard was announced as his replacement. Bishop's allies
in the cabinet, including his common-law wife, education minister Jacqueline
Creft, who was pregnant with his child, resigned and some were arrested.

Popular protests broke out, culminating in a large crowd that marched to
Bishop's house on Wednesday, October 19, and freed him and Creft. The
crowd, with Bishop, then marched to the fort and police headquarters in the
center of town, and took it over. But reinforcements from the People's
Revolutionary Army appeared, and fired into the crowd, causing them to
panic and run. Bishop, Creft, and several who were loyal to them were
trapped in the fort and killed, apparently by quick execution after capture.

Army chief General Hudson Austin, a boyhood friend of Bishop's, took
charge of the government from Coard, and declared on radio a four-day
round-the-clock curfew, during which anyone on the streets was to be shot
on sight. Understandably, fear and confusion gripped the island. Since Grenada has only 110,000 residents, almost everyone knew someone who had
been at the fort during the panic. As word of the shooting spread, people
knew only that their leaders had been murdered inexplicably, and that strangers
had taken over the government threatening to shoot anyone seen outside his
home. Scrawled messages of "No Bish-No Revo" appeared around the island,
indicating feelings that were pro-Bishop, but anti-Coard and anti-Austin.

In other words, if the Yankees had invaded two weeks earlier, when the
heroic if controversial Bishop had been in power—if we had attacked the
government our president had been criticizing all these years—we never
would have received the warm popular welcome we did. Possibly, because
the island is so small, we still might have prevailed, but not so quickly or
so comfortably or with so few casualties. We were overthrowing not Bishop,
but Bishop's enemies, the people who had *killed* Bishop and terrorized the
island.

Why did Coard take this unpopular action and make of himself a convenient target for the U.S.? Washington's explanation was that he did so at

the behest of the Cubans. Castro allegedly thought Bishop, with his possible plans for an election, was too soft. But Reagan's own envoys in the Caribbean didn't believe that—in fact, as will be explained in a moment, they believed exactly the opposite, that Cuba vehemently *opposed* Coard's coup. And Cuba pretty clearly *did* oppose it. Castro consistently reacted in shock and anger to each new blow Bishop suffered, issuing long and plaintive press releases on behalf of his friend. Castro appeared to be out of contact with the new government, and when it was formed, he began withdrawing personnel from Grenada. There seems no reason to believe he was bluffing, or that his regard for Bishop was not genuine.

The intriguing thing about the Coard coup, as one sees it from the facts now available, is that the only outsiders who stood to benefit from overthrowing Bishop were not the Cubans or Russians, but the policymakers in Washington. With U.S. military efforts in Central America and Lebanon in real trouble, and the president planning to run for reelection, the U.S. governing team needed a victory to justify its whole foreign policy attitude. Is it possible that Washington, acting perhaps through some *agent provocateur*, catalyzed the October coup on Grenada, paving the way for our intervention? Could Coard himself, who was quickly captured by the U.S. but not made available for public questioning, have been in U.S. pay? There is no evidence for saying so, except for the circumstances cited here, and the fact that such a scheme would have been no more exotic than others we have tried in the Congo, in Vietnam, in Iran, in Guatemala, in Cuba itself, and in other places. All the stranger, then, is the presence of one-time CIA operative and international *bête noire* Frank Terpil on Grenada right up to the time of the coup, when he returned to his haunts in the Middle East.

We can only hope that in years to come, some logical explanation will be forthcoming for why Bernard Coard did what he did.

Getting back to provable fact, what kind of government was General Austin running on Grenada at the time of the U.S. intervention, and what were its intentions? This is important, because the primary justification Reagan and Secretary of State Shultz gave for the invasion was that the lives of Americans, mainly the 700 or so medical students on the island, were being threatened. Only secondarily was the invasion's purpose to restore our idea of democracy to Grenada.

To try to evaluate the threat to Americans, I talked in New York to Geoffrey Bourne, the vice-chancellor of the medical school and its highest-ranking representative on Grenada throughout the coup and invasion. Then I went to Barbados for long and detailed interviews with three of the four main U.S. diplomats who were on Grenada just before and during the invasion. I also talked there with a high-ranking official of our embassy on Barbados, which covers Grenada and a few other islands too small to rate a U.S. diplomatic station; this official had helped relay communications between the Caribbean and Washington during the crisis. (He insisted on speaking for the embassy, rather than in his own name.)

These points emerged:

1. Austin's revolutionary military council was extremely solicitous of the welfare of the students. Dr. Bourne recalls that the morning after Bishop's murder and all the shooting, two armed security men came to his house. He remembers thinking at first that his visitors were going to arrest him. But instead, he says, "they wanted to know if the students had enough food and water for a four-day, twenty-four-hour curfew. That was the only reason they came. I told them that the True Blue campus [one of two the school had on Grenada] had water for only one night. And they had water trucks down there within a couple of hours."

Before long, Austin himself drove up to Bourne's house. On the first day after taking over the government, Austin chose to make goodwill calls, first on the British governor general, and second on Bourne, the resident chief of the medical school. The next day, Bourne says, Austin's government "released the curfew on one of our drivers" so he could get supplies for the school. Bourne was also granted a pass and a police escort, so he could travel about at will despite the curfew.

Throughout the curfew period, Austin and other high-ranking army officers repeatedly inquired about the welfare of the students, promising their safety and saying they could leave if they wanted.

2. Austin worked to initiate friendly contact with the U.S. government. That first morning, looking worn and talking apologetically, Austin told Bourne he had ordered the troops not to shoot at anyone the day before. He complained that his own daughter now wouldn't speak to him, and urged Bourne to invite U.S. diplomats to the island from the embassy in Barbados. For symbolic reasons, Reagan's ambassador, Milan Bish, had refused to present his credentials to Grenada, but several lower-ranking emissaries sometimes visited the island. Amazingly, though, the embassy hadn't sent any envoys to Grenada throughout the week of trouble because, in the words of the embassy official, their "schedules couldn't be worked out" and they "couldn't get away." Two diplomats, Kenneth Kurze and Linda Flohr, did try to fly in on a commercial flight Thursday, October 20, but the flight was canceled due to the establishment of the round-the-clock curfew that morning. On Austin's invitation, they chartered a plane and were admitted Saturday, October 22.

They met with Leon Cornwall, probably second-in-command to General Austin; the U.S. diplomats had been ordered by the embassy not to meet with Austin so as not to imply diplomatic recognition of the new government. Cornwall repeatedly offered assurances of the students' safety. When Bourne, who attended the meeting at Cornwall's request, suggested a two-week school holiday allowing everyone to go home and "come back when things settled down," Cornwall said, "it wasn't a bad idea."

3. The Austin government repeatedly pledged that it would authorize transportation to get the students out, and while this may have been a bluff, the U.S. never tried to put it to the test. Ironically, the main hang-up was over the inadequacy of the Grenadan airport that Reagan had previously insisted was perfectly adequate. Cornwall had stated from the beginning that chartered civilian planes would be allowed in, as many as necessary, to evacuate whoever wanted to go. But since the largest craft that could land on the abbreviated airstrip was capable of carrying only forty-six persons, U.S. officials argued that an evacuation by this means would take too long to assure proper security. They also noted that the road to the airport was long and difficult.

The U.S. suggested instead an evacuation by U.S. battleship, to be loaded by marine landing craft from Grenada's main harbor. Cornwall rejected that idea as tantamount to allowing a military occupation of his country, but agreed in principle to an alternative U.S. suggestion to bring a Cunard cruise ship into port and load it up. This suggestion, never reduced by the U.S. to a specific plan, was still on the table when the invasion occurred.

Bourne recalls Austin's calling him privately that Sunday, October 23, upset that the Americans insisted on evacuating all the students. Bourne had been telling Austin up to that point that only about 10 to 15 percent of the students had told the school that they wanted to leave. As Bourne recalls it now, "Twice each day I would go meet with the students at the two campuses and brief them as to what was happening and get their reactions, which in general were pretty controlled. A very small number were a bit inclined to get hysterical, raise their voices a bit. What I was doing was advising them myself that I felt it was pretty safe. We had been through one revolution, in '79."

4. U.S. diplomats meeting with students on the island in the few days before the invasion repeatedly encouraged the students to demand evacuation, even when most students had already indicated their preference to stay in Grenada. The public was told that our envoys merely offered neutral consultation. Envoy James Budeit acknowledges that when the first U.S. diplomats left for Grenada Saturday, October 22, no more than 15 percent of the students had indicated they wanted to leave, but that the Americans felt "there might be a snowballing effect if somebody actually came out there."

Budeit also says that at his first meeting with students, on Sunday night, October 23, "one student asked me point-blank, 'What would you tell your own son if he were down here?' I said I'd tell him to get the hell out." Even that night, though, he says, "they had not made up their own minds." The next morning, just eighteen hours before the invasion began, Budeit says, he and Flohr told the students, "You've got to make up your own minds. We're not going to stick around here forever."

That afternoon he visited homes of married students who lived near the radio station in town, warning them that it would be dangerous to stay there because in the event of a countercoup, the radio station would probably be a scene of action. He says he and a colleague "scared the hell out of those people," then went back to campus, where he later saw some of the wives he had talked to. "They were weeping, crying," he recalls. "I stayed the hell away from them. I had done my bit, and gotten them out of there."

Bourne remembers another factor, that on Sunday night there were "rumors from outside radio, mostly Caribbean stations, that the Caricom [neighboring] countries were going to invade Grenada. That stirred up the students quite a bit. They were scared, and that jumped the number who wanted to leave to over 50 percent" by Monday, Bourne says. Thus it may have been the invasion itself, and the salesmanship of the U.S. diplomats, that set off student panic—not any action of the Austin government. Budeit himself says, "I expected that some of the students were going to get killed."

Kenneth Kurze says there was never any doubt in his mind that a Grenadan-arranged evacuation wouldn't work anyway. "I felt going over to Grenada, and I felt coming back, that you could not have an orderly evacuation of large numbers of foreigners in a situation controlled by the military council, given their shakiness and the large chance of violence. Therefore, if you're going to do this, you have to secure control of a certain area." In other words, invade. "This was a group that killed their own people, their former leader. They were desperate. They would have done anything," Kurze says.

5. Austin made a radio speech announcing a political program built around Western capital and private property. Dr. Bourne says he found the program "very encouraging." Kurze heard the same speech, and recalls thinking that "it was bullshit, farcical, really. They were stalling for time."

6. On Sunday, October 23, the day before the invasion was finally authorized, Washington received alarming reports from its emissaries on Grenada, but these reports were groundless and inaccurate. For one thing, a plane carrying envoys Budeit and Gary Chafin was denied permission to land because of a communications foul-up. They were coming with Austin's approval to replace Kurze, whose mother had just died. The U.S. embassy telexed Bourne's office after their plane had been waved off and forced to land at a nearby island. Bourne, tracking down the problem, found that Austin's secretary was using a two-year-old telephone directory and had dialed the wrong number to alert airport personnel to admit the U.S. plane despite the curfew that shut down normal airport operations. Bourne says he supplied the right telephone number and the problem was rectified.

"I must admit to you that we were doubled up with laughter during this period," Bourne says. "It was just a bunch of people inexperienced at running that kind of operation and unable to make command decisions."

It wasn't so funny, though, when the embassy got a misleading account of it all from Budeit, a consular officer and former Navy man who had come to Barbados fresh out of the National War College, and who, before that, had been assigned to help direct the military evacuation of civilians from Beirut. Budeit and Chafin reported to the embassy by phone late Sunday afternoon from the airport in Grenada that they had been shot at while attempting to land—this on the word of someone their private pilot introduced them to in the control tower; none of them had heard or seen shooting. Budeit and Chafin also reported that they were being held at the airport by armed soldiers and that Kurze, the man they were to relieve, was mysteriously missing.

That, they now concede, was not true, although they say they were genuinely afraid because of the circumstances. It eventually turned out that Kurze was two-and-a-half hours late reaching the airport because a Britisher who was flying out with him had wanted to go home and pack first. The delay had been no one's fault but theirs. And Budeit and Chafin say, on reflection, that they could have left the airport for town any time they wanted, and in fact that the soldiers encouraged them to do so, but that they waited at the airport out of fear. Budeit says that if Kurze "hadn't come out, I wasn't going in."

The opinions of the senior embassy official who was relaying this information to Washington are still dominated by the scary tenor of that erroneous Sunday phone call. Nearly two months later, he cited it as evidence that the word of the Austin government couldn't be relied on. Apparently, he was never told or had forgotten that the whole problem was one of misunderstanding, not duplicity.

7. *The U.S. embassy on Barbados relayed to Washington a much more negative picture than our representatives on Grenada recall supplying.* The senior embassy official says that the message he got from Kurze and Budeit, and relayed to Washington, was that Cornwall would allow nothing but scheduled transport out of Grenada. Since all scheduled air service had been halted by the airline operating in the region, which was owned by the governments of Barbados and other neighboring islands that were boycotting Grenada, this appeared to leave no hope of exit for the students. The embassy official says Kurze and Budeit told him Cornwall had specifically rejected the idea of charter aircraft or a charter cruise liner; yet the diplomats who went to Grenada say Cornwall specifically *proposed* the charter aircraft, and Budeit says Cornwall okayed in principle the cruise liner. (Chafin remembers Cornwall skirting the cruise-liner issue noncommittally, with a joke about not wanting the students to get seasick, and that no one pressed him on it.)

The embassy official also maintains, contrary to all other accounts, that the Austin government "did not show any particular concern for the students. We did that. They were responding to our repeated requests for assurances. They did not, then or ever, offer *unsolicited* [his inflection] assurances on our people."

8. *The U.S. diplomats cold-shouldered friendly gestures by the Austin government.* When Cornwall greeted Budeit at the main hotel in town after

his arrival, and apologized for the mix-up at the airport, Budeit says, "I told him to wait while I get checked into the hotel." Then over beer in the lobby bar, Cornwall tried to tell the Americans of Austin's plans to form a civilian government and revise the constitution. "But," says Budeit, "I told him I wasn't there to talk about that. I just wanted to arrange for the Americans to get out." When Cornwall then tried to address that question, Budeit told him to put an offer in writing, and then "told him I've got to go eat, and left."

Chafin recalls a stunning offer from Cornwall that same evening. "He [Cornwall] said, 'We were planning to set up a civilian cabinet, and we would entertain suggestions as to the make-up of the cabinet.'" In other words, Cornwall was inviting U.S. suggestions on which Grenadans should be included in the new government! "We thought maybe this was just a ploy," Chafin says, "but maybe it was the opportunity to make a real break-through." Later, though, Chafin recalls, Cornwall went to a lengthy meeting of the military council and returned, "tired, eyes bloodshot, flexibility gone. He said they were going to maintain relations with Cuba and the Soviet Union. They were still debating the civilian cabinet. He said he needed to go home and get some sleep."

Late Monday afternoon, with the invasion already set, Budeit says envoy Linda Flohr told him to go meet Cornwall, as scheduled, at the foreign ministry. "He's going to be a little bit pissed because we don't have a response for him [an exact U.S. evacuation proposal]," Budeit recalls being told. "I said, I don't know why he'd be pissed. We never promised him anything."

The meeting itself seems strange. Budeit recalls that at about 4 P.M., he, Cornwall, and a secretary were the only ones in the foreign ministry building, and it was raining. "The roof was leaking and it [the rainwater] was running down my leg, and I pretended it wasn't happening. I don't know why he didn't say, 'Why don't you just move over?'"

Budeit says he explained that there was no reply for Cornwall because the Grenadans' message had taken a long time to be relayed to President Reagan. "He said, 'What can I tell the RMC [Revolutionary Military Council]?' I said, 'You can tell them to wait for a reply.' He said, 'Can you tell me, really confidentially, what do you advise me to do?' I said, 'I can't advise you anything. Wait for the response.'" A few hours later, the troops landed.

Budeit remembers that at the end of the meeting, Cornwall invited him to go together to the Sugar Mill, a local disco. Budeit declined. "I had to protect myself with my own government," he says. "I can't go to discos together. Our president called them a gang of leftist thugs, although Cornwall seemed a nice enough guy, and might not have murdered anybody. What he was trying to indicate was, 'We could be influenced along the way. There's no need to shake us up.'" Cornwall was being conciliatory, Budeit agrees.

Summing up, he recalls that Cornwall "kept asking for advice. I considered this a ploy to find out what we were doing." On the other hand, he says,

Cornwall's offers may have been genuine. "They may really have been over their heads and not knowing what they were doing. They couldn't go anymore to the Cubans for advice, so they went to the other side [the U.S.] for advice." Apparently no one took time to find out.

Budeit says he had no briefing or specific instructions before coming to Grenada, but "was basically winging it." He says he didn't know an invasion was coming until he got back to the hotel Monday night and, in a phone conversation with the embassy, caught a veiled reference to military aircraft.

9. *The U.S. diplomats on the scene, quite contrary to blaming Cuba for the October coup as Reagan and Shultz did, believed Castro was so angry at Coard and Austin that the Cubans might be planning a countercoup, which might endanger the students.* "The Cubans had already expressed their upset with the shooting of Bishop," Budeit observes. "They might have staged their own coup and put in somebody more to their liking, a Cuban-sponsored coup. After all, if you can't support the RMC [Revolutionary Military Council], you've got to put somebody in there you *can* support."

This, he says, is what made him urge the students to leave, despite the desire of both the school and the RMC to have them stay. "It was obvious the school wanted them to stay right there and continue to operate, and the RMC wanted them to stay right there and continue to operate," he acknowledges. But the military council's promises of protection had to be discounted, Budeit says, because Austin's men "weren't that firmly in control."

10. *Contrary to reports from Washington that Cuba was about to send reinforcements to Grenada, and that the marines got there "just in time," witnesses on the island saw Cubans packing up and going aboard homeward-bound ships in the days before the invasion.* Medical students said trucks had come in the middle of the night to the homes of Cuban technicians, to load up furniture and families.

11. *Throughout the invasion, Austin's troops had countless opportunities to harm or take hostage both American students and American diplomats; they never did.* Bourne recalls that a few hours before the invasion, Austin, evidently aware something was afoot, stopped by to say, "Thank you for your cooperation, and I won't forget it." Says Bourne, "I interpreted that to mean that the students would be safe even if there would be an invasion. I think he meant that the PRA [People's Revolutionary Army] would not harm the students. So far as I know, no one connected with the PRA ever fired at the students or anybody connected with the school." In fact, once during the invasion, PRA soldiers inadvertently burst in on a house where six medical students were living; they apologized, and left, saying they were going off "to fight the imperialists," Bourne says.

Budeit remembers eating breakfast in the hotel dining room with other guests during the invasion (they did their own cooking), and that the dining room was open to the road where truckloads of RMC soldiers would pass. Even though Cornwall knew exactly where the Americans were, no one paid them any attention. Nights, Budeit says, they spent raiding the hotel wine cellar.

THERE is, to say the least, strong reason to question the Reagan-Shultz explanation for Grenada. The diplomacy preceding the invasion doesn't show an overriding concern for the students' safety. The U.S. may not have landed on the island for the reasons given. On the other hand, the government of Hudson Austin represented almost no one. It would be hard to find very many Grenadans other than Austin himself who weren't better off after the invasion. Austin might (or might not) have proved able to set a right course if given time. But Reagan had found his lucky moment in history and exploited it. For three years he had sought that quick victory to reverse American fortunes. It finally came. But by the time it came, and small as it was, so much else had been lost around the globe that it still couldn't bring the administration even.

The U.S. had shown its "might" by defeating what may have been the weakest excuse for a government the world has seen in years. The message Washington sent may have reached the voters, but the rest of the world seemed to ignore it. Certainly it missed Castro. In fact, our bearded antagonist attributed the fall of Grenadan "progressivism" not to the U.S. army, but to the Austin–Coard coup. Castro did reduce the exposure of a few Cubans in a place called Surinam, but that apparently had no effect at all on what passes for a government there. The Sandinistas in Nicaragua continued to hand out automatic weapons to farmers, not a sign they doubted the loyalty of the Nicaraguan populace should Reagan get more ambitious with our GI's. The Moslem majority in Lebanon somehow did not seem cowed. The Russians continued to kill Afghans and snub disarmament talks.

Meanwhile, U.S. diplomats set about planning an election on Grenada, but ran into a problem. Eric Gairy, the witchcraft practitioner whom Bishop threw out in 1979, wanted to run for office again. And some diplomats conceded he seemed the favorite, principally because he was the only leading politician on the island who was not killed or imprisoned.

Plus ça change...

Still, even a bad policy can have favorable results in a particular and bizarre set of circumstances. The only really bad thing that can come out of the Grenadan invasion—besides the loss of life and limb—would be for such good fortune to be mistaken for good policy.

Of course, we may yet learn that there is much more to Grenada than has so far been made public.

AGAINST all the to-do over Grenada, the coup in Nigeria—far more important in the world scheme of things—got scant attention in the U.S. The primary reason we didn't feel compelled to learn much about what happened in Nigeria is that it seemed unlikely to make any great difference to us.

Again, we had stayed out of another country's internal affairs, so the new ruler, like the old one, wants to do business with us. There was even speculation he would lower the price of the oil we buy.

But democracy has been set back another few years, maybe another generation, in Africa. And while we don't know yet exactly what happened, the instant talk was that the democracy fell because of IMF problems. With the price of oil down, Nigeria couldn't comfortably meet the vast foreign debt payments assembled when the price of oil was up. Back then, the Western banks had wanted to lend money to Nigeria. Now the government needed to borrow money to pay the banks off. The IMF insisted that the country cut back its imports, raise prices for local goods and generally impose austerity on its citizens to meet these foreign obligations. The politicians were about to cave in to the Westerners' demands. So some soldiers thought they could do better. Democracy itself has not yet acquired value in Africa commensurate with price stability and well-stocked marketplaces.

You can search your atlas a long time, but you still won't find many places where the IMF and that American army of hard-selling bank vice-presidents have furthered the cause of political and market freedom.

ACKNOWLEDGMENTS

My greatest debt for this book is probably to the hundreds—by now maybe thousands—of people overseas who have graciously invited me into their homes to share a meal, or pass the night, so that I could learn a little bit about their lives and the ways of their countries. A few lines in a book could never begin to repay such debts, and most of the people who hold them are beyond reach of these words anyway. I only hope that when their countrymen visit the United States, they find the same warm hospitality and the same eagerness to exchange information that I have found all over the world.

Many of the travels that fed this book were undertaken as a team with my late wife, Martha Kwitny, who kept better diaries than I did. Beyond the broad inspiration that her courage and steadfastness gave to all who knew her, her wisdom and even her words have occasionally wound up on these pages. I trust she would think they were used properly.

A new generation of Kwitnys has taken up the rucksack. My daughters Carolyn and Susanna helped bridge many a cultural gap during reporting trips to Kenya, Nigeria, and China. Their companionship on the road and at home has contributed immeasurably to this work.

Tom Congdon, the editor and publisher of this volume, and Ellen Levine, my agent and loyal friend, went above and beyond professional duty numerous times to help bring this project to fruition in the best shape possible. Others had no professional duty here, but volunteered: John Emshwiller, Robert Sack, and David Thaler lent a lot of reading and discussion time to help me hash out many of the ideas herein. They gave vital advice. Each had a profound effect on the outcome (for which I, however, take full blame;

they tugged, sometimes successfully, sometimes not). Andrew Cockburn and Anthony Scaduto also put in long hours of reading to help make some critical editing decisions. John Marks was a bountiful contributor of ideas. And John Kelly of *Counterspy* magazine was amazing in his ability to corral documents. Sidney Rittenberg was a fountain of advice on China.

Translating for a very inquisitive person can be the world's most exhausting job; Laurie Cohen, Frances Ruddick, Janet Ter Veen, Liz Thurgood, and Anne Nelson did it superbly, always adding their own logic and curiosity to our door-to-door hunts; I hope they enjoyed the trips enough to make it all worth the effort.

Much of the research for this book was originally undertaken as reporting for the *Wall Street Journal*. The loyalty and support I've received over the years from managers and editors at the *Journal* have been more than a man could ever ask from a mere employer. For their help during the years this book encompasses, my thanks in particular to Stew Pinkerton and Jack Cooper, and also to Warren Phillips, Peter Kann, Fred Taylor, Larry O'Donnell, Mike Marks (for his work on the Cuban project), Bowen Northrup (Zaire), Glynn Mapes, and Seth Lipsky. A note on Cooper, who retired in February 1984: I and many others at the *Journal* may have had the privilege of studying under the best editor in the publishing business; at least I have heard of none near his equal. He could see through to the simple skeleton that underlay the most grotesque body of the most complicated story, and could reorganize things around it. He could find an easy phrase that was funny and memorable and yet caught the essence of a convoluted situation. He was relentlessly determined to be fair to everyone, and to be open to truths coming from strange directions. If on occasion an immovable prejudice caused him to mistreat a story, it probably happened with him as little as with anyone I know, myself included. His work will be sorely missed by all of us who learned from him and most of all by the readers, who, unfortunately, were mostly unaware he was there, providing the gifts they enjoyed. He deserves a lot of happy traveling and no more complaints about anything.

Cynthia Rigg once again came through with the index, and the reader can see the ingenuity of David Lindroth's maps on the endpapers.

A special thanks to Larry Stein, Lee Brody, Keith Gill, and the crew at Computermart who helped set up my IMS 5000, without which I can no longer imagine writing anything, and who patiently coached me through the initial trauma. Also to Marlene Harrigan, critical home support staff, who has waited all this time to see what the top of my desk will look like.

An additional dedication of this book to a new and yet unnamed Emshwiller, due to be issued at about the same time, who has very special parents; and to Michael Scaduto, who also does.

And, finally, special thanks to two people whose contributions have gone far beyond the definable; they are simply the best and most giving friends a person could ever hope to have: Dave Thaler and Janet Ter Veen.

INDEX

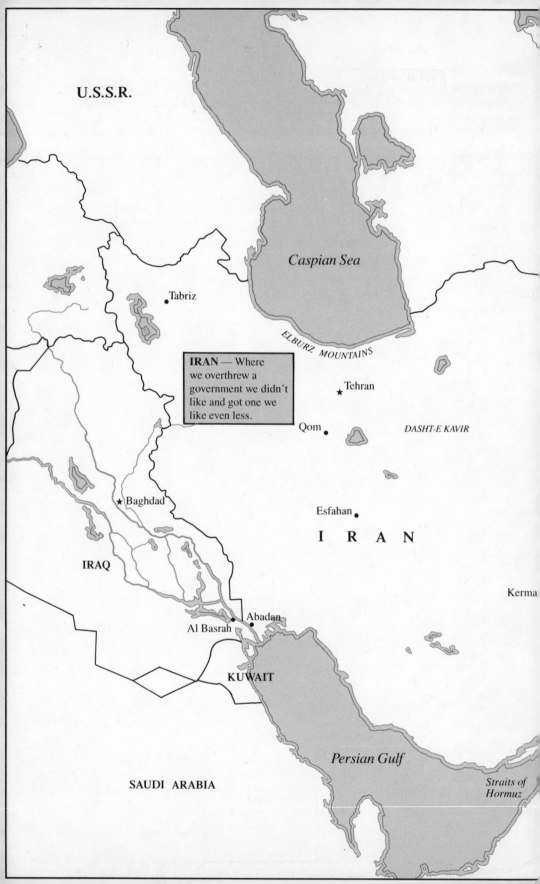

U.S.S.R.

Caspian Sea

Tabriz

ELBURZ MOUNTAINS

IRAN — Where we overthrew a government we didn't like and got one we like even less.

★ Tehran

Qom ● *DASHT-E KAVIR*

★ Baghdad

Esfahan ●

I R A N

IRAQ

Kerma

Abadan
Al Basrah ●

KUWAIT

Persian Gulf

SAUDI ARABIA

Straits of Hormuz